Fourth Edition

Europe and The Middle Ages

Edward Peters

University of Pennsylvania

PEARSON

Prentice Hall

Upper Saddle River, New Jersey 07458

Library of Congress Cataloging-in-Publication Data

Peters, Edward, (date)
   Europe and the Middle Ages / Edward Peters.
      p.   cm.
   Includes bibliographical references and index.
   ISBN 0-13-096772-6
      1. Europe—History—476-492.   2. Europe—Church history—600-1500.   3. Civilization,
   Medieval.   4. Europe—Social conditions—To 1492.   5. Crusades.   6. Material
   culture—Europe—History.   I. Title.

D116.P475 2004
940.1—dc21
                                                                              2003046014

To my brother Jack,
and to Ann, Heather, and John,
in memory of
EDWARD LOUIS PETERS (1964–1981).

Editorial Director: Charlyce Jones Owen
Senior Acquisitions Editor: Charles Cavaliere
Associate Acquisitions Editor: Emsal Hasan
Senior Production Editor: Barbara DeVries
Cover Design Director: Jayne Conte
Cover Designer: Kiwi Design
Prepress and Manufacturing Buyer: Sherry Lewis/Tricia Kenny
Line Art Supervisor: Guy Ruggiero
Map Artist: Maria Piper
Editorial Assistant: Adrienne Paul
Cover Art: Europa and the Bull, from "House of Jason" at Pompeii. Floor mosaic from a Roman villa at
Lullingstone in Kent. Fourth Century C.E. © The Heritage Trail.

This book was set 10/12 Galliard by Interactive Composition Corporation and
was printed by RR Donnelley & Sons Company. The cover was printed by
Phoenix Color Corp.

© 2004, 1997, 1989, 1983 by Pearson Education
Upper Saddle River, NJ 07458

Printed in the United States of America
10 9 8 7 6 5 4 3 2 1

ISBN 0-13-096772-6

Pearson Education Ltd., London
Pearson Education Australia PTY. Limited, Sydney
Pearson Education Singapore, Pte. Ltd.
Pearson Education North Asia Ltd., Hong Kong
Pearson Education Canada, Ltd., Toronto
Pearson Educación de Mexico, S.A. de C.V.
Pearson Education-Japan, Tokyo
Pearson Education Malaysia, Pte. Ltd.
Pearson Education, Upper Saddle River, New Jersey

Contents

Maps and Illustrations

Preface

Marking Time

The term "Middle Ages" is an instance of the historian's practice of dividing the past into distinct periods in order to focus more closely on the problem of continuity and change in the study of human experience.

When other disciplines use historical periodization, they usually possess reasonably specific and generally undisputed criteria for defining change. Measurable physical changes in the earth's structure, for example, account readily for geological periodization. Significant differences in the record of material culture account for periodization in archaeology. But the past of human societies offers a much broader and more widely debated spectrum of things to describe, measure, analyze, and explain. Our lives are short and our experience limited, but we have always desired a much greater—and greatly changing—access to the human past than our own personal experience and memory can provide. We have invented the discipline of history to provide us with that access.

Different methods of historical research and different ideas of historical periods came into existence precisely because of the different questions about the past that people asked, the reasons why they asked them, and the wider range of historical source materials that they used. In the late fourteenth century, as the last chapter of this book will tell, a number of literary moralists asked why the great power of the Roman Empire seemed to have collapsed around 500 C.E., or, as the greatest successor they ever had, Edward Gibbon, put it, why the Roman Empire "declined and fell." They also thought that in their own time they had managed to revive many of the linguistic, literary, artistic, and moral values of ancient Rome. These humanists came to call their own age (from the year 1350 or so) the period of rebirth, the "Renaissance" of Roman and later Greek values. With the glories of ancient Rome at one end, and the imagined glories of revived Roman and Greek culture at the other, the period from around 500 to 1350–1450 came to acquire a negative shape. What seemed to be conspicuous about it was its "un-Romanness," between two periods of "Romanness." And so people took to calling it "Middle"—middle between what seemed to them two more admirable periods of human achievement.

In the early sixteenth century, religious reformers like Martin Luther and John Calvin, and a number of Protestant historians, added to the humanist historical argument their accusations that at the end of the Roman Empire an authentic, evangelical Christianity had begun to be perverted by the Latin Christian Church and had not been purified until their own time, by themselves. This view reinforced the first definition of "the Middle Ages." It was itself reinforced in the seventeenth and eighteenth centuries by thinkers who argued that even if their age had not exactly recreated the glories of ancient Greece and Rome, it had done something even better—it had created a greater civilization, "the Modern Age." The new age professed to have discovered an absolute standard of rationality according to which all civilizations in the past and present could be ranked. "Antiquity," "the Middle Ages," and "the Modern Age" thus became standard divisions of the European past.

By all of these criteria, the millennium after 500 C.E. indeed seemed hopelessly remote, or, as many others called the period at various times, dark, rusty, monkish, leaden, dull, and barbarous, ruled largely, as the first great American medieval historian, Henry Charles Lea (1825–1909), once observed, by "superstition and force."

But during the nineteenth century, some of the very values that had created and characterized the "Middle Ages" themselves began to come under historical and cultural criticism. Romantic critics opposed seventeenth- and eighteenth-century claims to have discovered universal laws of human behavior and a single, narrow standard for judging the past. They argued that such a narrow view of both human nature and history made no allowance for historically derived differences among European peoples and between Europeans and other peoples. Another line of criticism came from nineteenth-century political reformers who urged a broader level of popular participation in politics and identified the people and its past with the nation-state. They attacked the Renaissance and early modern world of aristocrats, absolutist monarchs, state churches, extravagant wars, and rationalist philosophies of history, and turned back nostalgically to what they saw as a more inclusive, appealing, spiritual, virtuous, and less intensely governed medieval world.

The industrial revolutions of the nineteenth century appeared to have changed the lives of so many people so drastically and in so many ways, to have increased and redistributed wealth on such an immense scale, and to have changed the very nature of economic, social, and political experience so thoroughly, that the differences between the Middle Ages and the early stages of the modern period seemed to shrink to insignificance. Historians began to speak of *preindustrial* and *industrial* societies, of "Old Europe" and "traditional Europe," rather than of "Medieval," "Renaissance," "Reformation," or "Early Modern" Europe. In the light of the new long-range view, the French historian Jacques Le Goff and others have argued for a "long Middle Ages," from around the year 1000 to about 1800.

The original historical ideas that created the term and concept of the "Middle Ages" certainly no longer satisfy modern historical criteria of accuracy and appropriate methodology. Yet we still mark time with the term, not because we agree with the humanists, reformers, or eighteenth-century rationalists (and certainly not because we want to use the period as a cultural escape-hatch out of our own nostalgia or alienation from the present) but because even such concepts as "preindustrial" or "traditional" Europe encompass very broad and often unwieldy areas for concentrated study. Periodization also recognizes that there are limits to what a single historian or student of history can accomplish and the kinds of sources a single historian can master.[1] But we also acknowledge that one period cannot be hermetically sealed off from those the precede and follow it. The historian's problem remains that of balancing continuity and change.

A series of new scholarly disciplines for the study of human society were devised in the nineteenth century and greatly refined in the twentieth—archaeology, sociology, political science, anthropology, comparative religious studies, art history, and others. These approaches raised fundamental questions about the nature of life in the past that older historical methods, focused nearly exclusively on statebuilding, politics, and diplomatic history, could not readily answer. Historians themselves began to reshape their idea of their culture's past and to face the question of whether the Middle Ages or any early period of history might be a legitimate cultural past for the modern world. Might interest in it not be mere antiquarianism? Or nostalgic and escapist Romanticism? Because the modern (now, sometimes, postmodern) world in which we all live was really born much later, what did the remote past matter? Does the contemporary world have a past at all?

Historians and students of history still mark time, but their reasons for marking change. Periodization requires that we identify what changed and what did not, how and where change took place, and how the consequences of that change worked themselves out in human society. We ask sharper and more precise questions partly because we have increased and, we hope, more precisely defined the methods and subjects of historical research and partly because our own cultural experience has compelled us to.

Any distant historical period, however defined and labeled, must be seen as both very unfamiliar to us and at the same time accessible to our understanding. The unsettling combination of alienness and intelligibility is often difficult to negotiate, but it is also one of the most rewarding results of historical study. On the one hand, some historians are tempted to make the earliest history of Europe look less alien—largely by focusing on its economic and institutional features and emphasizing continuity rather than discontinuity. On the other, some historians are fascinated by many features of that alienness, arguing that these alone give legitimate voice to those people and groups about whom the sources are silent, those without power, the marginalized peoples of early Europe, or, as one historian identified them, "the people without history." The shift from the domination of narrow and often anachronistic political history to the history of societies more broadly defined has been one of the most important changes in historical inquiry since the middle of the twentieth century. Historians have begun to inquire about cultural history and the mentalities of both rulers and the people they ruled, about devotional life and lived religion instead of purely normative institutional religion, and about gender and the principle of inclusion rather than that of exclusion.

---

[1] The best introduction to the sources and methods of historical research, with a particular focus on early Europe, is now Martha Howell and Walter Prevenier, *From Reliable Sources: An Introduction to Historical Methods* (Ithaca, NY and London: Cornell University Press, 2001). Le Goff's essay, "For an Extended Middle Ages," is in Jacques Le Goff, *The Medieval Imagination,* trans. Arthur Goldhammer (Chicago and London: University of Chicago Press, 1988), 18–23.

By asking these new questions, historians have produced a richer history of medieval Europe, one that can no longer be turned quite so readily to the instrumental service of fashionable ideas, ideologies, confessional wrangling, simplistic reductionism, or the instrumental reinforcement of various kinds of power. In this role, the study of history has become a kind of intellectual martial art, and if we do not insist that it can and must be used legitimately, others will assertively misuse it, usually to our own confusion.

Human beings live in time, but, as novelists and physicists continually remind us, we perceive our own passage through time in subjective and distorted ways. Perhaps there is no other way of living in time. The study of history is an intellectual tool that permits us to observe others living through time in the past without the distortion that prevented them, and often prevents us, from perceiving what living in time means. And it makes our lives more interesting.

The distinguished English historian Alexander Murray once observed that, "Without any vision at all, history books are waste paper." Vision is not always expected or wanted in survey texts, but there is no reason to write them without some vision. The vision behind this book is simply that the Middle Ages is not the middle of anything, but that the period constitutes the first part of the history of a distinctive European and Atlantic civilization, and that even a survey text, when it bridges the gap between specialized research and popular understanding, may be a useful intellectual exercise.

Acknowledgments

The history of this edition began with an earlier book, *Europe: The World of the Middle Ages,* published by Prentice Hall in 1977. Many readers of that book—and of the first three editions of this book (1983, 1989, and 1997)—passed suggestions on to me that I have incorporated wherever feasible. I remain grateful to the readers invited by Prentice Hall: Donna L. Boutelle, California State University, Long Branch; John B. Freed, Illinois State University; and Larissa Taylor, Colby College; and to those inspired to comment by a sense of collegiality or pure reader's interest. For this edition I am especially grateful to Adel Allouche, Noah Caplan, Eugene N. Genovese, Robert Giegengack, John Pollack, Kris Rabberman, Larry Silver, Ivan Stoner, and Matt Smith. I am also grateful to the great library systems and librarians of the University of Pennsylvania and Yale University. Michael T. Ryan generously read the entire manuscript and made many helpful suggestions. Particular thanks go to Barbara DeVries, who edited a very large manuscript into a relatively sensible book.

Edward Peters

Prologue

Europa: Myth and Landscape

Between the ninth and the sixth centuries before the Common Era, Greek mariners and geographers identified first two, and then three continents, or, as they called them, "parts of the earth." They drew a line along the long waterway running from the Aegean Sea through the Dardanelles, the Sea of Marmara, the Bosporus, the Black Sea, and up the valley of the river Don. They called the land lying to the north and west of this divide *Europa,* and the land to the south and east, *Asia.* Later, they named a third great landmass, which they called *Libya* and the Romans later renamed *Africa.* Both Asia and Libya/Africa originally acquired their names by applying the names of small local districts in Asia Minor and North Africa to the larger land masses that we still call by those names today—Asia from a small area in what is now northwest Turkey, and Libya and Africa from small regions on the North African coast just to the west of Egypt. For reasons that no one knows, however (even later Greek and Latin historians and geographers wondered about it), Europe was the only continent until the Americas that was named after a human being, in its case a young woman from southwestern Asia who appeared very briefly, but dramatically, in early Greek mythology.

According to the myth, Europa was the daughter of Agenor, king of Tyre in Phoenicia on the eastern coast of the Mediterranean Sea in what is now Lebanon. Zeus, the ruler of the gods, saw her picking flowers and desired her. He disguised himself as a white bull and slowly won her confidence. He then mounted her on his back and swam off with her to the island of Crete, where, changed back into human form, he had three sons with her. Her brother Cadmus, who set out searching for her, was said to have

1

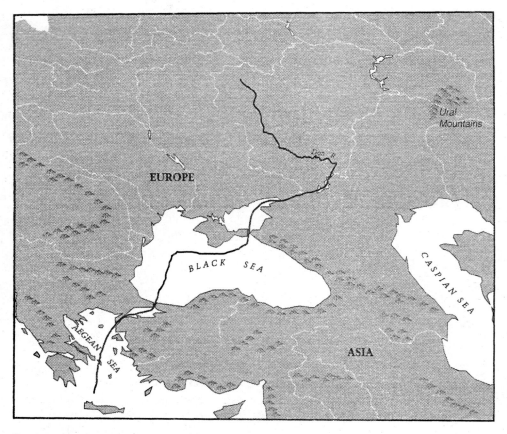

The original Greek division between Europe and Asia.

brought writing to Greece—perhaps, like Europa herself, representing a memory of the early cultural influences of Egypt and Phoenicia on later Minoans and mainland Greeks. One of Europa's sons by Zeus, Minos, became the legendary founder of the Minoan civilization on Crete.

Crete remained Crete, but Europa gave her name first to the Greek mainland and then to the entire land mass about whose extent travelers, merchants, and sailors began to learn in greater detail as they moved north and west, up the Rhone Valley, across the Alpine passes, or through the Straits of Gibraltar and up the Atlantic coast to Britain. Geographers and historians had to keep up with this new information, redefining the continent of Europe, and filling in their knowledge of the details of its interior until they decided—wrongly—that it was about the same size as Africa and about half the size of Asia. No geographer realized how far south Africa extended, nor how far east Asia extended. They acknowledged that Europe was separated from Asia by the great waterway and especially the River Don, and from Africa by the Straits of Gibraltar and the Mediterranean Sea. Africa and Asia were thought to be divided by the Isthmus of Suez or, figuratively, the Nile River. Geographers thought that the great River Ocean encircled all three continents.

The geographers' world remained small for a long time. "We live around a sea," said Socrates, "like frogs around a pond." The part of their world that was most important for the earliest sailors and geographers, and the area that they knew best, was the continents' meeting point in their own little world around the Mediterranean Sea.

The common designation *Europa* survived in the terminology of Greek and Roman geographers and ethnographers—originally for want or need of any better term, and eventually out of sheer habit. The story of Europa also survived in the works of mythographers and poets—since the story was familiar and appealing and could be re-told and pictorially represented in many different versions. But in Mediterranean antiquity the term never designated anything more than a young woman in an interesting old story and a convenient name to place in descriptive geographical texts and on maps.

The myth, like the geographical name, endured. One of the latest representations of Europa and the bull in antiquity was discovered in 1949 in a floor mosaic (a picture or design made of thousands of pieces of colored stone or glass, a medium that was immensely popular in antiquity) in the dining room of a Roman villa in Lullingstone, Kent, England, that dates from the fourth century of the Common Era, made for a cultivated local patron out of local materials by local craftsmen, near the end of Mediterranean antiquity and at the opposite end of the continent from that on which Europa first arrived.

But there was also some uncertainty about the name. As the Roman-Mediterranean world was slowly Christianized between the first and the fifth centuries of the Common Era, there emerged a kind of moral geography and history that attempted to coordinate biblical antiquity with that of the classical world. According to Genesis, after the Flood the whole world was peopled by the three sons of Noah: Ham, Shem, and Japheth (Genesis 9:1). Early Christian writers, preserving the Hellenistic tripartite division of the world, attributed the peopling of Africa to Ham, that of Asia ("to the Indian Ocean") to Shem, and that of Europa (from the river Tanaïs, the Don, to Gadeïra, Cadiz) to Noah's favorite son, Japheth, who was said to have possessed the middle part of Asia and all of Europa to the Britannic Ocean. The meeting point of the three parts could be seen to have a religious significance in the location of Jerusalem, which seemed to be the exact center of the known world. Geographers made schematic maps called T-O maps, showing the Don and the Nile, the rivers separating Europe, Asia, and Africa lined up as the crossbar of the letter T, with the Mediterranean Sea as the riser. Jerusalem was situated at the exact intersection of these, dividing the world into Asia, Africa, and Europa.

What seemed most important to Christian thinkers, however, was less the geographical and literary term Europa than the common Christianity, that seemed the most significant and useful term to describe a large, multicultural collection of peoples. And so, while geographers and poets could continue to use the term Europa, political theorists and theologians coined the alternative term *Christianitas*—"Christendom"—which served for many centuries as the cultural predecessor of the modern term "Europe."

Europa, especially its northern and western edges, had become better known by 600 C.E., and Europa it remained. But after the sixth century, Europa could be regarded

Isidorian T-O map, fifteenth-century version.

from two very different perspectives—one from the old Mediterranean world looking north, and one from the northwestern European islands and coasts looking east and south.

Three hundred years after the Lullingstone mosaic floor was laid, the old Mediterranean world and much of the rest of Africa, Asia, and Europe were beginning to be divided into the vast spheres of influence of the civilizations of Islam, the Byzantine Empire of East Rome, and Latin Christendom (below, Chapters 3–5); scholars on the far edges of northwest Europe were writing in Greek and Latin, and also in the vernacular languages that were taking shape among its old and new inhabitants. Late in the ninth century of the Common Era, an Irish monk recorded the death of the scholar Dubtach mac Maél Tuile, who was "the most learned of the Latins in all Europe." Ethnically, of course, Dubtach was not a Latin but an Irishman; Ireland had never formed part of the Roman Empire, and Ireland and the other nearby isles had long been spoken of as lying outside Europe at the very edges of the earth. The Irish monk wrote in Latin, not quite the Latin of Cicero, but a very adequate Latin. He also wrote a distinctive script using letter-forms that had been unknown in the Roman world, and he wrote on a surface, parchment—the treated skin of a sheep, goat, or cow—that had begun to replace the Roman papyrus. If he wrote by artificial light, his page would be illuminated by a wax candle, no longer the olive oil lamps of the Mediterranean. If he had an ivory inkhorn, it would be made of walrus ivory rather than elephant ivory. Both his language and his writing technologies are interesting examples of both continuity and change. By the ninth century, the old mythic name Europa still proved useful for describing the entirely new Europe that had come into existence since the fourth century but also still sensed its continuity with the remote past. This book deals with the early history of that new Europe.

* * *

Fortunately for writers of myths and early geographers and ethnographers, geology precedes mythology. Ancient mountain ranges extended across northern Europe from Scotland to the eastern Baltic region, and scattered low mountain chains existed in what is now Ireland, Spain, France, Belgium, and Germany, but these old and once high ranges had grown lower over long periods of time and wear. The youngest and highest mountain range in Europe lies to the south of these. Beginning around fifty-five million years ago, subduction of the African Plate under the southern margin of Europe crumpled up a thick section of moraine sediment, creating the range of the Alps. It also decorated the southern flank of the Alps with a belt of explosive volcanoes, still active today. To the south of the Alps it produced an immense trench in which the ground surface was pulled far below sea level. The floor of that trench remained a desert basin in which a great thickness of salt accumulated in recurring rainy episodes until five million years ago, when the bedrock sill at Gibraltar was breached, allowing a colossal flood from the Atlantic to fill the former trench, separating Europe and Africa by an inland sea, which the Greeks and Romans first called the Great Sea, and only much later the Mediterranean.

As sea levels rose in response to the melting of the ice sheets that covered northern Europe and Asia and the northern half of North America twenty thousand years ago, the Atlantic washed slowly over the northwestern coast of Europe, creating the English Channel and the Danish Sund, filling the Baltic depression with salt water and connecting it to the North Sea—and turning the old northwestern coast of Europe into the islands of Ireland and Britain, as well as the Scandinavian Peninsula. About 10,000 years ago, as melting glaciers released the vast amounts of water they had locked in for thousands of years, the level of the eastern Mediterranean rose and flooded catastrophically into the Black Sea, turning it from a freshwater lake into the northeastern arm of the Mediterranean waterway. This event displaced early agricultural societies in the region and dispersed them throughout eastern Europe. As the great Finno-Scandinavian Ice Sheet retreated to higher elevations and to the far north of Europe, it left behind a disorganized mass of glacial sediment, marked at its southern limit by the topographic feature of the terminal moraine. Another part of the Ice Sheet was the Laurentide Glacier, whose withdrawal created Long Island, Nantucket, Cape Cod, and the rest of the New England and eastern Canadian coasts and the Great Lakes at about the same time. These changes gave Europe the longest indented coastline in the world (about the length of the Equator) and a number of geographically distinctive internal regions. As a result of these enormous physical changes, Greek and Roman (and later Christian) geographers and mythographers could talk about Asia, Africa, and Europa as continents because by then they actually looked more or less like distinctive and separate large bodies of land.

These geological changes not only defined Europe, but they also gave it a number of distinctive physical features. Geographically speaking, Europe is not a continent at all, but a peninsula on the western edge of the great Eurasian landmass which lies on an east-west axis generally within the latitudes of 40° and 60° North, contains the longest continuous land distance on earth, and offers only slight ecological and geographic barriers to movement across it. South of the latitude 40° North, lies the Eurasian Arid Zone—or Saharasia—an area of low annual rainfall that marks the area of contact of pastoral, nomadic societies and sedentary, agricultural societies, the two great divisions of prehistoric and early historical societies.

Europe proper covers an area of 3.6 million square miles and is about one-quarter the size of Asia, one-third that of Africa, and about one-half that of each of the Americas. Europe's prehistory and much of its early history is therefore a function of greater Eurasian history, not only in terms of the movement of peoples, but also in terms of the age-old conflict between nomadic-pastoral and settled-agricultural societies and the long-range transfer of domesticated plants and animals, technologies, commodities, and ideas. The most important of the great migration routes that can be detected in prehistory and have been recorded in history are those from western Mongolia to eastern Europe through the Ural-Caspian Gate between the Caspian Sea and the southern tip of the Ural mountains and from the Ukraine southward toward the Mediterranean, around or over the Balkans and the Wallachian Plain and Bulgarian Plateau to the north and south of the lower Danube Valley. A second great set of transportation routes was the network of East-West roads linking a chain of oasis-cities along caravan routes that ran from Kai-feng and Ch'ang-an in China to Baghdad and the Crimea, through modern Afghanistan, Uzbekistan, Turkmenistan, and Iran, with spurs that ran to India and the Persian Gulf. Recent archaeological discoveries indicate that as early as 2300 B.C.E., a complex civilization grew up along the central part of these routes well to the west of China. By the late second century B.C.E. at the latest, these routes, only in the late nineteenth century collectively called "the Silk Road," carried a vast trans-Asian trading network across the Arid Zone in relays of caravans, linking both ends of Eurasia in relationships of exchange and cultural influence.

Europe's main geographical internal regions and their physical features are: the belt of mountains to the north of the Mediterranean (the Cantabrians, the Pyrenees, the Alps, and the Balkans), the great plain that rises gradually from west to east for 2400 miles from the Atlantic and North Sea coasts to the Ural Mountains, the large peninsulas of Iberia, Scandinavia, Italy, and the Balkans, and Europe's Atlantic and Mediterranean coasts, with their thousands of peninsulas and islands, from Crete itself to the Hebrides, Orkneys, Shetlands, Faroes, and Iceland.

Punctuating its long coastline, Europe is drained by a remarkable and regularly-spaced series of long and navigable rivers, making no part of it very distant from water transport and therefore offering effective internal communications over manageable

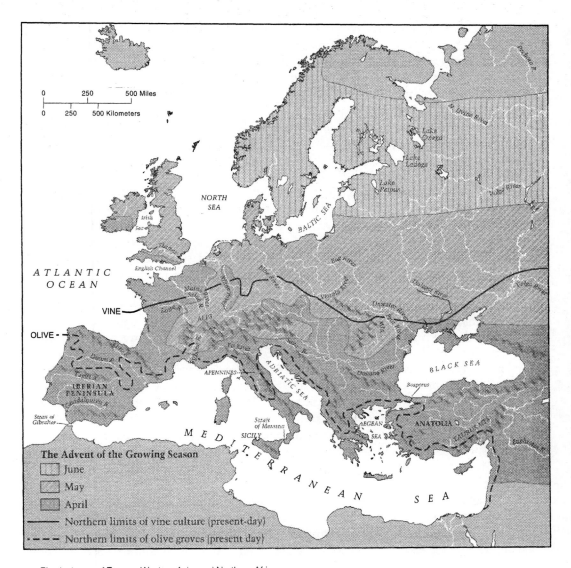

Physical map of Europe, Western Asia, and Northern Africa.

distances. These navigable rivers occur at nearly regular spatial intervals from what is modern southwestern France to the eastern Baltic region: the Garonne, Loire, Seine, Meuse/Maas, Thames, Rhine, Weser, Elbe, Oder, and Vistula. Although most of Europe's great rivers flow into the Atlantic, the North Sea, and the Baltic, a few flow into the Mediterranean—the Ebro, Rhone, Po, and Tiber. Two systems—the Rhine-Danube and the Dvina-Dniester—flow from near the North Sea and the Baltic Sea to the Black Sea. The maritime and riverine character of western and central Europe gives easy access to the sea, and, for seafaring people ranging from Bronze Age migrants to Vikings to later seagoing merchants, access to inland areas. North of the Mediterranean coast, the west-east chain of mountains never proved impassable—its passes and river valleys allowed for human movement across the mountains almost from the first recorded continuous presence of humans. The coastline, riverine, and climatic character of Europe is not duplicated anywhere else in the world.

The Gulf Stream (called by Europeans the North Atlantic Drift) carries warm water from the Caribbean to bathe the west coast of Europe, so that even the winter water temperatures off the North Cape of Norway are no lower than those off Boston, Massachusetts (35° F). Prevailing westerly winds, warmed by the Gulf Stream, blow steadily across the European Plain. Those winds maintain a moderate climate and provide regular year-round rainfall. The hot, dry summers and cold, wet winters of the Mediterranean basin give way as one moves north to less sharply contrasting climatic zones. Mediterranean seasonal rainfall did not leach out the mineral content of topsoil, requiring only light ploughing, but producing only a single crop per year. The Mediterranean warm summers favored such crops as the vine and olive, whose roots dug deep. Northern European soils had been created by the glacial moraine, with light soil on many uplands, soils of rich loam on lower elevations, and heavy clay soils which needed draining and turning to restore minerals to the topsoil. The regular year-round rainfall of northern Europe eventually permitted the production of two crops per year on suitable ground. Mediterranean forests are sparse, while those of northern Europe are thick, consisting mostly of hardwoods—oak, beech, and elm. Although much of the economic and social history of early Europe is the history of agricultural and pastoral development, the presence and economic usefulness of the great, thick forests was long a constant in European history and imagination virtually until the modern age. For a long time, the combined economies of *ager* and *saltus*—field and forest— played an essential part in the overall economy of preindustrial Europe, until the need to clear land for agriculture and an expanding population began to reduce the forests' extent.

Of all the physical features of Europe, the last to be adapted to the wills and needs of humans was the ocean. Atlantic civilization on the transoceanic scale did not begin to displace Mediterranean civilization until after the sixteenth century, of course, but well before 1500, Europeans were exploiting the eastern and north-central Atlantic. The Atlantic and the North Sea, far more stormy and capricious bodies of water than the Mediterranean, Black, and Baltic seas, offered Europeans many advantages that they were quick to adopt. The North and Baltic seas (like the Grand Banks off Newfoundland) teemed with fish, and the eastern Atlantic is not so difficult to sail that maritime cultures as early as the Bronze Age could not exploit the ocean itself as a means of transportation. When Europeans began to cross the Atlantic, they had two easy corridors. In the tenth century, the warmer north Atlantic and its reduced drift ice allowed Scandinavian sailors to reach and colonize Iceland and Greenland and to touch North America. In the late fifteenth century, Columbus and his successors had only to sail south to catch the easterly trade winds that blow steadily across the Atlantic.

Submitted to modern scientific analysis, the oldest physical features of Europe tell us much about these aspects of the past. The study of glacier movements, pollen analysis, dendrochronology (the reconstruction of past climatic history by the study of tree-rings, which indicate annual rainfall and tree growth), Carbon-14 dating, and recombinant and mitochondrial DNA have contributed to our knowledge of the changing physical profile of early Europe and early Europeans. So too have aerial and satellite photography, the modern earth sciences, and the archaeo-sciences—archaeology itself, of course, but also archaeobotany, archaeozoology, and archaeometeorology.

This last term reminds us that climate, too, has a history. From about 100 B.C.E. to 400 C.E. the general climate of Europe became warmer and drier than it had been earlier. From 400 C.E. to around 1250, the Atlantic Ocean was relatively free of great storms and drift ice. Writers in the Mediterranean area noted that it was possible to cultivate the vine and the olive tree much farther north and at higher elevations than is possible today. A mean summer temperature several degrees higher than at present reduced the dangers of May frosts and September freezes, two of the elements that determine the length and productivity of the agricultural year. Between 1200 and 1400, however, mean temperatures dropped several degrees, and rainfall increased considerably and erratically. The Northern hemisphere as a whole appears to have become colder, and records indicate erratic seasons of drought and flood, abundance and famine. During the crucial period of the opening of transalpine Europe to agricultural development, however, the climate was more temperate than it had been earlier and would be later.

The European ecosphere allows for a large variety of cultivable grains (initially wheat in the varieties of emmer and spelt, and barley from the Near East as well as rye and oats), domesticated large-bodied animals (cattle, horses, sheep, goats, and pigs), productive woodlands, high mountain pastures close to fertile valleys, accessible passes even across the highest mountain ranges, long navigable rivers, accessible mineral deposits, and the riches of the seas. From the first human settlements during the periods between successive Ice Ages (perhaps as early as 500,000 years ago) to the more consistent settlement of Europe after 7000 B.C.E., Europe proved to be a rich, diversified, and hospitable habitat for humans.

Until the invention of the hot-air balloon and the work of the Wright brothers and David Bushnell, all human activity took place on or under land and on or under water. The geophysical location and environment of Europe afforded certain material circumstances to its inhabitants, but they did not determine the uses that people made of them, nor did they relentlessly determine that people in Europe (or any other people anywhere else) became the kind of people they became. The physical environment is passive. To affect historical change, human technologies and cultures must encounter the environment. Connecting the broad and slowly changing features of environmental history with particular cultural characteristics, human actions, and events is a complex affair, and there is no more automatic or simple correlation between the two than there is for alleged (and imaginary) biological differences. There are environmental circumstances, but there is no environmental determinism.

This book deals with several groups of peoples in a particular physical location and type of environment and with some of the other peoples they encountered over a period of more than a thousand years. For the original Europa to become the Europe of history, the large landmass north of the Mediterranean had to be settled and cleared and establish regular contact with its other parts—Mediterranean societies and cultures, and later, the greater Eurasian and African worlds beyond. The process began with the expansion of the Roman Empire, first into the wider Mediterranean world, and then north and west into transalpine Europe.

1

The Beginning and End
of the Roman Peace

THE EMPIRE OF ROME FROM REPUBLIC TO PRINCIPATE

The empire assembled and ruled by Rome was the first political structure in the ancient world that centered on the whole of the Mediterranean basin and provincialized the Mediterranean hinterlands in North Africa, Europe, and southwest Asia. It differed greatly from the earlier, more eastern-oriented empires of Egypt and Persia and from the predominantly Greek but equally eastern-oriented empire of Alexander the Great (356–323 B.C.E.) and the kingdoms of his successors. Rome ringed the Mediterranean basin by building upon earlier colonizing efforts in the central and western Mediterranean that had begun before 500 B.C.E., when Greek city-states had sent out emigrants to establish new cities around the Black Sea and the northern Mediterranean coasts. The south shore of the Mediterranean was colonized from Phoenicia in southwest Asia. The most important colonial city in Phoenician North Africa was Carthage, from which colonists settled westward as far as the Iberian Peninsula. Because the Mediterranean is a sea with many islands and similar coastal areas but extremely diverse hinterlands, its shores had proved relatively easy for Greek and Phoenician migrants to colonize westward from Greece and Libya to the Iberian Peninsula, and travel between seaports was always easier, cheaper, and faster than travel overland. The Roman Empire brought under a single political and administrative unity both the culturally homogenized ruling classes of the diverse Mediterranean city-states and many of the inhabitants of their hinterlands.

The colonization movement of Greeks and Phoenicians not only ringed the Mediterranean with cities of a similar appearance and culture and crossed it with charted and familiar sea lanes, but it also resulted in the rise of the former Phoenician colony, Carthage, to the role of prosperous seaborne power. Greeks and Carthaginians also encountered and influenced other Mediterranean societies and their neighbors: Celtic-speaking peoples in northern Italy, southern Gaul, and Iberia; Etruscans, Latins, and Samnites in Italy; Egyptians, Numidians, Abyssinians, and Berbers in North Africa.

This territorial widening of the Greek cultural horizon also affected Greek ideas of human society and the world. For centuries Greek thinkers had conceived of the individual city-state, the *polis,* as the ideal form of human social and cultural life. But after the conquests of Alexander and the colonization movement westward, Greek writers began to speak more frequently of the *oikoumene* (the inhabited world), the familiar world of human cities, the inhabitants of which communicated with each other and shared many values, as the natural community for humans. With the spread of Greek colonies there also went Greek art and architecture, the Greek language, Greek literary, philosophical, and religious culture and the idea of a common world defined by the new Greek cultural standards. That world comprised the entire Mediterranean and Black Sea areas and those of their hinterlands in which the ruling orders of society could enjoy both an urban and rural style of life. Its symbolic capital was the large multiethnic city of Alexandria in Egypt. The Mediterranean basin was socially and culturally homogeneous in its ruling strata well before it became politically and militarily unified by Rome.

The elite culture of the Mediterranean world was based largely upon that of the Greek world after the death of Alexander the Great, and it is therefore usually called Hellenistic (the Greek word for Greece is *Hellas*). In spite of the imperial ambitions of a number of Alexander's successors during the late fourth and third centuries B.C.E., political power remained largely regional until the rise of Rome to political prominence in the Mediterranean after the third century B.C.E.

The small agricultural city-state of Rome was located in the west-central coastal region of the Italian peninsula—that is, on the western fringe of the Hellenistic world. Rome's legendary foundation date was 753 B.C.E., although remains of farms and villages on Rome's hills date from earlier than 1000 B.C.E. Rome was situated originally between two powerful cultures, both of which influenced it greatly. In the north, the civilization of the Etruscans long overshadowed and influenced that of Rome. In southern Italy and Sicily, colonial Greek-founded city-states (modern Naples, Syracuse, and Agrigento) brought Rome into contact with Hellenistic culture and mainland Greece. The hilly location of Rome was easily defended, and Rome was the first place upstream from the sea where the Tiber River could be easily forded or bridged. At the mouth of the Tiber was the convenient seaport of Ostia, and a number of peninsular trade routes passed through Roman territory.

Around 700 B.C.E., Romans began to drain and pave the lowlands between the hills, creating the public center that became the forum. They built temples and began to use stone and tile in their buildings. They developed a written Latin language. After throwing off the rule of kings, a title they never used for their rulers again, in the late sixth century B.C.E., Rome established an aristocratic republic, divided into two social orders—the patricians (a group of families possessing extensive political and religious privileges and offices) and the lower order of plebeians. Rome was ruled by two annually elected officials, called consuls, and administered by members of its leading families holding a variety of public offices, as well as by the tribune of the people, the spokesman and protector of the lower orders of Roman society. Roman military strength, based on an army of tough, well-disciplined peasant soldiers led by patrician officers, expanded Roman power in central Italy. Although Rome was besieged by Celtic forces from beyond the Alps in 387 B.C.E., the attack was repulsed, and by the third century B.C.E., Rome's military strength brought it into political contact and military rivalry with the Hellenistic and Carthaginian worlds.

In 265 B.C.E., Rome fought the first of three Punic wars to defeat Carthage, which finally fell in 146 B.C.E. The defeat of Carthage brought the Romans into North Africa and Iberia. At the same time, Rome was invited to participate on one side or another of local Greek wars, and by 146 B.C.E., Rome had also come to influence virtually all of Greece. Rome's involvement in Greece brought it into the affairs of a number of Hellenistic kingdoms in Asia Minor, where it created a province in 129 B.C.E. With the conquest of Egypt in 30 B.C.E., the Roman Republic had assembled an informal and disorganized Mediterranean-wide empire.

Because the Roman empire was put together piecemeal over several centuries, its "frontiers" were at first the frontiers of the territories that Rome had conquered. But with the advent of a single power in all these territories, frontiers had to be reconsidered. When the Romans conquered Iberia, for example, they recognized the importance of southern Gaul as a land route between Iberia and Italy. After defeating a confederation of Celtic Gauls in 125 B.C.E., Romans founded their first city in Gaul, *Aquae Sextiae* (modern Aix-en-Provence—Provence deriving from the Latin word *provincia,* "province") in 123. Between 123 and 118 B.C.E., southern Gaul became a Roman province, *Gallia Narbonensis,* and three characteristic Roman institutions were introduced: another city (*Narbo Martius,* modern Narbonne), the Latin language and colonists, and a road, the *Via Domitia,* connecting Roman Italy with Roman Iberia through what was rapidly becoming Roman Gaul. Other Roman towns in southern Gaul, *Arelate* (modern Arles) and the Roman absorption of Greek-founded *Massilia* (modern Marseilles), followed.

The settling of southern Gaul brought Romans into direct land-contact with the world of Celtic Gaul and northern Italy. Thus, Roman colonists and soldiers had to secure the new province in the north, and the needs of defense required the frontier to move northwards to strategically defensible ground, creating opportunities for daring political adventurers to gain reputations by waging military campaigns in new territory. Throughout most of its history, Rome had no grand strategy of defensive frontiers, but rather took advantage of the many occasions for military and colonial expansion whenever these presented themselves.

The Roman colonization of Gaul was not exclusively a military operation. Romans assimilated many Celtic Gauls into Roman provincial society, creating a distinctive Gallo-Roman culture that survived even the end of the Roman empire itself. The problem of the northern frontier of Gaul also offered considerable opportunities to ambitious Roman politicians and generals. One of these, Julius Caesar (100–44 B.C.E.), made his political reputation by a series of military campaigns between 58 and 51 B.C.E. that he recorded in his *Gallic Wars,* written around 50 B.C.E., a stunning essay in military tactics, political propaganda, and shrewd field ethnography. Caesar's adventurous conquest of northern Gaul and his brief expedition to Britain in 54 B.C.E., laid the foundation for the later Roman conquest of Britain, which Rome accomplished by 43 C.E. Eastward across the Channel, the Roman European frontier was gradually stabilized along the valleys of the Rhine and Danube Rivers, running to the Black Sea.

Elsewhere in the Mediterranean world Rome encountered similar problems. The conquest of Asia Minor and the establishment of the province of Asia brought Rome into direct contact with the peoples around the Black Sea and with the Parthian Empire of Persia, which remained a formidable enemy until the seventh century. The conquest of Egypt drew Roman forces far up the Nile River. The conquest of Libya and Numidia brought them to the edge of the Sahara Desert.

Between the third century B.C.E. and the end of the first century C.E., the Romans had come to dominate two worlds: that of the Iron-Age Celts and others in northern Italy and transalpine Europe and that of the Hellenized world of the Mediterranean basin. Rome was able to deal successfully with both of these worlds, because Rome, itself having developed on the margins of the Hellenistic world, had never become completely Hellenized. Rome also offered a relatively easy process of Romanization, often including Roman citizenship itself, to its provincial subjects and emancipated slaves in Europe and extended its influence beyond the Rhine-Danube frontiers through trade, tribute, and later military recruiting. Not only was the Roman Empire quite different from earlier Mediterranean and Near Eastern empires, but it was also very different from all empires that followed.

THE INVENTION OF THE EMPEROR: FROM FIRST CITIZEN TO LORD OF THE WORLD

Rome also underwent considerable internal changes with its acquisition of an empire. Latin literature, for example, which had begun (except in legal literature, where Rome showed a remarkable intellectual independence and originality) as a pale and often awkward imitation of a rich Greek literature, quickly developed a distinctive identity and power of its own. Latin became the language of imperial administration, law, and literature as well as the common spoken language of the western parts of the empire. Greek, however, remained the language of philosophy and much literature throughout the Roman world, as well as the common spoken language in most of the eastern part of the empire. At the height of the empire, most of its ruling classes were bilingual in Greek and Latin.

The creation of the empire also transformed Rome's older social structure and republican form of government. In addition to the consuls, tribunes, and other public magistrates, Rome was also dominated by the senate, an advisory body of former holders of public office. By the first century B.C.E., Roman society was divided into two broad groups, the nobles of the senatorial aristocracy and the rest of the people. The old distinctions that had rigidly separated the patricians and plebeians had faded away, and new groups had arisen. The most important group below the nobility was the order of equestrians, originally those wealthy enough to serve in war on horseback, who could now enter the senatorial aristocracy by moving up through the ranks of military commands and public offices.

Following a series of political and military crises in the first century which demonstrated that the republic could not survive as it had long existed and continue to rule the empire, the Romans created a form of government resembling a monarchy but preserving many of the republican elements that Romans had come to venerate. Civil unrest in Rome and its provinces in the first century B.C.E. led to the emergence of a series of contending military strongmen who arrogated extraordinary powers to themselves in the name of saving the republic. The most successful of these was the patrician Julius Caesar, who courted popular favor by means of his considerable powers as an orator and eventually overcame his political rivals. But Caesar also raised the fear that he would make himself king, a word and idea that Romans particularly detested, since they identified the Republic as having been created by ending the rule of kings in 509 B.C.E. and disliked and feared the rule of the kings they saw around them in the Mediterranean and Near Eastern worlds. Kings might have been suitable for foreigners and barbarians, but not for Romans.

An example of Caesar's political strategy was his creative use of his role as *pontifex maximus,* a priestly office that empowered its holder to adjust the public calendar. Revision of the calendar was periodically necessary because by the mid first century B.C.E., the inaccurate lunar calendar of early Rome had gotten ahead of the solar year by more than four months. With the advice of astronomers, Caesar added a single fifteen-month year of 445 days to 46 B.C.E., added two extra months to the old ten-month year, and for all following years added ten days to seven formerly 29-day months and included an extra day in February every four years, making the calendar relatively consistent with the solar year, a reform that lasted in Europe until the appearance of the Gregorian Calendar in 1582. Caesar was also said to have commissioned four geographers to create a map of the known world. Maps and descriptions of the world in the service of political power became commonplace in the Roman world and in later Europe.

Caesar was assassinated in 44 B.C.E. (the month *Quinctilis* was renamed *Julius* in that year to commemorate him—our July), and the Roman world was plunged into a series of wars among rival groups of nobles. The victor in these wars was Caesar's adopted son and heir, Gaius Julius Caesar Octavianus (63 B.C.E.–14 C.E.), who raised a private army from among Caesar's soldiers and paid them out of his own pocket. Octavianus also effected the most significant constitutional revolution in the history of the ancient world.

Having defeated and eliminated his political rivals and their supporters, Octavianus had a freer hand in Roman politics than had any of his predecessors. He shrewdly understood the willingness of war- and disorder-weary Romans to accept the rulership of a single man as long as such a man did not call himself a king. His titles reflected his genius for compromise. Octavian first took the title *princeps,* or "first citizen," and in 27 B.C.E., the Senate conferred upon him the title *Augustus,* a name suggesting his responsibility for the empire's growth, prosperity, and internal peace. The period of Roman imperial history from Augustus to the late third century is generally termed the Principate.

Augustan propaganda emphasized the restoration of republican liberty and traditional moral values. In 19/18 B.C.E., Augustus' triumphal arch erected in the forum identified Augustus with Romulus, one of the legendary founders of the city. In 14 B.C.E., Augustus divided the city into fourteen regions. Between 13 and 9 B.C.E., the Senate commissioned a monument in the same area of the Campus Martius which it called the Altar of Augustan Peace—the *Ara Pacis*—depicting Augustus and his family as upright and virtuous Roman republican citizens. Augustus' mausoleum was built in the same area. In 8 B.C.E., the Senate renamed the month *Sextilis* after Augustus (still commemorated in our own August). In 2 B.C.E., it designated him *pater patriae*—"father of the fatherland."

Augustus' insistence on observing traditional Roman moral values extended to his spending vast sums of his immense personal wealth on the building and restoration of temples and Roman public buildings, the repair of aqueducts and other public works, and the establishment of a small imperial civil service. The Forum of Augustus, dedicated in 2 B.C.E., created a new center of public space in Rome, including temples, colonnades, statues of Roman heroes, and elegantly decorated space for public activities. He temporarily stabilized the frontiers and enacted substantial land reforms for the benefit of the soldiers. Augustus also observed that rulers from places as distant as India, the River Don, and Persia—the edges of the known world—sought his (and Rome's) friendship.

While preserving the external forms of republican rule, and therefore acknowledging a number of constitutional norms that defined and ostensibly limited even his own power, Augustus assumed personally and for life a number of public offices, as well as the direct command of several key provinces, especially Egypt, and the armies. The confiscated wealth of his enemies made him the richest individual in the empire, and he used that wealth strategically. He established twenty-eight colonies for soldiers in Italy and over eighty in the provinces. He also imposed new taxes on the wealthy.

The title emperor (from the Latin *imperator,* the holder of *imperium,* the power of a magistrate to carry out the legal, financial, and military functions of his office) was joined to Augustus' own name and assumed by his successors, who were thus his personal heirs wielding his accumulated honors, offices, immense personal wealth, and both civil and military authority. But the *imperium* of Augustus was also recognized as being greater than that of any other magistrate, held for a longer period, renewable, and eventually attributed to his person, not requiring Augustus to hold any public office at all. Augustus also instituted the Praetorian Guard, the ruler's personal bodyguard which was modeled on the military bodyguard of a Roman general, and he stationed the guard in Rome, around himself. Augustan propaganda set the tone and at least the theoretical limits of later imperial styles of rule. But the problem of succession loomed large: Who but a virtual Augustus could direct the empire in the form that Augustus had created?

Augustus' reign also produced artistic and literary patronage on a new and much greater scale. The poet Vergil (70–19 B.C.E.), a Celt from northern Italy, in his epic poem *The Aeneid* produced a literary work that many Romans saw as a lightly veiled tribute to Augustus that rivaled the great epic poems of Homer. In Book VI of *The Aeneid,* Anchises,

Aeneas' father, defined precisely the role that Romans saw for themselves in the world:

> *Let others fashion from bronze more lifelike, breathing images—*
> *For so they shall—and evoke living faces from marble;*
> *Let others excel as orators, and others track with their instruments*
> *The planets circling in heaven and predict when stars will appear.*
> *You, Romans, never forget that government is your medium!*
> *Be this your art—to practice men in the habit of peace,*
> *To spare the humble and strike down the proud.*

Vergil's poem also predicted even further conquests for Augustus:

> *Caesar Augustus, son of a god . . . his empire shall expand*
> *Past Garamantes and Indians to a land beyond the zodiac*
> *And the sun's yearly path, where Atlas the sky-bearer pivots*
> *The wheeling heavens, embossed with fiery stars, on his shoulder.*
> *Even now the Caspian realm, the Crimean country,*
> *Tremble at oracles of the gods predicting his advent.*

Early in the poem Jupiter stated that he had given the Romans "empire without end." Rome, said one writer, will last as long as mankind endures. And the later poet Ovid (43 B.C.E.–17 C.E.) claimed that "Roman space encompasses both the city and the world."

By claiming to have preserved the republican forms of government and ancient moral values, Augustus and his successors asserted at least the decent fiction of the identity of the emperor and the senatorial order, whose composition Augustus had greatly widened, and some of whose members sat on his council. These marks of respect sustained senatorial support for most emperors of the first two centuries, except for those emperors who autocratically rejected it. Outside Rome itself, Augustus and his successors were regarded as world-kings in the manner of Alexander the Great and other earlier imperial rulers, and by the second century C.E. as gods. Since the emperors governed the empire chiefly with the advantage of Rome and Roman citizens in mind, Rome and central Italy were the original beneficiaries of the Mediterranean conquests; wealth poured into Italy. Eventually the other provinces benefited also. But the flood of new wealth also destabilized a Roman society that had already experienced profound political disturbances.

In the hinterlands and the remoter provinces, Romanization and Hellenization touched local elites, although a provincial form of Romanization developed and influenced both provincials and peoples living beyond the frontiers. Classical towns and country estates (villas) appeared first in Gaul, North Africa, and Syria, later in Britain, the Rhineland, and the valley of the Danube. Leading families in provincial towns, the populations of even the largest of which rarely exceeded 10,000 people, imitated those in the great cities, privately donating the expensive essentials of Mediterranean urban civilization—great amphitheaters and the games held in them, aqueducts, bridges, public baths, statues, gates, monuments, temples, paved streets, and market-places. They preserved the imperial cult and modeled their local public calendars on that of Rome. They willingly held public office at their own considerable expense, forming the *curialis* order that virtually ran the empire outside of Rome itself. Wherever possible, they built

The Rape of Europa, a first-century fresco discovered in Pompeii. (The Art Archive/Archaeological Museum Naples)

Roman-style houses of stone with open interior courtyards and tile roofs, decorated on the interior with wall-paintings and mosaics illustrating classical themes, including Europa. Augustus himself claimed to have found Rome a city of brick and transformed it into a city of marble. He had reshaped the city of around one million people, crowded into palaces and tenement-blocks, requiring an enormous food and water supply, and increasingly accustomed to privately provided public spectacles. Could ambitious provincials do any less for their own towns?

But the cities, especially in the western parts of the empire, were centers of administration rather than production, consumers of revenue and private largesse rather than producers of income. Except for the occasional early waves of wealth that came from new imperial conquests and imperial generosity, the empire depended on private initiative in both local public works and governmental administration. The number of imperial administrators was very small, and most of the empire in the first two centuries of the Common Era was administered by a combination of local effort and loose imperial supervision.

For the ruling elites, however, the empire offered a privileged and secure existence, homogeneous throughout a larger and larger world. The historian Peter Brown has characterized this aspect of imperial life:

> *For a short time an officer's mess modelled on an Italian country villa faced the Grampians in Scotland. A checkerboard town, with amphitheater, library, and statues of classical philosophers, looked out over the Hodna range, at Timgad, in what are now the bleak southern territories of Algeria. At Dura-Europos, on the Euphrates, a garrison-town observed the same calendar of public festivals as at Rome. . . . One of the main problems of the period from 200 to 700 was how to maintain, through a vast empire, a style of life and a culture based originally on a slender coastline studded with classical city-states.*[1]

So successful did Rome's internal and external affairs appear in the first and second centuries C.E., and so little were the frontiers troubled, that this period has often been termed that of the *Pax Romana*—the Roman Peace. In the midst of imperial aggrandizement, Cicero (106–43 B.C.E.), who appreciated the spread of Roman power and did much to popularize Greek philosophy in the context of Roman public service, remarked that under Roman rule, *orbis terrarum est civitas*—"the whole world has been turned into a single [Roman] city-state." To Cicero and others, the *orbis terrarum,* literally "the circle of the lands," was the Mediterranean and its shores and hinterlands. Poets, historians, and philosophers praised Rome's rule and took pride in it. They called the entire Mediterranean simply *Mare nostrum*—"*our* sea," just as they called the Mediterranean *oikoumene,* "*our* world."

ROMAN SOCIETY: FREE AND SLAVE

In the course of creating an empire, Roman society and the Roman economy underwent rapid and profound change. Rome had begun as a community of prosperous peasant farmers in which the male heads of households held absolute power, including that of life and death, over members of their own households. The original meaning of the Latin word *familia* included not only the domestic household proper, but also all dependents, including slaves. In law, the domestic power of the father was termed *patriapotestas*. The Roman economy was originally pastoral and agricultural—producing the essential Mediterranean diet crops of grain, olive oil, and grapes and the northern Mediterranean meat staples of beef cattle and sheep. Even urban patricians retained deep rural roots,

---

[1]Peter Brown, *The World of Late Antiquity* (1971; reprint, New York: W.W. Norton 1978), 11.

and the peasant armies of early Rome were recruited from among the holders of small farms. Roman aristocrats long affected this image of themselves as frugal, morally upright, paternalistic heads of agricultural households, and they preserved much of this self-image in Roman law.

Roman citizens of high rank were responsible for the legal affairs of both their households and socially inferior clients, and they took an early interest in the intricacies of the law. They also considered legal activity, along with the holding of public office, estate management, and military service to be the only public activities suitable to their rank and status. For them, any other kind of work, Cicero said, was vulgar—only for the *vulgus,* the lowest ranks of society—although slaves and freedmen could engage in manufacturing and trade on behalf of their masters. Therefore Roman law developed early and precociously, and much Roman social history is reflected in the law. *Patriapotestas* regulated much of Roman domestic life, initially allowing no independence—and hence no right to hold political office—to women and retained even adult married children in dependence on their father until he died. Marriage was regulated by male heads of households, and fathers and husbands originally possessed virtually complete legal responsibility for and power over the women, children, and dependents of their households.

Tutelage of this kind was originally continued even for adult women who had neither husband nor father. Cicero's daughter Tullia (79–45 B.C.E.), for example, was engaged at twelve, married at sixteen, and was a widow by twenty-two, still under her father's power. The women idealized by Roman writers were those like Lucretia in the sixth century B.C.E., who, in order to preserve her and her family's honor, committed suicide after having been raped, or Cornelia in the third century B.C.E., who, as a widow, refused a marriage proposal from the king of Egypt in order to manage her estates and raise her twelve children, two of whom, the Gracchi, became influential social reformers on behalf of the plebeian order. Several religious cults were open only to women, the best known of which is the college of the Vestal Virgins, and occasionally women were recognized as possessing prophetic powers. To the Romans, masculine identity entailed a primarily active and dominant role in social activities, including sexual relationships. Feminine identity was understood to be passive, domestically confined and family-identified. As one Roman (male) argued, opposing a law restricting the personal adornment of Roman women,

> *No offices, no priesthoods, no triumphs, no decorations, no gifts, no spoils of war can come to them; elegance of appearance, adornment, apparel—these are women's badges of honor.*

Such adornment and apparel identified Roman women according to family, social rank, and protected, passive social role, just as the width of purple stripes on the toga indicated male social status. Roman men also sexually used socially inferior concubines, prostitutes, and female slaves. Throughout Roman history, concubinage was recognized, although the social status of the concubine was lower than that of the man, and concubines never received the formal respect paid to Roman married women.

At the very lowest level of Roman society and Mediterranean society generally, stood the slave. The slave was the chattel property, a possession, of the master, whose rights over the life and labor of the slave were total. In earliest Roman history, most slavery was small-scale and domestic—the work of a few household servants and farm workers. As Roman power and wealth increased, larger numbers of slaves came from those captured in war from the ranks of defeated armies or captured territories. Other sources of slave supply were kidnapping and piracy, from which slaves could be sent to slave markets for resale to a final buyer. Slavery became more important in the Roman economy when wealthy Romans acquired more and more rural property as free peasants left it for the armies or the cities. The new owners required larger numbers of slaves to replace the free labor that had been lost. As long as the usual sources of slaves continued to provide them, slavery of this kind continued and increased. Domestic slavery continued to exist alongside the newer large-scale rural slavery. Around the turn of the Common Era it is estimated that there were around two million slaves in Italy, while the free population stood at around four million—that is, slaves made up nearly one-third of the population of the peninsula. During the first century B.C.E., several large-scale slave revolts occurred in Italy, and Roman slave law became considerably harsher as a result. Fear of slave revolts was persistent in later Roman society. In the early centuries of the empire, however, the usual sources of slaves began to dry up, and the price of slaves increased, since slaves had to be found and transported farther and farther from Italy. Slavery began to decline for other reasons as well, but rarely for moral reasons. It became more economical to employ inexpensive, depressed free labor on many rural estates, and although aggregate slavery declined for a long time, slavery itself—and the legal condition of the slave—survived into the early modern world.

Domestic and rural slaves were identical at law, but their lives were often quite different, as were the lives of slaves who were permitted to conduct business on behalf of their masters and serve them as independent business agents, accountants, secretaries, and managers. In this capacity, the life of some slaves was materially better off than those of many free Roman citizens. Some slaves were used in occupations that even the lowest ranks of free Romans refused—mining, work on the docks, and gladiatorial combat. Others might rise to high household positions.

Regardless of the identity or social condition of the slave before enslavement, once someone became a slave, he or she was regarded in Roman law and culture as having no honor, no kin, and unable to enter military service or marry. As in the rest of the Mediterranean world, most Roman slavery was domestic; slaves were considered part of the household, the *familia,* ruled by the power of the father, *patriapotestas,* although they were considered in very different terms from the children of the household. Slaves could be sold, given away, or freed, and if freed, they could become Roman citizens. Slaves who had been freed might hold slaves of their own. But no Roman citizen could be enslaved, except for conviction for certain crimes. Children born to slave mothers, even if sired by the mother's owner, became slaves themselves.

Because there was no "racial" difference between masters and slaves (as there later was in the case of African slavery in North America), and because slaves had usually been free human beings before enslavement, Roman justifications of slave status were derived from their attitudes toward human nature in general. Some humans (especially barbarians), thinkers argued, were natural slaves, deficient in reason and therefore suited only to be under the control of others. This was the rationale of the philosopher Aristotle. Other thinkers argued that slavery was a purely man-made institution, although it was also legal. Philosophers, jurists, and religious thinkers also drew important analogies from slave status: even a free man might become a slave to his uncontrollable passions; the body was sometimes considered as enslaved to the soul. Whether natural or man-made, slavery was built into both the mind and the laws of the Mediterranean world. There was never an argument for its abolition, and when slavery did decline, it did so as a function of other changing material conditions in the world that supported and accepted it.

In the course of the second and first centuries B.C.E. and the first several centuries C.E., the early Roman social and economic world was transformed. The immense influx of wealth permitted private financial resources, rather than traditional rank and status, to play a larger part in Roman economy and society and increased opportunities for upward social mobility. By the third century C.E., the structure of Roman society was recognized in law as consisting of four orders: the senatorial aristocracy, the order of *honestiores* (city officials, jurists, military veterans, teachers, physicians, and civil servants), the order of *humiliores* (merchants, traders, farmers, and small craftsmen), and slaves. The *honestiores* constituted a kind of professional middle stratum. They were the salaried managers of society who, when they could afford to, bought land and aimed at achieving senatorial rank.

The great estates of Italy tended to be used more for the raising of sheep and cattle, while the production of olive oil and grain was increasingly transferred to the vast fields of Sicily and North Africa. The greatly extended lines of communication between the new grain-producing regions and Italy became a major problem in later centuries, when interruption of the great grain fleets raised the threat of starvation in the vast cities of the empire. For the empire now began to provide food for much of its urban population. Free bread, and cheap wine and oil came to be regarded as a prerogative of the inhabitants of the cities of Italy. Public provision of food (and entertainment—as the phrase "bread and circuses" indicates) became one more responsibility of urban elites, just as did many public services and the maintenance and adornment of cities.

Although highly skilled craftsmen and artisans worked in Italy, most manufacturing was provincially localized and made for local consumption. In the European provinces, much production was done for the armies. Military camps, forts, and the services they required and provided often shaped and gave a distinctive economic and cultural stamp to towns and camps near the frontiers. For army posts, *castra*, also represented an important force in the process of Romanization of the provinces. A military camp with 6000 soldiers also had one or more civilian towns, *vici*, close by, thus imposing a significant population presence even close to the frontiers. They also offered a lower-level Roman culture, along with rough, practical literacy in Latin, and their needs were met by tanneries, brickyards, metalworks, textile-weaving centers, as well as potters and glassmakers. Retired veterans often settled near their old camps. In many cases, these settlements were larger than those of the native population in whose midst they were set. To produce leather for military needs and beef for the soldiers, vast herds of cattle had to be developed—the tents for a single Roman legion required 54,000 oxhides. To produce enough food, new fields of grain had to be cleared and cultivated. It is no accident that the first example of Latin written outside the Roman Empire is found in a bill of sale for a cow written north of the Rhine around 30 C.E., recording a transaction between a Roman merchant and a non-Roman cattle-breeder. Besides the country estates and provincial cities, extensive, utilitarian Romanization also occurred at this level.

The economic transformation also entailed a social transformation. The status of women, initially aristocratic women, gradually improved in both legal and social terms. Because marriages continued to be arranged by families throughout the imperial period (since marriages were arranged for political, social, or economic reasons) the institution itself was particularly vulnerable to changes in the political, social, or economic climate. These aspects of marriage turned out to work to the advantage of women. Gradually, in law, women were able to control their own property, separate property they possessed before marriage from the property of their husbands, and to acquire substantial rights in property, including their dowries, after the end of a marriage. Divorce and the woman's retention of her own property became more readily available for women as well.

A number of Augustus' successors conspicuously lacked his immense political skills and temporarily weakened the imperial office. Some of them alienated the senatorial aristocracy and permitted the administration of the empire to slip into the hands of inept favorites, the Praetorian Guard, the imperial civil servants, or the armies.

TRAJAN'S COLUMN AND HADRIAN'S TRAVELS

From 64 to 96 C.E., rival contenders for the imperial office raised armies and competed among themselves for the imperial title, until the succession of the elderly senator Nerva (96–98) inaugurated a revival of senatorial influence and a series of able and diplomatic emperors, the Flavians and Antonines, who ruled through most of the second century. It is not surprising that the Age of the Antonines (98–180) has long been regarded by historians as the golden age of the Roman world—when Rome seemed to have resolved the social, economic, and political crises attendant on the creation of the empire. So at least it seemed to the wealthy, privileged, and powerful orders of the empire itself—and to many later historians who looked at only one level of society. The world seemed to them to be ruled by conscientious, considerate, intellectually respectable, talented rulers who adopted promising protégés and trained them in imperial duties. Nerva's imperial successors accomplished internal pacification and a temporary stabilization of the troubled frontiers.

Trajan (98–117), an Iberian and Nerva's immediate successor, extended the frontiers to their farthest limits. By Trajan's reign, the Roman empire extended 1600 miles from north to south, from northern Britain to the edge of the Sahara Desert, and 2800 miles from west to east, from the Atlantic coasts of Spain and Morocco to the Caucasus Mountains and the valleys of the Tigris and Euphrates. The empire held around fifty million inhabitants, unevenly distributed, with the heaviest concentrations in the eastern regions, and with nearly a million of them in the city of Rome itself. In area, the empire was about the present size of the United States. Its population was about the size of Europe around the year 1300, and about one-fifth that of the United States today.

The accidental frontiers had been shaped into a generally well-defined border. Trajan and his advisers had realized the importance of the Pannonian plain north of the Danube as a migration route into Europe, and they secured the Danube frontier and its provinces with eleven legions of troops, nearly double the number that protected Britain and the Rhine valley combined, even though the troops stationed in Britain alone constituted a significant fifteen percent of the whole Roman army. Trajan's reign also saw Roman trading contacts extended from south Arabia and Upper Egypt to India and Ceylon (present day Sri Lanka) across the Indian Ocean. Within the frontiers, the Roman provinces had attained nearly equal footing with the capital of the empire, and by the early second century C.E., the imperial administration had achieved a certain degree of uniformity throughout the empire, but without destroying the vigorous local cultures and traditions.

The Roman view of the empire and its military triumphs is illustrated in the great column that Trajan dedicated in the year 113 to commemorate his victory over the Dacians and the triumph of Rome. In a spiral frieze 3 feet high and 670 feet long, climbing a 100-foot-high column, Trajan's artists skillfully illustrated the military victory of the conquering emperor. Under Trajan too, the internal peace of the empire was restored. The reign of Trajan's successor, Hadrian, is an ideal point from which to survey both the extent of the empire in the middle of the second century and some of its most important neighbors.

Hadrian (r. 117–138) was also an Iberian. By the end of the first century C.E., membership in the senatorial aristocracy had widened to include the elites of the older provinces. Just as Italy no longer exclusively provided senators, the reigns of Trajan and Hadrian proved that it no longer exclusively provided emperors. One of the chief results of Augustus' legacy was the slow process of transforming Rome from being the head of a group of subordinate territories to the center of an association of provinces, the oldest of which—Iberia, Gaul, and North Africa—considered themselves to be as ancient and respectable as Rome itself. By Trajan's reign, 40% of the senatorial order was made up of provincials, and by the end of the second century, the Senate represented the upper classes of the entire empire. One reason for the success of the Antonine emperors was that they, like the Senate, were cosmopolitans who moved easily throughout the empire. They were traditionally educated and spoke Greek as readily as they did Latin. More and more they thought of the empire as a whole and not simply as an appurtenance of the city of Rome.

And they did not rule exclusively from Rome. Trajan was a widely traveled aristocratic general; Hadrian was a widely traveled scholar and administrator, the first emperor to wear (and have himself depicted as wearing) the characteristic beard of the philosopher. Both emperors probably knew the empire from personal experience and inclination better than any of their predecessors. Hadrian spent nearly twelve years of his twenty-one year reign moving about the empire, accompanied by a retinue of officials, military advisers, architects, engineers, surveyors, and cultural and artistic advisers. Part of Hadrian's purpose was practical: he wanted to know first-hand how his administrators worked, how efficient or oppressive they were, how strong the defenses were, what his subjects desired and needed, and to make immediate changes on the spot where they

From the Frieze on Trajan's Column. Dacian warriors have retreated to the stone stronghold, showering projectiles on Roman troops, who are being protected by other Roman troops using their interlocking rectangular shields as a turtle-shell formation. (German Institute of Archaeology, Rome, Italy)

were needed. On the other hand, Hadrian also had an insatiable curiosity about the varieties of life and thought and religious beliefs and practices in the empire. When he traveled, he inquired about local customs, religious beliefs, and local history. The Christian apologist Tertullian (below, Chapter 2) sneeringly called him, a "seeker-out of trifling curiosities." He was bilingual in Greek and Latin, well read, and had excellent

Hadrian's Wall. Looking westward across northern Britain, the course and fabric of the wall suggest the achievement of the emperor-engineer after whom it is named. (British Tourist Authority)

artistic taste, as his villa at Tivoli and his tomb in Rome, now the Castel Sant' Angelo and the gateway to Vatican City across the Tiber, illustrate.

Hadrian's travels informed him about everything an emperor could learn, but they informed him most about administration and defense. His legal reforms gave the empire a uniform body of law. Much of his travel resulted in his pulling back and tightening frontiers. Perhaps his best-known legacy is Hadrian's Wall, which the emperor ordered built during a visit to Britain in 122. Hadrian and his architects personally surveyed the seventy-three mile distance across the width of northern Britain and designed the long stone walls linking sixteen forts and many smaller guard posts and watchtowers. The wall was not intended, however, to serve as an absolute barrier against the northern peoples. Its purpose was to divide the hostile northerners and regulate their coming and going as well as to put on an impressive display of Roman might on the far northern edge of the empire. From northwest Britain, the Roman frontier extended eastward along the Wall to the North Sea, and then, in a chain of frontier towns, military camps, roads, and forts, up the Rhine and down the Danube Rivers to the Black Sea. It then ran south to the Black Sea coast, down the valleys of the Tigris and Euphrates Rivers, and turned west across Syria and Palestine, Arabia, Egypt, Libya, and the rest of North Africa all the way to Morocco on the Atlantic coast.

Hadrian's visits to the provinces increased the sense of association among the provincial ruling classes, as did his commissioning of statues of the personified provinces for his museum, the Hadrianeum, at Rome, and his issue of coinage depicting the personification of twenty-five different provinces and cities. The provincial cities of London, Paris, Cologne, Trier, Mainz, Lyons, Mérida, Vienna, and Budapest decorated their provinces and carried Mediterranean patterns of urban life well into northern Europe.

GALLIA AND *GERMANIA*

The invasion of Rome by Celtic peoples from across the Alps in 387 B.C.E., other battles between Celts and Romans in Gaul in the late second century B.C.E., and Julius Caesar's ethnographic accounts in his *Gallic Wars* contributed to the general Roman understanding and classification of peoples who lived outside the empire and from time to time threatened the security of its provinces. Romans also borrowed earlier Greek ethnographic ideas about non-Greek peoples, whom the Greeks called *barbaroi* and the Romans *barbari,* usually translated as "barbarians." The Greeks thought that *barbaroi* were non-Greek speakers whose languages consisted of incomprehensible sounds, people who therefore could not be Hellenized, whose passions could not be governed by reason, who were incapable of living under law and were therefore natural slaves, and were therefore unchanging—part of the order of nature rather than the order of humanity.

Romans referred to peoples living beyond the frontier as *externae gentes*—"the peoples outside." But Romans also used different terms to describe different categories of these peoples. For instance, a people might be a *populus*—a word the Romans also used of themselves, designating a group very similar to Romans, having both an origin and a history, practicing agriculture, recognizing private property, and living in fortified cities. Or a people might be termed a *gens,* not yet culturally developed or politically organized; or a *natio,* or as we would say "a horde," a body of individuals suposedly related by descent from common ancestors, but lacking the technical and intellectual culture or socio-political organization of the *gens.* From the Roman point of view, a *populus* or a *gens* could be Romanized, but a *natio* could not. Romans used these classifications as much in political as in ethnographic senses.

Roman literary sources concerning the peoples of northern and eastern Europe are not very informative before the first century B.C.E., but archaeological research has greatly illuminated the societies and cultures of the *externae gentes* to the north of the Roman provinces. Archaeology dates late prehistory according to the dominant type of metallic technology and identifies periods in terms of locations at which particularly important discoveries have been made. These consist of graves, building foundations, debris, pottery, personal ornaments, and hoards of weapons as well as buried treasure.

By the end of the Bronze Age (2300–750 B.C.E.), many peoples inhabited western and central Europe, making distinctive tools, weapons, and ornaments and capable of adapting these to new technologies and designs. They engaged in mining and trading for the copper and tin needed to make bronze. Their societies were stratified, and they practiced agriculture, clearing and reusing the lands they needed. Linguistically they were— like Greeks and Romans—speakers of languages in the Indo–European family. They possessed rulers and complex social organization, constructing sophisticated fortifications on hilltops, as well as large and small villages.

The Iron Age (750 B.C.E.–300 C.E.) is generally considered in two broad stages, the first identified with remains discovered at Hallstatt in the salt-producing region of the present province of Upper Austria (750–500 B.C.E.), and the second with remains discovered at La Tène, a town on the shores of Lake Neuchatel in Switzerland (450–100 B.C.E.) and usually described as "Celtic."

Celtic Europe is distinguished by distinctive and highly complex art forms, iron metallurgy, an increased interest in acquiring Mediterranean-produced art forms and objects, and the appearance of large and prosperous settlements that Julius Caesar, at least, did not hesitate to designate with the Latin words *oppidum* and *urbs,* "town" and "city." Most of these were walled enclosures of between 100 to 250 acres, although a few covered a thousand or more acres. Greek geographers and ethnographers were the first to record the characteristics of the Celts—and to name them: *Keltoi.* Such broad and general names—which have survived to the present, often misunderstood, actually conceal a rich variety of languages and cultures. Names like "Celts" and "Germans" are descriptive only from the Roman or Greek perspective and cannot be interpreted in anything resembling a modern ethnic or cultural sense.

Late Iron Age society was based upon the kin-group and the somewhat larger "tribe" (even the word "tribe," deriving as it does from an internal designation in Roman society, is technically misleading). As Roman soldiers, settlers, and provincial administrators encountered the Celts in northern Italy, Gaul, and the Danube valley, they readily assimilated many of them, and provincial Roman European culture was a mix of central Italian and Celtic peoples. Vergil (70–19 B.C.E.), the greatest Roman epic poet and author of the *Aeneid,* was a Celt from northern Italy.

Celtic societies lived from both agriculture (chiefly barley, wheat, and oats) and stock-raising, chiefly cattle and pigs. Much of Celtic agriculture was the domain of women, as was the weaving of fine textiles. Celtic men were reckoned wealthy in terms of the number of cattle they owned and prestigious according to their skill in battle.

Initially, there was little to distinguish Celts from Germans. The earliest Latin usage of the term *Germani* was applied early in the first century B.C.E., to designate rebellious slaves who had come from east of the Rhine. Later in the century, Julius Caesar's *Gallic Wars* emphasized great distinctions between Celts and Germans, but probably to support Caesar's policy of establishing the Rhine as Rome's ideal eastern frontier in Europe (and explaining why he had not conquered the Germanic peoples as he had conquered the Celtic Gauls) by designating the eastern territory and those living in it as an impenetrable wasteland whose inhabitants were too savage to provincialize—*nationes* rather than *gentes.* Caesar probably picked up the term *Germani* from the Gauls, who used it to designate outsiders from the east who had conquered local Gallic peoples (*Gallic Wars,* VI. 11–28). The establishment of a Roman frontier after Caesar probably helped make these distinctions somewhat more substantial—that is, Celts east of the Rhine probably became "Germanized," while Germans living west of the Rhine became "Celticized." But the difference was the Roman provincial frontier, Roman provincial culture, and Roman political ethnography, not inherent ethnic characteristics.

By the reign of Trajan, the central European frontier of the Roman empire had fluctuated considerably. Caesar had indeed established it at the Rhine, but under Augustus it was pushed to the Elbe, from which Roman forces were driven back in the military catastrophe of 9 C.E., when three Roman legions and auxiliary troops, around 20,000 men, were ambushed and killed by a group of peoples from a number of communities led by a former Roman ally named Arminius. Augustus, and later Trajan, determined to hold the frontier at the Rhine and to penetrate no further east.

Around the year of Trajan's accession, 98 C.E., the leading Roman historian, Tacitus, produced a description of the peoples east of the Rhine in his short book, the *Germania,* that is the most important and influential evidence concerning Germanic life and society. Tacitus' *Germania,* considerably influenced by Caesar's *Gallic Wars,* is a short, but complex text. Parts of it do indeed contain descriptions of Germanic society, derived from the interrogation of direct observers, but parts also appear to consist of political propaganda and moral criticism of contemporary Roman society by idealizing the Germanic peoples to the disadvantage of the Romans. Tacitus was not the only Roman writer who used the barbarians as devices to criticize contemporary Roman society. In his second satire, the poet Juvenal had bluntly pointed out that,

> *Though our armies have advanced*
> *To Ireland, though the Orkneys are ours, and northern Britain*
> *With its short, clear nights, these conquered tribes abhor*
> *The vices that flourish in their conquerors' capital.*

Tacitus himself had done something similar in his essay on Britain, the *Agricola,* which is a commemoration of his father-in-law's provincial governorship of the Roman province of *Britannia,* and a rich source for Celtic society, but marked by the same political and moral considerations as the *Germania.* It must be checked against modern archaeological literature in order to assess its reliability for the historian. This is but one of many cases in very early European history in which—even for the historian—archaeological evidence must take precedence over the texts that historians usually work with.

Tacitus begins by emphasizing the unknown character of the inhabitants of *Germania.* They are isolated from other peoples and live in a region of endless swamps and trackless forests (here Tacitus is echoing Caesar's geo-political point). Some Germans are distinguished from others by noble birth, and after distinguishing themselves in battle, they might be admitted to the council that rules the folk. "They choose their kings for their noble birth," says Tacitus, "and their war leaders for their bravery," suggesting two types of kingship, of which the second is a military type. There is substantial evidence that the second of these types was displacing the first and that a new kind of rulership was emerging among the Germanic peoples, probably as a result of the proximity of the Romans. Tacitus says that the Germans venerate and often seek advice from their women, who accompany them into battle and encourage them in combat. The council decides ordinary issues and disputes, but actions that involve the whole folk must be debated in an assembly of warriors. In battle, leaders fight alongside their retinues, sworn bodies of young fighters who have taken oaths of personal loyalty to their leaders (the Latin term for this association of young warriors with a leader is *comitatus,* and it has a long later history in European society). Organized routinely for war, the Germanic peoples of Tacitus were fierce and formidable, but Tacitus is contemptuous of their laziness and lack of discipline during peacetime.

Tacitus' description of the Germanic peoples nearest the Roman frontiers is generally accurate—their fierceness, lack of discipline, and repellent lands are emphasized only in order to dissuade any Romans who might want to absorb them and their lands into the empire; that is, on the Roman scale, to imply that they are merely *nationes,* hardly *gentes,* and certainly not *populi.* Tacitus emphasizes his point as he describes peoples even farther away than those across the frontier as progressively more exotic, fierce, and barbarous, ending his description with the most distant people, known only as the Fenni:

> *They care for nobody, man or god, and have gained the ultimate release: they have nothing to pray for. What comes after them is the stuff of fables—Hellusii and Oxiones with the faces and features of men, but the bodies and limbs of animals.*

Although Tacitus' text was lost to Europeans until the fifteenth century, other ethnographic sources for his last remarks about the sub- or non-human character of peoples distant from the frontier in other parts of the world remained common "knowledge" in the fabulous geography and anthropology of Europeans.

The peoples whom Tacitus describes were already undergoing momentous transformations during the reign of Hadrian, and Tacitus is no longer a reliable source for Germanic society after the early second century C.E. Anthropologists and archaeologists have shown that the Germanic, western Asiatic, and Iranian peoples along the edges of the Roman world were not complete strangers to that world. The very creation of Roman provincial society and Roman frontiers had influenced Germanic culture. Moreover, it was in the Romans' interest partially to assimilate some Germans as immigrant farmers and soldiers, and to destabilize border societies by tribute, bribery, political influence, and trade. The proximity of Germanic peoples had in turn influenced Roman provincial culture. In short, from the second century on, the "barbarians" were not nearly as barbaric and primitive as modern novels, films, and too-literal attention to Roman sources often suggest. From the second century on, barbarians served more frequently in Roman military forces and were admitted as agricultural immigrants to depopulated parts of the European provinces. In the third, fourth, and fifth centuries, the influence of Romans on barbarians and barbarians on Romans became reciprocal. During these centuries, events along the frontiers and their repercussions in both the central Roman empire and the vast world beyond the Roman frontiers—even beyond the Danube, the Rhine, and the plains of northern Gaul—created a distinctive and enduring European civilization. Patrick Geary has put it neatly:

> *The Germanic world was perhaps the greatest and most enduring creation of Roman political and military genius. That this offspring came in time to replace its creator should not obscure the fact that it owed its very existence to Roman initiative, to the patient efforts of centuries of Roman emperors, generals, soldiers, landlords, slave traders, and simple merchants to mold the (to Roman eyes) chaos of barbarian reality into forms of political, social and economic activity which they could understand and, perhaps, control.*[2]

The Mediterranean center of the Roman empire had entailed a Roman presence in Europe, at least, that extended far from the Mediterranean coast. Although Romans tried (and for more than three centuries handsomely succeeded) to live a Mediterranean lifestyle in Roman houses and on a Roman diet (the Roman frontier may also be correlated with

---

[2]Patrick J. Geary, *Before France and Germany: The Creation and Transformation of the Merovingian World* (New York and Oxford: Oxford University Press, 1988), vi.

those areas in which it was possible to produce locally or import easily the fundamental grain, olive oil, and wine on which Romans preferred to live) in much of what is now Britain, France, Belgium, Germany, Switzerland, Austria, Hungary, Romania, and Bulgaria, the proximity of "outside peoples" came more and more to transform both Roman and "barbarian" life. The crisis of the third century greatly accelerated the transformation.

THE THIRD-CENTURY CRISIS

Hadrian's two immediate successors, Antoninus Pius (138–161) and Marcus Aurelius (161–180), continued Hadrian's administrative practices and his personal intellectual and artistic culture. Marcus Aurelius has even been claimed as the last classical Greek philosopher. The system of emperors' adopting the best-qualified men as their successors appeared to have corrected the shortcomings of dynastic succession. But events in the reigns of Marcus Aurelius and his successors suggest that the golden world of Trajan and Hadrian was already coming to an end.

For the first time in nearly two centuries a Roman emperor, Marcus Aurelius, had to fight three major defensive wars—one against the Parthian empire of Persia (161–180), and two against new types of large confederations of barbarian armies on the Danube River (167–175, 177–180), the so-called first and second Marcommanic Wars. In addition, a great plague struck the empire in 166. Marcus Aurelius completed his book of philosophical reflections, the *Meditations,* in a military camp on the Danube and died near Vienna in 180. He had appointed his own son, Commodus (180–192) as his successor, and Commodus ended the Danube wars only by making an excessively generous treaty with the invaders. He also displayed utter indifference to both the provinces and the armies. His lenient treatment of the Marcomanni certainly stimulated other groups' interest in making war on Rome again, and his indifferent treatment of the army stimulated a revolt. Commodus' assassination in 192 triggered a period of civil wars.

In 193, Septimius Severus (193–211), a general from the city of Lepcis Magna in what is now Lybia, defeated the last of his rivals and assumed the imperial purple with the backing of his Danube army. Severus did not come from the provincial senatorial elite that had produced the Antonines, nor did he possess universal interests. His wife was Julia Domna, a wealthy Syrian woman whose intelligence and wide religious interests mark her as one of the earliest imperial consorts who were intellectually distinguished in their own right. In this respect, she resembles the wife of Trajan, Plotina, who was the patron of the philosopher Epictetus of Athens. Julia Domna, her sister, and later her niece, played considerable roles behind the throne during the period of the Severan dynasty.

Unlike Commodus, Septimius Severus strove to retain military support. He restored the frontier defenses (including Hadrian's Wall), increased the size of the standing army to around 400,000 men, increased the army's pay by half (in effect, tripling the cost of maintaining the armies), and threw the imperial civil service open to favorites from all corners of the empire, creating new networks of patronage, dependence, and loyalty that further eroded the traditional social fabric. His greatest concern was to secure the imperial succession within his own family, a redynasticizing of the imperial office. He further eroded the influence of the senatorial aristocracy and began the process of militarization and bureaucratization that quickly came to dominate both government and public finance. He died in 211 in a military camp near York, in northern Britain, where he had gone to repress a local rebellion.

But the frontiers remained threatened. Neither Severus' son, Caracalla (211–217), who gave universal citizenship to all inhabitants of the empire in 212, nor Alexander Severus (222–235) was able to guarantee the security of the frontiers. An army revolt led to Alexander's assassination in 235, and from that year on, the next twenty emperors were created or unmade by armies. Until the end of the third century, no emperor ascended the throne without the support of his army; when a stronger candidate, backed by a stronger army, challenged his rule, civil war decided the issue. After 235, neither the Senate nor an imperial dynasty—the traditional sources of imperial legitimacy—played a significant role in the rule of Rome. Not only did the army make the emperor, but the emperor was usually a former soldier himself, sometimes born in a remote province, who had been a peasant farmer before joining the legions. Working his way up through the ranks, where military talent, rather than social status, was rewarded by promotion, a peasant soldier might become a general, and a successful and popular general who made the right promises to his troops had a ready-made faction to support his imperial candidacy. Sometimes generals were virtually forced to revolt because their very success and popularity made them appear to be a threat to the current regime.

A successful imperial candidate had to reward his troops. To do this and maintain troop strength along the frontiers, he had to raise more and more money. But even raising money cost money; the emperors now had to spend more on administration as well. Armies, imperial bureaucracies, and heavier taxes came to characterize public life in the empire. With them came debased coinage, inflation, and heavier burdens on those citizens who were forced to pay the new taxes. The costs of government had risen steeply without a corresponding increase in general economic productivity. Moreover, the wealthiest ten percent of imperial society paid virtually no taxes, with the burden and the heaviest punishments for tax evasion thus falling on the *honestiores* and *humiliores*.

Having imposed harsh financial burdens, the emperors also had to be ruthless in enforcing them. Lacking the social and intellectual preparation of earlier emperors, the third-century rulers and their officials lacked the means of negotiation, compromise, and dispute settlement of their predecessors and imposed instead both the grim discipline of the army and the ceremonial style of the absolute ruler. From the mid third century, the figure of the emperor in documents, court ceremonials, coinage, and sculpture grew more autocratic, remote, godlike, forbidding, and capricious. Dressed or represented in military uniform or elaborate ceremonial regalia, the third- and fourth-century emperors looked and were far different from Augustus, Trajan, Hadrian, or Marcus Aurelius. Within a century, the core of the empire, the imperial office, had been drastically transformed.

Between 235 and 270, however, emperor after emperor went down to military defeat or assassination. Decius (249–251) was lost with his army fighting on the Danube. Valerian (255–260) was defeated in battle by the Persian Shah Shapur II (241–272) and

The Majesty of Emperors. This colossal head of Constantine the Great, nine times life size, was once part of a gigantic statue of the emperor that stood in the Basilica of Constantine in Rome. The size and imperial facial expression suggest the remoteness and majesty of late imperial portraiture. (Hirmer Fotoarchiv)

led in Shapur's triumphal procession to his capital at Ctesiphon, from which he never returned. The victory was commemmorated in large and beautifully executed relief sculptures, some of which still survive. From the reign of Shapur II until the destruction of the Persian empire in 626, Persia proved the most formidable and threatening of Rome's enemies. No Roman emperor could rule or deal with a crisis anywhere in the empire without first covering the Persian front. Between 260 and 268, most of Gaul was seized by an imperial pretender, Postumus, who claimed to have established a "Gallic Empire." From 267 to 270 the great caravan city of Palmyra, under its ruler Zenobia, declared the independence of a vast stretch of the Roman-Persian frontier, including Syria, most of the rest of the Levant, and northern Arabia. Even the inner provinces of the empire felt the impact of these disasters, and not only in a financial way. In 271, the emperor Aurelian built a new fortified wall around the city of Rome itself—a grim reminder of just how deeply the empire perceived itself to be threatened.

Even the empire's enemies had changed after the late second century. In 224, the decaying Parthian monarchy of Persia was overthrown by the vigorous dynasty of the Sasanids. The Sasanid kings created a powerful, highly centralized state with a common religion, that of Zoroastrianism, and developed strong armies—as Valerian discovered, much to his peril.

The Germanic invaders of the Rhine and Danube valleys had also changed. No longer were they the small, militarily adventurous tribes described by Caesar or the settled, named peoples of Tacitus. By the late second century, much larger confederations of peoples were assembled under warrior-kings with large bodies of personal retainers or groups of warlords acting in concert—composite peoples whose collective identity was that of their rulers and who absorbed other peoples as they campaigned. Well-armed and trained to a life of war either in or against the armies of Rome, the new peoples were geared to a predominantly military way of life. Marcus Aurelius had encountered the first of these, the Marcomanni, against whom he constructed new border camps and increased the size of the Danubian army. In the third and fourth centuries, the new confederations of the Alamanni (not a conventional ethnic designation, but a term meaning "all men") and the Franks (a term meaning the "fierce," and later, "the free" men) threatened the Rhine and Danube frontiers. Migrating eastern Germanic peoples, like the Goths, also broke through the Danube frontier in the third century. Not surprisingly, the Roman armies on the Danube, comprised largely of tough Balkan peasants, provided the core of Rome's defenses. Nor is it surprising that a series of talented generals from those armies succeeded each other on the imperial throne from 260 to 305, reformed the army, stabilized the frontiers, and saved the empire.

By 260, the Roman army had increased to around 600,000 men, a fifty-percent increase over even the army of Septimius Severus. Barbarians as well as provincials were permitted to serve in the armies, even rising to field rank. Command of the army was placed in the hands of professional soldiers; after 260, members of the senatorial order were excluded from military command. As the old Roman legion disappeared, the army was redesigned. The legions, like the light border defenses of Augustus and Trajan, had worked well when Rome held the initiative but proved ineffective against new enemies. The emperor Gallienus (260–268) established a new, mobile strike force that did not depend on detachments from the frontier armies and could be dispatched quickly to any point at the frontier where it was needed. The emperor himself began to rule from Milan, in northern Italy, where he could command the northern armies more efficiently. The frontier troops now became the *limitanei*, permanently stationed on the frontier and intended to delay an invasion until the new troops, the *comitatenses*, made up of heavy cavalry, specially trained infantry, and archers, could come up from their bases deeper inside the empire. The *comitatenses* were elite troops; they could be deployed rapidly, and at their best were certainly the equals, and usually the superiors, of enemy forces.

DIOCLETIAN AND CONSTANTINE:
REFORM AND RECOVERY

The military, economic, and administrative crisis of the third century was reversed by the reform of the imperial government by the emperor Diocletian (285–305) and his successor Constantine (312–337). Although these reforms produced another century or more of general stability for the empire, in the long run they proved immensely expensive and eventually unaffordable. During the fourth and early fifth centuries, the eastern part of the empire, with its many prosperous cities, strong commercial economy, productive peasantry, and larger population survived in better condition than the western parts. The west felt the consequences of a smaller population, less productive and fewer cities, a less-developed economy, and more frequently attacked frontiers that were closer to the main centers of government. The western peasantry became more and more oppressed by powerful landowners who often served as their only safeguard against a demanding state bureaucracy, but who also increased the peasants' dependence upon themselves.

The 270s and 280s produced a series of military victories that for a time pacified the frontiers and allowed the emperors to turn to the pressing need for internal reforms in finance and governmental organization. In the hands of Diocletian and Constantine, the empire was transformed.

On the macro level Diocletian created a second *Augustus,* a partner-emperor for himself, and announced the division of the empire into two halves, the *pars orientalis,* or eastern half, and the *pars occidentalis,* or western half. One Augustus was to rule in each for twenty years and then retire. Each *pars* was divided into two parts, in one of which the Augustus was the direct ruler and in the other, the holder of a new office, that of *Caesar,* the assistant and prospective successor of the Augustus. In theory, when an Augustus retired, his Caesar would replace him as Augustus and appoint another Caesar under him. This system, called the *Tetrarchy,* or rule of four—two *Augusti* and two *Caesares*—proposed to solve the perennial problems of Roman imperial rule: the question of predictable succession and the needs of administration and defense.

Within each of the new parts of the empire Diocletian also reduced the size of many provinces to manageable proportions and created new provinces, until there were more than one hundred. The provinces were gathered into groups of twelve, each of which constituted a *diocese,* ruled by a *vicar.* Each vicar reported to one of four *praetorian prefects,* who were appointed directly by the emperors. There were not two empires: there was now a single empire with two equal rulers, although the senior Augustus was considered the more authoritative. The emperors were by now also autocrats, addressed by the title *Dominus,* "Lord," instead of the old Augustan term, *Princeps.* Their word was law, and it was issued regularly in rescripts and edicts. Closeness to the emperors was a guarantee of good fortune and privileged positions in imperial government. There also emerged a new senatorial nobility, consisting of the upper stratum of imperial civil and military servants, open to careerists and heritable within their families.

The new nobility lacked the local roots and local identity of the older senatorial order, however, and saw no need to continue the private largesse and patronage that had

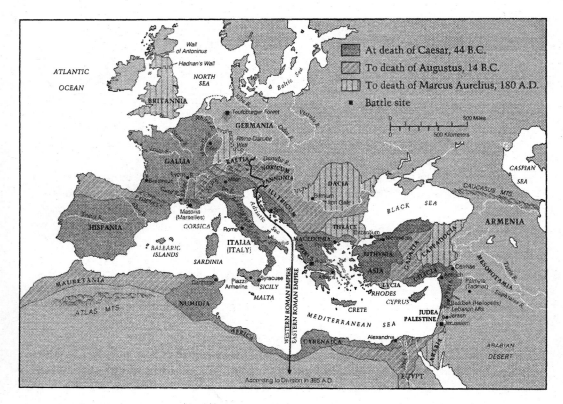

Roman territorial holdings under the Empire.

long characterized that order. Private largesse began to dry up, and public finance had to take its place, placing a great burden on the *honestiores,* particularly those in the *curiae* of cities, for they were responsible for local affairs, including the collection and distribution of taxes. Tax revenues were supposed to be divided into three parts—with one-third being spent locally, one-third going to the central authorities, and one-third to the army. The curial order was liable for the complete tax assessment of its district, and its ideal was to pay as little of it as they could and shift the rest of the burden onto the shoulders of others, while retaining the control of tax revenues expended locally. When demands for taxes became too high, or when there was no more money to be raised locally, the curial order had to pay the remainder out of its own pocket, a burden that inspired many to leave the cities entirely and retire to country estates. But the new order of Diocletian also made this escape difficult, since all positions in the empire were frozen by the emperors, and the sons of the curial order were required to become *curiales* in their turn.

So it was with the sons of everyone else. Diocletian attempted to freeze the structure of society by legislating that all sons had to follow in their fathers' work, whether members of the curial order or laborers, especially in key trades and professions, and on the land. Diocletian's edict thus contributed to further depressing the status of the tenant-farmer, the *colonus,* by tying him to the land, thus creating yet another degree of unfreedom to accompany slavery at the lowest level of Roman imperial society. Diocletian also attempted to set strict price controls on all goods and services, or at least establish the price which government officials and the army would pay. He stabilized the coinage, establishing the relative value of silver to gold at 10/1 and setting the price of a pound of gold at 72 *solidi,* or 72,000 *denarii,* a value that survived for centuries. In terms of buying power, a heavy cloak cost two-thirds of a *solidus,* a man's food for a year three *solidi.* In terms of modern costs, a *solidus* was worth around $190. By the time Diocletian retired in 305, the Roman empire had been subjected to the most complete overhaul of governmental and social institutions the ancient world had ever seen.

In 305, Diocletian retired to his villa at Split (in modern Croatia), having arranged, or so he thought, the appointment of the next four rulers. His arrangement, however, foundered on the equally perennial problem of dynasticism. Maxentius and Constantine, the sons of the first two Caesars, had been passed over by Diocletian, and upon the emperor's retirement and the not entirely voluntary retirement of his co-Augustus, the armies of Maxentius and Constantine revolted and proclaimed their leaders emperors. Constantine eliminated Maxentius in a battle at the Milvian bridge over the Tiber north of Rome in 312, and his other rivals and a large part of his immediate family over the next twenty years. Although Diocletian's plans for the tidy imperial succession failed at their first try, the rest of his reforms survived remarkably well.

For Constantine also continued the administrative redivision of the empire. Each *pars* was subdivided into prefectures. The four imperial prefectures were those of the East and Illyricum (for the *pars orientalis*) and those of the Gauls (Britain, Gaul, and Spain) and Italy (Italy and Africa) for the *pars occidentalis.* Rome and Constantine's new city of Constantinople each had its own urban prefect. Constantine continued and completed Diocletian's restructuring of Roman society.

Constantine also transformed the army high command, creating a master of infantry (*magister peditum*) and a master of cavalry (*magister equitum*). These new ranks commanded a greatly transformed Roman army. For the army, too, had become a hereditary occupation. Moreover, recruits native to the provinces in which they served also entered military service, strengthening the local identity of locally stationed troops, marrying local women, and dominating much of the local economy and governmental offices. When Caracalla granted Roman citizenship to all free subjects of the empire in 212 (not as an example of imperial affection, but as a device to increase the pool of those obliged to pay the new inheritance tax imposed on Roman citizens), citizenship itself enhanced the status of these newly localized and militarized provincial societies.

Increasing numbers of barbarians had long been recruited into the Roman army, originally as *laeti*—small groups permitted to settle in underpopulated provinces on the condition that they and their children agree to serve in the army. In the late third and fourth centuries, however, larger groups of barbarians—termed *foederati*—were allowed to settle inside the empire, also in return for military service. The practice of admitting barbarians into the European provinces for military purposes further contributed to the transformation of provincial culture. The increasing sense of localism in the provinces and the increasing numbers of barbarians living closely with Roman provincials created new provincial societies, with barbarians and Roman provincials sharing land, tax revenues, and responsibility for defense. The tendency to homogenize Roman provincial society in this way in areas close to the frontier paralleled the growth of the autonomy of great aristocratic private landholders in the older areas of the provinces. The aristocracy's interests, too, became more localized, and senatorial aristocrats were increasingly willing, when their own interests seemed to demand it, to support imperial pretenders during the periodic revolts of the third and fourth centuries, to serve barbarian rulers when it seemed in their best interests to do so, and to assume high office in the Christian church. The increasing cooperation between provincial aristocrats and barbarian rulers became a marked feature of Gallo-Roman society from the third century on.

The most important social consequence of these changes was the instrumentalization of all social orders in order to preserve the apparatus of government and defense. Although these changes pressed most heavily upon the poorest orders of society, they did not leave the aristocracy untouched. Its ranks were increased by the "new aristocrats" in imperial service, and its loyalties to the empire were severely challenged and ultimately weakened. As long as the peace of the frontiers and at least the outward form of the life of the inner empire could be maintained, however, the emperors and the aristocracy could avoid a direct conflict of interests. By the third quarter of the fourth century, however, new migrations and military conflicts subjected their relationship to a strain that it could not survive. In spite of the vast efforts of Diocletian and Constantine, the peace that was preserved through much of the late third and fourth centuries bore less and less resemblance to the *Pax Romana* that earlier writers had praised, and increasingly there was very little peace at all.

2

Religion and Society
in Late Antiquity

GODS OF THE HOUSE, COMMUNITIES, AND INDIVIDUALS

The oldest and most deeply respected deities of the Greco-Roman world were the domestic and local gods who protected the family, the house, the fields, woods, and groves. These "little gods" were the closest that the ancient world came to personal deities, although they paled beside the cult of the Olympian gods—powerful deities of the heroic age of Greece later adapted to Roman names and usage—whose worship survived and prospered until the end of the fourth century of the Common Era. Olympian gods, headed by Zeus, who became the Jupiter of the Romans, were very different from the lesser gods. They were eternal, but otherwise resembled superhuman beings. However, their memories contained all knowledge and made them immensely wiser and more powerful then even the greatest human heroes, and they were supremely beautiful. The proper human attitude toward them was deference and awe.

Besides their cults and temples, the great gods lived on in poetry and dramas, especially the epic poems of Homer and Hesiod in the ninth and eighth centuries B.C.E. and the tragedies of Aeschylus, Sophocles, and Euripides in the fifth century. By the sixth century, the increasingly philosophical concerns of Greek moral thought began to criticize the gods' conduct in these literary works. Tales of the gods' lusts (as in the case of Europa) and jealousies, their mad rages and vengeance on humans, and what seemed their petty vanity offended moral philosophers who began to develop a different sense of religion. The culture of the city-states turned strongly in the direction of ethical interests, and the Olympian gods came to be held to the same ethical standards as the best humans. An important means of reconciling the old narratives about the gods and the new ethical expectations was the argument that the stories of the poets were not intended to be understood literally, but figuratively; they concealed higher truths from ordinary human minds. Scholars in the fourth and third centuries B.C.E. developed learned techniques for explaining the figurative character of the Homeric poems and, particularly in the great city of Alexandria, worked out a means for the figurative interpretation of texts that later influenced both Jews and Christians in the interpretation of their own sacred texts.

Cult worship of the Olympian gods survived in Greece and Rome, but religious thinkers increasingly also speculated about the possibility of an ultimate, transcendent deity, a single god whose power might be expressed through a spectrum of lesser spiritual beings—lesser gods, spirits, or angels. These lesser divinities existed in a hierarchy: some gods lived above the earth, some on it, others below its surface. One text asks a question of the Olympian god Apollo: Who was really god? Apollo answers:

> *Born of itself, untaught, without a mother, unshakeable, not contained in a name, known by many names, dwelling in fire, this is god. We, his angels, are a small part of god.*

The movement toward monotheism, belief in a single god, characterized the religious temper of much of the Hellenistic world in the years around the turn of the Common Era.

Such speculation was generally the concern of philosophers, some of whom, like Epicurus (ca. 341–270 B.C.E.) and his followers, argued that although the gods existed, they were absolutely indifferent to humans and required no attention from humans at all. Most Greeks and Romans had other, more pressing, criteria for religious observance. There were many gods, and humans should revere them all, particularly those of one's own ancestors and city. To be a strict monotheist—to argue that there was only one divinity and no others—as Jews, and later Christians and Muslims did, was generally regarded as atheism and impiety.

Gods were believed to speak to their followers through their images, as well as through wonders, oracles, divination, omens, and dreams. Each deity required a cult—proper ritual attention paid to the god—and in this world, "religion" was everything one might legitimately ask of a god openly in a temple or shrine. If one followed the cults of one's ancestors and homeland (*pietas*) and respected the religious practices of other people doing the same thing, one's own gods might bestow health, beauty, children, wealth, freedom from servitude or other obligations, tax relief, protection from natural disasters, rescue from captivity, personal safety, booty (in the prayers of soldiers), the good fortune of the city, and other tangible rewards. These are the gifts most frequently asked of the gods in inscriptions and other religious records of the Hellenistic era.

Beyond piety lay impiety—improper behavior towards the gods. Impiety included *superstitio*—paying the wrong kind of attention to a god—and *magia*—seeking things considered improper to ask of gods, usually employing the help of charlatans or magicians who stood at the darker borders of religion, invoking lower and more dangerous orders of spirits. These last practices, especially magic, evoked the wrath of the gods.

These religions had no missionary component, nor did they have systems of defined belief. One "had" a god rather than "believed" in one. There is little evidence of the prospect of an afterlife in one's own personality in the gods' presence. From the second century C.E., however, the concept of the immortality of at least part of the self became more and more pronounced. In many religious cults the problem of the passage of part of the self through life and a series of ordeals and tests after death took on greater prominence.

Cults were supported locally by private endowments or contributions from followers or from the local public treasury, as part of that beneficence that characterized the aristocracies of cities and towns. Although cults and temples to the same god might exist in many different places, each place performed its own rites in its own way; there was no central religious authority capable of dictating either belief or behavior across a wide and religiously diverse world. In the Roman world, religion was also a component of good citizenship.

Although individual emperors might show devotion to one god more than to others, there is little evidence for anything resembling a Roman "state religion" before the end of the fourth century C.E. Because Rome's success in assembling an empire seemed to indicate considerable divine favor toward the city, Rome itself came to be considered a deity in some places. *Dea Roma*, "Goddess Rome," was first worshiped in the conquered provinces; from the end of the first century C.E., Roman emperors were also considered divine beings, again, initially in the provinces and only later in Rome.

Romans became more and more willing to permit an increasing number of cults to be observed in the city. Some features of outside cults, however—human sacrifice, ceremonial mutilation, or ritual prostitution—were not permitted by Roman law. Otherwise, the lively religious world of the Mediterranean basin continued to live on. The little gods, the Olympians, the philosophers' single god, and the many regional imported cults suggest some of the religious variety—and some of the limitations—of Hellenistic religion in the early centuries of the empire.

At the two poles of Hellenistic religious sensibility were the philosophical sensitivity and skepticism of a very small, literate elite on the one hand, and the devotional practices of a much larger number of ordinary people, on the other. The appeal of the philosophers was limited—to join them required a substantial income and leisure time, a rigorous educational and moral program of preparation, and commitment to an entire way of life, which varied according to the philosophical school that one chose to follow. Moreover, philosophical schools often contended with one another, pointing out each other's errors and undercutting each other's doctrines. From the late second century on, philosophy also helped contribute to its own discrediting in religious matters, regardless of how developed and complex its ethical and metaphysical claims became.

As an alternative to rigorous training, commitment, self-enlightenment, and debate with competing schools of philosophy, the religious sensibility of most people in late antiquity turned increasingly toward divine revelation, in which all that was necessary for humans to know was communicated to the initiate directly from the god through oracles or texts, or from the other initiated followers of the god. With the growing claims of divine revelation, philosophical inquiry concerning religious truth became less and less appealing during the third and fourth centuries, and the oracle and self-revealing god became more attractive.

Besides the growing appeal of monotheism and divine revelation, late antiquity also witnessed new forms of dualistic religion—the idea that in order to explain the presence and nature of evil in the world, one had to assume the presence of two equal gods, or at least a supreme god and a being only a little less powerful. The idea that evil was an active presence, rivaling the powers of good gods or of a good god, made the defense against evil an active element in religious sensibility. The Persian religion of Zoroastrianism elevated this principle to a major doctrine. Zoroaster, who probably lived in the sixth century B.C.E., taught that the world was created by a good god who was always in conflict with an evil god. Humans, caught in this cosmic struggle, will eventually be saved by the good god, some of them by purification after their deaths. This most complex and assertive statement of religious dualism influenced some later Jewish apocryphal scriptures and also affected both later pagan beliefs and some variants of Christianity—notably Gnosticism and Manichaeism—particularly in its dramatic personification of evil.

In the third and fourth centuries, even emperors reflect some of these changes. Some emperors restored and enhanced much of the traditional religion of the Olympians. The early third-century dynasty of Septimius Severus brought the worship of the Syrian sun-god Elgabal to Rome. Some third-century emperors also worshiped the sun, but under the name *Sol Invictus*—"The Unconquered Sun." Still others patronized the cult of Mithras, and others that of Isis. From Hadrian's curiosity about all religions, it is possible to pass into the next century and see the young emperor Alexander Severus actively worshiping many different and often unfamiliar gods, including, it was said, the god of the Christians.

Most of the so-called mystery religions relied on spectacles that were open to the public. They consisted of recitations of sacred texts, music, and dancing that demonstrated the revelation of a god to initiated believers and potential converts. These forms were also adopted by more recently arrived cults, like those of Isis and Mithras, and one of their most appealing features was the fact that they had no specific place of origin. They could be founded anywhere and did not depend on an original sacred location or a particular ethnic or civic community among their converts. In their geographical adaptability, the cults of Isis and Mithras reflect some of the general social characteristics of the later empire, especially the physical mobility of more people and the weakening of ties to cities of origin.

Mithras worship, for example, which had existed in some places since the fourth century B.C.E., and was adopted as the personal religion of the emperor Commodus (180–192), acquired increased popularity, most strongly among the physically mobile elements of the imperial population, particularly the army. Mithras was said to have slain a great bull in order to ascend to the heavens, and from the body of the bull emerged all the creatures of the world. A series of initiatory rituals carried out both above ground and in subterranean chambers introduced candidates and a graded hierarchy of adepts to a message of Mithras: ritual purification would enable the individual soul to pass safely through the ordeals that followed immediately after death and join the saved in a pleasant afterlife.

Far from consisting either of pure philosophy or of pure credulity, religious sensibility in late antiquity is striking in its widening scope, its attention to the whole of human life, its concern for the world of the spirit, and its conception of the individual soul and its place in the cosmos.

JUDAISM IN PALESTINE AND THE DIASPORA

Judaism resembled other ancient Near Eastern religions in its predominantly ethnic and regional character, in its possession of a central cult site in Jerusalem, and in the things it asked of the divinity. But it differed sharply from all others in its concept of the divinity, in its rejection of all images or pictorial representations of the divinity, in its insistence on the divinity's absolute transcendence, and in its use of a group of sacred texts to establish and regulate belief, behavior, ceremony, and ritual. The god of the Hebrew people was the creator of the universe and its only divinity. God had entered into a series of later covenants with the Hebrew people, whom he favored above others, in the persons of Noah, Abraham, and Moses. The divine name that humans used was YHWH, vocalized as Yahweh.

The terms of the covenant were established in the text of *Torah*—Genesis, Exodus, Leviticus, Numbers, and Deuteronomy—which became the first five books of the Bible (the term is derived from the Greek *ta biblia*, "the books," which originally meant scrolls). These books contain a history of the creation of the universe and the world, a history of the Hebrew people, the terms of the covenants between the divinity and the Hebrews, and the rules according to which they were required by the divinity to live. Although Torah is often termed a code of law, to Jews it has always been a summation of all wisdom. The full canon of Hebrew scripture that distinguished Jews from all other peoples, as it was formalized in the first two centuries of the common era, also included two other kinds of text besides Torah: the Prophets (*Nebi'im*) and the Writings (*Ketubim*).

The covenants were understood to have promised the Hebrew people an earthly kingdom of their own. The first kingdom was established around the turn of the first millennium B.C.E., under the kings Saul, David (1000–962 B.C.E.), and Solomon (961–922 B.C.E.), divided into the northern and southern kingdoms of Israel and Judah after the death of Solomon, and lasted until 587 B.C.E. The term "Jew" derives from the name of the kingdom of Judah. In 587, the Hebrew kingdoms were conquered, and many of the Hebrew people themselves were deported to Babylon, enduring what they termed the Babylonian Captivity. The faith survived the exile to Babylon, and the writings of the prophets, most strikingly those of the great poet known as Second Isaiah (*Isaiah:* 40–66), not only helped to preserve the faith, but also deepened and intensified it.

When the Babylonian Captivity ended in 537 B.C.E., many Jews remained in the Near Eastern World outside Palestine. For those who returned, since there was no king or royal dynasty, leadership was found in the temple priests and interpreters of the Law, thus actively restoring the centrality of the Temple at Jerusalem and Torah in regulating private and community life. Those Jews who remained outside Palestine shared the increasing mobility of many other peoples in the ancient Near East and Mediterranean worlds. This dispersal of the Jews, known as the Diaspora, located large Jewish communities in Babylon, Alexandria in Egypt, and in other cities that ringed the Mediterranean basin. Both in Palestine and in the Diaspora, Jews were subjected more and more to cosmopolitan influences from a rapidly changing world. If the texts of the Prophets focused on a dynamic, intensified Judaism, many of the texts in the Writings—especially the books of *Proverbs* and *Wisdom*—strongly resemble contemporary non-Jewish thought and parallel non-Jewish literature. Scripture itself was translated into Greek from the third century B.C.E. on, to serve the needs of Jews who knew no Hebrew. The most influential of these translations, the *Septuagint,* became the basis for later Christian understanding and use of Jewish scripture.

In the Jewish state after 537 B.C.E., priests and teachers urged obedience to the Law and reminded Jews that they were ritually separate from non-Jews (Gentiles) and must remain so. At the same time, the community was preserved under the influence alternately of Persia and Egypt until the early second century B.C.E. Then, the ruler of Syria, Antiochos IV Epiphanes (r. 175–164 B.C.E.), demanded that his own image be displayed in the Temple at Jerusalem and that Jews pay him divine honors. Jewish outrage led to a revolt that is chronicled in the *First Book of Maccabees,* and to the establishment of an independent Jewish kingdom.

The Hasmonean kings of the new state, however, began to alienate some of their earlier supporters, chiefly because they admitted some gentile social institutions and practices. One group, known as the Pharisees, became generally indifferent to the state, practicing the study of the Law, strictly observing the laws of purity and tithes, and remained hostile to outside religious and philosophical influences. Another group, the Sadducees, were a priestly party, equally committed to the supremacy of scripture and to the ritual integrity of Judaism, but differing from the Pharisees at some points and more closely tied to the monarchy and the state. Still other groups practiced cults of personal holiness, individual devotion to God, and emphasized the mystical interpretation of the Psalms rather than the strict and literal observance of the ritual laws.

Some Jewish thinkers in Alexandria attempted to combine Greek philosophical speculation and techniques of figurative literary interpretation with their understanding and observance of the Law. Philo Judaeus (25 B.C.E.–25 C.E.) devised a complex system of interpreting Jewish scripture according to which the literal sense of what scripture said was simply the first of several levels of meaning, each more esoteric than the last. Philo's technique did not immediately exert great influence among Jewish thinkers, but it later exerted enormous influence on Christian biblical scholarship and theology, because his system allowed Christians to incorporate much of the body of Jewish scripture accommodated to Christian understanding.

Yet another group, the Essenes, withdrew from society completely, retired to the desert, and waited for the act of divine intervention that they expected to occur at any moment. The discovery in 1947 of the Dead Sea Scrolls, the writings of a hitherto little-known Jewish sect at Qumran, has shed considerable light on the beliefs and practices of Essenes and similar groups. Still other groups focused more intensely on the apocalyptic dimension of Judaism—the idea that the end of time is at hand and that preparation for it is the greatest obligation of the believer.

Finally, besides various large groups and smaller sects, there appeared individual visionaries, prophets, and holy men whose teachings attracted groups of followers. The best-known of these to Christians was John the Baptist. Dressed in rough animal skins and living on the simplest of foods, John the Baptist taught that the judgment of God was soon to come upon His people and that repentance was essential. Repentance could be signaled by a symbolic washing in water—baptism.

These varieties of Jewish religious sensibility developed within a kingdom that came increasingly under the dominion of Rome after 67 B.C.E. Because the Jewish kingdom had allied itself with the winning sides in the Roman civil wars of the first century B.C.E., Rome recognized the Jews' unique status. Jews alone were exempted from the formal religious obligations that Romans imposed on other client states. In 37 B.C.E., Rome installed Herod, an Idumean, as king of Judea (r. 37–4 B.C.E.), and Herod began to rebuild the great Temple of Solomon, but also to admit outside cultural influences into the kingdom. When Judea became a Roman province in 6 C.E., Jerusalem remained its sacred city, but the port city of Caesarea Maritima became its Roman capital.

Jewish political opposition to the successors of Herod and to other Roman administrators made the Romans quickly suspicious of any movement, religious or not, that remotely resembled a political threat. In the mid first century, a group called the Zealots began to urge the expulsion of the Romans as the only way to preserve authentic Judaism. The Zealots participated in the great revolt against Roman rule in Judea that lasted from 66 to 73 C.E., and witnessed the destruction of the second Temple in the year 70 and the slaughter at Masada in 73. After a second revolt that lasted from 131 to 135, the emperor Hadrian adopted a strong anti-Jewish policy, founding the new province which he named *Palestina* in place of *Judea*. In antiquity, the term *Palestina* had been used chiefly for the southern coastal plain, but its use by Hadrian to designate the province, and Hadrian's renaming Jerusalem as *Aelia Capitolina* were part of a deliberate anti-Jewish strategy which included the exile of Jews from Jerusalem and the increasing of the size of the pagan and Christian populations of the area. Later emperors divided Palestina into three provinces, which remained part of the Roman empire until their conquest by Sasanid Persia in 614, their brief reconquest by Roman forces in 628, and their final conquest by Muslim armies between 629 and 640 (below, Chapters 4 and 5).

With the destruction of the Second Temple, the priestly caste declined, and teachers of the Law emerged as the primary guides to worship and conduct. During the late first and second centuries of the Common Era, the figure of the rabbi, the teacher, emerged as the chief official of each Jewish community, and the rabbinic office and the assembly—the synagogue—came to characterize Jewish life in Palestine as they already had in the Diaspora. Late in the second century, a revised law code called the *Mishnah* was established by a rabbinical court. Subsequent commentaries on the Mishnah by scholars in Palestine and Mesopotamia produced the *Talmud,* the great guide to rabbinic Judaism that formed, with Torah, the backbone of later Judaism. A second achievement of the early rabbinic period was the final determination of the canon of authentic Scripture, which also occurred in the late first and second centuries of the Common Era.

The failure of the kingdom, the destruction of the Second Temple, and the annihilation of the priests and political leaders by the Romans drastically transformed the

Jewish community after the early second century. Now scattered throughout the Greco-Roman and Persian worlds, possessing only Torah and Mishnah, Jewish communities, led by rabbis, preserved the faith of the Law and prayer in the face of increasing indifference on the part of gentiles and increasing hostility on the part of Christians. But a tormented history and religious genius were not the sole legacies of Judaism to the ancient and modern worlds. Among the varieties of Jewish religious sentiment that had developed around the turn of the Common Era, one set of beliefs took shape and grew in such a way that it transformed the entire Hellenistic world.

THE EMERGENCE OF CHRISTIANITY

Shortly before the middle of the first century C.E., a group of Jewish men and women in Galilee claimed that their master, Jesus of Nazareth, who had been tried and executed by the Romans, had been a messenger of God. They claimed that John the Baptist had so identified Jesus (Mark 1:2), and they interpreted the Prophets as having predicted the same thing. They recorded Jesus' sayings, circulated them among themselves, and taught them to others. They argued that Jesus had fulfilled the central prophecies concerning the *Messiah* (a Hebrew term with varying interpretations, ranging from a conquering king to a messenger of God: in Greek, *ho christos,* "the anointed one" [John 1:41]), and they embedded Jesus' sayings in a group of biographical narratives that were written between 64 and 110 C.E. These narratives, which were called *evangelia,* or "good news," were the Gospels, and they gave shape, consistency, and definition to Jesus' teachings, as well as inspiring great loyalty among his followers.

The problem of "the historical Jesus" has produced a vast and disputatious literature. From one perspective, Jesus as a historical figure must be understood in terms of the place and time in which he lived. The gospels illustrate much of the context of Jewish society in Judea in Jesus' lifetime. Sadducees, Pharisees, scribes, religious and political Zealots, the repentance and purification demanded by John the Baptist, guarded but sincere respect for the Temple and its priests, the urgent sense of prophecies about to be fulfilled, a filial relationship with God, and a sharp conception of sin and evil—all were current ideas in Judea during and after Jesus' lifetime. In this respect, Jesus may be understood historically as a charismatic Jewish teacher (a *hasid:* Matthew 7:28–8:1), not unlike John the Baptist himself (although Jesus personally baptized no one, his followers later did so in his name). His earliest followers were clearly rooted in the Jewish community: they practiced circumcision, worshiped at the Temple, paid temple tithes, observed Jewish dietary laws, and worked largely among Jews for the recognition of Jesus as the Messiah.

From another perspective, however, the life of Jesus represents a sharp break with this conventional Jewish identity. The biographies in the Gospels of Mark, Matthew, and Luke focus only on parts of Jesus' life: the circumstances of his conception and birth (which placed great emphasis upon the person of his mother, Mary, and the cosmological significance of the event represented by the appearance of angels to nearby shepherds, and the new astronomical phenomena that guided the astrological calculations of the wise men); his confounding the learned teachers of the Temple in preparation for his coming of age; his baptism by John the Baptist and John's proclaiming that Jesus was greater than he; and the final three years of itinerant preaching, working wonders, and attracting followers (initially according to the Gospels, twelve *apostles*—the term means "those who are sent"—and a number of *disciples*). In addition, the Gospels recounted the circumstances of Jesus' trial and execution, but they also stated that Jesus had risen from the dead after three days, resumed life among his companions for a short time, commissioned them to continue preaching his message, "even to the ends of the earth," and ascended into Heaven, from which he would soon return to judge the world. The sense of the immediacy of the Second Coming, the *parousia*, was very strong in the years following Jesus' execution, and it has remained a powerful aspect of Christianity ever since.

Although Jesus professed respect for religious institutions and ritual, he also insisted that love—between humans and God and among humans themselves—was the central religious law, as a number of rabbinical teachings had also asserted:

> *You must love the Lord your God with your whole heart, with your whole soul, and with your whole mind. This is the greatest and the first commandment. The second is like it: you must love your neighbor as yourself. On these two commandments rest the whole law, and the prophets also.*
>
> *(Matthew 22:34–40; cf. Mark 12:30–31)*

This message is reiterated in the single commandment that Jesus was said to have added to the original ten: "This commandment I give you: that you love one another" (John 15:16). Jesus' giving a commandment was consistent with the Gospels' insistence that Jesus was God.

Christians also argued that since the Godhead had long been described in terms of divine Power, Wisdom, and Love, and since the Gospel of Matthew (28:19) claimed that Jesus had commanded his followers to "baptize men everywhere in the name of the Father, the Son, and the Holy Spirit," the divinity was in fact three persons in unity and had been for all eternity. The doctrine of the Trinity became a centerpiece of Christian theology. The challenge of working out both the problem of the human and divine natures in Jesus (Christology) and that of the relation among the three persons of the Trinity (Trinitarianism) was the focus of much of the subsequent formation of normative Christian theological doctrine and the occasions for the most complex forms of theological disagreement. Thus, to the explicit Jewish assertion that there was only one god and that God had entered into historical covenants with the Jewish people, the followers of Jesus added a second specific historical dimension—the life, death, and resurrection of Jesus—and the assertion that as the supreme act of love, God had become human and given a new definition to the obligations of humans toward God. Although pagan gods were occasionally said to have assumed human form (as Zeus did in the story of Europa), Christians asserted that Jesus was a god who had suffered tortures and death in the flesh. They also believed that the death and resurrection of Christ had overcome the corruption of human nature that had been incurred by Adam and Eve when they had sinned against God and been expelled from Paradise.

The beliefs of Jesus' earliest followers spread slowly, first throughout the Jewish world of Palestine and later through the Diaspora. Their enthusiasm and certainty were surely one element contributing to the success of their message, but there were other aspects of Christianity that increased its appeal as well. The doctrine of a single God who had assumed human nature at a specific historical time and in a known individual proved compelling. Jesus' insistence upon love as the bond between the divine and human and among humans themselves (the Christians developed the little-used Greek word *agape,* poorly understood in the twentieth-century meanings of "charity," as a designation of this love) offered a new bond of community. Salvation itself became dependent upon repentance, belief, and a reformed code of conduct. Urging very close social bonds among believers in anticipation of the Second Coming appealed to a broad spectrum of Mediterranean society.

One of the earliest problems that Jesus' followers had to face was the question of the extent to which following Jesus was consistent with Jewish identity. Those followers who had known Jesus personally, especially Peter and James, clearly lived according to Jewish observance and preached chiefly to Jews. Resistance among Jews probably increased as the Christian message was spelled out more clearly and its implications better understood. With the increasing crisis of Jewish identity during the revolts against Rome in 66–73, the resurgence of Pharisaical Judaism limited the possibility of extending the Christian appeal among Jews, although various forms of Jewish Christianity survived in the Mediterranean world for several centuries.

The most dramatic change that came over the followers of Jesus in the decades following his execution was the increasing awareness that Christian (the term was first applied to followers of Jesus at Antioch around 66 C.E.) teachings were not to be limited to a Jewish audience but were meant for all people, gentiles as well as Jews. The central figure in this transformation was Saul, a Pharisee who had once persecuted members of the new sect, but after a vision of Jesus became an inspired interpreter and preacher of Jesus' teachings. Saul, who used the Greco-Latin form of his name, Paul, in dealing with gentiles, claimed that Jesus' teachings were aimed at all humanity, that they had entirely replaced the older covenants, even Torah itself, giving a "new law" for the "new man" that baptism had created. The earliest texts that Christians came to regard as scriptural were a series of letters that Paul sent to the various Christian communities he had visited or known, the *Epistles.* They emphasized both the universality of the Christian message and the necessity of peace and agreement within individual communities. The *Acts of the Apostles* depicts the missionary adventures of Jesus' followers, particularly in the light of Paul's ideas, and the principles of organization of the earliest Christian communities.

The appeal of Paul's message was considerable. Gentiles who became Christians were not obliged to assume a Jewish ritual identity. The command of charity broke traditional—and very strong—social and gender barriers. Jesus' earliest followers had been ordinary people, and the command of communal solidarity offered an alternative community to many gentiles, one based on love and devotion to Jesus rather than to conventional social divisions. Christians considered themselves to be a "new Israel," living under a new covenant, whose members would readily give up life itself for the sake of their beliefs. During the intermittent persecutions of Christians during the first three centuries, the steadfastness and brotherly love displayed by the martyrs ("witnesses" in Greek) attracted many converts and much respect from those who remained pagan. Tending their sick, caring for the poor and orphans, visiting prisons, sharing ritual meals, and providing decent burial for fellow believers also reflected the attractiveness of the Christian sense of community.

Besides ameliorating some of the most oppressive effects of social barriers—including the astonishing assertion by Paul that in Christianity there was no distinction between men and women, or between the slave and the free person—Christianity also broke gender barriers. Christianity offered women considerable dignity and status. Husbands were commanded to treat their wives with respect and love. Even the new Christian asceticism—the rejection of the appeal of this world in order to intensify spiritual life—offered dramatic new opportunities for feminine self-realization. Celibate virginity and widowhood became respected forms of feminine life within organized Christian communities, with particular eminence in liturgical life. Moreover, as benefactors, women who contributed property and patronage to Christian communities held a public place that was entirely new in the Roman world. The dissenting sect of Montanism included women as especially gifted prophets. Women also were notable—and extensively memorialized—victims of Roman persecution. An important text known as *The Martyrdom of Perpetua* is the authentic memoir of the last days, spent in prison, of Vibia Perpetua, a young mother executed at Carthage in 203. In the veneration of martyrs, who succeeded the apostles and disciples of Jesus as the most heroic representatives of authentic Christianity, there was indeed no difference between male and female. Although Paul himself reflected considerable ambiguity about the public role of women in Christian communities, and although this new ordering of gender identities and roles was greatly altered in the course of the next several centuries, the role of women in "living" Christianity throughout the early history of Europe constituted an original and immensely creative dimension of the Christian life.

SPIRIT AND FLESH, BODY AND GENDER

One important means by which Christians distinguished themselves from both Jews and pagans was the way they took up a theme that was prominent in late antique thought—the division between spiritual and material reality, or between the spirit and the flesh. A number of influential Christian thinkers applied this division in areas of religious life as different as the proper understanding of scripture (Christians were said to understand scripture "spiritually" while non-Christians, especially Jews, were said to understand it "carnally"), the authenticity of prayer and other forms of devotion (Christians prayed spiritually, others carnally), and sexual relationships. Although normative Christianity did not go to the extreme of utterly rejecting the physical body or human sexuality, it nevertheless insisted that these be lived and used in a properly spiritual manner. The body used in a spiritual manner could become the locus of holiness. Christians assumed that the earliest followers of Jesus had been holy, and that those Christians who had suffered martyrdom had also used the body in a spiritual way. Thus, the material bodies of these early Christian heroes (women as well as men)—that is, their relics as well as their burial places—retained that holiness, and many writers insisted that the material body as well as the soul would be resurrected after death.

Some Christian writers reinterpreted the Fall of Adam and Eve in the Garden of Eden as the result of improper sexual activity, and they interpreted the domestic dependence and preoccupations of Roman women in marriage as reducing the spiritual capacity of women. Therefore, many early Christian writers argued for the superior spiritual status of virginity and chastity in order to overcome the distractions of living in the world and the power of the senses, and to emphasize the need to spiritualize the body.

But not all early Christian writers agreed on these points. While some argued for an extreme rejection of the body and sexuality, others formulated a doctrine of legitimate Christian marriage. Some retained many of the Roman signs of gender differentiation, even in identifying masculinity as the true life of the spirit and femininity as signifying the flesh and the material world. Men, thus defined as having an active role, possessing power, and signifying the spirit, should rule in the Christian community. Women, passive, powerless, signifying the flesh, should be ruled and their spiritual experience guided and protected.

On the other hand, even the range of gender distinctions in ancient Christianity was potentially disruptive of Mediterranean tradition. Virgins could reject those aspects of marriage and domesticity that critics had argued limited and distracted them from true spiritual life. Freed from those burdens, they might confine themselves to a life of prayer and study—or travel and engage autonomously in all other activities of the new Christian life. Virginity and chastity (among the married, abandoned, or widowed) came to be seen as a kind of parallel to martyrdom, and hence holy. Both virgins (male and female) and the chaste were believed to possess a power of prayer that benefited the entire community. Christian marriage, chaste friendship, and virginity thus all contributed to the transformation of older gender roles in the late antique Mediterranean world. In order to become *new* people, aristocratic women might remain virgins or live in chaste relationships in order to acquire personal—and spiritual—freedom.

One spectacular instance of such renunciation from the highest ranks of Roman society was the life of Melania the Younger (383–438). A member of the ancient and wealthy family of the Valerii, Melania was married by her parents when she was fourteen and her husband seventeen. She bore two children and then convinced her husband to join her in renouncing the world. This meant providing for their children and then dispersing a fortune so vast that a separate department of the imperial treasury had to be created to handle it. Melania and her husband then devoted themselves to contemplation and study, and to travel to holy sites and holy men, who welcomed her, her biographer says, "as if she were a man." "In truth," the biographer continues, "she had been detached from the female nature and had acquired a masculine disposition, or rather, a heavenly one."[1]

At the other end of the social scale, prostitutes, too, could reject their former lives, styles of dress, appearance, and behavior, and their stories, too, became a popular component of early Christian devotional literature. Virgins and chaste men and women were thought to have produced spiritual children—their fellow Christians whom their own

---

[1]Elizabeth A. Clark, ed. and trans., *The Life of Melania the Younger* (New York: Edwin Mellen Press, 1984), 54.

devotion had inspired to lead more spiritual lives. Until the end of ancient Christianity, the debate over the limits and freedoms of the married, chaste, and virgin lives constituted a major element of Christian self-definition.

CONVERSION AND OPPOSITION

Christians believed that Jesus' death and resurrection from the dead freed them from the consequences of the Fall of Adam and Eve in the Garden of Eden. The Christian interpretation of the Fall insisted that all later humans carried in them original sin—the guilt incurred by Adam and Eve for disobeying God's command. In this reading of Genesis, as in others, Christians came to differ sharply from Jewish interpretations, which considered the Fall as having only personal consequences for the first humans, since the covenants with the Patriarchs had made no mention of collective consequences. Commitment to this doctrine through conversion, study, and baptism, made the Christian, as Paul said, "a new man," one who had literally turned his back on his old sinful life and nature, "the old Adam." Baptism was thought to remove the stain of original sin. Conversion stories thus came to play an influential role in understanding the Christian life, especially the story of Paul's own highly dramatic and miraculous conversion. Conversion and the new life of bearing witness to the truth (including suffering persecution and even martyrdom) became the center of Christian identity.

One sign of the attractiveness of Christianity is the nature of the hostility it generated. As the nature of its beliefs and practices was more precisely spelled out, its increasing distance from Judaism became apparent to Christians and Jews alike. Hostile pagans saw little out of the ordinary in Jesus' miracles, including the raising of the dead, since wonder workers were routinely thought to do this. Christians not only had to separate themselves from Judaism, then, but also from accusations of being the ignorant and gullible followers of an ordinary lower-class provincial magician. Christian arguments were made carefully on this point, and they also inform us about what it was that magicians were thought to do. Jesus had performed no divinations; he cured but did not inflict disease; he did not generate hostility and quarrels, but resolved them; he did not open locked doors without a key; he did not predict the winners of chariot races, nor did he inspire illicit sexual attraction. Later Christian definitions of and attitudes toward genuine miracles and magic (even in northern Europe, where non-Christianity was very different from the ancient pagan world) were shaped by these early experiences.

By the second century, learned pagans began to take hostile notice of Christianity's popularity. Some pagans considered it an eccentric offshoot of Judaism or yet another mystery religion—a "barbarian theosophy," as the philosopher Plotinus called it. One such writer, Celsus (ca. 180), produced a long diatribe against Christianity, suggesting that even intellectuals were compelled to take notice of it. One of the landmarks of early Christian literature is the long refutation of Celsus' work, the *Contra Celsum,* written by Origen (185–254), a priest of Alexandria and the greatest early Christian biblical scholar. By the middle of the second century many apologists (the term means "explainers," not apologists in the modern sense) were converts from paganism and intellectuals as well.

Besides Origen, the most influential of these were Justin Martyr (100–165) and Tertullian of Carthage (160–220). By the end of the second century, the appearance of Christian intellectuals who challenged pagan opponents on their own ground marks an important stage in the spread of Christianity in the Roman and Latin-speaking world. It is in the work of Tertullian, for example, that the Christian scriptures were first called the "New" Testament, thus equating them (but on a superior level) with Jewish scriptures (which Tertullian termed the "Old" Testament), and at the same time appropriating Jewish scripture for Christian use. Tertullian also challenged the value of ancient religio-philosophical thought. "What has Athens," he asked, "to do with Jerusalem?" What did all the profound learning in the world have to do with the life of the spirit and its duties to God?

The first Christian communities were loosely structured societies devoted to the commemoration of Jesus, which included a meal of thanksgiving (the original meaning of the term *eucharist,* the "good gift") as well as acts of charity. As Christian literature developed, communal readings followed, and Christians recognized the necessity of deciding which writings were to be considered authentically inspired, which were acceptable for purposes of increasing piety, and which were to be rejected. Considerable dissension arose over which of the many *Acts, Gospels, Epistles,* and *Apocalypses* attributed to various apostles were to be regarded as authentic. By 200, however, the present canon of Christian scripture was widely accepted, and the canon was formally closed at the Council of Carthage in 397.

The fact that Christian scripture was officially accepted by a council—a formal meeting of leaders of Christian communities—suggests the organizational articulation and definition of Christian communities between the mid first and late fourth centuries. The early Christians organized their communities (which were considered private clubs, as were synagogues—and hence subject to the official licensing of private clubs, one of the justifications for legal persecution) by consciously avoiding the religious terminology of both Judaism and paganism. They termed their group an *ecclesia* (Latin; in Greek *ekklesia*), a religiously neutral term simply meaning "assembly." Both the congregation and the private buildings in which it originally assembled were termed *kyriakos oikos,* "the lord's house (or household)"—a term that later became simply "church" in a number of modern languages. The first officers of these communities also had religiously neutral titles, including that of "overseer" (*episkopos, episcopus, bishop*), "elder" (*presbyter,* later *priest*), and "servant" (*diaconus,* later *deacon*). These titles originally designated managers of community property and organizers of meetings.

But even this sort of organization greatly concerned Roman officials. As long as Christians were considered part of Jewish communities, they were protected by the same religious considerations that Romans had extended to Jews. Once they became clearly distinct from Jews, however, Christians were considered members of illegal, because unlicensed, organizations. Roman imperial law was acutely sensitive to the dangers it perceived arising out of factionalism, and it regarded unlicensed groups of whatever kind as potential seedbeds of political dissent. Not all Roman emperors and magistrates were greatly concerned with the status of Christians, although after the late second century prosecutions became more frequent. But Christians also saw in martyrdoms (the phrase means "bearing witness" in Greek) like that of Vibia Perpetua and others, a new and powerful force of authentic Christianity. Tertullian called the blood of the martyrs, "the seed of the Church."

ORTHODOXY AND HETERODOXY: NORMATIVE CHRISTIANITY

In addition to intermittent legal persecution from the Roman state and intellectual attacks from Hellenistic philosophers, Christians also faced considerable dissension within their own communities. Some of this derived from debates on the degree of the Jewish character of Christianity; other issues followed, some of them supported by selective readings of scripture and acceptance of different versions of scripture.

In 1945, a library of early Christian literature was discovered at Nag Hammadi in Egypt. The discovery has proved as important as that of the Dead Sea Scrolls at Qumran. The fifty-two texts of the library reveal some of the profound differences that had arisen among Christians by the late first and early second centuries of the Common Era. Some of the religious ideas described in these texts are known as *Gnosticism*. A religious movement that probably predated Christianity, Gnosticism flowered when it was combined with selected texts of Christian scripture and the story of Jesus. As its name implies, Gnosticism offered *gnosis*, "revealed knowledge," to its initiates, specifically the true knowledge that was concealed in scripture and was unavailable to the average Christian. The Gnostic initiate, after studying highly selective versions of both authentic and uncanonical scripture, discovered that the Christian story was a veil of myth concealing the "true" story of the imprisonment of the spirit in material flesh and offering instruction that the spirit should follow to free itself and rejoin the divinity. For a time, the attraction of Gnosticism was very powerful, and recent studies have shown that the life and beliefs of the earliest Christian communities were far more varied and contentious than had once been thought, that there was less a single Christianity than several Christianities.

Nor did Christians simply ignore the appeal of Gnosticism and the criticisms of Hellenistic philosophers. In order to create a normative system of Christian thought, Christians had to draw on the learning of the Mediterranean world and its technologies of learning as well. For reasons that are still not clear, Christian writing tended to be contained in the *codex*, a manuscript book that contained a series of folded sheets of papyrus bound at the edges—the earliest form of the modern book—rather than in the *biblos*, the scroll. There were certain practical advantages to this choice, since the codex could hold more text, was easier to handle and store, and cost less to produce than the scroll. Pictorial images could also be placed closer to appropriate places in the text. The codex easily survived the shift of writing surfaces from papyrus to parchment in the seventh and eighth centuries.

Christians also adopted much of the philosophical terminology of the Greek language and a number of Greek patterns of thought. The Gospel of John and the sequence Luke–Acts are usually thought to be the earliest examples of such influences. One of the most important pagan influences on early Christianity was the movement known as

Neoplatonism, a philosophical development of Plato's ideas that reached its height in the third century of the Common Era. Its greatest pagan representatives, Plotinus (205–270), Porphyry (232–303), and Iamblichus (250–330), insisted on a rigorous program of disciplined study throughout one's life. Such study provided a philosophical approach to the relation between the invisible and immaterial world of pure spiritual being and the world of matter. They led the philosopher to perceive the subtle and harmonious links between the spiritual and material worlds, thus elevating the material world above the sharp condemnation of original Platonic thought, on the one hand, and Gnostic dismissal on the other. Neoplatonism thus helped to provide a conceptual vocabulary for some of the controversies of early Christianity, particularly in later debates over the relation between the divine and human natures of Christ. The greatest Christian representatives of Neoplatonism, Origen and Augustine, shaped the earliest theological terminology of Christianity.

The last formal assault by the Roman government on Christianity occurred during the persecutions of Diocletian and his associates between 298 and 312. When Constantine defeated his rivals for the throne in 312, however, he claimed that the god of the Christians had given him assistance. In 313, Constantine made Christianity a legal religion, although his so-called Edict of Milan did not make it the state religion. From the reign of Constantine until the end of the Roman Empire in the West, the emperors retained their appearance of supreme and awesome rulers, but they also underwent one momentous change. At the end of his life, Constantine proclaimed himself a Christian and was baptized. His successors, with the single exception of his nephew Julian (r. 361–363), were all Christians. Although the Christian Roman emperor could no longer call himself a god, he could—and all did—regard himself and act as God's representative on earth. The privileges and wealth that Christian emperors bestowed on the Church and the influence they exerted on the Church's structure altered the character of Christianity as well as the relation between religion and the Roman state.

With the passing of the generation which had known Jesus, and the apparent delay of the Second Coming, communities of Christians faced the problem of the location of authority, and the growth of profound divisions of opinion, belief, and practice within individual communities and between different communities. Since all Christians except Gnostics agreed that the apostles had received Jesus' authentic teaching, in both the "laying on of hands" and the appearance to them of the Holy Spirit at Pentecost, the "practices" of the apostles and the idea of the descent of teaching authority through the apostles came to be considered one kind of legitimation of authoritative teaching. By the second century at the latest, the figure of the bishop had come to be considered the local successor to the apostles, and hence the authentic teacher and interpreter of doctrine. The invention of the bishop was one of the most influential and enduring creations of Late Antiquity.

A number of texts also emphasized particular events in the life of Jesus that were interpreted as having universal importance to the individual Christian life. The baptism of Jesus was incorporated as a ritual for accepting new members into the Christian community; the Last Supper was identified with the eucharistic meal and later understood as a participation in the substance of Jesus; the act of making a bishop (originally locally elected, and later blessed by other bishops) was also regarded as deriving from Jesus' selection of the apostles. These ritual acts came to be called *sacraments,* and the right to administer them was restricted to bishops, although some of them might be delegated to presbyters, deacons, and, originally at least, to virgins and widows. Bishops therefore came to be thought of as possessing sacramental, magisterial (teaching), and governing authority.

On the basis of this process of organization and the emergence of the figure of the bishop, the agreement of the bishops of different communities created what has been called "normative Christianity," or "catholic (universal) Christianity"—that is, a set of doctrines, sacred texts, and ritual practices that were accepted by most Christians as determined by legitimate authority and passed on to successive generations as tradition ("that which is handed down"). Bishops agreed on short statements of doctrine to which their communities were expected to assent—creeds (from the Latin *credo,* "I believe"). Bishops assembled in occasional meetings, particularly after the legalization of Christianity in 313, that came to be called *councils.* Councils produced rules, or *canons,* that reflected widespread agreement about common matters, including the official, or "canonical" text of Christian scripture. Belief and behavior that agreed with the universal consensus was termed *orthodoxy* ("right teaching or opinion"). Increasingly, whatever belief and behavior that did not agree was termed *heterodoxy* ("different teaching or opinion"). Before the legalization of Christianity, these matters were internal to the Christian communities of the Roman Empire. After 313, however, and particularly after the conversion of Constantine and later emperors to Christianity, they became matters of state as well.

By the fourth century, forms of religious dissent within Christianity had proliferated and acquired new forms. Although Gnosticism ceased to be a problem by the end of the third century, other sets of belief had arisen to take its place, several of them not, strictly speaking, theological at all. And all of them troubled the new Christian emperors.

The first problem to emerge on an empire-wide scale was that of Donatism, a schismatic belief that originated in a disputed episcopal election in Carthage between 308 and 311. The devotional climate in fourth-century North Africa was extremely volatile, and nowhere more than in mixed attitudes toward Christian leaders who had collaborated with Roman officials during the persecutions of 298–305 by handing over the sacred books and thereby committing the sin of apostasy. By extension, Donatism posed the larger and more complex question of the nature of priestly orders and the efficacy of sacraments performed by morally unworthy clergy. Did such clergy lose its priestly functions? Did they need to be rebaptized? How could a community be absolutely certain of the moral purity of its clergy? A secret sin by a priest might wipe away his sacramental power and deprive his congregation of the grace needed for salvation. The normative response to the Donatist challenge became a fundamental ecclesiological doctrine of the Christian community. The efficacy of the sacrament was asserted to depend only on the canonical ordination of a cleric, not on his state of grace. With a little help from Roman law, one of the fundamental premises of ecclesiology took shape in the wake of the Donatist controversy, which was not formally settled until the Council of Carthage in 411, although the disputes continued through the fifth century.

The most significant doctrinal dispute centered on the problems of Trinitarianism and Christology. Between 315 and 318, Arius, a priest of Alexandria, maintained that Christ had been created by God and hence was a secondary kind of divinity to the Father.

The appeal of Arianism, especially to rulers, was considerable. Christ-founded institutions, for example, the Church and the sacraments, could be considered inferior to the power of the Father, or, by analogy, the emperor or other ruler. The ensuing debates brought into Christian theology the full force of the Greek philosophical vocabulary in a quarrel that lasted for more than two centuries.

In 325, the Council of Nicaea laid down what became ultimately the orthodox dogma, that Christ and the Father were *homoousios,* "of the same essence." Nevertheless, the divisions among the clergy, the contrary opinions of successive later emperors, and the philosophical arena that had been opened up by the free discussions of learned bishops heralded many of the later difficulties in definitions of theological orthodoxy. The imperial Christianity of the fourth century transformed both the empire and the church.

The regulation of religious dissent by invoking and supporting church councils and the aligning of ecclesiastical organization with the imperial civil service were not the only areas of imperial activity to benefit and trouble Christians. Christian emperors also drifted further away from the traditional civil religion of Rome and the priestly titles and offices emperors had once routinely held. By the third quarter of the fourth century, emperors had become consistently hostile to all manifestations of the old public religion of Rome. In 382, the emperor Gratian withdrew many of the funds that had supported other cults and priesthoods, and he removed the Altar of Victory, a venerable civic monument, from the Senate house. In spite of moving and articulate appeals from senatorial aristocrats, Ambrose, bishop of Milan (339–397), convinced the emperors to remove all such symbols from public places. The emperor Theodosius (379–395) outlawed all practices of old Roman religion in 392. As the aristocracy, the intellectuals, and the emperors themselves became Christians, the intellectual and social prestige and material benefits they had once brought to older religions were diverted to Christianity. Only the popular culture of the urban lower classes and the rural peasantry of the imperial provinces provided significant resistance to the process of Christianization by the end of the fourth century. *Pagani,* "those who live in the countryside," gave the later collective term to all of the older religions—their practitioners were now "pagans" in Christian eyes, whether they were rural peasants or urban aristocrats. The rural peasantry and their local gods provided both the last resistance of older religions in the ancient world and some of the most dymanic new movements within Christianity itself.

CHRISTIANS ABANDON THE WORLD: HERMITS AND MONKS

The problem of the conflict between the flesh and the spirit that produced such differing views of scriptural interpretation, prayer, conscience, and sexuality in ancient Christianity was not finally resolved by the Christianization of the Roman Empire. In fact, as tensions developed between imperially organized and culturally assimilated Christianity and individuals who feared that Christianity would be swallowed up by too close an identification with the "world," the ascetic element in ancient Christian thought became more and more prominent. To accept the world or to flee it in various ways was a choice that opened a division in Christian Roman society from the highest to the lowest ranks—both aristocrats and peasants could make the choice to withdraw from the world, even the new Christian world, and its temptations. The development of the ascetic Christian life constituted a second major consequence of the problem of Christianity and the world. One approach to it was the development of the idea of sainthood.

The apostles and other companions of Jesus were naturally revered among early Christians, as were the martyrs of the period of persecutions. Peter and Paul had long been venerated as saintly patrons of the Christian community at Rome. Late in the fourth century, Ambrose of Milan had discovered the relics of the martyrs Protasius and Gervasius, who then became the patron saints of the city of Milan. Later, saints became the patrons of individual cities and monasteries in northern Europe. Ordinary Christians considered the individual humanity of saints as more approachable and responsive in spiritual matters than the remote, majestic, and barely imaginable figures of God the Father and Jesus.

Saints' powers were believed to be preserved in their remains, their relics, which were a purified material connection to a world of spiritual power, left behind by the saint as a token for his or her community. The saint could be considered as owning property, could appear in visions, perform miracles, and administer justice, but the relics were the nodal point that materially demonstrated the connection of the saint to the community. They were housed in finely wrought containers called reliquaries, which were ceremonially displayed in processions on the saint's feast day, along with the public reading of an account of the saint's life. The concept of human sanctity is a useful framework for considering the transformation of the ascetic holy man and woman from the third century on.

Around the year 269, Anthony, a young man from a prosperous peasant family in Egypt, moved by Christ's injunction to "go, sell all that you have and give it to the poor, and you will have treasure in heaven, and come and follow me," left his family and the narrow agricultural belt of the Nile Valley and went out alone into the desert to live a life of self-mortification and prayer. From the period of the earliest Egyptian civilization, the desert had symbolized the utter absence of civilization and the habitation of demons. Anthony's self-imposed exile was both a literal and figurative rejection of both the imperial church and the ancient, deeply rooted Egyptian terror of the wasteland. The name that his contemporaries gave to Anthony's act was a Greek word, *anachoresis,* which was traditionally applied to those who had madly fled from the pressures of civilization into the hostile and forbidding wilderness—the dropouts, or to use the modern word, "anchorites." Anthony's devotional heroism soon attracted a number of followers, although he moved farther and farther away from the edges of the civilized Egyptian rural world. His struggles with the demons of the desert, themelves a combination of recent Christian belief and traditional Egyptian peasant folklore, attracted much admiration, and by the mid fourth century, the image of the isolated holy man had developed as a successor to the more dramatic and final ideal of an earlier Christian age—that of the martyrs and confessors, those who had suffered persecution, if not death, for the faith.

The *Life of Saint Anthony,* written in Greek by Athanasius, the pugnacious defender of orthodox Christian doctrine against Arianism, was translated into Latin before 386 and began a new genre of Christian literature, the life of the saint—hagiography. The lives and accounts of the passions of the early martyrs had constituted the most popular Christian literature outside scripture of the third- and fourth-century Church. At the height of the great persecution of 298–312, martyrdom came to be considered the highest manifestation of the life of the spirit, one that brought both men and women to the very threshold of heaven. The preservation of virginity out of devotion was considered an analogy to martyrdom. Anthony and the other hermits of Egypt and Syria offered another religious ideal, that of the monk (from the Greek *monachos*, "the solitary"). Here was a "martyr" whose martyrdom consisted of making himself "dead" to the world and achieving in the desert—through rigorous self-mortification (Greek *askesis*, "training"), contemplation, combats with demons in the desert (Greek *eremos*, "desert," whence the word "hermit"), and, ultimately, mystical experience—that stage of the spiritual life that the early martyrs had reached by so different a way in so different a world.

The spiritual biographies of early monks, inspired by the vast popularity of Athanasius' *Life of Saint Anthony*, became the new literature of piety and the most reliable guides to the new spiritual life. Soon such works as Jerome's *Life of Saint Paul, the First Hermit*, and James the Deacon's *Life of Saint Pelagia the Harlot*, as well as collections of the sayings of the Desert Fathers, were also in circulation. Ironically, the spread of the popularity of monasticism attracted the attention of the very world that the monks had rejected so dramatically. Christians who had not left the world thronged out into the desert to consult and admire the holy men, just as they had once made pilgrimages to the sites of early martyrdoms, some taking up the monastic life themselves and some returning to the corrupt world invigorated by their brief contact with strenuous holiness in a living human.

Increasingly, as the historian Peter Brown has shown, holiness in late antiquity began to shift its location from things and places to persons—to holy men and women. Such figures were thought to possess not only divine favor, but literally, some of the power that characterized both divinity and the highest levels of human society. Holy men also became for a time, particularly in the eastern part of the empire, intercessors between local communities and the powerful authorities of the larger world. They replaced the aristocratic patron and the pagan oracle, and their power was thought to manifest itself through miracles, curses, and exorcism—the driving out of demons—as well as through the social and economic benefits that they brought to the communities that venerated them.

Anthony and Athanasius were both men, but the ascetic life was not restricted to men. Just as virginity and chastity offered new roles and a new degree of freedom to women, so did the ascetic movement. Aristocratic women, too, might divest themselves of their wealth and their social and domestic responsibilities in order to pursue a quest for religious freedom in much the same way as men. And although aristocratic women had a better opportunity to do this, women from other social orders could follow a similar renunciation of the world. Two of the most prominent literary motifs in this movement are conversions to the ascetic life of the aristocratic woman and the reformed prostitute, each of whom could become a new person, not by assuming male identity or power, but by changing their former lives in so radical a way as to find in one type of the Christian life an original form of religious expression. Jesus himself had given the example of the two sisters of Lazarus, Mary and Martha, whom later Christians interpreted as representing the contemplative and active lives, as they interpreted the biblical figures of Rachel and Leah, showing greater favor to Mary, the contemplative. Alongside the Desert Fathers there lived the Desert Mothers, who asserted that the ascetic life, virginity, chastity, poverty, and world-renunciation were an ungendered, neutral ground for both masculine and feminine religious expression.

The variety of forms of monasticism increased during the fourth century. Some recluses retired to caves in the desert; some, especially the Syrians, lived atop tall pillars for decades; some subjected themselves to extreme bodily mortifications and privations, eating and drinking little or nothing. Small communities had always tended to grow up around individual holy men, and these needed to become organized. Under the influence of Pachomius (286–346), a former soldier in the army of Constantine, an organized monastic life appeared first in Egypt. Later, under the influence of Basil of Caesarea (329–379), monastic organization developed in the east as well. By constituting a model, or "perfect" Christian society, a replica of heaven on earth, these communities offered a moral pattern whose elements might be absorbed slowly into the devotional life of Christians still living in the world. By the early fifth century, monasteries were flourishing in Gaul and Italy as well as in North Africa, Egypt, Syria, and Greece. The appeal of monasticism transcended the boundaries of learning, philosophy, and social class. In monasticism the devotion of the humblest man and woman was elevated to the highest level of the Christian life and therefore stood outside the increasing world-acceptance of the Christian community.

Henceforth, the Christian adaptation of pagan learning, the office of bishop, and monasticism were to be the chief supports of the spread of Christianity, both inside the Roman Empire and into the world of the barbarians. Like the bishop, the monk was the other remarkable invention of Late Antiquity.

CHRISTIANS ORDER THE WORLD: EMPERORS AND BISHOPS

During the third and early fourth centuries, the population of Christians came more and more to reflect the population of the empire as a whole. Christians and non-Christians lived in similar ways, observing the civil calendar of festivals, banqueting, attending the circus games and the theater. Constantine's legalization of Christianity in 313 largely acknowledged a fact of social assimilation that was already well underway. With the conversion of Constantine and the Christianity of all of his successors except for Julian, the process of assimilation continued even more rapidly, with many people converting to Christianity because of the imperial favor it carried. In turn, these numbers placed a considerable teaching and administrative burden on existing Christian communities and raised the specter of still further variant ideas about the nature of Christianity from un- or underinstructed converts. Just as the earliest Christianity had never foreseen the possibility of a Christian emperor (which, among other things, placed on early Christian thinkers the great burden of formulating a Christian political theory), neither had it foreseen large-scale conversion or the problems of assimilation that this entailed. The alignment of the orders of Christian clergy with the grades of the imperial civil service and the ensuing privileged status of clergy in Roman law left a permanent mark on ecclesiastical organization, laying the groundwork for the sharp distinction between clergy and laity that characterized later European Christianity until the sixteenth century.

Constantine and his family had donated substantial resources in the city of Rome and elsewhere to the Christian community and its leader, the bishop of Rome. The palace of the Laterani family became the residence and primary church of the bishop of Rome, St. John Lateran. The great shrine built over the supposed grave of the apostle Peter in the area across the Tiber River known as Vatican fields remained a holy site visited by pilgrims, but did not become the bishop's residence until the mid fifteenth century. Constantine's mother Helena built the church of the Holy Cross in Jerusalem (*Santa Croce in Gerusalemme*). In giving buildings to the Church and in constructing churches, Constantine and his successors contributed the architectural type of the *basilica* to the vocabulary of church building. The *basilica,* a general-purpose imperial administrative building, consisted of a long hall (the nave) terminating in a curved chamber (the apse), a shape that appealed to the sense of religious space that confronted the assembled congregation with the cleric who led it in prayer.

Constantine also adjusted Roman time in favor of Christianity. In 321, he commanded that the Lord's Day be observed by the suspension of public and private business and named it Sunday, thereby altering the traditional Roman period of nine market days in months otherwise marked by Kalends (first of the month), Nones (fifth or seventh of the month), and Ides (thirteenth or fifteenth of the month) into a seven-day week. From this point on, both the Julian calendar and the weekly and monthly cycles of the Christian year came to mark time for more and more of western Europe.

Churchmen became advisers to emperors as well, notably Hosius of Cordoba (ca. 257–357) and Eusebius of Caesarea (ca. 260–340). Eusebius' life of the emperor Constantine became a prototype of biographies of later Christian rulers and an important document in later Christian political theory. He was also the author of the first Church history, a remarkable account of the rise of Christianity that emphasized the identity and continuity between the church of the apostles and martyrs and the imperial church of the early fourth century. By stressing the succession of bishops from the apostles to the present and the unchanging orthodox belief of the episcopal church, and by appropriating the cult of martyrs as the foundation of the new golden age of Christianity under benevolent Roman emperors, Eusebius emphasized themes that became central in the church of the later fourth century and after: identity and continuity over time, the sharp distinction between orthodoxy and heterodoxy, and the cult of martyrs and other holy people under the aegis of the episcopal church.

In the Greek-speaking eastern part of the empire, the most influential theologians were a remarkable group of thinkers and writers known as the Cappadocian Fathers: the brothers Basil the Great (d. 379) and Gregory of Nyssa (d. ca. 395), their older sister Macrina the Younger who was their earliest teacher, and Gregory of Nazianzen (d. 389). Superbly educated in Greek classical culture, these four Cappadocian thinkers, three of them bishops and all of them writers, nevertheless criticized those elements in pagan learning that they found morally unacceptable and contrary to Christian truth, while at the same time preserving what they considered the best of it and urging other Christians to do likewise. They also signaled the intellectual and spiritual vigor of a province that had hitherto been remote from the centers of both Hellenistic and Christian culture. Their influence extended not only to developing monasticism and the theology of Greek Christianity, but even into the west in the later fourth and fifth centuries.

Bishops, elected by local congregations and consecrated by other bishops, held office for life. They came to possess considerable prominence through their legal control of ecclesiastical property and finances, their exclusive authority to ordain deacons, deaconesses, and priests, their exclusive right to baptize and preach, and their right to exercise ecclesiastical discipline (including excommunication). In the west, they also exercised control over individual holy men and the cult of the saints, as well as over monasteries located within their dioceses.

The most influential example of this kind of bishop was Ambrose of Milan (ca. 339–397). Son of the praetorian prefect of Gaul, Ambrose was born at Trier, entered the imperial civil service, and became civil governor of Milan, the most important center of imperial administration in the west. When the Arian bishop of the city died in 374, the orthodox population of the city acclaimed Ambrose as their new bishop, although at the time Ambrose, a Christian believer, had not yet even been baptized.

Ambrose at first protested his inadequacy, but he then devoted himself to his congregation for more than twenty years. He stoutly defended orthodox doctrine, maintained the independence of his church from the imperial government, and wrote what is still the most thorough guide on how to be a Christian bishop. In 390, after the Christian emperor Theodosius had ordered the massacre of the Christian population of Thessalonica because it had disobeyed an imperial command, Ambrose forbade Theodosius to participate in Christian liturgical ceremonies and forced the emperor to perform penance for his act. Ambrose may thus be regarded as one of the strongest early defenders of the superiority of the clergy over the temporal powers, at least in matters of belief and ecclesiastical moral discipline. Ambrose also emphasized the bishop's responsibility for the people in his care. He popularized the collective singing of hymns, and his discovery of the relics of Gervasius and Protasius and his construction of the city church over their graves gave Milan its patron saints. Ambrose's reputation, episcopal activity, and extensive writings made him the model Christian bishop. They also reveal in his life and thought the influence of late antique Neoplatonic philosophy (through his reading of the Cappadocian Fathers) and the continuing influence of traditional Roman concepts of public service, responsibility, and civic morality that had been expressed long before by Cicero.

Other fourth- and fifth-century bishops, including several bishops of Rome, also helped to shape and define the new imperial church. Although the bishop of Rome was originally no different from other bishops, Rome was the site of the first Christian community in western Europe and the city where the apostles Peter and Paul were allegedly buried. It was also the old imperial capital, and thus the leader of its Christian community could claim a certain precedence over other western bishops. Damasus I (366–384) increased the prestige of his see by renewing the history of Christian Rome, turning older Christian burial places (the catacombs) into shrines and patronizing the cults of

The Silver Plate of Theodosius. This plate shows a highly formalized scene of the emperor Theodosius investing an official with his rank of office, catching the extreme sense of hierarchy still present at the end of the fourth century. (Spain, end of 4th century, "Disk of Theodosius I (The Great)." Real Academia de Bellas Artes de San Fernando, Madrid, Spain. Copyright Giraudon/Art Resource, NY)

martyrs in the city. Damasus also cooperated with the emperor Theodosius' decisions on the nature of orthodox belief, and in return Theodosius formally recognized the preeminence of the bishop of Rome as successor to Peter the Apostle. No one at the time understood such preeminence as being much more than honorific, but later bishops of Christian Rome invoked, not only the succession to Peter, but also the dignity of the city, the antiquity of its Christian community, and its historical orthodoxy to support later claims to rule the spiritual affairs of the west, and indeed of the entire empire and all Christian peoples beyond its limits.

Damasus became the first bishop of Rome to use the title "apostolic" in connection with his see and began addressing other bishops as "sons" instead of "brothers" in his correspondence with them. His successors elaborated on these usages. Siricius (384–399) was the first to use the title *papa* (later, "pope," but at the time simply the Latin version of the Greek *pappas,* a term of reverence for a religious leader). Innocent I (401–417) claimed that important ecclesiastical cases should be judged only by the bishop of Rome. By the time of Leo I (440–461), the greatest of the bishops of Rome before the late sixth century, the office had clearly emerged as the successor of the senatorial guardians of imperial tradition and as the highest ranking churchman in the empire.

The prestige of a bishop like Ambrose and the gradual rise to prominence of the bishops of Rome were two of the forces that shaped the imperial Christian church between 350 and 450. A third was the emergence of a remarkable series of theologians writing in Latin, whose work marked the Christian absorption and transformation of earlier philosophical culture. As theologians, Ambrose and Leo I were two of these. But the most articulate and influential spokesman for Christianity was Aurelius Augustinus (354–430), professor of rhetoric in Rome and Milan, convert to Christianity, and later bishop of Hippo Regius in North Africa. Augustine was one of the "new provincials" whose secular and ecclesiastical career reveals much about both Christianity and Roman society at the turn of the fifth century.

Born at Thagaste in North Africa in 354, the son of free landowners, Augustine was reared by his Christian mother Monnica, although he rejected Christianity through much of his youth and early adulthood. His father was Patricius, a minor member of the decurion class, who could provide a comfortable provincial life, although he was not wealthy. Patricius and Monnica were unable to afford more than minimal schooling for their precocious son, but a wealthy neighbor undertook the expense of Augustine's continuing education at Carthage, where he easily mastered Latin, but not Greek. He also lived with a woman, whom he does not name, with whom he had a son in 370 or 371. The woman was a Christian, and Augustine later remarked that he was faithful to her as long as they were together. Augustine also became a follower of the dualist religion of Manichaeism, a derivative of Persian Zoroastrianism that had grown up in the third century C.E., and he also seems to have flirted with various mystery religions.

From Carthage, Augustine's academic success as a teacher of rhetoric brought him first to Rome, and then, under the patronage of the great pagan noble Symmachus, to the professorship of rhetoric at Milan, the city of Ambrose, the greatest city in Italy, and the western imperial capital.

Until Augustine was thirty, his career as a successful intellectual from the provinces had been a clasical example of "making it" in a social system that was increasingly open to talent and the right kind of patronage. From his professorship at Milan, Augustine became eligible for marriage into an aristocratic family. With his academic and social credentials and influential friends, he could have aspired to a high administrative post in the empire, a provincial governorship, or a position as tutor to the children of an emperor. A generation earlier, the Bordeaux professor of rhetoric, Ausonius, had parlayed his own status as tutor of the future emperor Gratian into a praetorian prefecture and a position of power behind Gratian's throne. There was no reason, save one, why Augustine's career should not have followed a similar path. That reason was Augustine's restless spirit.

In the course of his education and social success, Augustine had encountered intellectually and personally the rich spectrum of spiritual experience that the fourth-century imperial world had to offer: his mother's provincial Christianity, his father's non-Christianity, mystery religions, Manichaeism, and the surviving paganism of rural North Africa. But if Augustine was not to become another Apuleius, neither would he become another Ausonius. His mother had followed him to Italy, and the emptiness of his own heart, as he was later to say, made the varieties of spiritual experience he knew appear only dim and deceptive shadows. In Milan, Augustine also met Ambrose, and the influence of the older man combined with Monnica's deep devotion seem to have turned the professor's mind and heart back to that Christianity he had ignored for so long. After a sudden personal religious experience in 386, Augustine returned to Christianity, renounced his professorship, broke off relations with the woman with whom he had lived, and returned to Africa. He would pursue there, he thought, a life of prayer and contemplation with chosen companions in a company that resembled both the learned academy and the monastery.

We know the course of his life because of his *Confessions,* which he wrote in 397. The work is the first intellectual self-portrait in history; in it Augustine offered not only the external events of his life, but the "history of a heart," the story of his own religious experience told from the viewpoint of a middle-aged bishop. In the *Confessions,* Augustine offered yet a new version of the Christian conversion story, one in which the scheme of an entire life became the story of continuing struggles to come to terms with the traces of God—the *vestigia Dei*—in the human soul. For Augustine, the discovery of the will of God, which guides and patiently waits for the errant human will to recognize it, the conversion, was the climax of the human life. But the work was not one of saccharine spiritualism; the *Confessions* reads far more like "the account of a great spiritual disease and its convalescence" than like the heroic conversion or martyrdom stories of old. Augustine keeps constantly before the reader's eyes the full depth and complexity of the human condition. Nowhere, even after the conversion, does he betray that complexity, and nowhere does he offer an easy and confident life as a result of his conversion. Augustine was probably the first thinker to use himself to describe both the nature of the spiritual disorder that pervades the soul of anyone who ignores the will of God and the continuing burden of that disorder even after conversion, even after he had become the bishop of Hippo Regius (395–430).

Augustine witnessed the great religious reforms of the emperor Theodosius and his successors, but his role was never that of an imperial adviser like Ambrose. Augustine ruled his North African city as its bishop, wrote commentaries on scripture, treatises on points of doctrine, sermons, and letters—more than 270 of them to correspondents across the Latin-speaking Roman world—on all aspects of Christian belief and practice. More than any other Latin Father, Augustine shaped the future intellectual development of western Christianity.

Augustine's vast literary output made him the foremost Latin theologian of his day. His work also exerts its influence on our own present, just as it has on all periods of the past. His commentaries on scripture formed the basis of all later Christian biblical interpretation, and his letters and treatises on particular topics became the starting points for all subsequent discussions of their subjects. One reason for Augustine's enduring influence was that as both theologian and bishop, he constantly looked at the human condition as he saw and experienced it himself. He saw humans as they were, with small victories and frequent failures of both reason and will, and neither as wicked nor as perfectable as other Christian thinkers saw them.

Augustine's concept of the human will is a major key to his thought. God, he said, had given humans free will, the power to choose what their instructed reason designated as good. Adam and Eve had asserted their will against God, and although baptism removes the stain of that original sin, the will itself remains defective, troubled by passions that it can scarcely resist, requiring grace from God to restore it. Sexual desire and activity, for example, were created by God with Adam and Eve, and Jesus possessed complete sexual capacity, for he was fully human as well as fully divine. For Augustine, the problem of human sexuality lay in the fact that before the Fall, Adam and Eve would have engaged in sexual intercourse undistracted by the passions that overwhelm the will and make it powerless to control desire. Jesus could, but did not, because his will was perfectly aligned with the divine will. Only humans, neglecting grace, lost control of their wills, subjecting themselves to random passions, creating a disruptive power that mirrored all the other disruptions to which fallen human nature was subject. Augustine's last disputes with other Christian leaders, especially the followers of the British monk Pelagius, focused on the problem of the perfectability of humans in this world. Augustine never reconciled himself to the idea that fallen human nature could be reconciled to God without the acceptance of divine grace.

As in psychology, so in history. Augustine's most complex work was the immensely long and intricate essay on history, time, and justice that he called *The City of God,* a work he produced between 413 and 426. The military reversals of the late fourth and early fifth centuries, including the sack of Rome by Alaric and the Visigoths (below, Chapter 3), caused Roman non-Christians to claim that Christianity had brought down the wrath of the old gods on the empire. Augustine took up the charge by reassessing the Roman past and laying down the principles of the ideal relations between earthly political orders and the spiritual community of Christian believers. He argued that there were "two cities," or societies. The city of God consisted of all Christians, past, present, and future, who live in this world for a time and make use of earthly institutions to attain temporal peace, but can give no ultimate loyalty or affection to any state created by defective human powers. The city of man regards this life and its needs as an ultimate goal and gives too much of its affection to this world, using human achievement as an end rather than as the limited means that it really is. No earthly society, not even a Christianized Roman Empire, is anything more than an unstable creation of mortals. The best that anyone can hope for from any earthly society, especially one ruled by Christian rulers, is that it curb the baser instincts of fallen human nature and preserve a modicum of earthly peace that is necessary for the conduct of a Christian life. Such rulers are more like "godly magistrates," than absolute sovereigns; their duties are regulatory and punitive, disciplinary and corrective, rather than constructive or progressive. No gods ever helped Rome, and God will allow no earthly state to become a heavenly city. Nor can even the worst circumstances of life in this world impose a moral stain on human nature. Augustine condemned the suicide of the idealized Roman woman Lucretia (above, Chapter 1) because she confused an insult to the body with a moral fault, falling into the sin of pride by defending an imaginary and transient honor.

The City of God became the first, and in many ways is still the most complex, expression of a Christian philosophy of history and political theory. As such, it remained one of the most influential works of the late antique world and a challenge to the absolute validity of any purely secular view of history or political theory.

The third Latin Father, very different from both, was Jerome. Born at Stridon, in the western Balkans, in 331, Jerome received a good literary education, became highly influential in aristocratic and learned circles in Christian Rome, and was a protégé of Damasus I, the bishop of Rome. Upon Damasus' death, Jerome was considered a potential successor, but social and literary enemies—Jerome made enemies easily—prevented his election and forced him to leave Rome entirely. Jerome settled in Bethlehem, where he devoted the rest of his life to doctrinal disputes and to his great project of translating into Latin and commenting on all of scripture, directly from the original Hebrew, Greek, and Aramaic texts. Jerome's knowledge of historical Greek and Hebrew was pressed into service as he undertook his work, and he finally translated both testaments into Latin, a monumental work of linguistic, historical, and interpretive scholarship. The Latin Vulgate (the Latin word *vulgus* means "the crowd"—and by extension "popular"), provided the entirety of Christian scripture in a language available to every literate person in the west. Jerome's choice of a middle-level, administrative Latin instead of an elaborate literary Latin made a great impact on both Latin theology and the later development of European thought.

3

The Roman and Other Worlds Transformed

OLD ROME AND NEW ROME: THE FOUNDING OF CONSTANTINOPLE

The original unity of the ancient Mediterranean world, that of a "slender coastline studded with classical city-states," was economic, cultural, and political, but it was felt most by a small set of ruling elites and their clients and servants. In the third and fourth centuries, the demands of the vast and increasingly troubled hinterlands that protected the coastline put great strains on both imperial power and the resources that held that world together. The diplomacy of Trajan and the universal curiosity and selective benevolence of Hadrian gave way, once the military and political problems of the third century had been temporarily settled, to the heavyhanded managerial techniques of Diocletian and Constantine and their successors. The duplication of the imperial office, abolished by Constantine, but restored by his successors, reflected not merely political and military conditions, but also a growing division between the eastern and western parts of the empire. More and more spheres of life were bureaucratized and militarized, with different results in different parts of the empire. While this chapter will concentrate largely on the western parts of the empire, events in the west can only be understood in terms of events in the east (below, Chapters 4 and 5).

Although some of Constantine's successors attempted to restore the civilian and aristocratic character of the empire, the emperors of the fourth century became more and more autocratic, not only in styles of governance, but in appearance and conduct as well. Constantine had begun the practice of wearing a purple headband decorated with pearls, clothing himself for public appearances in jeweled robes and sitting on a throne. Separated from both his courtiers and his visitors by a series of veils that structured his throneroom, the emperor governed through a rigidly defined hierarchy of officials. No longer a god, he became God's deputy on earth, the *autokrator,* the sole bearer of legitimate authority.

The divisions within the empire's Mediterranean core became even sharper in the fourth and fifth centuries. External threats grew stronger, not only from the Persian empire, but from new configurations of militarized peoples along many of the frontiers. The emergence of Islam (below, Chapter 5) in the early seventh century introduced yet a third force into that world. After the early seventh century, the most striking feature of Cicero's *orbis terrarum*—"the circle of the lands"—was its division into three distinct parts, each of which, as it expanded into areas that Rome had never controlled, became the core of one of the three great civilizations that have characterized the world of Europe, Africa, and Western Asia ever since: the East Roman, or Byzantine; West Roman/Northern European, and Islamic.

For six centuries the Roman empire ruled, but never fully absorbed, the Mediterranean world and governed, but never fully assimilated, its provinces. Local languages, cultural forms, and material technology continued to exist under the indifferent surface of imperial government and elite culture. In the late fourth and fifth centuries, imperial government made greater demands on all levels of imperial society, but it also eroded some of the structural elements that had for a long time sustained the universal character of the empire. During this period, local culture, economy, and technology broke through the surface of imperial civilization and reasserted themselves, often in the face of imperial resentment and impotence.

The network and functions of cities and the communication links among them, the observance of public calendars, and even the villas of aristocrats all changed. The cities, those "checkerboard towns" mentioned above, had long depended on the private support of both local aristocrats and the decurion order. Some of this generosity may be attributed to public-spiritedness, but most of it was the result of what the Greeks called *evergetia* and *philotimia* (generosity and love of honor) and the Romans called *magnanimitas* (great-spiritedness), that is, the desire for status, honor, and fame after death that was expressed in a spirit of competition with others who sought the same things. As long as this stimulus survived, the towns and cities of the Mediterranean world benefited greatly and preserved the distinctive functions and "look" that is their most striking feature.

As private wealth left the cities and public responsibilities and expenses increased, the maintenance of cities lost its chief support. Aristocrats and decurions (the *curialis* order) withdrew to their private estates when they could, and the country villa with its domestic interests, leisure, and servants replaced the city and public responsibilities in the life of the aristocracy. In the eastern part of the empire, where there were some 900 cities, this transformation was slow and never complete. In the western part of the empire, where there were only 114 cities, the transformation was drastic. The annual income of the eastern imperial court was 270,000 pounds of gold, of which 45,000 pounds were expended on the military. The annual income of the western imperial court was

20,000 pounds of gold (in a world where a single senator might have a virtually untaxable income of 12,500 pounds), with very little to spend on anything.

Although they were expensively built and usually over-engineered, ancient cities, like modern ones, were physically fragile and required considerable maintenance and repair. Roman donors, however, were usually more inclined to fund new buildings than to renovate older ones, unless the latter had significant public and historical importance. When donors ceased their civic generosity during the fifth century, the problem of repairs loomed large, not only in terms of buildings, streets, bridges, water supply, and baths, but also in those of town walls and fortifications. When building repairs were done in the west in late antiquity, they were expended largely on fortifications, churches, or private projects that interested emperors and imperial officials.

Imperial officials gradually replaced town councils. Exempted from the burdens of public office themselves, these officials directed their personal wealth to private projects. The diminished prestige that had characterized public generosity in earlier centuries increased the financial responsibilities and burdens on the former governing orders of the towns, and then directly on ordinary townspeople. This process worked more slowly in the area around the city of Rome itself and the vast lands of the senatorial aristocracy in southern Italy, but it proceeded more quickly elsewhere in the west.

The costs of empire—the imperial court itself, the army, the vast bureaucracy, imperial public works, and the provisioning of the cities—did not decline, but the tax base did, in the fifth century in the west and in the late sixth and seventh centuries in the east. To many western aristocrats and landowners, the financial demands and administrative pressure of the empire simply became too heavy. Accommodation with local Germanic rulers (who themselves became largely Romanized in the course of the fifth and sixth centuries) became easier and economically more attractive. Moreover, these rulers did not require nearly as heavy a system of taxation, because the greatest imperial need for taxes, the army, was supported instead by grants from part of the land revenues and did not require the high salaries of Roman soldiers. The cooperation of disaffected Romans and Romanized Germans characterizes much of the late fifth and early sixth centuries in the west.

The shape of the western city also changed during this period. When fortifications were built, they fortified only part of the older town complex, and the center of a reduced population shifted into them. Where new fortifications were unaffordable, several towns simply moved their reduced populations into the old arenas and amphitheaters. The city became the responsibility of its bishop, since bishops had assumed many of the civic responsibilities of the former governing classes, and many towns took on an increasingly clerical character, with church compounds, including cemeteries, protected by any new fortifications that were built.

The observance of a common imperial calendar also tended to disappear. The only surviving calendar from the Roman Empire is a splendidly illuminated manuscript describing both pagan and Christian festivals, prepared in 354 as a gift for a Roman noble named Valentinus. Its illustrations were the first full-page illustrations in any codex, and the volume contained much information on Roman history, the holders of high office, games and spectacles, and other facets of Roman life in the mid fourth century. In 389, an imperial law abolished pagan holidays, and Christian holidays in addition to Sunday were given legal status. Emperors detached public games and chariot races from the pagan feast days that had originally generated them. In 448/9 in Gaul, a Gallo-Roman named Polemius Silvius produced the other surviving calendar from the imperial period, dedicated to the bishop of Lyons, Eucherius. Polemius' calendar began on January 1, and it omitted many pagan festivals, preserving some of these only as neutered aspects of traditional Roman culture in an increasingly religious Christian present. The fifth and sixth centuries began to be called "Christian times."

Local calendars were observed in both cities and on country estates. These estates, the villas, which included the building complex of private family residence, cultivated fields and gardens, orchards, buildings for livestock, cottage industry, and fishponds, increasingly became the primary residence for the middling and upper orders of western Roman society. The rural estate itself was not new in the fourth and fifth centuries. Many wealthy Romans had long maintained rural residences as well as urban ones, but its more widespread and exclusive use was new. Nearly economically self-sufficient, and in many instances, securely protected and policed by the master's own private army, the villa offered the attractions of both urban and rural life—since the facilities of the greatest villas were designed and decorated on a lavish scale. It also offered protection to those too poor or weak to protect themselves. People who fled the tax burdens of the cities, as well as local farmworkers, the *coloni*, were increasingly willing to exchange their precarious and expensive urban and rural freedom for the protection and security that the master of a villa could offer. Gradually, the status of many of these people was lowered, as they became tied to the land they worked. At the same time, the increasing numbers of half-free laborers reduced the need for slaves, and the villas became the laboratories in which new kinds of unfree status for the rural labor force—later termed serfdom—developed.

One useful way of indicating the consequences of this long process is to consider a tale of two cities—Rome and Constantinople.

The emperors in the western part of the empire during the fourth century found that Rome was no longer an efficient capital, and they ruled instead from a number of different cities in northern Italy and Gaul: Trier, Milan, Arles, Sirmium, and finally, from 404 C.E., Ravenna on the northeastern coast of the Italian peninsula. Ravenna was a port city protected by strong fortifications and large marshes that gave easy access to the sea and to Constantinople from its port at Classe.

After his victory at the Milvian Bridge in 312, Constantine turned against the Roman senate and Praetorian Guard that had supported his rival Maxentius, dissolved the Guard forever, and departed Rome for the east. There, on the site of the small fishing town of Byzantium, he founded a new city named after himself: Constantinople, "Constantine's *polis*." Located on a triangular peninsula between the Bosporos and the Sea of Marmara, bodies of navigable water that link the Black Sea and the Aegean, and at the point at which Asia and Europe meet, Constantinople benefited from Constantine's generosity and that of his successors. It became a vast new city that rivaled and surpassed old Rome. In 450, Theodosius II expanded the city walls, creating masterpieces of fortification that withstood every invader until they were breached by Ottoman Turkish cannon in 1453 (below, Chapter 20). The location, wealth, and security of Constantinople proved crucial in ruling and defending the eastern part of the empire, and the eastern part of the empire remained attractive to those in the west, particularly during periods of insecurity and invasion. The sea route between Constantinople and Ravenna was, until the eighth century, the connecting water link between the slowly separating cultures of the two parts of the Roman Empire.

The founding of Constantinople was an act of Roman daring—and of Roman genius. Not only was the city strategically located, well managed to provide a high standard of living for most of its inhabitants, and securely fortified, but it was also a dynamic center that could deploy the vast resources of the Greek-speaking, urbanized, agriculturally prosperous, and intellectually developed East Mediterranean world, including those of the cities of Antioch, Alexandria, Beirut, Thessalonica, and Athens. In addition, it was the western end of the long trade routes that originated in China. After the late fourth century, the strength of Constantinople and the east Roman empire was demonstrated, as wave after wave of invading peoples broke through the imperial frontiers, crashed against the walls of the great city, and invariably receded, moving west to assault the weaker and less resourceful centers of the western part of the empire, often as a result of the diplomacy of Constantinople.

With the western emperors ruling from Ravenna, the city of Rome was deserted by the imperial court and those who had business with it. Its population declined steadily, the area of habitation shrunk to the banks of the Tiber river and the lowlands among its hills, and more and more of its administrative needs had to be met by the only organization remotely capable of dealing with them—the churches of Rome and their bishop. Churchmen also led in defense against and negotiation with new kinds of invaders of the western imperial provinces and of Rome itself.

MIGRANTS AND INVADERS

The relations between Romans and *externae gentes* had always been even more complex than writers like Julius Caesar and Tacitus cared to admit. The Romanization of Celts and Germans, the culturally mixed societies on either side of the Rhine-Danube frontiers, the existence of *laeti*, and the admission of whole peoples as *federati* (allied troops under their own commanders who were subordinate to Roman leaders) of the Roman state and army all blurred any clear line between Romans and "barbarians"—if such a line had ever existed anywhere but in the imagination of Roman writers and politicians. The Roman society that encountered Germanic and other migrants and invaders from the late fourth century on was very different from that which had created the empire in the first place, and its own circumstances must be understood in order to understand the impact of barbarian migrants and invaders in the late fourth, fifth, and sixth centuries.

One manifestation of the transformed concerns of Gallo-Roman aristocrats was their assumption of the role of Christian bishop—perhaps as a substitute for their failed former role as voluntary civic benefactors. The emergence of the aristocratic bishop and his assumption of many of the older civic responsibilities of city management was one consequence of the transformation of the fourth-century Roman provincial world in Gaul.

Others from lower social orders also fled the network of imperial bureaucrats, tax collectors, and soldiers to the protection of landed aristocrats. Even members of these orders contributed, as did their aristocratic protectors, to the increasingly private and local character of the Roman west. The new society at the end of the fifth century had two levels—aristocratic lords, patrons, and protectors, virtually independent of any public authority, and their politically and economically dependent clients and servants. Such a society could accommodate any public authority that did not make excessive demands and permitted it to go its own way, whether that authority was Roman or barbarian.

It is in this context that the problem of the "barbarians" in the late fourth, fifth, and sixth centuries must be understood. From the encounters in the late second century between Marcus Aurelius and the Marcomanni, it is clear that the formation of Germanic peoples beyond the frontiers had changed from its earlier character. Large-scale migrations from northern Europe moved southward, absorbing and restructuring existing peoples along the frontier into new and larger groups that consisted of migrating armies increasingly geared for constant war. Far to the east of the Roman frontier, still other "barbarian" peoples, Asiatic nomadic pastoralists and warriors, also assembled military empires in Central Asia, either absorbing neighboring peoples or driving them east or west, into China or western Eurasia. These migratory "empires" and the peoples they absorbed lived on tribute and the pillage of conquered lands. Peoples who were not absorbed or destroyed by them were driven ahead of them, looking for safety rather than conquest. Between the second and the sixth centuries, these two quite different transformations of peoples far from the Roman frontiers stirred all of Eurasia and moved both migrants and invaders toward the frontiers of the Roman empire.

The history of the "Goths" offers a telling example. In the late second and early third centuries, the small people known as the Goths assembled a powerful military force that threatened the Roman Danube frontier in the mid third century and was finally destroyed by the emperors Claudius II and Aurelian. In the early fourth century, two new Gothic kingdoms arose, both of which were led by a military king and his warriors, reducing the public role of the old free Germanic warrior who was not a member of these groups to an inferior and subordinate status.

Allied with Rome, one of these new-style Germanic confederations, the Tervingi (later calling themselves Visigoths) was itself threatened by the appearance of the Huns, part of a nomadic warrior empire from Central Asia that had plundered Persia and China in the late second century. By the beginning of the third century, the Huns occupied the steppe north of the Caucasus, and by late in the fourth century, they pushed farther west and south, where they destroyed the Visigothic kingdom on the Black Sea in 374/5 and sent its remnants fleeing toward the Roman Danube frontier seeking asylum and protection from their old allies, the Romans.

Although the Romans permitted the Visigoths to enter the empire en masse in 376 (the first time the Romans had ever admitted an entire people under its own leaders and preserving its own organization), Roman soldiers and officials mistreated them savagely. The Visigoths revolted in 378, destroyed a Roman army and the emperor Valens (r. 364–378) at the battle of Adrianople, and began their migration through the western empire, periodically concluding short-lived agreements with Roman imperial officials.

By 402, the Visigoths were in Italy itself, briefly capturing and sacking the city of Rome in 410, and then moving north and west into Gaul and Iberia. There, in 415, they patched up yet another treaty with Rome and settled down to establish an independent kingdom in Gaul.

From the second century to the fifth, the armies of Rome's enemies (except for Persia), were polyethnic confederations and miscellaneous mercenaries that assembled themselves into an identifiable military force and then often dissolved, with their smallest components either disappearing or joining new assemblies. These groups cannot be called "ethnic" in any modern sense of the term, but several of them, particularly at the level of the military elite, underwent a process of group formation and survived long enough as a group so that they experienced what has come to be called ethnogenesis— the fabrication of an ethnic identity. As the Roman Empire in the West dissolved into a patchwork of provincial kingdoms, the ruling dynasties of those kingdoms imitated some aspects of Roman imperial rule, used what they could of Roman institutions, usually cooperated with the Gallo-Roman aristocratic bishops and lay nobles, converted at different times from Arianism to Catholic Christianity, and established the identity of a people on the basis of its ruling royal dynasty. Their elites learned how to deal with Roman aristocrats, and they also learned from Roman rulers how to become more effective leaders of their own peoples in their new circumstances.

The next stage of ethnogenesis was to identify a collective people—however it had originally come together—with an older tradition, often by constructing genealogies that reached far back into the distant past, thus asserting that the people of the present, particularly the ruling family, had always been the same people. Success in war meant the acquisition of land, booty, new warriors drawn to the successful group, and glory for the war leaders. And if the new group survived, its leader needed to turn himself into a new kind of king, the king of a people, and one way by which kings did this was to issue collections of laws that applied to all members of the people. During the fifth and sixth centuries in western Europe, the answer to the old question as to whether kings make peoples or peoples make kings, was usually the first. But when rulers failed to maintain themselves or were defeated in battle, the reverse process to ethnogenesis set in—the disappearance of some earlier ethnic groups. Groups might dissolve, with their smallest components joining other groups as the process of ethnogenesis began again.

Another Gothic kingdom, more assimilated by the Huns, yet also preserving its own small collective identity, survived as part of the Hunnic confederation. It took the name of Ostrogoths and remained a component of the Hunnic threat to Rome. In the 420s, the Huns, who were not themselves ethnically or linguistically homogeneous, raided the Carpathian basin and the Balkans, plundered regional trade routes, and demanded tribute. Hunnic contingents also sometimes fought alongside Roman armies against other peoples. They possessed new and fearsome weapons, excelled in light cavalry warfare, and were remarkably successful at absorbing other peoples and holding their vast confederation together. Under their king Attila (r. 440–454) they received a large imperial subsidy from Constantinople to leave the Balkans, and they turned west, alternately making treaties with the western Romans for tribute and then launching raids again. In 451, Attila attacked Gaul, which was defended by an alliance of Burgundians,

Visigoths, Franks, and Romans. The defeat of Attila in Gaul turned the Huns toward Italy, where they took Aquileia and Milan. The Hunnic army, however, suffered from disease, problems of supply, and exhaustion, and diplomatic negotiations in 452, which included the bishop of Rome, Leo I (440–461), persuaded them to move northeast out of Italy, where Attila died in 454. The remains of the Hunnic army and peoples were destroyed and scattered in the Battle of Nedao, when a subject people revolted. The survivors were either absorbed into the local population along the Danube or migrated elsewhere, possibly joining the later Asiatic confederations known as the Avars (below, Chapter 8) or Bulgars (below, Chapter 9).

In the winter of 405/6 other militarized confederations swept across the Rhine and penetrated deeply into Gaul. For two years, these invaders—calling themselves the Vandal, Suevian, Burgundian, and Alan peoples—sacked most of Gaul and then settled there. The Burgundians occupied a large part of eastern Gaul around Lake Geneva and the middle Rhone Valley, while the Vandals and Suevians crossed the Pyrenees into Iberia, where the Suevians remained in what is now modern Galicia in Iberia. One of the terms of the alliance of the Romans and Visigoths in Gaul had been the stipulation that the Visigoths would help the Romans to control the Vandals and Suevians. For fifteen years, the Visigoths fought the Vandals on Rome's behalf, until the Vandals crossed the Straits of Gibraltar in 428 and moved eastward, conquering much of Roman North Africa. During the next decade, under their king Geiseric, the Vandals systematically removed North Africa from imperial control, cut off the flow of grain fleets from Africa to Italy, and even launched seaborne attacks on the Italian peninsula, sacking Rome itself in 455. Augustine (above, Chapter 2) died in Hippo Regius in 430, as the Vandal army approached the gates of the city.

THE WORLD OF GALLA PLACIDIA AUGUSTA

When the Visigoths revolted and killed Valens, the *augustus* of the East, at the battle of Adrianople in 378, the surviving *augustus,* Gratian, appointed a retired Iberian general, Theodosius (r. 379–395), to replace Valens. By 392, Theodosius was the sole emperor. He established the Theodosian dynasty, the last imperial dynasty to rule both the eastern and western parts of the empire. In cooperation with Gratian, who had dropped the title *pontifex maximus* from the imperial title and confiscated the revenues and endowments of pagan temples and priesthoods, Theodosius completed the establishment of Christianity as the only legal religion in the empire in 392. Theodosius' sixteen-year reign is significant both for its success in temporarily controlling the problem of barbarian migrants and invaders and for making Christianity the Roman state religion. The history of his dynasty also reveals several shifts in power within the ruling circles of the empire, further localization and privatization of public interests, and the relative impact of barbarian migrations and invasions on the eastern and western parts of the empire.

One of the most striking features of the Theodosian dynasty—and of several other imperial dynasties that had preceded it—was the place of women in the domestic and public affairs of the empire. This place had been shaped by the changing position of women in Roman imperial society, briefly traced above.

From the fourth century on, female Christians in imperial dynasties played prominent roles. When successful military adventurers turned their families into imperial dynasties, the females of those families became important as well. They married for diplomatic advantage, served as guardians for minor children, and often influenced imperial policymaking. Helena, the mother of Constantine, was not only alleged to have discovered the cross on which Jesus had been crucified, but she also founded a number of churches (above, Chapter 2) and with her son, the Church of the Holy Sepulcher in Jerusalem itself. Justina, the wife of Valentinian I (r. 364–375) and mother of Valentinian II (r. 383–392) played a crucial role in military policy during the early reign of Theodosius I.

At his death in 395, Theodosius I left three children: Arcadius, *augustus* of the east, Honorius, *augustus* of the west, and a daughter, Galla Placidia. The world of Galla Placidia was one of both internal and external turmoil for the empire, and in that world, Galla Placidia proved considerably more intelligent, forceful of character, and able than her brothers, although she held an official title only briefly.

Galla Placidia was the daughter of the second marriage of Theodosius and was brought up at Constantinople and Rome, where she was probably educated in traditional Greek and Latin literature, trained in Christian morality to the degree suitable for an imperial princess, and given the stylized domestic education traditionally offered to aristocratic female children. She also remained unmarried far longer than was usual among imperial children, probably for political reasons. In 409, she was captured by the Visigoths, who kept her in respectful captivity. She witnessed the sack of Rome in 410 and then was taken by the Visigoths on their long trek northward out of Italy. Later in 410, the king Athaulf settled the Visigoths in western Gaul around Bordeaux and Toulouse, and in 414, the year before he entered a treaty with Honorius that stabilized the lands he controlled in Gaul, he married Galla Placidia.

Athaulf is an interesting figure in the early history of Europe. The historian Paulus Orosius, who had been driven from his home in Iberia by the events of 406–413, recounts a story in which Athaulf is alleged to have said that he once planned to replace "Romania" with "Gothia," but found that his people were too divided to live under law. He then decided to let the Visigoths become "Rome's shield," preserving Roman glory and restoring Roman power with Gothic arms. Whether or not Athaulf said this, and, if he did, what he meant by it, have been the subjects of considerable historical debate. Athaulf died in 415, having moved his people into northern Iberia in the face of pressure from the Franks (this chapter, next section).

The continued harassment of the Visigoths by Roman forces, the blockading of the ports on which the Visigoths depended for the importation of food, and the Visigoths' lack of success in attempting to move into North Africa, forced Athaulf's successors to come to terms with the Romans, who, in spite of Athaulf's proclamation of himself as a protector of Roman culture and his obvious affection and respect for Galla Placidia, had never ceased their hostility toward the Visigoths. After Athaulf's death, Galla Placidia was returned to her brother Honorius in 416, and relations between Visigoths and Romans improved considerably. In 417, Galla Placidia was married at her brother's orders to Constantius, an able general and Roman noble who had emerged as Honorius' most influential adviser. Through Constantius, Honorius managed to restore imperial influence even among the barbarian invaders of the west. But Constantius died in 421, leaving Galla Placidia twice a widow and mother of a son, who became the emperor Valentinian III (r. 425–455). During Valentinian's minority, Galla Placidia received the title *Augusta,* technically designating her the ruler of the western part of the empire. She died in 450.

Galla Placidia's brothers, Honorius and Arcadius, and her son, Valentinian III, proved far less competent than she, less and less able to wring tax revenues from the shrunken population, incapable of adopting a consistent diplomatic and military policy against enemies, their courts torn by rivalry among contending military and aristocratic factions. This incompetence was revealed again and again in the fifth century—after the Rhine crossing of 405/6, the sack of Rome in 410, the threat of the Huns in the 450s, and the Vandal sack of Rome in 455.

The pattern was similar in the provinces. In 446, a mixed group of armies consisting of Picts from what later became Scotland, Irish, and continental Saxons, invaded the Roman province of Britain, from which the defending armies had been removed shortly before 410 for service elsewhere. In the century following this invasion, Roman Britain slowly gave way to the Germanic kingdoms of Anglo-Saxon England (below, Chapter 6).

Theodosius II (408–450), *augustus* of the east, and Valentinian III (425–455), Galla Placidia's nephew and son respectively, were the last members of the Theodosian dynasty to rule the empire. Theodosius II's two most enduring achievements were the construction of the great fortified walls around Constantinople and a collection of laws, the *Theodosian Code,* issued in 438, which long served both as the law for Romans in Germanic kingdoms and as the model for early Germanic collections of written laws. On the death of Theodosius II, his sister, Pulcheria, elevated her husband Marcian to the imperial throne without bothering, as imperial law required, to consult her cousin, Valentinian III. This indifference toward the west suggests how far the divisions of the empire had widened by the middle of the fifth century.

From 445 on, both eastern and western imperial courts were dominated by barbarian masters of soldiers who became Emperor-makers and Emperor-removers for the rest of the century. In the east, however, imperial recovery proceeded more quickly. Under the emperors Leo I (457–474) and Zeno (474–491), the control of barbarian generals was slowly thrown off and the office of emperor restored to its former power. In the west, however, the masters of soldiers wielded much greater power for much longer, and a series of puppet-emperors succeeded each other under their supervision until 476. Then, Odovacar, the master of soldiers in the west and the effective ruler of all Italy, deposed the last western emperor, Romulus Augustulus, and sent the imperial regalia back to the emperor Zeno at Constantinople. Odovacar disingenuously observed that the empire needed only one emperor, and he appointed himself regent in Italy for the distant Zeno. Since Zeno was incapable of mounting a military offensive against Odovacar, he decided to use diplomacy against his irritating and presumptuous western "subordinate." His diplomacy introduced the Ostrogoths into Italy.

THE AGE OF THEODERIC: OSTROGOTHS, FRANKS, AND VISIGOTHS IN THE WESTERN EMPIRE

The Ostrogoths were a branch of the older Gothic peoples that had been absorbed by the Huns in 375. By the mid fifth century, however, they had shaken off Hunnic rule, recovered some of their earlier power, and, under their young and able king Theoderic (453–526), they attacked Constantinople itself. The emperor Zeno managed to divert them from the city by offering Theoderic a commission as master of soldiers and the invitation to move his people into Italy, destroy Odovacar, and restore Italy to the empire. By 493, Theoderic and the Ostrogoths had indeed invaded Italy, destroyed Odovacar, and established themselves as rulers of Italy, with Theoderic's palace located in Ravenna, the last imperial capital of the West. Theoderic deftly combined the official Roman titles of patrician and master of soldiers with his own title of king of the Ostrogothic people, which now settled in Italy.

But Zeno was only slightly less uneasy with Theoderic in Italy than he had been with Odovacar. Unlike Odovacar, Theoderic was king of his own people. Like the Visigoths, Theoderic had managed to keep his people intact, with himself as its king, but this time in Italy itself, the heart of the old western part of the empire. Unlike the Visigoths, however, Theoderic also had an official imperial position in regard to the Roman inhabitants of Italy. His problem was how to balance these two roles to his and his people's advantage.

The Ostrogoths had been Christians when they arrived in Italy, having been converted to an Arian form of Christianity by missionaries who had arrived among them to minister to Roman prisoners. One of these missionaries, Ulfilas (ca. 311–383), translated parts of the Bible into the Gothic language, the first written work we possess in a Germanic language. But the heterodox Christianity of the Ostrogoths only became a further cause of friction between them and the Romans and eastern Christians in Constantinople.

The debates over Arianism and other forms of heterodoxy had generated a number of criteria for determining religious orthodoxy. According to the popular definition of Vincent of Lerins (above, Chapter 2), orthodoxy was what had been believed "always, everywhere, and by everyone." That is, whatever could be demonstrated by tradition ("always") and universal consensus ("everywhere and by everyone") should be considered orthodox. The Greek word for universal was *katholikos, catholicus* in Latin. In the fourth and fifth centuries, this term was increasingly used to assert orthodoxy over and against heterodoxy, and it became used in this specialized sense to distinguish catholic Christians from Arians and others. This is the meaning of the term "catholic" in this and the following chapters.

Theoderic himself had spent part of his youth as a hostage at Constantinople, and he had received a Roman education. Able and intelligent, he found that he could establish his people in Italy relatively peacefully, something he could not have hoped for in the east. His use of high-ranking Romans in his administration and his refusal to claim a royal or imperial title over Romans made him initially acceptable to both the Romans and his own people. He ruled from Ravenna, not Rome, and his architectural works in Ravenna and elsewhere in Italy represent a significant effort to restore some of the damaged architectural fabric of Italy.

The Ostrogothic warriors were now the only military force in Italy. Civil government was restricted to Romans, and the Roman Senate still sat at Rome; public festivals and entertainments continued, and Theoderic's official proclamations to Romans were properly called *edicts*—that is, formal and traditional administrative Roman pronouncements issued by an official who was subordinate to the emperor. They were also deferential and respectful toward the Senate. The settlement and support of the Ostrogoths was conducted according to the Roman legal principle of *hospitium,* of sharing the tax income and revenues of the land, with two-thirds going to the Roman landholding "hosts" and one-third given to Ostrogothic "guests." The emperor's image continued to grace the coins struck in Ostrogothic Italy. Theoderic's mausoleum just outside the walls of Ravenna was built of massive stone blocks in a style that was perfectly consistent with Roman traditional architecture. His foreign policy was based on the principle of the advantage of Italy and its security from other kingdoms developing across the Alps. The security of Italy now had to be defended from Italy itself, and could no longer depend on armies stationed on the distant northern and eastern frontiers—there were no longer any such Roman armies.

Outside of Italy, the process of ethnogenesis was producing new kinds of kings and a new collective awareness on the part of the highest ranks of peoples in one of the most influential periods of political experimentation in human history. In southern Gaul and Iberia, the Visigoths were the first of the Germanic peoples to assert an ethnic identity, establish an elaborate royal state, and issue a collection of laws, the *Breviary of Alaric,* that distinguished Visigoths as a people exempt from the laws of their Roman subjects. Letters of the Roman aristocrat Sidonius Apollinaris (c. 430–479) describe a Visigothic ruler behaving much in the manner of a Roman emperor—although never claiming actually to be an emperor—distinguishing himself from his own aristocracy, receiving embassies while seated on a throne, and following Roman diplomatic protocols. Not all of these political experiments worked, but even those that failed helped to lay the groundwork for the mosaic of later European kingdoms and ethno-cultural identities.

Theoderic realized the need to balance the powers of the Visigoths, the Burgundians in the Rhone valley, and the powerful new kingdom of the Franks in order to preserve the security of Italy and the lands south of the Danube. Of these three peoples, the most ambitious and dangerous was that of the Franks.

The Franks were originally an assembly of unrelated peoples that constituted and reconstituted itself as it migrated south along the North Sea Coast during the third and fourth centuries. A group of Franks settled in parts of what are now the Netherlands and Belgium, occasionally serving in Roman armies as *federati*. In the fifth century, this group, known as the Salian ("Salty" or "Coastal") Franks, broke away from Roman imperial allegiance, harassed Roman towns in the lower Rhineland, and formed a small

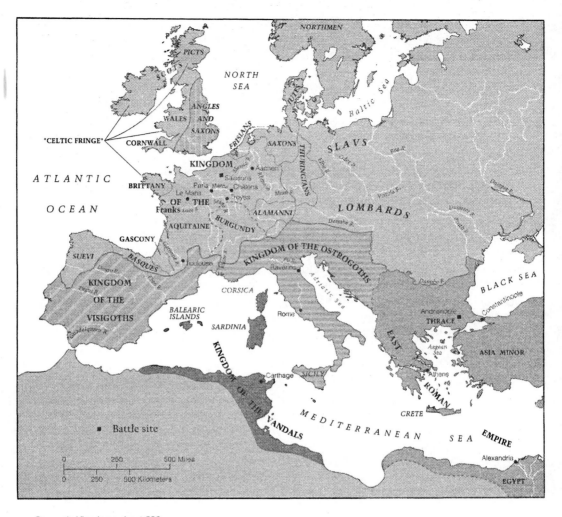

Germanic Kingdoms about 526.

independent kingdom in northern Gaul. The earliest recorded ruler of this kingdom was Childeric I, son of Merowech (from whom the name of the dynasty, the Merovingians, is derived: below, Chapter 7), who died in 482 and was buried at Tournai in what is now southern Belgium. In 1653, Childeric's tomb was excavated and its contents carefully described and illustrated. Weapons, rich garments, jewelry, hoards of coins, and the head of the king's warhorse were found in the tomb, along with an elaborately brocaded and jeweled cloak, which served as the pattern for Napoleon's imperial cloak just over thirteen centuries later.

The Franks settled and farmed as well as fought. Their farmsteads were scattered around older Roman provincial cities, most of them now religious centers. Small ports like Quentovic and Dorestad in Frisia (the modern Netherlands and Belgium) on the North Sea coast were trading emporia that connected northern Gaul, the southern Scandinavian territories, eastern Britain, and the Baltic Sea in the earliest days of the first commercial northwestern Euro-region.

After Childeric's death, the kingdom expanded rapidly under his son, Chlodovicus, or Clovis (r. 482–511). In 486, Clovis defeated Syagrius, a local Roman ruler near Paris, and proceeded to consolidate his power among several divisions of the Franks, including the Ripuarian ("Riverside") Franks. When he became king, Clovis was approached by Remigius, the bishop of Rheims, with an offer of support and the request to respect the church and protect the defenseless. This offer of support from Remigius and other aristocratic Gallo-Roman bishops as well as a number of lay aristocrats, and his own marriage to the catholic Burgundian princess, Chrodechildis, influenced Clovis' decision sometime around 500 to be baptized as a catholic Christian, rather than an Arian (as had the Visigoths, Vandals, Burgundians, and Ostrogoths). Clovis' military success and his support from his new Gallo-Roman co-religionists not only permitted him to emerge as the champion of catholic, Gallo-Roman Christianity against the Arianism of other Germanic rulers and peoples, but they also constituted yet another development in the character of Christian kingship.

The value of Gallo-Roman aristocratic support for Clovis' ventures is revealed in the letter sent to him by Avitus, the bishop of Vienne, on the occasion of Clovis' baptism:

> *We saw (with eyes of the spirit) that great sight, when, a crowd of bishops around you, in the order of their holy ministry, poured over your royal limbs the waters of life; when that head feared by the peoples bowed down before the servants of God; when your royal locks, hidden under a helmet, were steeped in holy oil; when your breast, relieved of its cuirass, shone with the same whiteness as your baptismal robes. Do not doubt, most flourishing of kings, that this soft clothing will give more force to your arms: whatever Fortune has given up to you now, this Sanctity will bestow.*

Avitus' rhetorical interpretation of Clovis' success as a shift from depending on random *Fortune* to more predictable *Sanctity* indicated what became a standard Christian interpretation of barbarian political success: fortune was uncontrollable and could vanish as suddenly and inexplicably as it came, but sanctity was a gift of God, continuously bestowed on righteous rulers, and it entailed the unreserved cooperation of the Gallo-Roman episcopate. Both the conversion and Avitus' interpretation of it go far to account for Clovis' image in the eyes of later generations of the Franks. Of all the barbarian rulers, only he seemed to have met with continuing success. Legends surrounding Clovis' baptism quickly began to circulate, the most enduring of them being that the Holy Spirit, in the form of a dove, had descended from Heaven with the baptismal oil. This legend and others were fleshed out by later kings of France, who were anointed at their coronations with what they thought was the same miraculous oil, and therefore claimed to possess alone the title of "Most Christian King."

Clovis' "fortune" had already been evident in his earlier successes, as well as in his conquest of the Thuringians, a federation of smaller Germanic groups, northeast of

Cologne in 491. The power of his "sanctity" quickly demonstrated itself in 506, when Clovis led his Frankish army against the Alamanni at Tolbiac, near Cologne, and defeated them, taking his conquered enemies as his subjects. In 507, Clovis defeated the Visigoths, with whom he had been contending since the 490s, at the battle of Vouillé in southern Gaul, driving them out of Gaul and confining their kingdom to Iberia. In 508, Clovis was officially recognized as a kind of honorary *consul* by the emperor Anastasius (491–518). Until his death in 511, Clovis resided principally in the old Roman city of Paris, consolidating a new Frankish kingdom in northern Gaul, to which his three sons succeeded. Its three sections, often ruled by different kings, were Neustria, the original kingdom of the Salian Franks, Austrasia, the old home of the Ripuarian Franks, and Burgundy, after Clovis' sons conquered and annexed it in 534. The kingdom was far enough from the Mediterranean centers of political conflict to retain its independence and strength, and it was sufficiently orthodox in its faith, or at least in the reputed faith of its rulers, so as to leave not only a memory, but also a legend of Clovis as "the new Constantine," an image that greatly benefited his successors, that is, when they were not being criticized by later Christian writers for having defected from it.

Theoderic correctly perceived the success of Clovis and his successors and the appearance of the vast, new Frankish kingdom as a power to be reckoned with. He himself had married Clovis' sister, but he also remained wary of Frankish expansion, particularly south of the Danube, where Theoderic had settled several Germanic peoples, including the Bavarians. Theoderic married his own daughters to kings of the Burgundians and Visigoths, and his sister to the king of the Vandals in North Africa, making himself a kind of elder statesman in the politically fragmented world of the western Mediterranean and northern Europe. He actively mediated between the Franks and the Visigoths after 507, and he was at least partially responsible for the survival of the Visigothic kingdom in Iberia.

But religious and political turmoil in Italy turned Theoderic's attention from Gaul and Iberia to Italy itself. For all of Theodosius' early diplomatic restraint in Italy and his efforts to pacify Gaul and the Danube Valley, the court at Constantinople intrigued in Italy against him, and worried about his growing power. The eventual failure of Goths and Romans to come to terms with each other over religious and social issues further destabilized the experimental Romano-Ostrogothic state. Mutual religious antagonism between Arian Ostrogoths and catholic Romans also made Theoderic's reign increasingly harsh. In 526, the year of his own death, Theoderic persecuted Pope John I (523–526) and demanded that all Christian churches in Italy be turned over to Arian clergy. In 524, he executed his Roman master of offices, Boethius, on a charge of treason. Theoderic himself died in 526 and was succeeded by his daughter Amalasuntha. Relations between Ostrogoths and Romans deteriorated rapidly after the assassination of Amalasuntha, who had attempted to restore harmonious relations between the two groups, in 534. The Gothic kings who succeeded Amalasuntha were unable or unwilling to improve relations either with Constantinople or with the local Romans, and they ruled their Roman subjects with increasingly heavy hands. Within a decade of Theoderic's death, the armies of Constantinople invaded Italy and began the long series of Gothic wars that destroyed the Ostrogothic kingdom and laid waste much of Italy itself (below, Chapter 4).

BOETHIUS AND CASSIODORUS

The attitude of Theoderic toward Roman culture and the new political uses to which it might be put, and the state of learning during his reign can best be illustrated by the careers of his two remarkable servants, Boethius and Cassiodorus. Both were highborn Romans, both were scholars of considerable achievement, and both were in effect "prime ministers" of Romano-Gothic Italy.

Anicius Manlius Severinus Boethius was a descendant of the highest Roman senatorial aristocracy. Born around 480 and orphaned young, he was raised in the household of another representative of the traditions of the senatorial order, Quintus Aurelius Memmius Symmachus. Boethius received the extensive classical and Christian education that was characteristic of his class, which had not abandoned the social, literary, and artistic traditions of ancient Rome when it adopted Christianity. Boethius married Symmachus' daughter, Rusticiana. He met Theoderic around 505, and from that date until his execution in 524, he became an important figure at the royal court. First a learned adviser on what seem to be purely complex technical matters—he designed, among other things, a sundial and a water clock that Theoderic presented to his brother-in-law Gundobad, king of the Burgundians—Boethius soon was appointed to a series of public offices, which culminated in his consulship in 510 (his own two sons became joint consuls in 522) and the post of master of offices in 523, which made him the highest civil official in Italy.

The relatively light demands of public office constituted only one side of Boethius' life. Like several of his contemporaries, he participated in the intellectual life of his day, including ecclesiastical deliberations. He wrote a number of highly accomplished works of Christian theology. In these works, he was among the first thinkers to attempt to apply the logic of Aristotle to the theological language of Latin Christianity. But he also wrote on music, and he translated and commented on Porphyry's *Introduction* to the *Categories* of Aristotle, a key work of technical logic that served for the next seven centuries as the introduction to Latin readers of the subjects of logic and introductory philosophy. He also translated another work of Aristotle, *On Interpretation*. In these last two works, Boethius seems to have had the ambition to translate the complete works of both Plato and Aristotle into Latin, which had never been done (and was not done until the period between 1150 and 1500; below, Chapter 16).

The importance of Boethius' work on logic is immeasurable. By beginning with broad questions dealing with the art of classifying objects external to the mind and by further classifying all statements that can be made on any subject, Boethius left one of the greatest intellectual legacies of antiquity. The nature of that legacy is often difficult for modern readers to appreciate. Essentially, it involved devising for the first time in Latin a vocabulary capable of discussing the intricate mental processes that had hitherto been written about only in Greek. By systematizing a Latin philosophical and logical vocabulary that could be applied effectively to the analysis of mental processes, the classification of valid arguments, the detection of logical errors, and the accurate description of the material world, Boethius left to the west the basic tools for the elaboration of theology, law, logic, and metaphysics. In this sense, both Thomas Aquinas and Descartes are his direct heirs, but the entire West also used these works of Boethius as its own introduction to formal logic. In the great revival of the study of logic that occurred in the eleventh and twelfth centuries (below, Chapter 13), the work of Boethius played a fundamental role. There are no more important intellectual legacies to the future from this period, in terms of Latin vocabulary and critical terminology, than Jerome's translation of the Bible into Latin (above, Chapter 2) and Boethius' translations of Aristotle and Porphyry a century later.

Boethius' best-known work, however, falls into neither of these categories. Deteriorating relations between Theoderic and Anastasius' successor, the emperor Justin (518–527), were intensified when Justin persecuted Arian Christians throughout the empire. Since the Arian faith of the Goths was one of the elements that Theoderic used to keep them separate from native Romans, he discouraged conversions from one form of Christianity to the other. The emperor Justin also attempted to restore Rome's ecclesiastical loyalty to the East after a short period of division known as the Acacian Schism. Boethius was considered a particular ally of both the bishop of Rome and the emperor at Constantinople, and his pro-senatorial sentiments could be easily misunderstood at Ravenna as disloyalty to Theoderic. When Boethius was accused of suppressing evidence in the case of a fellow senator who had been charged with engaging in a treasonable (to Theoderic) correspondence with Constantinople, Boethius himself was charged with treason, as was his father-in-law, Symmachus. He was imprisoned at Pavia and tortured and executed in prison in 524. Symmachus' execution followed in 526.

While in prison, Boethius wrote his best-known work, a dialogue between himself and the female personification of philosophy, *On the Consolation of Philosophy*. The dialogue begins with Boethius seeking means of consoling himself for the undeserved fate that has befallen him. Philosophy enters, and the remainder of the work is a dialogue in prose between the two characters, punctuated with moving interludes in verse, written in a strong and clear Latin. In the course of the dialogue, Philosophy leads Boethius through various logical steps to a consideration of the nature of true happiness and the highest good, which Philosophy identifies with God, although not with any specifically Christian aspects of God. In the dialogue, Boethius attempted to resolve the problems of misfortune and justice, good and evil, within a purely philosophical framework. The work culminates in a description of the philosopher's obligation to accept the essential justice of the divine plan and to interpret the particulars of personal experience in terms of it. The work became so popular among learned Europeans that it was translated in the ninth century by King Alfred of England, in the late fourteenth by Geoffrey Chaucer, and in the sixteenth by Queen Elizabeth I of England. With Vergil and Ovid, Boethius became the most widely read Roman author of the next ten centuries, even gaining a local cult of sainthood in Pavia as Saint Severinus and a place in paradise in Dante's *Divine Comedy* (below, Chapter 16).

But Boethius' later reputation for learning and his sainthood were not the only response to his enemies. After the conquest of Ostrogothic Italy by the emperor Justinian (below, Chapter 4), Boethius' widow, Rusticiana, received imperial permission to destroy many statues and memorials of Theoderic as an act of private revenge.

Cassiodorus, Boethius' successor at Theoderic's court, did not come from the same high senatorial circles as Boethius and Symmachus, although his family was aristocratic. He was a noble from a family of imperial civil servants, holding extensive lands around Squillace in Calabria, to which he later retired and where he built a semimonastic community of scholars.

Cassiodorus, too, had studied extensively, and one of his teachers had been Dionysius Exiguus (ca. 475–550), a learned and influential Greek scholar, translator, and an important figure in the history of western law. Dionysius was also a first-rate mathematician and became an expert in correlating the complex dating systems of the ancient world. In the process of calculating tables projecting the dating of Easter for several years to come (Easter is a lunar feast, and therefore movable—its exact date changes each year), Dionysius was reluctant to use the conventional dating of the reign of Diocletian as his starting point for calculation, because Diocletian had been a persecutor of Christians. Instead, Dionysius hit on the idea of dating from the Incarnation of Christ, which he incorrectly dated in 753 A.U.C. (from the founding of Rome), thus inaugurating the modern system of A.D./B.C. dating. Although his dating system was not immediately accepted, Dionysius' manuscript library passed on to Cassiodorus, who himself wrote about A.D. dating. From his reading of Cassiodorus, Bede, in late eighth-century northern England, adopted the practice in his own histories (below, Chapter 8), and from Bede, the system was taken up by the later Carolingian rulers of the Franks, who used it officially and established it as the most common chronology in the modern world (below, Chapter 8).

Cassiodorus was thus intellectually well prepared for his work for Theoderic, but both his work and his temperament were different from those of Boethius. As the writer of Theoderic's official letters from 506, and in a position much closer to the daily activities of the court than Boethius had been, Cassiodorus was confronted every day with the political events of early sixth-century Italy. He had neither the leisure nor the inclination to deal with the complex process of philosophical study, and he had the official obligation of explaining Roman culture to the Goths and the Gothic character and policies to the Romans. Boethius' major work required no knowledge of the Goths in order to be understood, but Cassiodorus' major work is wholly inexplicable without an acquaintance with the Gothic kingdom in the last years of Theoderic.

When he succeeded Boethius as master of offices in 524, Cassiodorus continued to produce the official correspondence that he had written in the name of Theoderic since 506 to rationalize the Gothic role in preserving what he called Roman *vetustas*—the ancient and traditional essence of Roman civic culture. These letters, the *Variae,* contain an amazing wealth of information, learned digressions on all sorts of subjects, expressions of Ostrogothic political theory, some of it pompous and hopelessly obscure, but much of it lively and infinitely interesting.

Cassiodorus also wrote a (now lost) history of the Gothic people, in which he extended the history of the Goths so far back in time that it became as ancient—and therefore as venerable and respectable—as that of the Romans themselves. Cassiodorus' Gothic history was the basis for the surviving history of the Goths by Jordanes. By showing that both Goths and Romans were of equal antiquity, Cassiodorus implied that they could legitimately and with equal dignity collaborate in preserving Roman civilization.

But the long and terrible war in Italy that followed the assassination of Amalasuntha in 534 (below, Chapter 4) proved Cassiodorus' hopes unfounded. In the 550s he retired with some friends to his estates near Squillace, where he spent his time in devotional reading and assembled his last work, the *Divine and Human Readings,* an encyclopedic survey and analysis of spiritual and secular literature that remained for many centuries a guide for European scholars through the literature of Christian and pagan antiquity.

The *Divine and Human Readings* marks another important feature of late antique learning, the process of organizing and classifying all knowledge into specific subjects. In the first century B.C.E., the Roman writers Varro and Cicero had developed the idea, from earlier Hellenistic learning, that the proper subjects of study for a free Roman citizen ought to be grouped and classified in terms of their place in the hierarchy of learning, their relation to one another, and their sequence in preparation for the study of philosophy. Although the number of subjects of learning varied between Varro's time and the sixth century, one literary work memorably numbered the subjects as seven. The fourth-century advocate Martianus Capella wrote *The Marriage of Mercury and Philology,* a very long and obscure, but also very influential allegory in verse and prose, which also designated the seven subjects as the *liberal arts*—that is, the arts suitable for a free man. Boethius divided the seven liberal arts of Martianus into two groups, the *trivium* and the *quadrivium.* The former was essentially literary, consisting of grammar, rhetoric, and dialectic (logic); the latter was essentially mathematical, comprising arithmetic, music, geometry, and astronomy. In the *Divine and Human Readings,* Cassiodorus repeated both Martianus Capella and Boethius, thus passing down to later European history the principles of the divisions of learning and the organization of knowledge that remained fundamental in western Europe until the seventeenth century and still echo in the modern expression, the "liberal arts."

THE EMPIRE AND THE WORLD

None of the political changes in the western part of the empire changed the idea of empire in the minds of the emperors at Constantinople. To them, the empire remained a unity, its western parts temporarily in the hands of imperially deputized barbarian kings. The diplomatic skills and strategically expended tribute money of imperial emissaries kept barbarian armies—whether steppe-nomads or other militarized confederations—well away from Constantinople itself. From the perspective of Constantinople, the folk-migrations in the north and west were far less dangerous than the great rival of the Roman empire, the Sasanid empire of Persia. Nomadic confederations might dangerously come and quickly go, but Persia and its immense resources remained.

Both empires stood at the western end of the great communications routes that led westward from China: the Eurasian steppe grasslands that supported the nomad horsemen and pastoralists, and the great network of trade routes and oases that carried luxury goods and ideas from eastern Asia to the Middle East. Persia, whose border ended at the eastern edge of the Iranian plateau, not far from the Indus River valley, and whose northern border enclosed the fertile lands along the lower coasts of the Caspian Sea and Khorasan, was a rival whose power the Roman emperors had to respect and take more seriously than it did the small bands of migrating peoples along their own northern borders. Persian victories in the late third and fourth centuries, culminating in the defeat and death of the emperor Julian (r. 361–364), brought hostilities to a temporary standoff. The Persian state religion was Zoroastrianism, but it was a religion of the Persian elite and not a proselytizing religion. Thus, it was far less appealing to the diverse peoples who lived between the two empires than Christianity, which did proselytize and became more and more strongly identified with Roman imperial authority during the fifth and sixth centuries. During the fifth century, both empires had had to turn their attention and military resources to migrating nomadic steppe peoples, Rome to the Huns, and Persia to the Asian Turkic peoples known as Kidarites and Hepthalites.

The worlds of Rome and Persia, like the rest of Europe and the Near East, lay at the western end of the steppe grasslands that extended from Mongolia to the Hungarian Plain, and they were intermittently, but often profoundly, affected by the steppe peoples until the middle of the eighteenth century. The steppes were an ocean of grass, inhabited by nomadic pastoralist peoples, Turkic or Mongol, who drove their vast herds of sheep and horses to seasonal grazing grounds. To the north of the steppe lies the great Russian Forest Zone, to the west, the dense forests of Europe, where nomadic cavalry tactics became less effective, and to the south, the Arid Zone. But the steppe itself is open, and although its inhabitants did not establish settled societies or agriculture, they benefited from exchange with sedentary peoples in the form of trade, tribute, or conquest. The steppe peoples could also quickly form militarized, predatory confederations that could turn against China or western Eurasian states, absorbing nearby peoples or driving them toward settled and temporarily safer places like the Roman Empire.

Nomadic tribes were socially stratified, with noble families ruling and commanding others. Frequently, one ruling kin-group would rise to power over others, organize a new state under the administration of its relatives and favorites, and then continue expanding until it could expand no longer, when a process of dismemberment set in. Each of these states was predatory—it had to expand in order to survive; it had to gain regular control of agricultural and commercial territories in order to sustain itself. Those territories were gained at the expense of the sedentary societies along the edges of the steppe and sometimes at that of other steppe peoples. The starting point of such nomadic state formations was usually in the east toward the Chinese Wall, and peoples who were displaced moved west, to the Volga Steppe between the southern Ural mountains and the Caspian Sea, the Ukrainian Steppe to the north of the Black Sea, or to the western end of the steppe, the Hungarian Plain. These migrants could not mount the massive, concentrated attacks that such peoples as the Hsiung-nu or the Juan-Juan (and later the Mongols) launched against China, but they remained formidable and were worth buying off or employing as mercenaries by sedentary civilizations like Rome and Persia.

Thus, the steppe peoples who invaded the Roman Empire and Persia—the Huns and later the Avars and Magyars (below, Chapters 4 and 9)—constituted one force to which both empires had to pay attention, but which also could not conquer them. The areas of most of this kind of contact were the Balkans, the lower Danube Valley, Transcaucasia, and Turkestan.

Between Rome and Persia, there were a number of small client-kingdoms, whose location exposed them to nomad raids and also made them attractive to both superpowers. The northernmost of these was Georgia, south of the Caucasus mountains between the Caspian and Black Seas, which had converted to Christianity in the mid fourth century, apparently persuaded to convert by Saint Nino, a captive woman from the Roman Empire. The western part of Georgia was strongly influenced by Constantinople, while the eastern part was generally more strongly influenced by Persia.

South of Georgia lay Armenia, at the eastern end of the Roman empire. With the conversion to Christianity of its king Trdat III (ca. 298–330), Armenia became the first Christian state in history, maintaining a distinctive cultural identity with its own alphabet and written language. Like Georgia, Armenia attempted to sustain its own semiautonomous status by playing Constantinople and Persia against one another.

Southwest of Armenia lay Syria, dominated by the great cities of Antioch, Edessa, and Damascus. Syria experienced great population growth and economic prosperity during the fifth and early sixth centuries, its wealth and value to Constantinople second only to that of Egypt, the richest mideastern province of the empire and its most productive source of grain. Syria had been thoroughly Christianized by the mid fifth century, and the patriarchs of Antioch and Jerusalem were two of the five highest-ranking prelates in the Christian world, along with the patriarchs of Alexandria, Rome, and, after the fifth century, Constantinople. From Syria, a line of Roman fortifications extended south to the Red Sea, intended to control desert peoples and offer a strong front to Persia.

East of Syria, in Upper Mesopotamia and the Syrian Desert, a number of Arab cities and principalities completed the buffer zone between Constantinople and Persia. The desert city of Palmyra, which had revolted against Rome late in the third century, had been greatly diminished by the end of the century, but other Arab principalities survived and thrived between the two empires. The small Arab kingdom of the Ghassanids was a Roman client-state in the fifth century and early sixth century until it was dismantled in the later sixth century. The Ghassanids also became Monophysite Christians (below, Chapter 4). The Arab Lakhmid kingdom was a client-state of Persia.

Around 500 C.E., the eastern part of the Roman empire was its wealthiest, most productive, and most thoroughly Christianized component. From Georgia to Egypt, Roman defenses protected its eastern and southern flanks. With the east in its possession, there was little reason for the emperors at Constantinople to be anything but confident that the empire would exist as it always had, that it could, when the time was ripe, recover direct rule of the west. Between 500 and 650, however, this confidence disappeared, much of the east was lost, and the empire at times reduced to the limits and walls of Constantinople itself. With this transformation of the eastern part of the Roman empire, the old Mediterranean world was divided and rebuilt along entirely new and different lines.

4

The Making of Byzantine Civilization

POWER AND DEVOTION IN THE EAST ROMAN EMPIRE, 450–527

The success of the emperors Leo I and Zeno in freeing the imperial court at Constantinople from the domination of barbarian masters of soldiers was as remarkable as their ability to head off threats of invasion into the West. Their successors preserved the unique character of the imperial office: Its holder was the ruler of the Christian Roman Empire, the successor of both Augustus and Constantine. After 450, the emperors were crowned by the patriarchs of Constantinople in a religious ceremony that gave them a quasi-priestly character. The emperor claimed a kind of authority that no other power in the world could equal, that of God's sole deputy on earth. The presence of the emperor, whether in the court ceremonies of the Great Palace on the Bosporus, in imperial portraits and statues throughout the empire, or on coins, reminded his subjects of both his power and his status. The coinage itself remained stable, and even imperial extravagance and the high costs of the armies did not impose in the prosperous East the crushing burdens they did in the West. The core of a civil service consisting of palace and city officials effectively civilized the highest levels of government. The nearly two thousand bishops in the east served, as one historian has called them, as "the emperor's watchdogs." The emperor's subjects, whether high aristocrats or commoners, paid their taxes, obeyed imperial laws, prayed publicly for the emperor's safety and prosperity, and loudly expressed their opinion of him when he appeared at the chariot races in the great Hippodrome.

The multiethnic and multilingual empire, its culturally diverse subjects speaking Latin and Greek, Phrygian and Cappadocian, Georgian and Armenian, Syriac and Coptic, Arabic and Hebrew, comprised what one historian has termed "an ethnographic zoo," all of whose inhabitants except Jews, whose status was further depressed as the empire identified itself more and more with Christianity, acknowledged their common Christianity and common loyalty to the emperor and empire. The liturgical rituals of the clergy sanctified the cities, and the local town councils kept them orderly. The great urban monasteries provided spiritual support. And ascetic holy men in remote districts settled local disputes, attracted pilgrims, and even intervened with the emperors on behalf of their localities. The most dramatic such holy man, Symeon Stylites (ca. 390–459), spent the last several decades of his life praying alone on top of a fifty-foot-high column near Antioch. His heroic austerities gave him enormous prestige in the area, attracting both pagan and Christian pilgrims, and sufficiently established him outside and above the local community to be able to reconcile enemies and promote orthodox beliefs among dissenting Christians.

In the western part of the empire around the year 500, the chief concern of churchmen was the Arian heresy of the Germanic peoples who occupied much of Italy, Iberia, and Gaul. But not all believers, then or now, were professional theologians, and Arianism served as much as a mark of collective identity that distinguished Goths and others from Romans as it did doctrinal differences. In the east, Arianism was a dead issue, and the western concern with Arianism was not echoed in the east. Doctrinal concerns in the east, however were more complicated. The adoption of a Greek philosophical vocabulary to define and articulate Christian dogma produced highly technical debates concerning the divine and human natures of Christ, and these technical debates often resonated in the provinces, where they became a component of regional Christian identity. As more of East Roman society was Christianized, so theological disputes touched wider and wider social groups and influenced imperial policies as well.

One of the most important dissenting doctrines was that formulated by Nestorius, who became patriarch of Constantinople in 428. Nestorius, and the school of Antioch from which he came, was greatly disturbed by the increasing popularity of the cult of the Virgin Mary and its implications concerning the divine and human natures of Christ. Called by many *theotokos* ("bearer of God"), the Virgin was rather, Nestorius insisted, *christotokos* ("bearer of Christ"), and Christ's nature could then be considered more human than divine, since a human woman should not be considered capable of giving birth to God.

The strongest opposition to Nestorianism came from a faction led by Eutyches of Constantinople, who insisted on a single (*monos*), divine nature (*physis*) of Christ. Eutyches' doctrine, termed Monophysitism, seemed to some churchmen to veer too far in the opposite direction from that of Nestorius, but equally far from the majority orthodox belief.

One response to these dogmatic conflicts was for the emperors to call Church councils to debate and resolve the issues raised by the dissenters. The First Council of Ephesus in 431 condemned Nestorianism. The Council of Chalcedon in 451 condemned Monophysitism, stating what became and has since remained orthodox dogma—that Christ had a completely human and completely divine nature:

> *Following the Holy Fathers, we teach with one voice that the Son of God and our Lord Jesus Christ is to be confessed as one and the same person, that He is perfect in Godhead and perfect in manhood, very God and very man, of a reasonable soul and a human body consisting, consubstantial with the Father as touching his Godhead, and consubstantial with us touching his manhood; made in all things like unto us, sin only excepted. . . . This one and the same Jesus Christ, the only-begotten son of God, must be confessed to be in two natures, unconfusedly, immutably, indivisibly, inseparably united, and that without the distinction of natures being taken away by such union, but rather the peculiar property of each nature being preserved and being united in one Person and subsistence, not separated or divided into two persons, but one and the same Son and only-begotten, God the Word, our Lord Jesus Christ, as the prophets of old time have spoken concerning him, and as the Lord Jesus Christ has taught us, and as the creed of the Fathers has delivered to us.*

Such a ringing assertion of orthodox belief had its implications. First, Christian religious orthodoxy was determined by the prophets, the teaching of Christ, the consensus of earlier church leaders, and the process of tradition by which these had been made known to the clerics assembled at Chalcedon. Other church councils cited the universality of belief (thus implying that heterodoxy was a local and not universal religious opinion) and its sameness over time (thus implying direct and unchanging continuity from Jesus to the present). This idea of universality (Greek *katholikos*, Latin *catholicus*, English *catholic*) was adopted as a means of defining orthodoxy in a specific historical setting, and that is how the word will be used in this book. By insisting on the inseparability of the divine and human natures in Christ, the Council of Chalcedon rejected one of the chief tendencies of early Christianity, that of denying the dignity of the material world and the human body as represented in Christ's human nature. On the other hand, the Council in effect elevated human nature so that it was deemed capable of sharing a single person and substance with the divine.

Theologians might debate, and councils vote, on highly complex dogmatic issues, but even these authorities did not convince everyone. The emperors played the central role in convening the Councils, and sometimes in managing their proceedings. Considerably fewer Latin churchmen attended them, and those who did often did not understand the Greek language in which they were conducted. Many canons of councils were not efficiently or widely distributed, and, particularly in the west, the need for translation from Greek to Latin often led to omissions or incorrect versions of council decisions, thereby exacerbating the increasing differences between eastern and western imperial societies.

Moreover, the condemnation of some heterodox views also appeared to condemn the ecclesiastical districts from which their proponents came; they seemed to challenge the ancient authority of such centers as Alexandria or Antioch and put forward what were considered excessive claims to authority over others on the part of the recent upstarts Rome and Constantinople. As Rome, for example, became the leading voice of the Latin Christian community, it appeared to some in the east to insult the wisdom and piety of eastern Christians. But Rome was also the only major non-Greek city in the empire, and eastern churchmen and emperors often turned to its bishop as a kind of umpire in their own internal disputes. There was far more involved in theological disagreement than technical points of dogma and the language in which they were expressed. Entire communities could rally to their representatives, whether they were triumphant or rejected.

Nor did the Council of Chalcedon solve the problems of Nestorianism and Monophysitism to everyone's satisfaction. The reigns of Zeno and Anastasius saw attempts at compromise with all sides, and several bishops of Rome, notably Leo I (440–461) and Gelasius I (492–496), took up strongly pro-Chalcedon and anti-Monophysite positions. Nor was the arena of doctrinal dispute confined to the formal sessions of councils or to the learned (and sometimes physically violent) debates of high-ranking churchmen. Some heterodox beliefs, particularly Monophysitism and Nestorianism were stoutly maintained in entire provinces. Egypt, for example, remained devoutly Monophysite, although it also remained intensely loyal to the emperor. Even in the imperial capital of Constantinople, dissent was often expressed by the factions that supported the Blue and Green chariot racing teams in the Hippodrome. Monophysites favored the Greens and orthodox Christians the Blues.

These Christological conflicts also underlined and tested the deep regional differences among the provinces and provincial capitals of the East Roman empire and the Latin West. Since Rome was the only Christian community in the western part of the empire that could claim its foundation by apostles—in Rome's case both Peter and Paul—the prestige of the Christian community and bishop of Rome was considerable, and the apostolic foundation of Rome was one of the bases of claims that the bishop of Rome had primacy, at least in Latin ecclesiastical affairs. At the Council of Constantinople in 381, the patriarch of the new city of Constantinople was raised by the emperor to a level of dignity equaling that of the leaders of the apostolically founded churches. Thus, a degree of rivalry became evident in the fifth century between the Patriarch of Constantinople and the older Christian communities in the east, as well as between the patriarchs and the bishops of Rome.

Nestorius had come to Constantinople from the church of Antioch. One of his opponents, who veered toward heterodoxy himself, was Cyril, Patriarch of Alexandria. Alexandria was a city with considerable Monophysite sympathies, and since it was also the ecclesiastical center of Egypt, its views made Egypt a largely Monophysite province, as was northern and eastern Syria and the Persian-dominated part of Armenia. In terms of political loyalties, much depended on the way in which emperors treated those who retained what had been condemned as heterodox theological opinions. Generally speaking, imperial coercion was not so severe as to break the loyalty of the dissenting provinces. When contrasted with the threat of Persia, eastern Christians found that they had much more politically and devotionally in common. Increasingly, the empire was a Christian state, and the devotional differences among its parts proved less important politically than their common Christianity.

Zeno's successors, Anastasius I (491–518) and the Illyrian soldier Justin I (518–527) managed to pacify the worst of the religious disputes, to reform the imperial fiscal and administrative systems, and to undertake considerable programs of public works and social welfare. By the accession of Justin's nephew Justinian, in 527, the East Roman Empire had escaped the domination of barbarian masters of soldiers and the greatest dangers of religious dissension. Its finances and economy were sound and its frontiers were, at least temporarily, at peace.

THE EMPEROR WHO NEVER SLEEPS

Flavius Petrus Sabbatius Justinianus (or Justinian, as he is generally known) was the first emperor since Theodosius II to have been trained in imperial administration. He spent his young adulthood observing the machinery of imperial government, and he probably knew it better than any emperor in the past seventy-five years. Justinian was also well educated, and he knew law and theology with the familiarity of a professional. Moreover, he had made an extraordinary marriage with one of the ablest women ever to share a throne in the Roman world.

Justinian's wife, Theodora, was born not into the aristocracy, but into the family of a bear trainer in the circus. Although the sources agree that she was strikingly intelligent and beautiful, and possessed a commanding presence, her role in Constantinople suggests other, more important qualities, including great personal bravery and a strong will. The world in which Theodora grew up was not the equivalent of a twentieth-century "circus world," however. The entertainment industry in the sixth century was an unsettling mixture of spectacularly erotic performances, athletics, and gymnastics. Much of our knowledge of Theodora's early life comes from *The Secret History*, a malicious portrait of Theodora and Justinian written by the court historian Procopius. Procopius, like Theodora's other enemies, made much of her past life, and one historian has called her portrayal in *The Secret History* "probably the most infamous and scurrilous piece of sustained character assassination in all of literature."[1] Ostensibly, marriage to Theodora might have been a great mistake on the part of the heir to the imperial throne. As things turned out, the marriage was probably the most sensible act of Justinian's life. Although Theodora held strong Monophysite sympathies, her contribution to Justinian's reign far outweighed the religious dissension she helped to perpetuate.

The importance of Theodora's presence became dramatically evident during the first great crisis of Justinian's reign, the famous Nika riots of 532. The factions supporting the Blue and the Green chariot-racing teams in the Hippodrome had waged a bitter rivalry through the early years of Justinian's reign, a conflict rendered more serious because the factions had been armed and made into an urban militia some years earlier and had decidedly different religious sympathies. In 532, Justinian imposed new and heavy taxes, and, for once disregarding their opposition toward each other, the Blues and Greens erupted in a riot in the Hippodrome against Justinian. The riot spread from the arena into the city, destroying most of the old town and killing thousands. Justinian, who fled from the Hippodrome, is said to have contemplated abdication and flight and to have been restrained only by Theodora's firmness, embodied in her alleged remark that "the [imperial] purple makes a glorious winding-sheet." The emperor regrouped his

---

[1]John W. Barker, *Justinian and the Later Roman Empire* (Madison: University of Wisconsin Press, 1966), 68.

scattered forces and quelled the riot with a force and thoroughness previously unsuspected. He then unleashed reprisals against the aristocratic leaders and their followers that may have killed as many as 30,000 people.

Immediately after the Nika riots (so called because of the rioter's cry of the Greek word for "conquer"), Justinian began to establish firmly his own imperial authority against the powers of both the aristocracy and the urban population. By the middle of his reign, he had destroyed most of the traditional powers in the empire and had made himself supreme, basing his strength on the vast fiscal resources of his predecessors and the support of the Christian provincial population of the empire. The necessity of rebuilding the shattered city of Constantinople and the need to reassert the political prestige of the emperor gave Justinian his opportunity.

In rebuilding Constantinople, Justinian gave it the shape it was to have throughout its long history. His triumph was the reconstruction of the great Church of *Hagia Sophia* (Holy Wisdom), in which the boundless architectural and engineering talent available in Constantinople created one of the most impressive buildings in history. Justinian's architects, Anthemius of Tralles and Isidore of Miletus, created an immense quadrilateral of four arches, on the top of which was set a vast dome, the lowest level of which was a circle of clear glass windows, so that the dome seemed to hover lightly over the heads of those far below.

Justinian's architects and engineers completed the physical form of the great city and nearly filled the space inside its eighteen square kilometers of fortified wall that had been built by Theodosius II in 450. The city contained a palace complex across the square from Hagia Sophia, many other churches, a hippodrome seating 60,000, and a population of around 350,000. Wide avenues and plazas carried ceremonial and commercial traffic though the city. The water and food supplies were supervised by competent city officials, as were the markets, ports, and labor organizations. The public services of Constantinople were greater that those of any other European city before the nineteenth century. Because of its prominence as the imperial capital, the city also thrived economically, becoming a great port and trading entrepôt.

Justinian's passion for thoroughness is reflected in many of his other achievements, particularly in his reform and codification of Roman law. Until the reign of the emperor Hadrian in the second century, Roman law had been the archaic Law of the Twelve Tables, the primitive law of the early Roman community, modified by the work of later officials called praetors and the subject of a distinctive literature of legal science. Under Hadrian's reforms, some of the changes that had developed under the pressure of new prosperity, and relations among the new classes, were regularized, and the influence of legal philosophy was recognized. The flow of imperial commands increased in the third century, however, and the administration of imperial law had by then fallen into the hands of bureaucrats who understood and appreciated little of Rome's earlier legal history or the principles of law. By the fourth century, private collections of imperial edicts were the most commonly used legal reference books, although they varied greatly in quality and availability. In 438, the emperor Theodosius II issued the *Theodosian Code,* an official collection of imperial edicts from the fourth and fifth centuries, systematized according to topic (above, Chapter 3).

Theodora and Her Attendants. This mosaic portrait of the empress Theodora and her retinue in the Church of San Vitale at Ravenna suggests the richness and majesty of the imperial court ceremonial and the deliberate invocation of these elements in churches in the far-flung corners of the empire. (The Court of Empress Theodora. S. Vitale, Ravenna, Italy. Copyright Alinari/Art Resource. NY)

In the East Roman Empire the study of law flourished, and Justinian knew it well. He commissioned the jurist Tribonian and a team of experts to assemble a new and systematic collection of imperial edicts. By 529, Tribonian had completed the *Codex,* the first part of what came to be known as the *Corpus Iuris Civilis,* "The Body of Civil Law." In 533, Tribonian and other jurists compiled the *Digestum,* or Digest, a systematic topical anthology of the writings of great jurists, to which Justinian now gave the force of law. In the same year, Justinian's commission produced the *Institutes,* an introductory textbook on Roman law. Finally, throughout the rest of his reign Justinian issued new edicts, the most important of which were included in the fourth section of the *Corpus,* the *Novellae,* or Novels (where new laws were to be included). Justinian's *Corpus Iuris Civilis* formed the basis of imperial law until the end of the Byzantine Empire in 1453, even though later emperors enacted additional collections of law. Moreover, because it was written in Latin, the *Corpus* was accessible to western European societies, although its great influence dates only from the late eleventh century. By the end of the Middle

Justinian and His Attendants. This portrait, a twin of that depicting the empress Theodora, stands across the apse of the church from the empress's mosaic. They are participating in the Mass itself. (Byzantine (476–1453). Justinian and his court and St. Maximian. S. Vitale, Ravenna, Italy. Copyright Alinari/Art Resource, NY)

Ages, Roman law had influenced every legal system in Europe, and it is arguable that the *Corpus* is Justinian's greatest legacy.

Justinian had many other able servants besides the architects, lawyers, and theologians with whom he surrounded himself. In fact, Procopius, in a more charitable mood, remarked that these talented individuals were God's greatest gift to the ruler. Among them, Justinian's generals were perhaps the most striking. Under his general Belisarius, Justinian destroyed the Vandal kingdom of Africa in 534, and under Liberius, he gained a strong foothold in Spain in 552. In 535, he began a war with the Ostrogoths of Italy under the commanders Belisarius and Narses that lasted twenty years and caused more damage to the old heartland of the empire than any of the other disasters of the fourth or fifth centuries. Justinian's ambition to reunite all the old parts of the empire was perhaps the only act of his reign in which the usually prudent emperor finally overreached himself.

After the great triumphs of the first fifteen years of his reign, Justinian witnessed new threats and disasters and spent his last twenty-three years doggedly trying to cope with them. In 540, the king of Persia broke the long truce that Justinian had so painfully arranged, and the eastern frontier once again became a troubled land—a land, moreover, with few soldiers left to defend it. In 542, a devastating plague struck the empire, weakening the population and dealing the economy a severe blow. In the 540s also, new immigrants to the Danube and the Black Sea began probing the frontiers and making tentative raids into Thrace and the Balkans. These Bulgar, Avar, and Slavic peoples plagued the northern frontier and occupied much of the time, money, and energy of Justinian and his successors.

The emperor's efforts to stem these new disasters and yet preserve something of the triumphs of the 530s shaped the contemporary image of his last years. To the chroniclers, he became "the emperor who never sleeps"—constantly vigilant, eternally deceptive, all day and night directing the vast and intricate process of salvaging an empire. Justinian gained this reputation by cutting costs, exhausting the treasury left by his

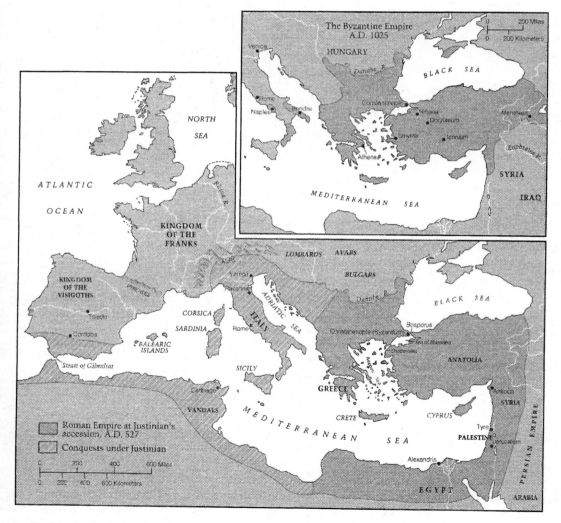

The Byzantine Empire (527–1025).

predecessors, keeping the western armies small, and experimenting constantly with new military organization and new techniques of diplomacy, restructuring the civil service, and drawing the provincial cities more tightly into the imperial fiscal system. At his death in 565, Justinian saw many of his greatest achievements still intact. Constantinople remained the greatest city in the world, and from it the emperor ruled Thrace and Asia Minor, Syria, Palestine, Egypt, and North Africa. Imperial rule was restored in Italy and parts of Iberia, and in the old imperial and Ostrogothic capital of Ravenna, a window on the East and the end of the sea route from Constantinople, a restored imperial Christianity glittered in the mosaics of imperial churches.

THE CITY

Constantinople—the city that Constantine founded, Theodosius fortified, and Justinian rebuilt—remained the largest, most complex city in Europe until its fall to the Ottoman Turks in 1453. Although it was often besieged and twice captured by invaders, it repelled its enemies far more often than it succumbed. Because of the role of Christianity in the life of its founder, Constantinople claimed a novel sort of Christian legitimacy, and its advocates argued that the city was particularly favored by God because pagan rites had never polluted it. If Rome may be said to have become the city of its patron Peter, and its bishop, Constantinople must be said to have been the city of Christian imperial rule, the city of the emperor. Thus, a look at the city as it came from the hand of its imperial restorer, Justinian, tells us more than just a piece of early European urban history. Constantinople was the center of the only Christian empire, and it generated great affection and loyalty in its citizens, as well as awe and envy in the hearts of others.

Its easy access to the Black Sea gave Constantinople control of all trade west of the Caucasus Mountains. By the tenth century the grain, fur, gold, amber, and slaves of the Slavic lands sweeping away to the north were flowing though its port, as did later Islamic trade. Its ready access to the Aegean made communications with other Mediterranean cities easy. From Constantinople across Thrace and the Balkans ran a network of roads, defense works, and frontier forts that protected Greece and dominated the eastern Adriatic Sea. Across Asia Minor ran the great road to the eastern frontier on the Tigris and Euphrates rivers. Constantinople became both a political and a commercial center, fed by the rich agricultural and fishing resources of Greece and Asia Minor, drawing on the populations of these lands for its armies and citizens. It proved a far more secure and strategic capital to the emperors of the east than did the city of Rome, the old center of the empire. From the late fourth century, its strategic value was proved beyond any doubt, as wave after wave of invading peoples broke though the imperial frontiers, failed to take Constantinople, and invariably moved west to assault the weaker cities of the western part of the empire.

One of the results of the Nika riots of 532, was the destruction of much of the physical fabric of the city; indeed, no building earlier than the sixth century can be identified today. One of the consequences of Justinian's success in quelling the riots was his replanning and rebuilding of much of the great city, which gave it the form it had for almost a

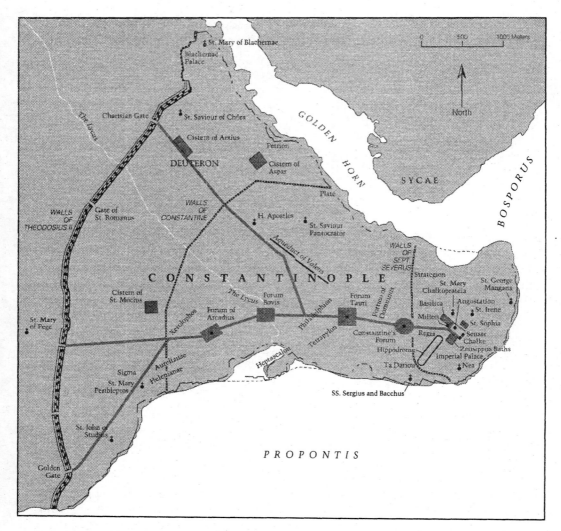

Constantinople. (Reprinted from Cyril Mango. *The Art of the Byzantine Empire, 312–1453: Sources and Documents* (Englewood Cliffs, NJ: Prentice-Hall, 1972), pp. 8–9.)

thousand years, a form that is still detectable in modern Istanbul. Justinian's success refurbished the great avenues and arcades of Constantinople, and he constructed immense underground reservoirs to improve the city's water supply—several of which are still in existence. Large public buildings, including hospitals and even the great palace complex itself, were rebuilt. Justinian's city, as archaeologists and art historians have reconstructed it, is clearly one of the most important examples of urban design in human history.

Constantinople was a sacred city as well. Its churches and monasteries were as important as its streets, squares, and walls. Justinian shaped the spiritual city as well as the material one. His triumph was the reconstruction of the magnificent church of

Holy Wisdom, *Hagia Sophia*. The historian Procopius remarked of the ceremony of inauguration of this striking building:

> *The great door of the new-built temple groaned on its opening hinges, inviting Emperor and people to enter; and when the inner part was seen, sorrow fled from the hearts of all, as the sun lit the glories of the temple. And when the first gleam of light, rosy-armed driving away the dark shadows, leapt from arch to arch, then all the princes and peoples with one voice hymned their songs of prayer and praise; and as they came to the sacred courts it seemed to them as if the mighty arches were set in heaven.*

The vast interior dimensions of the church indeed create the impression of other-worldliness. The diameter of the dome is 107 feet, and it rises 160 feet above the floor. Marble paving in a great variety of colors and patterns leads the eye to the great eastern and western apses and to the rows of pillars that support the north and south galleries, then upwards toward the four great arches. In the pendentives, the spaces where the arches join, the figures of great angels appear to float over the floor far below; with the row of clear glass windows at the base of the dome, the effect created is that the great dome is not supported by the arches, but is suspended delicately from heaven. No other achievement of Justinian captured both the variety of resources and talents available to the emperor and the emperor's intelligence in using them. Procopius summed up the impression the church made on the people of the city and the empire:

> *Whenever anyone enters the church to pray, he realizes at once it is not by any human power or skill, but by the influence of God that it had been built. And so his mind is lifted up to God, and he feels that He cannot be far away, but must love to dwell in this place He has chosen. And this does not happen only to one who sees the church for the first time, but the same thing occurs at each successive visit, as though the sight were each time a new one. No one has ever had enough of this spectacle, but when present in the church men rejoice in what they see, and when they are away from it they love to talk about it.*

The response thus described was surely not unanticipated by Justinian, nor was it limited to the sixth century. When in the tenth century, Vladimir, the prince of the Kievan 'Rus, was negotiating an alliance with Constantinople (below, Chapter 9), his envoys were shown the glories of the city's churches and were apparently swayed by them toward Constantinople:

> *The Greeks led us to the buildings where they worship their God, and we knew not whether we were in heaven or on earth. For on earth there is no such splendor or such beauty, and we are at a loss how to describe it. We only know that God dwells there among men, and their service is fairer than the ceremonies of other nations. For we cannot forget such beauty.*

The later strength of Constantinople lay in its economy, the strength of its armies, and the talents of its administrators. But when the city reached out to Slavs, Georgians, Armenians, Bulgars, and Rus, it was the spiritual and emotional power of the liturgy and hymns, the play of light across golden mosaics, and the sheer grandeur of such churches as Hagia Sophia that caught and held distant peoples' hearts in bonds as strong and enduring as the power of its emperors, the wealth of the empire, or the might of its armies.

Hagia Sophia, Interior. The interior of Justinian's great church, shown here with later Islamic additions, gives some sense of the awe with which its congregants were struck and helps explain its reputation as the greatest church in the Christian world. (Dumbarton Oaks, Byzantine Photography and Fieldwork Archives, Washington, DC)

And the city was known throughout the Eurasian world. Its own inhabitants called it simply "the city," or *Basileousa,* "the Empress-city." Westerners called it Constantinople and the Arabs *Konstantiniye;* to the Slavs it was *Tsarigrad,* and to the Scandinavians *Micklegard.*

In the city itself, schools of classical learning came under attack, but survived. Although Justinian had closed the Academy of Plato in Athens in 529, other centers of earlier Greek philosophical and scientific learning continued to flourish. In Alexandria, John Philoponos (ca. 490–ca. 570) became one of the greatest of all critics of Aristotle, and older Greek philosophical and literary works were widely read.

Materially, the city contained farmlands and orchards, as well as vast water reservoirs below ground. Churches and public buildings were well maintained. Public services included shelters for foreigners, orphanages, poorhouses, hospitals, old age homes, cemeteries for the poor, and homes for the blind. Private largesse contributed to many of these, as did the work of a salaried city bureaucracy.

The state controlled the guilds that different kinds of manufacturers formed. Prices for raw materials, the conduct of markets, and every other facet of economic activity was regulated by state inspectors. During Justinian's reign, the East Roman empire managed to import (or smuggle out) silkworms from China, and Constantinople became the center of a prosperous silk-weaving industry. The enmity of Sasanid Persia did not close the rest of the world off from the East Roman empire, but after the middle of the sixth century, Persia and other enemies had to be confronted. The confrontation transformed East Rome into Byzantium.

THE AGE OF HERACLIUS

Against Justinian's triumphs must be set his failures. The long and expensive military campaigns in the west brought few lasting results. The Visigoths in Iberia and the Lombards in Italy slowly extended their control into imperial territories, and in the sixth and seventh centuries they converted to catholic Christianity. The destruction of the Ostrogothic kingdom in Italy caused irreparable devastation and opened Italy to the Lombard advance. Even the immense wealth of the agricultural provinces, especially Egypt, and the fiscal legacy of Anastasius and Justin I could not meet the needs of Justinian and his successors. Around the year 500, the annual budget of Constantinople was 900,000 gold pieces. At the death of Anastasius in 518, the imperial treasury contained 320,000 pounds of gold, or 23,000,000 gold pieces—a surplus nearly twenty-five times the annual budget. No state west of China was capable of mobilizing wealth on such a scale. But between 527 and 627, all that wealth was spent, and more and more tax revenues had to be raised. By the end of the sixth century, the empire was virtually bankrupt. These figures give some idea of the scale of the challenge of the events in the later sixth century.

Natural disasters, too, took their toll. The plague that swept the empire in 542 returned in cycles later in the century. Earthquakes, too, took considerable toll. Even those parts of the empire that survived under the rule of Constantinople underwent a serious population decline. A smaller population meant a smaller tax base, but the need for money did not lessen. As Justinian's successors discovered, new hostilities in the Balkans and along the northern and eastern frontiers—precisely those areas that Justinian had left generally unattended—increased the need for money and troops. Justinian had also bought a temporary peace with Persia at the cost of a high tribute. The fiscal burden of that tribute grew heavier every year. When Justinian stopped paying it, the eastern frontier with Persia became another danger spot.

Justinian's successors thus faced the prospect of expensive wars fought on two frontiers. They also had to restructure a new society, one geared now for continual war. They turned to the vast reserves of manpower among the populations of Thrace and Asia Minor, and they maintained close control over the armies by means of a complex bureaucracy in Constantinople. This program of administration was financed by new forms of social organization and taxation.

Unlike the organized opposition of Persia to the east, the presence of migrating and invading peoples from the north was intermittent and has left few records. Slavic peoples had begun migrating into the empire after the mid sixth century, and the invasion of the Asiatic Avar people in the late sixth century drove the Slavs farther south and westward. Under their ruler, the Khagan, the Avars exacted immense sums of tribute from nearby peoples, including the emperors. By the end of the sixth century, the Slavic peoples were exerting steady pressure on Macedonia and Greece. Athens was sacked in 582. Thessalonica, the second largest city in the empire, was often under Slavic, and sometimes under Avar, siege. In 617, a combined Slav and Avar force unsuccessfully assaulted the city of Constantinople itself. Besides Macedonia and Greece, Slavic peoples migrated into eastern Bavaria, Moravia, and Bohemia during this period. Farther north, Slavic tribes extended along the shores of the Elbe River.

The threats along the northern and eastern frontiers tested both the abilities and resources of Justinian's successors. The most energetic of the late-sixth-century emperors was Maurice (582–602). After ten years of war, he achieved a temporary peace with Persia. Facing Lombard pressure in Italy and Slav-Avar pressure south of the Danube, Maurice reorganized the western frontiers. He turned the city of Ravenna into a frontier fortification. He also created the office of *exarch,* combining civil and military government in one official. Maurice also created an exarch at Carthage. These steps helped to turn the provinces into defensive societies protecting a frontier threatened on many sides.

Maurice was assassinated after a military revolt in 602, and a brutal and incompetent military officer, Phocas, usurped the throne. Phocas fiercely repressed political opposition in Constantinople, and his accession signaled a renewal of the Persian wars. After the first decade of the seventh century, the empire was plunged into a crisis that completed its transformation.

In 610, Heraclius, the son of the exarch of Carthage, led a fleet to Constantinople, captured and killed Phocas, and made himself emperor. The renewal of Persian hostilities under Shah Khosroes II (591–628) occupied most of Heraclius' attention. Facing a renewed Persian threat in the east, Heraclius withdrew Roman troops from the Balkans, leaving the area open to further Avar and Slav incursions. In a series of quick and thorough campaigns, Khosroes captured Roman Mesopotamia and western Syria, and he conquered Antioch and Damascus in 613, Jerusalem in 614, and Egypt in 620. From 620 on, he assaulted Constantinople directly. In combination, the problems posed by the Slav-Avar coalition and the Persians seemed insurmountable. By 618, Heraclius was seriously considering moving the imperial capital from Constantinople to Carthage. At the same time, other peoples migrated into the Balkans. The ancestors of the modern Croats entered the western Balkans around 600; around the same time, those of the modern Serbs had settled in the southern regions of what is now Serbia. Both peoples assimilated to the local Slavic population, and by 700, the ethnic mix of Balkan populations was in place.

The growing power of both the Avars and the Persians meant that the Roman empire was threatened from two directions, by powers that aimed to capture Constantinople itself and finish the empire off entirely. In 626, the forces of the Avars and Persians joined in an alliance and began the siege of the city. The population of Constantinople, however, resisted. The church and the citizens submitted voluntarily to even the most stringent economic measures. They had already produced enough money to enable Heraclius to buy off the Avars for a short time, and in 624, they raised enough to enable Heraclius to leave Constantinople and raise a new army in Armenia and among the Turkish steppe-nomads, which he took into Persia in a dramatic and unexpected move, leaving Constantinople's own citizens to defend their city against the last and greatest combined offensive of Slavs, Avars, and Persians in 626/7. Heraclius' "new model army" carried all before it. His victories in Persia culminated in the defeat of the Persian army near Nineveh and the destruction of the shah's palace at Dastgerd. Khosroes II, humiliated by the unexpected reversal of his fortunes, was assassinated in 628. As Heraclius fought his way through Persia in 627, the citizens of Constantinople achieved a victory as great as their emperor's. They destroyed the barbarian fleet that lay before the city, and with it the other great threat to the empire's survival. The defeat weakened the Avar khaganate permanently.

But the victory proved to be immensely costly. It had exhausted the empire economically and militarily, and it proved that Justinian's dream of a restored Mediterranean Roman Empire was gone forever. The western frontiers proved less important than the north and east. Facing the greatest crisis in the history of the empire, Heraclius and his successors turned away from the Latin west, converting the peasantry of Thrace and Asia Minor into a citizen army and mobilizing the empire for a different kind of life in a new world.

FROM THE EAST ROMAN TO THE BYZANTINE EMPIRE, 627–718

And they did so just in time. With the new threats from Arabs and Bulgars beginning in the seventh century, the empire faced formidable new enemies, one of which remained a threat until the fall of the Byzantine Empire in 1453.

Molded into a new kind of cultural and political force by the religion of Islam (Below, Chapter 5), Arab armies began to move out of the Arabian peninsula, and by 636 they posed a threat to both the East Roman and Persian worlds. Disaffected imperial provinces in Egypt, North Africa, and Palestine either could not or would not put up significant resistance to the conquerors, and the shrunken military resources of Heraclius were not sufficient to stem the invasions. The major Arab defeat of an East Roman army at Yarmuk in 636 cost Heraclius the provinces of Syria and Palestine, and shortly afterwards the Arabs swept into the ruins of the Sasanid Persian empire and conquered it entire. During the next thirty years, Arab commanders prepared to assault Constantinople itself. The first major siege came in 674–678, when Arab fleets managed to blockade the city but failed to breach the walls. In 717–718, Arab armies and fleets assaulted the city again. This time an able Syrian general turned emperor, Leo III (717–741), successfully directed the defense of the city. But even such victories as these cost the empire dearly; much of its southern and southeastern Mediterranean empire vanished. Arab armies and fleets swept across Egypt, North Africa, and into the Iberian Peninsula, which they conquered between 711 and 720. From the beginning of the eighth century, Arab and East Roman forces struggled along a mountainous frontier in southern Asia Minor. The eastern frontier had come once again to dominate the energies and attention of the East Roman Empire.

The emergence of a new Arab empire in some of the richest parts of the East Roman empire and all of Persia created a new political, economic, and cultural world that extended from the Atlantic Ocean to northern India, a dynamic configuration that had never existed earlier and that affected all the societies that it touched.

In the Balkans another Asiatic people, the Bulgars, established themselves around 680. After having checked the earlier advances of Slavs and Avars, the empire found itself unable to prevent the establishment of a Bulgar kingdom. The defeat of the emperor Constantine IV in 679 by the forces of the Bulgar khan Asparuch guaranteed Bulgar control of the lower Danube valley. With the establishment of the kingdom of the Bulgars and its recognition by the emperor in 681, the local Slavonic population came under Bulgar domination. Although the new state experienced dynastic conflicts and rivalries for the kingship in the later seventh and early eighth centuries, a strong kingship emerged from the mid eighth century on, based on a high degree of integration of Bulgar and Slavic elements in the population. The Bulgarian kingdom, like the empire of Islam, became a permanent force in imperial foreign relations.

The crises in imperial defense of the late sixth, the seventh, and the early eighth centuries were not without their internal consequences. The horizons of the empire had shrunk to the eastern Balkans and southern Asia Minor, and the empire had exhausted the last resources of its people to defend and preserve itself. Heraclius had invoked the aid of supernatural powers to defend Constantinople against the Slavs and Avars, but the appearance of yet newer and more threatening enemies seemed to indicate God's anger at the Christian empire. The permanent war-footing of the imperial economy and the importance of orthodox religious observance helped shape the transformation of the East Roman into the Byzantine Empire, a process that was well under way by the early eighth century. An eastern Mediterranean Christian state, the Byzantine Empire depended for its survival on stringent economy, military alertness, and religious uniformity. Its horizons were limited to the lower Danube valley, the Black Sea, the eastern Balkans, northern Greece, and Asia Minor.

In spite of the wars, political upheaval, and religious crises of the seventh and eighth centuries, there is striking evidence of a powerful cultural revival that reflects the transformation of the East Roman into the Byzantine Empire. Although many of the greatest cities of the empire were either lost to Islam or devastated from war, Constantinople itself thrived and became in effect the only city in its empire. And the empire existed because of the city. Officials in the city collected taxes in cash and kind. Army commanders were appointed at the imperial court, and the city thus became the source of both wealth and power, as nowhere else in the empire. Atttachment to the imperial court and the holding of public office became a sure path to noble status. A core of educated aristocratic civil servants and churchmen in the city preserved some of the traditions of older learning and generated new cultural interests. The Greek language and Orthodox Christianity that had been shaped between the sixth and the ninth centuries constituted the basis of Byzantine civilization.

One of the most striking features of Byzantine civilization is the character of its most representative figures. Churchmen and civil servants, they came from the ranks of urban Constantinopolitan society, received similar educations, and often followed similar careers in the civil service until their paths divided into the church and government. Such similarity between churchmen and government officials was not to be found in the west until much later, and thus it is possible to speak of an educated class consisting of both churchmen and government officials that formed the basis of Byzantine civilization. Schools appear to have increased in number and improved in the late eighth century, and a new, more efficient form of handwriting appeared. The study of the Greek classics was resumed, and although Justinian had closed the academy of Plato in Athens in 529, influences of Platonic philosophy remained strong among the highly developed philosophical interests of Greek Christian theology.

A second feature of Byzantine civilization is the dedication of artistic talent and innovation to liturgical ceremonies and church decoration. From the sixth century on, Syrian musicians helped create liturgical services that were marvels of ritual and aesthetic achievement. The public and communal character of eastern Christianity was dynamically effective in the formal liturgical services in which material objects were made holy by the actions of ordained clergy, in the buildings and hymnologies of the great churches, in the devotions of monks, and in the processions through the city on holy days. All of these were believed to have been ordained by God. Privately, eastern Christians venerated individual holy men, the relics of saints, and especially religious icons. The icon was a picture of Jesus, the Virgin, or one of the saints, that Christians believed was infused with a spiritual power, one that led the eye and the mind from the material holy image into the realm of unchanging spiritual truth. But the veneration of icons also raised questions as to their own holiness. Were they aids to piety or objects to which their worshipers attributed an unsanctioned kind of holiness—a kind of idol? Defenders of icon veneration claimed that some images had indeed been given by God—Christ's own image imprinted on a cloth at Edessa—or had originated in the earliest moments of Christian history—Luke's alleged portrait of the Virgin. During the early eighth century, the dispute over icons came to a head, and the movement known as *iconoclasm* developed in order to challenge the worshipers of icons, the *iconodules* (below, Chapter 9).

In spite of the threat of iconoclasm, the Byzantine genius for pictorial representation survived and indeed triumphed in the new programs for church decoration that were called for in the ninth and tenth centuries. Although Byzantium has sometimes been criticized for its traditionalism and lack of innovation, its culture was, in fact, more highly differentiated than any European culture until the nineteenth century. Imperial court ceremony, like the liturgy of churches, reflected Byzantine philosophy, and the emperors remained energetic patrons of the arts.

Third, Byzantium had sustained—and survived—what were probably the most sweeping changes that occurred anywhere in the ancient Mediterranean world. In the West, much of the civilization of antiquity was swept away, and rulers and churchmen could create a new world with fewer restrictions and simpler forms. In the East, however, the legacy of both antique and Christian culture managed to survive in spite of transformations that were as profound as those in the West. The old urban aristocracy gave way to a new aristocracy of generals and civil servants; an old society that depended heavily on slave labor gave way to one in which a free peasantry sustained the economic strength of the state. With the removal of the older aristocracy, the imperial government taxed its population directly, and, except for the great city of Constantinople itself, that population was largely ruralized. Many of the great eastern Mediterranean cities declined in the sixth and seventh centuries, and in their place remained Constantinople alone, ruling an empire of villages and towns and defended by an army that was controlled from Constantinople, under the central authority of the state.

In a sense, this transformation may be regarded as the price paid by East Rome for the survival of the state on a new economic and social basis. Under this new state control, orthodox religious belief, directed from Constantinople, became more rigorous against dissent. Even as it lost territories, the East Roman Empire also lost dissidents. Like the Greek language, orthodox Christianity became a major support for the state.

It is in this light that Byzantine political theory ought to be understood. Although the Byzantine emperor is often accused of "caesaropapism"—that is, imperial rule of the Church—it is important to note that the highly developed cosmological ideas of the Byzantines provided a special place in God's favor for the emperor, as ruler of the world and "head of the family of rulers" of all peoples. Moreover, the integration of spiritual and temporal culture meant that the emperor, churchmen, and civil leaders were allies. The genius of Byzantine culture lies precisely in the spiritual bonds that held the secular state together. Byzantines considered their state to be a holy community, charged by divine command to preserve the true faith. This attitude produced the rich ecclesiastical culture that absorbed much of the Byzantine genius that seems so foreign to modern eyes.

And all of this was defended by the armies. The governmental control of coinage and taxation meant that military service, paid in coin, remained an attractive career opportunity for large parts of the population. In the wake of the seventh-century political disasters, the armies of Constantinople, *themes*, as they came to be called, were withdrawn into Asia Minor, where they were originally stationed in four areas under their own generals, side by side with a civil administration. After 750, the generals tended to assume civil as well as military authority. The armies were recruited from Armenian and other Caucasian peoples, but also from the population of Asia Minor itself. Manuals of military science continued to be written and studied, treating both field tactics and fortifications. The Byzantine navy also remained effective, especially when armed with "Greek Fire," a combustible substance that could be fired or sprayed to ignite enemy ships.

The mosaics, icons, sculpture, and architecture of Byzantine civilization should be regarded from the perspective of the late seventh- and early eighth-century transformations of the whole empire. The army protected, and the empire was ruled from, a sacred city. Beneath the glittering, superbly arranged decorative surfaces lies a spiritual ideal, which literally charges each picture with meaning. In the sonorous, intricate liturgy of the Orthodox church is reflected a whole theology. And through ecclesiastical art and liturgy the ideals of Byzantine civilization were expressed to all classes of the empire. Indeed, it may be said that Byzantine civilization was more deeply and thoroughly rooted in its population than either the civilization of the ancient world or that of the Latin west.

5

The House of Islam
and the House of War

THE ARAB PEOPLES AND THE ROMAN
AND PERSIAN WORLDS

In the deserts of the southern Near East and along the desert frontiers of the Roman and Persian empires there lived Arab peoples, Semitic-speaking desert nomadic pastoralists and village- and town-dwellers who had long played a prominent role in Near Eastern history. The word *'Arab* originally designated the nomadic tribesmen (*arabiyē*) who inhabited the region from the Red Sea to the upper Tigris and Euphrates valleys. Arab peoples are mentioned by the Greeks as early as the fifth century B.C.E., where they are also called *Sarakenoi,* later Latinized and vernacularized as "Saracens." They appear in Jewish scripture slightly earlier. The nomadic Arabs, the *bedouin,* herded flocks of sheep and goats on the edges of the desert, or, if they were wealthier and deeper in the desert, camels, for their meat and milk, and traded or raided more sedentary peoples for women, grain, dates, and slaves. In the deserts, small-scale agriculture could only be practiced at oases, and the bedouin were therefore also tied commercially to northern agricultural regions in the Fertile Crescent. Arab society was based on the small kin-group or clan and the larger tribe. Kin—and tribal—loyalty took precedence over all other social obligations.

During the long conflict between Rome and Persia, many Arab peoples lived in trading cities along the Roman-Persian frontier, and several Arab kingdoms, notably Nabatea and Palmyra, had risen to considerable prosperity in the third century C.E. on the borders of the Roman and Persian empires. Two of the northern Arab peoples, the Ghassanids and Lakhmids, were important allies of the Roman and Persian empires in the desert areas along the frontier. A number of Arab peoples had also converted to Christianity, and the early fifth-century Christian historian Sozomen says not only that there had always been among the Arabs a kind of primitive monotheism similar to that of pre-Mosaic Judaism, but also that some Arabs in these regions had recently encountered Jews and learned and accepted the idea of Arab descent from Abraham through Hagar and Ishmael (Genesis 15–16, 21:8–19). The *Qur'an* (below, this chapter) emphasizes again and again the lineal descent of the Arabs from Abraham and mentions Abraham's prayer for a later Messenger from God. The question of pre-Islamic Arab contacts with monotheistic religion has generated considerable scholarly debate, although it is clear that there were Jewish and Christian communities in the Arabian peninsula during the lifetime of Muhammad (ca. 570–632). What Sozomen's argument about the Arab acceptance of a very early form of Abrahamist monotheism did reflect, however, is the self-conscious antiquity of the Arab peoples themselves and their sense of cultural unity.

During the same period, the southern part of the Arabian peninsula came to be dominated by the nomadic tribes of bedouins that had long flourished in the north of the peninsula. By the sixth century C.E., in spite of the prosperity of some segments of northern Arab society, the majority of Arabs remained bedouins, and the "bedouinization" of Arabian society between the fourth and sixth centuries C.E. is a feature marked by all historians of the period. The nomadic tribe under the direction of its elected chief (the term *shaykh* is used in this sense only much later) became the module of Arab society. The tribe was characterized by its fierce independence, warlike character, sense of honor and fear of shame, devotion to the tribal gods, contempt for the life of the urban Arabs, and its adherence to the concepts of *'asabiyya*, tribal solidarity. Arabic tribal culture was oral, consisting of poetry of praise of patrons, invective against enemies, love, elegies for the dead, glorification, description, and riddles, as well as a rich tradition of storytelling passed down from generation to generation.

In the fifth and sixth centuries C.E., some Arab cities became more prominent and wealthy. The trade routes followed by camel caravans between South Arabia and Persia, made dangerous by the wars between Rome and Persia, and the trade routes between Ethiopia and Egypt, made dangerous by the more frequent attacks of bedouins, declined in importance. The third route of trade, between the Mediterranean and Yemen, ran down the western edge of the Arabian Peninsula, the *Hijaz,* and this route may have increased in importance as the other routes declined. Although the towns along the western Arabian route were not the equal of the earlier great cities of South Arabia or northward along the Fertile Crescent, several of them grew prosperous, and one, Mecca, became a pilgrimage site as well.

Increasing wealth from trade and the presence of a number of important shrines made Mecca attractive to the desert peoples as well as the urban Arabs. Mecca was a *haram,* a neutral ground or sanctuary where members of feuding and predatory tribes and pilgrims to its many idols might meet in safety. The city's most important shrine was a black meteorite kept in a sanctuary called the *Ka'ba,* and the city was eventually dominated by the Quraysh tribe. The desert tribes that came to Mecca brought their fierce independence with them, and the presence of the bedouin along with the growing commercial wealth and the limited ability of traditional Arab culture to deal with such pressures made sixth- and seventh-century Mecca a highly volatile boom town.

THE MESSENGER

Around 610 a middle-aged Meccan caravan manager, Muhammad (ca. 570–632), began to receive visions and commands from God in Arabic through the angel Gabriel (*Jibril*). In the following years, Muhammad delivered the "recitations" that God had commanded, the *Qur'an* (the term comes from the Arabic root meaning "to read" or "to recite"). Muhammad had been born in Mecca, the son of 'Abd Allāh, who died before Muhammad was born, a poor member of the Hashim clan of the important Quraysh tribe. Orphaned by the age of six, Muhammad was brought up in the lively and turbulent world of Mecca, first by his grandfather, 'Abd al-Muttalib, and then by his uncle, Abu Talib. As a young man, he became a successful caravan manager and later married his wealthy employer, the widow Khadija (555–619). But he did not simply retire to the prosperity that his marriage offered. He had been extremely devout all of his life, frequently retiring to a nearby cave to meditate, and his experience of Mecca made the spiritual fate of the Arabs in that turbulent society his chief concern.

Muhammad's message directly addressed that concern. He announced that the single God (Allah in Arabic), the same God who had spoken to Abraham, Moses, and Jesus, had been the source of his message, and the Arabs its intended recipients. The *Qur'an* expressly calls the Arabs "the best community" (Q. 3. 110). He reported his "recitations," the *Qur'an,* as a body of instructions concerning the only acceptable life a subject of God was to live. Although God had partially revealed himself to Jews and Christians though the prophets Moses and Jesus, only Muhammad received the final and ultimate revelation of divine truth. Muhammad was the Messenger (*al-rasūl,* messenger, or *an-nabi,* prophet), and the "seal of the prophets" (*khatam*). The *Qur'an,* which was compiled after Muhammad's death and was arranged in 114 *suras* (steps, or chapters) subdivided into verses (*ayas*), declared Allah, "the Merciful, the Compassionate," the only God, and therefore the God to whom humans must subject themselves.[1] The religion Muhammad proclaimed, *Islam,* means "subjection to God." The term *Muslim,* which derives from the same Arabic root, *-slm,* means "the one who has subjected himself to God," and, by implication, entered on a covenant of peace with others who have done so (Q. 3. 60). Like Jews and Christians, Muslims were considered "People of the Book," *alu-l-kitab,* but only Muslims were given the final revelation of God's will. The injunctions contained in the *Qur'an* attacked the ills of contemporary Arab society and professed to forge all believers into one great *'Umma,* an expanded conception of an

---

[1]The best English translation of the *Qur'an* and the one cited here and in later chapters (as Q, followed by the numbers of *sura* and verse) is that of A. J. Arberry, *The Koran Interpreted* (New York: Simon & Schuster, 1996).

Arab tribe, to which all the faithful would feel primary loyalty, regardless of former ties and allegiances to kin or to others.

At first Muhammad gathered around him a few followers from his family and clan, but he encountered opposition from the ruling aristocracy of Mecca. Possibly fearful of the decline of the city as a pilgrimage center, and certainly disapproving of Muhammad's low social origins, the Meccan rulers were at first indifferent to the new faith and then actively hostile to it. In 622, Muhammad and a number of followers moved to the city of Yathrib, where Muhammad had been invited as an outside arbitrator of the city's internal conflicts. The flight from Mecca to Yathrib, which thereafter changed its name to Medina (*Madinat,* "the City"), was called the *Hijra* ("Migration"), and the official calendar of Islam (a lunar calendar adopted around 640) is dated from its beginning, September 24, 622.

At Medina, Muhammad was able to give his conception of the Islamic *'Umma* a practical political form and to establish the alliances among his original followers, the population of Medina, and the neighboring bedouin tribes. After initial cooperation with local Jewish communities, Muhammad expelled them from Medina and sent his forces to establish his power in other parts of Arabia. In 624, in the battle of Badr (Q. 3. 119), Muhammad's followers defeated a force from Mecca. From Medina, Muhammad led his followers back to Mecca in 630, where he was recognized as a religious leader to whom most of the population of the cities and many more of the desert tribes now offered their allegiance. Using the ethical force of his religious visions to overcome the divisions that separated the desert Arabs from each other, and both from the Arabs of the cities, Muhammad began to forge a new society of all Arabs united on religious grounds. In this sense Muhammad may be said to have created the Arabs as a people.

ISLAM

Although it responded to the cultural, social, and political circumstances of Arabs, Islam was unquestionably a religious revolution. Like other religious revolutions, it established a new role for religion in the lives of its followers. Unlike Christianity, Islam offered no distracting theological problems, such as that of the Trinity or that of the relation of the two natures of Christ, that might detract from the absolute single majesty of God. It possessed no clergy with sacramental authority. Unlike Judaism, it had no complex history of theological and eschatological movements, nor was its practice limited by intolerant Christian rulers. The intensity and directness of Islamic belief gave the faith an appeal to peoples at all levels of social and theological development. The attractiveness of Islam to both the ferocious Berbers of North Africa and the subtle theologians and country gentlemen of Persia is powerful testimony to the personal force of Muhammad and the eloquence of his spiritual message.

At the core of Islam is the *Qur'an* and its great message: There is one God and Muhammad is His Messenger (Q. 3. 137: *lā ilāha illa llāh muhammadan rasūlu llāh*), the "Seal of the Prophets" (Q. 23. 40). Consistent with Abrahamic monotheism, God is unique, eternal, the creator of all worlds, omnipotent, and has no needs (Q. 3. 92, 39. 9).

God is also merciful and compassionate (Q. 1. 1), and that is His consistent designation in the *Qur'an*. Islam rests on five pillars (Q. 2. 172-3):

> True piety is this:
> to believe in God, and the Last Day,
> the angels, the Book, and the Prophets,
> to give of one's substance, however cherished,
> to kinsmen, and orphans,
> the needy, the traveller, beggars,
> and to ransom the slave,
> to perform the prayer, to pay the alms.
> And they who fulfill their covenant,
> when they have engaged in a covenant,
> and endure with fortitude
> misfortune, hardship and peril,
> these are they who are true in their faith,
> these are the truly godfearing.

The first of the pillars (*ash-shahada*) is the acknowledgement of God and of Muhammad's authentic prophetic role. This acknowledgement, when recited sincerely in Arabic before two adult male Muslim witnesses, is what makes an unbeliever a Muslim. The second pillar is the ritual prayer (*al-salat*) performed at first three, and later five, times a day at fixed hours, with the proper formulas and physical gestures, with the great public communal prayer at midday on Friday. The third is the observation of the holy month of Ramadan (the month in which the *Qur'an* was revealed; Q. 2. 180) by fasting (*al-sawm*) from dawn to sunset. The fourth pillar is almsgiving (*al-zakat*). The fifth is making the pilgrimage (*al-hadj*) to Mecca at least once in a lifetime, if possible (Q. 2. 192). These elements of Islam are the same for Muslims today as they were in the early Islamic period.

Since the *Qur'an* asserted the existence of an afterlife, Paradise for the faithful and the fires of Gehenna for the unfaithful (Q. 2. 198), faithful observance of the law gives the Muslim a place in paradise (Q. 81. 1-14). Besides God and humans, the only other beings in Islam are angels and *jinn*. Angels are pure light; *jinn* (plural; sing. *jinni*, English "genie") are spirits who may, like humans, accept or reject Islam. Some *jinn*, notably Iblis (e.g., Q. 2. 32-34, 7. 10, and frequently elsewhere in Q.), refused to humble themselves before the newly created Adam and now seek to deceive and mislead men. A species of *jinn* is the *shaytāns*, "Satans," who are consistently malevolent. But these created beings never acquire the dynamic role of the Christian Satan, and they will end in the fire.

The history of Islam in the *Qur'an*, and its prophetic future in later Islamic thought consists of a constant falling back into corruption and erroneous practices by the community, which is then warned by a messenger from God. Abraham, anticipating this falling away, had even asked God to send a later Messenger (Q. 3. 60, 2. 123), Muhammad. Even after the Prophet, the 'Umma will again fall into conflicting sects leading to an apocalyptic end of time.

Islamic tradition describes Muhammad as having recited portions of the *Qur'an* during the years from 610 until his death in 632. These recitations were memorized and sometimes copied down by his secretaries and friends, perhaps with direction from the Prophet specifying to which part of the whole each recitation belonged. The entire *Qur'an* is believed by Muslims to have assumed its present shape around 648. By that time, the language of the *Qur'an* was regarded as sacred and absolutely authoritative. Its 114 *suras,* usually referred to by title, or catchword, rather than by number, were considered God's word and dictated by the angel Gabriel, and therefore no Muslim may read the *Qur'an* for spiritual benefit in any language other than Arabic (it is the *Arabic Qur'an;* Q. 20. 111, 42. 5), nor may the text be altered in any way. The expansion of Arab political power in the seventh and eighth centuries was therefore accompanied by the spread of the Arabic language, as new converts to Islam were made. The *Qur'an* became a spiritual guide, a language manual, and the greatest schoolbook in the Islamic world. It was also potentially a code of law and ethics, a book of political theory, and a guide to conduct.

But the *Qur'an* did not contain instructions for everything a Muslim should do, nor was its language entirely unambiguous. The textual history of the *Qur'an* and the development of Muslim religious law raise considerable scholarly problems. A number of recent scholars, using early non-Muslim sources and raising questions about the influence of later Islamic traditions on the interpretation of earlier Islamic history, have offered a somewhat different picture of the first two Muslim centuries. According to this version, the text of the *Qur'an* was not finally established until the ninth century, when a class of learned religious jurists (*'ulama*) began to expound and systematize religious law (see below).

Islam has long been much misunderstood and maligned in the West. In particular, the elements of Islamic law that reflect directly the customs of the seventh-century desert tribesmen—especially the predominance of the male, the prohibition of pork and alcohol, and the fleshy delights of the Muslim paradise—have deflected attention from other and ultimately far more influential Muslim beliefs. For the Muslim, no priest intervenes between the individual and God; there is no Islamic sacramental liturgy; the pictorial representation of living things is prohibited; and knowledge of the *Qur'an*—including the memorization of the entire text—is virtuous.

Two examples may suffice. The *Qur'an* mentions prayer and the house of prayer, the Mosque, but the later tradition designed the physical details of the mosque and distinguished the Congregational Mosque (*jami'*) from the everyday mosque (*masjid*). The Congregational Mosque was to be large enough to hold all the worshipers (originally men and women prayed together and were separated only in the eighth century) for Friday prayer. The *Qur'an* states that prayer must be oriented toward Mecca (Q. 2. 144-5). Later Arab mathematicians devised a trigonometric formula (*qibla*) whereby the exact direction to Mecca from anywhere in the world could be accurately determined. Tradition later stated that the mosque was to hold a *mihrab,* a prayer-niche, and a sounding chamber (*minbar*) so that the Imam's (the Prayer Leader's) recitation of prayers could be heard clearly. The mosque contained nothing resembling an altar, had no mediating priesthood, and a Muslim could pray anywhere in the mosque. The modern mosque was clearly a development during the first two centuries, not in existence at the death of the Prophet.

A second example is the status of women in Islam. In matters of personal status and law, women are not equal to men, and divorce is easy for a man and virtually impossible for a woman. In cases of adultery between unmarried people, which must be proved by the identical eyewitness testimony of four male witnesses, both parties are to be flogged (Q. 24. 2). Later tradition commanded the stoning to death of a married woman convicted of adultery. The *Qur'an* permits the male believer to take as many as four wives, whom he must treat equally. There are also a number of laws on ritual purity in which the burden falls on the woman. Women are to cover their bosoms (Q. 23. 59), although the *Qur'an* says nothing about covering the face (veiling a woman's head and face was a Byzantine practice, perhaps later adopted by Muslims). On the other hand, the *Qur'an* also greatly ameliorates the condition of women compared to the practices of the pre-Islamic period. Then, female infanticide had been widely practiced, but the *Qur'an* prohibits it (Q. 81. 1-14). All wives had to be treated equally and were to bring dowries to a marriage provided by their family. Widows had to be provided for for a year after their husband's death; they could inherit a portion of his estate, and they could remarry. Women shared in the inheritance system, being permitted also to inherit a share in their parents' and close relatives' estates.

THE PROTECTORS OF THE FAITH
AND THE SPREAD OF ISLAM

Muhammad died in 632. He had had four daughters by nine wives (although he married no other wife during Khadijah's lifetime), of whom several wives, but only one daughter, Fatimah, survived him. He left no instructions concerning a successor, and the *Qur'an* was vague on this point: "O believers, obey God, and obey the Messenger and those in authority among you" (Q. 4. 62). Because many of the tribes that had submitted to him considered their relation to him nontransferrable and his death the severance of their bond to Muhammad and to fellow Muslims, the problem of a successor became crucial. Such a leader could not be called Messenger or Prophet, for that title could designate only Muhammad. Abu Bakr (r. 632–634), father of Muhammad's beloved and influential wife A'ishah, was elected by the other Companions of the Prophet as Muhammad's "Deputy" and assumed the title *khalifa* ("caliph," successor), although it was not at first clear as to what the role and powers of the caliph should be, nor whether the caliph should be chosen from Muhammad's own family, from among his original Companions, or from elsewhere in the community. Surviving tribal political values required extensive recognition of and consultation with prominent elders and acknowledgment of an ancestral nobility. Such a view seemed to be confirmed in the *Qur'an* (Q. 33. 6, 49) and appealed to tribal societies that later came under the influence of Islam in Central Asia and sub-Saharan Africa. The royal and imperial—or "patrimonial"—tradition of Sasanid

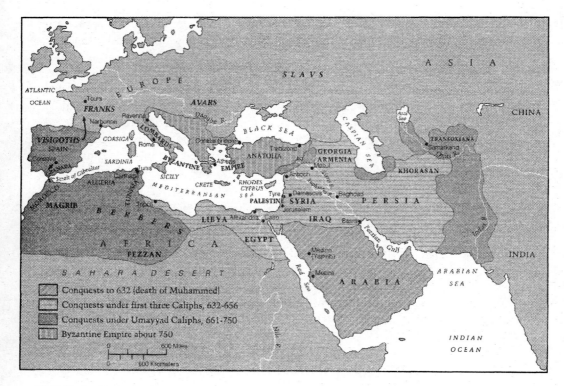

The expanding Muslim zone.

Persia offered the model of an autocratic ruler, especially appealing to caliphs who had to raise and pay armies and officials and reward their own followers and supporters. In addition, the new Islamic image of the Community of Believers implied a collective authority of believing adult males, detatched from Arab ethnicity, that fitted neither of the first two positions easily. The tensions among these ideals are reflected in subsequent Islamic political history.

Islamic historians recognize three major groups of caliphs between 632 and 1258; the "Rightly Guided" caliphs (*rashidun*), from Abu Bakr (632–634) to Muhammad's cousin and son-in-law Ali (656–661); the Umayyad Caliphate, from Muawiyah (661–680) to Marwan II (744–750); and the Abbasid Caliphate, from Abu-l-Abbas (750–754) to the end of the Caliphate in 1258. The Rightly Guided caliphs faced not only the problem of determining the nature of the caliphate and its powers, but also that of organizing Muslim society in the absence of Muhammad. The Umayyad Caliphate directed the continuing expansion of Islam from its capital at Damascus. The Abbasid Caliphate represented the culmination of Muslim expansion and the rise to prominence of nonethnic Arabs in the Islamic world, symbolized by its move of the capital to the new city of Baghdad (begun in 762). The caliph, first at Damascus and then at Baghdad, was the official orthodox protector of the faith and sometimes the temporal and spiritual leader of Islamic society.

JIHAD

Muhammad's small community of original followers at Medina had bitterly resented their exile from Mecca, and they adopted the old tribal custom of the *ghazwa* (raid or expedition) against those who had scorned them and driven them out. The *Qur'an* calls these activities "striving in the way of the Lord," or *jihad fi sabil Allah*. The *jihad*, misleadingly called the "Holy War" by Westerners, was a Muslim adaptation of the tribal *ghazwa*. Used against persecutors of Muslims, and later against pagans, the *jihad* became one focus of Muslim society under the first caliphs, although it remained a potent force in later Islamic political history. Raiding against infidels was permitted, then encouraged, by the *Qur'an* (Q. 4. 73–94, 22. 40 and elsewhere) so that the energies of the warlike desert tribes could be channeled. In Arabic sources, these wars are not called "conquests," but rather the "opening" (*fath*) of lands to Islamic obedience, to make the inhabitants of other territories submit to Muslim rule and pay taxes. From this perspective, the world was divided into two parts: the House of Islam (*dar al-Islam*) and the House of War (*dar al-Harb*). The plunder of the old *ghazwa* became the territorial conquests of the new *jihad*.

Only Christians, Jews, and Zoroastrians were entitled to the status of protected minorities if they surrendered to Islamic armies. They were called *dhimmis*, and had to pay a poll tax (*jizya*). For Muhammad and his successors, the conversion of the Arabs to Islam was the primary goal. Others were to be plundered and governed as the true worship of God expanded, but they were never faced with the choice of Islam or the sword, as western historians once believed. Although many non-Arabs became Muslims (*mawali*), they did not do so because they were forced.

In many respects, for much of Islamic history the military meaning of *jihad* was less important in Muslim political and ethical thought and less frequently discussed in religious literature than its interior meaning—the inner struggle on the part of the individual Muslim against his own tendencies to sin.

The direction of the Arab armies was in the hands of able caliphs and their talented generals, supported by an Arab military aristocracy comprising male Arabs who were given a stipend by the caliph if they fought or performed other work for the state. Relieving the Arab military forces of the need for other work and promising a place in paradise for anyone who died a warrior's death, the caliphs and their generals soon created a large, able, and dedicated army. Nothing in the Mediterranean or Persian worlds could match it. Further, the army was kept intact as it cut its way through the south and east of the ancient world. It was contained in separate camps when it conquered territory, isolated from the alien life and the temptations of the cities it conquered. The cities of Basra, Kufa, and al-Fustat (the earliest settlement of Cairo) began as such military camps.

Under Abu Bakr, Islam was consolidated among the Arabs, and tribes that had broken off from Islam after the death of Muhammad were brought back into the Islamic *Umma*. Under Abu Bakr's successor Umar (r. 632–644), father of Muhammad's wife Hafsah, and his great general Khalid, Arabic armies raided outside the peninsula into the Byzantine and Persian worlds. Exhausted border provinces, weakened enemies, and Arab military skills and experience, coupled with the disaffection of many of the provincials in Palestine, Syria, Egypt, Africa, and Persia, reduced local resistance and allowed many territories to pass quickly under Arab rule. The conquests created a political world in which majority non-Arab and non-Muslim populations were ruled by a minority Arab elite. Even the armies of the Byzantine and Persian empires, worn out after the long Byzantine-Persian war, fell before the skillful generalship and superior tactics of the Arabs. Antioch and Damascus both fell in 635. The battle of the Yarmuk (Jordan) in 636 destroyed Byzantine resistance, and the fall of Ctesiphon in 637 and that of Persepolis in 648 virtually wiped out Persian resistance. By 640, Syria was conquered. Alexandria was conquered in 642, and the rich Roman province of Egypt fell in the same year; Cyrenaica and Tripolitania (Northern Libya) fell between 643 and 647, Carthage in 698, and *Ifriqya* (Tunisia) by 700. By 700, all of North Africa was conquered. In 692, the caliph Abd al-Malik began construction of the Dome of the Rock in Jerusalem. These conquests resulted in an Arab overlay on local administrative structures and non-Muslim majority populations, which the Arab conquerors maintained, and on local cultures.

Military success was followed by initial political success, as the Arabs organized their newly won states into wealthy, tribute-paying provinces ruled by the caliphs at Medina, who adapted and used the existing structures of government and administration of both Rome and Persia. But the vexing problem of the nature of the office of caliph and succession to the caliphate once more came to the fore when Uthman (644–656), who was the husband of two of Muhammad's daughters, was murdered by dissenting soldiers. Opposition to Uthman was based on his alleged favoritism toward his own followers and his neglect of the legitimate claims of other tribes and clans. Uthman's opponents chose Ali as his successor in 656. Ali, the son of Muhammad's uncle Abu Talib, and therefore a cousin of Muhammad, had also married Muhammad's daughter, Fatimah. Ali's rule (656–661) encountered opposition from some of Muhammad's old followers, from the relatives of Uthman, and from some of Ali's own followers, who objected to his acquisition of the caliphate by negotiating with his opponents (relying on human resources rather than seeking God's will) after his victory at the Battle of the Camel, near Basra. These disaffected followers, the Khariji, who elected their own religious leader (Imam), demanded strict standards of religious understanding and conduct and legitimized war on all who disagreed with them. A Kharijite assassinated Ali in 661. Muawiyah (r. 661–680), the nephew of Uthman and governor of Syria, was elected to succeed Ali and was recognized by Ali's son, beginning the Umayyad Caliphate. The military turbulence of central Arabia (and the fact that Muawiyah had been governor of Syria for twenty years) inspired Muawiyah to move the capital of the empire to Damascus.

SUNNIS AND SHIITES

The assassination of two successive caliphs, Uthman and Ali, created divisions in the community of believers. Some remained neutral in the dispute between Uthman and Ali; others preferred to postpone a decision. The Khariji remained implacably hostile to both. At the invitation of the people of Kufa, who regarded the Umayyad caliph as illegitimate,

Ali's son, Husayn ibn Ali, rebelled against Muawiyah's successor Yazid I (680–683), and, with his army, was wiped out at the battle of Karbala in 680. The "martyrdom" of Husayn galvanized many followers of Ali who objected fiercely to Yazid's slaughter of Husayn, his disregard for the family of the Prophet, his autocratic conduct that seemed to violate communitarian ideals, and his betrayal of the Prophet's message shown by his impious and immoral conduct. They now claimed that Muhammad himself had designated Ali as his successor and that only a biological descendant of Muhammad could be the true Imam, or religious leader of the Muslim *Umma*, which meant only a descendant of Ali through Husayn, designated by his predecessor. In their eyes, no other caliph, no matter how powerful, possessed any legitimacy at all, nor had any earlier caliph except Ali.

Those who came to share these views called themselves the "Party of Ali," or *shiat Ali*, Shiites. They insisted on the combination of religious and political authority (*Imama*) in the Imam, and they recognized an independent line of Imams until 675. But under the leadership of Husayn's successors, they remained politically inactive and withdrawn. Shiites remained hostile to both the Umayyad and the Abbasid Caliphates and identified a different sequence of Imams. Upon the death of the sixth Imam, Jafar, in 675, a dispute about the succession broke out between different Shiite groups. Some, the Ismailis, believed that Muhammad ibn Isma'il, son of Jafar's son Ismail (who would be the seventh Imam, hence the term designating the Ismailis as "Seveners") was the true Imam and that he would return eventually as the Mahdi, the savior of Islam. Their main opponents, the Imamis, recognized a different line of succession (from Musa, the brother of Ismail) until 874, when they announced that the twelfth Imam, Muhammad al-Mahdi, had gone into hiding and would return during the Last Days and restore Islam. Imami Shiites are therefore called "Twelvers." In a Shiite society, the Imam had considerably greater powers than a Caliph, since his role combined religious authority derived directly from the Prophet with a derivative political authority legitimized by religion. Ali was the *only* religious heir of Muhammad and had been criminally deprived of the caliphate in 632—therefore all other caliphs had been and continued to be illegitimate. Shiism also developed its own *hadith* and traditions of jurisprudence, as well as a theory of open (through Muhammad) and secret (through Ali) Islamic religious doctrines.

Initially, Shiites comprised a minority of the Muslim population. The majority gradually came to call itself the people of the community and the tradition (*ahl al-kitab w l-sunna*), or Sunnis. Sunni Islam based its claim to legitimacy on its development of a full-fledged Islamic jurisprudence, the *Shar'ia*. Between 720 and 770, its scholars collected and recorded the sayings and records of the practices of the Prophet (*hadith* and *sunna*), and they produced the first biography of Muhammad, by Ibn Ishaq (d. 767). Collections of the sayings and practices of the Prophet began to be used to supplement the *Qur'an;* each of these attested by reference to an identifiable and trustworthy chain of transmitters (*isnad*) back to the lifetime of the Prophet himself. The science of *isnad* produced a series of large biographical dictionaries of the transmitters and influenced the later Arabic writing of history, first in the great epic *History of the Prophets and Kings* by al-Tabari, published in Baghdad around 915. Although the *Qur'an* was the absolute and primary authority, as the science of Islamic jurisprudence was worked out in the eighth and ninth centuries, if the *Qur'an* appeared ambiguous or failed to deal with a religious problem, a legal scholar could refer to the *hadith,* and if the *hadith* said nothing about the subject, the scholar should then turn to the consensus of respected earlier legal scholars (*ijma'*) or to the process of analogy to similar cases (*qiyas*). Finally, if all else failed, the jurist could use his own personal knowledge (*ijtihad*), but never as the independent basis for a judgment and always consistently with Islamic principles. The entire process constituted Muslim legal science, *fiqh* (understanding), and these principles were known as the "Roots of Jurisprudence," *usul al-fiqh*.

Those who acquired this knowledge of religious law became the *ulama* (those possessing *ilm,* knowledge), a new class of legal specialists whose interpretive authority in local society gave them a distinctive status and immense respect, as well as a predominance in religious authority in nonpolitical matters greater than that of the caliphs, who for the most part recognized the jurists and approved their work. The jurists became a meritocracy, their standing depending on their knowledge, not on family or social status. Distinctive schools under respected individuals trained these legal specialists. The two most important were those of al-Shafii (d. 820), a combination of rationalist and literalist jurisprudence, and Ibn Hanbal (d. 855), a literalist interpreter who had survived the theological movement to impose a rationalist theology over the literal interpretation of scripture (Mutazilism).

Revisionist interpretations of Islamic history between the death of the Prophet and the mid ninth century suggest that the earlier version of the first two centuries of Islamic history was shaped from a distinct and later Sunni perspective that idealized the Abbasid Caliphate and may conceal a much greater variety of early practices and internal conflicts—many more early varieties of Islam—than the tradition acknowledges. The selection of accepted *hadith* and *sunna* (and the rejection of others), a methodology of using them, the Sunni-Abbasid version of early Islamic history, and the formation and eventual triumph of a class of learned jurisprudents help to explain the variety of views of both early Arab monotheism and the transmission of religious tradition.

THE UMAYYAD DYNASTY AT DAMASCUS

The internal crises that established the Umayyad dynasty at Damascus and sowed the seeds of Shi'ite-Sunnite dissension in the Muslim world did not, however, slow the process of conquest for long. As early as 647, Muawiyah had begun raids into Asia Minor, and at the same time he began to build an Arab fleet so that Constantinople itself might be assaulted by sea and land. As we have seen, in 678 and again in 717–718, massive Muslim forces assaulted the great city. The frontier between the Byzantine Empire and the Caliphate at Damascus slowly stabilized in southern Asia Minor. At the other end of the Mediterranean, Arab armies swept across North Africa. In the first years of the eighth century, one military leader, Tariq, crossed the Strait of Gibraltar into Visigothic Spain, and between 711 and 720, Arab-led armies destroyed the Visigothic kingdom. Tariq's route has been memorialized in the name of Gibraltar, for the Arabic *Jabal Tariq* means "the Mountain of Tariq." The rapid Muslim conquest of Spain drove the last Visigothic rulers north, where the tiny kingdom of Asturias and the independent Christian Basques maintained a precarious independence.

From Spain, Arab raiding armies pushed into southern Gaul, and only the exhaustion caused by the long drive across North Africa and the conquest and settlement of Spain prevented a permanent Arab settlement there. Arab armies regularly raided Gaul until the tenth century, but resistance proved to be stiffer there than elsewhere. After several governors of Muslim Spain had lost their lives in raiding parties, Abd-ar-Rahman, the governor of northern Spain, made an initially successful campaign around Poitiers and then marched on the old city of Tours. Near that city, in 732 or 733, he encountered an army of Franks led by Charles Martel (the Hammer), the mayor of the palace of Austrasia (below, Chapter 7). Charles Martel's forces defeated the Muslim army, killing Abd-ar-Rahman and forcing the Muslims to withdraw to Spain for a time.

Although Charles Martel's victory has long occupied a prominent place in Western history, it was far more significant in increasing his personal power than in preventing the Arabs from conquering Gaul. In the latter respect, the successful defenses of Constantinople in 678 and 717–718 were far more important in the long run for Christian Europe. As later history shows, the area from the head of the Aegean Sea to the Caspian Sea was the real gateway to Europe from the Near East, and the centuries-long resistance of Constantinople played a very important part in controlling the northward expansion of Islam.

Damascus, the new capital of the Muslim Empire, quickly fell under the influence of Byzantine civilization. Greek mathematical and scientific learning, Syrian art, and the vibrant commercial and social life of Egypt, Palestine, and Syria attracted the conquerors, and was developed by prolonged contact with the institutions and cultures of the old Hellenistic world. Greek and Syrian Christian administrators ruled in the service of the caliph, and subject peoples supported the regime with their taxes. The court of the Umayyad caliphs, and even their coinage, were modeled after the imperial court at Constantinople. For centuries the gold *dinar* and the silver *dirhem* constituted the most stable metallic currency in the world.

The prosperity of the Umayyad Caliphate was also reflected in the building and decorative programs undertaken in Damascus itself, as the tribute of a conquered world flowed into the hands of the Arab ruling elite. Although two wars with the Khazars, a Turkic people settled north of the Caucasus, in 642–652 and 722–737, stopped the Muslim advance to the north, Islam moved far to the east with the conquest of Iraq and Persia and victories in Turkestan and Sind. An Arab army even defeated a Chinese army north of the Jaxartes River in 751, but the conquest of China was beyond Muslim resources. One advantage of the battle appears to have been the capture of several Chinese papermakers, and paper began to circulate as a writing surface in the Muslim world shortly after the mid eighth century. Only in the mid thirteenth century did Europeans acquire the techniques of its manufacture. From the capital at Damascus, the Umayyad caliphs ruled a vast, Saharasian empire, stretching from northern India westward to the Atlantic coasts of Morocco and Iberia, and they prospered from the material and cultural gains that the empire gave them.

The conquests of the late sixth and seventh centuries brought great power and wealth, and also a great stimulus for cultural development, to the Arabs. The desert warriors of the first conquests educated and acculturated their children in the complex and fascinating ways of the world they had conquered. Many of the inhabitants of that world sought in turn to understand and accept the message of Islam. In addition to the transformation of Arabic culture there occurred a change of even greater importance. Although Muslims did not proselytize among the conquered peoples, many of these converted to Islam nonetheless—so many, in fact, that by the early eighth century, the ethnic Arab element among Muslims had begun to decline sharply.

THE ABBASID CALIPHATE IN BAGHDAD

In 747, a revolt broke out in Iraq against Umayyad rule, outraged by its highly central-ized government and what appeared to be its impious rule, denounced by Shiite and Kharijite critics. By 750 Abu-l-Abbas had defeated and killed the last Umayyad caliph and exterminated the rest of the family, except for one prince, Abd-ar-Rahman I, who es-caped to Spain and founded an emirate (a local principality) and later an independent Umayyad caliphate at Córdoba. The Abbasid Dynasty founded by Abu-l-Abbas repre-sented not only a political revolution, but also a cultural change of great importance in Islam. The Abbasid caliphs greatly emphasized their religious orthodoxy and criticized the earlier secularizing tendencies of the Umayyads. In addition, they viewed Arab and non-Arab Muslims as equal, regarded the merchant, the judge, and the administrator, rather than the warrior, as ideal citizens, and fell under the progressively greater influence of the old Sasanian Persian culture. In 762, the Abbasids built a new city, Baghdad, on the Tigris River, far to the Persian east of Damascus. From the foundation of Baghdad dates the decline of Syria into a second-class province and the rise of what had been Sasanian Persia as the center of the Islamic Empire. During the first century of the Abbasid reign, large numbers of scientific, philosophical, and theoretical works were translated into Arabic from Greek, Syriac, Persian, and Hindi, and extensive building programs began to create the new face of the Near Eastern world.

The period 750–833 marked the highest achievements of the Abbasid caliphs. Sev-eral of them, notably Harun-al-Rashid (781–809) and his son al-Ma'mun (813–833), have become legendary figures even in the West, the former through the stories of the *Arabian Nights* (The Thousand Nights and a Night) and the legends of his wealth and personal style of rule, and the latter from his patronage of learning. The reign of Harun al-Rashid was indeed a kind of economic golden age, when goods from east Asia and Africa poured into Baghdad. But from the late ninth century, the Abbasid caliphs fell vic-tim to internal family rivalry and political intrigues as well as to external resentment against increasing taxes. They also turned to slave-soldiers (*mamluks*, usually Turkish) in order to create a loyal army. But they were gradually overshadowed by their powerful advisors and administrators, and local governors and princes often proclaimed their independence of Baghdad. Most significant was the establishment in 945 by the Persian Shiite family of Buwaih, the *Buyids*, of their control of the caliph in Baghdad. Until the arrival of the Sunni Seljuk Turks in 1055, the Buyids ruled what was left of the Abbasid Caliphate. By 1055, a new official called the *sultan* had become the effective head of the Abbasid state.

From the very beginning of the dynasty, Spain had broken away and later pro-claimed its very own Umayyad Caliphate. Other princely dynasties in North Africa proclaimed their independence. A Shi'ite caliphate of the Fatimid dynasty was proclaimed in Tunisia in 909, conquered Egypt between 969 and 973, and it lasted there until 1171, when it was overthrown by the Ayyubids under Saladin (below, Chapter 12). The Shi'ite Idrisids ruled Morocco independently, as did the Kharijite Rustanids in Algeria. Fatimid North Africa remained a great power in the Islamic world until the arrival of the Sunni Seljuk Turks in the eleventh century.

Political fragmentation of the Islamic world was thus a marked feature of the ninth, tenth, and eleventh centuries. The Abbasid Caliphate survived, much weakened and under Shiite domination, until 1258, when the Mongols captured the city and killed the last caliph, Al-Mustasim (below, Chapter 17). What survived the Abbasid power was no longer the political unity of an empire, but a politically divided world bound by a common religion, language, and culture. Islamic civilization replaced Islamic political unity.

ISLAMIC CIVILIZATION

The desert Arabs who had struck out at the Greco-Roman and Persian worlds in the middle of the seventh century became both their conquerors and their cultural heirs. As early as 700, the intellectual and artistic legacy of those ancient worlds began to influence Arabic culture. By the tenth century, Muslims had absorbed and put to their own uses, the cultures of the Byzantine and Persian worlds. And they had shaped a geographical-cultural world unlike any other ever seen. By extending their culture throughout most of the Mediterranean basin and well onto the Iranian plateau, Muslims assumed some of the older roles of both East Rome and Persia, permitting the interaction among different religious traditions and constituting the main route of long-distance trade between East Asia and the Mediterranean and Europe.

As the Arabic language became the cultural, as well as the religious, language from India to Iberia, it circulated among Muslims and non-Muslims alike, and as a consequence, a number of earlier local languages disappeared. Its attraction lay not only in its role of the language of a ruling group, but in the vitality of its lyricism in poetry and rhymed prose and the precision of its analytical and descriptive powers. It expanded, not only by borrowing terms from other languages, but also by internal development, making it capable of accepting translations from other learned languages. As early as the Umayyad Caliphate, works on chemistry were being translated from Greek, then medical books from Syriac. Under the Caliph al-Mamun (813–833), a "House of Wisdom" with a vast library was established in Baghdad for translators. Individual scholars also compiled very large personal libraries. From the House of Wisdom came the medical works of Galen and some of those of Hippocrates. By 1050, virtually all of the works of Aristotle were available in Arabic. By the eleventh century, there was far more literature originally written in Greek available in Arabic than had ever been available in Latin. The great wave of translation from Greek and Persian into Arabic, often through Syriac, was the greatest effort at translation in human history yet undertaken.

But Arab thinkers were not content with reading the works of earlier thinkers in Arabic. They began to comment on them, and to correct them, often based on their own experience and observation. The physician Rhazes (864–925) wrote an original treatise on smallpox and measles, and another physician, Ibn Sina (Avicenna, 980–1037), produced a medical encyclopedia that outlined the contagious character of tuberculosis and proposed a theory of the etiology of disease based on the contamination of water supplies. But in his theological writings, Ibn Sina appeared to some critics to have relied too heavily on Aristotelian rationalism, and his theology was refuted by the learned pietist theologian al-Ghazzali (1058–1111). The works of both Rhazes and Ibn Sina were later translated into Latin and greatly influenced the early development of European medicine. Arab medicine was especially successful in treating diseases of the eyes and plague. In addition, the Arab world also saw the earliest development of the modern hospital. In philosophy, too, Muslim thinkers absorbed and transformed the work, not only of Aristotle, but of Plato and the Neoplatonists as well. The greatest of all medieval commentators on Aristotle was Ibn Rushd (Averroës, d. 1199), many of whose commentaries were also made known to the west in Latin translations at the beginning of the thirteenth century.

Arab thinkers also studied the logical and scientific works of Aristotle and they surpassed the Greek philosopher in mathematics and astronomy. One of the greatest of them, al-Biruni (973–1048), was a physician, but also an astronomer, mathematician, geographer, chemist, historian, and physicist. From India, early in the ninth century, an Arab scholar interested in mathematics adopted Indian numerical notation (Greek and Latin numbers were written as letters). They adopted and perfected a new system of numeration (the Arabic numerals used today throughout the world) by place notation, and they introduced the concept of zero. Al-Khwarizmi (Latinized as Algorismus, the root of the modern term algorithm) wrote his *Treatise on Calculation with the Hindu Numerals* in 825, and another work, *The Compendious Book on Calculation by Completion and Balancing*. Al-Khwarizmi's term for "completion" was *al jabr,* the root of our term algebra. There were two Arab translations of Euclid's *Elements of Geometry.* Arab mathematicians also discovered trigonometry. Not only Arabic numerals, but also Arabic mathematics are the basis for the mathematics of the modern world. Muslim scholars discussed the possibility of the earth's rotating on an axis, and they mapped the skies, giving many stars and constellations the names they bear today. From their work in mathematics and astronomy, Muslim thinkers went on to new studies and discoveries in optics and experimental chemistry. In the latter field, they were the first scientists to perfect the process of distillation and sublimation.

On less formal levels of culture too, the Islamic conquests produced a thoroughgoing cultural revolution. The *Qur'an* was the basic textbook, as we have seen, for learning the Arabic language. The *shari'a,* the ethical law of the *Qur'an* shaped legal decisions and individual conduct, down to matters of personal hygiene and proper social behavior and responsibility. Thus, in spite of political divisions, the daily life and thought of most of the Muslim world centered on the *Qur'an;* it played an immensely important social and philosophical role as well as a major religious role. As a body of commentary and interpretation grew up around the text of the *Qur'an* and other religious literature that was regarded as pious (such as the *sunna* and *hadith,* words and practices of Muhammad), schools of formal theology and guilds of law created new intellectual elites who played prominent roles in the Islamic world. Independent devotional movements, such as Sufism, drew their inspiration from the *Qur'an* and created a mystical movement in Islam that proved immensely attractive to many people who had no part in the more formalized intellectual circles of the world.

Islamic civilization conquered worlds and opened markets. During the Fatimid period in Egypt (969–1171), gold *dinars* circulated so widely and were so consistently valued throughout western Europe, India, and even China, that they have been called "the dollar of the Middle Ages." During the Abbasid period, Arab trade left its traces far up the Volga River and into Scandinavia, and Baghdad became the western terminus of the Silk Road, from northern China to Iraq (see below, Chapter 17). Commercial exchange went hand in hand with agricultural exchange. Muslim agricultural adaptation and innovation brought many new plant varieties into the Mediterranean world, including hard wheat, rice, sugar cane, cotton, watermelons, eggplants, spinach, artichokes, sour oranges, lemons, limes, bananas, mangoes, and coconut palms. Agricultural engineering techniques developed new and extensive systems of irrigation, especially in the river valleys of Iraq and Persia.

In terms of material culture, Muslims created a physical "look" to their world that is readily identifiable today. Muslims were great city builders, and two of their early triumphs, Baghdad and Cairo, are still great cities. Even in modern Spain, the Islamic architectural influences are readily visible. The great city of Còrdoba held a population of around 450,000, with many mosques, baths, palaces, and libraries. Under Muslim rule around the year 1000, Palermo in Sicily had around 350,000 inhabitants. Throughout the Muslim world, the *masjids* (houses of prayer), with their distinctive courtyards and minarets, the *madrasas* (schools for the study of law), the baths, bazaars, and markets reflect a flowering of urban culture. The life of the cities was supported by a rich agriculture, scientific and innovative, which made material life for the better-off Muslims as comfortable as any people anywhere in the world. The Islamic development of such architectural features as the pointed arch, traceried windows, and decorative script, as well as fountains, gardens, and secluded courtyards, shaped the physical appearance of the Islamic world.

The economic, intellectual, and spiritual vitality of the Muslim world, particularly between the eighth and twelfth centuries, is a remarkable part of the rise of Islam. To some extent it is just as remarkable as the appearance of the faith itself, the influence of Muhammad, and the great early conquests. A religion of desert Arabs created armies, generals, and caliphs, plus a genuine cultural revolution that transformed, once and for all, not only the southern and eastern parts of the old Roman Empire, but the ancient Persian world as well, and extended well beyond the Caucasus, to present India, and later to southeast Asia. Where conquest went and religion followed, language circulated too. The present Arabic-speaking world is the world of Islamic belief, and beneath that belief lies a formidable culture. That culture shaped the golden age of Islam and later provided for western Europeans many of the scientific and philosophical tools and economic institutions that contributed to the numerous changes in European society in the twelfth and thirteenth centuries.

PART III THE EXPANDING LATIN WEST, 550–950

6

Rome and the West

ITALY IN THE SIXTH AND SEVENTH CENTURIES

The inner transformation and external downsizing of the East Roman empire in response to the Slavic, Avar, and Persian invasions in the early seventh century and Islamic and Bulgar invasions in the later seventh and early eighth centuries was not the only cause of its growing separation from the western Empire. In Italy, Gaul, and Iberia a new localism and new political crises also contributed to the division. Some of these circumstances can be seen in the consequences of Justinian's attempt to reunite the empire in the second quarter of the sixth century.

From 535 to 554, Italy was wracked by Justinian's campaign of reconquest against the Ostrogoths. Early imperial victories under the able generalship of Belisarius provoked stiffer Gothic resistance. Several able Ostrogothic kings, notably Totila (541–552), won back much of what had been lost. The twenty years of war, however, the increasing size and determination of the contending armies, and the refusal of either side to negotiate resulted in the physical and demographic devastation of Italy. In addition to the wars, widespread famine in 538 and the years following, as well as devastating plagues in 542 and 589, and a particularly savage sequence of floods, earthquakes, and other natural disasters further reduced the resources and population of Italy. After Justinian imposed a new peace in Italy with his Pragmatic Sanction of 554, Italy enjoyed only fifteen years of peace before another group of invaders, the Lombards, became a new and dominant force in the peninsula and remained aggressive for the next two centuries. The Lombards had converted to Arian Christianity, which heightened their opposition to local catholic Christianity. Lombard hostility to what remained of Byzantine power in Italy (chiefly in the east and south of the peninsula) led the bishops of Rome to assume the role of middlemen between the two hostile powers and eventually to become the focus of relations among Byzantines, Lombards, and Franks in central and northern Italy.

War, famine, plague, and new military conflicts also affected both the material fabric and the social structure of Italy. Many Italian aristocrats had fled Italy during the Gothic Wars, either to their estates in Sicily and North Africa or to Constantinople. Many of those who fled did not return. By 600, the Roman Senate had disappeared as a body. The last reported official meeting of a town council in the west outside Rome or Ravenna took place in 565. In those territories still controlled by the East Roman empire, military leaders took the place of the older local aristocracy. Although Justinian's Pragmatic Sanction had envisioned the separation of civil and military authority in Italy, the Lombard invasions and the disappearance of much of the older aristocracy made such a separation of powers impossible. Thus, although Justinian sent his new official collection of Roman law to the west, there is no evidence that its most important parts were ever used until the late eleventh century. Before then, written and learned law in Italy and elsewhere in the west remained the *Theodosian Code* and the scattered, private, and simplified collections that were adopted and used by local powers, both Roman and Germanic. There arose in imperially controlled Italy a closely integrated military ruling class, at the head of which, from the late sixth century on, was the *exarch,* who was directly appointed from Constantinople and usually resided at Ravenna, now the empire's window on the west.

Side by side with the new military aristocracy, there emerged the Christian higher clergy. During the sixth and seventh centuries, the clergy assumed more and more of the responsibilities for the civil administration of the cities. These included the supervision of urban food supplies, the distribution of charity, the maintenance of an urban infrastructure—walls, gates, aqueducts, and buildings, public spectacles, and the law courts. Bishops also made their cities centers of devotion to heavenly patrons by emphasizing the city's saints as part of the aristocracy of heaven that would not desert the city as many of its human aristocrats had. Although the churches of the leading cities—Milan, Pavia, and Ravenna—prided themselves on their local independence, the long-range consequences of these changes are best reflected in the position of the city and bishops of Rome.

The case of the city of Rome illustrates better than any other the effects of the sixth-century changes in Italy. Taken by Justinian's general Belisarius in 536, the city was besieged by the Goths and recaptured by them in 546. Much of the city was dismantled and the population scattered before the Goths abandoned it in 547. The Byzantine reoccupation lasted only until the Goths once more took the city in 549/50, and not until 552 were they driven out for good. Not only the sieges, but the deliberately destructive policy of the Gothic king Totila, which included prolonged blockades and deliberately induced famine, shredded the material fabric and life of Rome during fifteen years of unremitting conflict. The population of the city was well along in the precipitous decline from nearly one million in the age of Constantine to the twenty thousand of the late eighth century. As the population decreased, large, formerly inhabited areas of the city became vacant, giving way to farms, orchards, pastures, and wastelands within the city walls. Ancient palaces and disused public buildings crumbled, their structural elements often recycled into newer and smaller buildings. With the disappearance of consuls, urban prefects, most of the civil bureaucracy, the senate and the old aristocracy, the clergy undertook to provide what minimal public services were possible. By the late sixth century, the city of Rome had acquired the shape and character it was to possess until the seventeenth century.

Far from reintegrating the western and eastern parts of the Empire, Justinian's re-conquests marked the ultimate transformation of the world of antiquity. The former imperial provinces were now the setting for Germanic kingdoms in Iberia and Gaul. Italy itself was divided between the Lombards and Byzantines, with the clergy acting as a re-luctant, uneasy, and often mistrusted mediator among them. With the old aristocracy gone, the cities took on new physical shapes. Civil administration gave way to ecclesias-tical administration—where there were public affairs to be administered at all. A new world was emerging, one that can be seen most clearly in the life, thought, and writings of Pope Gregory I.

GOD'S CONSUL

Gregory I, commonly and accurately designated "the Great," was a Roman noble, born around 540 into one of the immensely wealthy aristocratic Roman families. Part of his childhood was spent on family estates outside Italy, where his family had fled to avoid the dangers of the Gothic wars. Rising in the municipal civil service, Gregory became head of the civil administration of Rome when he suddenly decided to turn his family prop-erty over to the Roman Christian Community and to enter, as a novice, a monastery that he himself had founded, St. Andrew on the Caelian Hill. Ordained a deacon in 579, Gregory was designated by Pelagius II (579–590) as *apocrisiarius* (since the early sixth century the office of legate of the bishop of Rome to the imperial court at Constantino-ple), and in 590, he was elected bishop of Rome.

A number of Gregory's sixth-century predecessors, notably Pelagius II, had con-tinued the ecclesiastical administration of urban offices and services in Rome—large-scale relief for the poor, partial maintenance of the physical fabric of the city, including its churches, the restoration of dilapidated buildings, and the organization and distribution of the increasing territorial wealth of the Church. Gregory I continued and routinized these practices as functions of the Roman episcopal office, but he went much further than this. Loyal to the empire, his view of the world entirely consistent with the view of Constantinople, he maintained respectful diplomatic relations with the empire and explored relations with the Lombard rulers of Italy. Finally, in his writings he examined in detail the character of clerical life and ecclesiastical office, and he opened new avenues of communication with Christians scattered throughout the fragmented world of late sixth- and seventh-century western Europe.

Such a range of duties carried out by a man with a traditional vision of his own world is remarkable. The register of Gregory's letters, the only collection of papal letters besides that of Leo I (440–461) to have survived complete from before the end of the eleventh century, reveals a strong sense of both missionary zeal and diplomatic propriety, and it maps Gregory's attempts to restore communication between Rome and the bishops and kings of western Europe. Gregory's letters contain both theological and administrative instructions, and they may justly be considered among the most important documents in papal history. Gregory also wrote cautious, discreet letters to barbarian rulers, and to emperors at Constantinople as well. This papal diplomacy constituted the first recognition that the barbarians were there to stay; that, in effect, the old frontiers of the western Empire were being reconfigured by the spread of Christianity to include new peoples and territories that had never been Roman.

Gregory's nearly 850 letters depict an ideal of clerical responsibility and conduct that had a great influence on later European civilization. Historians have called these letters and Gregory's treatise, *The Book of Pastoral Care,* a "mirror for bishops." They embrace the most influential definition of episcopal office written since the work of Ambrose in the fourth century, a definition reflected in later papal regulations, in canon law, and in later biographies of saintly bishops. Gregory argued that churchmen's spiritual care of themselves trained them to the spiritual care of others. He had little patience with churchmen who tried to elevate their status above that of others. When a patriarch of Constantinople referred to himself as an "ecumenical patriarch," Gregory rejected the title on the grounds that it diminished the local authority of every bishop. In his letters he referred to himself only as the *servus servorum Dei,* "servant of the servants of God." The straightforward and practical *Book of Pastoral Care* has as its theme Gregory's favorite maxim: "The guidance of souls is the art of all arts." It is largely through Gregory's work that the episcopal ideals of the Church between the fourth and the seventh centuries were transmitted to later centuries, and these ideals still define clerical standards in most modern episcopal churches. Gregory himself, through his responsibilities for administering extensive ecclesiastical properties, knew from experience the practical requirements of ecclesiastical leadership, and, like many talented Roman administrators, he was able to apply his own experience in a treatise written for the instruction of others.

Gregory also wrote a voluminous commentary on the Book of Job, the *Moralia.* In it he adapted for a far less learned and less sophisticated audience both the fourfold allegorial technique of interpreting Scripture, which had begun with Philo and Origen (above, Chapter 2), and the theological works of his great predecessors Jerome and Augustine. Like *Pastoral Care,* the *Moralia* played an immensely important role in passing down to later centuries the scriptural interpretive techniques and the body of theological knowledge developed in the great age of the fourth and fifth centuries. Gregory has often been accused of simplifying the rich complexities of earlier doctrine, but it may also be said that he passed down these techniques and beliefs in the only form that made them usable in a world that increasingly needed readily comprehensible, basic books.

Gregory's Rome had become the Rome of Peter, overlaying a Christian understanding of the city and its past upon the memory of the Rome of Augustus and Hadrian, and even the Rome of Constantine. Gregory played an important role in the devotional history of the Latin West by his cultivation of the lives and stories of saints, miracles, and holy places. Gregory's approach to the saints, however, placed more emphasis on dramatic miracles and aid than had earlier saints' lives. In 593/4 Gregory wrote a long work called the *Dialogues*, which, in the form of a series of saints' lives, purports to be conversations between himself and the Deacon Peter about saints, relics, and miracles. The *Dialogues* too had a great influence on later hagiography, the pious and edifying accounts of the lives of saints. Gregory's interest in miracle, the drama of sanctity, and the manifestations of God's power in the physical world made his stories simpler, more imaginative, and more widely appealing than many earlier lives of saints, and thus played an important role in the history of Christian biography and lived religion.

Gregory's thought also addresses some other important concerns of his age and treats those concerns with great care and native intelligence. For example, strong anti-Jewish attitudes appeared in the western and eastern parts of the empire in the sixth century, part of the process of making the empire and Christianity coterminous. Visigothic kings of Spain issued the first anti-Jewish laws in European history, and a notable anti-Jewish strain became conspicuous in much Christian literature. Gregory, however, strongly and publicly opposed the forced conversion and oppression of Jews.

Although Gregory conceived his world in terms consistent with those of traditionally Christianized imperial Rome, and always deferred to the emperor at Constantinople, the worlds of western Europe and Byzantium were drifting rapidly apart. Nowhere does Gregory's thought reflect this drift more than in the transformation of his doctrine of conversion. His early statements on the conversion of rural pagans and heterodox Christians inside the empire are consistent with the view of the Christianized Roman Empire after the fourth century: Christendom and the Roman Empire are identical; clerics and powerful men together must bring about the conversion to Christianity of all within the empire. Gregory expected landowners to banish pagan shrines and practices from their own property and attempt to win their tenants and dependents to Christianity by building churches and spreading the Christian cult. He expected emperors to disestablish all pagan cults and practices by issuing appropriate laws and enforcing them harshly. This view had developed at a time when Romans were relatively unconcerned about the Christianization of peoples outside the empire, whose conversions were the work of individuals who originally came among them to serve only the few already-Christian communities of Romans in barbarian territories.

Jesus' last words to his followers in the Gospel of Matthew (Matt 28:19) had been:

> *Go therefore and make disciples of all nations, baptizing them in the name of the Father and of the Son and of the Holy Spirit, and teaching them to obey everything that I have commanded you.*

Other passages in Christian scripture, as well as Christian inrterpretations of several passages in Jewish scripture (Matt 24:14, Psalms 72:8, Zechariah 9:10) echoed the language of this text. As the empire was Christianized in the fourth and fifth centuries, the task of internal conversion became central. Some thinkers, like Augustine of Hippo, argued that in theory Christianity was intended in the literal sense of Matthew 28:19. Augustine, and later Gregory I, expressed such ideas chiefly because of their strong sense that the world was nearing its end and since the conversion of "all nations" was generally understood to have been postponed until the end times. Less apocalyptically minded thinkers continued to consider Christianity as an appropriate faith for Romans, but not for barbarians.

A number of Christian thinkers, including Origen, had argued that God permitted the creation of the Roman Empire only so that Christianity could spread more easily in a world at peace—a Roman world. Here, the ethnography of late antiquity reinforced the distinction bretween Roman and barbarian in terms of Christianity. As if to prove the truth of the Roman view, when barbarians did convert to Christianity, they converted to the heterodoxy of Arianism. And for several centuries the problems of converting the Roman cities and countryside, the public and private spheres inside the empire, had seemed formidable enough. Even the term "catholic," which in Greek meant "general" or "universal," was originally used chiefly to distinguish orthodox Christians from Arian heretics. It did not originally mean "universal" in terms of applying to all people everywhere. This view characterized Roman attitudes toward the conversion of outsiders until the sixth century.

The populations of the kingdoms of the Visigoths in Iberia, the Ostrogoths in Italy, the Vandals in North Africa, and the Burgundians in southeastern Gaul consisted of a majority of Romans and a minority of Arians. When the Vandal kingdom was overthrown by Justinian, imperial Christianity returned briefly to North Africa, and Justinian's reconquest of Italy destroyed Ostrogothic Arianism. The surviving Arian kingdoms in Iberia and Burgundy also witnessed the success achieved by the Franks under the catholic Clovis with the support of the Gallo-Roman population. When the armies of Justinian achieved a partial reconquest of southeastern Iberia in 552, and later supported a catholic pretender to the Visigothic kingship in 580–584, the Arian king of the Visigoths, Leovigild (569–586) realized that his kingdom needed the support of the Hispano-Roman population in order to survive. His son Recared (r. 586–601) converted to catholic Christianity in 587 and established the city of Toledo as the ecclesistical center of the kingdom. At the Third Council of Toledo in 589, Recared formally condemned Arian belief, and from that date, the alliance of kings and ecclesiastical councils characterized the Visigothic kingdom. As for Burgundy, the kingdom appears to have been largely catholic Christian since the fifth century, although at least one Arian king, Gundobad (474–516), became a successful ruler. In any case, catholic Christianity became the norm in Burgundy after it was taken over by the sons of Clovis in 534.

Although the Lombards did not convert to catholic Christianity until the mid seventh century, by 600, the new Christian kingdoms inside the old western part of the empire were in religious and doctrinal agreement, local churches in deferential communication with the bishop of Rome. To be sure, there remained pagan barbarians outside their areas of influence, but the tide had turned: Christianity was now eminently suitable for barbarians as well as Romans, and it was as catholic Christians that Romans and their Germanic rulers began to fold into single peoples.

Gregory's loyalty to the empire did not preclude his interest in converting non-Roman peoples, but this idea only dawned slowly. In his handling of the conversion of peoples outside the empire he gradually adapted earlier, rigid imperial conversion policies to a set of more flexible approaches to a complex problem. In this sense, the bishops of Rome adapted their policies of conversion to individual novel circumstances both inside and outside the empire and laid the foundations for the idea of Christendom as the unifying bond among the different societies and kingdoms of a fragmented western Europe.

Other aspects of Gregory's thought are equally striking. Sixth-century Christianity demonstrated a heightened interest in demons, miracles, and holy men and women. Although Gregory could not do away with this new fascination, his stories could at least show that demons were always defeated by simple Christian practices. Demons and sorcerers were a vivid part of Gregory's universe, but they were kept firmly under control by no more than simple Christian practices and demonstrations of sanctity. When the souls of the dead or visions of saints appeared in Gregory's writings, it was usually to inspire, not to terrify, the living.

Gregory taught by other means as well. At his urging, the visual depiction of scriptural scenes on the walls of churches (and, later, on church windows) took on a new role; they were to become "the scriptures of the unlettered," the teachers of the illiterate. The motifs of Romano-Christian visual art, like the principles of late Roman ecclesiastical administration, were transformed into instructional materials for the new world taking shape in western Europe. By his death in 604, at the end of a life wracked by physical illness and exhausting concern for the Christian world, Gregory had succeeded in beginning the reorientation of the Latin Church toward its new members. He had taken steps to define principles of missionary work and conversion, reestablished papal contact with the far-flung churches, from Iberia to Britain and from Italy to Alexandria, and shaped the mold of Christian understanding and devotion in forms that lasted for a thousand years. His epitaph, a long Latin tribute to his work and saintliness, calls Gregory "God's Consul." There is no more succinct expression of Gregory's Christian and Roman antecedents, nor a better description of his service to his own and future generations.

THE DESERT IN THE WEST: MONKS, MISSIONARIES, AND CULTURE

Among the forms of abandoning the world and taking up the ascetic life that emerged in the late third and fourth centuries, monasticism (the word comes from the Greek *monos*, "one," or "alone") was creative, enduring, and influential in later European history. One sign of its creativity has already been noted—the tendency, well underway in the late fourth century, first in eastern, and later in western Christianity, to create communities of monks under the leadership of a single abbot (the word derives from the Coptic *apa*, "father") and following a common rule of life. This form of monasticism, called cenobitism, permitted the establishment and continuity of monastic institutions.

Among Gregory I's major achievements was his support of monasticism in the Latin Church. Between the sixth and the twelfth centuries, monks and missionaries not only shaped the dominant forms of Christianity and achieved the conversion of western Europe, but also passed down the only legacy of the ancient world that early Europeans possessed.

As we have seen, hermits and monks became a conspicuous feature of Christianity in the third and fourth centuries, first in Egypt and then in Syria and the eastern Mediterranean. The group of monasteries at Mt. Athos at the head of the Aegean Sea is a striking example. Another is the monastery of St. Catherine at Mt. Sinai, fortified and patronized by Justinian. The appeal of a life of prayer and isolation from a turbulent world spread quickly, and in the fourth century, many individuals withdrew from the world, seeking such a life in the wilderness of Italy and Gaul.

Martin of Tours (ca. 335–397) was a striking and influential example of such a career. Martin was a Roman soldier who converted to Christianity, left the army, wandered through several Roman provinces, and settled in Gaul, where he soon attracted followers and began to convert the rural population around Tours. He became bishop of Tours in 372, and patronized the spread of other monastic communities. Martin was quickly regarded as a saint by the people and clergy of Tours and as the heavenly patron of the city. Sulpicius Severus (363–420) wrote an account of Martin's life and miracles around 396 that became immensely influential as an example of the life of a remarkable holy man, an ascetic very different from the usual aristocratic Gallo-Roman bishops.

In the early years of the fifth century, a Gallo-Roman named John Cassian (385–440) made a journey to the monastic centers of the east and returned to Gaul with a plan for an ideal monastery and a large literature on monastic life that he had acquired in his travels. Cassian introduced ideals of monastic organization that had developed in Egypt, Syria, and Cappadocia. His own influential writings, the *Institutes,* attempted to homogenize into a single ideal system the different rules and practices that he had found. By the sixth century, there was no single standard form of monastic life; individuals and groups followed a wide variety of practices throughout Latin Europe. The most substantial contribution to Latin monasticism was that of the community founded by Benedict of Nursia (480–547) at Monte Cassino, south of Rome. Benedict came from a prominent Roman family, but he rejected the education and plans for a public career that his family had made and withdrew to live a hermit's life in central Italy. Benedict, like many other holy men, soon attracted followers, and early in his life he demonstrated considerable organizational ability, as well as penetrating insight into the minds of those who wished to become monks. He established a successful community on Monte Cassino, and for it he wrote his *Rule,* one of the most influential organizational programs in the history of human society.

Another sign of the creativity of monasticism in the West was the range of its appeal to very different kinds of people. The appeal of Martin of Tours, for example, rested not only on his effective conversion of the countryside, the last bastion of rural paganism in Gaul, but also on the immensely popular *Life of Martin* written by Sulpicius Severus, which depicted Martin as a devout bishop-monk and a model for the religious life of bishops as well as monks. Another aspect of Martin struck the Frankish king Clovis (above, Chapter 3), who not only saw in Martin a saintly warrior, but a personal patron who aided in battle. Clovis' sponsorship of the cult of Martin dramatically increased the appeal of the *Life* and the dedication of more communities to Martin's ideal. Clovis even took Martin's cloak, the *capella,* back to Paris with him, where it gave its name to the room in his palace that contained it—the royal chapel.

The monasteries founded under the influence of Cassian (particularly that of St. Victor at Marseilles) and his contemporary Honoratus on the island of Lerins at the mouth of the Rhone river, presented yet another kind of appeal. Both Cassian and Honoratus were extremely learned, and their communities appealed especially to aristocrats, particularly those displaced by the turmoil in northern Roman Gaul. The intellectual influence of these Rhone-area monasteries was considerable. Monks from these centers were often chosen as bishops and archbishops by neighboring communities, and some of them produced influential theological literature, introducing the important component of learning to communities that were best suited to preserving it during periods of political and religious turbulence. A monk of Lerins, for example, and later bishop of Arles, Caesarius (469/70–542), produced the first rule of monastic life for women, and female religious communities sprang up quickly in Gaul, located near shrines and churches containing the relics of venerated saints, and often under the protection and authority of the local bishop. The Lerins tradition, too, emphasized the subordination of the monastic community to the local bishop. The relations between monastic communities and episcopal religious authority became a continuing source of tension throughout the early history of Europe. Other Roman aristocrats also turned bishop, one of the most influential of whom was the former soldier and imperial administrator Germanus of Auxerre (375–446), who twice traveled to Britain and may have been responsible for sending Palladius, the first cleric known to have been sent to the Christians in Ireland.

The appeal of such figures as Martin and Benedict and such institutions as Lerins was spread by networks of friendship and patronage, texts, and cult, from levels as different as that of Gregory the Great and that of the itinerant holy man Martin. Their effectiveness in converting local rural populations, offering new social roles to dislocated Gallo-Roman aristocrats, and developing new forms of the religious life for bishops was considerable. Their role in the conversion and the organization of the religious life of key areas of northern Europe, particularly Ireland and Britain, suggests an even greater importance from the late fifth century on. In these areas, churchmen for the first time began to undertake the conversion of barbarians outside the old imperial frontiers.

THE CONVERSION OF IRELAND

Since the Irish were the first people to undergo such a conversion, it is useful to consider the character of Irish society and culture when the conversion began.

In the fifth century C.E., Ireland lay outside the worlds of both the Roman Empire and the Germanic migrants and invaders. Other Celtic peoples had long since been absorbed into the empire in Italy, Gaul, Iberia, and southern Britain. But by 600 C.E., Celtic culture had been reduced to the "Celtic Fringe" of western Europe—Ireland, Scotland, Wales, Cornwall, Brittany, and Galicia (in northwestern Spain)—where it is ethnically traceable today. But Ireland was not Celtic only. Westward-moving migrants had kept arriving at the small island at the western end of the known world since 8000 B.C.E., and in the fifth century C.E., some surviving archaic social and cultural forms predated even the arrival of the different groups of Celts during the first millennium B.C.E., which gave Ireland its language and its most distinctive cultural features.

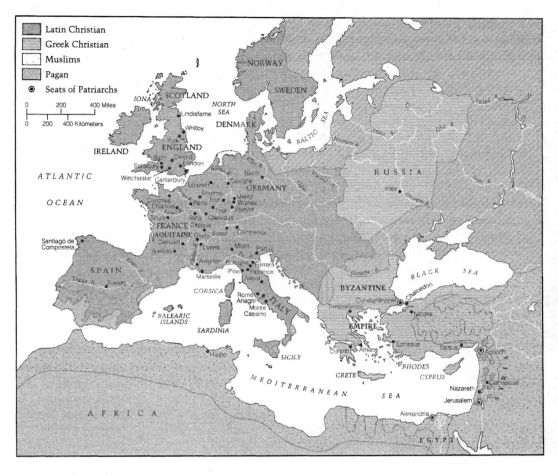

Legend:
- Latin Christian
- Greek Christian
- Muslims
- Pagan
- ⊙ Seats of Patriarchs

Medieval Christianity.

Greek ethnographic accounts provide limited information concerning the island and its peoples, but with the coming of the Romans to Britain in the first century C.E., there is evidence of regular contact in trade and technology transfer (including the use of iron) from Roman Britain to Ireland, which greatly changed Irish material culture. There is also evidence of increased Irish mobility, whether as exiles, refugees, mercenary soldiers in Roman service, or as pirates. Irish groups settled in western Britain—in Wales and Cornwall—and in southwestern Scotland at *Dál Riada* in the late fifth century C.E., which became the core of the later kingdom of Scotland.

Irish society in the fifth century was organized on the basis of the *derbfine,* or "true-kin," a clan with a common great-grandfather in the male line. Property was held by the collective *derbfine* and could not be alienated from it unless the clan became extinct. The economy was based on herding and dairy farming, with cattle the common medium of exchange, and arable farming whose chief crops were oats, barley, and wheat. The economy was supplemented by raiding, and the oldest Irish epic poem, the *Táin Bó Cúailnge,* "The Cattle Raid at Cooley," presumably set around the turn of the Common

Era, describes a raid on the province of Ulster by the people of Connaught, led by their queen Medbh and successfully resisted by the hero Cú Chulainn. The *Taín* and its related tales comprise the "Ulster Cycle," the earliest Irish epic tradition.

The basic political unit was the small "people," the *tuath* (pl. *tuatha*), ruled by a petty king, the *rí*, always selected from the particular *derbfine* of the *tuath* that was considered royal. Each *tuath* recognized its own king, nobility, free farmers, lesser free social ranks, and those tied to the soil. The *tuatha* were small, since there were generally 100 to 150 of them in existence at any one time. Frequently, a strong king of one *tuath* asserted himself over lesser kings, claiming to be a "king of kings," a *ruiri*. When a single ruler claimed to be master of an entire province, he was termed a *rí ruireg,* and when one king claimed to rule over all the kinglets of the entire island, an *ard rí,* or high king.

The affairs of both small and larger kingdoms were dominated by a warrior aristocracy (the *flaith*). The aristocracy measured its status in honor, fame, and wealth, usually in land and cattle. Although the kings lived on a somewhat larger scale than the aristocracy, their authority and power were limited. The status of lords was measured by their birth and wealth and by the number of their clients. Status was also measured by honor-price, *lóg n-enech,* the amount to be paid for offences against a lord. Fifth-century Irish society comprised three kinds of status: kings, lords, and commoners, with different degrees of status and wealth in each kind. Clients were men bound to a lord by his giving them land and cattle (also termed a *rath*) in return for rent, service, or hospitality. Clientage might be free or base. Free clientage provided the lords with their military support. Base clientage consisted of manual labor and the payment of goods to the lord. Beneath the level of clients, base or free, were landless men who worked for others, and beneath them were slaves.

Some of the most important early Irish texts are collections of laws, which describe a highly articulated social structure, but also give the impression of a society much more static than it really was. People and kin-groups might move higher or lower in society very rapidly.

Although women appear in heroic roles in some epic poetry, wisdom literature, and later saints' lives, Irish society was clearly male-dominated. Women were under the domestic authority of their fathers until marriage, their husbands during marriage, and their sons during their widowhood. They could make no independent contracts without the agreement of the man who had authority over them. Irish law recognized different forms of union between a man and a woman, from lawful marriage to the daughter of a social equal to lesser unions that afforded the woman a lower status, and the higher ranks of Irish society also practiced polygyny. The continuing polygyny of the Irish in later centuries remained a sore point with later ecclesiastical reformers and was held against them as making them deficient Christians. Divorce and remarriage, even serial marriage, were frequent. But a woman who divorced her husband without what was considered an appropriate reason also lost status and rights.

The law was preserved in memory by a class of men known as *brithemin* (English: brehons), who were specially trained in reciting the law and able to establish the procedures for adjudicating the legal relations of feuding clans and powerful aristocrats. Besides the brehons, noble houses also patronized the order of scholars, including the *fili,* a class of poet-historians who composed oral histories of their patrons, and songs praising their bravery and generosity, as well as songs defaming and cursing their patrons' enemies. The order of druids, and later that of the Christian bishops which replaced it, was equal to that of the king. These higher ranks possessed status recognized throughout the island, while members of a *tuath* were secure only in their own lands.

The first evidence of Christianity in Ireland is the record of Palladius, a priest who was sent from Gaul to some Christians in Ireland, allegedly by Germanus of Auxerre, in 431. But the best-known (and least generally understood) figure of the fifth-century conversion is Patrick (ca. 390–461), the son of Romano-British Christians. In his short autobiography, the *Confessions,* he states that he was kidnapped as a child and kept as a slave in the west of Ireland for six years before escaping and returning home. In a vision, Patrick states, he heard the Irish people calling for him to return. It was a remarkable moment in the history of early Europe. For the first time, a Christian set out from Christian territory to convert pagans outside Christian territory. Patrick's *Confessions* make his motives clear: he took the scriptural injunction of preaching Christianity to all nations quite literally, as had none of his predecessors, but many of his successors. Patrick returned to Ireland sometime after 431 and began the conversion of the island. Patrick had to work from *tuath* to *tuath,* since there was no single ruler whose conversion meant the conversion of an entire people.

Although Patrick may also have been trained and sent to Ireland by Germanus, the details of the mission and the process of conversion are obscure. It is clear that the first organization of Irish Christianity was modeled on Continental patterns; bishops and priests led the people, and the church at Armagh emerged as a central authority. Yet Continental Christianity had been shaped by Roman society, and ecclesiastical institutions by the administrative institutions of Rome. Ireland, however, had no cities, no provinces, none of the structures that had supported the spread and established the character of Christian organization elsewhere. Moreover the culture of Ireland soon imparted distinctive characteristics to Irish Christianity. One of these characteristics was the Irish passion for asceticism—a life of world-rejecting austerity. A second feature was the growth of family monastic settlements, perhaps as a result of asceticism combined with the technical difficulties of Irish land law which located the ownership of land only in the *derbfine,* which made family monasteries easier to establish than bishoprics. These two features soon made Irish Christianity predominantly monastic, and made the abbots of family monasteries the most powerful ecclesiastical figures in Ireland. The bishops were relegated for the most part to subordinate sacramental roles within the monastic community.

By the middle of the sixth century, large monastic foundations were being built. Clonmacnoise on the River Shannon was founded around 550, Bangor in the north around 560, and Clonfert around 570. By the end of the sixth century, Irish monasticism had absorbed most other forms of Irish asceticism and had begun to reflect another distinctive characteristic of Irish culture, its fascination with learning. The Irish had never had to fight the fierce intellectual battle against learned, literate paganism that the churches and churchmen in Italy, North Africa, and Gaul had, and the Irish took eagerly and quickly to Greek and Latin learning. After the monks at Lerins, Irish monks were the first in European history to make schooling and learning a major part of the monk's life.

Learning, of course, entailed writing, and with Christianity, writing entered Irish life. The distinctive handwriting and elaborately illuminated calfskin manuscripts produced by Irish monks testify to the resources, learning, devotion, and talent of Irish monastic culture.

Another distinctive feature of Irish monasticism was the emergence of penitential exile. Because Ireland was a society of clans, the identity of an individual was established by the place he or she held in the structure of a clan. One of the most severe punishments in Irish law was exile from the clan, for exile meant a removal of part of a person's identity, since one could never attain full membership in another *derbfine* or *tuath*. In monastic communities, such exile was undertaken voluntarily as a sign of penitence— "exile for the love of God." Irish monastic exiles, however, did not simply go off alone into remote regions for a life of isolation.

In 565, a monk named Columcille, better known as Columba (521–597), left Ireland in the wake of a clan feud to found a monastic settlement in exile on the island of Iona, off the west coast of Scotland. From the community at Iona, a missionary movement traveled into northern Britain and began one phase of the conversion of its Celtic and Germanic inhabitants. Shortly after the founding of Iona, another exile, Columbanus (ca. 550–615), a rigorous ascetic driven to missionary work, moved onto the Continent itself, wandering through eastern Gaul and founding monastic communities at Luxeuil in what is now Switzerland and at Bobbio, northern Italy. A disciple of Columbanus founded the great monastery of St. Gall. Bobbio became one of the most important devotional centers of the seventh and eighth centuries.

The impact of Columbanus' form of monasticism was considerable. Although it was, like all Irish monasticism, rural, it did not withdraw from the world, but maintained contact with powerful lay patrons. Those patrons could be assured that their family gifts to a monastery would commemorate the family in the prayers of the monks. His form of monasticism asserted the independence of the monastery from the local bishop, and it offered a form of Christian religious life to the Franks that was not based on the culture of the Gallo-Roman aristocracy that had monopolized ecclesiastical office until the seventh century. Through the influence of Columbanus, the Frankish aristocracy began to take its place in the network of ecclesiastical offices, acquiring saints in its families, and taking a family interest in the establishment and patronage of particular ecclesiastical foundations. Columbanus died in 615, eleven years after Gregory the Great, the other great representative of the rich and varied religious culture of the early seventh century. In 635, another Irish ascetic, Aidan, moved to northeastern Britain and founded the monastery of Lindisfarne. The distinctiveness of Irish Christianity, both in Ireland itself and on the Continent, suggests a new experience of northwest Europe—the adaptation of monasticism and Continental forms of Christian devotion to the customs and minds of a non-Roman and non-Germanic society.

ANGLES AND ANGELS

Among the many pressing concerns of Gregory the Great was his vision of bringing to Christianity all the peoples of the old western provinces of the Roman empire. In 596, Gregory began his best-known attempt at conversion, the mission of Augustine of

Canterbury to England. Gregory may have felt particularly compelled to conversion missions because Arian Lombard pressure on catholic Christianity in Italy had recently increased, and in 590, the year Gregory became bishop of Rome, the Lombard king Aistulf had forbidden Lombards to be baptized as catholic Christians. Gregory had already urged Italian bishops to use preaching more intensively as a means of converting the Arian Lombards, and his close relations with a catholic queen of the Lombards, Theodelinda, increased catholic influence. At first, as we have seen, Gregory was not opposed to the use of coercion along with preaching, especially in the case of those who had backslid from orthodoxy to heterodoxy and lived under Christian rulers. During the conversion of England, however, Gregory adopted a more moderate approach and rejected the use of force as a means of conversion to Christianity.

When Gregory set about planning the mission to England, so legend has it, he was inspired by the sight of some Anglo-Saxon prisoners in Italy being sold in the slave market. Asking who these striking people were, Gregory was told that they were Angles. "Not Angles," Gregory is supposed to have replied, "but angels."

Gregory undertook the mission to England seriously. All Gregory knew of the island, however, was what he found in late Roman geographical lore and administrative literature—and that was not much. Gregory's younger contemporary, the Hispano-Roman Isidore of Seville (ca. 560–636), wrote a large and very popular encyclopedic work called *The Twenty Books of Etymologies,* in which he noted that "Britannia is an island set in the sea, wholly separated from the world." Besides such information as this, Gregory knew only of England's provincial organization under the late Roman Empire, an organization that had been totally destroyed by the end of the sixth century.

Germanic invaders from the Continent had begun to attack the rich province of Roman Britain in the 440s. The Roman parts of the island contained more than six hundred stone villas, a mint, and around one hundred walled towns. The province was divided into thirty *civitates,* many based on earlier tribal centers. The full apparatus of a Roman province included roads, canals, public buildings, temples, baths, bridges, and sea- and river-ports. The walls of Roman *Londinium* (later London) enclosed 330 acres. Christianity had probably arrived on the island in the second century. The martyrdom of Alban occurred in the third, and by 314, there were Christian bishops, Christian decorations in several villas, and Christian inscriptions on tombstones. During the second century, fully fifteen percent of the Roman armies were stationed in Britain, a sign of the province's importance. But Britain had begun to lose troops in 383, when the imperial usurper Magnus Maximus made his bid for the throne. Imperial masters of soldiers moved more troops out in 401, and in 407, another imperial pretender took troops with him to Gaul. In 408, came the first raids by continental Saxons, and when the Romano-British provincials wrote to the emperor Honorius in 410, they received his famous reply that they must defend themselves, because he had no troops to spare. Hadrian's Wall was evacuated around 400, and the territory north of the Humber was quickly lost.

Romano-British resistance to the invaders was remarkably tough—it lasted through most of the fifth century. The great British victory at Mount Badon around the year 500 is only one indication of this. As the invaders moved west and south, they began to carve out small kingdoms throughout the island. The most powerful of these from north to south were Northumbria, Mercia, and Kent. The Romano-British moved west into Wales, where their presence is attested in the small kingdoms of Gwynedd, Powys, Dyfed, and Deheubarth.

The best-known archaeological evidence for the culture of these Germanic kingdoms is the early seventh-century ship burial at Sutton Hoo. The ship had been hauled to the top of a one hundred foot-high bluff from the river Deben, and placed in a trench that had been excavated for the purpose. There was a cabin amidships for a coffin. When the ship had been filled and furnished, the trench had been filled in and a mound of earth erected over it. Although the ship and the trench were important in themselves, the furnishings are the most striking. They include weapons: a helmet, a sword, and a shield. There were also ornaments of gold with garnet inlay, silverware, kitchen equipment, and an object usually called a "ceremonial whetstone." On the body of the buried man was a purse with thirty-seven gold coins that had been struck in the Frankish kingdom, none later than the 620s. The craftsmanship of all of the furnishings was extraordinarily accomplished. The ship held cloisonné shoulder-clasps, a buckle whose design and decoration indicate that it came from eastern Sweden, a large silver dish made in Constantinople around 500, ten silver bowls made in a Mediterranean style, a bronze bowl made at Alexandria in Egypt very recently before the burial, and a number of hanging bowls of Celtic design. The riches of Sutton Hoo give some indication, not only of the attraction of Britain to raiders and settlers from outside the island, but the very wide geographical range that produced the objects in the tomb.

Of the Germanic kingdoms, Gregory chose that of Kent, in southeastern England and most accessible to Gaul, as the destination for his mission. To lead the mission, Gregory appointed Augustine (d. 604), prior of the monastery of St. Andrew in Rome. Dispatched in 596, Augustine and his companions traveled through Gaul and arrived at Kent in 597. Kent was ruled by the pagan Anglo-Saxon king Æthelbert (561–616), whose wife was Bertha, a Christian Frankish princess. Permitted to settle and preach, Augustine and his companions soon converted the king and a large part of his following. In several letters of 601, Gregory announced that he was sending Augustine more help, wrote a letter instructing Æthelbert in the duties of a newly converted Christian king, and described for Augustine the principles of establishing a church in lands newly converted from pagan practice. In these last letters, Gregory abandoned force as a motif in conversion and urged Augustine instead to convert people gradually by persuasion, using their old shrines and sacred places as sites for new Christian churches.

Roman Christianity spread from Kent northwards into other kingdoms, notably Northumbria, whose king, Edwin, married the daughter of Æthelbert and Bertha in 619. In the course of the seventh century, the Roman mission encountered other forms of Christianity that had long been at work in the northern part of the island. Celtic Christianity was well established in Wales, and the Irish kingdom of *Dál Riada*, in conjunction with Columba's monastery at Iona, had begun to spread Irish Christianity into the north of the island, which had never been effectively Romanized. The resulting form of Christianity that took shape in England drew heavily from both Celtic and Roman traditions, and it marks a second distinctive example of the role played by Christianity in the transformation of the life of the new Europeans. Among the conflicting issues that divided Roman and Celtic Christianity were the Celtic concept of private, repeatable, and individual, rather than public and communal confession of sins, and the widespread use of penitentials—books of meticulous lists of penances to be performed for various sins. In addition, the tonsuring of Celtic monks differed in form from that used in Rome, and the Celtic churches celebrated important Church feasts, notably Easter, according to a calendar different from the one in use at Rome.

These differences led to friction between Celtic and Roman Christians, and their disagreement came to a head at the court of Oswy, king of Northumbria (641–670). Oswy, a Celtic Christian, and his wife, a Roman Christian, found themselves celebrating Easter at different times, and they therefore sponsored a debate between representatives of Celtic and Roman Christian practices. Oswy called for a conference of clergy from the two sides at the monastery of Whitby, which had been founded and ruled by the widowed noblewoman Hild (614–680). At the Synod of Whitby, held in 664, the liturgical authority of Rome was recognized by the king and by most of the Celtic clergy. The first encounter of two varieties of Christian practices outside the Roman Empire had been resolved in favor of Roman practice.

From 664 until the end of the eighth century, the fusion of Celtic and Roman Christianity under the guidance of Roman-inspired ecclesiastical organization produced a church that was thoroughly loyal to Rome, yet retained many of its distinctively Celtic features. Like Celtic Christianity, English Christianity developed a powerful monastic culture, although under the influence of an episcopal organization. At the head of the English church was the archbishop of Canterbury, Augustine's own center. The most influential of the early archbishops of Canterbury was the Syrian monk Theodore (abp. 669–690), whose patronage of devotion and learning exerted a strong influence over the entire English church (below, Chapter 8). Later, a second archbishop was appointed at York. Dioceses for bishops, which had not taken root in Ireland, did so in England, although several diocesan centers were changed or abandoned before the late eleventh century. Asceticism and learning became prominent features of English monastic life as they had in Ireland. So did the ideal of exile and missionary work among pagans.

The result of those missions included not only the conversion of other, still-pagan peoples on the Continent, but also the beginnings of the reform of the Christian church in Gaul. English loyalty to Rome gave Rome's bishops a new voice in northern Europe and laid the foundations of ecclesiastical renewal among the Franks and other Germanic peoples that so marked the age of Charlemagne in the late eighth and early ninth centuries (below, Chapter 8).

7

Land, People, and Kings
in Merovingian *Francia*

FROM *GALLIA* TO *FRANCIA*

The geographical focus and narrative perspective of much of this book so far—and of the history of the ancient world generally—has been the Mediterranean basin, the societies around it, and the frontiers drawn by Romans to defend it and them. By the beginning of the eighth century, the Mediterranean Basin no longer housed an ecumenical culture and society, but rather three contending cultures, each with significant internal variations, those of Islam, Byzantium, and the Latin West. In addition to the transformation of the Mediterranean, northern Europe for the first time ceased to be either a frontier province of a Mediterranean Empire or the setting of a number of Iron Age, preliterate Celtic or Germanic cultures. The growth of new, settled societies that began to clear more land and increase the agricultural production of northern Europe was well under way by the eighth century.

Those peoples were now organized into low-intensity kingdoms in which hereditary nobles and kings lived directly from the produce of the land and the labor of a peasant population, with few intermediate bureaucratic or urban structures: those of the Lombards in parts of Italy, the Visigoths in Iberia, the different Celtic and Germanic kingdoms in Britain and the neighboring islands, and the Franks in Gaul. Each of these kingdoms was catholic Christian, and except in Italy, the local Roman population at all levels had begun to blend with the new peoples, assuming collective identities as Visigoths and Franks. The most successful of these ethnogeneses was the creation of *Francia*.

In the fifth century, the Visigothic king Athaulf said that he had once fancied replacing *Romania* with *Gothia* (above, Chapter 3), designating territories simply by the names of the people who dominated them, Romans in *Romania*, Goths in *Gothia*. Although Athaulf also said that he gave up on the idea, the changes of territorial names proceeded in any case. The old Roman provinces that we and they collectively designate *Gallia*, "Gaul," began in the sixth century to give way to distinctive areas called by localized names. The southwestern part became *Aquitania*, or Aquitaine, and its people continued for a long time to be called "Romans." The near southwest along the Mediterranean coast became *Gothia*, or *Septimania*. Part of northwestern Gaul had always had a substantial Celtic population that was increased by migrants from Britain around 500 and again in the later sixth century. Not surprisingly, this area became *Brittany*. Both Aquitaine and Brittany long retained distinctive regional identities. The part of *Gallia* lying to the north of the River Loire became simply *Francia*, "the land of the Franks." The Frankish kingdoms created, divided, and reassembled by Clovis and his successors became the most powerful, stable, and enduring territories in the west until the tenth century. *Francia* is a necessary focus for seventh- and eighth-century European history.

Francia and all other political structures in these centuries drew their resources directly from the land, and the kinds of political order that could be created, depended heavily on the land itself and the peoples who lived on it and ruled those who worked it. In order to understand the political history of *Francia* it is necessary to understand the material, social, and cultural circumstances of that history. For the land, those who worked it, and its produce determined both the extent and character of all forms of rulership.

LANDSCAPE AND FOLKSCAPE

The fragile balance between population levels and agricultural production in the Mediterranean region had long been destabilized by natural disasters, disease, war, and social turmoil, but the world of northern Europe was little better off. In that world of dense forests and rivers, in which less than ten percent of the land was under cultivation, societies remained small and lived precariously.

Much of transalpine Europe was thinly settled, with small, densely populated communities of farmers and warriors widely separated by thick forest, swamp, and ridge. Until the eleventh century, the material circumstances of the transalpine environment set firm upper limits to population growth and increased agricultural productivity. A glance at the population trends in England from the Roman period to the seventeenth century (see graph) suggests the difficulty of sustaining population growth and the vulnerability of populations to natural disasters, such as the invasions of the fifth century and the wave of plagues in the fourteenth century (below, Chapter 17). Although England is not typical of the European demographic experience in all details, it does reflect some common elements. The population remained small, averaging no more than two to ten persons per square kilometer. Small villages containing 50 to 150 inhabitants, tiny markets and fairs, small areas of rational, careful cultivation, and large areas of wasteful, unproductive

England: Population in Millions, 100–1650

	ROMAIN BRITAIN	550	1066	1325	1400	1650

cultivation constituted the physical profile of transalpine Europe between the sixth and tenth centuries.

The small societies of early medieval Europe sustained themselves by cultivating at first a very small portion of the land available to them. Their productivity was low, and their resources—from tools to theory—were few. For most people, the village or the isolated farmstead constituted the social horizon, and growing and finding food the principal occupation. Economic historians have suggested that in this period, not enough land was in cultivation to feed even the small population of Europe, and that stock raising, hunting, and fishing played an essential part in forming the European diet. The bulk of that diet was cereal-grain products in the common forms of bread, porridge, and beer. Wheat was the most desirable grain, but barley, rye, and oats were easier to raise and had better prospects of coming to harvest in the northern climate. Meat and fish were not as common, and meat, at least, was usually available only seasonally, when those animals which could not be fed over the winter were slaughtered in the fall. Otherwise, what meat was eaten at other times (and fish except when freshly caught) was usually dried and heavily salted. When peasants had access to meat, it was usually small game and domestic animals, often pigs. All animals were considerably smaller and leaner than their modern counterparts.

Studies of human skeletal remains reveal considerable dietary deficiency, and the diet appears to have been relatively uniform throughout most social ranks. Vegetables were consumed mostly in season, except for those few that could be preserved in root cellars. Few spices were then cultivated in Europe, and some that are now common—particularly pepper—were imported and expensive delicacies. The only sweeteners were honey and those few fruits native to transalpine Europe. Diets of rich and poor were heavy on carbohydrates, largely deficient in vegetable protein until after the tenth century, and seasonally overloaded with animal protein and fat. One difference between rich and poor was that the rich ate more, but not necessarily healthier, food.

Because of the difficulties of plowing the heavy, damp soil of northern Europe, cultivated acreage expanded only slowly. Because there was generally no fertilizer, fallowing (letting a field lie idle for a season, fertilized by the droppings of grazing animals) was the chief way of restoring at least some of the land's fertility. The process known as marling, working ground limestone into the soil, was another method of soil restoration, but only where limestone was readily available. These limitations point to the very low ratio of yield to seed, the standard index of agricultural productivity. Throughout the Middle Ages, one measure of seed yielded about three measures of grain, a ratio that rarely changed. Twentieth-century farmers are accustomed to getting at least twenty measures of grain from one measure of seed. In addition, agricultural tools were few and generally of poor quality. They usually had to be made locally. Although the eleventh and twelfth centuries saw the development of the water mill and windmill on a relatively large scale, the period before the eleventh century knew only animal power as a supplement to human effort. The largest carts could hold only a quarter ton.

The rhythm of the agricultural calendar is the oldest of Europe's social rhythms. The agricultural calendar dominated individual and social life, and the ecclesiastical calendar was pegged to it. But local agricultural and landholding customs varied considerably from place to place. Thus, there was not only great seasonal variation in Europe but considerable regional variation as well. The need of small communities for the cooperation of all their members at critical times during the agricultural year imposed considerable village solidarity, but at the price of restricting personal freedom.

Above all, these societies were vulnerable to a wide scale of natural disasters. A failed harvest brought the threat of hunger. A series of bad harvests brought the threat of local famine. Geological evidence indicates that between 450 and 750, glaciers once more advanced, and the climate grew colder. Dietary deficiencies made early Europeans more vulnerable to many more diseases than later Europeans, including scurvy and rickets as well as diseases derived from mold and from the close proximity of animals. Modern palaeoepidemiological studies indicate that in the long run, some of these circumstances built up the collective European immune system, but in individual lifetimes, vulnerability to epidemic disease remained high.

Both Romans and Germans suffered high infant and maternal mortality rates and a very short life expectancy. Both societies produced many children, many of whom died very young. The survivors were exposed to high mortality risks throughout their youth, as well as the general shortcomings of medical science and the ordinary, high traumatic risks of the warrior's or farmer's life.

Even for those increasing numbers who survived birth and youth, the physical experience of life itself was different from that of people in modern industrialized nations. Many people were familiar with prolonged periods of illness, including low-grade fever, blood poisoning, and pain from improperly healed wounds. They were unable to correct defective eyesight and hearing problems, and they were routinely subject to intestinal sickness, including amoebic dysentery and worms. Skin disorders and other forms of disfigurement were common, and there were very few effective painkillers. Moreover, the results of illness and other physical disorders were everywhere visible; people saw the worst results of the physical human condition before them in both rural and urban areas, and they accommodated themselves to what they saw more readily than modern people do.

Because early Europeans depended for most of their life support on field and forest, they tended to overuse the land they had. Inefficient early medieval agriculture required large areas of land to support relatively few persons. The land also had to produce trees for building and toolmaking, hay and oats for animal feed (there were no fodder crops), grazing land for sheep, and ploughed areas for flax growing—the latter two needed for the production of wool and linen clothing.

Although the agricultural riches of northern Europe were beginning to increase by the eighth century, they did not yield much, and they did not yield it easily. The archaeology of population and settlement in this area reveals a small world living precariously on a limited agricultural economy, subject to the ravages of disease and natural disaster. This world was hard, and making it marginally less hard took centuries of labor.

Control of that labor force by landholders, whether churchmen or lay lords, was essential to both their survival and their status. The landholder had control over all cultivated land and pasture, as well as rights over everyone and everything on the land—its people, livestock, and buildings. Land was valued in terms of the rights that went with it and the income it produced. The lowest rank of the labor force was occupied by slaves.

Slavery might be hereditary, imposed penally by powerful men who controlled the law in a district, or the result of capture in war or simple kidnapping as in the case of Patrick. Slaves appear to have been used most widely in domestic service, sometimes highly specialized, and often agricultural. Slaves tended to live near their owners, and households holding slaves might range from having only one or two to several dozen. The domestic intimacy of owners and slaves indicates that although owners held virtually limitless power over slaves, they generally resorted to violence infrequently. Slave life and the slave regime were extremely harsh in any case. Individual slaves or small groups of slaves might murder a particularly vicious owner, but organizing slave resistance beyond the household was difficult. In lesser cases, slaves might decrease their labor output by working slowly or selling off the owner's goods on the sly when they had the chance. Slaves could, of course, run away, perhaps joining warbands or escaping to places where they weren't known to be slaves, or be manumitted by their owners so that they became freemen. Current research indicates that the overall number of slaves decreased in the sixth and seventh centuries. More and more, western Europe was creating at its economic base a peasant society ranked in varying degrees of partial freedom.

The fifth and sixth centuries also recognized several statuses that are generally described as "half-free." Lombard law, for example, recognized the *aldius,* a person who did not have the full legal status of a freeman and was tied to the land he worked, but not regarded as the personal property of someone else. The Lombard *aldius* seems similar to the Frankish *litus,* also a person of half-free status and also tied to the land rather than to an individual owner. One point of origin of such a status seems to have been the *coloni,* the dependent free laborers on the vast estates of Roman Gaul and northern Italy who had conceded much of their freedom in return for the protection of the great landowner. From the fifth through the eleventh centuries, however, formerly free Germanic individuals also appear to have lost considerable freedom and themselves become dependents of powerful landlords. The process seems to have worked at different rates of speed in different parts of western Europe, and its causes, rate of occurrence, and geographical distribution are not yet matters of scholarly agreement.

Both free and half-free peasants lived on small individual holdings called *manses,* cultivating their own food in a garden and attached small plot of land, and usually paying rent in cash or kind and also labor services to the lord of the land, who might be a prominent figure whose properties were scattered in different parts of the kingdom, traveling from one to another to consume their produce and leaving them in charge of a bailiff or steward when he departed. Free Franks, too, might be humble peasants, although they owned their own land and could be called into military service. They might live on individual farmsteads or in small villages of wooden or clay houses with thatched roofs close to woodland and water. Not all Franks were powerful or well connected to those who were. To be a lord of any importance in sixth- and seventh-century Europe required being a lord of land—and being related to other lords of the land.

LORDS OF THE LAND

The material limitations—in terms of population levels and technology—on early medieval transalpine society contributed to the shape and structure of that society. So too did the historical experience of migration and settlement in the Roman provincial world of Gaul, Iberia, and Italy and the emergence of new political and social structures as a result of these. Contact with the empire itself offered new models of social organization. Not only were the political structures of the empire, the Roman armies, and the Roman provincial governments available for imitation, but the pattern of life suggested by Roman landholding practices, agricultural technology, communities, and cities offered prospects that had been unthinkable in the old world beyond the imperial frontiers. The decay of Roman governmental and administrative institutions and the formation of a sub-Roman culture among the Germanic immigrants meant that both societies were becoming more like each other and less like their own individual remote and even recent pasts. And just as the late Roman Empire barely resembled the empire of the first and second centuries, so the Germanic peoples of the fifth, sixth, and seventh centuries bore little resemblance to their predecessors, whose way of life had been described so extensively by the Roman writer Tacitus at the end of the first century.

For the Germanic inhabitants of seventh-century Europe, the most important social bonds were those between lords and followers and that of the kin-group. Early Europeans used several different words to describe what moderns would call the "family," and these words possessed distinct meanings. *Parentes* or *parentela* designated a group of relations, or kin descended from a putative common ancestor, while *familia* (the word from which the modern term "family" is derived) originally designated the individual household, including marital and blood relations, other dependents, and slaves, but it could also designate the entourage of a bishop or a monastic community.

Whether grouped in villages or isolated in farmsteads, those who worked the land thought in terms of household work units and the wider group of fellow villagers. Villages were generally isolated and separated from each other by forest or meadow. They also had to be virtually economically and technologically self-sustaining, since no single village could support technical specialists. The decreasing number of districts that it took to support, for example, a highly skilled blacksmith or a well-armed fighting man, may be an indication of improving micro-regional economic formation and development. Those who did not have to work the land thought in terms of their membership in a kin-group which gave them high status, of how to preserve their status or make it higher, of strategic alliances with other powerful families or the royal court. Such ambitions could be achieved by marriage strategies, the exchange of gifts, the conduct of feuds, the shared experience of warfare, and the acquisition and distribution of plunder. The most prominent member of this nobility was the *dominus*, the lord who ruled his own property and house, "who has many riches," who was a powerful man, a *potens* who held his land from no one, although he might add to it by accepting gifts of land from the king.

The legal texts of Germanic peoples reflect some of the chief features of their social structure. Much of the terminology that describes military service or tax assessment tends to measure society in terms of households. In several early law codes the *mansus*, the land and possessions required to support a household, are terms used frequently. These may be considered the elemental social forms of early European society.

In the legal codes, the kin-group and household are generally assumed to comprise free individuals—that is, fully fledged members of "the people," the largest group to which any individual professed loyalty. Freedom entailed the right to carry weapons in the wars of the people, the right to participate in the settlement of legal cases and disputes according to the laws of the people, and the right to participate in community decisions at assemblies. In other words, freedom meant full membership in a named group larger than the kin. In day-to-day experience, the free peasant was a fully privileged member of an agricultural community. Membership in the village community also meant full membership in the larger people, which was signaled by the right to be judged by the law of the people, whether Visigothic, Frankish, Burgundian, or Lombard, no matter in whose territory a legal dispute was heard. It also meant the right and obligation to fight—either in the expeditions of occasional war leaders or in the wars of the king. For many centuries, one sure sign of personal freedom was the right to carry weapons and the knowledge of how to use them.

We know far more about those in the higher orders of society during these centuries than we do about those at the middle or bottom. Even these orders varied in degree. The term "noble" might indicate a well-off freeman, a *potens*, the somewhat higher ranking *illustris*, or at the very highest, the *proceris*, a man close to the king. One way to recognize the different statuses below the nobility is to look at the institution of *wergild* in the early law codes. *Wergild* (literally, "the money for a man") was the assessed value of individuals of different social status. Because most Germanic law was personal (the members of a people could be judged only according to the law of that people), and because most legal disputes were treated as matters involving personal injury (or tort, in modern legal terminology), the focus of Germanic law was compensation rather than punishment. Thus, the way by which compensation was determined reveals the "worth" of different members of society. The slave (or rather the slave's owner) received the lowest amount of wergild, the *aldius* somewhat more, the freeman much more, and the noble—in some instances the noble in the king's service—most of all. Formally, at least, the law codes give us an approximate profile of social rank and offer a rudimentary terminology for distinguishing among members of society.

The society of the codes, however, was not fixed forever. As the conquests slowed down and stopped, as society was transformed by settlement, and as individual circumstances changed, the legal categories had to be adapted to new circumstances. One general trend after the seventh century was the gradual emergence of the institution of lordship and the "dependence" of different kinds of individuals upon a lord. A second trend was the general lessening of formal slavery and the general depression of the status of many peasants who were technically free. With this general leveling among the lower ranks of society, the dependent agricultural worker, or serf, tied to the land and under the rule of a local lord, became a characteristic social type. The process is complex and certainly occurred more rapidly in some areas than in others, but by the eighth century at the latest, the institution of serfdom was in the process of formation.

The *gens* (plural, *gentes*), or "people," was both the acknowledged aggregate of a kin-group, and all free individuals who lived under the same law and fought in the same armies. Thus, one could speak both of the *gens Merovingorum* as the dynasty of Clovis, or the *gens Francorum* for the Frankish people as a whole. The term *gens* meant something more than a spousal household and something less than a state. It reminds us that the focus of Germanic culture was the individual and his or her membership in a larger group, reflected in personal law, rights within that group, and rule by a common king. The *gentes* were loosely structured, however, and membership in them was not the same as either citizenship or subjecthood in a later form of kingdom. In general, public organized life existed on a small scale.

As many free peasants shrank into half-free status, the idea of freedom came to be restricted to powerful men who dominated others—the first European nobility. Originally, the Germanic nobility consisted of the most successful warriors, the richest men, and relatives and favorites of the kings of the *gentes*. If families managed to retain their wealth, connections to royalty and to each other, and remained prominent over several generations, they were considered *nobilis*, or noble. As one writer of the time put it, "They had a known name," that is, their ancestors had established themselves and their descendants as prominent. Such status depended originally more on recognition by others than on legal definition—everybody "knew" who was noble and who was not. The surviving sources are good at telling who was recognized as noble, but rarely how such people had become noble in the first place. Their wergild was far higher than that of other persons.

One means of maintaining noble status was marriage to members of other powerful families. Another was royal favor and service, which might entail holding a royal office. Powerful men who served the king and acted as his representatives could easily dominate others and pass to their heirs at least some of the wealth they had acquired. Although the seventh and eighth centuries witnessed great family fortunes rising and falling, the most powerful, wealthy, and fortunate great families of the Frankish kingdoms came slowly to constitute a generally recognized social rank having special wergild and privileges, a special first name (last names were not used then) or set of names that the kin-group alone used, and an increasing consciousness and general recognition of their superior status. But that noble self-consciousness also had to be maintained. In most cases, the core of the kin-group consisted of a group of people most closely descended from an important grandparent. The core kin-group might then discriminate against those of the kin's members who were more distantly related, and these relationships and perceptions changed with every generation. The perspective of any particular member of the wider kin-group was thus determined by his or her position in a network of close and distant relatives and might be altered by marriage into another group, which could be of higher or lower status than the original.

This nobility spent its time moving from estate to estate attending to their lands and maintaining their skills as warriors. A man might be born with noble blood, but the most respected noblemen were those who showed bravery in the hunt and in battle, who had family connections with others like themselves, who generously feasted and rewarded their followers, and who married the daughters of their equals or superiors.

GENDER AND POWER

Kin-groups were sustained and expanded by marriage. This was a matter for negotiation between families. The account of the life of Gertrude of Nivelles (621–653: the great-great aunt of Charlemagne) describes such a negotiation:

> When her father Pippin had invited King Dagobert to his house for a lordly meal, the son of a duke of the Austrasians arrived . . . and he had entreated the king and the parents of the girl that this girl be promised to him in matrimony . . . for the sake of his worldly ambition and mutual alliance. This pleased the king and he persuaded the father of the girl to call her with her mother into his presence.[1]

Gertrude, however, at the time about eleven years old, flew into a rage and declared that she would have no husband but Christ. She eventually did enter the religious life, founding the convent at Nivelles, and later became widely regarded as a saint. As a young girl from a prominent and wealthy family, Gertrude was just the sort of bride an ambitious young man from another similar family in Austrasia would want. Such a marriage not only required a brideprice from the man's family, but also established "friendship" with them, a connection to a potential set of allies who were on friendly enough terms with the king to invite him to dinner, and finally, children to continue the line.

Nor was the dinner merely a dinner. Such ceremonial occasions had little room for surprises. It is possible that the boy's father had mentioned the idea to the king and perhaps to Gertrude's father beforehand, and the idea of the match may have initially appealed to all three. But Gertrude quite vocally chose otherwise, and her father supported her choice.

In the event, Gertrude's sister, Begga, did marry a powerful noble (although probably not the ambitious one in the story), Ansegisel, and so continued the line of Pippin that would later produce the family known as the Arnulfings and the Pippinids, and later

---

[1] *"Vita sanctae Geretrudis,"* in Paul Fouracre and Richard A. Gerberding, *Late Merovingian France: History and Hagiography 640–720* (Manchester and New York: Manchester University Press, 1996), 320.

as the Carolingians (below, Chapter 8). Gertrude's objection to marriage in favor of the chaste religious life also raises an important point.

The biological differences between men and women have not changed through human history, but the extrapolation of biological differences to the definition any culture makes about what constitutes masculine or feminine identity—the problem of gender—has changed considerably. Some of these changes were reflected in later Roman history and in the ideals of masculinity and femininity in the early Christian communities, at least until the assertion of a definition of masculinity that coincided with the location of male authority within the church, around the sixth century.

The law codes also tell us something of perceived gender differences. They indicate that Frankish women, for example, were valued by men chiefly for their ability to bear children to continue the family line and to forge alliances with other noble families. The ideal Frankish woman was the obedient daughter and the obedient spouse, and obedient female spouses and unmarried women were protected by the laws. Insult, rape, and the seizure of free women, particularly those unmarried and those of childbearing age, were harshly punished, not only because they violated a woman's greatest value, but because they also violated the woman's father's or husband's *mundium,* his right of protection. Marriage transferred this right from the woman's father to her husband, usually in return for the brideprice—originally the price paid by the groom's family to the bride's father, and the main support for the bride's widowhood if the husband predeceased her. Brideprice was later transformed into dowry, wealth that passed from the bride's family to that of the groom. *Mundium* was not only a right of protection, but the right to represent the woman in court and to manage her property. The morning–gift, paid from the groom to the bride, was presumably a price for her virginity. But brides could also exert some control over their dowries, and they could receive gifts of land from their husbands. Childless widows could manage their dowry lands in whatever ways they wished. Even a woman in religious life might inherit the property of parents or male siblings and dispose of it, either as a gift to her religious house or as gifts to private persons.

Masculine identity, then, was construed as that of a protector, lord, and disposer of women. Masculinity was a gender to which violence was permitted and even expected, just as sexual activity such as concubinage with a free woman not his wife or sexual activity with female slaves was permitted to men, but not to women. Men were supposed to be generous gift-givers to friends and followers.

In spite of the powerful restraints imposed on early medieval women by gender definition and normative clerical misogyny, they were not entirely without resources, and on occasion, power. Gertrude's father, after all, conceded to her wishes for the religious life. As converters of pagan husbands to Christianity, founders or patrons of monasteries and churches (like Gertrude), patrons of candidates for appointment to a bishopric or abbacy, or links between different kin-groups, women were certainly capable of exerting influence. In royal marriages, queens were given considerable authority in managing the affairs of the royal household, the palace, and the royal estates, representing absent royal husbands, guarding the treasure of the royal house, and during the minorities of their children, often serving as regents of the kingdom. In one well-known instance, Balthild, an Anglo-Saxon slave girl (of apparently noble birth), was given to Clovis II (638–657) of Neustria by her owner (who had briefly fancied marrying her himself), the king's mayor of the palace, Erchinoald. At the death of her husband in 657, Balthild served as regent of the kingdom for her young son Chlothar III (657–673), actively ruling with a council of advisers, and obviously respected by the Frankish nobility, until her son came of age in 664, when Balthild retired to a life of religion at the convent of Chelles and was regarded very soon after her death in 680 as a saint.

More than queens, however, holy women suggest an inversion of the very characteristics that defined most early medieval European women. The lives of female saints are remarkably abundant from the fifth through the eighth centuries, and they reveal a creative adaptation of the very features that defined and limited women in the world. The female saint preserved virginity because she rejected the lusts of the flesh; her humility conquered pride; her meditation on scripture suppressed the desire for visual delights. She chose an immortal, rather than a mortal husband. And although she might leave a normal feminine role in the world, she might take property with her into the religious life, often serving as a kin-group's representative in controlling monasteries or churches that the kin wished to keep in its possession. The holy woman, too, gave gifts—but to the poor and to the churches, and she and her ecclesiastical property offered shelter and hospitality. And holy women could construct communities of spiritual kin.

Women generally had a shorter life expectancy than men, and throughout the early Middle Ages the practice of men about to be married to bring gifts and payments to their bride's family upon marriage may serve as evidence that noble women suitable for marriage were not only fewer in number but also shorter-lived than men. Women were also a means of enhancing a man's social status by marriage, and a number of prominent families in the early Middle Ages reckoned their descent from the family of a prominent female rather than that of a male, even naming their children according to naming patterns in the female line rather than the male. At the highest levels of society, women could inherit and control property, and by the eighth century (and probably even earlier) queens undertook a number of responsibilities in the management and disposition of royal property. The first coronation ceremony for an empress occurred in 816, and for a queen in 856.

In the religious life, women in early Frankish and Anglo-Saxon society enjoyed considerable power and status, not only as wives of bishops and priests (the active and successful enforcement of clerical celibacy dates only from the eleventh century), but also as patrons and founders of monasteries. Such figures as Hild of England (above, Chapter 6), who founded the monastery of Whitby and patronized the poet Cædmon, and Radegund of Poitiers (518–587) played crucial roles in the spread of literacy, the transmission of intellectual traditions, and the patronage of unmarried women—women who deliberately chose a celibate life, women who had persuaded their families that they preferred the cloister to marriage, or women who were deliberately cloistered by their families in order to keep them from an undesirable marriage market. Radegund, like Balthild a century later, is an important example. Captured from her home in Thuringia by Frankish invaders, Radegund, a prisoner of war and therefore a slave, was compelled to marry Chlothar I (511–561), the son of Clovis. After ten years of extremely unhappy marriage, Radegund left Chlothar, entered the religious life with his grudging permission, and was ordained a deaconess around 550. She established the convent of the Holy Cross at Poitiers, where she remained until her death. Her life was written by a disciple in the convent, Baudovinia. Although the formal ecclesiastical orders of widows and the female diaconate were later abolished, the kind of religious authority assumed by women like Radegund remained possible—and significant. Merovingian kings sometimes married slave women like Balthild and Radegund, perhaps so as not to tie themselves too closely to one or another of the great families or family factions of the kingdom.

Radegund also patronized the traveling Italian poet Venantius Fortunatus, later Bishop of Poitiers, who wrote for her convent the texts of two of the greatest of Christian hymns, the *Vexilla regis prodeunt* ("The banners of the king of heaven go forth") and the *Pange, lingua, gloriosi* ("Sing, my tongue, the glorious mystery"). But women also read and wrote. Female religious houses had libraries—and women in them, who worked as copyists and illuminators of manuscripts. A ninth-century abbess of the house at Chelles was called "a woman of great wordpower," *femina verbipotens*. The works of a number of women writers constitute a small, but no less important, literature than those of male writers.

Apart from celibacy and widowhood, women experienced a variety of different forms of association with males. The early Merovingian rulers of the Franks appear to have practiced polygyny, and the older Roman form of concubinage also survived, as well as the Germanic institution of *Friedelehe,* a form of marriage conspicuous among Frankish royalty and nobility when they married socially inferior women, in which the woman remained under the rule of her own family, along with her children. In spite of the ecclesiastical restrictions on the ministry of women and the formal male control of women in the law codes and legislation, it is clear that both the status and the function of women were considerably higher and more varied than the sources immediately reveal. As guardians of minor children, as patrons of monastic and other ecclesiastical institutions, and as wives of powerful men whose own status protected that of their wives, as religious, and as scholars, even royal women in Merovingian *Francia* experienced a series of exclusions from formal authority in ecclesiastical and lay environments; at the same time, their status and the informal exercise of power on their part reflected the transformation of late antique and early Germanic society and offered opportunities for control over much of their own lives, usually in spite of the dictates of gender distinctions and the legal limitations on female independence.

RELIGION AS THE FRAMEWORK OF CULTURE

If a barbarian could become a catholic Christian, could he also become a monk, abbot, or bishop? Or could he or she become a saint? In one respect, such questions became moot upon conversion, because the barbarian ceased to be a barbarian on becoming a catholic Christian. Later usages of the word "barbarian" almost always implied "pagan" as well. By the late sixth century, there were clearly bishops of Frankish or of mixed descent who maintained a collective identity resembling that of their Gallo-Roman predecessors in the office. Particularly under the influence of Columbanus, Frankish men and women also entered the religious life. Royal and noble families built, endowed, and patronized churches and religious houses and often provided them with their own members as rulers of those houses. Around the year 700, there were 550 monasteries in *Francia*. Of these, 320 had been founded since 600. Of the 320, 90 had been founded in the southern part of the kingdom, 230 in the north. Christianity had spread north dramatically during the seventh century.

The emergence of a concept of Christian kingship among the Germanic peoples of sixth- and seventh-century western Europe is one striking sign of the fusion of Christian-Roman and Frankish cultures that marks these centuries. When Clovis, king of the victorious Franks, called a council of the Gallo-Roman higher clergy in Orleans in 507, he began a tradition of royal patronage of the Church—and royal interest in seeing that the Church was properly organized—that ran through the Middle Ages and early-modern European history. But regular meetings of Church councils that represented all the bishops of *Francia* were not always possible, either among the Franks or among any other Germanic people, except the Visigoths in Spain, where frequent councils met at Toledo until the extinction of the kingdom in 711. Frankish kings and their clerical advisers might preserve the ideal of a well-organized church, but, as in many other Christian communities, the church tended to become localized.

By the late seventh century, Frankish bishops were routinely connected by family or faction to the royal court, and although the king might permit the election of a bishop by local clergy, the king always had the final say in episcopal appointments. Once appointed, the bishop acquired control of ecclesiastical property in his diocese and played a necessary political as well as an ecclesiastical role in regional affairs. Such a role often involved the bishop in large-scale political conflicts, and bishops who lost out or were killed in these were often commemorated as saints who had suffered martyrdom. The written lives of these sainted bishops and other sainted nobles are an important source for the history of the period, since the lives are often apologies for the saint's political activities and a condemnation of the saint's enemies.

Saints, alive or dead, were regarded as powerful patrons in heaven, of private individuals or of whole communities. In *Francia,* saints were heavenly counterparts of the *potens*—the local great man—who took an interest in the communities that venerated them and interceded on their behalf with God himself. The Franks understood the role of patron saints in terms of their own social structure. Whatever else it meant, sanctity always meant power. And saintly power protected both individuals and communities.

Originally, transalpine Europe had few local saints from the early centuries of Christianity, and the need for relics usually led to their importation—via purchase, gift, or pious theft—from the Mediterranean world. The spread of the cult of Peter, for example, is a useful measure of the spread of the influence of Rome and its bishop in the northern world. The spread of the cult of Benedict is partly responsible for the growing popularity of Benedictine forms of monastic life. But local saints and their cults also appeared in the fourth and fifth centuries—first that of Martin of Tours, then that of Patrick in Ireland, whose cult was carried to Britain and the Continent by Irish monastic exiles. The first Continental mention of a cult of Patrick, in fact, occurs in the life of Gertrude of Nivelles. Although clerics, including bishops, were now male, sanctity was open to women as well, and Gertrude is only one of the many female saints, most of them noblewomen, venerated in Merovingian *Francia*.

The transfer of relics and cult observances also aided the battle against paganism, since saints could replace local deities in popular veneration. Many sermons of the sixth and especially the seventh centuries were based on the histories of saints and martyrs who were venerated locally. They were also directed against surviving pagan beliefs and practices, which the cult of the saints replaced. Much of the tone of Christian culture in this period is combative—designed to prove the superiority of Christianity through the actions of its holy men and women over pagan beliefs, or to Christianize pagan practices. Thus, much pagan practice was simply redesignated as worship of demons, and the saints conveniently replaced the "demons," although the muscular Christianity of the seventh century always showed the demons defeated by Christian holiness. Lists of "superstitions" forbidden to Christians appeared regularly down to the twelfth century. Among the most original legislation of Germanic kings was that dealing with violations of Christian practices on the part of their people.

One result of such legislation was the imposition of Christian interpretations upon older non-Christian customs. Thus, the legal procedure of the ordeal, in which an individual was subjected to physical injury and later examined to see if the injury had miraculously disappeared, slowly acquired Christian liturgical patronage. Because the outcome of the ordeal "proved" guilt or innocence of a criminal charge, and because Christians, like pagans, believed in "immanent justice"—that is, in the direct intervention of God in human life—a Christian liturgy for the preparation, execution, and interpretation of ordeals slowly developed in the sixth and seventh centuries.

The canons of Frankish Church councils always represent an ideal state of the Christian community, but they do not describe actual practice. The purest forms of devotion were to be found in some monasteries, which usually survived less touched by the world than did the higher clergy, who were still in it. But even monasticism was fragmented by a multiplicity of rules and by the problem of monastic subjection to the local bishop or to family interests. The creation of rural parishes brought religion to some of the population, but it also fragmented the unity of the diocese. Bishops on the whole were inconsistent in their devotion and often indifferent or inept in their administration. Therefore, the chief concern of conscientious clergy was to impose uniform religious practices on the people. By substituting orthopraxy (correct religious practice) for the ceremonial aspects of paganism, seventh-century churchmen, and the cult of the saints, could embrace more and more aspects of social consciousness and social life. By influencing consciousness and conduct—emphasizing the community significance of baptism and penance, the social community of the mass, a common local calendar of saints' days and their attendant observances—they were able to form a distinctive Frankish culture whose base was constituted by Frankish Christianity at all levels of society.

It is in the realm of popular belief—in this instance belief shared by all levels of society—that early medieval Christian culture is most striking. Christians, like pagans, wanted, above all, security in this world and salvation in the next. Security in this world had originally been a matter of appeasing the proper god, and much of the tenor of missionary Christianity in this period was to prove the superiority of the Christian God in providing help in this life in terms of more abundant harvests, fewer natural disasters, cures of illness or injury, and protection from the forces of the other world. Such fears were overcome by changes in practice, which facilitated changes in belief. Even the saints came to acquire specialized functions and to be localized; each region venerated its own proven saintly patrons, and those patrons in turn protected those who venerated them. Just as certain kinds of conduct distinguished a member of a *gens* from members of other *gentes,* so certain kinds of conduct separated a Christian from non-Christians. Early medieval Christianity is characterized by behavior rather than by belief, and the king's responsibility for proper behavior in the Church was the sole guarantee of preserving divine favor in a turbulent world.

The image of God in the early Middle Ages was that of a remote and terrible judge, always ready to strike down humans for their sinful lives, yet willing to show mercy if attempts at reform were made. By extension, the theory of immanent justice applied to divine wrath as well, and the causation of events was seen as a manifestation either of divine favor or of divine anger. God was a power to be appeased rather than loved, for only by faithful observance of His commands could a society expect earthly peace and some assurance of heaven, however slight. In a world characterized by the worst effects of fallen human nature, plagued by demons, full of uncertainty and insecurity, the Christian first wanted help and protection. In their search for help and protection for everyday cares, men and women turned to the local saints, through prayers and liturgies, and through the saints to God, remote and barely approachable. Saints' and holy men's triumph over demons, illustrated in sermons and stories and art, was the visible proof of God's mercy in a world that regarded itself as existing precariously under the dominion of Satan.

THE LONG-HAIRED KINGS

At the head of these societies stood the king, but the office of king had also changed. It too had been subjected to the cultural pressures of migration, war leadership, models of Roman office, and the demands of ruling a newly settled and religiously unified society. By the eighth century, kings were no longer priests and symbolic tribal chiefs, nor were they simply successful war leaders who had managed to conquer a territory and hold on to it for a sufficient length of time. The kingdoms of the Lombards in Italy, the Visigoths in Iberia, and the Franks in what was rapidly becoming *Francia* each developed a distinctive political culture and had a distinctive political history.

The Lombard kingdom in Italy, initially hostile to Roman forces and Arian in its Christianity, converted to catholic Christianity only over a long period ending in the mid seventh century, and therefore never built up a cadre of clerical supporters as had the kings of the Franks and Visigoths. Since many Roman institutions survived in Italy, the Lombard kings controlled considerable resources and based their rule on cities, with their capital at Pavia. They also developed a number of precocious public institutions based on late Roman administrative practices and preserved a good deal of Roman learning, one notable example being the use of formal documents in governmental affairs.

Large parts of Italy remained outside Lombard control, and large parts of Lombard Italy remained outside of the king's control until the conquest of the kingdom by Charlemagne in 774 (below, Chapter 8).

The Visigothic kingdom in the Iberian Peninsula represented yet another type of early state development, the close association of kings and bishops meeting in regularly held church councils at Toledo, the royal and sacral capital of the kingdom. Visigothic kings were anointed with holy oil in a liturgical ceremony, and their claims to divine legitimacy made it easier for the nobility to support the royal armies and maintain the peace. The kingdom was plagued, however, by royal minorities and periodic revolts, the latter reflecting the conflict between the extraordinary consensus about religious and royal insistence on uniformity and its contrast to local diversity. The strong centralizing process created by king and bishops, however, had one disastrous consequence: When a mixed army of Arabs and Berbers invaded Iberia in 711, they only had to defeat a king and his royal army and capture Toledo in order to overcome the whole kingdom. Large numbers of Visigothic Christians, as well as Jews, remained under Arab rule, but some Visigothic nobles withdrew to the far north of the peninsula, where they began to build the small Christian kingdoms of Asturias and Leon.

The most successful kingdoms of the period are those that emerged during the sixth and seventh centuries in Anglo-Saxon Britain and in *Francia*. The distinctive political, intellectual, and religious culture of what would much later become the kingdom of England, long viewed as growing out of Irish and Roman missionary efforts, was once thought to have reinvigorated the culture of Gaul, which had allegedly declined from its originally high levels in the fifth and sixth centuries into a state of political weakness, ecclesiastical corruption, and aristocratic chaos. Recent research, however, regards the kingdom of the Franks as an essential element in the conversion of England and sees in the Merovingian dynasty of Clovis, "the long-haired kings," as contemporaries called them, not the series of murderous despots and incompetents that their Carolingian successors portrayed (below, Chapter 8), but energetic kingdom builders on whose work the later, more extensively documented kingdom ruled by the dynasty of Charlemagne (r. 768–814) creatively built (below, Chapter 8).

The kingdom created by Clovis (above, Chapter 3) before his death in 511 was a wholly new entity in the experience of the different peoples who made up the Franks. Clovis created a new form of catholic Christian kingship, coming to terms with the Gallo-Roman inhabitants of his new lands, including the powerful aristocratic churchmen. His conquests gave him all of the formerly imperially owned land in Gaul and the income from what was left of the Roman fiscal system. Even though he and his successors distributed much of this wealth to their relatives, servants, favorites, followers, and to the Church, they just as often replenished it by means of conquest, plunder, tribute, and the confiscation of the wealth of their internal enemies. Clovis and his successors also based administrations on the old Roman *civitates,* or administrative districts, and they continued some forms of Roman taxation. Finally, Clovis issued the first written law collection of the Franks, *The Law of the Salian Franks,* written in Latin, probably between 507 and 511, in this instance, too, imitating both earlier Roman rulers and other Germanic kings.

Clovis also had to deal with the new problem of succession. Although Frankish law held that privately owned land had to be divided equally among the surviving sons and sometimes daughters of a deceased father, there is no indication that the Franks considered the kingdom itself as private property in this way. It is likely that contemporary dynastic and political considerations dictated Clovis' solution—a division of the kingdom into four parts, each ruled by one of Clovis' four sons as king. The survival of four legitimate sons (by two different wives) to maturity and the pressure of their and their followers' claims that each was equally "royal" may have determined Clovis' decision. Except for brief periods between 558 and 561 and 613–639, when a single ruler governed all the kingdoms of the Franks, the realm was usually divided among three or four closely related, rival, and usually mutually hostile kings. In any one of these kingdoms, a king might die childless, be conquered by a neighboring king, or be forced to exclude his own sons from succession because of the risk of continually subdividing the kingdom. One result of the first division in 511 was the subsequent Frankish understanding that any legitimate male member of the Merovingian dynasty was entitled to a share of the whole kingdom of the Franks, and no revolt could succeed without the backing of a member of the dynasty.

During the reign of the generation following Clovis, new territories were added to the Frankish orbit, particularly Thuringia and Burgundy (above, Chapter 3). Military conflicts with the Visigoths continued into the 540s, particularly in the area between Aquitaine and the Pyrenees known as Septimania, with its cities of Nîmes and Carcassonne. During the Gothic Wars (above, Chapters 3 and 4), Frankish forces also intervened in northern Italy. During the sixth and seventh centuries, several of these Frankish kingdoms acquired a sense of regional continuity and identity. Gradually, three regions became customarily recognized. The territory of Neustria ("The New West Land"), with its capital at Soissons and later Paris, emerged out of the old Romanized western Frankish lands. The kingdom of Austrasia ("The East Land") took shape in the more Frankish and less Romanized northern and eastern lands. Its center moved from Rheims eastward to Metz. The third kingdom, Burgundy, survived as one of the three until 613, when it came under the permanent influence of Neustria and ceased to have its own kings. Even its nobles appear to have gravitated into the network of noble factions of Neustria; its last royal servant, the mayor of the palace, died in 626 and was not replaced.

One way of interpreting the divisions of the kingdom of the Franks between the death of Clovis and the reigns of Chlothar II (584–629) and Dagobert I (623–638) may be to regard Clovis' single reign as the exception, and the inability of the monarchy to rule a large kingdom effectively, as a norm, until the early seventh century. But the surviving sources must be read very closely in order to understand the different perspectives that informed them. The greatest narrative source for the period, the *Ten Books of Histories* of the Gallo-Roman aristocratic bishop, Gregory of Tours (538–594), certainly paints a grim picture of the rivalries and feuds of Clovis' successors, drawing the historical actors in stark black-and-white contrast. But Gregory's *Histories* is not an account of the Frankish kingdom as much as it is a use of events in Frankish history to illustrate the principles of an ideal, divinely prescribed order in Christian society. Gregory's central concerns are the divine framework of all human history, divine approval of those who support normative religious dogma, the sins of society that call down the wrath of God, the danger to society of godless kings, the ideal relationship of king and bishop, and the significance of these from the perspective of the Last Judgment. But in spite of its schematic program, Gregory's narrative is also powerful, vivid, and memorably anecdotal, and so it must be read very cautiously as an eyewitness account of the political events of the later sixth century. Gregory had many axes to grind, and he ground them sharply.

But the Merovingian kings had more pressing things to worry about than Gregory's view of salvation history. The reign of no individual ruler was ever entirely secure, either in inheriting a kingdom or in holding on to one after he had acquired it. Membership in the dynasty, approval by the powerful higher clergy and at least a significant faction of the nobility, assured a succession, but civil war, rebellion, or assassination might as quickly remove a ruler, particularly when failure to remove him offered the prospect of the complete loss of property and prestige on the part of one or more factions of the nobility. When heirs were minor children, Merovingian queens also played prominent political roles in the succession and in the early years, at least, of the royal administration.

An instance of this instability was the feud between Chilperic I (r. 561–584) and his queen Fredegund, of Neustria, against his brother, Sigibert I (561–585) and his queen Brunhild, of Austrasia. The feud began with the brothers' dispute over the inheritance of their dead brother Charibert I (561–567). Fredegund had persuaded Chilperic to kill his wife Galswintha, Brunhild's sister, generating bitter enmity between the two queens. The result of the wars between the Neustrians and Austrasians was the survival of the son of Chilperic and Fredegund, Chlothar II (r. 584–629), as king over only a small part of western Neustria along the Channel, and the installation of two of Sigibert's and Brunhild's grandsons, Theudebert II (r. 595–612) as king of Austrasia, and Theuderic II (r. 595–613) as king of Burgundy. Both kings ruled under the control of their grandmother, Brunhild, who induced Theuderic to kill Theudebert and then to attack Chlothar and acquire the entire kingdom.

At the same time, the resistance of a local Burgundian noble faction to Brunhild and Theuderic, evidently in collaboration with several prominent Austrasian nobles, led to their invitation to Chlothar II to attack Burgundy. For these years, two narrative historical accounts, *The Chronicle of Fredegar* and the *Book of the History of the Franks* offer different but very helpful accounts. The Austrasian nobles mentioned in the chronicle of Fredegar were Arnulf, bishop of Metz, and a landholder named Pippin of Landen, the father of Gertrude and Begga, who had once invited a king to dinner. As a consequence of this war, the prominence of the Arnulfing-Pippinid faction of the Austrasian nobility began slowly to increase. Chlothar's invasion succeeded. Theuderic died during the war, and Brunhild was captured, terribly tortured and publicly executed. Cholthar II succeeded alone to the three kingdoms in 613.

But Austrasia requested its own Merovingian king, and Chlothar II sent his young son, Dagobert, but he also appointed officials there with strong connections to Neustria. The Arnulfing-Pippinids had to wait. The first Pippinid to become mayor of the palace of Austrasia was Pippin I's son Grimoald, who controlled immense territories from Frisia south to the area between the Moselle and Rhine rivers. When Dagobert succeeded his father in Neustria in 629, he in turn appointed his own infant son, Sigibert III (d. 656), to the throne of Austrasia. Dagobert was succeeded in Neustria by his other son, Clovis II, the husband of Balthild.

During these reigns, it became clear that Neustria was rising to the role of the chief kingdom of the Franks, with Austrasia assigned to minor children, and that any noble faction that wanted power at the center had to secure its position in Neustria, and particularly in the royal court. The court consisted of the royal family and its household officials, recruited from among the favored noble families. The court was itinerant, moving from royal estate to royal estate in the valleys of the Seine and Oise rivers. The court was also a cultural center, dominated by a network of friendships and alliances that had been built up during the reigns of Chlothar II and Dagobert. At public assemblies held in the spring, the ruler and his closest associates among the magnates organized military affairs and announced policy and legal decisions to those assembled.

The court was headed by the king, but access to the king was controlled by his chief adviser and official, the mayor of the palace. The mayor in turn became the focus of the loyalty of the prosperous and increasingly powerful and self-conscious regional nobility. The most powerful of the mayors of Neustria in the late seventh century was Ebroin (657–683), who was generally hostile to the Austrasians, but during the same period some of the Austrasian nobility began to acquire lands and influence in Neustria. The most prominent—and ultimately the most successful—of these was the kin-group Arnulfing-Pippinids; Their leader was Pippin II "of Herstal" (the son of Begga and Adalgisel), whose own wealth in land was greatly increased by his marriage to the heiress Plectrude, who possessed large estates in the areas of Cologne and Trier. Pippin II asserted his military supremacy over Neustria at the battle of Tertry in 687. From that date, the Pippinids usually controlled the succession of Merovingians to the throne of Neustria.

Pippin's son, Charles, later called Martel, or "The Hammer," succeeded his father as mayor of the palace after a bitter struggle with the Neustrians in 716 and 717 and a struggle with his father's widow Plectrude, whose grandchildren he disinherited. Charles Martel successfully waged war on a number of peripheral territories that had asserted their independence from the Frankish rulership, and he also defeated an Arab-Berber expeditionary force in Aquitaine, at the battle of Poitiers in 732 or 733. At his death in 741, Charles Martel was virtually the undisputed ruler of the Franks in Austrasia, Neustria, and Burgundy. He left his lands and his office to his two sons, Carloman and Pippin III (below, Chapter 8). *Francia* was once again united, now under the real power of the mayor of the palace acting in the name of the last Merovingian kings.

The history of the Merovingian kings of the Franks illustrates important features of kingship and political order generally between the fifth and the mid eighth centuries. One justification for kingship was descent from a single family from which the kings had long been chosen. Dynastic right, a right as member of a royal kin, rather than individual right, was one of the most important bases of kingship. Second, kingship was regarded as distinguishing a people, a *gens,* from other societies that did not have kings or had different kings. The Merovingian kings of the Franks wore their hair long and flowing as a visible sign of their royal rank. They and other kings were expected to give gifts to their loyal followers, an echo of the division of booty in the war band. One source of royal treasure was inheritance from the previous king, but another was tribute paid by neighboring peoples and plunder from those they conquered. The kings and their guardianship of the law of the *gens Francorum* were living embodiments of the common origin and history of their peoples, however recent that history might have been in fact, and they were rulers of peoples, not of land. Early European monarchy was generally not based on territory, as in the modern state. Although the king could and sometimes did make new laws for the *gens*, he was regarded far more as the protector of the people's law. This law, as we have seen, remained essentially private, settling disputes between equally free litigants, often with the personal intervention of the king as settler of disputes among the powerful. The king was expected to protect the people from outside invaders and to maintain the peace internally. He was also expected to protect and expand the Christian faith in his kingdom.

With the Christianization of the Germanic peoples, kingship began to be regarded partly in terms of Old Testament institutions and partly in terms of the late imperial concept of the Christian emperor. The figures of David, Solomon, Hezekiah, and Josiah frequently appear in the sources as models to be imitated by sixth- and seventh-century Visigothic and Frankish kings, and such Old Testament practices as anointing the king at his accession and creating prayers specifically for the king slowly appeared among the elaborate rituals of kingship between the sixth and the eighth centuries. Biblical prophets became the prototypes for the bishops who advised the kings. The Franks regarded themselves as a chosen people, very much in the image of the Hebrews, thus locating themselves in a tradition of salvation history that began with the Book of Kings. The new, larger territories of the kings of the Franks and Visigoths in the sixth, seventh, and eighth centuries strengthened the concept of kingship, and the use of Latin in royal documents and in the writing of law codes suggests the Roman influence on Germanic institutions in a changing social and political world. The two influences of Christianity and Roman imperial ideas and institutions worked on the kings of the seventh and eighth centuries in their new circumstances in settled kingdoms far larger and more differently structured than ancient Germanic composite societies.

The role of king also came to include the protection and patronage of the Church, and the royal office and its functions were often included in liturgical prayers and ceremonies. Sometimes kings themselves or members of their families were venerated as saints, thereby adding luster and sanctity to the whole dynasty, and Christian chroniclers held before contemporary kings both historical and contemporary examples of good and bad royal behavior. Although one cannot say that the chroniclers' world-views directly influenced royal conduct, through them we may observe the formation of new kinds of political theory and political communities in seventh- and eighth-century western Europe. Superimposed upon the social realities of *gens* and tough-minded self-interest, the idea of a Christian people ruled by a Christian king came to be commonplace by the eighth century.

8

The Book and the Sword

AN ISLAND SET BEYOND THE WORLD

The link Gregory the Great forged between Rome and England with the mission of Augustine in 596, resulting in the conversion of the Angles and Saxons to Christianity, was strengthened by the victory of Roman customs at the Synod of Whitby in 664. The English church became the first northern European community to have been shaped by both Roman and non-Roman influences. As such, it exerted great influence on the communities near it, particularly the still-pagan Germanic peoples in northwest Europe and the Frankish kingdom. The influence of English churchmen on the Frankish kingdom in the first half of the eighth century was an important component of the reforms of Pippin III and the triumphs of Charlemagne.

In 668, four years after Whitby, Pope Vitalian consecrated Theodore (d. 690), a native of Tarsus in Asia Minor and part of an exodus of Greek churchmen to seventh-century Italy, as archbishop of Canterbury. Theodore traveled to England with Hadrian, a north African monk, and together they completed the organization of the English church into dioceses. They also encouraged the development of monasteries and reaffirmed the close connection between England and Rome. Learned men both, Theodore and Hadrian established a series of monastic schools that became the best in western Europe.

The widowed Anglo-Saxon noblewoman Hild, a contemporary of Theodore and Hadrian and the founder of the abbey of Whitby in 657, gave learning and study a major role in the monastery at Whitby and in other ecclesiastical centers her influence reached.

Study of the Scriptures was, of course, the focus of monastic and cathedral schools, but in addition it constituted a framework for the preservation of the liberal arts. It also influenced the devotional lives of those who knew no Latin. Hild patronized the first known poet in vernacular English, Cædmon. Under her patronage, Cædmon produced Old English poems on religious topics, thereby bridging one of the gaps between the literary Latin culture of ecclesiastics and some nobles and the oral, vernacular culture of Christian lay people.

The influence of these individuals is seen in the next generation of ecclesiastical leaders, particularly in the careers of Benedict Biscop and Wilfrid of Ripon. Benedict Biscop was born around 628 and spent his youth in the service of King Oswy of Northumbria. At about the time he turned twenty-five, Benedict left royal service, distributed his property, and undertook a pilgrimage to Rome. He traveled with Wilfrid of Ripon, another wealthy young noble who became a controversial and influential churchman. Benedict made five pilgrimages to Rome during his life, and he traveled to monastic communities on the Continent, where he observed different customs and took monastic vows himself. He was in Rome when Theodore was made archbishop of Canterbury, and he accompanied Theodore back to England. Benedict founded a monastery in Northumbria at Wearmouth in 673, and a second monastery at nearby Jarrow a few years later. Under the abbacy of Ceolfrid, another Northumbrian nobleman who left secular life to become a monk, the two monasteries founded by Benedict Biscop exerted spiritual and intellectual influences as far away as Ireland and the Continent.

The extraordinary intellectual and spiritual vitality of late-seventh-century England is exemplified by the careers of Aldhelm and Bede. Aldhelm was born around 640, and studied with the Irish teacher Maeldubh until he was about thirty. He then went to Canterbury and studied under Abbot Hadrian, acquiring great learning and proficiency in Greek and some Hebrew. Around 675, following the death of Maeldubh, Aldhelm was elected abbot of the small monastic community that had grown up around Maeldubh, which became the abbey of Malmesbury, long an important monastic community. In 705, when the diocese of Wessex was divided, Aldhelm became bishop of the western part, at Sherborne. He died around 709. Throughout his life, he produced literary works of considerable learning in an extremely ornate and difficult Latin style. Poems, letters, and theological treatises flowed from his pen, and his career suggests the high level of ecclesiastical culture that characterized England in the late seventh century.

Bede (ca. 673–735) was born a few miles from Benedict Biscop's monasteries of Wearmouth and Jarrow, which he entered as a small boy around 679. He spent his entire life at Jarrow, chiefly as a teacher of young monks, and most of his literary works were pedagogical. He wrote, around 701 or 702, an essay on versification, as well as other works introducing students to the technical problems of the primarily literary subjects that they studied. Bede later wrote two longer works on chronology, the science of coordinating ecclesiastical calendars with astronomical observation, as well as many biblical commentaries and lives of saints. His greatest work, however, and one of the greatest histories ever written, was his *Ecclesiastical History of the English People,* which he completed in 731.

Bede consciously shaped a unified history of the English people within the framework of England's conversion to Christianity. But Bede's England is also Roman, and the figure of Gregory the Great, whom Bede calls the "apostle" of the English, clearly dominates the early part of the history, which preserves many of Gregory's original letters to the members of the English mission. From the early martyrdoms, through Saint Augustine's mission, to the portrait of Oswald of Northumbria as the ideal Christian king, Bede's *History* is a remarkable intellectual document. The level of learning achieved by Bede in a life spent at a small monastery in a remote part of "an island set beyond the world" was nearly equalled elsewhere in England during his lifetime—at the monasteries of Hexham, Ripon, Malmesbury, Canterbury, and York. This cultural revolution may be considered the basis of the first European culture. It is reflected in the epithet that Boniface applied to Bede later in the eighth century—*candela ecclesiae*, "the light within the Church."

The society of England between the arrival of Augustine of Canterbury in 596 and the death of Bede in 735, was divided into a number of kingdoms descended more or less from the leaders who had conquered sub-Roman Britain by the early sixth century. In the kingdom of Kent, where Augustine landed and began the conversion of the south, the archaeological evidence shows a willingness to adapt older British arts and crafts, while its literary records indicate that it had extensive contact with the Franks in Gaul. The wife of Æthelberht, king of Kent, for example, was the Frankish princess Bertha (above, Chapter 06). At least one Kentish bishop attended a mid seventh-century Frankish Church council.

Letters of Gregory the Great and later bishops of Rome to the kings of Kent and other kingdoms in Britain reflect the progressively successful clerical and lay attempt to turn pagan kingship into a Christian office with predominantly moral and legal responsibilities. This became a powerful theme in the later writings of Bede and other Anglo-Saxon churchmen. Æthelberht also issued a code of laws for his kingdom, the first laws written in a European vernacular language—Old English. Although not all of Æthelberht's successors subscribed to Gregory's ideals, the history of a number of English kingdoms in the seventh and eighth centuries is marked by close cooperation of rulers and churchmen, and the literary sources, particularly Bede's *History,* regard this collaboration as essential to the stability of the kingdoms.

Like the contemporary and later laws of the Franks, Æthelberht's Kentish laws and later English legal collections reflect special concerns with the security of ecclesiastical property rights, violent acts, and trade. In these laws, wergild reflects the higher status of the noble, and the later laws of Ine of Wessex (688–694) recognize three or four levels of society below the king, each indicated by the amount of wergild that must be paid for killing a person at each level. Other offenses besides killing also reflect different social ranks. The breaking of a promise of surety, or the breaking of protective rights over women (the English version of *mundium*) also were graded according to the status of the victim.

The highest status in the English kingdoms after the kings were the ranks of *ealdorman* and *thegn*. The *ealdorman* was a royal officer, apparently responsible for much local government and military service, progressively bound closer to the kings in the late eighth and ninth centuries. The *thegn* was originally a servant, but as in other kingdoms, the term was gradually transformed into the designation of an official who possessed respectable wealth and was responsible for some military matters and the maintenance of the peace, and took a leadership role in local assemblies.

Below the *earldorman* and the *thegn* were the free *ceorl* and the merchant. Members of both these latter groups could achieve *thegn* status if they acquired enough wealth and property. Throughout free society the kin-group was an important element in social structure, particularly in raising compensation, or *wergild*, and in pursuing the feud against enemies of the kin. Along with the ties of blood and responsibility that connected members of the kin-group, there also existed the ties that bound leaders and their followers. Much early English literature deals in one way or another with the rituals, responsibilities, and heroic ideals of the fighting group of leaders and followers, and one stunning lament, *The Wanderer,* is written from the point of view of a warrior who has lost his lord and has failed to find another.

In the late seventh and eighth centuries, the most powerful of the kingdoms in Britain were those of Northumbria, Mercia, and Wessex. Offa, king of Mercia (757–796), was the first ruler in the island to call himself "king of the English." Although Offa was a powerful ruler, his claim was premature. Bede had envisaged the English as a single people, but not a single kingdom, and not until the early tenth century could a single king make the plausible claim to be king of the English (below, Chapter 9).

The influence of Benedict Biscop, Wilfrid of Ripon, and Bede made Northumbria the most productive literary and cultural region in northwest Europe. But the work of Aldhelm and his successors in Wessex and Theodore's successors at Canterbury was also important. Under the archbishops Egbert (abp. 735–766), Ælberht (abp. 767–780), and Eanbald I (abp. 780–796), an important school developed at York, whose most famous alumnus was Alcuin (ca. 735–804). The most influential of all Charlemagne's advisers, Alcuin was the chief transmitter of Anglo-Saxon culture to the Frankish royal court. Alcuin's *Poem on the Bishops, Kings, and Saints of the Church of York* is a brilliant description of the region and the school, its history, and his gratitude for its teaching.

Although the ideals of rulership preached from Gregory the Great to Bede and Alcuin did not always direct the organization of English society, they, helped shape significant changes in English society from the seventh century through the tenth, and constituted an influential presence during a critical moment in Frankish political history.

PIPPIN'S REVOLUTION: THE LAST OF THE LONG-HAIRED KINGS

The rise of the the family of Charles Martel and its Austrasian noble supporters in the Frankish kingdom in the late seventh and early eighth centuries coincided with a vigorous missionary movement on the Continent launched by English churchmen. Their primary purpose was to convert the still-pagan Germanic peoples in Frisia, Saxony, and Thuringia. Their secondary purpose was to reform the Frankish church. In the event, they also provided unexpected support for the new dynasty of Charles Martel.

The power of Charles Martel and his sons Pippin and Carloman was not unlimited. Rival families and factions, with their kin-related bishops and abbots of family monasteries, and hostile historical accounts like *The Book of the History of the Franks*, as well as some saints' lives, reveal stiff opposition to the dominance of the Pippinids. This opposition was expressed in extensive warfare, and in the course of that warfare, Charles attacked both lay and clerical enemies, confiscating (sometimes temporarily) church lands in order to support the larger armies he needed to raise. In the face of such opposition, some of it from enemy bishops and sainted (one historian has termed them "self-sanctified") aristocratic opponents, Charles Martel needed an alternative source of ecclesiastical support, and he increasingly turned to the missionaries from England. Charles also faced the problem of some regions having made themselves more independent during the period when he was consolidating his power. Some territories, like Aquitaine, Brittany, and Bavaria, had long asserted distinctive identities and a sense of independence. Others, particularly Frisia (the modern Benelux countries), with its access to the North Sea, had slipped into and out of Frankish control for several centuries. And it was in Frisia and Bavaria that some of the earliest Irish and Anglo-Saxon missionaries began to work. Frisia had long been important to the Franks, and under Dagobert I the bishopric of Utrecht had been established to further the Frisians' conversion to Christianity. The process took just over a century.

In 690, Willibrord (658–739), a student of Wilfrid of Ripon, asked permission from the bishop of Rome, Sergius I, to evangelize the Frisians. But Willibrord also needed Frankish aristocratic support for the mission, which he received from Pippin II and his son, Charles Martel. Willibrord had considerable success, even managing to ordain several native Frisians as clergy.

In 718, a monk from Wessex, Winfrid, also undertook a mission to convert pagans on the Continent. In 719, he went to Rome to receive approval of his mission from the pope, and during that visit, the pope seems to have changed Winfrid's unpronounceable English name to Boniface. Between 719 and 722, Boniface worked in Frisia, Bavaria, Thuringia, and on the edges of Saxony. His most memorable and dramatic accomplishment was the destruction of a Saxon shrine, the sacred oak tree at Geismar, in 722 or 723. In turn, he built a chapel dedicated to Saint Peter from the wood of the fallen tree. In 722, he went once more to Rome, where he was made bishop. He became an archbishop in 739 and ended his life as archbishop of Mainz. At the pope's recommendation, he received the protection of Charles Martel, thus strengthening the new link between the Pippinids and the popes. During the next several years, Boniface's independence, his sharp criticism of the Frankish higher clergy, and the hostility of the Frankish clergy often blocked his attempts at missionary work and church reform. Nevertheless, under Charles Martel's sons, Pippin III and Carloman, an alliance between the English missionaries and the Frankish mayors of the palace was firmly forged. In 742, Boniface presided over the first of the reform councils of the Frankish church, where his denunciation of the worldliness of Frankish aristocratic bishops probably reflects his own (and English bishops' generally) monastic perspective. In 744, Boniface established the important monastery of Fulda. In 746, with Pippin's blessing, the Frankish bishops sent a series of ecclesiastical questions to Rome, and in 747, Pippin and the Frankish aristocracy sent a declaration of faith to Rome.

Turning to his Frisian mission late in life, Boniface was killed in a pirate attack in 753. After his death, he was revered as the "apostle to the Germans." He had called himself *exul Germanicus*—"the exile in Germany." Missionary and reformer, Boniface brought to the Continent a sense of proper ecclesiastical order and secular religious responsibility, as well as the link to Rome that contributed to the shaping of the kingdom of the Franks after Pippin's revolution and throughout the life and reign of Charlemagne. Nearly one hundred letters by, to, and about him survive, as well as a *Life of Boniface,* written by his disciple Willibald.

In 751, Pippin III, son of Charles Martel and mayor of the palace of both Neustria and Austrasia, placed the last Merovingian king of the Franks in a monastery and ascended the Frankish throne in his place. To effect his revolution, which had immense consequences in Western political history, Pippin used his own power, an alliance with some of the Frankish aristocracy, his relationship with Boniface, and his new relationship to Rome. The association between the new Frankish ruler Pippin III and the English missionaries contributed several important elements to the new conception of kingship. A chronicle entry gives what became the "official" version of Pippin's revolutionary act:

> *Burghard, Bishop of Wurzburg, and the chaplain Fulrad of St. Denis were sent by Pippin to Pope Zachary to ask him about the kings in Frankland, who at that time had no royal power. Was this right or not? Pope Zachary replied to Pippin that it was better for the man who had power to be called king rather than one who remained without royal power, and, to avoid a disturbance of the right ordering of things, he commanded by apostolic authority that Pippin should become king.*

The seeming naturalness of this text must not cloud its genuinely revolutionary character. Pippin invoked ecclesiastical support at the highest level to deny Merovingian claims to kingship by blood right. His supporters devised a new kind of liturgical ceremony to make him king. He consulted the pope in a matter about which no pope—or any churchman—had ever been consulted before. In short, Pippin applied to the archaic dynastic form of Frankish kingship the very ideals that earlier Frankish kings and bishops had helped to create, but with an intensity that they had never foreseen.

A near-contemporary account suggests the diverse elements he and his supporters combined to create the new model monarchy of the Franks: "Pippin was a pious king . . . raised to the throne by the authority and order of Pope Zacharias . . . by anointing with the holy chrism at the hands of the blessed bishops [and] by the choice of the Franks." No longer did simple blood right and long hair make a Frankish king, but energy and zeal for the welfare of his people and his church. If he is indifferent to power, dissipates wealth, and neglects his people's spiritual welfare, he loses his title to legitimacy. Much of the interpretation of the history of the Merovingian dynasty derives from Pippin's and later Carolingian propagandists' smearing of the reputations of the last long-haired kings. Only recently has that reputation begun to be restored.

THE ARTICULATION AND EXPANSION
OF FRANKISH POWER

From the reign of Pippin (r. 751–768) to that of Charles the Bald (r. 843–877), the Carolingian kings of the Franks stabilized and increased the monarchy's resources and expanded Frankish power throughout Europe on a scale not seen since the days of Roman expansion. Within half a century the Franks controlled all of western Europe except for the British Isles, most of the Iberian peninsula, and southern Italy. Their frontiers marched against those of the pagan Frisians, Saxons, Danes, Balts, northern and southern Slavic peoples, Christian Greece, and Muslim Spain. The immediate driving force behind this expansion was the Frankish army, but the organization of the kingdom by Pippin and his son Charlemagne (748–814) played an equally important role. From their reorganization of the royal household, which they grandly called the "royal palace," to their institution of counts and dukes as royal representatives throughout the kingdom, and their patronage and support of the Frankish church, the kings reshaped the political order of Frankish society.

Among the royal resources available to govern the kingdom, the greatest was land. The income, often in food and goods, that the land produced supported the king, his household, and his officials. In order to obtain the regular services of the nobility, the king granted lifetime tenure of part of the royal lands to those who served him. When the person so rewarded was a bishop, the lands and income he received were called the *epsicopatus*. When the servant was a count, these were called the *comitatus*.

The count (*comes*, or *grafio*) was the essential unit of royal administration outside the household itself. Counts had existed under the Merovingians, and in old Roman territories they had come to control the former public services and sources of income of those districts known as *civitates* that had become the property of the Frankish king. They combined the functions of judge, provincial governor, military commander, court clerk, and royal representative. Under the later Merovingians, many counts had assimilated their royal duties and resources to their own personal and family property, thus alienating much of the royal wealth. Under Pippin and Charlemagne the counts were controlled more effectively. They were made to serve in areas where they had no personal connections, their offices ceased to be heritable by their children, and their duties were spelled out in directive after directive issued by the royal court. Traveling circuit inspectors called the *missi dominici* ("those sent by the king") reviewed the counts' activities and corrected them when necessary. Charlemagne also made the counts work harder, especially in administering the law courts and assembling their local contingents of soldiers and supplies for the army campaigns of the summer. The counts had small staffs of assistants, including the *vicecomes*, or viscount, and the *scabini*, or *judices*, men learned in the law. But the count, like the king, worked out of a household rather than an office.

Although the system of administering the kingdom by counts (and in particularly troublesome places by margraves and dukes, counts with increased powers and resources) is clear enough in theory, it had many shortcomings, even under Charlemagne. Ideally, the system would have required around 2500 officials, including at least 600 counts, to operate efficiently, but it is doubtful that Charlemagne ever assembled nearly that many. Many of the ills that had plagued Merovingian governance could only be checked, not overcome. Long distances, the tendency of counts to localize themselves, the inefficiency of supervision and communications—all worked to reduce efficiency, and the kings often reiterated their demands that loyalty be the count's primary virtue.

Fidelity—and its opposite, treachery and breaking faith—dominate the literature of the ninth century. As early as 779, Charlemagne insisted that oaths sworn on sacred objects be made only to the king, and he repeated a demand for oaths to himself from all his subjects in the first years of the ninth century. The limitations of the ethical world of both royal servants and subjects are shown nowhere more clearly than in the constant emphasis on personal loyalty to the king. The Carolingian record of Pippin's revolution emphasizes that the pope had released Pippin from the oath of loyalty he had made to the king whom he deposed. Later citations of the deposition in canon law continued to emphasize the release from the obligations of the oath, even when they mention little else about the event. One of the most remarkable examples of ethical literature in the generation following Charlemagne was the *Manual,* written for her son by Dhuoda, a Frankish noblewoman in Aquitaine. The *Manual* focuses on the ideal of manners and piety in a youth of high rank, but Dhuoda's greatest emphasis falls on the obligation of loyalty to God and the king. Personal loyalty and disloyalty are themes that run through European society for centuries. As late as the thirteenth century, treason itself was understood chiefly in terms of personal disloyalty to a lord to whom one had taken an oath of allegiance.

Out of these limited resources and on the tenuous foundations of personal oaths of loyalty, the Carolingian rulers of the Franks built their extensive kingdom. Its fabric consisted of the church and the palace household, the local courts, the *scabini,* the vicars, and the counts. The great frontier lords were conceived as a kind of supercount, and the seven marches that they ruled—Spain, Brittany, Bavaria, Pannonia, Friuli, Nordgau, and Swabia—guarded the edges of the expanding kingdom. Through these territories traveled the king's *missi,* his household servants, ecclesiastical officials going back and forth to Rome, pilgrims, and strangers.

The new and insistent tone of the Frankish king's ecclesiastical mission makes the ecclesiastical reforms under Pippin and Charlemagne an illuminating aspect of the character of Carolingian kingship. The divisions of ecclesiastical administration created in the last years of imperial rule in the Roman West had virtually disappeared by the late seventh century. Episcopal offices were left vacant for long periods, fell under the control of powerful noble families, or were given to royal relatives and favorites often without consideration of personal qualifications or the ecclesiastical legality of their elections. The ecclesiastical reforms urged by Boniface changed the course of the Frankish church in the late eighth century, but the power of Pippin and Charlemagne prevented the Church's establishment of an autonomous hierarchy. Part of the royal mission was the assumption of responsibility for a Christian people, and the Carolingians retained considerable power in the matter of ecclesiastical appointments. The reorganization of the Church, however, was now sponsored powerfully by the kings themselves, and the restoration of the old archbishoprics, the creation of new ones, the subordination of bishops to their metropolitans and of local clergy to bishops, and the frequency of ecclesiastical synods and councils contributed to the restoration of administrative order within the Frankish church, and constituted simultaneously a new kind of organized support for the king. Not only were older sees reconstituted, but new ones were founded, and some, like Salzburg in 798, were raised to metropolitan status. This vigorous, newly organized episcopate, many of whose members were drawn from the greatest families of the kingdom, became one of the strongest supports of the monarchy and eventually, a nearly independent group in the complex ecclesiastical and political atmosphere of Charlemagne's son and successor, Louis (r. 814–842).

Besides the bishoprics, Pippin and Charlemagne restored and enriched the monasteries of Gaul and founded new ones in other parts of their territory. The monasteries, whose reform was continued brilliantly through the reign of Louis, provided the norms of religious life in the rough Frankish kingdom, personnel for royal service, scribes, advisers, and allies to the ruling dynasty. Such monasteries as St. Denis, near Paris, Corbie and its daughter house to the east, Corvey, St. Gall in Switzerland, Echternach (founded by Willibrord), and especially St. Martin at Tours are the best-known of Charlemagne's day. Under Louis' ecclesiastical adviser, Benedict of Aniane, the influence of the Benedictine rule grew much greater in the Frankish kingdom.

The internal stability created by the king's use of counts and dukes, bishops and abbots, enabled Pippin, and still more Charlemagne, to turn to the expansion of the kingdom. The frontiers moved slowly outward toward Spain, Italy, Germany, the Slavic lands, the Low Countries, and Scandinavia. Territories that had been in the kingdom but had continually proved restive whenever a crisis troubled the royal authority—areas such as Aquitaine, Bavaria, and Brittany—received particular royal attention, and the commanders of the marches were in a state of almost continuous military preparedness. The Carolingian kings also developed the ability to conduct different military operations on different fronts at the same time. During the period 752–759, Pippin fought both the Lombards in Italy and the Arabs in Septimania in far southern Gaul. Later, kings were often recalled from one area of military activity in order to quell a local rebellion or defend another frontier from invaders. The ability of Pippin and his successors to repeatedly raise armies and wage war, sometimes on two fronts simultaneously, and sometimes in serial campaigns in different parts of the kingdom in the same year, was one sign of the increasing political control of the dynasty.

The driving mechanism of Frankish expansion was the 8000-man military force that the Frankish kings could assemble every spring, after a winter's military planning. The army consisted primarily of infantry, well armed and highly disciplined, and some cavalry, wearing mailed coats and helmets and armed with sword and spear. Depending on the area of campaigning, some parts of the kingdom contributed more fighting men, some less, from year to year.

After putting down local revolts in Aquitaine, Brittany, and Bavaria, Pippin and then Charlemagne directed Frankish power primarily toward Spain, Germany, and Italy. In 778, Charlemagne entered Spain. His failure to take Saragossa became the kernel for the epic poem *The Song of Roland,* but he captured Gerona in 785 and Barcelona in 801–803. In addition, he established the Spanish March, a durable enclave of Frankish power south of the Pyrenees that protected the frontier against the Muslim forces to the south.

The conquest of the Saxons proved to be Charlemagne's longest and most costly campaign. The nobles from the eastern parts of the kingdom and the missionary churches along the eastern border had long faced the power of this Germanic people settled between the Elbe and the North Sea. Small groups of Saxons had migrated into the Frankish kingdom in the fourth century, and some had migrated to Britain in the fifth. The Saxons were really a group of peoples, having no single leader or ruler, and some of them had served in earlier Frankish armies. The most important Saxon settlements, however, were east of the Rhine, where some Saxon groups were tributary to the Franks. But Saxon hostility sharpened in the early eighth century, at the same time as a number of other tributary peoples asserted their independence from Frankish hegemony. The Saxons also remained pagan, although the nature of their practices is not well known, and religious differences exacerbated the political tensions created by Saxon expansion toward Austrasia and Frankish resistance. In the first of his campaigns against them in 772, Charlemagne destroyed an important Saxon shrine called the *Irminsul* and despoiled it of its considerable treasure. But defeating one group of Saxons did not entail the conquest of all the Saxons. Charlemagne directed a substantial campaign into Saxony virtually every year between 772 and 785. Frankish victories were followed by Saxon rebellions, and Charlemagne's early policy of forcing Saxons to convert to Christianity helped to maintain their resistance. By 804, however, Charlemagne was able to add the vast territories of Saxony to his domain and to adopt a more moderate and systematic campaign to instill Christianity among them. The fall of Saxony made it easier for Charlemagne's armies to overcome Frisian resistance in the Low Countries, and the conquest of these two areas brought Charlemagne's borders to the base of the Jutland peninsula and face to face with the Danes.

To the southeast, Charlemagne defeated Tassilo, duke of the Bavarians, in 787 and incorporated his realm into the Carolingian kingdom. The conquest of Bavaria led Charlemagne to Carinthia, and thereby into the affairs of the southern Slavs and the Avars. The Avars, as we have seen, entered the Danube valley in the sixth century, divided the Slavs and incorporated many of them into their kingdom, and participated in the great assault on Constantinople in 626. Their military capabilities had been considerably reduced by the late eighth century, however. Charlemagne's armies destroyed their capital, the *Ring*, in 796, removing the great, centuries-old accumulation of Avar treasure to Aachen and causing the Avars, like the earlier Huns, to disappear from history.

The military successes of the reign were not the only manifestations of Frankish royal power. Since Charlemagne based his rule on his acknowledged sense of obligation to maintain a Christian society pleasing to God, he regarded his internal legislation as a form of *correctio*—a returning of morals and behavior to idealized traditional Christian practices. Earlier Frankish church councils in the eighth century, and several of the advisers of Pippin—Chrodegang of Metz, for example, and Fulrad of the monastery of St. Denis—had accelerated this process. Charlemagne continued it by issuing collections of royal legislation, called *capitularies* (collections of legislation divided into *capitula*—chapters), the first of which, the Capitulary of Herstal in 779, dealt primarily with the obligations of clergy. The next major capitulary, the *Admonitio generalis* ("The General Notification") of 789, was a much more ambitious and comprehensive program addressed to clergy and laity alike. A letter of the same period from Charlemagne to Abbot

Charlemagne's Palace Chapel at Aachen. Borrowed from a Roman church at Ravenna, the design for this chapel (now a part of Aachen cathedral) suggests visually Charlemagne's heightened sense of Christian rulership. (Ann Munchow Fotografin)

Baugulf of Fulda called *De litteris colendis* ("On the Cultivation of Letters") lays out a program of the ecclesiastical responsibility to teach all in the kingdom who were capable of learning.

THE CAROLINGIAN RENEWAL

Charlemagne accompanied his successes as a king and a warrior by a heightened conception of himself as having a divinely ordained mission that included responsibility for the quality of spiritual as well as temporal life. This was hardly a new idea among Christian rulers, but Charlemagne pursued it with an intensity of purpose and backed it with such extensive resources that it became a fundamental component of all subsequent conceptions of Christian rulership. The quality of spiritual life turned upon the quality of the clergy, and Charlemagne's clerical reforms gave rise to a vigorous Latin literary and artistic culture often called the Carolingian renaissance, but perhaps more properly designated the Carolingian renewal. Charlemagne's first steps were to continue his family's patronage of Frankish church reform and to secure accurate texts of essential items of Christian literature—the Bible, canon law, a reliable sacramentary, and the Benedictine rule. From this essentially practical emphasis on proper learning for the purpose of improving the intellectual and moral quality of the clergy, there quickly grew up active book-producing centers that copied the works of classical writers as well as those of church fathers, borrowing books to copy from Spain, Italy, Ireland, and England and, in turn, circulating copies to other monastic and episcopal centers. It is not intellectual profundity or originality, but the sheer volume of book production in the late eighth and early ninth centuries that characterizes the reigns of Charlemagne and Louis as critical in the intellectual history of Europe.

The Carolingian literary renaissance was marked not only by the increasing circulation and standardization of basic Christian literature, but also by striking changes in the techniques of book production, particularly decoration and handwriting. Book covers of jewels and precious metals adorned the most important sacred writings. A new and much more easily legible form of handwriting, the Carolingian minuscule, replaced the irregular and difficult-to-read Merovingian script, and durable vellum and parchment replaced papyrus. The organization of the scriptoria (writing rooms) of the monasteries included the selection of works to be copied, the assignment of works to copyists, and the training and supervision of new scribes. The head of the monastic scriptorium became an important figure in the monastery and not uncommonly, when the abbot himself happened to be a learned man, produced literary works whose importance cannot be overestimated. The Carolingian bishops constituted administrative and disciplinary support for the new Frankish monarchy, and the abbots of the major monasteries constituted its intellectual and literary complement. In order to promote these intellectual reforms, Charlemagne developed the palace school, transforming an older institution for the training of young boys into an academy where literary learning and other forms of training were combined under the watchful care of the king himself and the scholars he brought to court.

Carolingian scholars' search for authentic texts of fundamental documents had important consequences. The *Dionysio-Hadriana*, the collection of ecclesiastical law sent to Charlemagne by Pope Hadrian I in 774, became the foundation for later collections of canon law. The copy of the Roman Sacramentary that the king received in 786 became the foundation for Continental liturgical practice. The copy of the rule of Benedict that Charlemagne ordered from Monte Cassino in 787 became the basis for the monastic reforms of the next several centuries. Charlemagne charged Alcuin with revising the standard Latin text of the Bible.

The Carolingian choice of the Rule of Benedict had momentous consequences. It gave most of Latin monasticism a single pattern to observe, and it brought into the mainstream of European thought and sensibility one of the most remarkable influences they ever experienced. The rule of Benedict differed from earlier monastic rules in several ways. First, most eastern monastic rules were aimed at the individual monk, whereas Benedict's was directed at the monastic community. Second, many early rules were noted for their ruthless breaking of the human spirit by a rigid pattern of self-denial; Benedict's rule struck a remarkable balance between penitential discipline and human relations within the community. Third, many earlier rules reflected their regions of origin; Benedict's rule is clearly patterned on the needs of Latin Christians in general and reveals strong traditional Roman influences. Finally, many earlier rules were aimed at cultivating an exotic piety that frequently exceeded human endurance; Benedict's rule aimed at shaping the devotional life of the monk within the context of an organized community, carefully and conscientiously administered by its leader, the abbot, and intended to keep the monk from falling into vices rather than cultivating devotional excesses.

The chief emphasis in Benedict's rule is on the cornerstone of monastic life: the vows of poverty, chastity, and obedience. The individual monk owns nothing, is celibate, and gives up his individual autonomy to the community under the abbot. Thus prepared, the monk, by living a temperate life characterized by a balance of contemplation, prayer in community, and manual labor, could avoid some of the extremes of eccentric behavior that were sometimes encouraged by other rules. By setting the monk's sights toward a less rigorous, but more achievable level of self-discipline, Benedict prevented the despair that individual hermits or extreme asectic communities experienced when they could not live up to their often unrealistic expectations.

The Rule of Benedict is as important a document in the history of psychology as it is in the history of religion. It shows considerable concern for what today we would call the monk's personality. Its main thrust is toward a kind of psychological conditioning, dependent upon a careful balance of different kinds of activity, sensible dietary regulations, and strict but charitable discipline. Regularity, consistency, order—these are the keys of Benedictine monasticism. The earliest use of the concept of "revolution" in modern Western thought, in fact, comes from this monastic environment. Here it meant, not social disorder or reversal, but the repetition day after day of the same patterns of monastic devotional life. Indeed, one reason for the later success of the Benedictine rule may have been that it helped create the most stable personalities in the West between the sixth and the eighth centuries.

Charlemagne sought out scholars from the far reaches of his empire and beyond. Peter of Pisa and Paulinus of Aquileia, both grammarians, and Paul the Deacon, the historian of the Lombards and of the church of Metz, all came from Lombard Italy in the 770s and 780s. Theodulf of Orleans was a Visigoth. Dicuil, the geographer, and Dungal, the astronomer, came from Ireland. The man associated most closely with the Carolingian renaissance, Alcuin of York, was intellectually a product of the great growth of learning in England in the late seventh and eighth centuries. On a trip to Rome in the service of the archbishop of York, he met Charlemagne at Parma in 781 and was invited to the king's court. From the 780s to 796, Alcuin was Charlemagne's major ecclesiastical adviser and perhaps the most influential scholar in the kingdom. His influence can be seen in the intellectual tradition of his students who became teachers and abbots in the great ninth-century monasteries. For twenty years the most powerful ruler in the West and this individual who, probably more than anyone else, was his guide and consultant on the most important intellectual issues of his day, shared an extraordinarily close relationship.

In 793, Einhard (770–840), a young layman from the Main valley, came to Charlemagne's court, participated in its intellectual and administrative life, and much later, after Charlemagne's death, paid the king the tribute of writing his biography, the first biography of a layman in many centuries. Although much of Einhard's style and approach derived from Roman and later Latin sources, his portrait of Charlemagne is invaluable. In it one can see a semiliterate Frankish prince, a second-generation king who rose from a coup d'état of doubtful legitimacy, dressing and acting much like those around him, fond of hunting and baths and fighting, but abstemious in food and drink. One can see something more, too. Something in Charlemagne's imagination made him view his conquests and power as more than private acquisitions. With his conquests there grew in him a mighty sense of personal responsibility for the lives and the souls of his subjects. The legacy of this vision influenced the thought of Europe for centuries to come. Warrior and king, Charlemagne was also Christian Europe's first great lay patron of religion and the arts, and perhaps its first political idealist.

Some of Charlemagne's intellectual legacy is tangible. Around 8000 manuscripts survive from the late eighth and ninth centuries, and many more are known to have been produced. These books are usually clearly written—many of them in the new style of handwriting called the Carolingian minuscule, which spread throughout Europe in the ninth century—usually well edited, brilliantly illuminated, and sturdily made. They consist not only of the expected ecclesiastical treatises, saints' lives, and chronicles, but also of the work of earlier Latin writers, many from the classical period. Under Charlemagne, the system of dating from the Incarnation of Christ, the modern C.E. system, was patronized by the royal court in official documents and by chroniclers in recording significant events in annals and chronicles.

Two examples may suggest the range of the revival of learning under Charlemagne. In the first half of the ninth century, several collections of Church law appeared that are known to have been forgeries. The most famous of these is the collection called Pseudo-Isidore. Many of them purported to contain documents as old as the second and third centuries. Although they were forgeries, the skill of those who made them, the wide range of ideas they contain, and their sheer bulk testify to the technical and intellectual abilities even of the forgers, themselves a product of the Carolingian renaissance. Many of the documents they skillfully fabricated played a prominent part for centuries in European intellectual history.

A second indicator of the renewal of learning is the degree of sophistication found in the theological disputes of the ninth century. On several occasions, Frankish churchmen and the king asserted their own religious orthodoxy against what they considered the heterodox opinions of others. One instance of this was their rejection of Adoptionism, a Spanish Christian view that Christ had merely "adopted" human nature. Another was the great debate over the validity of religious images, a Frankish component of the great Byzantine debates over iconoclasm. One of the most prominent participants in later debates in the ninth century was the Irish scholar John Scotus Eriugena, who taught at the court of Charlemagne's grandson, Charles the Bald, knew Greek, and translated the important sixth-century treatise *On the Celestial Hierarchies* by Pseudo-Dionysius, into Latin. Carolingian theological disputes ranged from the nature of the sacrament of the eucharist to predestination, reflecting the continuing influence of Carolingian educational reforms in the monastic and court schools through most of the ninth century.

And the Carolingians also built—between 768 and 855, they built seven cathedrals, 232 monasteries, and sixty-five royal residences, including Charlemagne's ambitious palace complex at Aachen. The Carolingian intellectual and artistic renaissance played as important a role in European history as the political and military achievements of the eighth-century Franks.

THE "KINGDOM OF EUROPE" AND THE EMPIRE OF THE ROMANS

Around 776, the Anglo-Saxon monk Cathwulf referred to Charlemagne's kingdom as the *Regnum Europae,* "the kingdom of Europe," invoking the obscure Roman geographical designation *Europa* to indicate the breadth of his new power. In the last decades of the century, Charlemagne's relations with the kings of Northumbria and Mercia indicated their deference to him, as did the tribute from the increasingly powerful King Alfonso II of Asturias in northern Spain. Shortly after 780, Empress Irene of Constantinople negotiated with Charlemagne concerning a marriage between his daughter Rotrud and her son Constantine VI. This recognition, along with the embassies from Harun al-Rashid, the caliph of Baghdad, and overtures from the patriarch of Jerusalem, who sent Charlemagne the keys of the city in 800, indicate one level of his position. The prestige of the king of the Franks was greater than that of any other Christian ruler.

Charlemagne's immense prestige and power in northern Europe were also well known to the popes, and during his reign, the link between the Franks and the popes grew considerably stronger. To understand Charlemagne's unique position in papal eyes, we must consider some important crises in papal history during the second half of the eighth century. Of these, the most important were generated by the Lombards and the iconoclastic controversy in Byzantium. From the early eighth century, a restored, ambitious Lombard monarchy, first under Liutprand (712–744) and then under his tough successors Ratchis (744–749) and Aistulf (749–756), moved against the powerful and largely independent Lombard duchies of Spoleto and Benevento, to the east and south of Rome, and against Ravenna itself. The tactical importance of the position of Rome and the weakness of the unsupported Byzantine garrisons in central Italy made the independence of Rome precarious, and when in 751, Aistulf finally captured Ravenna, which for two centuries had been the chief seat of Byzantine imperial power in Italy, he threatened to place Rome under his own authority.

The popes, who were unable and perhaps unwilling to treat with the Lombards, sought allies beyond the Alps. As we have seen, the middle of the eighth century was a period of crisis and instability in many parts of Europe, and the papal approval of Pippin's revolution in 751 drew the bishop of Rome and the king of the Franks closer together. In 754, when the Synod of Heireia pronounced firmly against the cult of images, when only Byzantine emissaries, not troops, were forthcoming from Constantinople, and when Aistulf's forces were threatening Rome more ominously, Pope Stephen II (752–757) made his way to the kingdom of the Franks. There he anointed Pippin again and implored his aid, which he obtained in spite of considerable resistance among the Frankish magnates and Pippin's doubtful security so soon after his revolution. Stephen had also crowned Pippin's sons Carloman and Charles kings in perpetuity, making Pippin *patricius Romanorum,* a title implying the status of special protector of Rome. The relationship between the pope and the king of the Franks—tentatively begun earlier in the century, established firmly by the approval of Pippin's revolution in 751, and cemented by the meeting between Pippin and Stephen II in 754—had enduring consequences, both for the future history of Italy and the papacy and for the concept of Frankish protection of the Latin church. The lands that Pippin guaranteed to the pope comprised large parts of the old Exarchate of Ravenna and the Duchy of Rome. Pippin's donation of these lands, later confirmed by Charlemagne, became the Papal States, a block of territory in central Italy under the direct rule of the bishop of Rome. They played an important part in medieval history and survived until the invasion of Rome in 1870. Not until the papal concordat with the Italian government in 1929, which preserved only the independence of Vatican City, did the popes formally acknowledge the loss of these territories.

Around the middle of the eighth century, perhaps as late as 778, a document began to be cited by papal scribes that had a great bearing on the constitutional history of European Christian society. This document, the *Donation of Constantine,* professed to have been issued in the year 313, in which the Emperor Constantine extended many privileges to the pope and clergy, chiefly in the matter of rank, possessions, and privileges. The most important statement in the document, however, was a passage that could be interpreted as granting rule over the entire western part of the Roman Empire to the bishop of Rome. The document probably was intended to provide independent legitimacy for the Papal States and to shore up the position of the bishop of Rome in the face of Byzantine, Lombard, and Carolingian pressures. Although little used in the eighth and ninth centuries, the Donation became a key document in twelfth-century collections of canon law and a foundation for the claims of some later popes to control the rulers of Europe. Although its authenticity had been doubted since the tenth century, it was not formally disproved until the philological analysis of the scholar Lorenzo Valla in the fifteenth century. The donation of Pippin and the Donation of Constantine both contributed to the strengthened relations between pope and ruler of the Franks in the later eighth century.

Between 754 and 790, the popes ceased sending notification of their election to the emperors at Constantinople and sent it instead to the kings of the Franks. Imperial portraits disappeared from Roman coinage and were replaced with portraits of the issuing popes; popes ceased dating their official documents in terms of imperial reigns, doing so instead in terms of their own pontificates. In spite of continuing Byzantine opposition and Lombard resistance, the popes in the second half of the eighth century reconstituted their territories as a distinctly Latin power and slowly removed the lingering traces of Byzantine imperial authority from central Italy.

By 780, new negotiations appear temporarily to have restored good relations among the pope, Charlemagne, and Byzantium. The Papal States had come into being, and the

Carolingian Empire and Anglo-Saxon England.

extension of Charlemagne's power had brought him not only the kingship of the Lombards but a newer and closer relationship with the pope and a renewed official status in the eyes of Rome and the Roman church. This aspect of the expansion of the Frankish kingdom opened the way not only to a double royal title, "King of the Franks and the Lombards" and the Roman title *Patricius Romanorum,* but also to the idea of a new title appropriate for all of the lands Charlemagne ruled, a renewed imperial title in the west.

We have already seen how Charlemagne's concern with ecclesiastical questions began early in his reign and, if anything, increased markedly toward the end of the century. The 780s witnessed extensive ecclesiastical reforms in the capitularies (ordinances issued by Charlemagne). The first suppression of iconoclasm in Byzantium had taken place in the Council of Nicaea of 787, whose canons, agreed upon by Pope Hadrian I but badly translated into Latin, reached the Frankish kingdom and elicited a complex response written principally by Theodulf of Orleans. This response, the *Libri Carolini,* strongly criticized the iconodule position, challenged the right of Irene, as a woman, to rule the empire, and undercut the claims to universality of imperially sponsored church councils in Constantinople. At the same time, it reiterated the traditional orthodoxy of the Franks, Charlemagne's conversion of infidels, and the traditional ties between the Franks and the pope, the true authority for the determination of orthodox beliefs.

At the Council of Frankfurt in 794, the Carolingian king and high churchmen dealt with the heresy of Adoptionism, a dispute concerning the natures of Christ that reflected a rivalry between the Christian churchmen of Muslim Spain and those in the Christian kingdom to the north. Throughout the 790s, the correspondence of Alcuin, Charlemagne's closest adviser during these years, reflected a great concern for the survival of orthodoxy and the dangers to orthodox belief posed by various movements in Spain and Italy. In 797, Charlemagne issued the *Capitulare Saxonicum,* a broadly conceived and diplomatic approach to a program for the peaceful introduction of Christianity among the Saxons and Slavs, a program very different from the earlier, more brutal policies of Christianization that the king had insisted upon.

From 795 on, another ecclesiastical crisis confronted the king. Pope Leo III (795–816), Hadrian's successor, encountered formidable opposition in Rome, was accused of crimes, and was kidnapped, imprisoned, and brutalized. Both Alcuin and Charlemagne were particularly concerned about the situation of the pope and the consequent welfare of the Church. These ecclesiastical concerns, which show a steady sharpening of Charlemagne's concept of his own role, as well as the influence of articulate advisers, occurred at the same time as the first successes of Carolingian educational reforms and the building of the palace at Aachen, which had been under way since 794 and reflected a new concept of a palace capital for the king. Echoes of the difficulties of both Byzantium and Rome resound in a remarkable letter written by Alcuin to Charlemagne in 799, at the height of the crisis:

> Until now, there have been three men of highest rank in the world. The first is the apostolic sublimity, governing from the throne of the blessed Peter, prince of the apostles, as his vicar. . . . The second is the imperial dignity and power of the other Rome [Constantinople]. . . . The third is the royal dignity which by the dispensation of our Lord Jesus Christ is conferred upon you as the governor of the Christian people.

After remarking on the present weakness of the papacy and the crimes of the empress Irene, he concludes:

> The royal dignity is more excellent than the other dignities in power, more shining in wisdom, more sublime in rank. Now on you alone rests the tottering safety of the churches of Christ. It is for you to avenge crimes, to guide the erring, to console the sorrowing, and to raise up the good.

In Alcuin's view at least, Charlemagne, the just king, must now act alone and imperially.

Pope Leo was kidnapped by his Roman enemies in April of 799, but he escaped and made his way to Charlemagne at Paderborn. In November 800, Charlemagne arrived outside Rome and was greeted by the pope with the ceremonial procedures appropriate for an imperial entrance into the city. In December, Leo cleared himself of all charges by a unilateral oath of purgation (swearing that he was innocent of the charges against him, but technically prosecuted by no one), and the ensuing synod that he held seems to have decided to make Charlemagne emperor, possibly at the urging of Frankish clerics then present. On the evening of December 25, 800, following the third mass of Christmas, Pope Leo placed a crown on Charlemagne's head and declared him emperor of the Romans. The imperial *laudes* (formal prayers for the emperor) were chanted, and the pope prostrated himself in the *proskynesis* (ritual prostration) before the emperor.

The coronation, acclamation, and public veneration of Charlemagne as emperor of the Romans has long vexed historians as a problem of interpretation. Its primary sources consist of texts that themselves describe liturgical acts. These acts contained meaning for those who performed them and for those who witnessed them or heard them described. From late antiquity, the public life of the empire had been conducted according to an increasingly elaborate ceremonial, and from the fourth century on, that ceremonial had acquired a liturgical dimension, including participation by the clergy. Such ceremonial influenced the early Germanic kingdoms, from that of the Visigoths in Spain to those of Anglo-Saxon England and Francia as well. In addition, imperial inauguration ceremonies existed in the East Roman Empire. In Charlemagne's world—and for long after—many basic political ideas were expressed through ceremony and the verbal, musical, and pictorial representation of ceremony rather than through explicit texts of law or political theory. Significant stages in human life—marriage, birth, coming of age, entering one state of life or another, coronation and formal visits (*adventus*) in the case of kings, and death were all accompanied by rituals whose meaning was understood by all concerned. The coronation of Charlemagne was part of that process of the ritual expression of significant sacramental, social, and political stages of life that characterized Europe from late antiquity until early modern times.

The ritual order of Charlemagne's coronation differed from that of contemporary Byzantine rulers. In Constantinople, the ruler-to-be was first acclaimed by the Senate and the army (originally in a military camp), then crowned by the patriarch (originally in a palace or public square, later in the Church of Hagia Sophia), and finally was publicly "worshiped" by the people in the ritual of *proskynesis*. In Charlemagne's case, the coronation by Leo III preceded the acclamation (the imperial *laudes* that were chanted by Romans and Franks together in St. Peter's basilica). These were followed by the *proskynesis*, which was performed only by Leo III himself. From 801 on, Leo III issued documents that were dated from Charlemagne's coronation, and he issued coinage in Rome with Charlemagne's portrait. By May of 801, Charlemagne and his court had settled on the exact form of the imperial title: "Charles, Most Serene Augustus, crowned by God, great and peaceful emperor, governing the Roman Empire, and, by the mercy of God, King of the Lombards and the Franks."

In the eyes of some, at least, of Charlemagne's followers, his coronation as emperor was the result of the recognition that God had so favored Charlemagne, that Charlemagne had created a new era of peace and just government, extending so far beyond the traditional achievements of the Frankish and Lombard kings that it deserved the renewal of the old imperial title. Charlemagne probably shared this view, as well as the extraordinary and novel responsibilities it imposed. In the years after 801, he made a particular effort to organize the ecclesiastical and secular legal systems of his empire and to intensify the Christianization of his subjects. Later diplomatic negotiations with Constantinople also emphasize the legitimacy of Charlemagne's status as emperor and the identity of his title with that of the early Christian emperors. In 802, Charlemagne required a new oath of allegiance from his subjects—this time to him as emperor—and throughout the last decade-and-a-half of his life, many of his accomplishments and aims are phrased in terms of a *renovatio*—a renewal—of idealized earlier times.

Although the coronation conferred no additional rights, lands, or wealth on Charlemagne (except, conceivably, in parts of central Italy), it did serve as a contemporary recognition of his extraordinary career and the impact it had on a wide variety of late eighth-century peoples.

CHARLEMAGNE: THE SUCCESSION, THE SUCCESSORS, AND THE LEGEND

Charlemagne's triumphs did not guarantee enduring political or military stability to the Franks and the other subject peoples of his empire, nor was Charlemagne under any delusion that they would. Toward the end of his life, he is even said to have asked "whether we are truly Christians." Throughout Charlemagne's last years, he faced the reality that the imperial title (and the imperial idea he shared with Alcuin) had been chiefly the concept of a small aristocratic and ecclesiastical elite close to him personally and not widely, if at all, understood or accepted by most of his subjects. Others, including the rest of the aristocracy and clergy, still thought in terms of a more traditional and regionalized Frankish monarchy and society.

Charlemagne had five wives in succession, and he also had children by several concubines. He never permitted his daughters to marry, probably for political reasons, and two of them became abbesses of religious houses. His first son Pippin "the Hunchback," by his first wife, Himiltrude, was gradually excluded from the king's favor to the advantage of his three sons by Hildegard (d. 783): Charles the Younger, Pippin of Italy, and Louis the Pious. The names indicate something of Charles's original intentions: Pippin was named after Charlemagne's father, and Charles the Younger was named after Charlemagne's grandfather, Charles Martel, whose prominence and fame had transformed the family name from that of Pippinids to that of Carolingians. Louis, however, received a Merovingian name (Louis, *Ludovicus* in Latin, is the Latinization of Clovis). Ironically, the son with the Merovingian name ultimately succeeded Charlemagne. Pippin the Hunchback was implicated in a revolt against Charlemagne and confined in a monastery, where he died in 811. Pippin of Italy, for whom Charlemagne had created the subkingdom of Italy, died in 810, leaving a young son, Bernard. Charles the Younger also died in 811, leaving only Louis (for whom Charlemagne had created Aquitaine as a subkingdom) as Charlemagne's only legitimate surviving male heir. By dynastic accident, for a remarkable fourth generation in succession, the power of the now greatly expanded Frankish kingdom and empire rested in the hands of a single ruler.

Charlemagne died in 814 and was buried simply and quickly in his chapel at Aachen. Einhard wrote his biography in the 820s, already idealizing the reign and the ruler. Around 884, Notker, a monk of St. Gall, wrote a longer life of Charlemagne, one in which the elements of folklore and legend are much more conspicuous. Indeed, the legendary history of Charlemagne was well underway at the end of the ninth century, magnifying the ruler into a just and powerful king of epic proportions, whose mere appearance terrified his enemies. Later legends quickly accumulated: of Charlemagne's journey to Jerusalem and of other activities on an epic scale, culminating in the eleventh-century epic poem *The Song of Roland* (below, Chapter 12). Long before King Arthur—and long after—Charlemagne became the king against whom all later kings were measured and with whose legendary memory they identified themselves.

Louis the Pious (773–840, r. 814–840) was named king and crowned as emperor by his father in 813. Not until 816, did Louis permit Pope Stephen IV (816–817) to crown him emperor as Leo III had crowned Charlemagne. On that occasion, Louis' queen, Ermengaud, was also crowned *Augusta*, empress, the first time such a crowning of a woman occurred. In 817, their son Lothar was crowned coemperor with his father, and his two brothers were made subkings. In an attempt to prevent the further subdivision of the kingdom, Louis also insisted that only the firstborn son could succeed his father—one of the earliest examples of the idea that some political units ought to be indivisible, in contrast with Frankish laws of private inheritance and earlier Frankish royal tradition of dividing the kingdom.

Under the influence of Benedict of Aniane, his chief ecclesiastical adviser, Louis vigorously continued his father's policy of church reform, issuing capitularies and holding church councils during the first ten years of his reign. From the thirteen years of Charlemagne's reign as emperor, there survive around twenty pieces of legislation, of which six or seven are originals. For Louis' reign there survive around 500 pieces of legislation, of which around twenty are originals. Charlemagne, of course, was constantly on the move, traveling throughout Europe, one historian has claimed, more than any other ruler until Napoleon. Louis had the leisure and freedom from war to manage the apparatus of governance more deliberately—preserving the structure of counts, *missi*, and other officials, and incorporating the bishops as imperial agents.

But Louis' independence, native intelligence, and unquestioned devotion to the responsibilities of a Christian emperor were offset by problems his father had never had to face. The costs of war rose, and there were fewer clear-cut victories. The expansion of the vast Frankish-ruled territories slowed, then ceased, and the Frankish lands soon went on the defensive against new external enemies. The Frankish armies had been far more successful on offense, when they could plan and carry out long campaigns, than on defense, when they might be called without much notice to different parts of the empire.

Louis also had to establish his own court and advisers in the face of opposition from some of his father's powerful servants.

Finally, Louis, unlike his father and grandfather, faced the problem of dividing his empire among several legitimate sons. There is no better test of the differing concepts of the empire and of dynastic right to kingdoms in the two generations following that of Charlemagne than the problem of a divided succession to the Frankish kingdoms and the imperial title. Civil wars among Louis' sons and between his sons and himself clouded the last years of Louis' reign. After Louis' second marriage, to Judith, and the birth of their son Charles (Charles the Bald, 823–877; r. 843–877), Lothar and his brother Pippin revolted against Louis, and in 830 attempted to depose him and confine Judith in a convent. Although the sons' support failed them, they rebelled again in 833, but again their alliance collapsed, and Louis resumed the kingship and emperorship. But the political and dynastic damage had been done. After Louis' death in 840, further fighting among his sons, now Louis, Lothar, and Charles (Pippin had died in 838, leaving a son, also Pippin, as ruler of Aquitaine), led to the Treaty of Verdun of 843, when three new kingdoms, not based on the old Frankish divisions but recognizing the greatly expanded extent of the kingdom of *Francia* and the acquired territories, were created in the old Frankish kingdom and the conquered territories. These divisions signaled the resurgence of independent kingdoms, the tripartite division of royal wealth and aristocratic allies, and hence the fragmentation of the empire. One contemporary account of the agreements between the brothers known as the Strasburg Oaths, records the oaths in the vernacular languages that Louis the German and Charles the Bald swore to each other's followers: Louis speaking the oath to Charles's supporters in a language that became Old French, Charles speaking the oath in a language that became Old High German. By the mid ninth century, vernacular linguistic differences added to the division of the kingdoms.

Of Louis' three surviving sons: Charles the Bald (r. 843–877) received the western part of Louis' territories, which became the kingdom of West *Francia;* Louis the German (r. 843–876) received the eastern portion, the kingdom of East *Francia;* Lothar (r. 840–855) received the central portion, the "Middle Kingdom," extending from just south of Rome to the North Sea, that included both Aachen and Rome, as well as the imperial title. But the division of the empire according to the politics of inheritance meant that in spite of Louis the Pious' order, these kingdoms, too, might be subdivided among the surviving sons of their own rulers. The first instance of subdivision was the division of the Middle Kingdom upon the death of Lothar I in 855 into a northern kingdom, ruled by Lothar II and called after him ever since, *Lotharingia,* or Lorraine, and the southern kingdom of Italy, ruled by Louis II. The subdivisions and ultimate disappearance of the Middle Kingdom played a powerful role in the later history of France, Germany, the Low Countries, Luxemburg, Switzerland, and Italy.

In the years that followed the Treaty of Verdun, a strong new sense of regional loyalties weakened the idea of central royal authority. The empire had ceased to expand, and the grandsons and great grandsons of Charlemagne had to surround themselves with local nobles in their kingdoms, with reduced resources in land and offices to distribute among their followers. This nobility was not as mobile across central and western Europe and was therefore much more locally bound than its Carolingian predecessor nobility. It put down local territorial roots and developed its own local groups of dependents. The kings of West *Francia,* East *Francia,* Lorraine, and Italy could not move their royal servants across as broad an expanse of territory as could Charlemagne. From the ninth century, the interests of the nobles could best be served by acquiring specific lands and powers in a single territory, preserving these for their heirs, and beginning the process of narrowing the kin-group to a patriarchal lineage focused on particular properties and succession to them, increasingly in opposition to the interests of the kings and the old wider kin-groups.

The title "Emperor of the Romans" usually went to the strongest of these kings or, failing strength, to the one who seemed most likely to protect central Italy. Thus, the imperial title followed Louis II to Italy when the Middle Kingdom was divided in 855, and remained at the disposal of the later ninth-century popes, who tended to award it to whichever Carolingian (and later, non-Carolingian) candidate appeared to offer the best chance of protection and order to central Italy. As early as 862, a Frankish monastic chronicle referred to Louis II only as the "emperor of Italy." Not until the papal coronation of Otto I in 962, did the imperial title once more evoke the idea of a transalpine empire (below, Chapter 11).

After 888, the disintegration of the late Carolingian kingdoms proceeded swiftly. Non-Carolingians assumed crowns in West *Francia* and Provence. The imperial title itself was assumed by non-Carolingian warlords in Italy. In 911, the last Carolingian king of East *Francia* died, and the local dukes elected one of their own number, Conrad of Franconia, as king. In 987, the last Carolingian king of West *Francia* died, and a non-Carolingian, Hugh Capet, was elected ruler of the shrunken kingdom in his place. Although the later kingdoms of Germany and France did not yet exist, their origins lie in the disintegration of the Carolingian monarchy in the late ninth and tenth centuries.

9

Europe Emerges

THE NEW INVADERS: ARABS AND MAGYAR

During the ninth and tenth centuries, the local nobility grew stronger still, as a new wave of invasions pierced the once secure Carolingian world. During the late eighth and ninth centuries, Arab sea power had grown considerably stronger, and from bases in North Africa, Spain, and southern Gaul, Arab raiders penetrated most of the southern areas of Europe, reaching even the passes of the Alps. The raiders were not in all cases interested in the expansion of Islam, but rather in the opportunities for loot, tribute, and ransom. By the 830s, Sicily had fallen to Arab raiders, and most of the Carolingian defenses in northern Spain were in ruins. These Arab armies consisted mostly of independent forces operating in their or their leaders' self-interest from their bases in North Africa against Sicily, Italy, and the northern Mediterranean coastal areas, and they were often used as allies in wars between Christian warlords.

In eastern Europe, another people, the Magyar, proved more dangerous than even the Muslim raiders of the Mediterranean. The Magyar were a Finno-Ugrian people from the steppes of western Asia (their later name, *Hungarians,* derived from the name of one group of them, the Onogurs). In 896, the Byzantine Empire, long engaged in military struggles with the Bulgars, employed their customary diplomacy in the lower Danube valley and the steppes north of the Black Sea to persuade the Magyar to attack the Bulgars. But the Bulgars persuaded another steppe people, the Pechenegs, to attack the Magyar, and the latter fled west into central Europe, establishing themselves in the Carpathian basin. From there, they defeated the neighboring Moravian and east Frankish powers, and launched lightning cavalry raids into Germany, France, and Italy. Like the Avars before them, the Magyar presence divided the Slavic population of the area. The Bulgars, Serbs, and Rus drew closer to Byzantium, while the Bohemians and Poles were drawn more closely to the church and kingdom of East *Francia*.

Between 898 and 920, Magyar war bands descended into Italy, Burgundy, eastern France, and especially Germany. Only stiff resistance put up by the Saxon kings of East *Francia*, Henry I (r. 916–936) and his son Otto I (r. 936–973), the latter spectacularly in 955 at the battle on the Lech river in what is today Austria, stopped the worst of the raids. Magyar warlords continued to dominate their own people and the local Slavic population until the end of the tenth century, but at the same time the Magyar themselves were turning from the life of nomadic warriors to that of sedentary farmers and pastoralists. In this social transformation, it became easier for a royal dynasty to assert itself in place of the warlords. When the Arpad dynasty began to establish its own superiority, it converted to Latin Christianity and began to create and stabilize the kingdom of Hungary.

THE NEW INVADERS: THE VIKINGS

The raids of Muslims and Magyars hastened the political disintegration of ninth- and tenth-century western Europe. The raids of the Vikings nearly completed the process. The third and ultimately the most influential group of invaders, the Vikings, were bands of Scandinavian warriors who sailed south in their long wooden ships in the summer, looted and pillaged freely along the coasts and river valleys of western Europe, and sailed home in the autumn. Scandinavian traders and fighters had been known in eighth-century Europe and Asia, but in the ninth century, their raids became more frequent. Their superbly built ships were not only the finest ocean-going vessels of the age, but their shallow draft allowed them to sail far up the western European rivers, attacking Rouen and Paris on the Seine and Trier on the Moselle, as well as the commercial ports of Quentovic and Dorestad in the Low Countries. The Viking dragon ships, carrying fifty to one hundred men and propelled by a single great sail and banks of oars, devastated the European seaboard. Like many of the Arab raiders in the Mediterranean, they sought loot, tribute, and heroic reputation. To get these, they ravaged undefended ecclesiastical lands, looted churches and monasteries of their movable wealth, took captives for slavery and ransom, defeated the small armies that local lords and kings sent against them, and sacked the little towns that lay in their path.

The weakness of local resistance to these raids gave plenty of opportunities to powerful local lords to protect weaker people from the Vikings and, in return, take over several of the functions of governance that had once been only the king's to give. In many cases, what the Vikings left, or never even touched, including ecclesiastical property, also fell into the hands of powerful warlords. This secondary effect of the Viking, Magyar, and Arab raids should not be overlooked. Carolingian Europe was weakly defended, but this situation did not prevent opportunities for strong and ruthless

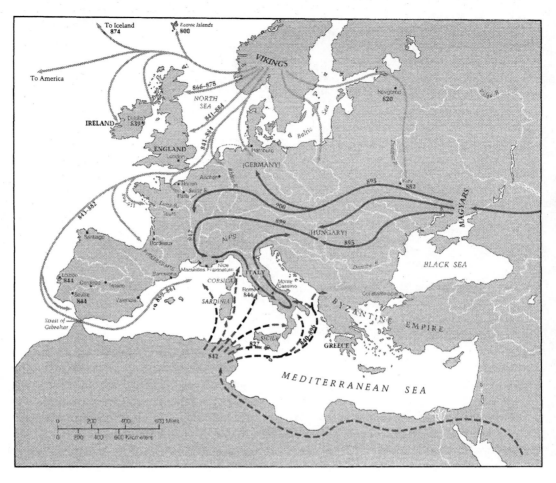

Invasions of Europe, seventh through eleventh centuries.

warriors to increase their own power and prestige at the expense of both the victims of the Viking raids and their own neighbors.

There were many paths of Scandinavian expansion. Norwegians moved chiefly into Ireland and the islands and coasts of western Britain. Swedes moved into the eastern Baltic and across northwestern Russia to Lake Ladoga, then down the great north-south river systems of Russia and the Ukraine to Novgorod and Kiev, trading and raiding alike, until they came into contact not only with Byzantium across the Black Sea but with Arab merchants on the Volga and the Sea of Azov. The Danes attacked eastern England, Frisia, and the Rhineland and then penetrated upriver into the heart of the old kingdom of West *Francia* itself.

By the middle of the ninth century, the patterns of raiding had changed. Groups of Scandinavians began to establish winter quarters in Europe, and the raiding parties grew larger, turning into settling parties. They turned, in fact, into expeditionary armies

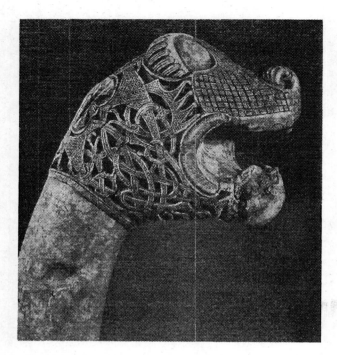

The Oseberg Dragon Head. Viking artistic skills are strikingly evident in this dragon's head on a cart found in the Oseberg ship burial. (Early Medieval Art: The Academician's Headpost from the Oseberg Ship Burial. Wood, 9th century. University Museum of National Antiquities, Oslo, Norway)

seeking land to take and settle. By the 850s, there were Norse settlements in Ireland, and in 865, the famous Great Army landed in England and stayed. By 878, a substantial part of northeastern England had fallen under Danish rule; it was known for centuries afterward as the Danelaw. English kings raised large sums of money by taxation to offer to the Danes as tribute. The Danegeld, as this money was called, played an important role in later English royal finances.

The Vikings clearly knew something about the lands they raided and captured. There is strong evidence that they had advance intelligence on defenses and military preparations and raided accordingly. By the tenth century, they had begun to settle on the Continent as well as in the Isles. In 911, the king of West *Francia,* Charles the Simple, formally ceded to one Viking leader, Hrolf (Rollo in Latin), some land at the mouth of the Seine in order to protect the territory and the river route to Paris from other Vikings. Under Hrolf and his successors, this territory was greatly expanded to become the eleventh-century Duchy of Normandy.

The Vikings and other Scandinavians did not confine themselves to island and continental territories, however. Between 860 and 865, they sailed westward across the North Atlantic, and in 874, they settled Iceland. Not only did the strong egalitarian sensibility of the Icelandic settlers survive the settlement, but their privately owned farms, their wide-ranging and highly skilled seamanship, and their public assembly laid the foundations for the oldest democratic community in western Europe. In 984, Erik, an exile from Iceland, discovered the island of Greenland, and small settlements sprang up there as well. In 1000, Erik's son Leif sailed even farther west and made a landfall at a place he called Vinland, which scholars now agree was located in North America. The archaeological evidence, principally from L'Anse aux Meadows ("Jellyfish Creek") in northern Newfoundland, discovered in 1961, strongly indicates an eleventh-century temporary occupation by Greenlanders. By the end of the tenth century, western Europe had been subjected not only to the ravages of Viking raids but also to the pressure of Viking settlements. It had received a new maritime vocabulary and been drawn closer to the northern Atlantic than ever before, and it had been expanded enormously by the wide-ranging voyages of the Vikings.

From the mid ninth century on, royal dynasties in Denmark, Norway, and Sweden began to increase the authority and control of the king over the marauding bands of chieftains, pirates, and raiders. Some Viking leaders fled to England, the Continent, or Iceland rather than live under a royal rule that increasingly tended to direct and limit their raiding activities. With the expansion of royal authority and the Christianizing of the Scandinavian kings in the late tenth century, the great age of Viking expansion came to an end. By the twelfth and thirteenth centuries, the early tales of the Viking period, particularly of Iceland, had begun to be worked into heroic tales called sagas, the last genuine European epics. Preserving their rough history in this form, the Scandinavians joined the Magyar as the newest peoples on the edge of Christian Europe.

There is another aspect to these raids that proved immensely significant in the history of Europe. As the great historian Marc Bloch pointed out long ago, they were the last outside invasions of western Europe until the allied landings in 1944 during World War II. That is, western Europe was the only territory in the world free of outside invasions for the nearly thousand years between 955 and 1944. This long absence of invasion from outside is certainly not the least important aspect of the history of western Europe after the tenth century.

KINGS AND WARLORDS

The most successful defenders of western Europe in the tenth century were the kings of England and East *Francia* on the one hand, and on the other, the tough warlords of West *Francia,* who protected their little territories with ruthlessness and skill. Late Carolingian-style monarchs and illiterate warriors, kings, and lords survived with the help of churchmen and the labor of peasants. In their age, the history of Europe becomes the histories of two successful monarchies and several hundred territorial principalities. In these territories were the beginnings of recovery. Old landholding systems, archaic social forms, and much custom had been swept away by the shock of the invasions. The land was fertile, however, and the small populations of warriors and peasants, most of the latter tied to the land more closely than ever but secure once more, began to increase. Once the greatest military threats to their rule had been removed, lords began to explore ways to assert and legitimize their titles and powers. Churchmen sought ways of ensuring peace in a society that had become more warlike than ever before.

The tenth century has long rivaled the seventh for the title of the "darkest" of the "Dark Ages," but recently, historians working with very different kinds of sources have changed the conventional picture of this period, just as historians have begun to rehabilitate the reputation of the seventh century. The economic historian Robert Lopez, basing his case on the signs of steady population growth and new economic developments, even postulated a tenth-century renaissance. In a book dealing chiefly with political culture, Geoffrey Barraclough noted:

> *The ninth and tenth centuries were a formative period in European history, every bit as much as the better known periods which preceded and succeeded them, and it was out of the anarchy and tribulation which men and women of that generation suffered that a new Europe took shape.*[1]

Indeed, the great debate among historians of early Europe centers largely on the problem of dating the emergence of a distinct and continuous European culture—in the eighth, or the late tenth and early eleventh centuries.

Because political history has long offered scholars an attractive organizing theme for different periods in the past, it has been tempting for historians to interpret many other aspects of social life in terms of modern standards of political stability and instability. Thus, since the experience of most of the peoples of tenth-century Europe (England and East *Francia* excepted), have been that of decentralized political institutions, it has been tempting to interpret broader social and economic aspects of tenth-century society in much the same light. But social and economic growth do not always require political stability over large areas, and the tenth-century growth of Europe is most easily traceable in small areas. In the early tenth century, there was a swamp outside the gates of Paris (which occupied only the islands in the middle of the Seine and small settlements on the right and left banks of the river), and there were forests and unworked fields inside the walls of Rome and Milan. Cultivatable land did not have enough hands to work it. But by the end of the tenth century, population growth is traceable in the records of the expansion of cultivated land. The older Carolingian landscape of densely populated settlements separated by forest and waste slowly gave way to a more regularly developed landscape devoted in greater proportion to agriculture, the founding of new villages and monasteries (themselves capable of stabilizing agricultural demand and production), and the appearance of local trade fairs. Such growth of population and expansion of cultivated land constituted the strong substructure for the political and longer-range trade developments of the eleventh and twelfth centuries, and those who first benefited from it were not kings and emperors, but the secular and clerical lords of the land.

In two notable instances, however, those of England and East *Francia*, strong central rulers began to take advantage of the ending of the invasions and the stirrings of local growth and expansion.

THE EMERGENCE OF *ENGLALAND*

The tide of invasion began to turn in Anglo-Saxon England with the victory of Alfred the Great (871–899) over a large Danish army in 879. Alfred, originally the king only of Wessex, proceeded to consolidate his authority in other English kingdoms, and his

---

[1]Geoffrey Barraclough, *The Crucible of Europe* (Berkeley and Los Angeles: University of California Press, 1976), p. 7.

tenth-century descendants proved to be strong, able monarchs. By the reign of Edgar (959–975), the English monarchy was the most highly developed in Europe. England was now a single kingdom, which its ruling groups began to refer to as *Englaland*. The kings and the nobility cooperated, and the old units of local government, the hundreds and shires, provided a broad base of support. The English church, under the leadership of a remarkable group of prelates, notably Dunstan of Canterbury (909–988) and Aethelwold of Winchester (abp. 963–984), patronized learning and the arts and placed their skills at the service of the monarchy. During the tenth century, the Old English language, the most precocious recorded vernacular language in Europe, experienced its greatest age. Epic and lyric poems, sermons and scriptural commentaries, and the first vernacular national history—the *Anglo-Saxon Chronicle*—were produced, as were continuing compilations of royal laws and translations from such Latin writers as Gregory the Great and Boethius.

But the strength of England depended on the cooperation of the kings and the nobility, and renewed Scandinavian threats weakened that cooperation at the end of the tenth century. Ethelred II, the "Ill-Counseled" (978–1016), lost his nobles' loyalty when he proved incapable of resisting a renewed invasion by the king of the Danes. England was conquered by Svein Forkbeard, king of Denmark (r. 987–1014; r. England 1013–1014). Svein, however, was not a Viking: he and his successor Cnut (r. 1014–1035; r. England 1016–1035) continued the English-style monarchy and preserved English laws, language, and other institutions.

When Cnut's line died out in 1042, Edward the Confessor (1042–1066), the last surviving son of Ethelred II, became king. But Edward's reign did not stabilize the relations between king and nobles, and it attracted the attention of still other peoples to the English scene. During the reign of Cnut and his sons, Edward had been raised at the court of the Dukes of Normandy—the precocious state-builders descended from the Viking invaders of the ninth and early tenth centuries. The continuing connection with Edward the Confessor gave the rulers of Normandy a unique interest in the fortunes of the English crown, and at Edward's death in 1066, the Norman invasion marked yet another transformation of the English kingdom.

THE PROBLEM OF "NATIONAL" ORIGINS

It has long tempted politically minded scholars and politicians with a taste for historical scholarship and historical mythology to see the beginnings of modern nation-states in the patchwork of kingdoms and territorial principalities that succeeded the Carolingian empire. But the limited scope of tenth- and eleventh-century political life warns against such anachronistic interpretations. Carolingian forms of kingship survived until the late eleventh century, and late-Carolingian kingship consisted of personal relations among great men, whether kings or territorial princes, with such elements as ethnicity and widespread public ethnic or political consciousness coming into play among other levels of society only much later.

The Carolingian kingdom of East *Francia* was the part of Charlemagne's empire that had been most recently conquered—not completely until the first years of the ninth century—and still preserved a distinct sense of folk identity on the part of the different peoples that had been brought under Carolingian power at different times. Bavaria and Saxony had been worked into the fabric of the Frankish kingdom slowly, but deliberately, in the late eighth and ninth centuries. Having had a substantial tradition of independence, both territories preserved a sense of Bavarian and Saxon identity, and Charlemagne recognized the distinctive legal customs of Saxon and Bavarian law.

Frankish rulers had also recognized the identity of some eastern peoples like the Saxons when they assigned officials known as *duces* (dukes) to govern them rather than the ordinary *comes* (counts). Although many of the duchies were suppressed at the end of the late eighth century, they appeared again a century later, with men using the old ducal title now firmly identified with the people for whom the duchy had been originally created. The ducal title, with the wealth, prestige, and opportunities to reward followers and allies that went with it, was also worth fighting for among rival great families. In Franconia and Swabia, such competition was prolonged into the tenth century. In Bavaria and Saxony, the dangers of borders exposed to pagan Magyar or Slavic peoples in the east may have hastened the process, for strong ducal families appeared in both territories in the ninth century.

With the death of the last Carolingian king of East *Francia*, Louis the Child, in 911, the dukes of the Saxons, Bavarians, Franconians, Thuringians, and Swabians, desiring to preserve the kingdom as a kingdom, elected one of their own number, Conrad I of Franconia, as king. Conrad attempted to rule as a Carolingian king, but his former fellow dukes rejected his pretensions, regarding him simply as one of themselves. Conrad's reign was ineffective and short. He declined to establish a dynasty and urged his brother to recognize the elective choice of the other dukes, Henry the Fowler, duke of Saxony (r. 919–936). Henry, however, was elected only by Conrad's Franconians and by his own Saxons, since the Swabians refused to participate, and the Bavarians elected their own duke as king and only later recognized Henry. Henry I founded the Saxon royal, and later imperial, dynasty, which lasted from his own reign to that of Henry II (1002–1024) and achieved considerable success, but it never molded Germany into the compact kingdom that England became. Henry I and his able son and successor Otto I (r. 936–973) both had to rule with far less autocratic power than Carolingian kings had wielded, and behind even the royal self-awareness of Otto I there lay a world of complex consensus politics. Alongside the basis of royal wealth and noble support in Saxony, there survived the general independence of the other duchies and their own local nobility. Carolingian kingship could not be reconstructed in the east, and it took considerable time to discover precisely what kind of kingship could.

The Saxon kings were responsible for the defense of a very large kingdom against both outside invaders and local rebellions, and they had to create a new kind of legitimacy because they were not Carolingians. They also faced other problems: They could not, unlike the Carolingians, reward their local followers with lands and titles throughout a large kingdom, as Charlemagne had. Although they were kings, there were large areas of the kingdom beyond their control, and their resources were almost entirely based on their family properties in Saxony. Therefore, they could not partition the kingdom among their sons. Much of the Saxon nobility that might have aided the kings in other parts of Germany could not be spared from the wars with the Slavic peoples on the eastern border of Saxony. Moreover, other dukes as well as local nobles did not forget that the Saxon kings had once been dukes themselves. Their only resources for ruling all of East *Francia* were the lands and incomes they controlled personally as dukes of Saxony.

Lacking regular sources of men and money, the Saxon kings turned to the church of East *Francia,* and that institution became one of their most important sources of support. To maintain themselves, the Saxon dynasty had to acquire other duchies by marriage or inheritance, or control appointments to high church offices. Usually they tried to do both. The vast size of their kingdom, and their widely scattered possessions throughout it, meant that they spent most of their lives in the saddle. Their only means of imposing their rulership was to practice itinerant kingship and travel constantly, being seen by their subjects, giving judgments, bestowing rewards and punishments as effectively they could, and trying to stem the strong sense of independence, particularism, local rivalries, and resistance to their rule.

The most successful Saxon king was Otto I (r. 936–973). In 955, on the River Lech, Otto led an army that annihilated a large force of Magyar invaders, thus turning the tide in favor of East *Francia.* In later successful campaigns against pagan Slavic peoples, Otto restored older missionary bishoprics like Hamburg-Bremen and founded a number of new missionary bishoprics, notably Magdeburg, Brandenburg, and Havelberg, that played an important role in Christianizing the northern Slavic and Scandinavian peoples.

Otto I also intervened in Italy, conquering the north in 951. His immense personal power and prestige led to his coronation as emperor of the Romans in 962 by Pope John XII. For the remainder of his own reign and those of his son Otto II (r. 973–983) and grandson Otto III (r. 983–1002), the Saxon king/emperors faced the challenges of managing the large and difficult-to-control kingdom of Germany and the smaller but historically very different kingdom of Italy and defending the unstable eastern frontier against Slavic peoples.

Unlike England and East *Francia,* the kingdom of West *Francia* had shrunk considerably by the late tenth century. In 987, the early Capetian kings of West *Francia* ruled directly only a small territory surrounding Paris. Although their titles made them the nominal lords of the powerful territorial princes whose lands surrounded theirs (and in some cases were far larger), they possessed no effective control over the warlords and territorial princes of their kingdom. These men were the real powers in West *Francia.*

Although the idea of dependence and service had originally been repugnant to free Germanic warriors, the wealth, glory, and prestige derived from serving a Carolingian king or other powerful lord slowly overcame such cultural reluctance. The very terms that came to designate the institutions of lordship—*dominus* (lord) and *vassus* (vassal)—reflect the humble roots of the bond among fellow fighting men and between fighting men and their war leaders. The English word "lord," for example, derives from the Old English term *hlaford,* "the giver of the loaf," or provider of food. *Vassus* is a Latinization of an old Celtic word meaning "boy" or "menial servant." One psychological root of lordship and vassalage, then, is reflected in the acceptance in certain advantageous circumstances by members of relatively high social status of a terminology that had once designated functions of a very low social status. Even in Carolingian royal household service, performed by men of very high social status indeed, such terms as *constable, marshal,* and *seneschal* all derived from older Latin and Germanic words designating menial domestic service. The language of lordship described an old domestic relationship between superiors and inferiors that rose in social esteem and increased in acceptability as it became a specialized description of relationships among powerful persons.

The strongest, and sometimes the only, bond between lord and follower was the power of the mutual oath of loyalty. In some instances, the vassal commended himself to the lord by offering an act of homage (becoming the *homo,* or man, of the lord) and later fealty (from the Latin *fides,* meaning faith or loyalty). Upon receiving homage, the lord swore to protect the vassal and be loyal to him in turn. In theory, this mutual assertion of personal loyalty could be nullified by either party if either thought that the other did not fulfill his promises. The lord might also show his favor by conferring on his new man a conditional gift of land, money, or rights. Such a gift was called a *beneficium* ("good deed" or "benefice") or a "fief." This practice, however, was distinct from the ties of homage and lordship and was not the practice in many parts of Europe.

Upon the vassal's death or breaking of faith, his benefice reverted to the lord, who might then grant it to another vassal. On the lord's death, the old vassals had to become vassals of the lord's successor. Increasingly, pressure from vassals led to the possibility of the vassal's son (or, in some cases, daughter) succeeding the vassal in the benefice. The complex bonds of these personal relationships were often confusing, especially when land received as a benefice was confused with land held privately, or when lands held from two different lords became the object of mixed loyalties.

Originally, the chief value of a vassal was his military ability and in the prestige his oath and loyalty gave to the lord. As vassal of a lord (whether supported within the lord's household, or perhaps as the domestic lord of a large household himself), he was able to maintain the expensive equipment and specialized training of a mounted warrior and to take the time to fight in his lord's wars. Socially, lords and their vassals constituted the class of fighting men that came to dominate the composition of the European nobility in the eleventh and twelfth centuries. The turbulent ethos of these warlords led churchmen to try to impose the sanctions of morality upon their relationships with each other. One way of doing this was to surround the occasion of the oathtaking of lord and vassal with liturgical rites.

The growth of the ninth- and tenth-century nobility and of territorial principalities is as much a chapter in the history of European communities as is the history of European invasions and post-Carolingian "anarchy." In imposing their own rule, the small and great lords who controlled lands ranging from tiny single castles in Castile to the great duchy of Bavaria made themselves responsible for keeping the peace, maintaining the privileges of diverse communities, and protecting the Church. In return they received, sometimes grudgingly, loyalty and prestige. They ruled the most manageable territories that the tenth and early eleventh centuries could create. They also patronized the beginnings of the agricultural revolution and the eleventh- and twelfth-century spiritual revolutions (below, Chapter 12). Often enough, they were brutal, greedy, suspicious, abrupt, and ferocious. Yet they were devout after their own fashion, efficient, and ambitious for their dynasty and their territories. Often possessing no family history, they made up histories and genealogies; lacking traditional legitimacy, they appropriated titles for themselves; they cultivated and patronized the monasteries and the holy men of the tenth century. Unlike the newly Christianized rulers of Norway, Denmark, Bohemia, and Hungary, they themselves were not often venerated as saints. But they cultivated those saints they could find, and they did make pilgrimages, sometimes at politically risky times.

In 1035, for example, a seven-year-old boy familiarly called William the Bastard succeeded to the duchy of Normandy because his father, Robert, had died on a pilgrimage to Jerusalem. Some lords went on long pilgrimages two or three times, and to Compostela and Rome as well as to Jerusalem. They ransacked land and labor alike for their fortresses, but they also gave away favorite hunting lodges to monks, allowed exceptional privileges to colonizing peasants, and sometimes entered the religious life themselves after a lifetime of looting and fighting. In practice, they became successful warlords; in theory, they retained spiritual horizons and ideas of loyalty to higher powers that held the germ of wider social bonds.

The fragmentation and very different circumstances of England, East *Francia*, and West *Francia* graphically illustrate the variety of political paths from the Carolingian world to that of the territorial principalities and monarchies of the twelfth and thirteenth centuries. As western European kings, lords, and peoples explored those paths, it is necessary to consider at the same time the circumstances of the two other civilizations that had emerged out of the old Mediterranean world, those of Byzantium and Islam, on the eve of the western European economic revolution and the age of the Crusades.

SAILING TO BYZANTIUM

The Byzantine Empire was also wracked by invasions and internal revolts in the eighth and ninth centuries. From the early eighth century until about 840, it faced virtually annual attacks from an Islamic empire that was ten times its size, with a budget fifteen times greater, and with armies five times the size of its own. If that empire had ever been completely mobilized against it, Byzantium would have fallen. But the caliphs' greater interest in Persia and the political crisis of the mid eighth century that replaced the Umayyad dynasty with the Abbasids (above, Chapter 5; below, this chapter) deflected the caliphs' concentration from Byzantium. Substantial Byzantine military successes in Asia Minor and Syria under the emperors Leo III (717–741), Constantine V (741–775), and Leo IV (775–780) greatly strengthened Byzantine resistance. During the same period, however, Byzantium was also internally divided over the issue of icons, the iconoclastic controversy, which ended in 843. The rhythms of the internal Byzantine debate over icons are linked to the intensifying and lessening of the Arab threat between 717 and the 840s. Arab victories over God's chosen empire raised the question among Byzantines as to why God seemed to have abandoned them; the disputes over icons were an attempt to answer that question.

In the Greco-Roman world before the coming of Christianity, gods and humans gazed at each other across the porticoes and marketplaces of every city. Statues and pictures of gods, heroes, and emperors filled the temples, public spaces, and audience halls.

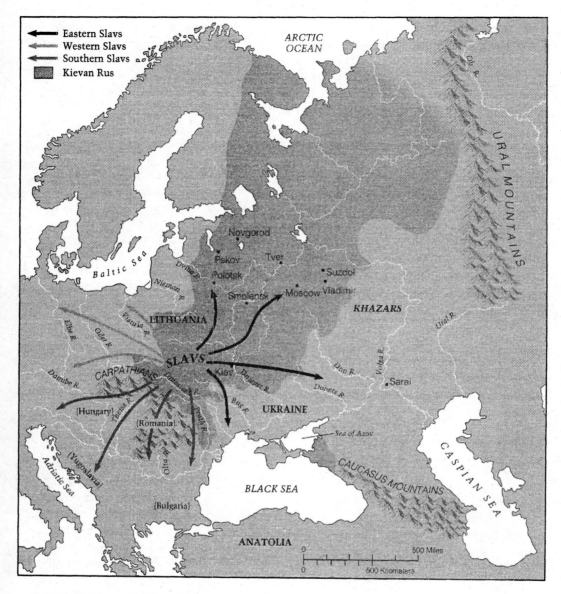

Spread of the Slavs and the Kievan Rus.

To Jews, as later to Muslims, the idea that divinity could be depicted in material form was anathema and a violation of the Second Commandment, as, indeed, it was to many of the early Christians themselves, whose art was sparse and often simply decorative. Exodus 20:4 was explicit:

> *Thou shalt not make unto thee any graven image, or any likeness of anything that is in heaven above, or that is in the earth beneath, or that is in the water under the earth.*

The rapid growth of Christianity in the Roman Empire, however, generated a new kind of Christian art, with the pictorial representation of biblical scenes, martyrdoms, holy men, and then God the Father, Jesus, and the Virgin Mary. This was one way by which Christians defined themselves as non-Jews. Jews in turn accused the Christians of idolatry (the paying of *latreia,* the worship due only to God, to an *eidolon,* or image). The veneration of holy images painted on icons became particularly popular in Greek Christianity.

Spiritually troubled by Arab military victories and increasingly concerned with the popularity of icon veneration, the emperor Leo III (r. 717–741) dramatically removed an icon of Christ from the Chalke gate of the imperial palace in 726, and his son Constantine V (r. 741–775) called a church council in 754 to condemn icons formally. At the same time, the military victories of Leo and Constantine against Arab armies appeared to justify their theological position. But icons also found articulate defenders among both theologians and political leaders. When the emperor Leo IV (r. 775–780) died, he left a young son, Constantine VI, and a widow, Irene, who served as regent for her son. Irene, however, arrogated more and more power to herself and in 797, had Constantine VI blinded and made ritually unfit to rule. But Constantine died from his injuries, and although Irene arranged for a church council in 787 to restore image veneration, she was removed in 802, and her immediate successors returned to iconoclastic policies. Only the articulation of a theology of icon veneration by such major theologians as John of Damascus (ca. 675–753/4) and Theodore, abbot of the important monastery of Stoudios (759–826), and the military failures of iconoclastic emperors during the first half of the ninth century moved Byzantine society finally toward an iconophile policy.

In 843, icons were formally restored to their places of prominence. Michael III (r. 842–867) restored the icon of Christ to the Chalke Gate, and in 867, a program of icons was introduced to the church of Hagia Sophia itself and from there to the rest of the empire.

The reign of Michael III also witnessed the beginnings of Byzantine military recovery. One of the most significant changes in the structure of the armies had begun in the reign of Constantine V, when a military revolt led the emperors to create a new imperial guard, formed by placing several armies directly under imperial control and forming an elite force called the *tagmata.* Later emperors enlarged this force, and gradually it assumed a central place in the Byzantine military structure, relegating the armies of the *themes* to second-class status and turning their generals to local territorial administrators. The *tagmata* cavalry was particularly effective in Transcaucasia and southeastern Anatolia, where the new troops and sophisticated defensive tactics virtually ground Arab incursions to a halt by the end of the ninth century.

Michael III's great minister Bardas succeeded in mobilizing the resources of the empire and introducing remarkable reforms in secular education, ecclesiastical life, the military, and the peasant economy. The schools at Constantinople came under the direction of Bardas himself, educating a highly literate cadre of government officials in a combination of classical Greek and Christian education. Under Bardas' great contemporary, Patriarch Photios (858–867, 877–885), a new energy was given to religious studies as well. Such men as Bardas, Photios, Leo the Mathematician, and the linguist and missionary Constantine (Cyril) led an intellectual renaissance easily comparable in importance and influence to the military and social reforms of the imperial administration. The restoration of icon veneration under the aegis of these learned civil servants may represent their appropriation of a form of devotion that had once been associated exclusively with monks.

The Byzantine revival of the 860s was not, however, without its darker side. The end of the iconoclast controversy in 843 did not end the difficulties within the Greek Church, nor did it lead to improved relations with the Latin Church. Internal struggles over the office of patriarch of Constantinople at the accession of Photios in 858, led to a faction of the Byzantine clergy appealing to Pope Nicholas I (858–867), a brilliant and ambitious man. The problem of Photios and the arrival of a letter to Nicholas from the khan of the Bulgars, Boris (r. 852–889), in 864, asking the pope about Rome's view of certain liturgical and theological problems, led to a clash between pope and patriarch over the direction of Christianity in the Balkans.

In the course of the dispute, Photios accused the pope of heresy, on the ground that the Latin Church had erred in adding to the passage in the Nicene Creed that originally stated that the Holy Spirit proceeds from the Father, the single word *filioque,* "and from the Son," that is, the assertion that the Holy Spirit proceeded from both the Father and the Son rather than from God the Father alone—an issue that still divides the Greek Orthodox and Roman Catholic communions. The Photian Schism, as the division between pope and patriarch is known, shows the strains in the relationship between the eastern and western branches of the Church and the increasing tendency of both pope and patriarch to make claims that were very close to universal authority.

Indeed, the problem of Christianizing the still pagan Slavic and Balkan peoples of eastern Europe made the question of the competition between the Greek and Latin spheres of religious influence even stronger than it had been in the days of Charlemagne. The exchange of correspondence between Nicholas I and the khan of the Bulgars signals the creation of defined spheres of influence in eastern Europe of Latin and Greek Christianity. The Bulgars had invaded the northern and central Balkans in the late seventh century and created a kingdom that incorporated the local Slavic population. In 681 and again in 811, the Bulgars successfully fought off Byzantine attacks. In the late ninth century, Khan Boris converted to Greek Christianity, thereby closely linking Bulgarian religion, politics, and culture to those of Constantinople. The most significant aspect of the conversion of the Bulgars was the missionary work of two brothers, Constantine (ca. 827–869), who later took the religious name Cyril, and Methodios (ca. 815–885). Not only did these missionaries preach Christianity, but they also devised an alphabetic script (as earlier missionaries had for Georgian and Armenian) for the language that became Old Church Slavonic. But Bulgaria retained its political independence, and the powerful khan Symeon (893–927) launched yet a new Bulgar attack on the empire.

Byzantine civilization, however, proved extraordinarily resilient. The new Macedonian imperial dynasty, under the emperors Leo VI (886–912), Constantine VII Porphyrogenitus (913–959), and Basil II (976–1025), succeeded in reducing the power of the empire's external enemies and restoring internal stability to the troubled cities and provinces. The expansion of missionary activity and diplomacy, the collaboration of the patriarchs of Constantinople with the emperors, and the great patrician civil servants of the ninth and tenth centuries constituted the foundations of Byzantine survival and triumph. Palace revolutions, usurpations of the throne, and military blunders in the face of new enemies failed to undo the work begun in the mid ninth century. The administrative and legal genius of Leo VI and Constantine VII was augmented by skillful generals, several of whom even usurped imperial rank temporarily, yet at the same time strengthened the defenses of the empire. Under the first of these, Romanus I Lecapenus (920–944), the threat of the Bulgarian ruler Symeon was finally turned back. During the last years of Romanus' reign, Byzantine forces defeated the Bulgars. Basil II launched the final war to suppress the Bulgars, which took place between 986 and 1019 and gave Basil II his historical epithet: *Bulgarauctonos*—"Slayer of the Bulgars."

The ecclesiastical difficulties of the 860s were accompanied by new military crises. Faced with a hostile and permanent Arab threat from the east and increasingly from the sea, Byzantium looked for allies in the steppelands north of the Danube valley and the Black Sea and in Transcaucasia, among the Georgian and Armenian peoples. In Transcaucasia they encountered a rival Arab influence which slowly weakened during the tenth century, drawing Georgians and Armenians, like the Bulgarians, more closely into the orbit of Byzantine influence.

In the steppelands, Byzantium made a series of alliances with different Turkic peoples, initially the Khazars. The assembly and disintegration of a number of Turkic empires in northern Mongolia between the sixth and the ninth centuries scattered parts of these empires westward across the steppes. One of these, the Khazars, whose center was the steppeland north of the Caucasus mountains, had allied with the emperor Heraclius in 626. By the mid eighth century, the Khazar empire was immensely prosperous and powerful, and its ruling elites converted to Judaism. But the Khazar empire became more and more vulnerable to attacks from neighboring peoples. Late in the ninth century, one of these, the Magyar, established an independent territory between the Don and Danube rivers. In 895, Byzantine diplomacy encouraged the Magyar to attack the Bulgars from the east. As we have seen, however, Symeon of Bulgaria induced another steppe people, the Pechenegs, to attack the Magyar, and in their flight, the Magyar drove not south toward Bulgaria, but west toward Moravia. Between 896 and 909, the Magyar armies destroyed the Great Moravian Empire and settled on the plains of Transylvania, from which they proceeded to raid Germany, Italy, and Poland. The Pechenegs moved west to take the lands north of the Danube that the Magyar had vacated.

The Byzantines then turned to another people north of the Black Sea, the Rus. The Rus was a mixture of Scandinavian, Baltic, Finnic, and Slavic peoples who had consolidated a federation on the northwestern edges of the Khazar kingdom, initially mobilizing, then becoming part of the local Slavic population in the Dnieper Valley. By 940, the center of Rus power was based in Kiev. In 860, a fleet of Rus attacked Constantinople, but was repulsed. In 911, a Rus leader agreed to a treaty with Byzantium concerning trade relations, and in 980, a prince of the Kievan Rus, Vladimir (r. 980–1015), began to extend Rus power southward and westward into Poland. In 987, the emperor Basil II solicited Rus military support in his war against the Bulgars, which Vladimir promised in return for the emperor's sister as his wife. In 988, the marriage took place, and Vladimir, and eventually his people, converted to Christianity. The conversion was momentous: The last lines of division between Latin and Greek Christianity were now in place in eastern Europe, where they remain today. The steppelands north of the Black Sea and the northern Balkans were either under direct Byzantine rule or under that of the princes of Kiev. With the Kievan absorption of the Khazar khanate in 965, and the increasing Byzantine control of Armenia, the Arab threat to eastern Europe via the Caucasus vanished, and the northern and western edges of the Byzantine empire were secure.

But the Arab domination of the eastern Mediterranean, their occupation of Sicily, their landholds in south Italy, and their control of the island of Crete also posed a threat to Byzantium. In 904, Arab raiders sacked Thessalonica, the second city of the empire. But after the early tenth century, Arab attacks took the form of raids rather than invasions, and Byzantium fended them off regularly.

10

Material Civilization

THE POPULATION GROWTH OF MEDIEVAL EUROPE

Between Scandinavia and Spain, Ireland and Kiev, the population of late tenth-century Europe was around thirty-eight million people, most of them living in irregularly spaced, isolated, densely populated rural communities. Most of these communities lacked the resources to make their agriculture more efficient, and they required extensive cultivated land to feed a very small number of people. By the mid fourteenth century, the population of Europe stood at around seventy-five million, before it was decimated by the wave of drought, famine, plague, and war from which it did not fully recover until the eighteenth century. The population of mid fourteenth-century Europe cultivated far more land than that of tenth-century Europe, and it did so far more efficiently. The food surplus helped the population to grow, to break old patterns of settlement, to intensify the cultivation of land, to undertake the cultivation of new lands, and to build much larger cities. Thus, the population growth between the tenth and the fourteenth centuries transformed the way of life and rearranged the demographic and economic map of Europe.

The population growth after the tenth century did not occur at the same rate all over Europe. A glance at an approximate population table for different areas of Europe between the years 500 and 1500 reveals two striking features of this population growth: First, the population grew most rapidly between 1000 and 1300; second, the repopulation after the disasters of the mid-to-late fourteenth century occurred even more rapidly.

In preindustrial societies, population growth may occur because fertility rates increase, because sexual activity coincides closely with a woman's actual childbearing years, because mortality rates decrease, or because of a combination of these factors. In all cases, the key to growth is the number of female children in an age cohort who survive into their childbearing years. For growth to be sustained, children who are born must survive, and the amount of food available per person must either remain the same or increase. For social diversification to occur on an appreciable scale, significant numbers of people must be freed from the time-consuming task of producing their own food. All of these elements played important roles in European population growth after the tenth century.

But the circumstances of population growth are not the same in all cultures. In early Europe, some distinctive features, both natural and cultural, must also be taken into account. Serial monogamy, the sexual union of one male with one female, whether institutionalized in marriage laws or simply cohabitation, usually acts as an element of population control, even when the possibility exists that the male may have children with other women. The amount of landed wealth conventionally required to support a married couple may increase or decrease, thus lowering or raising the age of a couple at marriage. If mothers breast-feed their own children, the time between pregnancies is lengthened; if wet nurses are used, the same time is shortened. If women's mortality rate while in the childbearing age cohort declines or shifts to a later age cohort and life expectancy increases, the production of children is likely to increase. Although early Europeans appear to have used few methods of contraception and not to have practiced abortion on a significant scale, it appears that infanticide occurred regularly, usually in the cases of sickly infants and in terms of gender, more often in the case of female infants.

Celibacy, too, played a role in population control. Although clerical celibacy had always been an ideal in Latin Christianity and greatly emphasized by the Carolingians, it was rarely possible to enforce until the eleventh century. But from then on, clerical marriage as well as clerical cohabitation of any kind with women was not only more widely denounced, but actually appears to have declined.

Although early Europeans were fertile and prolific, infant mortality remained high, and many women died in pregnancy and childbirth or succumbed to related diseases shortly after giving birth. In addition, mortality rates remained high for both sexes through adolescence and into early adulthood. Although cemetery evidence is always very localized and must be used with caution, some of it indicates that in the age group 14 to 19, there were 114 females for every 100 males, a relatively small ratio. But the proportion of women to men in regional populations changed over time and from place to place. The ratio that demographers find to be the norm is around 104 males to 100 females. Mortality also differed between the sexes in terms of age groups. Male mortality after age 20 was greatest in the age cohort 40 to 59, whereas female mortality after age 20 was greatest in the age cohort 20 to 39—the ideal childbearing years. Statements about average life expectancy can be extremely misleading, particularly when they sometimes include the very high mortality rates of birth, infancy, and childhood. Better evidence comes from the studies of J. C. Russell and others on the life expectancy of males and females over age 20 in terms of the percentage of each sex that survived to age 60. Russell's results are set out in the Table on next page.

Average Percentages of Males and Females Aged 20 and Older Who Survived to 60 Years of Age

PERIOD	MALE	FEMALE
1–540	15.9	17.4
541–750	6.0	5.1
751–1000	16.9	16.4
1001–1345	9.3	10.5
1346–1500	7.9	10.8

Better diet, the reduction of infanticide in the case of female children, and more resistance to disease probably account for much of the increased demographic balance in favor of women after age 20 beginning in the year 1000. The greatest age might be extremely advanced; we know by name a great many individuals who lived into their eighties and nineties and a few who reached 100.

Besides celibacy and monogamy, other elements contributed to the specific profile of age and sex in medieval Europe. Europeans tended to marry later than other peoples, and the high rates of mortality in different age groups meant that frequently an older man might marry a younger woman and that an older woman, often a widow, might marry a younger man. This too influenced the pattern of female childbearing. A number of religious regulations, notably specified periods of abstention from sexual relations, probably reduced the childbearing period even further. In general, the population of Europe remained far younger in the aggregate than that of the modern world. In 1980, about twenty-five percent of the population was under fourteen years of age. In the thirteenth century, this figure was as high as forty percent.

The high proportion of the young in the population meant that a smaller percentage of the population was economically productive. On the other hand, it also meant that the young had to be included in the work force early. The birth rate tended to stay just slightly ahead of the mortality rate, and people tended to remain in the work force late in life. If too many people in a society grew too old to work, the burden on the work force increased because it had to support both youth and age.

The second element in medieval population growth, the availability of food per capita, will be discussed in the next section of this chapter. Here it may be noted that food production did, in fact, increase considerably, that existing arable land was cultivated more intensively, that new lands were brought under cultivation, and that the generally mild European climate during the period 1000–1300 may well have improved agricultural conditions. So too did the ending of the tenth-century invasions and the return of security, perhaps the essential requirement of a peasant society.

The final element, the freeing of part of the enlarged population from the necessity of producing its own food, led to the possibility of social diversification, to the formation of specialized occupations and the growth of the nobility and clerical orders, and to the expanding population of towns. It also permitted new settlements to grow up within the vast, largely empty lands of western and central Europe. Forests could be cleared, marshes drained, and lands reclaimed even from the ocean (as occurred in the Low Countries). Scholars have estimated that by the end of the thirteenth century, more land in Europe was under cultivation than at any time before or since. Specialized crops like grapes could be grown exclusively in one area, because people could depend on markets to provide them with the food they did not grow themselves and the means to buy it. The population expansion between the tenth and the fourteenth centuries is the basis for the development and articulation of medieval European civilization, from the specialization of agriculture to the diversification of the nobility, clergy, and urban centers and crafts.

THE AGRICULTURAL TAKEOFF

Agricultural communities were the basis of European society and the original centers of population growth. Essential to survival, trampled over by invaders and defenders, worked by serfs and free peasants, they altered the rhythm of county and kingdom alike. Their essential product was grain. In the forms of bread, porridge, and ale, grain constituted the primary diet of Europeans. Milk from cows or goats provided the calcium that grain products did not. Because they did not yet have sugar cane or sugar beets, their sweeteners were honey—which meant that beekeeping was an important part of their activity—and dried fruits, raisins from grapes and prunes from plums.

Many fruits and vegetables entered Europe from Arab agriculture. The innovation and productivity in Iraq and Iran moved west to North Africa and Muslim Spain, from which many of its results entered Christian Europe. Sugar cane was introduced by the Arabs into Sicily in the thirteenth century and into Spain in the fourteenth. Sour oranges, lemons, and limes entered Italy and Spain in the thirteenth century, as did spinach.

The more land that was cleared and the more productively the cleared land was worked, the more grain was grown. The increased availability of grain sustained population growth, and slowly vegetable proteins—legumes and radix crops like turnips, beets, radishes and rutabaga—meat, and fish supplemented the grain diet. Improved methods of planting led to the introduction of vegetable proteins and soil-renewing crops at the spring planting. Markets traded in food and spices as well as craft and luxury goods. Dairy and stock herds were sustained by increased fodder production, sometimes by seeding the fallow field with clover and chickpeas. There is considerable evidence that the abundance of large-bodied animals in Europe was greater than in any other part of the world. Not only did these animals provide nonhuman power and rich fertilizer, but large numbers of them could be killed for food in late autumn, while the rest were preserved to reproduce and replenish the meat supply the next year.

There was much work to be done, but from the eleventh century on, there was also a new kind of help. From this century, date the earliest references to the new sources of nonhuman power and the new labor-saving devices that constitute such a distinctive feature of western European history from the seventh to the nineteenth century. By the sixth century there is evidence of the increased use of waterpower. At first used chiefly to turn millwheels, by the twelfth century it was employed in a remarkable variety of ways. The sixth-century volume of saints' lives by Gregory of Tours mentions one of the earliest examples of its use:

> *The Abbot Ursus (d. ca. 500) . . . had the idea of [diminishing] the labor [of his brethren] by establishing a mill in the bed of the river Indre. Fixing rows of stakes in the river, with heaps of great stones to make dams, he collected the water in a channel and used the current to make the wheel of the machine turn with great speed. By this means he diminished the monks' work and one brother could be delegated to this task.*[1]

The water mill had been used sparingly by the Romans. In the tenth century it began to be used more regularly in the heavily rivered areas of transalpine Europe for a variety of tasks.

As important as the wider use of the water mill was the revolution in the use of animal power for plowing. The development of the stirrup and the breeding of the great and expensive war horses that appeared in Europe early in the eighth century represent another new power source. Less spectacular, but ultimately more important, were two further ways in which the horse was employed in society. Widespread use of the faster and more versatile horse in agriculture had been hampered under the Romans and in the early Middle Ages by the limitations on the weight a horse could pull, limitations imposed by the traditional system of harnessing. A tight collar around the horse's neck choked off the animal's air supply if too great a weight were attached to it. A new system of harnessing horses appeared during the tenth century. The new horse collar allowed the pressure points of the load to be placed on the horse's shoulders instead of the throat, which increased the pulling power of the animal. The horseshoe, too, appeared around this time. It complemented the increased pulling power of the horse by improving both footing and traction and by protecting the hooves against the damp, heavy clay soils of northern Europe. Thus, an animal of hitherto limited military and domestic use suddenly became the second great nonhuman power source available to Europeans.

The third source of power was wind. By the end of the twelfth century, windmills had appeared. The animal-, water-, and wind-power revolution of the tenth through the twelfth centuries was the first major development of nonhuman sources of power since the domestication of oxen and the invention of the ship, and the most important before the discovery of steam power in the eighteenth century.

These new sources of power were soon put to work. By the twelfth century, water mills and windmills were used in different phases of the process of cloth manufacture, and soon after, they were turning saws and releasing triphammers. The horse and the ox were now harnessed in tandem to pull an equally important complex machine, the heavy plow. The plow of the Mediterranean and the Near East had been developed for the soils of that world—light, sandy soils that were easily broken and pulverized, in which soil chemicals did not leach down into the subsurface. The agricultural engineering of the ancient world was not concerned with plowing techniques, but with water

[1] J. N. Hillgarth, *Christianity and Paganism, 350–750: The Conversion of Western Europe* (Philadelphia: University of Pennsylvania Press, 1986), 43.

engineering—the complicated business of keeping the dry soils moist, either through irrigation or planned flooding—and with terracing and supporting fragile hillside fields. But the Mediterranean scratch plow proved barely effective against the heavy, poorly drained clay soils north of the Alps. Although literary references suggest that the sixth century witnessed the appearance of a new kind of heavy plow, archaeological research indicates that it may have been invented even earlier. This new plow, called *carruca* by the sources (as opposed to the Mediterranean *aratrum*), appears to have begun to circulate widely after the ninth century.

Several features of the new plow bear closer examination, because they helped transform social as well as mechanical relationships. The new plow consisted of three parts: The coulter cut the sod; the plowshare lifted and turned the earth to a considerable depth; and the mouldboard shaped the turned earth into a furrow. These three parts, in other words, cut the earth, raised important soil chemicals to the surface, and provided for essential drainage. In order to operate efficiently, the new plow required considerably greater power than the older plow; not one or two oxen or horses but six or eight were needed to pull its load. The thinness of early medieval population and the unlikelihood that a single peasant would possess eight oxen suggest that a pooling of plough teams was necessary. Second, the ideal way to plow a field was to move in a straight line as far as the pitch of the field would permit in order to reduce the considerable time lost when the plow had to turn. The long narrow fields of the world of the heavy plow contrasted sharply with the square fields cultivated by the cross-plowing techniques utilized with the older scratch plow. Thus, the heavy plow introduced a degree of peasant cooperation, a redesigning of fields, and an increase in labor productivity that made faster headway in lands hitherto unsettled or vacated rather than in lands crowded with peasants who had divided their fields in traditional ways. The new plow required a long field (measures of field lengths varied greatly—the "furrow-long," or furlong, measured 66 feet by 220 yards), a headland at the end to permit the plow to make its great turn, and a layout of fields that saved time for peasants going to and from work.

The old and new systems of plowing operated on land whose use had been developed over centuries. Because animals were few and were often turned out to graze when not working, much animal manure was lost. The necessity of fertilizing the heavy soils of Europe or letting them rest fallow in order to restore their fertility directed that early plow lands generally be divided into two parts. One field was planted in the fall and the other left fallow, the process being reversed every year. Thus, half of all the arable land lay fallow at any one time. The fallow field was restored in part by animals grazing over it, leaving their manure to restore its soil. Around the eighth century, however, possibly earlier, another system appeared. Instead of two fields, one of which lay fallow, the new system provided for three. One field was planted in the fall with grain, one was planted in the spring with spring grain and peas, beans, and vetches, and the third lay fallow. Both winter and spring plantings were harvested in the summer, at which point the cycle altered: the fallow field became the winter field, the winter field became the spring field, and the spring field turned to fallow.

The advantages of the three-field system are obvious: The amount of arable land that was out of use was reduced from one half to one third; the varieties of vegetable protein from the spring planting improved and varied the diet; the beans yielded by the same spring planting returned valuable nitrogen to the soil; and the rotation of crops made the exhaustion of the land by exclusive grain growing less likely. The two- and three-field systems were not, of course, separate in time. Both coexisted with other kinds of agricultural practices. Land might be cleared, sown for a few seasons, and then left fallow indefinitely; some land might be cultivated intensively and continuously while most of the rest was cultivated and left fallow in alternate years, or planted one year and left fallow for two or three. To impose uniformity on early European agricultural practices, whether in the form of an "ideal" manor or a single system of cultivation, is to distort seriously the variety reflected in, and the chronology of, agricultural history.

Agricultural life consisted, of course, of far more than the men's work of plowing fields and working the the nearby woodland, meadow, and grazing lands. This world of peasant work also had the important dimension of rural household economy, and this component was largely directed and undertaken by women. In great and small households, women generally controlled domestic management, the accumulation and distribution of food supplies, and the rearing of children. But women's role in the household economy did not end there. If men cleared land, sowed, plowed, and reaped the fields, women made hay, sheared sheep, washed and carded the wool, spun it into cloth, milked animals, brewed beer, and harvested grapes and other fruits. Originally, the distaff was portable, and women could spin anywhere in the company of other women. But the distaff, like the hearth, moved into the house in the course of the eleventh and twelfth centuries as looms became larger, tending to isolate and restrict women to the domestic scene.

In the house proper, women assured the essential supplies of fire and water, maintained the hearth—which also moved into or close to the house in the eleventh and twelfth centuries—and often milled grain before baking it into bread. They also worked the household, or kitchen, garden, where much of the household's food was grown. Outside the house, women congregated at the local mill, at the place where community laundry was done, and at communal ovens when the hearth had not yet moved indoors. When they had to work for the lord of the manor, women worked in the *gynaeceum*, the women's workshop, where they made clothing or performed other required labor. Agricultural societies do not live by plowing and reaping alone, and writers of agricultural treatises always recognized the autonomous sphere of what they termed *opera muliebria,* the essential work of women in an agricultural economy.

THE RHYTHMS OF THE WORKING YEAR

In the book of Genesis, when Adam and Eve were expelled from the Garden of Eden, Adam was told that he would now have to work by the sweat of his brow, and Eve was to suffer the pains of childbirth and also to labor with her hands. In most pictorial representations from the ninth century on, Adam is depicted as plowing and digging, and Eve holds a child or a distaff. One of the most commonly illustrated themes in books containing prayers and calendars of saints' feast days was the depiction of peasant labor appropriate to each month. These illustrations are often important evidence of the changing practices of labor, the transformation of tools, and attitudes toward peasants.

The work calendar was synchronized with the ecclesiastical calendar, and both emphasized seasons, rather than days, weeks, or months. Significant moments of the day were marked by the sound of church bells, which had become widely used throughout Europe during the eighth and ninth centuries. No one worked for an hourly wage, and people tended to think and feel in terms of larger blocks of time than we do—mornings, afternoons, evenings, mealtimes, weeks, months, and seasons. Since there were no vacations, the only time off from work was provided by holidays and half-holidays, and holidays were, as the name implies, religious festivals. Although there was a standard yearly cycle of Christian seasons and feasts, there was also room for immense local variety. The universal ecclesiastical calendar alternated seasons of penitence and celebration. The liturgical year began in Advent, the fifth Sunday before Christmas, a season of penitence. From Christmas to Ash Wednesday was a season of celebration, followed by the forty penitential days of Lent, ending at Easter. The summer season was the second season of celebration, ending the year as Advent approached again. But within the two cycles of penitence and celebration there were many local feasts—of locally venerated saints—and often many profane activities on some religious holidays. Shrove Tuesday, or "Fat Tuesday"—*Mardi gras,* in French—the day before Ash Wednesday, the beginning of Lent, was usually wildly celebrated, as was the end of the twelve days of Christmas, January 7, called in England Plow Monday.

The work year began and ended at Michaelmas, 29 September, when the harvest was in, accounts totaled up, stock and produce moved into barns, and fields rearranged for the next plowing. Planting and sowing had to be completed by All Hallows (November 1) or Martinmas (November 11). November was "Blood month," the time for slaughtering the winter meat and threshing, winnowing, and bundling the harvested grain.

At the end of Advent came the holiday season of Christmas, the twelve days between December 25 and January 6. The great feast of Yule, or Yole, was an opportunity for heavy eating and drinking, carousing, exchanging gifts, and performing mummeries—celebrations that parodied the authority structure of the community, with such figures as the Lord of Misrule and in England, the "Boy Bishop" and the St. George's plays. The Lenten season was the time of sowing the spring seed, marked by Candlemas, February 2, the feast of the Purification of the Virgin. At Candlemas, women who had borne children were "churched," ritually accepted back into the devotional community. Seed was sown by Lady Day (the feast of the Annunciation, March 25). The great feasts of the summer season were Mayday (May 1), and the work calendar ran from Hocktide (the first Tuesday after Easter) to Lammas (August 1).

The rhythms of penitence and celebration, labor and rest, characterized everyone's year until very recent times. In the twelfth and thirteenth centuries, other means of marking time were introduced (below, Chapter 16), but some of these rhythms still echo even in the modern world.

(a)

(b)

The Labors of the Months. Scenes showing the different occupations appropriate to different months of the year often decorated astronomical manuscripts, as in this tenth-century example. (Bild-Archiv der Österreichischen Nationalbibliothek, Vienna)

RURAL SOCIETY: MANOR AND VILLAGE

The agricultural economy of medieval Europe bound lords and peasants alike into communities of enterprise and management. The term manor describes the single estate. The term includes the laboring community of serfs and free peasants each of whom lived in an individual *mansus* with its house and garden and worked the land, as well as the cultivated fields, meadows, and forest. The peasants would have shares in the cultivated land, and they also worked the *demesne*, the land reserved to the lord who held the manor, who might be a person or an institution like a monastery. A manor might be so small as to be part of a village, or so large as to include several villages. The manor and village were also legal communities, and the customs of the manor, ruled on in the manor court, constituted the only law that most rural people knew. But peasants, although they might be tied to the land, could also have families and had security in their tenure. Any increase in their rents or services required negotiation, and sometimes lords found it in their interest to convert servile dues and labor services into a cash rent.

The village church and the parish also constituted a community. It compelled the parish community's attendance at religious feasts, the mass, baptisms, penance, marriages, and funerals. After the Fourth Lateran Council in 1215, the parish also compelled yearly confession and communion. From the eighth century, all parishoners had to pay a tithe, one-tenth of their income, to the parish, and so the boundaries of parishes as tithing units became firmly fixed. The patron saint of the church was also the patron of the village community. Most villages also possessed at least one rural confraternity—a lay organization whose members banded together to care for their sick, bury and pray for the dead, and celebrate its annual feast together, distributing food and clothing to their members once a year.

The lands of the manor, of course, stretched beyond the village center, extending out into, and including, the woodland, forests, and meadows that surrounded rural villages and constituted the other major component of the woodland-field economy. These settlements were usually linked by a path or rough track, rarely by roads. In theory, each manor consisted of enough land to support a lord's household and peasant tenant farmers; in fact, many lords had several manors, and traveled from one to another throughout the year, leaving each manor to be supervised by a bailiff or reeve. The manor required not only a house for the lord and houses and barns for the lord's tenants, but cultivated land, pastures, meadows, and woodland as well. The outer woodland provided kindling, rooting ground for the village pigs, berries, timber, and hunting—the last a privilege usually reserved for the lord alone. The lord commonly controlled the appointment of the village parish priest. This person was obliged to cultivate his own plot of ground, which was given him by the lord in return for his services. On most manors, the lord took a percentage of the harvest, since his own demesne land was scattered throughout the manor fields. Villagers took their own percentages, based on the number of pieces of land they held.

Manor, village, and parish thus overlapped and together constituted the social framework for almost every person's life cycle and death. At the end of the eleventh century in England, for example, ninety percent of the population lived in small rural communities; four centuries later, even in highly urbanized areas, more than sixty percent of the population continued to live in such communities. The world of developing western Europe was emphatically and predominantly rural. Its history can be constructed from written documents—especially those from large institutions like monasteries—archaeological remains, the modern earth sciences, and place names. Its dimensions are social, economic, legal, and devotional.

In spite of the rough similarity of manors and villages, the European landscape was socially diverse. Several features of eleventh- and twelfth-century life contributed to this variety. First, large areas beyond the local village woodland began to be opened up for greater agricultural production. Second, lords' new interest in exploiting the economy of their property often led to changes in peasant status and obligations. Third, the settlement of hitherto sparsely populated lands along the edges of Europe offered new opportunities for lords and peasants alike. The eleventh and twelfth centuries saw both the internal and the external colonization of western Europe.

As new regions in settled areas were opened up for cultivation, and as unsettled areas attracted settlers, the shape and structure of manor and village slowly changed to accommodate the new character of agricultural enterprise. Such changes often benefited both lords and peasants. When lords with uninhabited lands supervised their colonization, as they did in northern Germany, Ireland, and northern France, the patterns of settlement in the new lands resembled those of the old and involved similar conditions of service and social status. When lands were let by remote lords and ecclesiastical establishments, individual entrepreneurs would be empowered to offer attractive terms to the colonists, acquire such concessions as milling and baking rights for themselves, and guide the new inhabitants to their new land, rather like the wagonmasters in the nineteenth-century United States. Cities, too, required a steady increase of settlers from the countryside. Traditionally, cities do not replace their own populations; steady immigration is required if urban populations are to sustain their numbers or grow. Migration to the cities—indeed, the entire urbanization of early Europe—took place between 900 and 1300.

RURAL SOCIETY: SERVITUDE AND FREEDOM

The agricultural development of western Europe also poses complex problems of personal legal status. These focus on the categories of servitude and freedom. Included in the category of servitude is slavery, but slavery was not the only form of servitude. In the ninth century, the abbot Irminon of the monastery of St. Germain des Prés just outside Paris, made an inventory of the lands held by the monastery, a *polyptich*. Irminon designated the dependent *mansus*, the elementary unit of landholding, according to whether it was free (*ingenuilis*), part-free (*lidilis*), or servile (*servilis*). That is, the monastery had acquired authority over lands once worked by free peasants, half-free peasants, or slaves. These estates had different obligations—the free estates had the fewest, the servile estates the heaviest. But not all the servile estates were worked by slaves. The institution of slavery depends on a regular supply of slaves, whether in the biological reproduction of a slave population or acquisition from an outside source, as well as an economic rationale for slavery. In the late Roman Empire, where slavery was either domestic or agricultural, slave populations tended not to reproduce themselves, and outside supplies of slaves became intermittent, then dried up. At the same time, landowners attempted to make their holdings self-sufficient, ensuring themselves a labor force, but also offering security in its tenure to that labor force, as well as its own housing and plots of land. Although slavery continued in many aspects of economic life into the twelfth century—and longer in the Mediterranean world—the largest part of the labor force came to consist of the half-free or partially free rural peasantry. The old Latin name for a "slave"—*servus*—became the word for the half-free serf. For chattel slaves, the term *sclavus*, from "Slav," the largest ethnic group in the later slave trade, was adopted.

By the eleventh century, the rural working population consisted mostly of serfs and free peasants, whose proportions in the population varied greatly depending on location. The organization of servitude and freedom on great estates of kings or ecclesiastical institutions was far different from that in a region consisting largely of free peasant households or a manor ruled by a single lord and consisting of a mix of slaves, serfs, and free peasant proprietors. It was often far less degrading for a free peasant to convert himself and his family into the serfs of a great landholder in return for security of tenure and the opportunity to work more land for his own benefit than to be coerced by a predatory lord into servile status.

Nor was the history of status change all in one direction. In some areas, notably Catalonia and much of eastern Europe, free peasant populations were reduced to servile status between the eleventh and the fifteenth centuries. In Catalonia, only a substantial and successful peasant revolution in the late fifteenth century reversed a process that continued to last in parts of eastern Europe until the nineteenth century.

While from the year 1000 on, chattel slavery does seem to have greatly diminished, except for its survival in domestic slavery, much of the free peasant population did experience the depression of its status into half-freedom. From the eleventh century, however, opportunities also arose to exchange servile status with its attendant mandatory labor services for free status and the payment of rent for land. Conditions in the market, as well as legal status and moral theory, influenced social mobility. That mobility was in the direction of a free peasant society. But not all of that society remained peasants—much of it moved into towns and cities.

TOWN AND CITY

The small rural village and the slightly larger country market town were the largest societies in which most medieval people lived. In the eleventh and twelfth centuries, the differences between villages and market towns, and cities, began to stand out more sharply as the latter began to grow larger and form different kinds of societies from those in the village. The cities were more densely inhabited, ranging from 100 to 200 people per 2.471 acres (one hectare). The most striking feature of the early European landscape was probably the ruins of old Roman cities and fortifications. Even they housed only very small populations, but they made useful defensive sanctuaries in time of invasion, and they were located on communication routes that were still in use. In the sixth and seventh centuries, some of them became ecclesistical centers with the specialized needs of bishops and their clergy. In the eighth and ninth centuries some fortified towns grew more attractive to merchants, and many a *portus,* centers of transportation and market facilities, grew up at their edges. Especially along the great rivers of France and Germany, trade, communications, and fortifications all contributed to the continuation of some forms of urban life.

Outside of northern Europe, however, city life survived in more clearly marked ways. The Islamic cities of Spain thrived at the two ends of the Mediterranean. In southern Italy, particularly after the Byzantine reconquest of the ninth century, such towns as Bari, Amalfi, Salerno, and Naples remained in contact with northern Italy and Byzantium. In central Italy, Rome remained a shell of the old imperial city, although the popes and the ecclesiastical affairs of the city sustained its small population and steadily attracted large numbers of pilgrims. Such port towns as Genoa and Pisa recovered slowly from Lombard and Arab domination, but by the end of the tenth and the beginning of the eleventh centuries, the small fleets of both cities had begun to regain some maritime success.

One extraordinary example of urban growth took place in the West. A region of lagoons, islands, and marshes at the head of the Adriatic Sea had long sheltered a population of fishermen and small seaports. The invasion of the Lombards late in the sixth century drove many wealthy Italians into these regions, and by the end of the eighth century the town of Venice had emerged. Under Byzantine control, and always maintaining its close maritime and commercial ties with the Byzantine Empire, where it gained increasing commercial privileges, Venice developed a mercantile fleet. Throughout the ninth century, it engaged in trade with Byzantium and the Islamic world and with the hinterland of the Po Valley. Salt and slaves constituted the earliest bases of Venetian prosperity, and by the tenth century, Venice was the central trading depot in the West for Byzantine and Islamic commerce.

Other medieval cities, however, were much more a part of the local economic and political life than was Venice. They drew on neighboring rural areas for population, food, and labor. Towns also existed as parts of larger territorial lordships, and many lords failed to treat the cities any differently from the way they dealt with their other lands. However, the lords quickly found that cities desired greater autonomy and different treatment from other forms of society. From the eleventh century on, associations of nobles and urban patricians, sometimes helped by rebellious clergy, often wrested administrative and legal control of their cities from the counts or bishops.

The new communes, which were often bitterly and savagely resisted, regulated town law and institutions, appointed their own town officials from among an urban aristocracy, and distributed their new authority across a system of offices and powers that aimed to increase the prosperity of at least that part of the population that counted as citizens. By the twelfth century, communes had begun to acquire charters from royal and episcopal authorities that specified their newly won rights and powers. Within the cities there was an increasing regulation of both economic and political affairs, as well as the beginnings of a new kind of social mobility.

Some lords, however, saw an advantage in granting to cities those rights and privileges that the citizens wanted. London, for example, was an old Roman city that had fallen on hard times after the fifth century, being displaced as the capital of England by Winchester in the Anglo-Saxon period. Like that of York, its population was around 8000, and London and York were two of only ten cities in Anglo-Saxon England with populations larger than 3500. By the end of the eleventh century, however, London had begun to grow as a commercial center, while nearby Westminster served as the center of royal government. At the death of Henry I in 1135, Londoners proudly proclaimed that it was they alone who determined who would be king of England. Actually, Henry I (r. 1100–1135) had issued a charter of privileges to London's citizens during his lifetime. This charter freed the city from the jurisdiction of Middlesex County and permitted its leading citizens, as a municipal corporation, to be solely responsible for paying all fees and taxes owed by the city to the king. In the twelfth century, London won the privileges of burgage tenure (the right to transfer ownership of land, usually as collateral for credit) and the farm of the town (to arrange internally the collection of all dues owed by the city), and the right to administer its own law courts.

The kings of England, however, like many other lay and clerical lords in the twelfth century, were never quite comfortable with town liberties. William the Conqueror (1066–1087) built the Tower of London to demonstrate that he could control the city when he needed to. But English and French kings also found it to their advantage to increase the liberties and privileges of townspeople, especially since grants of liberties increased their own revenues and offered allies in the king's dealings with the landed nobility. By the end of the twelfth century, London had a population of 30,000, a charter, a corporate seal, a mayor, more than 130 churches, and a growing collection of neighborhoods, trades, and crafts. It was the greatest city in England.

The movement for town independence in Europe was greatest where the rule of lords was weakest—in northern Italy, southern France, the Low Countries, and the Iberian peninsula. The hardy frontier society of Castile and Aragon needed settlers and fighters more than it needed traditional forms of lordship, and the towns of the Iberian peninsula won considerable rights and privileges as a result. The urban Spanish *fueros* (municipal codes of local law) and the powers of municipal representatives in the *cortes* (representative institutions of the kingdoms of Castile and Aragon) made Spanish towns early examples of virtually independent municipal corporations. In southern France, where traditional territorial lordship was difficult to establish because of the large number of small, ferociously independent lordships and because of the survival of Roman cities, towns also showed a remarkable degree of independence. The city of Narbonne, for example, was governed by its own consuls as early as 1056. In Flanders, the organization of woolen cloth production developed a number of precocious cities—notably Bruges, Ghent, Lille, Ypres, and Arras—which took advantage of the superb network of waterways and the agricultural and pastoral resources of the surrounding countryside in order to assert their independence, even, on occasion, from their own count.

The most striking examples of the movement toward urban independence are to be found in the cities of Lombardy and Tuscany in northern Italy. These cities were generally ruled by a count, a bishop, or both. Often, nobles built castles within the city and ruled the countryside from them. The cities' resistance to the invasions of the ninth and tenth centuries often permitted urban groups to bypass the powers of count and bishop and undertake corporately the defense of the city. In the eleventh century, the citizens of the northern cities played prominent roles in instituting ecclesiastical reforms that reduced the authority of the local bishop. In general, the lords of the northern Italian cities were not as powerful as the kings of England and France or the counts of Flanders or Champagne. During the eleventh and twelfth centuries, municipal corporations took over more and more rights of governance, usually with charters from their bishops or the emperor authorizing them to do so.

The new municipal corporations, with their roots in recent military, political, and religious change, invented new political offices through which to rule themselves. The office of consul, for example, appears in many northern Italian towns from the late eleventh century: in Pisa around 1085, in Asti in 1095, in Milan in 1097 after a revolt against the archbishop's authority, in Arezzo in 1098, and in Genoa in 1099. The consuls ruled what came to be called the commune. They were elected by those citizens possessing the franchise (members of the municipal corporation) and served as rulers of the cities for a specific period. Votes on important matters were often presented to the citizens at larger assemblies, and the consuls were frequently more like city managers than city rulers. The need for the municipal corporation to delegate authority to consuls, or to representatives of the city in its dealings with other cities, the pope, or the emperor, created a constitutional climate in which corporate authority, delegated power, representative government, and other aspects of a new political order became highly developed. Although none of the communes was democratic and all continued to be ruled by a corporate patrician elite, the nature of political authority in them was novel in the eleventh and twelfth centuries.

By the end of the twelfth century, urban corporate lordship was far advanced in northern Italy, and its experience widened the political horizons of Europeans for centuries to come. Not yet democratic, barely republican in a classical sense, the northern Italian cities nevertheless were genuinely new political communities that disturbed traditional ideas of hierarchical political order. Even though they were closely governed, their political power was distributed more widely and used more versatilely than anywhere else in Europe. With the new political order came increased population growth, a commercial revolution, and even new forms of urban spirituality and lay culture. Cities also prided themselves on their autonomy in the face of claims from the rural nobility. Some jurists claimed that a serf who managed to get to a city and dwell there for a year and a day lost his servile status. German historians coined the phrase, *Stadtluft macht frei*—"The air of the city makes a man free"—to characterize the urban idea of personal liberty in northern Europe as well as in Italy. In the fourteenth century, the Italian jurist Bartolus of Sassoferrato coined a formula that seemed to a world of kings, lords, and princes the troubling embodiment of urban freedom: *civitas sibi princeps*—"the city is a prince unto itself." The new reality of independent city-republics was thus cast in the constitutional language of revived and transformed Roman law.

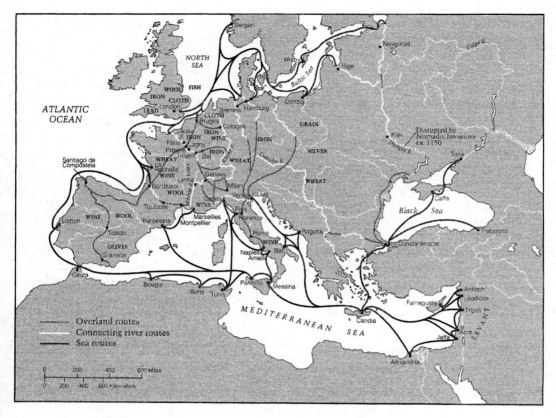

Medieval cities and trade routes.

THE ADVENTURE OF TRADE

In the Byzantine and Islamic worlds, trade played an important and recognized role in social, legal, and economic life. Merchants' journals, their correspondence, and descriptions of trade and travel conditions from North Africa across the Middle East as far as the Baltic Sea and the Volga illuminate whole regions and classes of people about whom no western source speaks until the late tenth century. In the matter of trade, as in many other areas, eleventh-century western Europe was far less developed than Byzantium and Islam.

The strangers who came to trade in the small western European ports, markets, and fairs were sometimes pirates and thieves (as were the Vikings) who shifted their activities from plunder to trade as it suited them. More often, however, they were hard-working small-scale caboteurs, traders in wool, foodstuffs, craft goods, and slaves, often trading over short distances. *Homines duri* ("hard men") they were called, and their lives involved far more risks than pleasures. Like all strangers in the early Middle Ages, they possessed no legal identity in the towns and markets they visited and at first received little protection from local authorities. They needed protection from robbers, arbitrary confiscation of their wares, and the frequent tolls that private authorities imposed on their goods. They had to deal with the infinite variety of local weights and measures, as well as coinage, which differed from region to region and were important signs of the particularism of eleventh-century Europe. Their activities were confined to specific places; they might sell their goods only for the duration of a fair; they had to deal fairly, pay their bills, and leave when their work was done. Before the eleventh century, European communities had no place for people who possessed no local identity, who had no status (in the anthropologist's sense of the word), who were not part of the local community.

By the end of the eleventh century, trading conditions had improved. Some lay and clerical authorities worked out the rudimentary privileges of merchants who visited their markets and fairs and began to create a protected identity for merchants. The *homines duri* became a more common sight, and the image of the merchant began to change from that of a "hard" man to that of a "sly" man. Ecclesiastics worried more about the moral consequences of the merchant and the spiritual dangers of his wealth than about his sword and his wrath. The changing adventure of trade in the period between the tenth and the twelfth centuries reflects not only economic growth and diversity, but also the alteration of a warrior and peasant society into a society with room for merchants, administrators, and townspeople.

Lords and communities that did not accommodate merchants soon found themselves at a disadvantage with those who did. The most striking example of aristocratic patronage of trade is the series of great fairs held annually in Champagne, where the trade of southern Europe met that of northern Europe. The counts of Champagne, ambitious and astute territorial princes, offered protection to visiting merchants, having devised novel legal procedures for this purpose, and they regulated commercial practices carefully. In the twelfth and thirteenth centuries, Champagne developed a cycle of six fairs a year, from the fair at Lagny in early January through fairs at Provins and Bar-sur-Aube to the "cold fair" at Troyes in December. These fairs represent the first regular large-scale commercial enterprise in European history.

With the development of the Champagne fairs, luxury goods and exotic items became part of a large-scale trading network that included raw and finished wool, furs, crafted goods, grain, and wine. The variety of regions represented at the fairs helped begin the long process of standardizing weights, measures, coinage, and law. A specialist mercantile law spread from developed fairs to places just beginning to establish their own markets. Like the travels of pilgrims, those of merchants opened up new routes of communication and exchange throughout most of western Europe. In fact, the fairs held by the monks of the monastery of Saint-Denis, near Paris, combined the pilgrimage to the shrine of the saint with the sale of the wine produced on the monastery's lands.

European agricultural conditions and the European climate both created demands that could be satisfied only by manufactured goods. Iron tools, wine, building materials, and wool for clothing were not usually produced locally; they had to be bought from their manufacturers or from traders. More than the expensive consumption of luxury goods by aristocrats and high clergy, this necessary domestic trade marks a distinctive change in European life. Sometimes the two kinds of trade were combined.

Venice began its great commercial career by trading salt from its own region, then by shipping grain and timber to Constantinople and slaves to Muslim lands, and then by bringing back luxury goods from the East.

In many areas of Europe the towns signaled the new importance of trade. In Flanders, northern Italy, and southern France, urban centers became centers of economic exchange. The rich wool of England and Flanders was processed in the Flemish cities and sold at fairs. It even passed to northern Italy, whose merchants then transported it to the Near East and traded it with Muslim merchants. Both the urbanization of trade and the kinds of goods being manufactured at this time help explain another feature of European economic development—technological innovation and its rapid influence on all forms of life.

The early history of the water mill reflects this characteristic of European culture. By the eleventh century, not only had this method of grinding grain spread more widely than ever before, but new applications of its physical principles were continually appearing. The principle of water-powered rotary motion was adapted to the creation of reciprocal motion from the same power source. Thus, by the twelfth century, water mills were being used for the fulling of cloth and the powering of sawmills. The extent of the use of these new devices suggests a propensity for the application of technological developments to industrial use very quickly, more so than in earlier periods and in other civilizations. The organization of new monasteries and settlements in former wasteland, the increase in the demand for such products as cloth, iron, and spices, and the existence of a complex market system all contributed to the spread of technological developments and their application across a broad band of the labor spectrum. Although the scale of such development was very small by modern standards, its mere existence is significant. Agriculture on a very large scale and small local centers of industrial and commercial enterprise were the driving forces of the medieval economy.

11

Power and Society

LORDSHIP AND KINGSHIP

The most common formula that people in the eleventh century used to describe the structure of their society was that of the three orders—those who pray, those who fight, and those who labor. The idea that society was divided into three functional parts had appeared earlier, for example in King Alfred's translation of Boethius's *Consolation of Philosophy* late in the ninth century: "A king's raw materials and instruments of rule are a well-peopled land, and he must have men of prayer, men of war, and men of work." This idea of a tripartite society reflected both an idealized conception and a descriptive set of functional norms.

The prayers of the clergy, in an age when most lay people—whether fighters or laborers—usually feared that they were too sinful and inarticulate to pray for themselves, were essential for the spiritual well-being of the men of war and the men of work. In turn, the men of war fought to protect the men of prayer and the men of work. Finally, the men of work labored to feed the men of prayer and the men of war. About a century after Alfred, Abbo of Fleury took up a version of the theme again, this time using a model of two orders, laity and clergy:

> *Concerning the first order of men, that is laymen, it must be said that some of them are farmers, others warriors. Farmers sweat at agriculture and other crafts in a rustic manner, whereby they sustain the multitude of the whole Church. The warriors, supported by the dues of military service, ought not contend with each other in the womb of their mother [the Church], but by their military skills contend against the enemies of the holy Church of God.*

For Abbo, the men of war and the men of work were two subdivisions of the laity in a society conceived of as "the Church," parallel to and supporting the other order, the clergy. In Abbo's view and that of other writers who followed him, the laborers' work was essential, for it fed everyone else, even if it was always grossly undercompensated, usually disrespected, and often scorned. He is critical of the men of war because they sometimes inflicted violence on each other instead of using their skills against their proper object.

In spite of its conventional popularity, however, Abbo's shorthand image of the tripartite society concealed great differences within each of the orders. The men of work might be successful merchants, highly skilled craftsmen, prosperous free peasants, upper-level serfs who performed administrative services for their lords, half-free rural laborers, or slaves. A man of prayer might be an immensely wealthy and powerful prince-bishop of Durham or Cologne or an impoverished bishop from a tiny Italian diocese; he might be an abbot of a vast network of monasteries like the abbot of Cluny (below, Chapter 12), or an isolated scholar at a very small monastery like Guibert at Nogent (1055–ca. 1125, below, Chapter 12). Among men of war were emperors, kings, and great lords, but also poor knights living in their lord's castle or in houses that he gave them, and owing him military service. What is most striking about Abbo's discussion of the laity, is his assumption that laborers did not fight, and fighters did not labor.

Thus, no matter how low on the scale of warriors a knight stood, he was considered to have more in common with all other warriors, no matter how much more noble or powerful, than he did with even the most prosperous and skilled "laborer." The first concern of all fighting men was to distinguish themselves (and be recognized as distinguished) from peasants, merchants, or craftsmen. The same distinction made it possible for the order of fighters to acknowledge their military skills as creating a common bond among their members. That bond was strengthened by changes in the expense and technology of military activity and by the concept of knighthood. In order to understand the character of eleventh- and early twelfth-century power, it is essential to understand the relationships among the men of war.

In the preceding chapters, we saw a new nobility take shape in the late ninth and tenth centuries. The members of this nobility combined the social status of high birth with old royal titles of service (count, duke, viscount) and landed wealth that enabled them to bind subordinates to them by oaths of fidelity. The creation of this new form of lordship transformed older social relations and made the bond between the lord and his man more important than that between king and subject. In order to rule effectively, kings had to control lords, who in turn controlled their own men. One way for kings to do this, was to make themselves the lords of the lords. But to do this, was to transform the older Carolingian and Anglo-Saxon ideas of kingship. Such a step required assistance from the clergy, who emphasized the sacred character of kingship, and from the nobles themselves, who had to recognize the king's hierarchical superiority over them in order to justify their own superiority over their inferiors. Kings first had to become effective lords in the lands they ruled personally—their royal *demesne*—before they could hold sway over distant and independent lords who preferred to exercise their inherited or invented authority untroubled by royal interference.

Older noble families also changed their structure, inheritance patterns, and consciousness of family in the eleventh and twelfth centuries. Around the turn of the year 1000, many noble families, like kings, began to think of their lands as indivisible and to pass them down to a single heir, usually the eldest son, in a process that came to be called primogeniture. Each generation looked back to a dynastic line traced from father to son, assuming a patrilineal memory that excluded collateral relatives and usually the family of the mother. The lands of the lineage were consolidated into compact areas, more and more of whose inhabitants were protected and dominated by the family castle.

Around the turn of the eleventh century, there occurred a transformation of the noble residence. Counts and others began to build castles, defensive residences of wood or stone, both functional and symbolic indications of their power. The castle was ruled by the castellan, who might hold the castle under a greater lord or in his own interest. The castle dominated the land and people around it. Ambitious territorial princes often built a number of castles to demonstrate their power and defend themselves from neighboring and equally predatory lords, but even a single castellan owing allegiance to nobody was a formidable neighbor. He could subject local inhabitants, servile or free, to the payment of dues for his protection and force them to swear oaths of allegiance to him. Increasingly, the nobility identified with and named itself after the castle that held its domains together.

Sons excluded from the landed inheritance increasingly had to fend for themselves, usually at the courts of powerful men or in careers in the church. Such unmarried and landless fighting men who hoped to gain favor in the courts of more powerful men were called "youths," regardless of their actual age. They might enter the service of a landed lord or wander from place to place seeking fame at tournaments that might move a lord to accept them in his service. Daughters did not entirely lose the power they once held; a daughter could sometimes inherit in default of a male heir or marry and bring the inheritance to her husband, who himself might be a nobly born "youth" but could only restore his fortune by marrying an heiress.

In most cases, descent in the male line increasingly dominated noble society. The lands as a unit often gave the new, identifying name to such patrilineal dynasties: Men in the line of inheritance assumed the name "of"—*de, von,* or *of*—the name of their castle or territory, further distinguishing themselves from more remote relatives who could not use the identifying place name. If a male line died out, the title and territorial lordship might pass to a male relative, as happened in Flanders in 1119 when Baldwin VII died childless of a battlefield wound, designating his cousin Charles of Denmark (later Charles the Good of Flanders) as his heir and successor. When the childless Charles the Good was murdered in 1127 by low-born officials who feared that he would reimpose servile status upon them, only then, with the male line virtually exhausted, did the right to appoint the next count of Flanders finally revert to its lord, Louis VI, the king of France.

The authority of the eleventh- and twelfth-century nobles derived from their claims of noble lineage and the older private and public wealth and offices that they had accumulated from the weakening of late Carolingian kingship. In addition to consolidating and perpetuating land and income, they assumed control of older public financial obligations that had once belonged to the king and his servants. Such rights, from the collection of fines in courts that they ruled to the collection of old and sometimes forgotten taxes, made the aristocracy of the eleventh and twelfth centuries a group of private lords wielding what had once been "public" authority.

For more than two centuries, historians have characterized the infinitely varied practices of lordship and dependence discussed in this and later chapters by the blanket term "feudalism." The term, however, has been used to describe so many different things for so many different purposes, implying a uniformity and consistency in social and political relationships that certainly did not exist anywhere, that historians who know the sources have become extremely reluctant to use it at all, particularly since it was never used during the period to which it is usually so carelessly applied. Instead, historians now use terms like "power," "lordship," and "dependence"—terms that people did use of themselves and their relationships. For example, it was once fashionable to characterize "feudalism" as the existence of "public authority in private hands," based on the bestowing by a lord of a "fief" (Latin *feodum*, whence the term "feudalism") on a vassal who had sworn allegiance and acknowledged the obligation of performing military service to him. But lordship, fief, vassalage, and military service were rarely connected to each other, especially before the twelfth century. Historians now prefer to study particular relationships without the unnecessary and misleading baggage that the term "feudalism" brings with it.

Instead, historians have analyzed the different kinds of lordship that were exercised. Three in particular are worth noting. *Domestic lordship* was a relationship between a lord and individuals who were directly attached, but infinitely subordinate, to him, generally serfs. There was no oath of fidelity between them. A second type, *landlordship,* was based on control of land rather than individuals. Tenants of a lord's land owed him services and rents because they held land that owed these things, not because they were personally bound to him. A third type was *banal* lordship (derived from the power of the *ban,* a kind of public authority). Here, the rights of lordship that had survived from older public authority were wielded by individual lords for their own benefit. When differentiated in this manner, lordship is seen as the essential basis of the different kinds of power that the "men of war" had come to exercise by the eleventh and twelfth centuries.

Although warfare had been one of the phenomena that created the noble order, the changing character of warfare helped give that order its new shape and potential inclusiveness of all fighting men. The men of war increasingly fought on horseback, riding specially bred warhorses, wearing long shirts of chain mail over hardened leather and protective caps made of iron or steel plates. The horse was shod, and the saddle included stirrups, which enabled the mounted warrior to charge with a long lance instead of a light spear, since the impact of the striking lance would be absorbed by the stirrups. The knight's weapons also included a sword, a long shield, and a mace, a weighted club. To acquire such a warhorse and such weapons required considerable wealth, either one's own or a gift from a superior. To use them effectively, required long years of training. Military training and engagement required more and more of the warrior's time and style of life. The days of the peasant militia were temporarily over.

The new power of the warrior order and the social conditions of the eleventh and twelfth centuries made violence an increasingly normal fact of life. However, indiscriminate violence was also widely challenged after the tenth century. From that time on, movements of clergy and laymen sprang up in a number of different places, with the intention of curbing private warfare. It was not for nothing that warlords gave lands and income to the Church, undertook penitential pilgrimages, and sometimes became members of monastic communities at the end of their lives. The nobility that saved Europe from the invasions of the late ninth and tenth centuries was hardly less efficient than the invaders at enforcing its own rights and wants, whether real or imagined.

The idea of peace had been surrounded with spiritual legitimacy in the Gospels and the writings of the Church fathers, and it echoed in the canons of ecclesiastical councils down to the tenth century. At a council at Charroux, near Poitiers, in 989, an assembly of bishops pronounced a solemn condemnation, over relics, of anyone who attacked a cleric or robbed the poor. From that date on, longer and longer lists of specific prohibitions against attacking certain classes of people were issued by ecclesiastical assemblies, frequently with local laymen joining in the pronouncements. By the mid eleventh century the Peace of God had become formalized; it designated protected classes of persons and regulated the character of violence. The Truce of God, which soon followed, protected certain times of the week and year. These assemblies prohibited violence, at first during the periods of Easter, Lent, and Advent, and later the period in every week from sundown Wednesday to sunrise Monday. These rules were enforced by sworn members of the local peace associations.

These movements did not consist simply of pious pronouncements by ecclesiastics. Laymen joined in the acts of proclamation, and by the end of the eleventh century, the peace associations had emerged as powerful local groups, joined by a common oath and secured by a willing armed force. In some areas, these groups grew powerful enough to be considered local governments in themselves, and in strong local principalities such as Normandy, the Peace of God became the Peace of the Duke, a new means of expanding the local ruler's power over independent nobles. The emperor Henry III (below, Chapter 13) publicly preached a peace sermon in Constance in 1043. As the end of the century approached, peace movements, peace associations, and the concepts of the Peace and the Truce of God themselves acquired great emotional and institutional strength. The lords against whom many of these movements were directed often found themselves either facing strong resistance or being invited to participate in the movements themselves. In the latter instance, lords could further legitimate their military prowess by casting an air of spiritual legitimacy over themselves as warriors and over their particular warlike functions.

Although the peace movements reduced one early prerogative of the nobles, they did so by justifying the use of limited violence against breakers of the peace and large-scale warfare against infidels. Along with the private and banal rights of the aristocracy there emerged a new form of legitimizing noble status—that of protector of the peace of the Church. It is in the light of such movements and the nobility's efforts to justify its social superiority that the institution of knighthood ought to be understood. Once the skills of the fighting man were dedicated to a set of values approved by the clergy, one obstacle to the elevation of his status was removed—the traditional Christian ban on violence. From the tenth century on, in art, saints' lives, chronicles, and cult, the figure of the warrior dedicated to God became prominent. Otto I's church at Magdeburg was dedicated to the soldier-saint Maurice. Other cults of warrior saints—George and Theodore, for example, as well as Michael the Archangel—also flourished, and the cult of Martin, which had long ignored his military history, now also became the cult of a warrior-saint. The act of receiving arms was ritualized into a religious ceremony, and weapons and other accoutrements of war were blessed and dedicated to Christian service. Thus, the men of war—whether wealthy hereditary rulers or simple knights—constituted something more than a functional "order" within a tripartite society. They created social and economic divisions among themselves, but at the same time, linked the highest and wealthiest group with the lowest and poorest. The ethos of this change came to be called chivalry, from the French term for horse—*cheval*—characterized (at least in its self-idealizing literature and books of manners) by bravery, fame, generosity, and the manners of the court, the lordly household whose rules of behavior became the model for all fighting men.

Knights and lords transformed the character of political power within society, and they posed to kings the problem of transforming lordship over individuals and territorial principalities into territorial monarchy.

EAST *FRANCIA* AND THE IMPERIAL TITLE

Under the first four Saxon kings the kingdom of East *Francia* achieved a sense of identity that was not substantially weakened by the frequent revolts by members of the royal family and the leading nobles. Otto I had insisted that if he should die without an heir, the kingdom ought to remain within his wider family and that it was indivisible. Even the considerable attention paid to the affairs of Italy and Rome by Otto II and Otto III and their pronounced interest in the imperial title did not alter the separate conceptions that their most powerful subjects held of the kingdom and the empire. The failure of later Ottonian policies in Italy, however, did cause unrest in the kingdom of East *Francia*. Otto III had taken for his motto "The Renewal of the Roman Empire." But Otto's successor, Henry II, (1002–1024), the last of the male line of Saxon kings, adopted as his motto the phrase "The Renewal of the Kingdom of the Franks" and devoted much of his reign to affairs north of the Alps.

The last Saxon rulers managed to establish generally stable territorial frontiers to the west, through negotiations with the new Capetian dynasty of the kingdom of West *Francia,* and in the east, by establishing diplomatic and ecclesiastical relations with the rulers and the churches of Poland, Hungary, and Bohemia (below, this Chapter). In the southeast, they converted part of the old Carolingian East March, originally erected to defend against the Avars, into an "eastern region," or *Ostarrichi,* an increasingly Germanized area that formed the core of the later duchy of Austria. Within the East Frankish kingdom, Henry II added his own domains in Bavaria to the older Saxon and Franconian resources of the Saxon dynasty. He also laid the groundwork for the claim of his successor, Conrad II, to the throne of the kingdom of Burgundy. During his reign, Henry II relied heavily on the Church. He supported monastic reform programs and continued to recruit talented clergy for service in the royal chapel, from which they could be promoted to high ecclesiastical office throughout the empire. However, he also exploited ecclesiastical property for the purpose of royal service and controlled the appointment of bishops in the duchies he did not rule himself.

In spite of his two titles of king and emperor, Henry II also faced difficulties that were characteristic of Saxon East *Francia*. He had to be careful about delegating power and territory, for these tended to slip away from the kings and into the private control of those who received them. Lacking a consistent system of communication with his officials, the king had to travel constantly—and over a much larger territory than that of any other ruler in Europe. In East *Francia,* where ducal power was strong and growing stronger and where the inhabitants were acutely conscious of their own local legal traditions, the frequent physical presence of the king was essential. Although Bavaria naturally saw much of the king, Saxony was the duchy in which Henry II traveled the most. The rich ceremonial trappings that accompanied the king's travels were enhanced by the support of ecclesiastical ritual, invoking every possible image of the divine grace and favor that were often assumed to distinguish the kings from powerful nobles. Henry II also cultivated the memory of Charlemagne as the ideal Christian ruler, as his motto suggests.

In spite of their attempts to assert themselves over and above the dukes and great nobles, the Saxon kings were regularly drawn into private feuds, faced rebellions, and were forced to compromise with mighty subjects. Lacking adequate institutions and having little control over duchies of which they were not the rulers, they were forced to work personally, usually against formidable opponents and interests. The Saxon dynasty had to conciliate, honor, and use members of different ethnic groups—Saxons, Franconians, Bavarians, Swabians, Lotharingians and others—and therefore no single group could claim a monopoly on royal closeness, service, or benefits. Because of this, loyalties tended to remain local rather than be extended to the kingdom as a whole. Paradoxically, as the king and some of the high churchmen became less localized and spoke more regularly from the eleventh century on of a "Kingdom of the Germans," the powerful inhabitants of the duchies remained local minded and could only with difficulty be persuaded or coerced into thinking in kingdomwide terms.

When Henry II died in 1024, leaving no male heir and designating no successor, the question emerged once again of the elective principle becoming an instrument against the power of a single dynasty. But both candidates for the throne were cousins by descent from Liutgard (931–953), a daughter of Otto I, and the election of Conrad II (1024–1039), whose mother Adelheid also claimed descent from the Merovingian dynasty of the Franks, was peaceable. Anointed and crowned by the Archbishop of Mainz, Conrad was crowned king of Italy in 1026, won the imperial title in 1027, and successfully established his claim to the kingdom of Burgundy in 1033. Geographically, Burgundy greatly strengthened Conrad's access to Italy. The possession of the three crowns of Germany, Italy, and Burgundy, as well as the imperial title, greatly added to the prestige of Conrad II. Conrad also continued the practice of strong kingship of Henry II, visited Aachen, and sat on Charlemagne's throne. His biographer, Wipo, remarked that "Charlemagne's stirrups are suspended from Conrad's saddle."

No matter how great his titles and prestige, however, Conrad II also faced the divided great nobility as well as new groups that asserted themselves as possessing rights that the nobility could not fail to oppose. In a dispute in northern Italy in 1035, Conrad came out in full support of the lesser nobility against the greater nobility and the powerful churchmen, assuring the lesser nobility that its own family interests would be protected by making landholdings heritable and by assuring them that their relations with greater lords would be regulated by courts of their own equals.

During Conrad's reign, a class of men, ministerials, who performed knight service and performed other administrative services to greater lords but were themselves serfs and therefore unfree, claimed certain rights that derived from the dignity of the kinds of service they performed. The term *ministerialis* appears to have been applied to them first in episcopal service and later in the service of lay lords and kings. Although the rise of the ministerials was slow and unsteady, here too a new force was located in the lesser nobility and service knights that later shaped the internal political culture of the kingdom.

At the beginning of Conrad's reign, the people of the city of Pavia in northern Italy destroyed the royal residence there on the grounds that the last king had been dead and there was no king at the time of the destruction. To this argument, Conrad II asserted that, "If the king is dead the kingdom remains, just as the ship remains even if the helmsman falls overboard." In this assertion of the indivisibility and continuity of the kingdom apart from the lives of individual kings, Conrad was asserting the enduring and indivisible character of kingdoms in eleventh-century thought. The kingdom was an entity apart from local duchies and leading families, apart, too, from the normal patterns of private inheritance and division of property common in many legal systems. Conrad combined this view with a powerful dynastic awareness, associating both his wife Gisela and his son in the rule of the empire with him. This awareness of the existence of the kingdom, an equal awareness of the existence of the empire, and a strong dynastic consciousness mark the reigns of Conrad II and his son and successor, Henry III (1039–1056). These first two Salian kings of the *regnum Teutonicorum*, the "Kingdom of the Germans," continued the policies of their Saxon predecessors, elevating the ideal of kingship to the highest in Europe, and acknowledging their responsibilities in ecclesiastical and imperial affairs. But the cases of the lesser nobility and the ministerials indicate that there were other forces in the kingdom as well, forces that included the great "tribal" dukes and the higher nobility, as well as reform-minded churchmen and disruptive local interests. Beyond the Salian triumph there lay problems that the kingship was ill equipped to solve.

THE PRINCIPALITIES AND KINGDOMS OF CENTRAL EUROPE

Bulgaria and Russia entered the orbit of Byzantine influence in the tenth and eleventh centuries, but Hungary, Bohemia, and Poland, as well as the Scandinavian kingdoms, entered that of the Latin church and the powerful influence of the kings, territorial princes, and bishops of East *Francia*. The result was the creation of Latin Christian kingdoms in these areas, which became ecclesiastically independent of German prelates and at least initially stablized their territories. The victory of Otto I at the Lechfeld in 955, signaled the end of the Magyar raids into western Europe. But Otto I and his successors did not conduct only defensive campaigns against Slavic and Magyar military threats. Otto I created several large eastern command areas, or Marches, that extended his power east of the Elbe river; he also established bishoprics in the north and east, subordinating those in the north—Aarhus, Ripen, and Schleswig—to the archbishopric of Hamburg-Bremen and those in the northeast—Brandenburg and Havelberg—originally to that of Mainz. Additionally, Otto also received permission from the bishop of Rome, John XIII, to elevate his favorite foundation of Magdeburg to the rank of archbishopric in 968, which absorbed Brandenburg and Havelberg as well as the newly created bishoprics of Merseburg and Meissen.

Both the southern German archbishopric of Salzburg and the bishopric of Passau were energetic in proselytizing among the Bohemians and the Magyar. The work of Pilgrim, bishop of Passau (971–991), and Adalbert of Prague, led to the conversion of Vaik (r. 997–1038), son of the Magyar duke Geza, in 996. Otto III stood as Vaik's godfather, and Vaik took the Christian name Stephen, marrying Gisela, the sister of Duke Henry of Bavaria. He also arranged with the bishop of Rome, Silvester II (998–1003) in 1001, that the Magyar kingdom should have its own archbishop at Esztergom, thereby making Hungary a metropolitan province ecclesiastically independent of the bishops of the kingdom of the Germans. Vaik/Stephen also reputedly received a crown from the bishop of Rome and was locally revered as a saint in 1083. Stephen became the patron saint of Hungary, and the crown of Stephen remains the most treasured symbol of the modern Hungarian state.

Adalbert of Prague (ca. 956–997), who had participated in the conversion of Vaik/Stephen, was a Slav noble born in Bohemia. Several Bohemian princes had converted to Christianity in the late ninth and early tenth centuries under the influence of Bavarian missionaries, and one of them, Vaclav (ca. 907–929, Wenceslaus, Wenzel), a member of the Premyslid dynasty, became the national saint of Bohemia, the "Good King Wenceslas" of the carol. Wenceslaus' brother Boleslav promoted the local cult of his brother and moved his remains to the prosperous town of Prague, which was made a bishopric around 960. Boleslav I's sister, Dobrava, married Miesko I (ca. 922–992), a duke of the Poles (the name refers to the agriculturally rich plains of modern central Poland) of the Piast dynasty, around 964. Through Dobrava's efforts, Miesko was baptized in 966, and the first Polish bishopric was established at Poznan in 968.

Adalbert of Prague studied in Magdeburg and was made bishop of Prague by Otto II in 983. But the opposition of his family to the ruling Premyslid dynasty and his prickly insistence on rigorous religious observance encountered the opposition of Boleslav II and drove Adalbert from Prague to Italy. Adalbert was invited to Poland, where he was martyred on a conversion mission to the Prussians in 997. Adalbert's remains were buried at Gniezno, and in 999, he became one of the first saints to be canonized by a pope. The cult of Adalbert attracted widespread interest, especially that of his old friend, the emperor Otto III, who made a ceremonial journey to Gniezno in the year 1000.

Otto's pilgrimage to Gniezno was also a significant diplomatic gesture. He raised Gniezno to the status of bishopric, and he formally recognized the Polish duke, Boleslav Chrobry "the Great" (r. 992–1025) as "brother and coworker of the empire."

Poland, Bohemia, and Hungary remained in the orbit of the empire, but their kings' and bishops' independence from direct German political and ecclesiastical rule gave them a degree of autonomy that permitted local economic, ecclesiastical, and political development under native kings and clergy. Poland especially, under Boleslav Chrobry, expanded considerably to the east, fought a series of wars with Henry II, and finally was recognized as king by the pope shortly before his death.

By 1025, the principalities and kingdoms of central Europe had been formed, converted to Latin Christianity, and stabilized.

FROM WEST *FRANCIA* TO FRANCE

Unlike East *Francia,* West *Francia* possessed few territories in which local history gave a sense of common identity to their inhabitants. To be sure, the territories of Brittany and the Basques possessed both an ethnic character and former royal designations as marches. Aquitaine and Burgundy also possessed a strong historical and political identity. Other territories, however, were the products of the successful ambitions of holders of the titles of counts and dukes and of the progressive divisions and redivisions to which West *Francia* had been subjected after the death of Louis the Pious in 840. Such were the counts of Anjou and Maine and the dukes of Normandy.

By the late tenth century, the term *Francia* might mean one of the three broad sections into which the old Carolingian kingdom was divided (along with Aquitaine and part of Burgundy), or, more commonly, it referred to that part of the old kingdom of West *Francia* that had shrunk to the region between Beauvais and Orleans, the *Ile-de-France* in the middle Seine Valley, centered on Paris and ruled by the last Carolingian kings but largely under the control of powerful local nobles and independent castellans. Aside from the kings, the nobility of tenth-century West *Francia* was largely descended from the earlier Carolingian nobility. However, its concept of its place in the kingdom, its relation to its own local lands, its strategies for dealing with neighbors (whether more or less powerful than itself), and its attitude toward the king and the kingdom were all different from those of the eighth and early ninth centuries. Other divisions separated the old Carolingian West *Francia* from the tenth-century kingdom, including those of vernacular language and the different experience of outside invasions.

The last Carolingian king of West *Francia,* Louis V (d. 987), ruled only a fraction of the former kingdom, and even within his own lands was rivaled by other families, notably that of the Robertines, the "*duces* of the Franks," who had already provided a king in West *Francia* earlier in the tenth century. But even in the diminished territory known as *Francia,* the kings faced further erosions of older royal authority. Some of the great peripheral territories—Normandy, Brittany, Aquitaine, and Burgundy—had to all intents and purposes broken away under their own rulers. Large territories in the east were disputed with the kings of East *Francia.* Still other territories, under leaders who proclaimed themselves princes, dukes, marquesses, or counts—Flanders, Maine, Blois, Champagne, and Anjou—existed in virtual independence of the king, and sometimes of other large territorial rulers. They rarely visited the royal court or witnessed royal charters, and the king never entered their territories. Territorial and banal lordship was also claimed by rulers of even smaller territories, castellans and simple knights. In many parts of the kingdom, bishoprics and the estates and control of monasteries fell into the hands of ambitious territory-building families.

When the last Carolingian king died in 987, the Robertine family, unlike Conrad I of Franconia or Henry I of Saxony, had already seen one of its members on the throne of West *Francia* since 888. The only Carolingian claimant, Charles of Lorraine, the uncle of Louis V, was not attractive to the nobles and prelates who had to decide on a king. The election of Hugh Capet in July 987, permanently changed the dynasty of West *Francia*.

Hugh Capet (987–996), his son Robert II (996–1031), and his grandson Henry I (1031–1060) had to fight hard to preserve the shrunken monarchical possessions of West *Francia*. Chronicles and official documents suggest strongly that the kings were surrounded by local subjects only, with few distant lords appearing at their courts. Ties of vassalage to the king weakened among higher clergy as well during the first half of the eleventh century.

During this period, the kings of West *Francia* were effective kings only where they were effective lords, and this meant strictly on their own properties and the royal demesne lands around Paris. The counts or dukes of Champagne, Blois, Chartres, Anjou, Maine, Normandy, and Flanders were individually far more powerful than the kings of *Francia,* but they were also rivals with each other for greater territories, and they never collaborated against the weaker kings. Even this nominal recognition of the distinctiveness of the royal title helped preserve the kingship of *Francia*. In theory at least, some of the surviving characteristics of Carolingian theocratic kingship, for example anointing in a liturgical ceremony and their claim to rule by the grace of God, differentiated the kings from the other great lords. During the reign of Robert II, the legend of the king's power to cure certain diseases by his touch began to circulate. The ecclesiastical literary patronage of Robert managed to preserve the memory of some of these important traditional attributes even in the most difficult days of the kings, when they were hard put to establish their lordship even in the heart of their own demesne. Unlike his contemporaries in East *Francia*, however, Robert stopped short of making for himself the strongest Carolingian imperial claims.

Hugh Capet and Robert II spent their reigns trying, without marked success, to enforce their lordship over their own territories and to expand their dominion over neighboring lands. Elected to the kingship, the early Capetians strengthened their hand by associating their sons (and later their wives as well) in their rule. Thus, although the monarchy of France was not formally declared hereditary until 1223, the Capetian dynasty was strengthened by the continuity provided by the genetic good fortune of eleven monarchs having sons usually old enough to share power from the beginning of a reign. Indeed, much of the legitimacy of the Capetians was acquired through sheer endurance and genetic good fortune. The early Capetians also allied with the church.

The reign of Philip I (1060–1108) marked the advance of effective royal attempts to establish lordship securely in the region of *Ile-de-France,* to establish royal justice against arbitrary local lords, and to establish royal authority within the royal demesne. The process of creating a strong lordship within the compact territory ruled by the king was the real beginning of the French monarchy. Exploiting both ecclesiastical and temporal resources, Philip paid little attention to the wider movements for ecclesiastical reform that stirred Europe within his lifetime (below, Chapter 12). Unlike William the Conqueror (r. 1066–1087), he had little to gain by supporting the ecclesiastical reformers, and like his other contemporary, Emperor Henry IV (1056–1105), he had much to lose. Excommunicated from 1092 to 1108, because he dismissed his wife and married the wife of one of his nobles, Philip went on no crusade and kept his political horizons narrow. He made himself lord in his small domain, and his descendants built upon that lordship in expanding the horizons of French kingship.

The struggles between popes and emperors in the last quarter of the eleventh century and the first half of the twelfth (below, Chapter 12) made the kingdom of France an attractive ally for the papacy. Philip's son Louis VI the Fat (1108–1137) and his grandson Louis VII (1137–1180) further cultivated this relationship. The close connection between France and the popes lasted until the end of the thirteenth century (below, Chapter 15). It greatly increased the strength of the royal dynasty while affording the popes reliable allies in their struggles with emperors.

Louis VI and Louis VII also had the services of the remarkable abbot of St. Denis, Suger (1081–1152), who wrote an admiring biography of Louis VI and served as regent of the kingdom when Louis VII was fighting the Second Crusade in 1147 (below, Chapter 12). In Suger's view, Louis VI possessed legitimate authority over all nobles in the kingdom, whether they had sworn oaths of loyalty to him or not, for the king was responsible for maintaining the peace. Suger also stated that the king's obligation to protect the church and the poor gave him added legitimacy. The work of Suger signaled the long identification of the monastery of St. Denis with the interests of the Capetian dynasty, a role later taken up by historians at the monastery who produced the royal history of France, the *Grandes chroniques de France.*

ANGLO-NORMAN ENGLAND

The last Anglo-Saxon king of England of the house of Wessex, Edward the Confessor (1042–1066), succeeded to the throne after the extinction of the Danish dynasty of Cnut. Edward had spent much of his life outside of England, a good deal of it at the court of his cousin, the duke of Normandy, with whom he maintained generally good relations. But Edward was not able to retain the loyalty of the greatest magnates of England, and some of the most powerful English families increased their independence during his reign. Harald Godwinson, a member of the greatest of these families and Edward's brother-in-law, claimed the kingship of England for himself upon Edward's death without heirs in 1066. One source states that Edward did name Harald as his successor, and that the *witan,* the king's advisory body, had concurred. Across the English

Channel, William, duke of Normandy, who had acquired the neighboring county of Maine in 1063, claimed to have been designated his cousin Edward's legal heir, and prepared to back his claim by force. For additional legitimation, William also claimed that the English church had failed to reform itself, and he received a papal banner from Pope Alexander II that empowered him to reform it.

In September 1066, William of Normandy assembled a fleet and a large army, crossed the Channel, and challenged Harald for the Crown. Harald, who had just routed a Danish invasion in the north of England led by Harold Hardrada, another claimant to the crown, hurried two-hundred-and-fifty miles south, gave William battle at Hastings, and fell under the swords and spears of the Norman invaders on October 14, 1066. At Christmas, William was crowned king of England in London, and a new era of English political history began.

The reign of William the Conqueror (1066–1087) began as a continuation of the reign of Edward (William always claimed to be the heir of Edward, not the conqueror, of England), but William soon imposed a different style of kingship. His need for resources, his obligations in Normandy, and the turbulence of his subordinates forced him to impose a stronger personal rule in England than that of the last Anglo-Saxon kings. In doing so, William created a stronger English monarchy. Not only had he inherited the lands formerly owned by Anglo-Saxon kings and the lands confiscated from rebellious nobles, but he had conquered the island and become lord of England in a novel way. Keeping about one-fifth of England under his personal rule, William gave the rest to his nobles and churches, thus ensuring that every piece of land in England was held directly or indirectly from the king. The Anglo-Norman aristocracy stood in a different relation to the Norman kings of England than had the Anglo-Saxon aristocracy to the Anglo-Saxon kings. About 180 great lords held land directly from the king as tenants-in-chief, and several hundred lesser nobles held land from the king's tenants-in-chief. The massive transfer of nearly all the land of England from Anglo-Saxon kings with limited territory and great independent landed families, to a hierarchy of nobles holding ultimately from the king himself, transformed the nature of English kingship and nobility. William's disposition of the landed wealth of England to nobles whose lands were scattered throughout the kingdom gave to the new Norman aristocracy a perspective more "national" in character than that of the more localized Norman or French aristocracy, sometimes by encouraging the marriage of his nobles to Anglo-Saxon heiresses.

Disputes concerning landholding and the obligations attached to it led William to order a remarkable inventory of the kingdom in 1086. Teams of officials fanned out across the kingdom, making what the sources term an *inquisitio,* an inquiry or inquisition, about the extent, resources, and obligations of each estate, both at the time of the death of Edward the Confessor and the present. The result was the monumental survey called Domesday Book, which was so thorough, said *The Anglo-Saxon Chronicle,* "that not a cow or a pig escaped notice" and its judgments would last until Doomsday. William also consulted natives about traditional English law. In addition, William decided to keep using earlier English units of local government, such as the shire (redesignated as the county) and hundred, which became integral parts of the new Anglo-Norman state.

The military and judicial powers of the sheriff (the shire reeve) continued, and the attendance of all the free men of the shire made the county courts extremely influential in the development of English Common Law. William continued to issue the characteristic and extremely efficient Anglo-Saxon written royal command, the *writ*, but now in Latin rather than Old English. The writ was a brief written command from the king that ordered a sheriff to do something on behalf of someone who had applied to the king for assistance. It was an extremely effective instrument of royal intervention.

Although much of the old Anglo-Saxon culture was preserved in local administration and law, much was also swept away in the twenty years following the Conquest. The genius of the Old English vernacular literary language slowly changed in the face of the conquering aristocracy's Norman French; the unique calendar of Anglo-Saxon saints and liturgy sometimes gave way to the tough-minded reform ecclesiology of the Norman churchmen. The rebellious Old English aristocracy slowly disappeared before the numerous and powerful Normans. The material resources of the north of England were devastated by William's putting down of political uprisings. Nor was the kingship of England the only concern of William and his successors. Political affairs of Normandy and the Continent occupied them consistently. Not until the thirteenth century did England by itself become the primary concern of its kings. Moreover, English trade was closely tied to the ports of northwestern France and Flanders. Both churchmen and nobles maintained closer ties with the Continent.

Upon William's death in 1087, his possessions were divided among his sons, in keeping with the Norman law of inheritance. Robert, the eldest son, inherited Normandy and Maine, William II Rufus (1087–1100) inherited England and the crown, and Henry received land and money. At William Rufus' death in 1100, Henry inherited England and made a strong bid for the control of Normandy as well, which he achieved by defeating Robert at the battle of Tinchebray in 1106. The reign of Henry I (1100–1135), the last of the Conqueror's male children, witnessed the strengthening of royal lordship in England and the shaping of a system of governance that later came to characterize English monarchy and the role of kingship in English society.

Faced with pressing financial needs for his defense of Normandy, Henry I raised a group of men from the lower nobility—or sometimes from no nobility at all, "men raised from the dust" the nobles complained—to serve his interests in England. These royal servants, like the *ministeriales* in German lands, dependent solely upon the king's favor and backed solely by his power, turned their attention and energies not to traditional structures of privilege and the acquisition of great landed fortunes, but to the institutions of uniquely royal governance—the courts, tax systems, wardship (the right of guardianship of heiresses and often the determination of whom they married), and administrative office—in order to funnel as much money as possible to the king. As a result, they strengthened these institutions and made the royal court focus on governance and administration as well as power and prestige. By making the royal law courts recognized centers of recourse for injuries, the servants of Henry I offered wider opportunities to those who resorted to law, and created a structure that was easily supervised by the king and his chief servants. With few exceptions, the strength of the English monarchy was built up by royal servants working for—and owing their careers and fortunes to—hard royal taskmasters.

The energy and skill of William the Conqueror and Henry I managed both to preserve Anglo-Saxon monarchy and to impose a style of lordship very much like that of Normandy upon England. By the middle of the twelfth century, a native English culture had begun to revive, a culture that at first lacked the earlier brilliance of Anglo-Saxon culture but was distinctive in its own right and drew more heavily on French and Mediterranean influences. Moreover, in the late eleventh and twelfth centuries, the Continental concerns of England's kings drew the country more and more into Continental affairs and created for it the role of treasury for their personal Continental enterprises. Not until the thirteenth century did England's role among its king's possessions change significantly.

Henry I, who had lost his one legitimate son in a shipwreck in 1120, left his kingdom and duchy and their cares to his daughter Matilda (1102–1167), who had been successively the wife of the Roman emperor Henry V (r. 1105–1125) and of Geoffrey Plantagenet, count of Anjou (r. 1142–1151). At Henry I's death in 1135, however, his nephew Stephen of Blois (the son of William the Conqueror's daughter Adela and Stephen, count of Blois) was acclaimed by some of the English nobility and crowned king in 1135. The nobles who had chafed under Henry's strong rule took the opportunity offered by Stephen's easygoing disposition and his need for support to rebel against him and encourage his rivalry with Matilda, whose own title was "Matilda Empress, daughter of Henry the King and Lady (*Domina*) of England." A series of civil wars resulted from the competing claims, and a final compromise established Matilda's son Henry Plantagenet Fitzempress as the successor to Stephen. Upon Stephen's death, Henry II Plantagenet (1154–1189) became king of England. Henry II had far more extensive possessions on the Continent than his grandfather Henry I. He was count of Anjou, Maine, and Touraine, duke of Normandy, king of the English, lord of Ireland, and, through his marriage to the heiress Eleanor of Aquitaine, duke of Aquitaine. The history of England in the later twelfth century is inextricably bound up with the Continental empire of the Plantagenet house.

THE OTHER ISLES

English history is also bound up with the political affairs of the other parts of the Isles. The first wife of Henry I, Edith (or Matilda, since the name varies in different sources), was the daughter of Malcolm III Canmore, king of the Scots (1031–1093) and Margaret, a descendant of Æthelred the Ill-Counselled and a great-neice of Edward the Confessor (above, Chapter 9). The kingdom of the Scots had grown from the small Irish settlement at Dalriada, ruling the Inner Hebrides and the territory of Argyll, expanded to the south, north, and west by a number of vigorous rulers, notably Kenneth mac Alpin (ca. 843, traditionally the first king of the Scots). Like England and Ireland, Scotland (at first called the kingdom of Alba) was threatened, not only by Viking raids in the ninth century, but by the creation of a strong Viking principality that controlled the Orkneys and the Shetlands and regularly raided the Hebrides, Scotland, and Ireland. The rule of Macbeth (r. 1040–1057), a strong and generally successful king (in spite of the later propaganda campaign against him that resulted in Shakespeare's inaccurate, but terrifying play) was ended by Malcolm III, who established a royal dynasty that ruled Scotland for nearly 150 years.

Under Malcolm III and Margaret (canonized as Saint Margaret of Scotland in 1249), the local Celtic church was reformed, and Anglo-Norman aristocrats began the transformation of Scottish society. Under David I (1124–1153) provincial lordships were created for royal favorites, and administrative structures similar to those of Anglo-Norman England were created. The Canmore dynasty, however, also maintained Scotland's autonomy and independence, and the survival of local culture served as a means of controlling the Normanization of the kingdom.

The four principalities of Wales were also troubled by Viking raids in the ninth and tenth centuries. The four principalities varied in power, with one sometimes emerging as superior to the others, as did the kingdom of Gwynnedd under Rhodri Mawr (844–878) and his successors. His grandson, Hywel Dda (ca. 909–949/50) acquired three of the four principalities, Gwynnedd, Powys, and Dyfed, and his name is associated with the codification of traditional Welsh law. The church in Wales developed along distinctively Celtic lines.

The unification of the Anglo-Saxon kingdom of England in the tenth century increased English pressure on Wales, whose princes, including Hywel Dda, often acknowledged English overlordship. Welsh princes continually faced the problem of negotiating relations with a much richer and politically strong neighbor, the kingdom of England. Occasionally, a very strong Welsh prince like Gruffyd ap Llewellyn (1039–1063) could achieve power in all of Wales and even repulse English invasions.

The Norman Conquest of England posed additional problems for Wales. The first of these was the creation by William the Conqueror of the border earldoms of Chester, Shrewsbury, and Hereford. William's friend William fitz Osbern and later Robert de Montgomery also built a powerful line of castles and manors for the Norman military force along the border with Wales from which invasions could be launched regularly. These Anglo-Norman border areas became known as the "March of Wales." William the Conqueror made a ceremonial tour of Wales in 1081, but the strongest Anglo-Norman influence was the enterprise of individual ambitious nobles. Gradually Anglo-Norman nobles settled in Wales, as they did in Scotland. In addition, Welsh princes themselves might willingly submit to English kings in return for their aid against local political rivals, as Grufydd ap Cynan (d. 1137) did to Henry I in 1114, and as one of the Irish princes would to Henry II in 1169.

Ireland, too, was transformed by the Viking invasions, both in the devastation of ecclesiastical and other properties on the island and the intrusion of Viking allies and enemies in local political disputes among the petty kings. In the course of these wars, the most powerful of the royal dynasties of Ireland, the Uí Néill, was greatly weakened, making way for the rise of later dynasties. The Vikings also added a strong commercial and maritime dimension to Ireland, founded Dublin, and made it one of the richest cities of the northern world. Bitter rivalries among the Uí Néill opened the way for the rise of Dál Cais of north Munster, whose king, Brian Bóruma (or Brian Boru, r. 976–1014) became the founder of the line of O'Brien kings of the eleventh and twelfth centuries. Brian Boru called himself "the emperor of the Irish" and created an Irish kingship that for the first time potentially encompassed the entire island. But Brian himself was killed at the battle of Clontarf on Good Friday, 1014, by a coalition of Viking and Irish enemies, and his successors set about building infrastructures of kingship—administrators, tax collectors, castellans, and military strategists—much in the manner of state building in other parts of Europe.

The greatest of the successors of Brian Boru was Turlough O'Connor (1106–1156), who made himself effectively king of all Ireland. But in the disputes following Turlough's death, one of the contending parties, Dermott MacMurrough, ruler of Leinster, fell from power in favor of Rory O'Connor. He then fled to Henry II of England for aid, and in doing so changed the course of Irish history. One of Henry's barons, Richard fitz Gilbert, called "Strongbow," undertook the support of Mac Murrough, leading a mercenary force into Leinster in 1170, which he then took over for himself. Henry II, who would not tolerate independent principalities ruled by overmighty subjects, entered Ireland in 1171–1172 and received the submission of both Strongbow and the Irish princes. The Anglo-Norman penetration of Ireland, as of Scotland and Wales, was now underway.

THE IBERIAN PENINSULA: CONQUEST OR *RECONQUISTA?*

The Muslim conquest of the Iberian Peninsula between 711 and 720 had destroyed the kingdom of the Visigoths and brought all but the extreme northern mountains and coast into the economic, cultural, and religious orbit of the vast southern Mediterranean and Iranian empire of Islam. *Iberia* was the name the Greeks had given to the peninsula; the Romans and their Visigothic successors had called it *Hispania* (whence modern *España,* Spain), and its Islamic rulers termed it *al-Andalus* ("the land of the Vandals"). Although the contrast between *al-Andalus* and *Hispania* is a convenient one, neither Islamic nor Christian Spain was a unified and closely governed whole. Dissent within the Islamic community and rivalry among the Christian princes of the north reveal profound dissensions within each part of the peninsula. The great vision of the reconquest, the *Reconquista,* of formerly Christian Spain from its Muslim invaders inspired a number of Christian writers (and a large number of modern historians of medieval Spain) to characterize Iberian history from the late eighth century on as largely or exclusively the progress and momentary setbacks of the *Reconquista.* Such a view, however, neglects the actual circumstances of the peninsula between the eighth and the mid twelfth centuries.

The early decades of the new Muslim state witnessed severe internal conflicts between Arab and Berber Muslims, and not until the reign of Abd al-Rahman I (756–788) was there a single emirate in Spain. Abd al-Rahman established his capital at Córdoba and began the construction of the Great Mosque, one of the monuments of Islamic architecture. During the eighth century, occasional Muslim attempts to secure the far north of the peninsula were checked, as were Muslim incursions into southwestern Gaul. In 721 Odo, duke of Aquitaine, repelled a large Muslim raid. In 732 or 733, Charles Martel, mayor of the palace of the Frankish kingdom, defeated a Muslim expeditionary force (above, Chapter 7). In the late eighth century Charlemagne established a Frankish defensive zone, the Spanish March, north of Barcelona, which became the territorial basis for the later county of Catalonia, which itself was later absorbed into the Crown of Aragon. To the west of the Spanish March, lay a number of small territories governed by petty Christian rulers: the county of Aragon, the largely Basque county of Navarre, and the larger and more important kingdom of Asturias, with its capital at Oviedo.

Under the vigorous rulership of Abd al-Rahman III (912–961), *al-Andalus* became a full-fledged caliphate, rivaling Baghdad and Cairo in its claims to legitimacy within the Muslim world. From the reign of Abd al-Rahman III to that of al-Mansur (977–1002), *al-Andalus* reached the height of prosperity and power. The cities of Córdoba, Valencia, and Seville boasted great wealth and large populations, Cordoba itself approaching the size and splendor of Constantinople and Baghdad, with a population over 300,000. The city contained many mosques, schools, public baths, libraries, bazaars, and lavish private residences. The productivity of Muslim agriculture was legendary, and *al-Andalus,* too, began to grow rice, melons, oranges, lemons, and other new European crops in abundance. Leather, steel, and other manufactured goods became known as the best of their kind in both the Muslim and Christian worlds. Wool, cotton, and silk came from Andalusian looms, and papermaking was introduced to Europe. Spanish Muslims recognized Jews and Christians as *ahl al-kitab* ("People of the Book"), possessing legitimate revelation from God in their religious traditions, and therefore treated as a special class of subjects, *dhimmis* ("protected ones") and taxed at a different rate from infidels.

Although Muslims in Spain, as elsewhere, were generally tolerant of Jews and Christians, not many conversions appear to have taken place. Thus, substantial populations of Jews and Christians survived in *al-Andalus* and shared some of its material prosperity and rich cultural life. Some Christians adopted Muslim culture, if not Islam itself, and spoke Arabic. These individuals were called *Mozarabs.* Although they developed their own unique Christian liturgy and Christian culture, they were regarded with suspicion by the Christians in the north of the peninsula and by Christians elsewhere.

Muslim Spanish devotion and learning were well known in the Islamic world. Extensive libraries and large schools preserved in Spain the Muslim versions of Greek philosophy and scientific thought. Ibn Rushd (1126–1198; Averroes to the Latins), the greatest of all commentators on the works of Aristotle, lived in *al-Andalus*. With devotion, learning, and prosperity went art and architecture, particularly the latter. Such buildings as the Alhambra at Granada and the Great Mosque at Córdoba, with their delicate structural elements, brilliantly colored and arranged tiles and mosaics, and exquisite ivory and rare wood inlays, have survived to the present and give even modern Spain its characteristic Muslim architectural flavor. In spite of the political rivalry between *al-Andalus* and Baghdad, Muslim Spain continued to be nourished by contact with the rest of the Islamic world.

In the early eleventh century, internal dissensions led to the downfall of the caliphate and to the emergence of a number of small Arab states and rulers, the *reyes de taifas,* "kings of parts." The fragmenting of the caliphate gave opportunities to the rulers of the Christian states in the north to expand at the expense of the divided and weakened Muslim powers. These small, tough states, whose force depended upon an alliance between fighting kings and small-proprietor freemen, enabled some kingdoms to grow and change. The old kingdom of Asturias became absorbed in the larger northwestern kingdom of León, and in the course of the twelfth century, León was absorbed into the north-central county, and later kingdom, of Castila, as its name suggests, "the land of castles."

Growing population pressures, especially in the north, brought Muslims and Christians into frequent military contact during the late ninth and tenth centuries. The northern Christian kingdoms, particularly Castile, began to press south against the frontiers of the Muslim caliphate. The caliphate of al-Mansur proved to be the last of the great Muslim reigns in the peninsula. In the eleventh century, the Muslims lost about a third of their territory in northern Spain, and the young Christian kingdoms of Castile, Aragon, León, and Navarre emerged as substantial Christian powers, calling their expansion a *reconquista,* a "reconquest" of old *Hispania* from the Muslims. Under the patronage of the apostle Saint James (*Santiago Matamoros*), whose cult was centered in the northwestern town of Compostela, they appealed for aid from Christians across the Pyrenees and mobilized their own forces for expansion to the south.

The *reconquista* provided a focus for the expansion of these northern Iberian kingdoms, and its publicizing north of the Pyrenees appealed to fighting men and pilgrims who were beginning to see, in war against the infidels, a means of legitimizing their own warlike cultures. During the eleventh century, legends of "Saint James the Killer of Moors," of Pelayo, the legendary successor of Roderigo, the last Visigothic king, and of Fernán Gonzalez, a great warrior of Castila, helped develop the Iberian awareness of the sacred character of the *reconquista.*

The kingdom of Navarre, under Sancho I (1000–1035), achieved considerable success and preeminence in the north. The division of Sancho's lands at his death in 1035, made kings of his three sons, and the kingdoms they created—Navarre, Aragon, and Castile—became strong Christian powers. The earlier kingdoms of Asturias and Galicia united to form León, and the old Spanish March became the county of Barcelona. The division and recombination of these small kingdoms continued into the later eleventh century. Under Ferdinand I of Castila (1035–1065), León and Castila were united into a single kingdom.

The reign of Alfonso VI of Castila (1065–1109) proved Castila's endurance and ability. The Muslim south paid tribute and yielded booty to Alfonso's warriors. Alfonso also opened communications across the Pyrenees; French aid, warriors, monastic foundations, and clergy assisted his efforts in the south. In 1085, Alfonso captured the city of Toledo, the old Visigothic capital and ecclesiastical center of Spain, a triumph that increased his reputation at home and in the north.

Alfonso's greatest servant, Rodrigo Diaz de Vivar, who was called El Cid (from the Arabic word *al-siddi,* meaning "chief"), led his master's armies heroically, but other aspects of El Cid's career suggest the kind of life northern Spain offered in this period of turbulence. El Cid fell out with Alfonso VI in 1081, entered the service of some Muslim princes, was briefly reconciled with the king, and then undertook to conquer Valencia for himself. The independence and occasional indifference of El Cid to Alfonso's political difficulties, his willingness to serve under Muslim leaders, and his political adventurousness in Valencia suggest that the ideal of a Christian warrior fighting God's war was not his unvarying self-image. However, the epic poem in the Castilian vernacular produced in the late twelfth century, *El Cantar del Mio Cid*, tried with considerable success to remake the frontier adventurer and local warlord into a model Christian warrior.

The enemies against whom Alfonso VI and El Cid fought were no longer the great caliphs of *al-Andalus*. With the collapse of the caliphate in the first half of the eleventh century, about the same time as the Abbasid Caliphate collapsed in Baghdad, petty rulers of small regions and individual cities, the *reyes de taifas* ("kings of parts") now constituted the political and military strength of *al-Andalus*. Strong at home, they were nevertheless vulnerable to the forces of Christian expansion, and with the fall of Toledo, several of these kings invited the puritanical warrior sect of the Almoravides into Spain from North Africa. The victory of the Almoravides over Alfonso VI at Zalaca in 1086 temporarily halted the *reconquista* and briefly unified *al-Andalus* under Almoravid rulers, but they did not win back much territory from the Christians.

Even this temporary unification of Muslim *al-Andalus* could not prevent the kings of Castila, Navarre, and Aragon from consolidating their earlier gains and even expanding more slowly. In 1139, a noble adventurer named Afonso Henriques established Portugal as an independent lordship and began to build it into a monarchy with himself as king.

The rudimentary institutions of governance and the rivalry among different Christian rulers during the late eleventh and early twelfth centuries make it difficult to see the ideal of *reconquista* as anything more than an occasional rallying cry in particular instances. The idea of *reconquista* became rationale for the Christian rulers and nobility of the north, but it was hardly a reality. Before the late twelfth century, during the reigns of Alfonso VI, his talented and able daughter Urraca (1109–1126), and Alfonso VII (1126–1157), population pressures, the economy, and individual ambition characterized both internal relations among the Christian rulers of Spain and their relations with their Muslim counterparts.

FROM LORDSHIP TO KINGSHIP IN SOUTH ITALY AND SICILY

One of the most spectacular instances of the shaping of royal lordship was the creation of the Norman kingdom of Sicily and South Italy, not out of older Visigothic, Anglo-Saxon, or Frankish traditions, but out of fragments of Byzantine and Lombard institutions through the dynamism and ruthlessness of an able Norman dynasty. "The Other Norman Conquest," as historians sometimes call it, created a state where none existed before, a state whose wealth, character, and power made it the most powerful kingdom in Europe by the end of the twelfth century and a major point of contact among Christian, Jewish, and Muslim cultures.

In the tenth century, Byzantium had regained control over much of south Italy, including its restive Lombard principalities and its largely Greek population. The eleventh-century crisis in the Byzantine Empire (below, Chapter 12), however, weakened Byzantine control and sparked a Lombard revolt. The Lombard rebels engaged a number of Norman pilgrims as mercenary warriors, and between 1017 and 1029, Norman military power led the Lombard resistance to Byzantine authority. In 1029, Rainulf, a Norman leader, won for himself the countship of Aversa, and in the following two decades, other Norman leaders also carved out territories for themselves.

In 1053, Pope Leo IX sent a military force into South Italy, intending to displace the Normans and reassert papal claims to the territory south of Rome. The papal force was soundly beaten by the Normans at Cividale in that year, however, and the pope himself was taken prisoner. In the negotiations that followed, Leo IX recognized certain Norman rights in South Italy, and in 1059, Robert Guiscard, the Norman count of Apulia, formally received Apulia and Calabria from Pope Nicholas II, who recognized Robert's title as duke. From 1059 until his death in 1085, Robert Guiscard continually enlarged his territory and consolidated his control in South Italy. Robert's younger brother, Roger, "the Great Count," wrested Sicily from its Muslim overlords between 1061 and 1091. In 1071, Bari, the last Byzantine stronghold in South Italy, fell into Robert's hands. In 1081, Robert Guiscard launched an attack against the western coast of Greece itself, but the campaign had to be interrupted when Guiscard was called back to Italy to rescue Pope Gregory VII in his struggle with the Emperor Henry IV (see Chapter 12). Robert Guiscard died shortly after his rescue of the pope, and his lands went to his son, Roger Borsa.

At his own death in 1101, Roger the Great Count left his widow Adelaide of Savona (d. 1118) and a young son, Roger II (1095–1154). Adelaide maintained a successful regency for her young son until he legally came of age and was knighted in Palermo cathedral in 1112. With Palermo as Adelaide's and Roger's capital, Sicily was welded into a territorial principality during the first years of the rule of Roger II. In 1127, at the death of his cousin William of Apulia, Roger II succeeded to the mainland possessions of the family, and he was invested as Duke of Apulia by Pope Honorius II at Benevento in 1129, thus uniting all of Sicily and South Italy under a single ruler. The antipope Anacletus II crowned Roger king of Sicily, Apulia, and Calabria on Christmas Day, 1130. Roger also sponsored many of the architectural projects that made Norman Sicily one of the wonders of the world. The cathedrals at Palermo and Cefalù, the Palatine Chapel at Palermo, and many other religious and secular buildings began to take on that unique combination of Greek, Arabic, and Norman style that has characterized the area ever since. In 1140, Roger II promulgated the Assizes of Ariano, one of the more thorough law codes of the twelfth century and the basis of later thirteenth-century legislation.

More effectively and dramatically than any other twelfth-century ruler, Roger II had transformed lordship into kingship.

12

Christendom East and West

THE IDEA OF REFORM

From the fifth to the eleventh century in western Europe, both lay lords and clerics had two main goals: the conversion of pagans to Christianity and the establishment of proper order within the Christian community. The tools for this mission were to be an educated missionary clergy supported by royal and aristocratic patrons. The expansion of Frankish power and Christianity under Charlemagne, and the Carolingian insistence on clerical reform and education illustrate both goals at a moment in early European history when they seemed closest to achievement. In spite of the disasters of the late ninth and tenth centuries, the process of conversion went on, including that of the Viking and Hungarian invaders and many of the princes of central Europe. By the end of the eleventh century, most European pagan peoples had converted to Christianity, and one of the religious aims of Christians from Gregory the Great to Nicholas I had been accomplished. One sign of this change is the decreasing frequency with which ecclesiastical writers described forbidden pagan customs and superstitions in their works on penance in the twelfth century. They concentrated instead on the second goal: proper beliefs (orthodoxy), attitudes, and practices (orthopraxy) of Christians within a Christian society.

When Christians began to reorder the Roman world in the late fourth and fifth centuries, they became aware that the passage of time would inevitably, given the human condition, dilute the apostolic and evangelical purity of the earliest days of the church. They developed the idea of reform to counteract the spiritually deteriorating effects of the passage of time and their own increasing distance from apostolic Christianity. Texts from the fifth century on spoke of *reformatio,* "reformation," and *renovatio,* "renewal." By the eleventh century, the concept of reform was built into Christian consciousness as a means of assessing a particular time and as a justification for change. Cries for reform were usually framed in terms of violent criticism of the problematic present and directed against the moral defects of the unreformed clergy. Against the newly revived ideal of apostolic perfection, few clergy could come up to that standard.

The period between the late tenth and the late twelfth centuries witnessed a new stage of European religious consciousness, one that reflected a heightened awareness of the importance of the proper ordering of Christian society. Nearly at the end of its long duel with paganism, Christianity confronted the problems of order and disorder inside the Christian world. Among the main aspects of these problems were the monastic life, the perception of abuses within the Church, the relation between lay and clerical authority, and lay piety.

The first signs of the new temper are to be found in the strongest centers of early European Christianity, the monasteries. The most influential and best known—but not the only—center of monastic reform was the monastery of Cluny in Burgundy. Established in 910 by Duke William the Good of Aquitaine, Cluny was exceptional from its very origins. The duke gave the monastery not to an individual abbot or lay protector but directly to Saint Peter. The monastery was therefore independent of all local ecclesiastical and lay authority and directly subordinate only to the pope, Peter's representative on earth. The power of the spiritual attraction of Rome was considerable, and some of Cluny's early prestige may have derived from its particular connection with Rome.

A series of distinguished abbots—Berno (910–927), Odo (927–942), Aymard (942–954), Mayeul (954–993), Odilo (993–1048), and Hugh (1048–1109)—supervised the development of Cluny into a reformed monastery in which the closely regulated life and training of the monks, the richly embellished liturgical services, and the independence of the monastery from all outside influence made Cluny an attractive model of monastic reform. The monastery greatly emphasized liturgical reform, and its liturgy became a model for monastic liturgies throughout western Europe. Local and distant nobles came under the influence of this dynamic institution, and asked for instructions about reforming their own monasteries along Cluniac lines. Cluny also developed a network of donors who gave it lands and revenues, making it one of the largest landholders in western Europe. Because its lands were inalienable, Cluny also developed a rationality and continuity in its practices of land management that impressed its neighbors as much as its church services. Many other monasteries were slowly put under the direct control of Cluny by their lay patrons, and the Cluniac influence began to reach out into corners of Europe where there had been few previous signs of monastic reform.

The constitution of Cluny was also unique. Even after many monasteries had become affiliated with it, the abbot of Cluny remained the only abbot in the order; all other monasteries controlled by Cluny were governed by subordinate officials called priors. The fact that the abbot could select his own successor and that he was the single abbot among the 1500 or so monasteries that were eventually attached to Cluny, enabled the houses of the Cluniac system to work together for reform and to coordinate their activities closely.

It also made the abbot of Cluny one of the most influential churchmen in Europe. The abbots traveled extensively, and they were as familiar in Rome and northern Italy as they were in France. Toward the end of the tenth century, the kidnapping of Abbot Mayeul by Arab raiders in the Alps appears to have been the rallying point for the final southern French assault that destroyed the powerful Arab stronghold of La Garde Freinet.

There is no greater monument to the synthesis of aristocratic reform monasticism represented by Cluny than the great monastic church, now destroyed, called Cluny III. Begun in 1088, and financed largely by gifts of King Alfonso VI of Leon-Castila, the building was completed after many delays in 1130. Until the rebuilding of St. Peter's Church in Rome in the sixteenth century, Cluny III was the largest church building in Latin Christendom. It was a church in which not only monks but clergy and laity alike could see God worshiped with devotion, elegance, and purity that were achieved in few other places in western Europe. In a culture that valued the purity of ritual highly and was all too aware of the distractions of secular life on other "men of prayer," Cluny and its great church offered the fulfillment of the Carolingian ideal of enlightened lay patronage and protection that enabled disciplined men of religion to perfect the art of liturgical prayer, to struggle against the forces of darkness in their unceasing liturgies, and to accept and shelter the bodies of their patrons and pray for their souls after death.

The abbots of Cluny also invoked images of an earlier, more peaceful, Christian world. But they were not the only monastic reformers of the late tenth and eleventh centuries, nor was their form of monasticism the only model followed by their contemporaries. At Camaldoli in Italy and elsewhere, a rigorously ascetic form of monasticism was developed and, in conjunction with this, new forms of the religious life of hermits and anchorites. These practices often sacrificed the earlier ideals of study and manual labor (and, in later forms, even the liturgical richness of Cluny) in favor of a life of silence and contemplation. In order to fulfill the devotional needs of some of these rigorous communities, groups of lay brothers were admitted. These brothers, "converts," or *conversi*, became a major part of monastic life in the late eleventh and twelfth centuries.

Other monastic movements sought out remote and unsettled areas in which to build and to separate themselves from lay society. Besides the life of the "new desert," yet other centers of monastic reform worked more closely with the reforming elements in secular society. The Norman monastery of Bec, for example, was extensively patronized by the eleventh-century dukes of Normandy and became the source of much ecclesiastical reform after William I had conquered England. William's first two archbishops of Canterbury, Lanfranc and Anselm (below, Chapter 13), were both former monks of Bec. At Gorze, near Metz, an important reform monastery remained closely tied to local episcopal and noble society, exerting its influence especially in Lorraine and southwestern Germany. Emphasizing the necessity of cooperation with pious earthly rulers, Gorze gave great impetus to the reforms of the Church in Germany and Italy on the part of the later Salian emperors and their servants.

Reform monasteries at Cluny, Gorze, Camaldoli, and other centers offered models of the devotional life that influenced other clergy and much of the laity, and their influence sharpened the perception of the need to carry reform even farther than the monasteries themselves. Abuses in the clerical life outside monasteries were now perceived more sharply. Among these, two in particular stand out: clerical sexual purity and clerical dependence on lay power.

Although the Latin Church (unlike the Greek) had long forbidden clerical marriage, the circumstances of clerical life between the fifth and the eleventh centuries made the prohibition a dead letter outside of monasteries. With the demand for a purer clergy that emerged in the eleventh century, however, and with the increased influence of monastic standards on reformers' thought, there rose the question of clerical marriage and concubinage. The charge of "Nicolaitism," the technical term for clergy who were married or otherwise lived with women, was hurled with increasing vigor at clergy throughout the eleventh and twelfth centuries. Popes legislated against it, councils forbade it, and individual bishops were urged to combat it. In many cases, clerical marriage became a weapon with which lay people attacked nonreformed clergy, and the problem generated a large literature in the twelfth century. Behind the growing distaste for clerical marriage was the ideal of a ritually unpolluted clergy, separated sexually as well as by its sacramental powers from the laity.

One profound social consequence of the new emphasis on clerical celibacy was the enforced separation of priests from their wives, which turned many women and children out into society alone, unprotected, and usually unsupported. In a very short period, the status of priest's wife changed from being one of local honor to one of scorn.

Of equal importance was the second great abuse of the century, the perceived problem of the dependence of the clergy on the laity. Several elements had contributed to the lay domination of the clergy. One of them, obviously, was the clergy's need for defense and protection against rapacious neighboring lords or invaders. A second was the influence of Old Testament thought on early medieval political theory and the resemblance of early medieval kings—at least in their own and the clergy's minds—to David and Solomon, the great kings of Israel. Other elements were technical and legal. Germanic law had permitted privately owned churches, called *Eigenkirchen* (literally, "churches of one's own"), whose owners appointed clergy, often in return for a gratuity or fee. In the wider world, kings and emperors often determined the appointment of bishops and abbots. The altar, according to this view, was the province of grace, but the church building, property, and income were the province of the patron. As we have seen in the case of Cluny and elsewhere, the power of a dedicated, reform-minded lay patron could be the easiest path toward reform; on the other hand, an indifferent or wicked lay or clerical patron could cripple devotional life. In the eleventh century, the general practice of laity dominating clergy came to be called *simony*, after the figure of Simon Magus, the charlatan who allegedly attempted to buy religious power from Saint Peter (Acts 8:9–24).

By the second half of the eleventh century, two distinct attitudes toward reform had become predominant. The first, traditionally Carolingian and continued by the Saxon emperors, left it to the emperor and his clergy to rectify abuses, even, if necessary, to the point of removing from office canonically consecrated prelates, from abbots to popes. This great responsibility was justified by the emperor's sacral status as God's deputy. The second view, which necessarily possessed political as well as spiritual dimensions, attacked the entire concept of lay authority of any kind over clergy, whether that of a local lord or that of the morally best-intentioned emperor himself. This view was maintained by radical reformers in the name of *libertas*, the freedom from interference of any sort that was guaranteed by God to the Church so that it might carry out its sacred mission. In the first half of the eleventh century, the two views did not necessarily find themselves in conflict, for the agenda of reform was vast, and badly needed imperial and other lay assistance. From the middle of the century, however, their ways divided, and the one view opposed the other with increasing sharpness. The polarizing of views on Church reform, and the great conflict between spiritual and temporal authority that they generated toward the end of the eleventh century, constituted a major departure from the spiritual ideals of Carolingian and Saxon Europe and opened new horizons for both the government of Christian society and the definition of clergy and laity.

POPES, EMPERORS, AND CHRISTIAN SOCIETY

The first centers of religious reform had been the monasteries of France, Lorraine, and northern Italy. The high standards of some imperial German churchmen and emperors and the popular religious sentiment in Flemish and Italian towns contributed other elements to the reform movement. But the papacy had been slow to change. From the reign of Otto III, however, emperors had occasionally installed reform-minded churchmen on the throne of Peter. Otto III installed Bruno as Gregory V (996–999), the first pope from German lands. Upon Bruno's death, Otto installed his old teacher and friend, Gerbert of Aurillac, who took the name Sylvester II (999–1003). From the late tenth century, popes, upon their election, began to take the names of former popes, probably in imitation of the monastic practice of taking a new name to signal a new life. Often, the choice of papal name was significant because it suggested an indentification with an earlier pope. The name "Sylvester II" is an example, since the first Sylvester had long been (mistakenly) associated with the conversion of Constantine and was alleged to have been the recipient of the Donation of Constantine. In 1046, when a particularly offensive scandal produced three claimants for the papal title, the emperor Henry III (1039–1056) convened the Synod of Sutri, outside of Rome, at which he and a group of sympathetic higher clergy declared all three claimants deposed from the papacy and installed the first of a series of German reformers as pope. Although the first two reform popes after Sutri died soon after their election, in 1049 Henry III's cousin, Bruno of Toul, was elected and took the papal name of Leo IX (1049–1054). Leo brought with him to Rome representatives of the reform movement in Lorraine and Burgundy, traveled back across the Alps to hold reform councils and synods in France, and by his own reputation for holiness, greatly increased the prestige and presence of the papacy in the reform movement of the late eleventh century.

Among the reformers who rose to prominence under Leo IX and his successors was Humbert, Cardinal of Silva Candida, the most articulate and radical proponent of reform. Humbert's treatise *Against Simoniacs* argued not only that bishops who had purchased their ecclesiastical offices should be deposed, but that priestly ordinations that they had performed were not valid. Other reformers, such as Peter Damian (1007–1072), one of the best-known proponents of ascetic monasticism and a strong proponent of lay rule in both secular and ecclesiastical affairs, argued a more moderate position that allowed for the participation in reform of pious lay authorities.

Humbert's work was not confined to western Europe. Byzantine intervention in southern Italy and increasing Byzantine criticisms of Latin orthodoxy had greatly strained diplomatic relations between Constantinople and Rome. Leo IX sent Humbert to Constantinople in 1054 to investigate what he considered the high-handed conduct of the patriarch, Michael Keroularios (1043–1058). The deteriorating relations between the two churches and the two individuals came to a head on July 16, 1054, when Cardinal Humbert and his delegation entered the church of Hagia Sophia and placed a statement condemning the patriarch on the altar. The patriarch in turn anathematized the Latins, and the incident abruptly launched one of the many schisms that further separated Latin and Greek Christendom. As the two churches learned more about each other in the ensuing debates, each acquired a sharper sense of its differences from the other. The mutual condemnations of 1054 were not lifted until 1965!

The sense of universal mission on the part of the reform popes is illustrated by Alexander II (1061–1073), who sent a papal banner to William of Normandy as he was departing to conquer England, urging him to reform the English church and thereby link Normandy and England with Rome. Alexander also sent papal banners with Robert Guiscard during his invasion of Greece in 1072. In 1064, Alexander granted the forgiveness of sins to Spaniards assaulting Muslim strongholds in Spain. The church of Aragon adopted the Roman liturgy instead of the older local Mozarabic liturgy, thereby forging another kind of link with Rome. Nor did the reform papacy neglect the workings of the church in Rome. In 1059, during the vigorous pontificate of Nicholas II (1059–1061), a new rule for electing popes was adopted. Henceforth only the cardinal clergy and the people of Rome itself were to have the right of electing and installing the pope, although the "due honor and reverence" owed to the emperor were to be respected. The decree of 1059 also forbade for the first time, a cleric's acceptance of a church from the hands of a lay patron.

The most active and controversial of the reform popes was Gregory VII (1073–1085). Unlike some of his predecessors, Gregory saw the causes of abuses in the Church not in specific faults that might be corrected one by one, but in the defective ordering of the Christian world. Gregory's pontificate launched a great debate about the nature of Christendom, *Christianitas,* between the two great powers that claimed responsibility for the ordering of spiritual and temporal life, the pope and the emperor. Against the old Carolingian-Saxon idea of the emperor's ultimate responsibility for Christian society, Gregory set an alternative vision of two contending societies on earth—Christian society and the city of Satan—thus echoing one aspect of Augustine's fifth century work *The City of God* (above, Chapter 2). According to Gregory and his supporters, only the pope at the head of Christian society, authorized by the merits of Peter, could fulfill God's plan for the world. Even the emperor was necessarily subordinate. Any challenge to such a plan was a threat from the forces of Satan and had to be countered by whatever force was required.

Thus, a large part of Gregory's pontificate was devoted to outlining systematically the nature and history of papal authority. To this end, he had some of his subordinates search out old collections of ecclesiastical laws and treatises to substantiate his case. The work of earlier eleventh-century reformers in building a doctrinal basis for the attack on clerical marriage and simony had already produced a significant body of research on doctrinal and papal history, and some of it had begun to be organized in the form of legal texts. The *Collection in 74 Titles*, compiled in Rome, first asserted papal authority over the entire Church in the form of a legal code. Earlier searches, various new collections, and the renewed efforts of Gregory VII turned up a vast amount of older literary material, and much of the late eleventh and twelfth centuries was spent in shaping it into a constitutional theory of Latin Christendom, largely through the increasingly important discipline of canon law (below, Chapter 13). Some of this material came from the great ninth-century collections of forged material, particularly that of Pseudo-Isidore, which, as we have seen, contained the text of the Donation of Constantine. The *Dictatus Papae,* a list of papal privileges and powers intended to serve as an index of the diverse aspects of papal authority, was included in the official register of Gregory's correspondence, the first full surviving register of papal correspondence since that of Pope Gregory I, who died in 604.

In the process of organizing the theory of papal authority, describing it in collections of canon law, and building an administrative system that would distribute and apply it regularly and effectively, Gregory VII contributed substantially to the foundations of papal authority in the twelfth and thirteenth centuries. Not only did he increase the workload of the staff of the popes in Rome, but he dispatched papal legates, representatives for special missions, throughout Europe; in some places he established permanent legates. The clergy of the city of Rome, hitherto important chiefly for its role in assisting the popes in their many liturgical functions throughout the city, grew into an administrative body. The cardinals, titled priests, deacons, and bishops of key churches in the area around Rome slowly grew into an administrative body that directly handled papal affairs. In both the realm of ideas and the translation of those ideas into institutions and programs of action, Gregory VII transformed the papacy and made himself the spokesman for a new vision of Christian society.

Although Gregory VII began his pontificate on good terms with the emperor Henry III's successor, Henry IV (1056–1106), the pope's vision of the respective places of pope and emperor soon led to direct conflict. Gregory, for example, supported the reform-minded citizens of Milan who rejected Henry IV's candidate for archbishop. The position of archbishop of Milan was an important imperial office in northern Italy, since Milan itself was a rich city and it controlled the southern end of the passes across the Alps that the emperor and his army had to use. Moreover, resistance to Henry's methods of governance in Germany had grown stronger, and Gregory found allies among the German nobility when he pressed further with new regulations against the lay appointment and investiture of clergy. In 1076, after Henry and a synod of imperial bishops at Worms had announced Gregory himself deposed from the papacy, Gregory declared Henry excommunicated and suspended from the imperial office. In the winter of 1077, in one of the most dramatic moves of the conflict, Henry IV suddenly crossed the Alps and presented himself as a penitent at the Tuscan castle of Canossa, where Gregory VII was staying on his own way into Germany, asking forgiveness from the cleric who had excommunicated him. Gregory reluctantly agreed to absolve Henry, thus weakening the opposition to Henry in Germany, which nevertheless proceeded to elect an antiking on its own and wage civil war against the emperor for the next three years.

Relations between Gregory and Henry quickly broke down again, but Gregory's censures had far less effect the second time they were used, and by 1080, Henry had overcome his opponents in Germany and turned his full wrath on Rome. The synods of Bamberg and Mainz in 1080 renounced obedience to Gregory and elected an antipope, the archbishop of Ravenna, in his place. With the antipope in his train, Henry IV invaded Italy in 1084 and forced Gregory to flee Rome and go to Salerno, where he was protected by the Norman dukes of Apulia (above, Chapter 11). Gregory died in exile at Salerno in May, 1085.

Gregory's immediate successor, Victor III (1086–1088), the former abbot Desiderius of Monte Cassino, was a far less volatile prelate whose brief pontificate ended too soon for him to achieve reconciliation with the emperor. Victor's successor, however, Urban II (1088–1099), unlike Gregory, was a nobleman and had been prior of the monastery of Cluny. By compromise, diplomacy, and a reorganization of papal administrative practices, Urban II undercut much of the support of Henry IV and greatly strengthened the prestige of his own office. The intransigence of Henry IV, who died in 1106, and of his son and successor, the last Salian emperor, Henry V (r. 1106–1125), dragged out the formalities of the conflict between pope and emperor. Not until the pontificate of Calixtus II (1119–1124) was the formal aspect of the conflict finally resolved. In 1122, pope and emperor agreed to a treaty, the *Concordat of Worms,* according to which the emperor retained the right to oversee the election of high churchmen, to decide between disputed candidacies, and to confer the temporal privileges of ecclesiastical office by means of the scepter. He gave up the right to invest prelates with the ring and the crozier, precisely those ceremonial rights that had appeared to confer spiritual as well as temporal authority upon a churchman. The end of the conflict also had profound consequences on the political character of imperial authority in the German lands (below, Chapter 15).

The Concordat of Worms formally ended what historians have long termed the Investiture Conflict, but it did not conceal the real triumph of modified Gregorian ideals that the papacy and its supporters had achieved. Never again could an emperor successfully invoke the old Carolingian idea of the emperor as God's vicar on earth, responsible for laity and clergy alike. Only the popes could now make such a claim. The image of a tripartite society comprising men of prayer, men of war, and men of work became less important in reformers' eyes than that of a bipartite society. "There are two kinds of Christians," said a popular text often quoted by churchmen in the twelfth century— "laity and clergy." Of the two, the clergy now claimed the ultimate responsibility for the spiritual welfare of humanity. This legacy of Gregory VII led to a widening of the idea of reform, new monastic and clerical movements, and new forms of lay piety.

Church of St. Peter, Mosaic: Tympanum. The tympanum is the part of the church façade just above the doors. Romanesque tympanum imagery is particularly striking. In this tympanum, Christ in Majesty is represented as in the Apocalypse with the symbols of a widely understood pictorial religion. (H. Roger-Viollet/Getty Images, Inc-Liaison)

NEW MONKS IN A NEW DESERT

By the late eleventh century, a new ascetic spirit was inspiring a number of monastic leaders to try once more to remove monks from close contact with the world and restore what they understood to be the rule of Saint Benedict to its place of supremacy over local privileges, customs, and diverse practices. The most successful of these movements was that begun at Citeaux in Burgundy. Founded in 1098 by a group of monks who sought a stricter observance of the monastic rule than existed at their old monastery of Molesmes, Citeaux (*Cistercium* in Latin, whence the common name for the order—Cistercians) prospered under the directorship of Stephen Harding (1070–1134) and the immense prestige of Bernard of Clairvaux (1090–1153). By the late twelfth century, a Cistercian Order was in place; there were nearly three hundred Cistercian religious houses, as well as several hundred more that followed one variation or another of the Cistercian rule. That rule, drawn up by Stephen Harding in 1114 and called *Carta*

Caritatis (The Charter of Love), was a modified version of the rule of Benedict. It organized and regularized the liturgical life of Cistercian houses, their relationships with one another, and the relations between the order and the world outside, and it emphasized the development of the spiritual discipline of the monks.

Principles of monastic organization were not, however, the greatest legacy of the Cistercians. The order offered not merely a rigid austerity and a puritanical view of the dangers of worldly temptation, but the prospect of a new interior spirituality, a wholly new relationship between humanity and God. In their scriptural commentaries and devotional writings, the Cistercians opened new avenues of spiritual awareness that exerted profound and enduring influences on the world around them. Both in organization and spirituality, the Cistercians illustrate the role of monasticism in the age of Gregorian reform.

One of the most striking features of the *Carta Caritatis*, although not fully in effect until the end of the twelfth century, was the constitutional principle of Cistercian organization that it laid out. The abbot of Citeaux was, like the abbot of Cluny, the head of his order, but there were far more checks on the former than on the latter. First, Citeaux developed a strong sense of the relationship between motherhouse and daughterhouses. The abbot of any Cistercian monastery that had directly sent out monks to found other monasteries was required to inspect those monasteries and in turn be inspected by their abbots at the motherhouse. The abbot of Citeaux, for example, had the right to inspect the four daughterhouses of La Ferté, Pontigny, Clairvaux, and Morimond, and the abbots of those four houses had the right to inspect Citeaux. In addition, all Cistercian abbots were to convene annually at Citeaux to make collective decisions about the order, a reflection of a considerable corporate awareness in the governance of the order.

Cistercian recruitment was also versatile. Those who seemed less suitable than others for participation in the full austerity of the monastic program were enrolled as *conversi*, or lay brothers. They worked and managed the farms and granges of the order and lived their own regulated devotional life separate from that of the monks. For the Cistercian monks themselves, life was strict. Only the most severe decorations were permitted in Cistercian churches. Clear glass alone filled the windows. Bernard of Clairvaux denounced the bright colors, intricate sculpture, bell towers, and metal crucifixes, the most distinctive features of Cluniac and other church decoration, as "deformed beauty and beautiful deformity." All these were banned from Cistercian churches. The cloisters too were stripped of their architectural ornament. A "typical" Cistercian style of church architecture carried the aesthetic and devotional principles of the order into the farthest corners of Europe as the order itself spread south to Italy and Spain, northwest to England, and northeast to Germany and Poland.

The greatest attraction of the Cistercian movement, however, was its creative role in developing the new spiritual outlook of twelfth-century Europe. Traditionally, monasticism was a defensive institution, consciously isolating its members from the temptations of a fallen world by placing them, through self-discipline and community life, in a tiny earthly duplication of heaven. In Cistercian spiritual writings, there appears less emphasis on the defensive character of monastic life and much more on its role of developing the inner spiritual life of the monk, enabling him to reach out and grasp God's love for humanity. This new spirituality is also reflected in the way artists from the tenth century on depicted the crucifixion of Jesus. Instead of a remote, majestic being superimposed on a cross, they depicted an anatomically accurate suffering figure who aroused the viewers' sympathy and affection, not merely their awe and dread. Depictions of the Virgin and the Child Jesus became more popular at the same time. No longer in art and spirituality was all of humanity depicted as fighting a hopeless rearguard action against the inevitable triumph of the devil. Rather, devotional writers described people as following a path, conducting a quest, or climbing a figurative ladder—all these images appear frequently in the twelfth century—toward inner spiritual growth. This new sense of God's affection for humanity and the obligation of interior spiritual development in order to embrace it was largely an invention of twelfth-century Cistercian writers.

The most prominent individual in the Cistercian movement—indeed in the religious life of all western Europe—in the twelfth century was Bernard (1090–1153), abbot of Clairvaux. Part of the importance of Bernard lies in the extent of his personal influence outside as well as inside the cloister. Bernard was born to a noble family near Dijon. In 1112, with his brothers and a large group of other young noblemen, Bernard suddenly left the lay life and joined the still young community of Citeaux. Bernard's arrival traditionally marks the surge of the order; indeed, Bernard's growing prestige greatly increased the attractiveness of the order throughout France. In 1115, Bernard was sent out to found the third daughterhouse of Citeaux, at Clairvaux. Throughout his life, he remained devoted to the ascetic ideals of the Cistercian program. Bernard's physical austerities became well known and widely admired throughout Europe. His flawlessly ascetic character, the burning lyricism of his devotional works, his concept of human dignity, and his explorations in the psychology of devotion establish him securely in the great exemplary tradition of Benedictine monasticism. Yet Bernard was also the most widely respected holy man of the twelfth century, and it is as one of the last and most outstanding examples of the holy man, a type that developed in antiquity, that Bernard is perhaps best understood.

Bernard played a role outside the cloister as extensive as his role in it. In 1128, for example, he was the secretary for the Synod of Troyes, where he composed a work in praise of the new orders of monk-knights in Jerusalem (below, Chapter 14). In 1130, his support determined the outcome of a disputed papal election. In 1140, he attacked the new theology of Peter Abelard at the Council of Sens (see below, Ch. 13). In 1144, he preached the Second Crusade and even traveled to Germany to put a stop to the persecution of Jews and to persuade King Conrad III to join the crusading expedition (below, Chapter 14). In the last decade of his life, he wrote an influential handbook for his protégé, the Cistercian pope Eugenius III (1145–1153), on how to be a pope. In 1145, Bernard traveled to southern France to preach against heresy. In addition to these personal journeys, Bernard poured forth a stream of correspondence, treatises on devotion, prayers, and meditations, and instructions to diverse groups and individuals in European society.

The success of the Cistercians and similar monastic movements also inspired many secular clergy—those who lived in the world and served the laity—to reform their lives along the lines of monastic reforms. Because individual clerics often found it impossible

Cathedral of Autun, Tympanum: The Torment of Souls. The great tympanum of Autun depicts salvation and damnation. In this detail, the signed work of the sculptor Gislebertus, demons are tormenting the souls of the damned. (Ets. J. E. Bulloz)

to live reformed lives without the support of a religious community, groups of pastoral clergy (those actually serving the spiritual needs of lay people) began to organize themselves in communities. There they lived according to a rule, as monks, but served the laity as priests. One such group, the Augustinian Canons, took their rule of communal life from the rule for religious that Augustine had produced in the fifth century. As Canons Regular (pastoral clergy who lived communal lives like monks), they became a very effective pastoral branch of the clergy. The Premonstratensian Canons, founded by Norbert at Laon in 1120, were a second important group of Canons Regular. The form of life of both groups of canons greatly improved the quality of the ministry in areas where they worked, and they began the long labor of improving the quality of the secular clergy. They thereby made themselves a bridge between the new monasticism and the ill-educated and poorly trained parish clergy that ministered to lay people.

LAY PIETY ON THE EVE OF THE FIRST CRUSADE

The eleventh-century movement of monastic, clerical, and papal reform was not restricted to the men of prayer. Lay patrons and the inhabitants of cities had both supported and opposed clerical reform. In Milan, a group called the Patarines, an alliance of rich and poor, layfolk and clergy, attacked clerical wealth and opposed an imperially appointed archbishop. They, too, received a papal banner and support from Alexander II.

The reformed clergy, now marked off from the laity by its canonical celibacy, also dealt with a lay population whose participation in the spiritual life of the church now became a matter of greater concern. Although the reform movement had increased the distance between clergy and laity and asserted the sacramental powers of clergy that no layman could possess, it also emphasized the clergy's moral and spiritual responsibility for the laity.

The new emphasis in both art and devotional texts to the humanity of Christ, especially in representations of infancy and the passion—the most defenseless and vulnerable occasions of that humanity—suggests another aspect of a shift in religious sensibility that affected laity as well as clergy. Penitential pilgrimage, undertaken by increasing numbers of people over increasingly long distances—to Santiago, Rome, and Jerusalem—is another sign.

The sacramental role of the secular clergy was also expanded. Sacraments were liturgical ceremonies, in which—with the exception, in cases of emergency, of baptism and the last rites—only a priest possessed, through his ordination, the power to administer God's grace to lay people. The most important of these were baptism, the consecration of the eucharist at mass, the administration of penance, and the ordination to holy orders. Liturgical ceremonies drew in the laity as participants—for example, as godparents at baptism—or as pious observers, in the case of the mass.

But the case of marriage is probably the most important sign of the new relationship and responsibility. Marriage had long been, as we have seen, purely a matter of alliance between families. Clerical participation was limited chiefly in determining whether the spouses were related within the forbidden seven degrees—that is, whether they had a common ancestor within seven generations, later reduced to four. The prohibition of marriage to the clergy, however, also required a change in the clerical attitude toward marriage among the laity. During the twelfth century, clerical participation in the ceremonies of betrothal and marriage increased, until marriage was finally declared a sacrament at the Fourth Lateran Council in 1215 (below, Chapter 15). So did clerical thought about marriage. One of the major intellectual concerns of eleventh- and twelfth-century thinkers was the problem of responsibility: Were people responsible only for the consequences of their acts or for the intentions behind them? Earlier views in terms of both penance and law had emphasized the consequences of the act alone. But in the eleventh century, thinkers began to concentrate on intentionality, a reflection of a general interiorizing of personal identity as well as religious devotion. In the case of marriage, this meant that the consent of the individuals, and neither the agreement of the families nor sexual intercourse, was the constitutive element in marriage. Increasingly, the changes in religious sentiment among both laity and clergy in the late eleventh and twelfth centuries transformed the assessment of the spiritual value of more and more aspects of the lay life.

This is part of the context in which the events of 1095–1099 should be considered.

THE ISLAMIC AND BYZANTINE WORLDS
ON THE EVE OF THE FIRST CRUSADE

The power of the Abbasid Caliphate at Baghdad began to fragment during the ninth century in favor of local territorial rulerships that nominally acknowledged the caliphs' authority, but in fact functioned autonomously. One of the strongest of these was the federation ruled by the Islamic, but Iranian-speaking Samanid Dynasty in Mahwara'n-Nahr south of the Aral Sea to the east of Khurasan during the ninth century. The Samanid state was economically prosperous and culturally dynamic, governed by an elaborate administrative system and defended by an army that was comprised of slave-soldiers, *ghulam,* mostly of Turkic origin from the steppelands northeast of the Aral Sea. The movement of Turkic peoples from Central Asia is one of the marked demographic features of the place and period. Abbasid caliphs, too, increasingly used slave-soldiers from the same sources, at least from the caliphate of al-Mu'tasim (r. 833–842). The use of such armies tended to divide the military and civilian populations, link fiscal and military power, weaken the traditional military aristocracies and the influence of towns, and pose the perennial danger of military rebellions.

The Samanid federation was defeated by Turkic armies under the Ghaznavid dynasty around the year 1000, and the Ghaznavids themselves by a Turkic people called the Seljuks, or Saljuks, in 1040. Their leader, Tughrul Beg, proclaimed himself *amir* and negotiated for approval from the caliph. By 1053, the Seljuk power was recognized by the Abbasid caliphs. Having adopted Sunni Islam, the Seljuk *sultan* (power), Tughrul Beg, was welcomed by the caliph when he marched on Baghdad in 1055, defeated the Shiite Buyids, proclaimed himself a "deliverer" of the caliph, and assumed effective control of the Abbasid Empire. Two of Tughrul Beg's successors, Alp Arslan (1063–1072) and Malik Shah (1072–1092), threatened both the Byzantine Empire and the Fatimid Caliphate of Egypt. The rapid rise of the Seljuk Turks was thus not only an event of major importance in the caliphate of Baghdad, but also in the world of the Byzantines, since the lands the Seljuks now ruled abutted Georgia, Armenia, and Anatolia, and the eastern frontiers of the Byzantine empire.

The achievements of Basil II (976–1025; above, Ch. 9) included the securing of the borders of the Byzantine empire by a professional army, at the core of which stood the emperor's personal troops, the Varangian Guard. Basil also tolerated considerable religious diversity in permitting assimilated peoples and newcomers to the empire to continue to follow their own versions of Christianity. But Basil's rule was also autocratic and highly personal, and he neither married nor left provision for a successor. Byzantine aristocrats and churchmen increasingly resented the religious diversity of the empire, which they considered to be the toleration of heresy. This growing resentment at religious difference lies behind the bitterness in relations with Rome, culminating in the condemnations of 1054.

Basil's brother and successor, Constantine VIII (1025–1028), ruled only briefly and left two daughters, Zoe and Theodora, to succeed him. Zoe, who had no children, outlived two husbands and was succeeded by her third, Constantine IX Monomachos (1042–1055), who in turn was succeeded by Theodora (1055–1056), with whose death the Macedonian dynasty ended. During the reigns of Zoe, Constantine Monomachos, and Theodora, Turkic peoples migrated into both Armenia and Anatolia. The last Macedonians turned for internal support to the aristocratic families and the population of Constantinople. The military apparatus became more expensive, as wars on the Danube and local rebellions drained the last of the immense treasure that Basil II had left.

By the late eleventh century, the Byzantine Empire was wracked by political rivalry between the imperial civil servants and the landowning rural aristocracy. The extinction of the Macedonian dynasty in 1056 gave rise to a series of civil wars, which only the accession of Alexius I Comnenos (1081–1118) was able to stop. Byzantine economic and military power had declined, moreover, at the moment when new invasions threatened the empire again. The greatest threat had come from the Seljuk Turks. In 1071, the armies of Alp Arslan destroyed a Byzantine army at Manzikert. In the same year, the Normans under Robert Guiscard captured the Byzantine city of Bari in southern Italy and soon crossed the Adriatic to invade Greece itself. For the next two decades, Byzantine foreign policy was dominated by the twin threats of the Normans in South Italy and the Seljuk Turks in Baghdad and Anatolia. With the death of Malik Shah in 1092, however, Seljuk power became divided among several competing princely houses and therefore decentralized. In Anatolia itself, an independent Seljuk sultanate, that of Rūm (East Rome, Anatolia) was established. During the eleventh century, following the death of the Fatimid caliph al-Hakim in 1021, Egypt, too, fell under rival contending powers. Alexius I's request for western mercenaries was made with a view to exploiting the breathing space that Islamic disunity seemed to have given him.

THE EXPEDITION TO JERUSALEM

Throughout the early years of his pontificate, Urban II (1088–1099) made extensive reforms in the operation of papal government. He designated it as the *curia*, or court, and he continued the diplomatic struggle with the excommunicated emperor Henry IV. He also entered into friendly relations with the emperor at Constantinople, Alexius I Comnenus (1081–1118), attempting to heal the breach caused by the mutual excommunications of pope and patriarch that had taken place in 1054. In 1095, Alexius sent legates to the Council of Piacenza in northern Italy, requesting papal aid in enlisting mercenary soldiers for the defense of the Byzantine Empire. As Urban moved across southern France during the summer of 1095, holding local reform councils, he decided on his response to Alexius. At the Council of Clermont in November, 1095, Urban made no call for mercenary recruits. Instead, he appealed to a large assembly of laity and clergy to impose peace everywhere in Christian Europe and to turn Christian weapons only against infidels who threatened the safety and security of eastern Christians, and infidels in possession of the Holy Land. Urban proposed a large armed pilgrimage to Jerusalem, offering forgiveness of sins to those who undertook the journey from pure motives. In proposing the armed pilgrimage (which he and his successors always called a "journey," "expedition," or "pilgrimage," and not until around 1200 "crusade"), Urban II created a new form for the expression of the growing piety of the lay warrior class. Indeed, the First Crusade, which Urban's plea created, was first and foremost a vehicle for lay warriors to participate in a renewed Christian society in the one capacity for which they were ideally suited—controlled violence in God's service against non-Christians.

The response to Pope Urban's proclamation of the "expedition to Jerusalem" was not that of a mercenary army. The very first groups to march east were an ill-assorted assembly of fighting men, townspeople, and peasants led by the independent preacher Peter the Hermit. The "Crusade of the Poor," as Peter the Hermit's expedition is often called, suggests the depth of response stirred by Pope Urban's call for a campaign in the Holy Land. Peter's army terrorized the Rhineland and Hungary as it passed through, massacring Jewish communities and looting its way east until it passed through Constantinople and met its destruction in Turkish Anatolia. Whatever Alexius had wanted and whatever Urban II planned, Peter's expedition was not it. The next phase of the expedition better fitted Urban's expectations, but not those of Alexius.

In 1096, four well-organized armies of western fighting men set out for Constantinople. They were led by great nobles and directed by Adhemar, bishop of Le Puy, Urban's legate, or representative, on the expedition. Alexius I Comnenus, a skillful diplomat, worked out treaties of agreement with each leader, forcing some of them to swear allegiance to him personally and extracting promises from them to return any conquered lands that had belonged to the empire. He then escorted the huge army across the Bosporus, where it captured the city of Nicaea. After marching south through Anatolia, the westerners encountered and defeated a Turkish army at Dorylaeum and marched east to Antioch. The siege and subsequent defense of Antioch lasted from late 1097 to the end of 1098 and exacted a terrible toll in human life on the part of both the armies and their opponents. Not until January 1099 did the final march to Jerusalem begin. Led by Raymond of St. Gilles, count of Toulouse, who was barefoot and clad as a penitent and a pilgrim, the armies first sighted Jerusalem on June 7. After a fearful five-week siege, the city fell on July 15.

Two principalities had already yielded to the Crusaders before the siege of Jerusalem began. Antioch had fallen into the hands of Bohemund, son of Robert Guiscard of Sicily. Edessa, an Armenian principality to the east of Antioch, had fallen to Baldwin, brother of Godfrey of Bouillon, one of the expedition's leaders. The capture of Jerusalem and of two other independent principalities immediately raised the question of the organization of the captured territories. Many members of the expeditionary army left Palestine and Syria to return to Europe, their mission completed. The occupying forces remaining in the Holy Land shrank dangerously. Byzantium made several claims concerning its own rights to captured territories, especially Antioch, exacerbating the alienation between Greek and Latin Christians that had been heightened in 1054.

In 1099, Godfrey of Bouillon was elected advocate of the Holy Sepulcher, but that meaningless title could not be made to work effectively as a force of governance. When Godfrey died in 1100, his brother Baldwin of Edessa succeeded him and formally became king of Jerusalem. By 1111, most of the important coastal cities had been taken by the Crusaders; the last, Ascalon, fell to them in 1153. During the reign of Baldwin I (1100–1118), four principal Crusader states took shape: the principality of Antioch; the county of Edessa; the county of Tripolis in the center of the Holy Land; and the kingdom of Jerusalem in the south. A new Christian kingdom had taken shape far from western Europe, among the hostile powers of Egypt, Baghdad, and Constantinople.

* * *

The news of the victory and the conquest of Jerusalem had an enormous impact on western Europeans. It seemed to justify the highly pitched religious ideals of the reform movement, to demonstrate an unmistakable sign of God's favor, and to cast the devout fighting man in a new light. Guibert of Nogent, writing in a small monastery in northern France, spoke to returning crusaders and read some of the early accounts of the crusade before writing his own account, which he entitled *The Deeds of God Performed Through the Franks*. In it, he summed up the opinion of most of his contemporaries about the significance of the victory:

> *God ordained holy wars in our time, so that the knightly order and the erring mob, who, like their ancient pagan models, were engaged in mutual slaughter, might find a new way of earning salvation. Thus, without having chosen (as is customary) a monastic life, without any religious commitment, they were compelled to give up this world; free to continue their customary pursuits, nevertheless they earned some measure of God's grace by their own efforts.*

The First Crusade generated more narrative accounts than any earlier event in European history, and it eventually produced a series of epic poems in vernacular Old French whose subjects ranged from the siege of Antioch to the legendary ancestry of Godfrey of Bouillon.

The crusade did not, however, meet with universal approval. One of the most interesting accounts of part of the Crusade is the *Alexiad,* the epic history of her father, Alexius I, that Anna Comnena wrote in early twelfth-century Constantinople. To Anna, the crusade was simply an attempt on the part of the Latins to subvert and conquer the empire, an attempt that was foiled only by the wisdom and heroism of Alexius. Anna had been around sixteen at the time the crusaders passed through Constantinople in 1096, and she was writing in her old age. But her remarkable work offers a vivid Byzantine perspective and memorable evidence of the impact of the events of 1095–1099, events that shook both the Latin and Greek Christian worlds.

THE CRUSADER STATES AND THE FALL
OF THE LATIN KINGDOM

The Kingdom of Jerusalem, the counties of Edessa and Tripoli, and the principality of Antioch constituted an unusual Christian political and social complex in a world of fragmented Muslim principalities. The armies of the First Crusade had walked through a window of military and political opportunity of whose existence they were not even aware. Dependent on both Byzantium and the Italian port cities for supplies, the transport of pilgrims and soldiers, and military assistance, the turbulent crusader states were internally divided by political and dynastic rivalries within its ruling groups and rarely agreed on a single policy. Although the king of Jerusalem was nominally the ruler of the crusader states, he had to respect the interests of the local aristocracy and the independent military orders of the Knights of the Hospital of St. John and the Knights Templar, as well as the energy and enthusiasm of new crusaders. Internal dissension in the lands that the Europeans had begun to call simply *Outremer* ("Overseas") usually influenced military and diplomatic policy.

In addition, Muslim resistance grew measurably after 1125—the window of opportunity began inexorably to close. In 1127, a talented Seljuk prince named Zangi established a strong Muslim principality in the city of Mosul and expanded his territory at the expense of Muslim, and then of Christian, neighboring states. In 1138, Zangi captured Damascus, and in 1144, he assaulted and captured Edessa, the first Christian principality to fall back into Muslim hands. The capture of Edessa prompted the pope, Eugenius III, to call another armed pilgrimage and to send out preachers and promise spiritual benefits on a large scale to all who participated. From this point on, the legal privileges of a fighting man who had taken up the cross became both more extensive and more precisely spelled out. As we have noted, among the preachers of the Second Crusade was Bernard of Clairvaux, whose fiery eloquence stimulated many, including King Conrad III, to go to the East. But increasingly specified crusader privileges and a more systematic preaching campaign were not the only results of the capture of Edessa. Bernard received, from the pope, permission for northern European fighting men who engaged the still pagan Baltic and Slavic peoples to be considered crusaders as well. Thus, crusading legitimacy was added to the old conflict between expansionist Christian lords and non-Christians in northeast Europe.

The Second Crusade of 1147 was very different from the First. Led by the German King Conrad III and King Louis VII of France, the two main armies were virtually uncoordinated and far more poorly organized than the noble armies of the First Crusade. Although some of the English, Flemish, French, and Portuguese crusaders managed to capture the city of Lisbon while en route to the Holy Land, the crusade itself, except for a futile assault on Damascus, achieved very little. Both king and emperor headed home without any of the glory that had covered the leaders of the First Crusade half a century before. Human sinfulness, said Bernard of Clairvaux, had lost the Crusaders God's favor. Human wickedness and cunning, said apologists for the king of France, had betrayed the Crusaders. Louis was particularly enraged at the Byzantine emperor Manuel I, who he believed had betrayed him in alliance with Conrad III. This attitude sharpened the growing Latin suspicion and dislike of Greek Christians and contributed to the deteriorating relations between Byzantium and the West, already aggravated by the frictions caused by the First Crusade and the rise of Venice.

As relations between the Crusaders and Byzantium deteriorated further, the new lands were especially dependent upon the Italian maritime cities for their lifeline to western Europe. Genoa, Pisa, Lucca, and Venice grew wealthy from the concessions they won in Palestine and Syria, and their new wealth played an important role in their drives toward independence from domestic powers in Italy. The prominence of Venice in both the Crusading and Byzantine worlds grew particularly quickly in the twelfth century, and Venice, like the Crusader states, experienced a deterioration of relations with Byzantium, although Venetian importance in Byzantine commerce grew during the same period.

One result of the new energies of the Italian cities and the Crusader states was the economic undercutting of Byzantium. The loss of lands and manpower to the Seljuk Turks in Anatolia, the continuing high expenses of Byzantine imperial government, heavier taxes drawn from a diminishing tax base, and a debasement of Byzantine coinage weakened Byzantium considerably during the twelfth century. Besides threats from Norman Sicily and South Italy, Byzantium faced the economic powerhouse of Venice and the sullen distrust of the Crusader states. Although the twelfth-century Byzantine Empire profited from the abilities and good sense of the Comnenian imperial dynasty from Alexius I to Manuel I (1143–1180), it failed to recover fully from the crises of the eleventh century and the shift in wealth and power to the Latin West.

Although Zangi was assassinated in 1146, his son and successor Nur ad-Din (r. 1146–1174) assisted in the defense of Damascus against the armies of the Second Crusade, and by 1154, he had acquired Damascus for himself. For the next twenty years, Nur ad-Din strengthened his state and profited from the dissensions and political crises in Outremer, which put the Christian states at a distinct disadvantage. Disputes over the

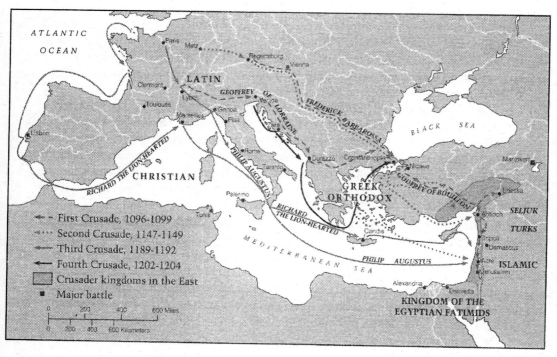

The Crusades.

succession to the kingship of Jerusalem, conflict between the noble families and the kings, and the important role played by the Military Orders (communities of knights who took monastic vows and lived a life of war and prayer) all weakened the stability and strength of the Crusader states in the face of growing Muslim resistance.

Although some collaboration between the kingdom of Jerusalem and the Byzantine Empire held off Muslim forces in the 1150s and 1160s, their combined efforts were achieved only at great expense. In 1176, the Byzantine army under the emperor Manuel was crushed at Myriocephalum by the Seljuk Turks, a defeat that lost the whole of Anatolia and exposed the Crusader states to a powerful Muslim enemy. In addition, the forces of Nur ad-Din grew stronger elsewhere in the Muslim world. Under the vigorous leadership of one of Nur ad-Din's officers, the Kurd Saladdin (1137–1193), his army conquered Egypt. After Nur ad-Din's death in 1174, Saladdin succeeded him and directed his combined forces at the Crusader states. In 1187, at the Battle of Hattin, Saladdin routed the Crusader forces, and shortly afterward he captured the city of Jerusalem. The Christians were left with a few coastal cities and the island of Cyprus, to which the kings of Jerusalem moved.

The triumph of Saladdin ended the century of the Crusader states, but it did not stop the Crusade movement or the idea of Crusade. The vigor and initial triumph of the First Crusade had created an image and a hope in European minds that the disasters of the twelfth century did little to diminish.

13

New Art and New Learning

A WHITE ROBE OF CHURCHES

The spiritual concerns of reformers and new forms of devotion were not the only signs of a revived religious culture in the eleventh and early twelfth centuries. Writing in the early eleventh century, the chronicler Radulphus Glaber noted that shortly after the year 1000, Europe began to be covered with "a white robe of churches." A new wave of church building and a new consciousness of the meaning and representation of the church building and the priestly order accompanied the spiritual concerns of the eleventh and twelfth centuries and gave them an important visual dimension.

The new and larger churches that appeared in eleventh-century Europe were based on several tenth-century architectural innovations and a new and informed interest in late imperial Roman architectural technique. Among the former influences is the appearance in several tenth-century churches of stone vaulting, the construction of a church ceiling completely out of stone arches instead of the timber framing that had characterized Carolingian architecture, especially in northern Europe. Among the latter influences are the size of late Roman buildings, particularly the basilicas, the thickness of their walls, the use of the rounded arch, and the dignity and solemnity of late antique architecture. The early eleventh century also reveals the earliest sources for ceremonies surrounding the dedication of a church, as well as depictions of the role of the priest in art that suggest a new respect for the sacramental powers the clergy claimed. This enhanced sense of the dignity of the church building and the person of the priest and

The Church of St. Philibert, Tournus: Interior. This is a good example of Romanesque church architecture. Note particularly the rounded vaults and small windows, as well as the ambitious formality of the design. (Les Archives Photographiques d'Art et d'Histoire)

liturgical ceremonies helps to explain the enthusiasm with which church builders constructed their new churches in the eleventh and early twelfth centuries.

Late-tenth- and eleventh-century builders also considered church building as a penitential act, as did William the Conqueror when he built Battle Abbey at the site of his victory over the forces of King Harold at Hastings in 1066. In thanks to God, the monks who had escaped from the Vikings and settled at Tournus built the church of St. Philibert shortly after 950. The patronage of the German emperors and the ambitions of imperial German churchmen accounted for a wave of large, new churches appearing in Germany throughout the eleventh century, particularly the churches of Speyer, Worms, Basel, and Bamberg. These churches were deliberately modeled on late Roman basilicas, and their large naves, high, rounded stone arches, and generous interior spaces were livened by a lavish use of color in their interior decoration. One of the most striking of these is the Church of St. Michael at Hildesheim, which was begun by Bishop Bernward in 1010.

Still other churches were the result of rebuilding programs. That of the monastery of St. Savin-sur-Gartempe, rebuilt in 1021, had its ceiling covered with remarkable frescoes depicting scenes from the Old Testament. Such churches as these, first in Germany, then in France, Spain, and Italy, and finally in England, reflect not only the development of tenth-century techniques and an imitation of Roman monuments and ruins but also internal influence within western Europe and architectural influences from the Byzantine and Muslim worlds.

The new churches of Romanesque Europe are testimony to the new ease of communications and the popularity of pilgrimage during the period in which they were built.

Church of Ste. Foy, Conques: Interior. An important pilgrimage church, the Church of Ste. Foy suggests the increased architectural solemnity of Romanesque church architecture and an impressive command of building techniques. (Art Resource, NY)

As the pilgrimage to the shrine of St. James at Compostela in northwestern Spain became more and more popular, many towns along the routes to Compostela built, or rebuilt, churches to accommodate the large numbers of pilgrims who wished to visit as many holy places and venerate as many relics of saints as possible on the long and dusty road to their destination. A fine example of one such church is that of St. Sernin in Toulouse, begun in 1060 and consecrated in 1096. Churches of this type were constructed in the form of a cross, with a nave large enough to hold a considerable crowd. The high side aisles of the nave continue around the north-south arms of the cross and meet in the apse at the east end of the building. This route inside the church is called an ambulatory, and it was a prominent feature of Romanesque church architecture. Its purpose was to offer a path for pilgrims walking around inside the church that would take them as close as possible to the relics they had come to venerate. The new appearance of churches, their size, and the increased degree of veneration people felt for them contributed an important visual dimension to an age of spiritual unrest and reform.

Monastery of St. Martin, Canigou. Perched high in the Pyrenees, this monastery and others like it witnessed the monastic reforms of the tenth and eleventh centuries. It was founded by a layman, Wilfred of Cerdana. (Max Alexander/Dorling Kindersley Media Library)

THE SEARCH FOR THE SCHOOLMASTER

Guibert of Nogent (ca. 1055–ca. 1125) wrote his history of the First Crusade, *The Deeds of God Performed through the Franks* (above, Chapter 12), as well as his remarkable autobiography, the *Monodiae*, at a small monastery in northern France around 1108. He had painfully acquired his learning over many years, and he once remarked on the difficulty of finding any teachers at all:

> *In the recent past, and even partly during my childhood, there had been such a shortage of teachers that you could hardly find any in the towns and rarely in the cities. When one did happen to find some, they knew so little that they couldn't even be compared to the wandering scholars of the present day.*[1]

Guibert was born into a family of minor knights, but had been promised to monastic life after his mother's difficult pregnancy and birth. Guibert's mother persuaded the not very accomplished tutor of one of his cousins to teach him, and so his education began. Once he entered the monastic life, his education continued in monastic schools. These schools, whose curricula were designed for monks, although they might also offer elementary instruction to other children, were one source of learning in the late eleventh century.

Monastic schools, libraries, and scriptoria had played a significant role in Charlemagne's revival of ancient Christian learning. In Carolingian monasteries, the old curriculum of the *trivium* and *quadrivium* (above, Chapter 3) governed the primarily literary education that monasteries provided. From the tenth century on, changes in thought took place largely in the context of monastic literary education. One of the first signs of change was a new style in the interpretation of scripture in the context of the increasing sophistication of grammatical and rhetorical education. The high literary quality of eleventh- and twelfth-century monastic literature is eloquent testimony to the improved status of these traditional subjects. The second change was the growing interest in the study of dialectic, or logic.

An example of both changes may be found a generation earlier than Guibert, in the career of Otloh of St. Emmeram (ca. 1010–ca. 1070). As a young boy, Otloh was sent to monastic schools at Tegernsee and Hersfeld to acquire a rudimentary education in the liberal arts, although he was not destined for monastic life. The superior quality of his handwriting led to his employment as a scribe by the bishop of Wurzburg and by others until he was around thirty-two. Then, a conflict with a rival drove Otloh to the monastery of St. Emmeram in Regensburg, where he taught in the external school operated by the monastery for young boys who were not to become monks. Otloh then entered the monastery as a monk, and he began instructing the young monks in the monastery school proper. Unlike many contemporaries, however, Otloh greatly admired the seven liberal arts in spite of their pagan origin, and the monastery boasted of being a "second Athens" because of the reputation of Otloh.

---

[1] *A Monk's Confession: The Memoirs of Guibert of Nogent*, trans. Paul J. Archambault (University Park, PA: The Pennsylvania State University Press, 1996), 14–15.

But Otloh also worried about the growing influence of dialectic, logic, an intellectual discipline that based its authority on reason rather than scripture, in conflict with the contemplative tradition of monastic education. Otloh thought that those who use dialectic excessively set themselves—or Aristotle—as authorities independent of and superior to scripture, therefore courting the vice of pride. A passage in Otloh's autobiography suggests how early and in what manner logic had begun to challenge grammar and rhetoric for primacy even in monastic education:

> *I call more learned those who are instructed in sacred scripture rather than dialectics. For I have found that certain dialecticians are so simple that they judge that all the passages of sacred scripture ought to be bound according to the rules of dialectics and in many passages, believe in Boethius, rather than the holy fathers. Whence these followers of Boethius condemn me for ascribing the name of "person" to anything but rational substance. If this condemnation be just, then it is also just that every name and word found in sacred scripture, used differently than dialectics would teach—as, for example,* substantia, genus, sentire, habere, *and many others—should be condemned.*[2]

Otloh was a gifted scholar and teacher and a sensitive and troubled spirit. He was also a good prophet, for the formal study of logic challenged traditional ways of understanding Scripture. It also offered critical means of comparing apparently conflicting statements in Scripture and the writings of the church fathers. Throughout the eleventh and twelfth centuries, considerable tension existed between the logical and literary analysis of key texts, especially in the monastic world and the study of scripture. Part of the solution to the growing popularity of logical study was the formation of new kinds of schools and scholars with aims different from those of monastic teachers and students.

A generation after Guibert of Nogent, Peter Abelard (1079–1142), born in Brittany into the same kind of military family as Guibert, also had to work hard to find teachers:

> *My father was a man who had acquired some literary knowledge before he donned the uniform of a soldier, and he retained such a liking for learning that he intended to procure for whatever sons he was to have a training in letters before their military service.*[3]

Abelard's father, although destined for a military career, had somehow acquired a reading knowledge of Latin (as probably had Guibert's mother) and an interest in learning, and passed that interest along to his son. The case suggests that the literacy of knights may have been more widespread than once was thought. We know nothing of Abelard's early education, but we do know that he took to it so enthusiastically, that with his father's permission he left Brittany and a military life to become one of those "wandering

---

[2]Irven M. Resnick, *"Scientia liberalis,* Dialectics, and Otloh of St. Emmeram," *Revue bénédictine* 97 (1987), 241–252, at 249.

[3]J. T. Muckle, *The Story of Abelard's Adversities* (Toronto: Pontifical Institute of Mediaeval Studies, 1964), 11.

scholars" that Guibert noted. Abelard's travels took him to whatever towns and cities had teachers of logic. He moved in and out of a world of cathedral schools—the second kind of late eleventh-century school—which offered a broader curriculum, based on the seven liberal arts, than the monastery schools, and ultimately to private teachers who had established their own schools—the third kind of education increasingly available in the late eleventh century. Outside the world of monastic education, in the schools attached to cathedrals and in the schools founded by private individual teachers in the eleventh century, the study of logic moved faster, partly because it could be applied in areas of study and thought that were not always prominent in monastic curricula. These schools became more and more popular in the late eleventh and twelfth centuries, and represent a second stage of the transformation of the setting for European learning after the improvement of the study of grammar and rhetoric. Under talented and dedicated bishops and individual teachers, such cathedral schools as those at Reims and Chartres, Laon and Paris, took advantage of their urban setting and their wide appeal to build an educational tradition that did not always rival, but certainly complemented, that of the monastic schools.

In the absence of widespread lay literacy and with limited means of communicating ideas, the schools of the eleventh, twelfth, and thirteenth centuries played a more prominent role in the history of thought and literature than modern schools usually do. As the relationships between literary and oral culture became more complex, the schools influenced wider areas of society and even lay thought. This influence may be seen in the thought of prominent theologians at monastic schools, in the schools of private masters in the twelfth century, in the appearance of new subjects, and in the tapping of new sources of learning.

An English contemporary of Abelard's, Adelard of Bath (fl. 1116–1142), acquired some early learning in England, then went to Tours in France and then taught at the cathedral school in Laon, where Abelard had also briefly studied. But Adelard became even more of a wandering scholar than Abelard. He left Laon and traveled for seven years to Salerno and Sicily, Cilicia and Syria, and perhaps Palestine. On his travels, he encountered Arabic learning and learned Arabic. Adelard translated the astronomical tables of al-Khwarizmi (below, Chapter 16) and Euclid's *Elements*, conveying to western Europe for the first time the results of Greek and Arabic astronomy and geometry. Later in life, Adelard was a clerk of the Exchequer in England and tutor to the future king Henry II. When he returned from his travels, Adelard, too, wrote a brief memoir in which he criticized the state of learning in the western Europe of his own day and praised the superior learning of Arabic scholars.

The two generations of Guibert, Abelard, and Adelard witnessed several transformations of education and learning that had immense consequences during the twelfth century. Monastic schools intensified their curricula, cathedral schools taught more and more students, individual masters opened their own schools wherever they could, and Arabic learning began to circulate in Latin translations. The twelfth century began with a search for the schoolmaster and ended with the invention of an institution for organizing teachers, students, and knowledge itself—the first universities.

ANSELM OF AOSTA, BEC, AND CANTERBURY

The career of Anselm (1033–1109) reflects many facets of the learning of the eleventh century. Born in Aosta in northern Italy, Anselm withdrew from the world and sought the contemplative life in the monastery of Bec in Normandy, then newly patronized by the rulers of Normandy. He eventually became schoolmaster and abbot of Bec, and then archbishop of Canterbury. Anselm was primarily a monastic theologian, and his literary works focused on the monastic life and monastic devotion. But in some of those works Anselm gave considerably more importance to the use of reason in devotion than had earlier monastic theologians like Otloh. His best-known expression of this use of reason is the phrase *fides quaerens intellectum,* "faith seeking understanding." Anselm proposed logic not as a road to faith or as an alternative to it, but rather as an important dimension of human nature that could be used only in conjunction with faith: "I do not seek to understand in order that I may believe," he once wrote, "but I believe in order to understand, for I also know that if I did not have faith, I would not be able to understand anything." Or, as he wrote elsewhere, "I want my understanding to comprehend in a certain way that same truth that my heart believes and loves."

Although he subordinated reason to faith, as most thinkers did, Anselm greatly opened the role of reason in theological discourse. In a work called the *Proslogion,* Anselm demonstrated that the truths of faith were not incompatible with reason. In his famous "ontological argument" about the proofs of the existence of God, he claimed to discover a proof of God's existence based on the argument that existence is an essential attribute that needed no further proof outside itself. Here again reason reaches the same conclusion as faith and revelation.

PETER ABELARD AND HELOISE

Peter Abelard (1079–1142), as we have seen, was the son of a literate knight in the service of the count of Brittany. Instead of taking up his father's profession of arms, he left the little town of Le Pallet and traveled through northern *Francia* studying under private teachers, including Anselm of Laon, a student of Anselm of Bec and a prominent logician and biblical commentator. Having a quick mind and a striking personality, Abelard soon claimed to have surpassed his own teachers. He became a professional teacher himself and moved to Paris. Although Abelard belonged to no monastery and had no formal right to teach theological matters, he began to lecture on precisely that subject. He soon became the most popular teacher in *Francia,* attracting students from England, Germany, and Italy as well as from the provinces of *Francia* itself. Latin, the language of learning, was spoken everywhere in western Europe, and students could move freely from a school in one place to a school in another without encountering a language barrier.

But Abelard made enemies as well as friends and admirers, as much because of his sometimes abrasive personality as because of the novelty of his thought and teaching.

The Faces of God: Christ as Teacher. The image of Christ in a majestic setting, but in the posture of a teacher, is taken from the ninth-century Lorsch Gospels.

Those who agreed with Anselm could hardly take Abelard's statement that "Nothing can be believed unless it is first understood" as anything less than a direct challenge. Fulbert, a canon of the Cathedral of Notre Dame in Paris, invited Abelard to tutor his niece, Heloise, a brilliant student and later an eloquent and important writer. The teacher and student soon became lovers. After she became pregnant by Abelard, Heloise and Abelard were secretly married. Fulbert, outraged at the secrecy of the marriage and Heloise's pregnancy, hired a gang of thugs, who broke into Abelard's living quarters and beat and castrated him. Both Heloise and Abelard withdrew from the world and took religious vows, Heloise at the convent of Argenteuil and later at Abelard's own foundation of the Paraclete and Abelard at the monastery of St. Denis. After a brief retirement, however, Abelard resumed teaching, and again students flocked to hear him. Although some of his theological ideas were condemned at the Council of Soissons in 1121, he became once more the most popular thinker in Europe. Condemned again at the Council of Sens at the urging of Bernard of Clairvaux (above, Chapter 12) in 1140, Abelard started out for Rome to plead his case directly before the pope. On the way, he stopped off at the monastery of Cluny and entered it, under the influence of its genial abbot, Peter the Venerable. He died in one of Cluny's houses in 1142. He recounted his earlier career in his autobiographical *History of My Troubles.*

Individual teachers of logic had stepped into theological speculation before Abelard, and some, like Anselm and Bruno of Cologne, who founded the Carthusian Order in 1084, left the world for monastic seclusion, but none had acquired his reputation or encountered as violent an opposition. During Abelard's own lifetime, such theological doctrines as the Eucharist (the real presence of Christ in the consecrated bread and wine of the Mass), the reasons for Christ's Incarnation and Crucifixion, and the nature of conscience all attracted much discussion, some of it traditional but some of it extremely novel.

The most important novelty in the new theological literature was the question of realism and nominalism, or the problem of universals. Late antique Neoplatonic thought had speculated on whether individual things, species, and genera exist as substances or as mental abstractions. In one influential work, the sixth-century thinker Boethius had followed Aristotle and stated that existence can be predicated only of real things; mental categories were mere abstractions, convenient cognitive devices and nothing more. In another work, however, Boethius followed Plato, arguing that such categories as species and genera were real things that existed in the mind of God, and that this existence was superior to the material imperfection of individual earthly things. This problem had troubled Otloh of St. Emmeram, and it continued to trouble thinkers in the twelfth century. Some twelfth-century thinkers argued for the Aristotelian approach: Only individual things have reality; the groups into which we classify them are simply *nomina* (names) and possess only a cognitive reality. Others argued for universalism, the Platonic notion that only the ideas in the mind of God were real, that individual things possessed only an inferior reality. Nominalism in its broadest sense argued that truth could be discovered only by the study of individual things and material creation; realism argued that truth could be discovered only by the contemplation of universals. Abelard himself adopted a modified nominalist position. Begun in the late eleventh century, this debate continued through the fifteenth century. It was one of the most significant frameworks for theological and philosophical discourse down to the seventeenth century.

Abelard's most important works were the *Ethics* and the *Sic et Non.* The former is subtitled *Know Thyself,* and it was this knowledge that Abelard regarded as the cornerstone of good and evil actions. Echoing the current theological emphasis on the love of God for humanity and the necessity for humans to participate actively in achieving their own salvation—the latter also a topic in Anselm's writings—Abelard stressed the importance of human intention in any estimate of the gravity of a sin or the virtue of a good act. He thereby contributed to the psychology of the twelfth century a view of human motivation that greatly widened the concept of the human personality and also played a role in new conceptions of marriage. In addition to his emphasis on intention and consent, Abelard stated that contrition, internal sorrow for sin, was the first essential stage of penance.

The *Sic et Non* ("Yes and No") is a teaching manual in which apparently contradictory passages from Scripture and the writings of the Church fathers are placed side by side. The method was designed to facilitate the problem of reconciling apparent conflicts among the diverse texts on which Christianity based its beliefs. In his preface to *Sic et Non*, Abelard laid down the criteria for systematically reconciling the apparent contradictions and, as in many of his other works, insisted that the application of logical method was the key to understanding the self, the self's relation to God, and the complexities of revelation. Aside from the colorfulness of his career, it is in this insistence on the supremacy of logical method that Abelard's originality lies and his influence is seen most clearly. Indeed, in his logic, his moral theology, and his autobiography we see one of the most remarkable and original thinkers in European history.

The case of Heloise reflects another aspect of twelfth-century learning—the perceived dangers of learning when the learned person was a woman, and the limited circumstances in which learned women might express their thought. Whatever her domestic background, Heloise came from a family with ecclesiastical connections that anticipated that women in it would be taught to read and write. Her uncle's invitation to Abelard to tutor her indicates a respect even for higher learning on the part of women in such families. It is also clear, from Abelard's own account and from the letters of Peter the Venerable, abbot of Cluny, that Heloise's learning was widely known and admired. Heloise's own first letters to Abelard in response to *The History of My Troubles* reflect a powerful mind and spirit, lively emotions conveyed in excellent Latin prose, and a wide range of literary references. They also reveal a determined and highly individualized perspective on their relationship and on Abelard's duties to Heloise and her sisters.

The correspondence begins with Heloise's recriminations against Abelard, but it then shifts focus to the role of religious women, a role that Heloise accepted reluctantly and appears to have exercised brilliantly. In the twelfth century, the convent offered a place, not only for unmarried women and widows, but also for female study and writing. Religious women who possessed and expressed distinctive personalities appeared in many convents in twelfth-century Europe. These women were literate, could write and illustrate manuscripts, commission literary works, give and receive dedications of literary works, and read aloud to their sisters in the convent. They were also considered more likely (and safer because of their communal and often cloistered life) to receive special revelations from God. Although Heloise never professed to receive divine visions, a number of other professed religious women did.

Hildegard of Bingen (1098–1179), from a noble family in the Rhineland, followed the religious life from childhood, chiefly at the convent for noble women she founded at Rupertsberg near Bingen on the Rhine. There she produced a series of encyclopedic literary works, including three books of visionary writings that had wide influence and brought her into contact with the rulers and popes of her time.

Hildegard's visionary writings were recognized and approved by Pope Eugenius III, chiefly because they were orthodox and explicitly attacked contemporary heretical movements and because Hildegard posed no threat of independence to the structure of the Church and Empire. The same was true of her friend and correspondent Elizabeth of Schonau (1128/9–1164/5), also a member of the Rhineland nobility, whose visionary works also circulated widely.

The cases of Heloise, Hildegard, and Elizabeth indicate something of women's participation in the intellectual world of the twelfth century. Noble families in courts and convents could offer women both access to and a distinctive role in the new learning. Their work did not alter clerical misogyny or improve the status of women in society, but it did express a feminine mind and voice that achieved considerable recognition from the twelfth century on.

LAW AND LEARNING IN THE TWELFTH CENTURY

The development of early European legal institutions had produced a body of law very different in complexity and purpose from Roman law. From the earliest Germanic law codes to the customary legal arrangements of individual manors, villages, and towns, early European law possessed little of the philosophical and professional attraction of Roman law. In addition, the fragmenting of political authority in the ninth and tenth centuries had tended to turn legal institutions into the private property of lords who controlled law courts, pocketed the fines they awarded, and administered a heavy-handed kind of local justice. Some legal systems, such as that of Anglo-Saxon England, were relatively highly developed, but Anglo-Saxon law was subsumed under the oppressive legal practices of William the Conqueror's Norman aristocrats. In most of the principalities that made up eleventh- and twelfth-century France, regional customs determined legal practice. Moreover, much law operated under heavy procedural limitations and according to the theory of immanent justice—the belief that in certain cases,

Christ Pantocrator. The image of Christ Pantorator, "the Judge of all," was of Byzantine origin. This dome mosaic from the church at Daphni, near Athens, influenced the West at a time when church decoration was being developed in order to overawe the spectator. (The Metropolitan Museum of Art, Gift of J. Pierpont Morgan, 1917. [17.190.678])

divine intervention is required to indicate the guilt or innocence of the accused. Thus, various forms of the ordeal and trial by combat were practiced, because it was believed that in them the will of God was revealed.

But the same intellectual revolution that had affected rhetoric and logic, bible study, and philosophy, also came to influence the law. The revolution had both ecclesiastical and secular sides. On the secular side, the revolution of learned law is generally attributed to the Bolognese rhetorician Irnerius (fl. 1088–1125), who began to expound the recently rediscovered text of Justinian's *Digest* (above, Chapter 5), the great volume of Roman philosophical jurisprudence, to his students. As the explanation of this law-book grew beyond the stage of simply explaining the meaning of obscure words, the great intellectual achievements of Roman law began to generate independent interest, and schools devoted exclusively to the study of Roman law began to grow up, first at Bologna and later throughout western Europe.

By the mid twelfth century, the students of Irnerius known as the "Four Doctors," Martinus, Bulgarus, Jacobus, and Hugo, had developed the techniques of explaining the texts of the law by writing marginal glosses, composing short treatises on legal reasoning, and writing summaries of individual titles in Justinian's collection. Medieval teachers of Roman law believed that the law was binding throughout Italy and the Empire, although students studied it as much for its scientific character as for its alleged authority, and the cities of Pavia and Bologna became especially well known as centers of Roman legal study. After more than a century of scholarship on Roman law, the jurist Accursius (d. 1260) arranged the long tradition of commentary on the law into a single systematic commentary that became known as the *glossa ordinaria*, the ordinary gloss, of Roman law. In time, the *glossa ordinaria* was routinely taught in schools of Roman law along with the text of the law itself.

The rediscovery of Roman law threw traditional practices into sharp relief. Twelfth-century teachers of Roman law tried to fit it into the law of the towns of northern Italy, southern France, and parts of the empire. Naturally, they encountered a great many difficulties, but their efforts tended to make law more rational and systematic. Ranulf de Glanvill's treatise *On the Laws and Customs of the Realm of England* (1188) suggested for the first time that English law was susceptible to explanation in an orderly and logical manner, just as Roman law was. At the same time, King Henry II of England was engaged in sweeping away the variety of jurisdictions and practices in English law and imposing instead the law practiced in the royal courts, which later came to be called the common law of England. In the thirteenth century, a royal justice, long considered to be Henry De Bracton, wrote the most sophisticated and rational analysis of a national legal system in European history, *On the Laws and Customs of England*. Between 1279 and 1283, Philippe de Beaumanoir wrote a treatise *On the Customs of the Beauvaisis* (the region around the city of Beauvais in northern France) that showed mastery of the principles of Roman law and applied them to a body of regional law totally different in origin and development. The great compilation of learned law in Castile, *Las siete partidas*, "The Seven Parts," issued by Alfonso X (1221–1284) between 1256 and 1265, derived directly from Roman law and played a long role, not only in Spanish history, but in that of the New World and the United States as well.

During the late twelfth and thirteenth centuries, the formalized teaching and examination process of the law schools created the first European legal profession. Educated jurists increasingly filled administrative and legal positions in the kingdoms of Europe, regardless of whether or not those kingdoms used Roman law. In one way or another, learned law touched more and more of the little, local laws of Europe.

The revival of Roman law coincided with a growing distaste for the confusion and archaism that many thinkers found in eleventh- and twelfth-century European law. Even in those legal systems that formally remained outside the orbit of Roman law, such as the common law of England, the rationality, systematization, and regularity of Roman law made a great impact. Twelfth-century theologians protested against the use of the ordeal and the trial by battle, on the grounds that they tempted God and were a kind of blasphemy. When the Fourth Lateran Council in 1215 forbade clerics to participate in the administration of the ordeal, the older legal procedure was well on its way to becoming a dead letter. In its place, theologians approved the collection of evidence, its analysis, and a decision based on rational process. So did the teachers and students of Roman law, who also worked as scribes, agents, judges, lawyers, and consultants for the towns, principalities, and monarchies of western Europe. Even those students who did not intend to become lawyers often studied Roman law for a time in order to acquire the intellectual training and discipline that the study of Roman law offered.

CANON LAW AND THEOLOGY

The revival of Roman law and the slow spread of its influence to the customary laws of different regions in Europe illustrate the appeal that systematic, consistent thought exerted on a society that had suddenly become aware of its own lack of system and the inconsistencies of its own law. The growth of theology and canon law in the twelfth century also reflect that perception.

With the spread of learning and the production of more manuscripts and new works, thinkers became aware of the inconsistencies that also existed in the vast body of religious literature that the eleventh and twelfth centuries had inherited from the past. Peter Abelard's *Sic et Non* was an ambitious attempt to illustrate the conflicts in interpretation in the sources and to devise a reliable method for resolving them. In spite of opposition to Abelard's theology, his method attracted more and more followers, for it offered an irresistible tool for solving the problems that had entered the awareness of thinkers. In addition to Abelard's logical study there was, as we have seen, a transformation of the substance and temper of theology, illustrated in Anselm's linking of reason and faith and in Abelard's sophisticated psychological analysis of intention and consent. Moreover, such theologians as Bernard of Clairvaux paved new ways in devotional literature, sharing with Anselm and even with Abelard a new sense of the love between God and humankind, a fascination with the human nature of Jesus, and a new emotional dimension to theological thought. It is in the light of these three developments that the rise of the study of theology and canon law ought to be considered.

Others besides Abelard had long worried about the apparent conflicts that seemed to exist in equally ancient and authoritative texts. Ivo of Chartres, a contemporary of Abelard, prefaced one of his own collections of ecclesiastical legal texts with a set of interpretative rules that was very similar to that of the *Sic et Non*. Shortly after 1140, Gratian, a monk at Bologna, compiled a collection of ecclesiastical texts arranged in such a way that apparently conflicting statements dealing with the laws of the Church could be reconciled with each other. He arranged these conflicting texts in a logical sequence in order to solve a systematic set of problems of ecclesiastical law and an expanded version of his work was called *The Concordance of Discordant Canons*, or the *Decretum*. Far more than Abelard's work, Gratian's *Decretum* was informed by a mind both legally acute and devout. From the beginning to the end of his work, Gratian imposed order, principle, and coherence upon the previously undigestible materials of ecclesiastical law. He marshaled over four thousand different texts from dozens of church councils and authors, sometimes using as many as seventy quotations to clarify and illuminate the diverse sides of a single topic. Between the texts, introducing them and bringing each topic to a conclusion, is Gratian's own commentary, a model of lucidity and economy. Although it always remained unofficial, the *Decretum* became the model for later official collections of canon law and for the system, used in subsequent theological works, of grouping thematically related texts and analyzing them.

A number of popes and church councils in the twelfth and thirteenth centuries also issued legal provisions, in most instances echoing the methodology and influence of Gratian. Several private collections of these began to circulate, and in 1209, the collection by Petrus Beneventanus known as the *Compilatio tertia* was sent to the law faculty of Bologna by Pope Innocent III (below, Chapter 14), the first collection of canon law promulgated by a pope. The *Compilatio tertia*, but not the *Decretum* of Gratian, was supplanted in 1234 by the *Liber Extra* of Pope Gregory IX, also sent to Bologna. In 1298, yet another collection of legislation subsequent to the *Liber Extra*, the *Liber Sextus*, was issued by Pope Boniface VIII. From the early twelfth century on, canon law became a systematic professional discipline, with Roman law one of the "two laws" that theorists claimed to be the essence of learned law in Europe.

Around 1150, and probably under Abelard's and Gratian's influence, Peter Lombard (ca. 1100–1160), a canon in the cathedral of Notre Dame, master in the Paris schools, and in 1159 bishop of Paris, produced his *Book of Sentences*, a systematic collection of scriptural texts and writings of Church fathers and masters that dealt topically with theological problems. Peter's work, which displayed an enormous grasp of both earlier and contemporary thought, became the standard text of theological teaching.

As the tools of logic and philosophy became the tools of theology, specialization, training, and formal expression became necessary for theological study. At the Fourth Lateran Council in 1215 (below, Chapter 14), the number of the sacraments was finally set at seven and their nature was defined; the complex questions of nature, grace, sin, and salvation now received firm definitions. In teaching theology, the master now proceeded to treat texts, no matter how traditionally authoritative, in terms of the questions they illuminated, and the choice of these questions and their complexity directed the thrust of study. In time, such questions became the principal form of theological exposition.

The creation of canon law was as significant as the development of the new theology. From Gratian's *Decretum*, through the unofficial, and later official, collections of papal legal decisions that appeared in 1234, 1298, and 1314, scholars and popes shaped a body of law that laid down a new, juridical view of the relationship between the individual Christian and the Church. This body of law remained valid and in use throughout Christian Europe until the Reformation of the sixteenth century and in the Roman Catholic Church until 1918. Part of its influence doubtless lay in Gratian's organizing principles, which clearly displayed where the greatest legal problems lay, and in the fact that the lack of a fundamental organization comparable to that of the *Corpus Iuris Ciuilis* left teachers and students much room to add their own thought to the body of scholarship on the law or to criticize Gratian's. From a course in the liberal arts, including dialectic, students moved on to read Roman law. They might then proceed to canon law, their minds sharpened by logicians, Romanists, and their own teacher of canon law. The first commentaries on Gratian's collection are hesitant and elementary. Longer commentaries quickly appeared, however, modeled on those produced by teachers of Roman law—summae, questions, and rules. Several of the early canonists, or decretists, greatly influenced later approaches to the teaching and the creation of church law. Such twelfth-century figures as Rufinus, Stephen of Tournai, and, the greatest of all, Huguccio of Pisa, were followed in the early thirteenth century by Richard of England, Alan of England, Tancred, and Johannes Teutonicus, who composed the *glossa ordinaria* to the *Decretum* around 1215.

THE INVENTION OF THE UNIVERSITY

The schools of Paris in the days of Peter Abelard and for decades afterward consisted of assemblies of students grouped around individual masters who owned the schools and either owned or rented the rooms in which they taught. These assemblies came under the ecclesiastical jurisdiction of the bishop of Paris and his chancellor. In Paris and Bologna, the experience of large numbers of individual teachers and students coming together to study in a strange city far from their homes was a social and legal novelty, and the very presence of the schools and their lack of legal status rendered the students vulnerable to much of the hostility generated by the inveterate localism of the twelfth century. Unprotected by local citizenship, status, or privilege, students were subject to price and rent gouging, a lack of legal protection, and the perennial distresses of underfinanced strangers.

In 1158, the emperor Frederick I Barbarossa (below, Chapter 15), issued a law known as the *Authenticum Habita*, in which he extended his protection to students in imperial territories and which he commanded be included in the official text of Roman law. In particular, the document granted students free travel and legal immunities, and it acknowledged that their study profited the emperor and his subjects. It is the earliest document in the history of academic freedom. As a professional social consciousness grew among teachers and students, so did formal recognition of the status that formal study conferred. In the late twelfth century, there appeared the ceremonial inception, a public defense of one's learning that has parallels in the formal rites of initiation into the order of knighthood, the oath of citizenship in the corporation of citizens of a town, and the ritual recognition of the status of master in a craft guild.

Thus, students and teachers slowly created a collective identity for themselves in a society that jealously guarded its status ranks and left the stranger without status unprotected. They formed corporate bodies called guilds, which were similar to religious fellowships and craft associations. These defensive measures taken by the late twelfth-century schools consisted of creating for scholars a recognized corporate status. *Universitas*, the Latin term used to designate the schools, was a common word indicating any collectivity, from craft guild to confraternity to body of citizens, and the formal designation of the universities was *Universitas societas magistrorum discipulo-rumque*, "the university, or society, of masters and students."

The term *schola*, from later Roman imperial and Byzantine tradition, meant any particular group regarded simply as a group. *Schola* in academic terms remained the designation of a master and his students together. A group of *scholae* working in close proximity and having a similar character was called a *studium*, and certain *studia* were given the exalted status of *studium generale*, which meant that their subject coverage and reputation were great enough so that their graduates could be permitted to teach anywhere. These terms possessed no collective legal status, however, and privileges such as the *Authenticum Habita* applied to scholars individually, giving them no collective rights and recognizing no collective legal existence. The key events in the history of the universities occurred between 1200 and 1220, when popes, emperors, and kings began to issue papal, imperial, and royal privileges entitling the scholars to act as a legal corporation, a *universitas*. They thereby had the right to act and be represented legally as a corporation, to possess a seal, to collect and administer common funds, to establish their own bylaws, set their own calendars, and to sue and be sued collectively in courts of law. In some places as in Paris, the *universitas* was one of the masters alone; in others, such as Bologna, the students alone constituted the *universitas*. Through such societal and juridical changes, the universities came into legal as well as social existence by the middle of the thirteenth century.

In 1200, King Philip II Augustus of France provided an extensive charter of privileges to the *universitas* at Paris, a document generally regarded as the foundation charter of the present university. In 1231, Pope Gregory IX issued the decree known as *Parens scientiarum*, "the mother of knowledge," which afforded ecclesiastical privileges to the University of Paris. The universities of the thirteenth century, possessing legal existence, often suffered from the same organizational problems as other "universities": disputes between masters and students, among masters, students, and the officials of the diocese, and between scholars and townspeople. Possessing legal identity, universities could leave a city, negotiate with another city for accommodations and move there, supervise lower schools in the vicinity, issue collective pronouncements on public questions, and regulate areas as diverse as the book trade and the rate of rents charged to students and teachers. For the universities existed only legally, and not physically, except for their members. There were no university campuses, no libraries, no buildings that were distinctly and exclusively a university's. Lecture rooms were rented in private buildings. Masters took students into their homes for residence and instruction; students who did not live in a master's house had to find private lodging. Only slowly, through gifts, did individual buildings become university property. Even the earliest colleges consisted simply of endowed funds that paid for the housing, feeding, and instruction of poor students under masters' supervision; they were more charitable trusts than physical places. For example, the Sorbonne, the popular designation of the University of Paris, derived from the gift by Robert de Sorbonne in the thirteenth century of a charitable endowment for the support of poor scholars. The first buildings belonging to Oxford, Merton College, were left by Robert Merton. He had acquired them from Jews in Oxford, who had renovated them and thus helped originate what is commonly called the collegiate Gothic style of academic architecture in the United States.

Within these legal and physical circumstances, the schools developed their curricula and played out their role in terms of the new and the old learning. The triumph of logic, the subordination of the subjects of the *trivium* to the increasingly professional disciplines of theology and law, and the creation of the degree, the *licentia ubique docendi*—"the license to teach anywhere"—shaped their internal intellectual processes, just as their privileges, legal status, and endowments shaped their physical and social character.

The universities prospered because society needed them. Churchmen, faced with increasing business at Rome and in the great dioceses after the Investiture Conflict, felt an increasing need for capable, loyal, specially trained assistants, and the church had the great power to attract the men it needed. The twelfth century was probably no more fond of legal disputes than the eleventh, but the new law courts of the towns and the courts of kings and princes and prelates had to be staffed. Moreover, lesser princes and prelates began to find that when their clerical business was not kept up, their revenues and status declined perceptibly. All of these potential patrons helped generate a new demand for learning and letters.

When Abelard returned to Paris in 1136, one of his students was a young Englishman who had been born about 1115, raised in the old episcopal town of Salisbury, and then sent to Paris to study. In 1147, after completing his studies, John of Salisbury joined the papal court. He remained there until 1153 (during which period he wrote an important and fascinating account of papal history), when he became the secretary of Theobald, archbishop of Canterbury. Europe in the 1140s and 1150s was full of opportunities even for men from places as remote as Salisbury, or, for that matter, England. The chancellor of the papacy in 1146 was Robert Pullen, the English theologian, and from 1154 to 1159, the pope himself was the Englishman Nicholas Breakspear (Hadrian IV), who had previously spent many years in papal service throughout Europe. John of Salisbury worked closely with Theobald and his successor, Thomas Becket. Exiled in the 1160s, John was present at the murder of Becket in Canterbury cathedral in 1170. In 1176, he was elected bishop of Chartres, a post he held until his death in 1180.

Becket, a friend and patron of John, was the son of a prosperous Norman citizen of London and also went to Paris to study. Becket, too, became a clerk of Theobald's, and became chancellor of England and then archbishop of Canterbury under Henry II.

Becket fell out with Henry II over the question of the freedom of clerics from Henry II's legal reforms, and relations between the two continued to deteriorate. In 1170, four of Henry II's knights took the matter into their own hands, assassinating the archbishop on the altar of the cathedral while he was saying Mass. Becket immediately became widely venerated as a martyr and a saint, and his cult spread rapidly throughout Europe Although Henry did not order the assassination, he performed a public penance for it. The Becket case itself became a matter of debate in the schools.

Such careers as these—and there were many more as striking—illuminate the changing conditions and new opportunities in the world of governance and power. Learning could lead to a kind of success until then greatly restricted, although many students failed to achieve the careers they sought and hurled bitter charges against those they thought prevented it. Even successful men such as John of Salisbury condemned the intellectual extravagance and bombast that sometimes passed for learning; they and others complained that true learning was bypassed and that flashy superficial talents seemed to make all the headway. These criticisms have much substance, as did the twelfth-century complaint that "Galen gives riches, and Justinian gives wealth"—the complaint about excessive study for selfish professional purposes and the gaining of wealth. But they also remind us of the explosion of the new learning and the new institutions that came along with it as well as what they offered to ambitious, brilliant, or merely glib and aspiring scholars and officials.

Nor were the new scholars only those whose social origins made them more mobile and adventurous than the rest. John of Salisbury, Nicholas Breakspear, and Heloise came from ecclesiastical families, Abelard from a knightly family in the backwoods of Brittany, Becket from London urban prosperity. One of Becket's contemporaries at Paris was probably Rainald von Dassel, a noble who later became provost of the cathedrals of Hildesheim and Münster and Archbishop of Cologne and, after 1156, Chancellor of the emperor Frederick Barbarossa, whose own uncle and biographer, Otto of Freising, had also studied at Paris.

Such opportunities afforded ambitious students considerable incentive to seek out the best (or the most popular) schools and teachers and to cultivate among their contemporaries those who gave promise of one day being able to dispense patronage. This early example of "networking" contributed to the patronage of learning and the spread and attractiveness of the schools. The schools and universities created a new style of learned official in the centers of power, and these officials patronized others like themselves. In a world that had hitherto been one of orders, ranks, and carefully graded statuses, they invented the professional career. Professors equated themselves to knights, counts, and dukes. In doing so they shaped the intellectual circumstances in which both educational and political institutions dealt with day to day problems, formed theories of law and governance, and contributed a new intellectual format for the reconsideration of old questions and archaic structures.

14

The Church and the World

PAPAL AUTHORITY AND THE PONTIFICATE OF INNOCENT III (1198–1216)

From the dramatic imperial attempt to reform the papal office in 1046, until the end of the twelfth century, the popes exerted an increasingly active leadership in Christian society. Depending originally on the support of the emperor Henry III, and then, during the Investiture Conflict, upon that of sympathetic bishops, abbots, prominent lay nobles, and kings, the popes slowly transformed their administration and strengthened their claims to supremacy in Christian society. By the second half of the twelfth century in western Europe, the pope was generally recognized as the highest-ranking churchman in Christendom.

Among the most important stages of this process were the revised laws concerning papal election, the reform of the papal curia (the immediate servants of the pope in Rome) by Pope Urban II, the growth of papal prestige through the Crusade movement, the establishment of papal legates (officials sent by the popes to different parts of Europe with special legal authority), and the frequent holding of church councils to publicize and legislate the ideals of reform. In less than a century, the popes convened six major church councils that drew representatives from across Europe: the First Lateran Council in 1123, the Second Lateran Council of 1139, the Council of Rheims in 1148, the Council of Tours in 1163, the Third Lateran Council of 1179, and the Fourth Lateran Council of 1215. In addition, the appearance of such works as Gratian's *Decretum,* subsequent papal and conciliar legislation, and later canon law scholarship strongly emphasized the constitutional and legal authority of the popes. The popes also gained in their ongoing struggles with kings and emperors, for in the twelfth century, neither of these powers could marshal arguments as sophisticated and persuasive as those of papal lawyers and publicists.

Finally, the areas from which popes were recruited also changed. In the early Church, a bishop had to remain in the diocese in which he first became a bishop; he was considered to be "married" to his see. Early popes therefore tended to come from diverse backgrounds in clerical life and not frequently from the ranks of the bishops. From the mid twelfth century on, however, this older view was relaxed and more popes came from the ranks of bishops and servants of the papal curia. Many of these men also had experience and training as lawyers, and thus their early lives prepared them very differently from those of most of their predecessors for taking an active role as pope.

Not every churchman was pleased at the new influx of business that occupied the time and the minds of the twelfth-century popes. Bernard of Clairvaux bitterly denounced the volume of legal business handled by the chancery, the legates, and the popes. Nor was Bernard the only critic of this intensified legal activity. Satirical texts, one of which was called *The Gospel of the Mark of Silver* and another *The Lives of St. Albinus and St. Rufinus* (The Lives of Saints Silver and Gold) circulated more widely than the warnings of Bernard. Lawyers even coined the expression that "cases at the court of Rome are like things eternal, having no end."

Not all popes, however, were the same, nor did they always rule in the same ways. The papal office was, of course, elective, and the election of a particular individual as pope depended on the inner workings of the cardinal-electors—of whom since 1179, a two-thirds vote was required to elect—and the particular candidates available. Because of the different combinations of personal experience, temperament, and interests on the part of different popes, it is not always advisable to think about "the papacy" as if it were an abstraction that absorbed the individuals who became popes and obliterated the differences among them.

Popes were first and foremost individual clerics whose pontificates were influenced by their earlier careers and concerns. The pontificate of the most active, energetic, and intelligent of the popes, Innocent III (r. 1198–1216), reflects a number of aspects of the nature of the papal office. Innocent had been born Lothario dei Conti di Segni in 1160 or 1161, to a family of minor nobility with property in Rome and the surrounding countryside. Dedicated early to the clerical life, he studied at several Roman schools and then at the schools of Paris and traveled through much of western Europe before being called to serve in the papal curia around 1187. When he was elected pope in 1198, Innocent was thirty-eight or thirty-nine years old, well-educated, widely traveled, and administratively experienced. In decretal after decretal, he spelled out with striking precision supported by juridical reasoning, his own conception of the principles of papal authority, assembling throughout his pontificate a formidable body of legislation that gave concrete legal shape to that authority. In the decretal *Solitae* to the Byzantine emperor (1201), Innocent made serious claims to universal authority over all Christians. In two decretals of 1202, *Venerabilem* and *Per venerabilem*, Innocent further defined his authority in cases subject to temporal jurisdiction. In the decretal *Novit* of 1204, Innocent claimed the right to intervene judicially in any case in which criminal sin was involved. At the same time, as a result of a disputed election to the archbishopric of

Canterbury, Innocent excommunicated King John of England and laid an interdict (the prohibition of all but essential liturgical services) on the kingdom. But Innocent negotiated with John, arriving at a settlement of the dispute and lifting the interdict in 1213. Innocent also saw to it that administrative records were meticulously kept, and his register of official letters is the first complete register since that of Gregory VII. It began a line of complete papal registers that extend down to the present.

Yet Innocent also possessed profound pastoral concerns. His biographer devotes considerable attention to Innocent's care for the well-being of the clergy and the Church—and of individual churches, on the restoration and decoration of which Innocent spent much money and time. He responded with surprising swiftness to the new devotional movements of the early thirteenth century, and should not be viewed solely as a lawyer and administrator acting within a narrow, legalistic tradition.

The pontificate of Innocent III, the busiest if not the greatest of medieval popes, revealed the broad spectrum of jurisdictional areas across which the theories of papal authority could be spread and the extraordinary ability of the pope and his curia to make such theories the basis for practical decisions in hundreds of particular cases.

THE FOURTH LATERAN COUNCIL AND THE COMMUNITY OF THE FAITHFUL

The work of twelfth-century theologians, canon lawyers, church councils, and popes culminated in the canons of the Fourth Lateran Council, held at Rome in November, 1215. The council was called by Innocent III to further the two aims of Innocent's pontificate: the reform of the Church and the recovery of the Holy Land. The council is a good focus for understanding the life of the faithful as it was envisioned by ecclesiastical specialists at the beginning of the thirteenth century. Making the ideas and rules of theologians and canon lawyers understandable to ordinary believers was generally accomplished in three ways: by the legislative and teaching authority claimed by pope and bishops; by the creation of new religious organizations directly aimed at the religious life of the average believer; and by the work of a remarkable group of moral theologians, many of them in Paris, who adapted the large and abstract theories of learned theologians and lawyers to everyday situations, theories which could become the teaching materials of confessors, preachers, and other clerics with pastoral responsibilities. The laity was reached by authority, by pastoral reforms, by sacramental duties such as confession and penance, and by teaching, especially by sermons.

The first canon of the Fourth Lateran Council was a general statement of Christian belief, a form of the *credo,* or creed, that all Christians were expected to memorize, just as they were expected to know the two most common prayers, the "Our Father" and the "Hail, Mary." The creed insisted on both the unity of God and the Trinity of three Persons, the Father, Son, and Holy Spirit; on God's creation of the world from nothing; and on Christ's divinity, humanity, and sacrifice in order to save humanity. It insisted on a single, universal Church, the repetition of Christ's sacrifice in the Mass, and the efficacy of the sacraments (which the Fourth Lateran Council numbered at seven in all). It asserted the reality of the last judgment and the bodily resurrection of the dead.

Moral theologians did not expect ordinary Christians to understand the complex workings of theology, but they did expect assent to simple statements of doctrine. Christians were also expected to participate regularly in the sacraments, those liturgical acts that facilitated the reception of divine grace. Baptism signaled the spiritual birth of the individual into the Christian community, providing him or her with spiritual kindred (godparents, or god-sibs, whence the English word *gossip*), which included the saints, particularly the saint after whom one was named, which was the general practice from the thirteenth century on. The Council legislated that every Christian had to attend Mass and confess his or her sins to a priest at least once a year. The Council also issued a canon on the Eucharist which stated in the new Aristotelian terminology of the schools (below, Chapter 16) that the bread and wine were *transsubstantiated;* that is, while their appearance as bread and wine was preserved, their *substance* had become the real body and blood of Christ. Later in the century, the feast of *Corpus Christi* was proclaimed in conjunction with the doctrine of devotion to the Eucharist.

The baptized Christian might marry or enter the religious life. Marriage was declared one of the seven sacraments at the Fourth Lateran Council, thereby asserting ecclesiastical authority in marital cases. The Council also prohibited secret marriages and marriages in which there were impediments, such as an already existing marriage to another spouse, or a marriage within the prohibited degrees of kinship, which the Council reduced to four.

Sins were generally categorized in terms of the vices to which humans were subject, and the theme of the Seven Deadly Sins was a popular organizing motif for the ordering of conscience. Of these, those sins that led to hostility against others and disrupted the peace of the community—Pride, Anger, Avarice, and Envy—were considered most serious. Penance for these might be harsh and prolonged and might include a long pilgrimage or a public display of penitential status. For some exceptionally grave or public sins, "criminal sins," as some theologians called them, private penance assigned by a confessor in the "internal forum" of conscience and the private confession was considered insufficient, and a hearing in the "external forum" of a canon law court was required. In some cases, an adverse decision might entail excommunication, as it had in the case of King John. Although by the thirteenth century, excommunication might mean no more than exclusion from the sacraments for a specified period, on some occasions it could entail severe spiritual and material penalties.

Death, too, was surrounded by ecclesiastical assistance, from individual counseling to the Last Rites and burial in consecrated ground. The ritual surrounding death was as elaborate as other rituals and, on the whole, the entire apparatus of belief and Christian life and death represented a joining of high doctrine and authority and the earthly affections and expectations of a large body of believers.

Even the spaces of the church building were used in versatile ways to reflect both the differences between spiritual and material life on the one hand and their merging on the other. On some occasions—marriage, the seeking of sanctuary, baptism, or the performance of religious drama—the porch, doorway, or side of the church building was used; on others, usually sacramental occasions, the interior of the building was used. The varied uses of the church building suggest the versatile ways in which the spiritual demands of Christianity accommodated themselves to the needs and expectations of the ordinary Christian.

Although most Europeans were Christians, not all Christians were thought of in the same ways. Theology also constructed a gender schematic that differed for women and men. Thinkers regarded men and women as being far more different from each other than mere biological and physiological differences might indicate. Thus, Eve was considered to have first succumbed to temptation herself, and then, through what some writers termed "women's language," persuaded Adam to sin. As temptresses and deceivers, women, as the daughters of Eve, were nevertheless also considered fragile, inconstant, and weak. Against the image of woman as Eve, the twelfth century had cultivated the image of the Virgin Mary, but many of the most devout adherents of Mary did not extend their devotion past her uniqueness—Marian veneration did not much change the situation of the other daughters of Eve.

Contemporary women were often urged to live a life of virginity, and theologians continually asserted that the spiritual rewards of the virginal life were far greater than those of the widowed or married life. Although the Fourth Lateran Council included marriage among the sacraments, theologians were reluctant to abandon the conventional misogynistic image of women and their uncertainty about the spiritual validity of sexual activity. During the twelfth century, for example, the legend of Mary Magdalene was created as the epitome of feminine lust and weakness who had transformed her sinful life into one of virginal purity. The cult of Magdalene, centered on the monastery church at Vezelay, was, like that of the Virgin, much more a cult of spiritualized ideals than a consideration of the nature and spiritual needs of real women.

But misogyny alone was not the whole story of the late twelfth and thirteenth centuries. The sacramental status of marriage stubbornly asserted the spiritual dignity of the married life and sexual activity within marriage, even though the nature and extent of advice to married women from confessors and preachers insisted on locating them within rigid and narrow frameworks, usually based on a denial or restriction of women's sexuality. Freedom of movement for women was thought to give dangerous rein to the characteristic female vices of inconstancy and envy—women were frequently discouraged from undertaking pilgrimages and were forbidden to go on crusades. Therefore, custody and restraint were urged on women—in the household, especially in public, in costume, bodily comportment, and speech. With the new interest in the spirituality of marriage, there also emerged the image of the good wife—again, an idealized type who was expected to be as much the "preacher to her husband" as his sexual and social companion and household manager. Although theologians evoked the creation of marriage by God in the Garden of Eden and commented extensively on Christ's first miracle—changing water to wine at the wedding at Cana (John 2:1–11)—the good wife was required to respect her in-laws in order to establish and preserve social peace, love her husband (but with the restrained conjugal affection that did not weaken the marriage, as too intense spousal passion was thought to do), and be submissive to her husband. The husband in turn would respond with the moderate and tempered affection appropriate to a man. The wife should not look for wealth or status in a husband (although a man could do so in seeking a wife). The wife above all must give no cause for scandal.

Since most female marriage partners were considerably younger than their husbands, even the principle that consent made a marriage was usually understood to mean the young girl's consent to her parents' choice of a husband for her. Those who objected were generally coerced, and only a few remarkable figures like Christina of Markyate (ca. 1097–ca. 1160) succeeded and were later venerated for their determined resistance to a forced marriage. Even then, Christina was venerated because she sought a higher spiritual life, that of the cloistered virgin.

Thus, even changes in cult and devotional modes—like the cults of the Virgin and Mary Magdalene—and the new spiritual dignity attributed to marriage did not realistically define the life of a Christian woman. But the cloister or the hermitage, as the cases of Heloise, Hildegard, Elizabeth of Schonau, and Christina of Markyate indicate, might indeed offer a setting for a feminine theology and what has been termed "women's religion." Early examples include the English Gilbertine Order, which was designed specifically for women. In other instances, several of the major religious orders accepted houses of religious women, as did the Franciscans and Dominicans later in the thirteenth century.

Women's devotion could be expressed not only in isolated hermitages or cloistered convents, but also in communities of religious laywomen who lived and worked in the world. Such communities began to appear in the lower Rhineland and the Low Countries in the late twelfth century. These women, called Beguines, followed no set rule of life and took no permanent religious vows, and they lived a life of chastity, although they could freely leave the community and marry if they wished. One of the earliest and most widely venerated of these women was Mary of Oignies (1177–1213), whose life was written and cult spread by the famous preacher and historian Jacques de Vitry (ca. 1160/70–1240), a contemporary of Innocent III. In their communities known as *beguinages,* women could work at cloth processing or lacemaking or serve in hospitals. Within the community, they found considerable freedom to explore the spiritual life, generally unrestrained by male authority or presence. But they could also confuse even well-intententioned observers. In 1274, the Franciscan Gilbert of Tournai remarked that, "There are women among us whom we have no idea what to call, because they live neither in the world nor out of it." The apparent anomalies of Beguine life led to considerable clerical opposition to it, even to charges of heresy and to a temporary decline of the movement in the early fourteenth century.

It is in these settings—the cloister and the community of women who took no vows and continued to work in the world—that the most original manifestations of the feminine experience of the medieval Christian religion has been found. Besides the controversies over sex and wealth that influenced both the image of women and male definition of their material and spiritual natures, there were other foci of religious experience. Some of these were located in religious symbolism, particularly that of food. The work of Caroline Bynum, for example, has suggested that food was central in women's material and spiritual existence because it was one of the few elements over which women had control; fasting on the part of women was, for example, the counterpart to the renunciation of wealth on the part of men. The stories of female saints involve intense eucharistic devotion, the giving of food to the poor, and the undergoing of extreme physical privations (including the denial of food to themselves) as a means of fusing their own humanity to the suffering of Christ. Such arguments imply that women in the twelfth and thirteenth centuries did not reverse gender roles to assert themselves as males, but elevated feminine nature by identifying it with the nutritive, redeeming, and suffering body of Christ.

Thus, although the canons of the Fourth Lateran Council reflect some of the transformations of Christianity from the ninth through the early thirteenth centuries, they are not exhaustive guides to such topics as personal devotion and the individual experience of religion. But they did reflect another movement that seemed at the time more complex and dangerous than the nature of feminine devotion—the threat of substantial dissent and the reawakening of the older terminology of heresy to characterize it.

DISSENT AND HETERODOXY

The devotional movements of the eleventh and twelfth centuries reflect the deepest strata of European language, consciousness, and culture. The successful struggle against paganism was virtually over by 1100 except in northeastern Europe. Monastic reforms, reform of the clergy, and the new prominence of the popes in European ecclesiastical and lay life all marked a new stage in the development of Christian society. But churchmen were not the only ones whose lives were touched by change. The transformation of lay piety was as important a phenomenon, and it was more complex. But for some clergy and laity, even the reforms of the eleventh and twelfth centuries and new expressions of devotion were not sufficient. These centuries witnessed the first recorded surge of popular religious dissent since the later Roman Empire. Religious dissent among the laity and clergy that reveals some evidence of popular interest and support appears in a few sources between 1000 and 1050, in virtually none between 1050 and 1100, and then in a great number and variety of manifestations from 1100 on.

Much of the dissent, as we have seen, was directed at unreformed clergy, particularly during the Investiture Conflict, and was concerned with one form or another of clerical purity. Married or concubinous clergy and clergy who had polluted themselves by paying for their offices were the main targets. In the twelfth century, a broader and deeper series of heterodox movements swept through Christian Europe. Not surprisingly, their causes have been the subject of much scholarly and confessional controversy. The term *haeresis* came into Latin from Greek, where it had originally designated the general concept of choice; later it referred specifically to the different beliefs of the Greek and Roman philosophical schools. In Christian Latin usage, it gradually acquired the meaning of doctrines held contrary to the normative teaching of the Church. The thirteenth-century definition of Robert Grosseteste, bishop of Lincoln, conveys both the contemporary and the original meanings of the term: "Heresy is an opinion chosen by human faculties . . . contrary to sacred scripture . . . openly taught . . . pertinaciously defended. Heresy in Greek, choice in Latin. " These meanings are important to keep in mind when considering the development, content, and spread of heterodox beliefs and churchmen's response to them by defining some of them as heresy. The individual whose opinions ran counter to those officially taught by the Church was not immediately guilty of heresy. He might be instructed, cautioned, asked to change his mind, or, in the manner used by Bernard, publicly denounced. For heresy to exist, it had to be openly maintained and taught; the concealed heretic did not emerge as a problem until later. Finally, the true heretic was one who, after being admonished and corrected, openly maintained and defended his opinion against all opposition, thus demonstrating both his contemptuous pride and unreason.

The use of the word heresy was extremely loose in the early twelfth century. Abelard applied it to persons who held incorrect theories of grammar, and much of the conflict between him and Bernard of Clairvaux leading to the condemnation of some of Abelard's doctrines at the Council of Sens in 1140, used the term in a way more reminiscent of the correction of an erring monk than of its later twelfth-century meaning. But the worlds of the cloister and the Paris schools were slowly drawing apart, and such conflicts grew sharper in the late twelfth and early thirteenth centuries.

However, the worlds of Abelard and Bernard were still closer to each other than either of them was to the popular world of devotion. Indeed, "learned heresies" were rarely attacked as bitterly as the spreading popular heresies, and scholars retained a considerably greater latitude in their freedom to teach a variety of opinions than did popular preachers or individual communities. One of the strongest condemnations made by the early churchmen, for example, was directed at astrologers. This hostility, which is reflected in the writings of the influential twelfth-century thinker Hugh of St. Victor (d. 1141), did not prevent astrology from becoming a popular learned pastime. Receiving the imprint of the Muslim thinkers, whose popularity grew as the twelfth century wore on, astrology seemed to account for the different physiological and temperamental characteristics of humans, since these were considered material consequences of the position of the stars and planets at conception and birth and had nothing to do with the rational mind and the soul. This kind of astrology slipped in the door of orthodoxy, as it were, just before that door slammed shut against heresy and other forms of the occult.

The roots of popular heresies, however, were more complex than scholars' disputes or monastic rivalry. Just as the tenth century had witnessed a turn to the more human aspects of the crucified Christ and depictions of the tender Virgin and Child, so the tenth, eleventh, and twelfth centuries saw increased veneration of the Virgin Mary. Yet side by side with this new sensibility and the new doctrines it inspired, another set of attitudes appears to have evolved, attitudes that savagely attacked what was considered to be the humanizing of divine power by representing it in earthly material images. In the eleventh and twelfth centuries, groups led by wandering preachers attacked churches, overturned altars, burned crosses, and bitterly denounced the local clergy. The general crisis concerning the extent of the reform movement, which worked itself out in the twelfth-century decrees of popes and councils, also engendered uncertainty in the believing public. Moreover, both progressive reformers and hostile, traditionalist critics heaped scorn on the burgeoning legal business of the papal chancery and the administration of the Church. The sharp reform distinction between clergy and laity placed great responsibilities on the clergy, which many clerics failed to meet. Bernard's attacks on the extravagance and materialistic Christianity of Cluny and the diversion of the papacy into the law courts found many ears. Some scholars have drawn the distinction between movements of reform and movements of heterodoxy. Reform and dissent that became heretical were defined as sharply by the definitions of orthodoxy with which church leaders met their challenges as they were by their own internal development.

The Faces of God: The Suffering Christ. One way to trace the changing forms of Christian piety is to study the depictions of Christ and the different moods they invoke. One of the most moving and revolutionary images is that of the suffering Christ crucified, an image that gained popularity after the tenth century. This is one of the earliest of such images known, the crucifix of Archbishop Gero of Cologne, from around 975. ('Gero Crucifix' ca. AD 975–1000. Oak crucifix, 6'2'. Cologne Cathedral Photo: Rheinisches Bildarchiv, Museen Der Stadt Koln)

The sources describing heresy and dissent from the first half of the twelfth century tend to reflect certain traditional views of their subject. First, they tend to assume that twelfth-century movements were simply revivals of what Bernard called "the heresies of old," that is, the movements of dissent and heresy that marked the first six centuries of the Church. Thus, most groups who believed in two supernatural powers, one good and one evil (dualism), were labeled Manichees (above, Chapter 2). In the course of the twelfth century, however, writers appear to have learned more about the new movements and to have regarded them more as "novelties," than as older heresies revived. In addition, historians have long debated the influence of heretical movements from outside of Europe. The most controversial of these was Bogomilism. Emerging as a heresy in the Byzantine Empire, Bogomilism found a home in Bulgaria and moved west on trade and Crusade routes in the early twelfth century. The Bogomils attacked much of the fabric of Christian orthodox belief. They echoed Manicheism by denouncing material creation and the creator as evil gods and in emphasizing the exclusive goodness of spiritual beings. Bogomil influence has generally been regarded as having arrived late in western Europe, however, and the roots of all Latin heretical movements have been located in the religious excitement of the twelfth-century conscience. Because churchmen had developed a much clearer, and more precise notion of orthodoxy, it became easier for them to identify heterodoxy.

The two best-known types of heterodoxy in the twelfth and thirteenth centuries—Waldensianism and Catharism—flourished primarily in Provence and Languedoc in the south of France, although Waldensians were also widespread in Austria and Bohemia. Although the two movements were closely identified with each other by heresiologists, they were entirely different. Waldensianism, named for the twelfth-century merchant Valdes of Lyons, was essentially a call for radical church reform, holding the doctrine of the corruption of the Church, the priesthood of all believers, the necessity of preaching and reading Scripture in the vernacular, and apostolic poverty (Matthew 19:21). This group, which resembled in many aspects other voluntary groups later accepted by the Church, differed from similar sects in its intransigence rather than in doctrine. Admonished, Waldensians would not accept ecclesiastical teaching; they were, in Grosseteste's term, pertinacious.

Catharism, whose name derives from the Greek word meaning "pure," was more complex and was, in fact, a different religion from Christianity. Particularly widespread in southern France, especially in Languedoc, Cathars in this area were called Albigensians, after the prominent city of Albi. Sharing the Bogomil concept of a material universe created by an evil spirit, Cathar dualism may also have shared the antimaterialistic revulsion that we have noted accompanying the growth of a "humanized" relationship between God and humans. The Cathars held that the evil god had created the world and human spirits were imprisoned in flesh. For them, the greatest sins were procreation and the consumption of meat, imprisoning another spirit in the material world or adding to the material chains on the spirit. They believed that God sent Jesus, who only appeared to take on the characteristics of a human being, to show humans the way out of the trap of material creation. None of the "human" aspects of Jesus—not the cross, not the passion, not the Church that was built on those symbols, or its clerical hierarchy—had anything to do with God. The Church, too, was a creation of Satan, and hell was earth, imprisonment in the material world.

One of the bitterest charges leveled by reformers, dissenters, and heretics, as well as by high churchmen and female visionaries alike was at the ineptitude and immorality of the clergy. Such charges had lain behind the success of the reform movement of the late eleventh century and the church councils and local prelates of the twelfth. To a large extent, many of these charges were true. Yet it is difficult to know where to lay blame for what is, after all, an anachronistic charge. There were no training schools for clergy; bishoprics often were awarded for petty temporal reasons and with ecclesiastical connivance or the clergy's submission to temporal power. The lowest clergy came untrained from the same class of people whom they served. Moreover, the rapid growth of towns and the settlement of new lands tended to make for a shortage of clergy, especially at the parish level. The growth of dissent and heresy posed acute problems to the Church and, because the Church touched the lives of all, to European society as a whole. Besides the problem of ongoing Church reform and that of the relation between spiritual and temporal powers, the problem of ordering the Christian life loomed large as the twelfth century came to an end.

THE ATHLETES OF GOD

Part of churchmen's response to dissent and heresy was to develop new approaches to pastoral theology—the care of souls. A group of moral theologians at the schools of Paris under the leadership of Peter the Chanter (d. 1197; so-called because he held the office of chanter of the cathedral of Notre Dame) adapted twelfth-century theology to specific real-life cases and addressed pressing social questions, thereby bridging the philosophical theology of the schools and the problems of daily living. They considered such problems as that of the just price, legitimate warfare, mercenary military service, taxation, commercial partnerships, and marriage law. By 1200, books of instruction for helping preachers and confessors perform similar functions had begun to appear. The popes also turned to traditional institutions within the Church, particularly to the Cistercian monks. But in spite of the occasional successes of a Bernard, monks proved unable to win a hearing from the busy lay and clerical world.

Some laymen and clerics, however, began a new kind of pastoral movement. Realizing that the heretics had adopted preaching in the vernacular languages, they too began to preach. In 1206, one of the canons regular of the Spanish diocese of Osma, Domingo de Guzman (1170–1221), having witnessed the ineffectiveness of Cistercians attempting to refute heretics in Montpellier, decided to organize a group of clerics who would be trained to preach and to live in strict poverty. For ten years Domingo—or Dominic—worked with a small group of trained preachers, and between 1215 and 1217, the group dispersed to carry out its mission in different parts of Europe.

Later thinkers saw a close parallel between Dominic and Francis of Assisi (1182–1226). Born to a wealthy merchant family in central Italy, Francis spent his youth and young manhood in the military and literary secular pastimes of his society. Suddenly, at the age of about twenty, he began to reject his own background and to circulate more and more freely with poor priests, lepers, and beggars. In 1206, he received his mission in a vision and began to preach. Francis and his first companions preached as laymen, rejected the ownership of property for themselves, and drew up a simple rule that attempted to translate the gospel into a program of action. Pope Innocent III, who was, as we have seen, both a capable and ambitious administrator and a man of great vision, accepted Francis' rule, and became a particular patron of the new group.

Both Dominic and Francis discovered in preaching and poverty two of the most effective keys to the pastoral needs of their age. Because of their poverty, the orders each man founded reached out to those who criticized the wealth of the established Church. Since members of the orders were compelled to beg even for their daily food, the orders established by Dominic and Francis are conventionally called the Mendicant (Begging) Orders. By bringing the license to preach, hitherto a prerogative of bishops alone, to priests who were specially trained for the task, they finally began to equal the appeal of the heretical preachers. In addition to the rights to preach of Dominic's Order of Preachers (popularly, the Dominicans) and Francis' Order of Friars Minor (the Franciscans), other individuals, even some lay people, were enabled to preach, although in doing so they were limited to exhortation to penitence rather than the exposition of dogma. The wave of preachers over the thirteenth and fourteenth centuries had an incalculable impact, and the literature of preaching influenced thought and secular literature for several centuries.

Yet another consequence of the development of the Mendicant Orders was the creation of second orders, cloistered communities of religious women following the rules of Dominic and Francis. The most famous of these, the Franciscan convent at

San Damiano, was directed by Clara di Offreducio, the first female follower of Francis, but Franciscan religious women were cloistered and not given the freedom of movement of those in the first order. However, the Franciscans also generated a third order—one of lay men and women living in the world but following Franciscan rules in their personal and public conduct. The emergence of these third orders helped to mold the communities of religious women living in the world—generally termed Beguines—that took shape in northern Italy and the Low Countries from the late twelfth century on.

HERESY, CRUSADES AGAINST CHRISTIANS, AND THE OFFICE OF INQUISITOR

The new orders of Franciscans and Dominicans captured the essence of the Church's new spirituality and employed it in a pastoral context. But there was also another side to the thirteenth-century church, a juristic one, and it was also called into play, particularly when the orders seemed less than successful. As we have seen, the work of episcopal and papal courts had grown in the twelfth century. The procedure they used borrowed more from earlier ecclesiastical procedure and Roman law than from the kinds of law used in the lay courts of the twelfth century. Early European law, both temporal and ecclesiastical, was based on the accusatorial process, in which a private accuser made charges before a judge and the accused party responded. This was the format of all trials, criminal and civil, including those decided by ordeal, by judicial duel, or by compurgation—the swearing of a required oath, often accompanied by a specified number of "oath helpers," individuals who swore the same oath. In ecclesiastical courts, another procedure, that of denunciation, was permitted, in which a respected member of the community could denounce someone anonymously, thus avoiding the responsibilities of the accuser in the accusatorial procedure. Yet another process was sometimes used, however, one that allowed the judge to act independently of an accuser when the accused was charged with an offense that entailed notoriety. Episcopal visitations—a bishop's formal visits to subordinate churches—throughout a diocese used this procedure. In the twelfth century, those newly familiar with Roman law discovered the complexity of the inquisitorial procedure, in which, unlike the accusatorial procedure, the judicial authority itself might begin a case and inquire into its facts. The decretal *Ad abolendam,* issued by Pope Lucius III (1181–1185) in 1184, ordered all bishops to inquire after heretics within their jurisdictions—to conduct, in effect, an inquest. Early legislation against heresy aided the spread of the inquisitorial process, but that process was still used loosely, and the chief punishment was anathema or excommunication.

In 1199, however, Innocent III issued the decretal *Vergentis in senium,* in which he increased the punishment of heretics to include the confiscation of goods and property. The chief importance of this text lies in its specific application of the old Roman legal concept of treason to heresy. In this decretal, heresy became treason to God, and the forfeiture of worldly possessions and excommunication were consistent with the penalties prescribed for treason in Roman law, though they did not yet lead to the death penalty. The longest canon of the Fourth Lateran Council summed up these new steps against heresy.

In 1208, the papal legate Pierre de Castelnau was murdered in Toulouse, and Innocent III decided to launch an all-out attack on the center of Catharism. Thus began the Albigensian Crusade against the heretics and their indifferent rulers, the counts of Toulouse.

The Albigensian Crusade lasted from 1209 to 1229; it destroyed the heretical culture of *Occitania* (the lands of southern France) and marked the turning of the Crusade against inhabitants of Christian Europe. Innocent recruited an army from the north of France, and during two decades of intense military conflict, acts of brutality on both sides, and the slaughter of heretics and orthodox Christians alike, the knights of the north battered and ultimately weakened the rich and varied civilization of the south.

But the military campaigns did not wipe out heresy itself, and Innocent's successors, particularly Gregory IX (1227–1241), doubled their efforts to urge bishops and councils to use inquisitorial techniques to discover hidden heretics. By 1233, Gregory had begun using the Dominicans and Franciscans as inquisitors, granting them powers that traditionally belonged to the bishops, particularly in those districts in which bishops seemed ineffective. By entrusting inquisitorial powers to the orders, Gregory moved a long way toward establishing a series of judicial functionaries directly under papal authority for discovering heresy by means of the inquisitorial process.

The continuous role of the Dominicans and Franciscans as inquisitors developed the inquisitorial process quickly. Inquisitors would travel to a town in which the presence of heretics was suspected, assemble the inhabitants to hear a sermon, announce a period of grace in which people might come forward and confess their own heretical beliefs or sympathies or inform on others who did not come forward, and then begin the interrogation of individuals. In most cases, especially those of confessed heretics, punishments were relatively light. For unrepentant heretics, however, or for those who had abjured heresy and returned to it, the punishments were stiffer. Long-term punitive imprisonment was one of these, for the first time in any European legal system. Although most of their earlier coercive power was psychological, financial, and sacramental, in the most severe cases, the inquisitors instituted the practice of "relaxing" or "releasing" recalcitrant defendants to "the secular arm," the lay magistrates who could inflict capital punishment—usually by burning—and shed blood without violating their canonical status. Convicted heretics and their families were also subject to the penalties of infamy, the legal infliction of public shame—their children could not inherit from them, they could not be buried in consecrated ground, their houses were often destroyed, and those convicted but not executed had to wear distinctive marks on their clothing.

The inquisitorial procedure soon developed its first oppressive procedural features: the concealment of the identity of witnesses and the specifics of evidence, the refusal of counsel, the obligation to identify accomplices as a sign of repentance, the admission of evidence from hitherto unacceptable witnesses, and, in Innocent IV's decretal *Ad extirpanda* in 1252, the admission of torture.

Judicial torture made its first reappearance in Europe since the Roman Empire early in the thirteenth century in the city-states of northern Italy, where it probably derived both from new kinds of crime and law enforcement and from the revival of Roman law. By 1252, it had become an instrument of inquisition in both clerical and lay courts. Since inquisitorial procedure could convict a defendant only by confession or the identical testimony of two eyewitnesses, no amount of what today would be called circumstantial evidence could ever amount to enough to convict. But such evidence could be considered sufficient to justify the use of torture to elicit confession, and this was the context in which torture entered thirteenth-century ecclesiastical and temporal judicial procedure. From the thirteenth to the nineteenth century, judicial torture, like punitive imprisonment and public execution, spread from the town courts of Italy and the inquisitor's chambers into most of the criminal courts of the Christian world.

Within a century, the newly armed inquisitorial office had crippled heresy in *Occitania,* and the Church had acquired a formidable and terrifying instrument for detecting and rooting out heresy. The new coercive powers of the Church were felt by others besides heretics, particularly by the Jews of Christian Europe.

JEWS IN CHRISTIAN EUROPE

Another canon of the Fourth Lateran Council had stated that all unbaptized Jews were to wear distinguishing marks on their clothing so that they could be easily identified as Jews. This canon represents the culmination of the deteriorating status of Jews in Christian Europe since the eleventh century.

In spite of increasing Christian hostility and the political weakness that followed the failed revolts of 66–70 C.E. and 131–135 C.E., the Jews of the Roman Empire preserved both their Roman citizenship and the privileges that their faith had been given from the days of Julius Caesar on. Settled in the cities of the Mediterranean world, Jews practiced a wide variety of trades and crafts as long as the Roman Empire survived in the East and West. Christian antagonism was expressed not only in terms of religious hostility, but probably in fear of conversions of Christians to Judaism, of which enough are documented to indicate Christian insecurity as long as the fourth-century emperors sustained the Jewish legal status within the empire.

Rules against different forms of social intercourse with Jews were first made inside the Christian community, as the canons of the Council of Elvira in 312 indicate. Imperial law, however, although it tended to restrict Jewish rights in regard to Christians, tended to preserve other Jewish rights, even in the face of increasing Christian hostility and the beginnings of a Christian anti-Jewish literature. Although such acts as the Christian destruction of synagogues in several Roman cities were individual expressions of violence, several emperors insisted that the synagogues be rebuilt. As the fourth century ended, however, attitudes toward Jews on the part of such figures as Ambrose of Milan (above, Chapter 2) reflected an ambivalence. On the one hand, Ambrose preached against what he considered the errors of Judaism and the insults to Christ that Judaism constituted, but he did not demand the abolition of Judaism, nor did he permit bishops to lead attacks on Jews. On the other hand, he appears to have urged imperial indifference to manifestations of popular Christian hostility toward Jews and to have thought that the Roman state should prevent the growth and development of its Jewish population.

With the disappearance of the Roman Empire in the West after the fifth century, privileged Jewish legal status became a matter for individual Germanic kingdoms either to preserve or destroy. Various kingdoms acted differently in this matter. In Visigothic Spain, for example, a number of rulers issued harsh, restrictive anti-Jewish legislation, as rulers in the Byzantine empire also did, although in other Germanic kingdoms there is little evidence of this and even considerable evidence of a continuation of distinctive Jewish legal status. During the same period, several formal doctrines regarding the Jews were adopted by Church councils and individual bishops of Rome, the most notable and enduring being the observation of Gregory I around the year 600 that, "Just as license ought not to be allowed for Jews to do anything in their synagogues that is not permitted by law, so also they ought to suffer no injury in those things that have been granted to them."

This legal doctrine was later joined by a several legal-historical doctrines. Judaism needed to be preserved in order to demonstrate that Christians were the "true Israel." Judaism needed to be preserved because it constituted a living testimony to the continuous history of God's plan for the world—in this sense Jews were "witnesses of the truth." Jewish learning needed to be preserved to assist Christians with Hebrew biblical scholarship. Finally, because prophecies of the Second Coming of Christ and the end of the world indicated that only at that time would the Jews be converted, Jews had to be preserved in their religion until that time, and therefore not forced to convert to Christianity or leave Christian lands. Together, these doctrines came to represent a formal Christian position, and until the twelfth century they seem to have been partly responsible for the growth of the Jewish community in Europe as the only non-Christian population of any significant size to be permitted to exist there.

From the second and third centuries, Jewish communities appeared in what became Hungary and in the Black Sea area, where the Khazars became the only steppe people to convert to Judaism. In the third and fourth centuries, Jewish communities clustered in southern Italy, Spain, and southern Gaul. These communities called themselves *Sephardim,* after one of the most distant points of Jewish migration in Syria mentioned in scripture. Other Jewish groups began to expand north and east, particularly into *Francia* and the Rhineland. The same process of collective naming designated these *Ashkenazim.* By the eighth century, southern Italy witnessed a Jewish revival of Hebrew studies, and Jewish population growth increased and became increasingly urbanized.

Such scant evidence as exists suggests that the average Jewish household consisted of parents and two children, and that rabbinic households, at least, were proudly aware of their lineage and of the learning and piety of their ancestors. Records of the decisions of rabbinic courts (*responsa*) indicate that the conjugal domestic unit was the primary social bond in Jewish society. Although Jews practiced much the same occupations as Christians in western Europe until the twelfth century, landowning, trade, artisanship, medicine, and moneylending—all largely urban economic activities—characterized most of the Jewish population of Europe after the eleventh century. But it should be noted that these activities were more generally urban than particularly Jewish. Historians have long overrated Jewish prominence in trade and moneylending.

Family law also indicates the urban character of European Jewish society. Especially in rabbinic families, which are usually the best documented, women married only with their own consent, preserved rights pertaining to dowry, and limited the powers of the husband over them. Women in rabbinic families were usually literate and might teach the

Strasbourg Cathedral: Ecclesia and Synagoga. (left) The figure of *Ecclesia* (Church) suggests the power of personified images and the techniques of Gothic sculpture. The female figure symbolizing the Church stands crowned, with cross and cup. (right) The figure of *Synagoga* (Synagogue), a personification of the Jews, holds a broken spear and disused book, items that correspond in symbolic value to the cross and cup of *Ecclesia*. Such visual juxtaposition of images reflects the paradox of art conveying social assumptions. (Bildarchiv Foto Marburg/Art Resource, NY)

law to other women and attend synagogue. In many families, women possessed somewhat more legal and economic autonomy than comparable women in Christian families. The cooperative character of the urban working family thus reinforced the distinctive characteristic of women's status in the rabbinic family.

The religious life of Jews in western Europe centered on the twin institutions of the synagogue and the rabbinic school. Prohibited from access to political power and increasingly restricted as to mobility and choice of profession, the Jewish communities developed strong domestic and communal bonds, and the level of Jewish devotional life and scholarship became extremely high. The *responsa*, decisions of individual rabbis and rabbinic courts, illustrate both the character of Jewish communities and the high level of religious and legal scholarship they enjoyed.

The great traditions of biblical and Talmudic scholarship culminated in the work of Rashi of Troyes (1040–1105) and—through Rashi's successor, Joseph Bekhor Shor—influenced the revival of Christian biblical studies of Andrew of St. Victor in the twelfth century, Hugh of St. Cher in the thirteenth, and Nicholas of Lyra in the fourteenth. The role of Talmudic scholarship and the work of the philosopher-theologian Moses Maimonides (1135–1204) in shaping thirteenth-century scholastic Christian philosophy were especially significant. During the twelfth and early thirteenth centuries, the domestic and urban stability and prosperity of Jewish communities, the high levels of biblical and Talmudic scholarship, and the expression of Jewish thought in poetry and philosophy—as well as the widely recognized Jewish skills in a number of professions, especially medicine—marked the high point of Jewish social and cultural life in western Europe between the fourth and the nineteenth centuries.

Christian society did not regularly or frequently express powerful and violent anti-Jewish attitudes until the later eleventh century, when some of the crusading pilgrims in the Rhineland in 1096 committed massacres in which entire Jewish families and communities were slaughtered by enraged warriors or destroyed themselves rather than undergo forced conversions to Christianity. From that time on, Christian behavior toward Jews changed. Although the formal doctrines continued to guarantee protection to Jewish belief, life, and property, and were frequently reissued by later popes and councils, the fury of individual clergy and lay people increasingly ignored them.

Two clear ideas appear to date from the early twelfth century: the principle that Jews had no legal rights except those granted them by the king, first outlined in England after 1135, and the necessity for firm pronouncements guaranteeing the safety of Jews from high ecclesiastical authorities. In 1120, Pope Calixtus II issued a decretal, *Sicut Judeis,* reminding all Christians of this responsibility, and Bernard of Clairvaux had to hurry to Germany in 1144 to stop new persecutions of Jews that attended the preaching of the Second Crusade.

By the second quarter of the twelfth century, the danger to the Jews appears to have distinctly increased. The new self-consciousness of Christendom, described in earlier chapters, may well have played a role in this new hostility. Certainly the anti-Muslim attitudes developed in the eleventh century came in part from the new Christian self-confidence. The new humanizing of the figures of Christ and the Virgin may also have contributed to the hostility to Jews, whose imaginary atrocities in twelfth century literature surely derive from this new devotional sentimentality.

Finally, the treatment of Jews in the twelfth and thirteenth centuries must be considered in terms of the broader religious and social turbulence of the period. Ruling and governed elements in a society and culture develop their own distinctive insecurities, which produce fear and hatred, and this fear is projected into whatever groups are the aliens of the moment. However deeply rooted and however indistinguishable from Christians Jews were, in law, religion, and culture they were the most visibly alien group, more so than the heretics.

In the late twelfth century, those who had long been acknowledged to have an obligation to protect Jews—the emperors, kings, and popes—began to issue formal statements of protection, but also to exact from the Jews what the letter of the law (most of which dated from the fifth and sixth centuries) permitted. The need for money on the part of thirteenth-century monarchies, the popes' furious attack on heretics and dissenters, and such legislation as the requirement that Jews wear identifying marks on their clothing, which dates from the Fourth Lateran Council of 1215, made these "protectors" less useful than a reading of the law and the theory about the protection of Jews might lead one to expect. Kings and popes, as it turned out, were dubious protectors at best. What Gavin Langmuir has called "the balance of contempt and toleration laid down in the Church's doctrines" was impossible to maintain. And when it was overthrown, it was always on the side of contempt, brutality, and sacrilege. The twelfth and thirteenth centuries marked not only a new hostility toward individual Jews and Jewish communities, but the development of anti-Semitism in its most manifold and wide-ranging aspects.

From the twelfth century on, two other significant transformations characterize Christian attitudes toward Jews. In the rhetoric of traditional Christian anti-Jewish literature, Jews were usually depicted as blind, stubborn, rooted in the flesh, unchangeable in time, and insulting to Christ and to Christianity. In the twelfth century, however, as Christian thinkers elevated reason to a greater height among the disciplines of learning—and identified reason and reasonableness with Christianity—anti-Jewish polemic now attacked the Jews as unreasoning and irrational, no longer merely blind and stubborn humans, but humans deprived of reason. In addition, increasing Christian familiarity with postbiblical Jewish literature, particularly the Talmud, led Christians to argue that the Talmud contained not only blasphemies against Christ and Christian beliefs and practices, but also heresies against biblical Judaism.

Besides the new attacks from learned Christians, the twelfth century witnessed a new intensity in popular anti-Semitism. Charges were made more frequently that Jews committed unspeakable crimes against Christians and the items sacred to Christians; that Jews murdered Christian children and used their bodies in abominable rituals (the "blood libel"); that present-day Jews were actively hostile to Christians and constituted an underground enemy of Christian society. The occasional popular outbursts of earlier periods now increased in frequency and savagery. Jewish quarters in cities became targets for rioting mobs, sometimes, as at York in 1190, destroying the Jews so as to wipe out their own financial obligations to them. And individual Jews, marked out by distinctive costume and badges, became more routinely visible as Jews at the same time.

Late in the 1230s, much of this new hostility culminated in a series of trials of the Talmud in France and elsewhere. Nicholas Donin, a former Jew, accused the Jews before Pope Gregory IX of having replaced Hebrew scripture with Talmud. In several trials, alleged Talmudic excesses were condemned, and only edited versions of the Talmud were permitted to be used in Jewish communities. At the same time, Christian definitions of "forced" baptism of unwilling Jews became extremely restricted, to the point that only physically forced immersion into the baptismal water accompanied by specific verbal protests on the part of the unwilling "convert" constituted technical forcing. By the fourteenth century, charges of performing magic were leveled more frequently against Jews, and in 1324, when a millennialist panic seized France, Jews and lepers were accused of poisoning water supplies, charges that were repeated after the onset of the Black Death in 1348/49 (below, Chapter 17).

In the wake of intellectual and emotional changes in the character and intensity of Christian anti-Semitism, the large and prosperous Jewish communities of the eleventh and twelfth centuries were drastically transformed. As Jews lost rights and lives, wore distinctive clothing and were restricted to distinctive quarters of cities, and to a limited number of occupations, were persecuted by sporadic mob violence, and exploited by greedy and hostile rulers, Christian doctrinal obligations often became virtually a dead letter. Afflicted with Talmudic censorship, exiled from England in 1290, from France in 1306 and in 1394, from some territories in Germany by 1350, and from Spain in 1492, the Jewish communities of Europe were attacked, herded, and forced into the role of a despised and largely impoverished minority. By the fourteenth century, their religion, humanity, and culture had been brutally caricatured in the earliest wave of anti-Semitic literature, art, and propaganda.

THIRTEENTH-CENTURY CRUSADES AND CHRISTIAN ATTITUDES TOWARD MUSLIMS

The attitudes of Christians toward Muslims developed largely in the atmosphere of Crusade propaganda and legal discussions, even after the fall of the Latin Kingdom of Jerusalem to Saladdin in 1187. Late in that year, Pope Grgory VIII issued the decretal *Audita tremendi,* the most extensive and detailed of all papal calls to crusades. The shock of the loss of Jerusalem ignited widespread response. The kings Richard I of England and Philip II Augustus of France, Leopold, duke of Austria, and the Emperor of the Romans, Frederick I Barbarossa all assembled the largest army in European history and launched the third crusade. But it, too, was a failure. Uncontrollable rivalries between the kings of England and France and between the king of England and the duke of Austria, as well as the emperor's death by drowning in a river in northern Syria all weakened the determination of the crusading host, and what was left of the armies and their leaders returned to Europe having achieved very little.

Early in his pontificate, Innocent III had stated that the two aims of his life were the reform of the church and the recovery of the Holy Land. The Fourth Lateran Council was his great attempt at achieving the first of these. The fourth and fifth crusades were attempts to achieve the second. Soon after his election, Innocent sent out crusade preachers, not to kings or the emperor, but to the nobility of France, the descendants of the victors of the First Crusade and Innocent's hope for victory in the next. Large numbers of warriors took the cross and elected leaders, who appointed a delegation to find a port city that would transport the armies by sea. The delegation contracted with the doge and council of Venice for a fixed sum for a fixed number of troops and their equipment, including horses. But many crusaders made their own way to the east, and when the armies assembled at Venice in 1202, they did not have the numbers or the money for which they had contracted with the Venetians. The Venetians, who had invested virtually an entire year of their commerce and shipbuilding capacity to construct and man the fleet, offered the crusaders the option of helping them conquer the city of Zara on the Dalmatian coast, which had rebelled against Venetian dominance in favor of the king of Hungary. The conquest of Zara alienated a number of the crusaders, who left the army and sailed to Palestine themselves.

At that moment, a young pretender to the throne of Constantinople, Alexius Angelos, promised the Venetians and crusaders that if they would restore his father and himself to the throne, he would arrange the reunion of the Latin and Greek churches under the pope and underwrite the rest of the costs of the expedition to the Holy Land. Taking Alexius at his word, the Venetians and crusaders sailed to Constantinople, from which the reigning emperor fled, installed Alexius and his father Isaac to the throne, and then demanded that they fulfill the conditions of their agreement. Since there was little suppport in Constantinople for the Angelos Dynasty, the new rulers could not possibly fulfill either promise, and the crusaders and their Venetian allies attacked, sacked, and captured the city for the first time in its history on April 12, 1204. The Fourth Crusade ended with the capture, not of Jerusalem, but of the holy city of Constantinople, which the crusaders looted for relics and wealth and where they elected a Latin emperor and established the Latin church. Far more than the condemnations of 1054, the events of 1204 sealed the division between the Latin and Greek churches.

Although Innocent III condemned both the taking of Zara and the conquest of Constantinople, he also took advantage of the opportunity to reunite the Latin and Greek churches. The Latin empire lasted until 1261, when Byzantine forces were finally able to retake the city.

Innocent III had come to the papal throne in the wake of the disasters of 1187 and the failure of the third crusade. His plans for the fourth were careful, but its failure—and Innocent's failure to maintain control of the crusade—suggest the limitations of even the most able and farsighted of popes. Innocent's turning of the crusade against the heretics of Albi and their sympathizers in 1209 suggests the versatility with which he could deal with European crises, and at the Fourth Lateran Council he planned yet another crusade to the Holy Land, but he died before it could be launched.

The fifth crusade (1217–1222) took up one idea of the fourth—travel by sea—and introduced a new tactic: invasion of the Holy Land by way of Egypt, which had weakened considerably following the death of Saladdin and rivalries among his successors. There was also to be a papal legate present on the crusade to maintain control and single direction of the enterprise. But the fifth crusade failed as well. Dissension and delay postponed attacks at critical moments, and conflict among the leaders created a diplomatic impasse that could not be broken. The repeated crusade efforts—and the astonishing numbers of soldiers who were willing to go—are a striking characteristic of the twelfth and early thirteenth centuries. Innocent's interest in the crusade suggests that he, too, saw the movement as one having great potential, but he lacked the means of harnessing it to his purpose. Ultimately, the Holy Land was too far away, its enemies too strong and numerous, its resources too few, and its means of communication with western Europe too irregular for such an enterprise to be sustained for any length of time. But the idea of crusade—as well as strong criticism of the crusade—survived the pontificate of Innocent III as well as the fall of Acre, the last Christian territory in the Holy Land, in 1291. For the next several centuries, the crusade idea worked best when it was applied to the defense of the margins of Christian Europe, rather than to the distant Holy Land.

15

The Political Culture
of Christian Europe

KINGSHIP AND THE POLITICAL COMMUNITY

The "history" of modern states is often erroneously extended backwards in time to remote periods and based on an idea of the political community and its components that was developed only in the nineteenth and twentieth centuries. The main components of modern political societies are geographical definition and continuity in space and time, community of language, impersonal institutions of governance and the impersonal loyalty of subjects and citizens, political sovereignty, and the various aspects (some nonpolitical) of ethnicity or national sentiment. Neither modern nationalism nor the modern sovereign state appeared in the twelfth and thirteenth centuries, but some extremely important components of them did. These were strengthened over the long span of time in which European political communities could develop without significant outside interference. Such diverse elements of a political community as the collective awareness of a "people" with a common history and language and the identification of the kingdom with a dynasty of legitimate rulers coalesced with the expanding claims and real powers of kings and helped to identify kingship with the early idea of the large political community.

By the end of the tenth century, the older tribes, warbands, *gentes,* and *populi* of early European society had virtually disappeared. The idea of a single Christian people, the *populus Christianus,* one of the legacies of the age of Charlemagne, still survived, and both popes and emperors claimed certain ordinary governmental rights (and at the very least a kind of honorific preeminence) in respect to it. But neither the regional principalities nor a universal Christian society determined the dominant political forms of Europe between the twelfth and the fourteenth centuries. That distinction was reserved for the city-republics, especially those of northern Italy, and the territorial monarchies of England, France, the Iberian peninsula, and elsewhere in western and central Europe that produced a new kind of political culture.

Not all kingdoms that had been established between the sixth and the twelfth centuries survived. Some simply disappeared, as did the old Carolingian Middle Kingdom and Burgundy, part of which was absorbed into the Roman Empire and part into the kingdom of France. But other kingdoms, many of them much smaller and with fewer resources, survived vigorously into early modern times. A good example is Scotland (above, Chapter 11), which developed a strong and enduring national identity under several royal dynasties in spite of its small size and relative weakness in comparison with England or France.

In 1247, King Hákon of Norway was planning to add Iceland to his kingdom. From its discovery and settlement (above, Chapter 9), Iceland had been a commonwealth whose internal public affairs were dealt with by an assembly, the *Althing*, composed of the heads of prominent households and elected law speakers. In support of Hákon's plan, the papal emissary Cardinal William of Savoy wrote that although Icelandic society was civilized and Christian, it was not proper for Iceland to be the only land without a king. However immediate and particular Hákon's political aims may have been, the opinion of the papal legate put them in a wider constitutional context: It was part of God's ordering of the world for a people to be subject to a king. According to this view, the old commonwealth of Iceland, like the increasingly independent city-republics of northern Italy and other teritorial principalities not directly under royal rule, was an anomaly. Kingship was an essential component of the divinely ordained hierarchy of authority in the world. In 1262, Iceland finally did become part of the kingdom of Norway, although many of the city-republics and some territorial principalities elsewhere in Europe held onto their independence much longer.

Kingship might be elective or inherited (dynastic). But in most cases, kings were inaugurated, crowned, and anointed in a liturgical coronation ceremony, and they took a coronation oath defining the limits of their powers and acknowledging their responsibilities toward God, the church, and their subjects. As early as the tenth century, some kingdoms came to be regarded by both kings and nobles as indivisible, and in the eleventh century, Conrad II stated that kingdoms were entities that endured even during those periods when there was no living king (above, Chapter 11). In order to account for both the mortality of individual kings and the enduring character of the kingdom in spite of that mortality, many twelfth- and thirteenth-century political theorists developed the idea of the crown as the abstract repository of the kingdom. And many rulers transformed the funeral ceremonies of kings so that they demonstrated the continuity of crown and kingdom.

But within each kingdom, the actual resources and the operation of royal governance differed greatly. The common measure of any king's rule was whether he was a just ruler, or on the other hand, tyrannous or incompetent. In the latter cases, political theorists gradually worked out constitutional theories for removing an incompetent ruler or even justifying the assassination of a tyrant. Differences in the style of royal governance might be indicated by a king's willingness to develop a class of professional administrators instead of giving offices to men who claimed them by right of noble birth and custom. Some rulers commanded their subjects to attend assemblies in order to circulate policy decisions or receive advice. Some kingdoms benefited from a developed vernacular literary language and literature. Some determined that only the king's subjects should occupy high ecclesiastical offices. Some founded local universities so that their subjects would not create a brain-drain by leaving the kingdom and studying elsewhere. Some learned quickly how to exploit new sources of wealth; others did not. The extraordinary variety of governmental structures within kingdoms must be kept in mind along with the common features of all kings and kingdoms during the twelfth and thirteenth centuries.

The mobilization of state resources, a general test of modern states, occurred on a far smaller scale and for shorter periods of time in twelfth- and thirteenth-century polities. The concept of citizen patriotism or, conversely, that of a state with resources so great that universal coercion was possible for its rulers, were both far in the future. The words *politics, polity, police,* and *policy*—all of which were derived from the Greek word *politeia* as it was used in Aristotle's *Politics,* an influential work that began to circulate in Latin in the thirteenth century—appeared in most western languages in the late thirteenth and fourteenth centuries, but it took a long time for both the words and the ideas later built on them to become part of people's common vocabulary.

For much of the twelfth century, great territorial principalities such as Normandy, Lorraine, Bavaria, Toulouse, Flanders, and Champagne remained indigestible to centralizing monarchies. This is but one indication that the road from medieval monarchy to modern nation-state was long and difficult, and it helps to explain the distinctive regional character of parts of many modern European states. The transformation was not inevitable. In the examples considered in the rest of this chapter, which focuses on kings and their servants, the two streams—political and cultural—in the evolution of a political society should be kept in mind. For only by developing monarchical power on the one hand, and on the other, a collective consciousness of belonging to a political community on the part of a widening circle of social orders and individuals, did some of the medieval kingdoms lay the foundations of the modern state.

Early European kingdoms also developed with one further key element. In spite of the strength of hierarchical arguments on behalf of monarchical legitimacy—whether that of emperors, kings, or popes—an equally important theme was the obligation on the ruler to rule according to law. However autocratic many early European rulers might seem in practice, and however much they seem to have used what we would call public resources to further dynastic and personal ends, no ruler professed to rule without the law. Even in cases when lawyers argued that "the Prince is above the law," or "what pleases the Prince has the force of law," they usually referred only to the positive law that the rulers themselves had made. But no ruler could fail to acknowledge himself to be subject to the law of nature, divine law, and even in some areas, custom. If law, and lawfulness, was one of the supports of monarchical authority, it was also, perhaps paradoxically, one of its great checks.

The twin developments of territorial monarchy and the rule of law shaped early European political culture. In them lay the kernel of both royal power and its limitations, both practical and theoretical. In the twelfth and thirteenth centuries, the older political order that conceived of political society as Christendom and based the legitimacy of rulership on the offices of pope and emperor was transformed into a new one based on territorial royal authority or the corporate autonomy of city-republics.

THE OLD ORDER: THE CONFLICT BETWEEN THE POPES AND EMPERORS

The Concordat of Worms of 1122, the First Lateran Council of 1123, the death of Pope Calixtus II in 1124, and the death of the emperor Henry V in 1125, brought to a close several aspects of the Investiture Conflict and inaugurated a new stage in the relative authority of popes and emperors in Christian society. The Investiture Conflict had generated a large literature of political theory and propaganda, most of it supporting or attacking the claims of popes or emperors to supremacy within Christendom. In the course of the conflict, the old Carolingian-Ottonian imperial ideal was defeated. Theorists and practitioners of papal authority transformed the figure of the pope from the chief liturgical officer of the holy city of Rome to a legitimate constitutional authority supreme in many respects over all other Christian powers. Although new claims for and against papal or imperial authority were made during the next several centuries, the rivalry between the two became a less significant focus of political theory and discussion. After the mid thirteenth century, the old polarity between papacy and empire gave way to a consideration of the rights and powers of princes, city-republics, and territorial monarchies, even against the rights of popes and emperors themselves. By the late thirteenth century, a new political order, one that considered the respective spheres of authority of popes and territorial monarchies and republics, had become the framework of European political culture.

The imperial office also changed during the later part of the struggle. The emperors of the Romans were also the kings of Germany, Italy, and Burgundy, and the Investiture Conflict had revealed that the two kinds of offices were not as separate in fact as they might be in theory. The needs of the kingdom of Germany colored both the functions of the imperial office in the later twelfth and thirteenth centuries and the policies of the kings of Germany as emperors of the Romans. Although much of the earlier prestige and memory of the emperors from Charlemagne to Henry V survived in imperial policy and propaganda and was even strengthened by the rediscovery of imperial Roman law in the twelfth century, the actual facts of imperial rule changed nearly as much as the actual problems of papal governance.

A number of characteristics of the monarchy in German-speaking lands help to clarify the changes in both kingship and emperorship during the twelfth century. In an age when the physical presence of the king counted for much, the very size of the German kingdom, five or six times that of England, meant that the king of Germany had to be constantly on the move. Tracing the itineraries of these rulers is an important part of the historian's work, not only because the itineraries reveal how often and how extensively the kings traveled, but where they could travel—where they had enough personal property or loyal subjects to afford them the extraordinarily expensive and burdensome hospitality that traveling kings required. The kings of Germany also had to rely on their personal wealth to pay the costs of governing the kingdom. This wealth, usually in land, was not distributed evenly throughout the kingdom. In some areas, notably the eastern borders of Saxony, nobles had conquered and opened up extensive lands in which the kings had never possessed any property or claims at all, and thus were virtually excluded from visiting or exploiting financially. The limits of royal resources left the German kings three sources of support: the royal ministerials, the local church and aristocracy, and whatever financial rights they might claim as kings and emperors in the German lands and especially in that part of northern Italy known as Lombardy.

The ministerials were unfree knights who administered royal and ecclesiastical property. Like the lowborn royal servants of the kings of England and France in the early twelfth century, they tended to rise into the local nobility as time went on. In order to control them efficiently, the German kings would have had to possess a sophisticated system of supervision, but they were never able to develop one. They did not establish an official archive of their documents until the fourteenth century. What some historians have called the "low intensity" of the German monarchy meant that kings rarely had systematic or efficient communications with, or effective control over, their local servants. The German aristocracy, unlike the aristocracy of England and France, possessed extensive lands that it owned privately and therefore did not hold from the kings. Most of the aristocracy's power base was out of the king's reach, and many nobles had no need of even nominal contact with the king. One way for the kings to achieve some control over the aristocrats was to give them lands that carried obligations of service, but many noble families were reluctant to accept these. Even when they did, they tended to merge their new lands with lands they already owned privately. Indeed, dynastic territory building characterized German aristocratic society in the twelfth century. Even the old tribal duchies, while retaining their former names, became the territories of princely dynasties in the twelfth century and bore little resemblance to their Carolingian origins.

Ultimately, the kings of Germany had to leave a great deal of power in the hands of the higher aristocracy, upon whose loyalty and cooperation they depended. This necessity, coupled with the expansion of German princely power to the east, created a powerful class of princes who effectively governed their smaller territories and expanded their lands into areas in which the kings had less and less authority. The best example of this aristocratic independence is the famous *Drang nach Osten,* the "push to the East," which developed steadily in the twelfth and thirteenth centuries, but under the direction of the princes, not the kings.

The long history of northern Germany as a base for territorial expansion to the east and for missionary efforts to convert pagan Scandinavians, Balts, and Slavs is the main political and cultural theme of northern European history from the tenth to the fifteenth century. With the foundation of the archbishopric of Lund in 1108, Scandinavian Christians developed an autonomous ecclesiastical center, free of German episcopal control. The German bishoprics of Magdeburg, Bamberg, and Hamburg-Bremen all launched missionary efforts in pagan Slavic lands, sometimes encountering opposition from the Christian Slavic kingdoms of Poland and Bohemia. In 1147, Bernard of Clairvaux obtained papal permission for German crusaders to battle the pagan Wends instead of going to Jerusalem.

Warriors followed missionaries, as did merchants and settlers. The expanding population of western Europe permitted not only the internal colonization of older territories, but expansion into new ones. The Cistercian monks were particularly zealous in settling remote lands. The founding of the city of Lübeck in 1158/9, the development of a community of merchants in Gotland during the twelfth century, the success of Albert, bishop of Livonia (1199–1229), in founding bishoprics and monastic orders in the newly conquered lands and establishing military orders to support them, and the territorial ambitions of Henry the Lion (ca. 1130–1195), duke of Saxony and Bavaria, and the margraves of Brandenburg furthered the expansion. By the early thirteenth century, trade flourished in the North Sea, the Baltic Sea, and the Rhine Valley. This trade linked England, the Low Countries, Denmark, Sweden, the towns along the Baltic coast, and Novgorod in northern Russia. The economic developments attending this trade, the growth of towns along the Baltic coast, and the large markets of Poland and Russia underwrote the great financial cost of the new German expansion and colonization.

In 1226, the Teutonic Knights, one of the military orders originally founded in the Holy Land, moved to northeastern Germany, where, with the support of Emperor Frederick II (r. 1220–1250) and under the leadership of Grand Master Hermann von Salza, they conquered and occupied Prussia. In 1236, the Knights incorporated the Livonian orders, and from the mid thirteenth century on, they governed Prussia and pushed frequently into Poland and Russia. In 1309, the city of Marienburg became their headquarters and the seat of the grand master of the order.

The military aspect of German eastward expansion was not dominant everywhere. Often, lords attempted to fill up their sparsely populated new lands with the mass immigration of German settlers. Migration and settlement were more often peaceful than forceful, and the competition for settlers was brisk among lords of all sorts. The local adoption of western European agricultural technology made the lands more productive, and the introduction of brickmaking and large-scale architecture by the Cistercian Order began to create the modern appearance of northeastern Europe. By the thirteenth century, a specialized group of men known as *locatores* organized movements of settlers from western Europe to the east, being rewarded with their own special privileges in the new settlements they founded. By the end of the thirteenth century, the balance of wealth and political power in Germany had shifted from its Rhineland origins far to the east. This movement was signaled by the rise in power of the King of Bohemia, the growth of Prussia, the influence of Cistercian ideas on eastern Germany, and the rapidly growing wealth of the Baltic and Rhenish cities and the city-foundations of Danzig (modern Gdansk), Riga, and Breslau (modern Wrozlaw). The rise of the Bohemian and Polish kingdoms and the eastward expansion of Germans during the twelfth and thirteenth centuries was thus a complex process, one that has far more political and economic characteristics than ethnic or racial ones. Dynastic difficulties and a limited economy, more than German hostility or influence, contributed to the weakening of the

Polish Piast Dynasty in the thirteenth century and the growing local Bohemian resistance to the Luxemburg Dynasty in the fourteenth.

A second difficulty—perhaps initially less important than the consequences of princely dynastic territory building—was the constitutional problem of election versus dynastic succession in the kingship. In spite of the electoral character of the early East Frankish monarchy that had been established in 911 and 919, the Saxon and Salian dynasties had established the fact, if not the constitutional principle, of dynastic succession of son to father in the kingship, even though each of these sons was elected. The death of the last Salian, Henry V, without an heir, in 1125, however, permitted the greater nobility and clergy once again to decide between candidates from two particularly powerful families, the Staufer and the Welf. Their choice of the Welf-sponsored candidate Lothar III (r. 1125–1137) suggests that the electoral principle was becoming more active, as did the election of Conrad III (r. 1138–1152), a Staufer, after the death of Lothar, also without an heir. The elections of 1125 and 1138 appear to have been an attempt on the part of the higher lay and clerical nobility to balance the power of two great families that themselves were rivals on other fronts as well.

The election of Frederick I Barbarossa (r. 1152–1190), a nephew of Conrad III who had both Welf and Staufer blood, appears to have been a compromise designed to satisfy both dynasties. Moreover, the electoral process now came to mean that the elected king had to make compromises with his electors in matters of property, privilege, and even in his recovery of usurped rights. The newly built castles of the princes and the extension of their political authority over their territories were not to be curtailed. The electoral principle may have been less dangerous as a principle than it was as a practical means of the ambitious territorial nobility's assuring itself that dynastic royal power could not be used to dislodge it from its expanded possessions and its own recently acquired powers. But the rivalry between the Welf and Staufer families endured long after the election of Frederick Barbarossa, coloring Barbarossa's long reign, and influencing royal politics and papal relations into the first quarter of the thirteenth century. It was a large-scale echo of other family rivalries that marked German aristocratic society through the thirteenth century.

The imperial title gave the German kings opportunities to exploit territorial and financial resources in Burgundy and Italy, which were not available to them as kings only of German lands. The reign of Frederick Barbarossa suggests how skillfully (although with only limited success) the imperial title might increase the resources of the German monarchy. Through his wife, Beatrice of Burgundy, Barbarossa obtained extensive private lands and revenues in Burgundy. Because Barbarossa badly needed the financial resources of the northern Italian cities, he boldly asserted his imperial rights, not only claiming the precedents of Charlemagne and of Saxon and Salian traditions of imperial rule, but also invoking Roman law and Roman history. These imperial claims encountered stiff opposition from the independent Italian cities, which formed the Lombard League against him in 1167, and from the popes, particularly Alexander III (1159–1181). Barbarossa had to compromise with both forces at the Peace of Venice in 1177.

Barbarossa also attempted to forestall the growth of his strongest aristocratic opponents, particularly Henry the Lion (ca. 1130–1195), duke of Bavaria and Saxony and the leader of the Welf family. Henry operated as an independent prince in his territories, investing bishops, using ministerials extensively, and expanding his power into Slavic territories. Having failed to obey a summons from Frederick Barbarossa, Henry was stripped of his lands and titles, although Barbarossa redistributed these to his own noble supporters. Even before the conflict with Henry the Lion, in 1156 Barbarossa issued an imperial decree later known as the *privilegium minus*, the "lesser privilege," which created the imperial duchy of Austria out of some of Henry the Lion's eastern territories, thus launching both a new kind of territorial state within the empire and creating the territorial foundations of modern Austria. By allying himself with other nobles, enriching them, enhancing their power in return for their oaths of loyalty, Barbarossa succeeded in destroying the vast power of Henry the Lion, but even this triumph resulted in the emperor's recognition of the growing power of the other German princes.

In 1186, Barbarossa arranged the marriage of his son, later the emperor Henry VI, to Constance, heiress to the kingdom of Sicily. When Barbarossa drowned in Syria in 1190 while on the third crusade, Henry VI succeeded him in Germany, as emperor of the Romans, and, in his wife's right, was also king of Sicily and south Italy. Although Sicily proved a difficult kingdom to govern, it promised Henry VI precisely that base of financial and military power that had largely eluded his predecessors in Germany and northern Italy. But the sudden death of the thirty-two-year-old Henry VI in 1197, plunged Germany, Italy, and Sicily into a succession crisis far more momentous than those of the twelfth century. Henry left a three-year-old son, Frederick Roger, to succeed him. The child's two names are those of his grandfathers Frederick Barbarossa and Roger II of Sicily, and the kingship of Sicily was not elective, but dynastic. But Frederick's minority and the unleashing of rival forces in Germany and northern Italy plunged both royal offices and the imperial office into chaos.

In 1198, a Welf-dominated electorate chose Otto IV of Brunswick, the son of Barbarossa's old enemy, Henry the Lion, and Matilda, daughter of Henry II of England, as king. Supporters of the Staufer dynasty backed Philip of Swabia, the brother of Henry VI, until his assassination in 1208, and for ten years the political worlds of Germany, Sicily, and Italy were plunged into political conflict. Innocent III took such an interest in the debates areound the election of 1198 that he opened a special papal register for documents pertaining to it, *The Register Concerning the Affairs of the Empire,* the first such specialized papal register ever compiled. In 1201, Innocent recognized Otto's election, but he also required Otto IV to take an oath not to invade Sicily, thus drawing the papacy into the dynastic struggles around the German crown.

The growing ambitions of Otto troubled the peace of Italy and the empire virtually from the moment of his imperial coronation in 1209. When, contrary to his promise, Otto's forces crossed into the Sicilian kingdom in 1210, Innocent III excommunicated the emperor, who died in 1218. Innocent, with the cooperation of some of the princes in Germany, then approved the candidacy of his ward, Frederick II, son of Henry VI and insecure ruler of the beleaguered kingdom of Sicily. Frederick quickly traveled to Germany, rallied more support in the face of considerable opposition, and was crowned king at Mainz at the end of 1212. In 1213, with the consent of the German princes, Frederick issued the Golden Bull of Eger, in which he confirmed the autonomy of the papal states, echoed promises made earlier by Otto IV, and gave up those rights in the

NORTH SEA

BALTIC SEA

Danzig

POMERANIA

Elbe R.

POLAND

Vistula R.

SAXONY

BRANDEN-
BURG

Rhine R.

Weser R.

Saale R.

Elbe R.

Oder R.

SILESIA

Meuse R.

LOWER
LORRAINE

• Cologne

Aachen

• Prague

MORAVIA

Mainz •

Trier

PALATINATE

FRANCONIA

Main R.

FRANCE

Strasbourg •

Rhine R.

SWABIA

Augsburg •

BAVARIA

Vienna •

Danube R.

STYRIA

Constance •

Adige R.

TYROL

HUNGARY

BURGUNDY

LOMBARDY • Milan

Pavia •

Po R.

Venice •

Genoa •

Canossa •

Ferrara •

Bologna •

Ravenna •

Zara •

Rhône R.

ROMAGNA

ADRIATIC
SEA

Avignon •

Pisa •

Florence •

TUSCANY

Siena •

Assisi •

CORSICA
(Pisa)

Rome •

Anagni •

SARDINIA
(Pisa and
Genoa)

Naples •

APULIA

*Tyrrhenian
Sea*

CALABRIA

Palermo •

SICILY

	Holy Roman Empire
	Papal States
	Burgundy
	North Italian states
	Kingdom of the Two Sicilies
	Boundary of the Holy Roman Empire

0   200 Miles

0   200 Kilometers

Medieval Germany and Italy.

selection of bishops and abbots that the Crown had retained in the Concordat of Worms of 1122. After promising to keep the German and Sicilian kingdoms separate, Frederick II was crowned emperor of the Romans at Rome in November, 1220.

As king of Sicily and emperor of the Romans, Frederick had very different sets of powers, and from 1220, he directed his immense energies and considerable talents to the restoration of the southern kingdom. Frederick founded the University of Naples in 1224, chiefly to provide his kingdom with the scholars and administrators he needed. Naples was the first state university to be established purely by royal decree. In 1231, Frederick issued a law code for his Sicilian kingdom, the *Constitutions of Melfi*. With his subordination of the South Italian nobility, the development of a strong military and naval force, the recruitment of able administrators, and the imposition of a sound and efficient financial system, Frederick II shaped the kingdom of Sicily and South Italy into the most thoroughly governed, and most secularized state in Europe within little more than a decade. A symbol of this achievement was Frederick's striking of gold coinage—the magnificent *Augustalis*—in 1232, the first gold coinage struck in Europe since the early ninth century.

Frederick's adventurous calculation is also reflected in his crusading policies. Although to everyone's surprise he had agreed to go on Crusade, Frederick was forced to postpone the expedition several times, and in 1227, when he had to postpone it again because of illness, Pope Gregory IX (1227–1241) excommunicated him. Undaunted, Frederick sailed to Jerusalem the next year and quickly signed a remarkable treaty with the Ayyubid sultan al-Kamil of Egypt in 1229. According to the treaty's terms, the holy sites of Jerusalem, Bethlehem, and Nazareth, along with a strip of coastal territory and certain other rights in the city of Jerusalem, were ceded to Frederick. The excommunicated emperor had won more rights in the Holy Land than any other crusader in the past century.

Relations between pope and emperor continued to deteriorate, and Frederick's concentration on South Italy and Sicily weakened his power in Germany and led Gregory IX to forge alliances with the Lombard cities of northern Italy, who also felt their autonomy threatened by Frederick's energies and ambitions in the south. In addition to these political circumstances, Frederick's own royal style tended to cost him sympathy in the north. The splendid court life in Sicily and South Italy, which had developed from both Byzantine and Norman court ceremonial, appeared (as Frederick did personally) alien and exotic both to Germans and to the citizens of the northern Italian towns. The emperor surrounded himself with immense wealth and splendor, ranging from Muslim bodyguards and a multiethnic court population to the imperial harem and the zoo with its elephants and other exotic beasts.

Frederick's considerable intelligence and curiosity drew learned men from all parts of the Mediterranean world—Muslims, Jews, and Christians alike—to his court. Michael Scot, a well-known translator of Arabic philosophical works, an astrologer, and a reputed sorcerer, was Frederick's frequent companion. Pier della Vigne, Frederick's chancellor, produced the most elaborate Latin political correspondence of the century. Speaking several languages with ease, Frederick was an integral part of the intellectual life of his court, not merely its pageantry-loving master. He corresponded with the mathematician Leonardo Fibonacci of Pisa (who gave his name to his discovery, the Fibonacci series). A poet himself, Frederick supported a school of court poets among his courtiers and administrators. So influential was the court poetry of Frederick II and his school, that at the end of the century the poet Dante proclaimed Frederick the father of Italian vernacular poetry (below, Chapter 16). A patron of the arts as well, Frederick left a powerful personal legacy throughout South Italy in his castles, public works, and sculptures. Frederick's new golden coins, the *Augustales,* reveal a quality of minting art and a metallic purity of an extraordinarily high character. To his subjects as well as his enemies, Frederick II was the *stupor mundi,* "the wonder of the world," who was regarded more in awe and fear than in affection and respect.

Frederick's ambitions in the south led him to make concessions not only to the popes but also to the German princes. In 1220, his *Confederation with the Ecclesiastical Princes* recognized the territorial lordships of the ecclesiastical princes, and in 1232, his *Statute in Favor of the Princes* removed several important imperial rights over the great magnates. Although these concessions were not of vital importance as long as Frederick's personal political power was intact, they became immensely influential after the emperor's death, and strongly influenced the growth of virtually independent princely territorial authority in Germany from the late thirteenth century on.

In 1237, war finally broke out between Frederick II and the great northern Italian cities. Although Frederick was initially successful, destroying the Milanese army at the Battle of Cortenuova in that year, Pope Gregory IX, alarmed by his ambitions and victories, excommunicated the emperor for a second time in 1239, and Frederick turned his forces against Rome itself. Gregory died in August, 1241, and local Roman nobles began to assert their own claims to authority in Rome, most dramatically when the Senator Matteo Orsini locked up the ten cardinals who had assembled to vote for a new pope in the fortified palace called the Septizonium and kept them locked in under unbearable physical conditions for nearly three months. The elderly theologian whom they elected, Celestine IV (1241), died after a pontificate of seventeen days, and the surviving cardinals fled Rome, where they waited two years to elect his successor. From the mid thirteenth century, the Roman nobility virtually ruled the city, constructing tall, fortified family towers to dominate their neighborhoods, and later popes ruled from nearby towns like Orvieto, Anagni or Viterbo, where some papal palaces still stand. The process of establishing orderly papal elections after the horrors of 1241 was formalized later in the thirteenth century when Pope Gregory X (1271–1276) ordered that the cardinals must assemble in locked quarters within ten days of a pope's death and were to be fed decreasing rations for as long as they delayed the election. This procedure, known as a *Conclave* (from the Latin word *clavis,* key), remains the norm for papal elections.

In 1243, the cardinals, meeting at Anagni, elected the Genoese canon lawyer Sinibaldo Fieschi as Pope Innocent IV (1243–1254), and at first, the election seemed to indicate a change in imperial-papal relations. A member of a proimperial family, a superb jurist, and a man wholly lacking in what Frederick II considered the irritable majesty and mystical intractability of Gregory IX, Innocent IV appeared to be an ideal candidate for compromise.

Innocent turned out instead to be Frederick's most resourceful and formidable opponent. Innocent rallied the Lombard cities and Frederick's other enemies. Escaping to the city of Lyons, he called a church council, the First Council of Lyons, and the first council since Lateran IV, and pronounced the excommunication and deposition of the emperor as a tyrant, a heretic, and supporter of heretics in 1245. Innocent's decretal deposing Frederick, *Ad apostolice sedis,* summed up fully and eloquently the canon law tradition of papal authority over the emperor. In spite of a battle of pamphlets designed to wear down papal support—and even a series of complaints against Innocent's action by other European rulers—Frederick was unable to overcome Innocent's opposition. He resumed the war in northern Italy in 1248 and even began a march on the city of Lyons in the same year. But military reversals in the Italian campaign prevented Frederick from capturing the pope, and when the emperor died of dysentery in 1250 at the age of fifty-four, the great German-Sicilian polity began to disintegrate.

Frederick's son, Conrad IV (r. 1250–1254), failed to hold his father's inheritance together. The succession crisis of 1198–1215 and the conflict of 1245–1254 between popes and emperors permitted many lords, clerical and lay, and many Italian cities, great and small, to assume virtually sovereign power over their own territories while holding only a nominal obligation of allegiance to higher authority. After the death of Frederick II, the *Confederation With the Ecclesiastical Princes* and the *Statute in Favor of the Princes* gave the greater nobility a virtually free hand. Groups of cities formed mutually protective and commercial leagues. The Hanseatic League dominated the trade of the Baltic Sea and the North Sea; the Rhenish League and the Swabian League, founded in 1254 and 1331, respectively, dominated western and southern Germany. With local princes and towns increasing their practical autonomy, the power of the nobles whose votes officially elected the king of Germany increased greatly. The electing nobles, a group whose number varied from election to election, as has recently been shown, were all descendants of Otto I through the female line. When the electoral college was formally defined by the emperor Charles IV in 1356, these lay nobles numbered four: the Duke of Saxony, the King of Bohemia, the Count Palatine of the Rhine, and the Margrave of Brandenburg. Three ecclesiastical electors were also named in 1356: The archbishops of Mainz, Cologne, and Trier, the chancellors for Italy, Germany, and Burgundy. With the elimination of the Staufer Dynasty, the electors turned to candidates who could buy votes or submit to control by the electors.

Innocent IV, now able to separate Sicily from Germany, formed an alliance with Charles of Anjou, brother of Louis IX of France, promising him the Sicilian crown if Charles could drive the last Staufer, Frederick II's illegitimate son Manfred, out of Italy. At the battle of Benevento in 1266, Manfred's forces were defeated and Manfred killed, and Charles of Anjou accepted the crown of South Italy and Sicily. The German electors, with a confusion of imperial candidates, simply left the kingship vacant from 1254 to 1273 and then elected a series of weaker rulers in the late thirteenth and fourteenth centuries. The old order had come to an end.

ENGLAND: FROM ANGEVIN EMPIRE TO ISLAND KINGDOM

The reign of Henry II Plantagenet (1154–1189; the name comes from the *planta genesta,* the broom plant, which Henry's father used to wear in his hat) illustrates both the building of royal institutions of government and law in England and the wider, less specifically English interests of a continental lord. Henry II's titles reflect the personal empire of an ambitious and fortunate king in the late twelfth century. Henry had inherited the county of Anjou from his father Geoffrey in 1149. He became duke of Normandy in 1151. He became duke of Aquitaine as a result of his marriage to Eleanor, heiress to the duchy, in 1152. He inherited the throne of England as a result of the treaty between his mother Matilda and King Stephen (above, Chapter 11) in 1154. Later in his reign, Henry received the title of lord of Ireland from the pope. Henry also held other territories as a vassal of the king of France: He was lord of Maine, Brittany, Touraine, Berry, Poitou, La Marche, Auvergne, Quercy, and Gascony. As king of England in his own right and as vassal of the king of France for the rest of his lands, Henry II assembled a vast personal "Angevin" (named after Anjou) empire that included the entire western part of what later became France. He ruled territories that extended unbroken from the Scottish border to the Pyrenees. He also exerted considerable political influence in Scotland, Wales, and Ireland.

Henry's father had advised him to preserve local customs and institutions of governance in the lands he acquired, and in fact, Henry's different titles and different kinds of rights in different parts of his empire prevented him from creating a homogenized state. Nevertheless, he was a talented and ambitious ruler. His judicial and administrative reforms in England and Normandy began the creation of some degree of uniformity between the two most important territories of his empire. Even though he had sworn fidelity to the king of France for much of his territory, Henry treated this relationship casually. On the other hand, he watched his own lands like a hawk. He spent twenty-one years of his thirty-four-year reign as king of England on the Continent, and he spent his energies where he spent his time, but not until he had put England itself to rights. If Henry had succeeded in establishing his rule on the Continent more securely, and if his sons had been able to hold his territories together, the present-day political maps of France and England might look very different. But Richard I Lionheart (1189–1199) and John (1199–1216) could not hold Henry's empire together. Not only did they have personal shortcomings as rulers, but they encountered the stiff and successful opposition of two remarkably able and persistent kings of France, Louis VII (1137–1180) and Philip Augustus (1180–1223). The relations among these five kings from 1154 to the death of John in 1216 shaped the internal growth of both France and England and defined the territorial sphere of each king's authority.

The story of the creation and dismantling of the Angevin Empire of Henry II is the framework for the political history of England and France in the twelfth and thirteenth centuries. Within that framework, Henry's governmental reforms and King John's formidable political concessions to his nobles transformed the governance of England. At the outset of his reign, Henry faced the immense task of reconstructing royal authority in England after the nearly two decades of civil war and political anarchy caused by the succession contest between King Stephen and Henry's mother, Matilda (above, Chapter 11). The English nobles, by changing sides and demanding royal concessions at opportune moments during the conflict, had acquired a considerable degree of independence, greater than any the Anglo-Norman aristocracy had ever enjoyed. In addition, the English church had become involved in the dispute. But with his astute judgment of royal servants, his ruthless drive to impose his authority, and his sophisticated concept of kingly power, Henry reshaped the governance of England and laid the foundations of a new monarchical constitution for the kingdom.

One way of measuring the effects of the anarchy created by the wars between Stephen and Matilda is to note that by 1154, at the outset of Henry II's reign, the royal income had fallen from the thirty thousand pounds per year that it had reached under Henry I to around ten thousand pounds per year. Not until Henry II's death in 1189, did it attain the old level. In addition, the great magnates who held their lands directly from the king, the tenants in chief, had grown considerably more independent between 1135 and 1154. They had also had time to develop a strong hereditary interest in their holdings, regarding their lands and rights as a family possession that ought to descend to no one but a child of the grantee. These two developments made the Anglo-Norman nobility much more dangerous in 1154 than it had been twenty years earlier, as did the fact that most of the 180 tenants-in-chief also held lands in Normandy as well as in England. Furthermore, the movement for ecclesiastical independence associated with the Gregorian reform principles came to England early, during the tenure of Anselm as archbishop of Canterbury (1093–1109). During the civil wars of 1135–1154, the English church grew even more independent of royal control.

The royal response to these movements within the nobility and the church was at first one of concession. In 1153, the Treaty of Winchester recognized certain hereditary rights among tenants-in-chief and all vassals of the crown. Henry I had earlier tried to maintain control of the church after the death of Anselm in 1109. But the influence of reform made a strong impact on England, and most of Henry's senior clergy, even though he appointed them from his own household and from ecclesiastical establishments that he patronized, were imbued with reform ideals. During Stephen's reign, higher churchmen added a practical degree of independence from the king to the theoretical independence that reform ecclesiology had already given them.

Henry II's first task as king was to establish the rudiments of public order in England. From the outset, he insisted on the destruction of unlicensed castles and the curtailment of private warfare. His second problem was that of royal finance. Henry first recovered, and then reorganized, the income from the lands he ruled directly, the royal demesne. Then he turned his attention to the money due him as lord of his tenants-in-chief. He successfully converted the personal military service owed him into scutage— "shield money" paid to the overlord in lieu of this service, thus enabling the king to hire soldiers when and for however long a period he needed them. Although the costs of war rose rapidly in the second half of the twelfth century, Henry's financial basis for military affairs made him less dependent on the uncertain resources of his vassals. Henry also made selective grants from his own lands in return for payment, and he increased the fees charged to those who collected taxes locally throughout the kingdom. He sold charters to municipal corporations, although he always distrusted cities and their populations. His legal reforms greatly increased the royal income from fines and pardons. Henry also brought more and more judicial business into his own courts, including all cases involving land, and thereby weakened the judicial powers of his vassals. Henry knew well that royal officials might be even more rapacious than the king, and he supervised them closely. In 1170, for example, he held an investigation of sheriffs, dismissing and fining heavily those whom he found either incompetent or excessively greedy.

Henry also developed an institution begun by Henry I. In 1156, his treasury, the Exchequer, was permanently established at Westminster, outside London, and its practices regularized. By the end of Henry's reign, the institution was so efficient in keeping accounts of money paid to the king that one of its officials wrote a treatise about its operations, *The Dialogue of the Exchequer,* the first analytical treatise on institutional operation in European history. Henry's reign witnessed another mark of administrative significance. From 1156 on, the records of royal government survive for the most part in unbroken sequence, and for the period 1156–1220 they are numerous. Henry II's administrators proved to be able and inventive servants of the king. We can trace their work from year to year in thousands of documents, whose existence makes the reign of Henry II qualitatively different for study from any previous reign in England or elsewhere.

His finances revamped and regularized and slowly growing, Henry II turned simultaneously to legal and ecclesiastical reforms. Of course, the profits of justice and income from the church were part of the royal finances, and Henry's motives for his reforms in these two areas were financial as well as political. Henry II's legal reforms, however, did not consist simply of restoring to the king those judicial rights that most of his predecessors had possessed and had let slip from their hands. As we have seen, the late twelfth century witnessed changing ideas about law and legal procedure in general, and the revived study of Roman law and the increasing sophistication of canon law also influenced legal reform in England. Occurring when they did, Henry II's legal reforms greatly transformed English law in ways that would have been impossible several decades earlier.

The pattern of English law at the accession of Henry II reflects the pattern of the Conquest. Ancient local courts of shire and hundred (some of which had fallen into the private hands of great laymen or ecclesiastics) existed side by side with the banal courts of the Anglo-Norman aristocracy, for with most grants of land from the king had also gone the grant of jurisdiction on that land. Justice was local, and even the king's courts resembled the courts of any lord, dealing only with those matters that touched on the king's rights as lord. Judges made their decisions according to local custom or on the basis of extremely limited modes of accusation and proof. For any cause, it was necessary for one person to accuse another and for the court to decide between the litigants, not on the basis of evidence, but on the oath of one or the other (compurgation) or the successful outcome of an ordeal or trial by combat, when the procedure called for one. Such courts and procedures were much more instruments of social consensus and control than rational courts of law. For the most part, they regulated personal relations; they cannot be said to have administered "justice" in any modern sense of the term.

The king's court was like that of any other lord—with two exceptions. Because in England the king was everyone's ultimate lord, and because he was the king, possessing certain extraordinary rights, he had more freedom to claim jurisdiction in some cases, especially crimes so heinous that they were considered to violate the "king's peace," than any other lord in England or Normandy. Henry I had begun to exploit these conditions, but it remained for Henry II to make a major transformation in the law of the land. In 1166, Henry II issued a set of instructions to a group of royal judges about to set out on a tour, or *eyre* (from the Latin *iter,* a journey) of the kingdom. These instructions, the *Assizes of Clarendon,* are a landmark in English law and reflect the knowledge of the law that Henry and his servants had acquired during his twelve years as king of England. The *Assizes of Clarendon* and other enactments of Henry's reign greatly increased the number of offenses that had to be tried in the king's own courts and expanded the number of issues that could be tried in those courts. Henry offered the use of a royal writ that began the legal process, the assembling of a sworn jury of twelve free men to testify as to the rightness of the cause before them, and royal enforcement of the verdict. In this way, Henry II brought a great deal of criminal and civil law under the jurisdiction of his own courts. Moreover, he required that a local group of landholders in each locality publicly testify under oath about the criminal activities in their district since the last visit of the royal justices. This finding jury, the predecessor of the modern grand jury, removed the necessity of a private person's having to bring an accusation against a criminal and put the burden of supervising the peace onto the community itself. This is one step in a process that some historians have called "self-government at the king's command."

The legal procedures that Henry II developed for the courts of the royal demesne became models of superior efficiency and lesser cost to litigants. By emphasizing the rights of royal officials in shire courts, Henry associated these courts with the procedures in effect in the courts of the royal demesne. This slow legal revolution tended to homogenize the law of the two kinds of courts and constituted the basis of what later came to be called the Common Law of England. By the end of the twelfth century, a royal justice named Ranulf de Glanvill found English law to have become sufficiently rational and systematic that he wrote a treatise *On the Laws and Customs of the Realm of England.* Like the *Dialogue of the Exchequer,* Glanvill's treatise—and the superior treatise of similar title attributed to Henry De Bracton in the thirteenth century—reflects the systematization of one of the most important social institutions of twelfth-century England. The large numbers of royal personnel who had to administer English law also testifies to the institutional importance of the laws, as does the establishment of a permanent Exchequer office in Westminster in 1156 and the settling of the Court of Common Pleas at Westminster in 1178. The court of Henry II, like that of the kings of Germany, was largely itinerant, and the location of these two institutions in a permanent home with permanent record-keeping procedures and appointed administrators indicated that the character of monarchical government was in an important process of transformation. Soon the kings themselves would cease to travel and would rule from Westminster itself.

Not all of Henry's high officials proved as docile as Ranulf de Glanvill and the author of the *Dialogue of the Exchequer.* Thomas Becket, the son of a landowning knight of London, attended the schools of Paris and entered the service of Archbishop Theobald of Canterbury, where he rose quickly to a position of prominence. When Henry II ascended the English throne, he made Becket his chancellor and then, on Theobald's death, archbishop of Canterbury. But Becket proved to be more devoted as a churchman than as a king's servant. He experienced years of exile between 1164 and 1170 and earned Henry's hostility for his refusal to conform the English church to the king's legal reforms. In 1170, Becket was assassinated by four of Henry's knights, although without Henry's knowledge or approval. Henry undertook a severe penance for the murder, but his reform legislation overcame both Becket's opposition and the immense popularity of the cult that formed around his martyrdom and sainthood.

Henry's sons nearly ruined their father's work. Richard devoted himself to continental affairs, to the third crusade of 1189, and to his political rivalry with Philip Augustus of France. In Richard's prolonged absences from the kingdom, as in those of his father, however, the real strengths of Angevin governance became apparent. The busy, loyal agents who governed England in the king's absence developed the institutional character of English governance considerably.

Richard's brother and successor, John, was energetic and intelligent, but a bad general and a tactless and capricious king. John also had the misfortune to lose much of England's continental possessions to Philip Augustus, including Normandy in 1204, thereby giving his barons an immediate reason for opposing the king, such as they had not had since the days of Stephen and Matilda. To make matters worse, John's interference in the election of the archbishop of Canterbury in 1206 permitted Pope Innocent III to intervene and choose Stephen Langton, a brilliant and popular theologian at the University of Paris. When John refused to accept Langton, Innocent placed England under an interdict—an ecclesiastical discipline imposed on a region. While the interdict was in force, from 1208 to 1213, few religious services were permitted and Christian life was publicly suspended.

Having alienated his barons by the loss of Normandy and the pope by his rejection of Langton, John brought further difficulties upon himself by his rapacious attempts to raise money for the recapture of Normandy. When John's allies were defeated by Philip Augustus of France at the Battle of Bouvines in 1214, the barons turned against John and, on the field of Runnymede in June, 1215, forced him to issue a charter of privileges that promised to restrain the most offensive features of Angevin governance. The Great Charter, *Magna Carta*, was surely no Declaration of Independence, and it proved unacceptable to Innocent III, to whom John had given England in 1213. In its sixty-three clauses, however, even those dealing with technical problems of lordly rights, it is possible to discern some important principles. Subjects must be allowed to enjoy their customary liberties in peace; they were to be subject in law only to the lawful judgment of their peers according to the law of the land; government might be hard, but it must not be capricious, and it must use regular procedures in collecting taxes and administering justice. In short, the king must be consistent, and he must recognize the myriad rights and liberties of his free subjects. If he was not yet under law, he was now under custom. Although Angevin-style governance was not destroyed, it was brought face to face with principles that rendered its most offensive and irregular aspects less harsh.

Magna Carta did not say that free men and women would be ungoverned, nor did it say that they might govern themselves. Such ideas were unthinkable anywhere in Europe at the time—except for Iceland. But the charter did say that men and women would be governed by law and not by the whim of royal officials masquerading as law. Because the barons and clergy—with good reason—did not entirely trust the king's

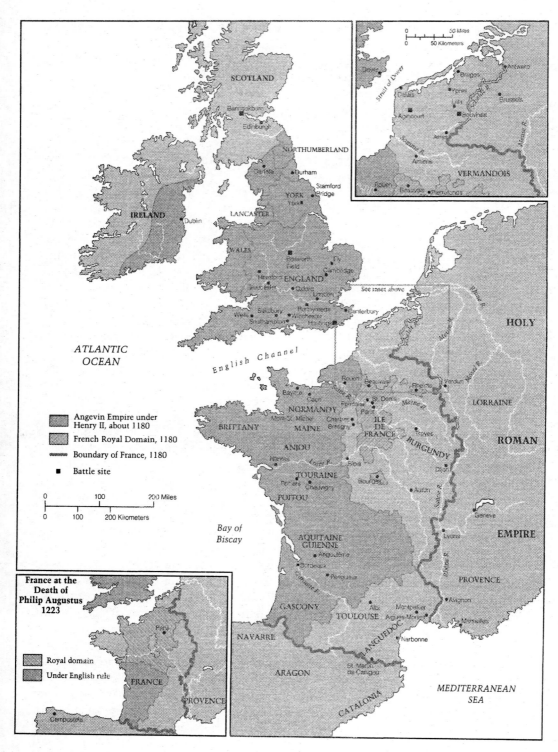

Legend (main map):
- Angevin Empire under Henry II, about 1180
- French Royal Domain, 1180
- Boundary of France, 1180
- ■ Battle site

0   100   200 Miles
0   100   200 Kilometers

Inset (lower left):
France at the Death of Philip Augustus 1223

- Royal domain
- Under English rule

Inset (upper right):
0   50 Miles
0   50 Kilometers

Medieval France and England.

word or seal (no one ever "signed" *Magna Carta* or any other royal charter; the keeper of the king's seal sealed it), the barons forced authenticated copies of the charter to be circulated. The charter was known only as the "charter of liberties" until around 1218, when an unknown royal scribe called it the *Great Charter,* probably to distinguish it from the contemporary and equally important Charter of the Forest. From that date, it has always been *Magna Carta* (never "the" *Magna Carta,* probably because Latin has no definite article).

In 1215, the charter had been forced upon John by his enemies, but when it was reissued in 1216 and 1217, it was done by his friends to insure the succession of John's young son, Henry III (1216–1272), during whose long minority, control of the government was disputed by both the barons and papal legates, and *Magna Carta* came to be regarded as both a kind of coronation charter of Henry III and the standard by which royal governance might be measured throughout the thirteenth century. By 1225, people spoke of it as containing "the fundamental law" of the kingdom. By 1237, Henry had reissued *Magna Carta* twice in order to get his subjects' agreement to increased taxation.

When Henry III came of age, he proved to be an ambitious but considerably less than competent ruler. The public servants of the crown became more efficient, and the king took lower ranking nobles into his service and extended his governance deep into the countryside. But the very efficiency of Henry's government and his use of low- or continental-born servants outraged many of England's great nobles. Their response went much farther than that of their predecessors at Runnymede; they forced the king to accept the *Provisions of Oxford* of 1258, which permitted royal governance to be controlled by a group of barons. Disputes between the king and the barons led to the intervention of Louis IX of France in favor of Henry III, but the barons, led by Simon de Montfort, rebelled and captured the king at the Battle of Lewes in 1264. A year later, however, Henry triumphed over the rebels at the Battle of Evesham and reasserted the king's supremacy in governance.

Henry was succeeded by his son Edward I (1272–1307), one of the strongest English kings. Edward took Wales and became its king by the Treaty of Rhuddlan in 1284, fought and temporarily established English royal dominance in Scotland, developed the few continental possessions left to the English king, especially Gascony, and systematically enforced the common law. He continually investigated and reduced the scope of baronial titles to jurisdiction and restricted the acquisition of land by the Church.

By stressing the law, rather than royal whim, as the test of rights and liberties, Edward greatly strengthened the political order of England. He continued Simon de Montfort's innovative practice of calling a Parliament—an assembly originally made up of two knights from every shire and two burghers from every town—to learn of the king's business and assent to his actions. These assemblies had roots in the full sessions of the royal court, which had been held from the twelfth century on. At first, Parliament met to give the king advice and to approve royal requests for taxation, but it was also the highest court in the kingdom, and it taught its members something about their common interests, sometimes against the wishes of the king. In the end, the reigns of Henry III and Edward I led England out of the difficulties created by the collapse of the Angevin style of governance without capitulating to the self-interest of the great nobles or depending on individual royal whim. Perhaps the phrase that best expresses the character of English governance in the thirteenth century is one that the people of that century invented: "the community of the realm."

The concept of the community of the realm is not as precise as that of the nation-state, but it accurately reflected the results of the innovations of Henry II and the crises under Henry III and Edward I. The reforms of Edward I expanded the principle of self-governance at the king's command. Royal justices sat, impaneled local juries, and administered the same royal law in all parts of the kingdom. Representatives of boroughs and knights of the shires attended Parliament, which was both a court and a representative assembly of the politically aware and financially responsible subjects of the king. In England, the law was the medium through which the king and his subjects arrived at definitions of their respective rights and responsibilities. Together, below the law, they constituted the community of the realm. That unique constitutional creation had been shaped by shrewd and greedy kings out of the rough mix of tradition and autocracy that survived the eleventh century. The association of local communal consciousness with a national monarchy was the great result of the Angevin experiment.

THE IBERIAN PENINSULA: ARAGON, CASTILE, PORTUGAL

Twelfth-century Iberian Christian rulers continued expanding their territories southward, although at a slower rate. Sometimes they had remarkable success. Alfonso I of Aragon and Navarre (r. 1104–1134) had to face both civil wars and the Almoravids, but he managed to capture several important towns in a series of able campaigns. In 1118, with help from southern France, he captured Saragossa. In 1119, Tarragona fell to him, and in 1120, Calatayud. This continued expansion and consolidation of territories already conquered created in Iberia a tough, highly mobile frontier society that developed differently from societies in England and France.

In 1229, James I of Aragon captured Majorca and the other Balearic Islands. In 1236, Ferdinand III of Castile captured Córdoba. In 1238, James captured Valencia, and in 1247, Ferdinand captured Seville. By 1247, only the Nasrid kingdom of Granada was left under direct Muslim rule, the last of the *taifa* kingdoms, protected by its contacts with the strong Moroccan kingdom and the many enclaves of Muslim power and population in reconquered Christian Spain. By the middle of the thirteenth century, the *reconquista* was nearly complete. The remaining Christian triumphs extended over two centuries—its most dramatic later moments were the capture of Algeciras in 1344 and the capture of Granada itself in 1492.

The *reconquista* was attended everywhere by two problems—a shortage of people for repopulation and the expansion of Christian settlements, and the need of the kings for money to finance their long and often costly campaigns. Although they shared these common problems, León-Castile and Aragon produced very different political cultures.

The development of Christian kingdoms on the Iberian peninsula may be considered to be a result of the ways in which land was conquered and became available for settlement and governance, and the particular characteristics of Iberian societies. Almoravid power lasted in Iberia until the 1140s, when another group of North African Muslims, the Almohades, invaded the peninsula. They remained the dominant force in Islamic Spain until the Christian victory at *Las Navas de Tolosa* in 1212, between the upper valleys of the Guadiana and Guadalquivir rivers. With this battle, Muslim power in Spain was broken, except in the far south, and Iberian society began to develop its distinctive forms. In León-Castile the powers of the warrior aristocracy and the privileged towns and associations of sheepherders grew great at the expense of both large-scale agriculture and commercial trade. The kings of León-Castile (the two kingdoms were united as Castile in 1230), lacking a permanent administrative class of servants, struggled to control a rebellious aristocracy and an ambitious church. They did control the *Cortes,* the representative assembly of bishops and powerful nobles in 1188, that included representatives of the towns for the first time ever in the history of Europe, and they occasionally succeeded in demonstrating potentially extensive royal power. Alfonso X *El Sabio* (1252–1284), for example, issued an elaborate and ambitious and extensive code of law, *Las siete partidas,* patronized a cultural revival, and offered himself as a candidate for the imperial title. But his reign ended in succession quarrels, and once again the privileged aristocracy and the economically underdeveloped countryside and towns failed to provide a workable basis for political centralization.

In spite of Aragon's expansion into the Mediterranean, to Sicily, and even to Greece and the Levant in the fourteenth century, its nobility and townspeople regularly opposed the king, limited royal authority severely, and defended their local immunities and customs. Aragon was in fact a confederation of states which included the kingdom of Aragon and the counties of Barcelona, Gerona, Vich, Besalú, and Cerdaña, that had been unified in 1137 and more properly called the Crown of Aragon. Two institutions in particular limited the authority of the king. The office of *justicia,* created in 1265, was a legal mediator between the nobility and the king of Aragon. The *Cortes* of Aragon, unlike that of Castile, also limited royal authority. Such restraints on the ruler constituted an important aspect of early Aragonese political culture.

Political instability, succession crises, and economic disorder plagued the Iberian kingdoms in the fourteenth and fifteenth centuries. However, the small frontier principalities in the northern part of the peninsula that had set out to "reconquer" Iberia from the Muslims in the eighth century had managed to create large, generally prosperous kingdoms. Under the banner of *reconquista,* these kingdoms slowly became diverse political communities possessing the most complex ethnic and historical legacy in Europe.

THE MOST CHRISTIAN KINGS OF FRANCE, 1108–1328

At the beginning of the twelfth century, France was a large kingdom in theory but a small and poor one in fact. Although the kings of France were technically the lords of the great territorial princes whose vast, thoroughly governed domains surrounded the small royal domain in the Ile-de-France—the dukes of Normandy and Burgundy and the counts of

Anjou, Blois and Chartres, Champagne, and Flanders—their lordship was usually recognized as a mere formality; most of their reigns were spent trying to impose order on the small territories that they ruled personally. Unlike the kings of England (who, as Dukes of Normandy, were among their most powerful and troublesome vassals), the kings of France possessed no land that they ruled directly outside the small royal domain; they controlled the appointment of few bishops and abbots outside the royal domain; and their courts were peopled by their own local vassals. Few signatures of powerful lords from the south, west, or east of the kingdom appear on royal documents from the eleventh or twelfth centuries. The best-known image of this diminished royalty is the remark said to have been made by King Louis VII when someone praised the great wealth of Henry II of England: "Now in France, we have only bread and wine and our heart's desire."

At the end of the thirteenth century, France was the largest, wealthiest, and most thoroughly governed monarchical state in Europe. Its king contended successfully with the pope and ruled directly a state that was forty times larger than it had been in 1100. Royal officials and relatives ruled most of the old territorial principalities; of the vast holdings of the Angevin Empire, only Gascony in the far southwest of France remained in the hands of the king of England. The city of Paris was an international center of learning and culture, and the kings of France had made it the first capital in modern political history. Toward the end of the thirteenth century, the lawyer Jean de Blanot proudly recognized that the king of France had come to possess qualities that had hitherto been attributed to the Roman emperor: "The king of France is emperor in his own kingdom, for he recognizes no superior in temporal affairs." By the end of the century, the king of France was indeed emperor in his own kingdom, ruling from a rich capital over a talented and energetic provincial administration, possessing most specialized instruments of governance, and, in spite of his conflict with the papacy, recognized by a title that set him off from all other kings and even the emperor: He was the "most Christian king," ruling a people universally regarded as defenders of the true faith. The bond between king and people in this most Christian kingdom was as strong as that reflected in the English phrase "community of the realm." The great transformation of the kingdom of France was the result of seven generations of hardworking kings and their servants, the particular configuration of French provincial governments and centers of power, and the rivalry between the kings of France and their powerful vassals who were also the troublesome kings of England.

The reign of Louis VI (1108–1137) illustrates both the limited power and the rudimentary governmental institutions of the early kingdom of France and some characteristic features of royal policy. Louis struggled chiefly to make his authority recognized throughout the Ile-de-France, a land full of independent warlords living in virtually impregnable towers and owing no allegiance to anyone. Louis' household was ruled by the great officers whose titles ran back to Carolingian Europe: the seneschal, chancellor, butler, chamberlain, and constable. These offices were hereditary in great local families, and the men who held them controlled the local royal administrators, the *prévots*. Such a system had more ceremonial value than practical effectiveness, however, and Louis relied on two other aspects of his authority much more heavily: cooperation with the Church and unremitting warfare within the royal domain. By claiming to be a defender of the Church, Louis preserved his own interests and invoked growing ecclesiastical support, witnessed by Abbot Suger's biography of him as a saintly defender of the faith.

The work of pacifying the royal domain and continuing the association between the king and the clergy was brilliantly accomplished by Louis VII (1137–1180) who also greatly increased the financial resources of the king and began to make royal authority directly felt outside the royal domain. Louis' patronage of the monastery of St. Denis and its abbot, Suger, gained the monarchy a strong source of support. Louis VII also made frequent expeditions outside the domain in order to defend ecclesiastical establishments elsewhere. As a result, he acquired several important ecclesiastical holdings, and several lay lords formally recognized his overlordship as well. Louis' role as a defender of the Church is reflected in his helping to protect Pope Alexander III from the emperor Frederick Barbarossa and in his reputation as a crusader, for although the Second Crusade (1147/8) covered no one with glory, the portrait of Louis that emerges from Odo of Deuil's *Journey of Louis VII to the East* is an admiring one.

Besides supporting the Church and receiving its support in turn, Louis began to develop Paris as the royal capital. He gave privileges to the Paris shipping merchants. (Their seal, bearing the picture of a ship, is still the official seal of the city.) Although Louis ruled the rest of the royal domain by the old system of household officers and *prévots*, he defined the powers of officeholders more sharply toward the end of his reign. By then he had increased his income to sixty thousand pounds per year, making himself the wealthiest territorial prince in the kingdom. Although Louis used no administrative institutions outside the royal domain, his presence as king was felt more regularly and with greater impact than that of any other early Capetian ruler.

Louis' son and successor Philip II Augustus (1180–1223) benefited from his grandfather's and father's efforts, and greatly strengthened royal rule and royal wealth in his own right. He is usually regarded as the first great king of France. Only fifteen years of age when he inherited the crown, Philip Augustus had already been associated in the kingship during the last year of his father's life. By 1190, when Philip Augustus issued instructions for the operation of the kingdom while he was away on Crusade, several marked changes in royal governance are noticeable. First, the *prévots* were instructed to come to Paris to render their accounts three times a year. Second, a new official, the *bailli*, was created to hear cases within the royal domain. Like the *prévots*, he reported three times a year to Paris. Together, the *prévots* and *baillis* brought in royal revenues of around 100,000 pounds for the year 1202/3, according to the first records that survive. Philip's *baillis*, then, were roughly comparable to the traveling justices of Henry II in England. In using Paris as a center of fixed governmental supervision, Philip Augustus continued the tradition established by his father. He made all citizens of Paris free townsmen, governed by a council of six and a provost. In 1185, Philip called an assembly of townspeople to discuss paving the streets of Paris, a considerable achievement of urban development at the end of the twelfth century.

Upon his return from the Crusade, Philip Augustus began to transform the archaic institutions of the royal household into a more modern system of governance. He ceased to fill the great household offices of chancellor (after 1185) and seneschal (after 1191). He drew more on the services of lesser nobles and less on those of the great families of the royal domain or nearby principalities. Other great household positions became merely honorific. Philip's increased use of *baillis* and low-born servants created a small, efficient, and loyal central royal court that was very well suited to the new and much larger administrative duties that the last two decades of Philip's reign imposed upon it.

Philip also knew how to use his great nobles to achieve his ends. In 1202, King John of England married Isabella of Angouleme, who was already betrothed to another royal vassal, Hugh of Lusignan. Before the royal court, Hugh accused John of bad faith, and Philip hailed John to appear at a hearing conducted by Philip's other vassals, in theory John's equals. John refused, arguing that the king of England could be no man's vassal, and Philip, invoking lordly privilege and utterly ignoring John's defense, declared all John's holdings from him forfeited, and invaded Normandy. Philip's able generalship and financial resources soon wore down John's opposition, and Normandy was lost to the English in 1204. Philip also enforced his rule in two other parts of the Angevin Empire, Anjou and Touraine, in 1206. Between 1192 and 1213, Philip acquired the large northern territorial principality of Vermandois and increased his powers in Flanders. These new and very large additions to the territories directly ruled by the king posed considerable problems for Philip. But by adapting his rule to local customs, adopting sophisticated Norman institutions, and sending his *baillis* to supervise the operation of provincial government in the new territories, Philip Augustus developed a full-fledged provincial administration and immensely increased both royal wealth and the prestige of the king of France.

Under Philip's son Louis VIII (1223–1226) and his remarkably able and talented queen, Blanche of Castile, royal institutions of governance were extended even further into the old independent territorial principalities of Poitou and Languedoc. By the reign of Louis VIII, there were three levels of royal administrators. The older offices of *prévot* and viscount had dropped to a second-level status. The new offices of *bailli* and *sénéschal* constituted a senior rank of officials. Drawn from the lower nobility, they were paid a salary and usually posted in provinces where they were not native. At the bottom, were numerous local royal servants called *servientes* or *gardes.* By the early thirteenth century, then, the royal governance of France had been greatly transformed, just as the territory directly and indirectly ruled by the king had increased immensely.

The early death of Louis VIII left the young Louis IX (1226–1270) in the care of Queen Blanche. For nearly thirty years, Blanche was the real ruler of France, both during Louis' formal minority, which lasted until 1234, and during his young manhood. When Louis departed on a Crusade in 1248, Blanche was regent of the kingdom, and she remained in control during Louis' capture and imprisonment in Egypt, which lasted until 1254. Blanche had to fight off coalitions of nobles anxious to take advantage of Louis' minority and absence in the east and the regency of a woman, in order control the royal government themselves. But together, Blanche and Louis successfully resisted baronial opposition and developed even further the administrative reforms of Philip Augustus.

Louis IX depended heavily on the *baillis,* and in 1247/8, he began to rearrange several of their jurisdictions, making them regularly territorial, dividing some into more manageable territories, and redesigning others. In 1247, Louis also introduced a new office, that of *enqueteur* (inquisitor), a royal official sent out to hear complaints of illegal

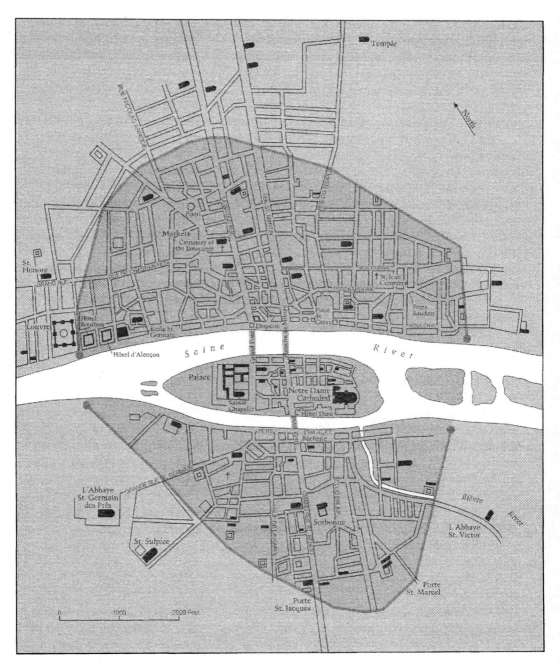

Thirteenth-century Paris.

activities on the part of *baillis* and other officials. Louis relied heavily on Dominicans and Franciscans to perform this duty, which he had created out of conscience and piety as well as a desire for more institutional supervision. So thoroughgoing were Louis' *enqueteurs,* especially after his return from Crusade in 1254, that Rutebeuf, a satirical French poet, complained that if Louis investigated his Dominicans and Franciscans as carefully as his *enqueteurs* investigated others, he, too, would find faults and errors. Among Louis' *enqueteurs* was Gui Fulquois, who later became Pope Clement IV.

Personally devout and imbued with a profound sense of royal moral responsibility, Louis IX was regarded for centuries as the ideal medieval ruler. His patronage of the Mendicant Orders, his crusading activities, his passionate desire for justice, and his personal life overshadowed even his administrative successes. Even though he developed his grandfather's institutions and increased royal revenues until they doubled those of Philip Augustus, Louis was remembered as a saintly ruler, and he was canonized in 1297 by a pope who otherwise had little good to say about the kings of France. Louis' canonization culminated the tradition of ecclesiastical support of the French monarchy. At Louis' death on yet another Crusade in Tunis in 1270, not only did the territory and wealth of the king of France surpass those of every other European ruler, but the prestige of the Capetian Dynasty and its most recent saintly representative had been vastly and permanently increased.

Philip III (r. 1270–1285) continued to develop both the royal administration and the royal crusading policy. But it was during the reign of Philip IV the Fair (r. 1285–1314) that the achievements of the Capetian monarchy were put to their severest tests. Although the kings of France had added to their territory by warfare in Normandy in 1204, and defended their gains at the Battle of Bouvines in 1214, they fought no major wars for the rest of the thirteenth century. Although their revenues had grown, their expenses had risen also, and the French king was in no position to make extraordinary military expenditures out of his normal revenues. Finally, France and the papacy had always been particularly close, and the French church had readily cooperated with the French kings without papal interference. But during the reign of Philip IV, war broke out once again on a wide scale. Royal finances were strained to the utmost, and the king of France and the pope entered a great contest to determine who in fact ruled the Church in France.

The king who faced these crises has always been an enigma to historians. Some have argued that Philip the Fair was a rational, calculating ruler who closely supervised all governmental activities; others argue that he was a nonentity whose policies were those of his assistants, particularly the many lawyers with whom he surrounded himself. One school of historians regards Philip as a "constitutional" king who recognized his duties to the law; another regards him as an autocrat who respected neither tradition nor law except when it was in his own interest to do so. Some regard him as an antireligious tyrant who tried to destroy the papacy and the faith, others as a devout Christian who merely resisted papal encroachments on his traditional rights. Not only the crises of Philip's reign but the problem of his character make his reign at once fascinating and ambiguous.

In 1271, the crown of France had been augmented by the acquisition of Languedoc, and in 1285, upon Philip IV's marriage to Jeanne of Navarre, the crown acquired the rich counties of Champagne and Brie. These immense territorial gains continued the meteoric expansion of the kingdom, but they put considerable strains on royal institutions and finances, and involved Philip more closely in the affairs of English Gascony and the urbanized region of Flanders. From the outset of his reign, Philip had to prepare for war, and his many campaigns against the English in Gascony and the Flemings in Flanders consumed his resources at a great rate.

Not only did Philip ruthlessly push his *baillis* and *sénéchaux,* but he also turned the *enqueteurs* into financial agents, whose new functions continued into the fourteenth century. Philip tightened control over his financial office, and laid the foundations for its reorganization and permanent settlement in Paris as the *Chambre des Comptes,* the French equivalent of the English Exchequer. He also systematized his royal court of appeals, the *Parlement* of Paris, which became the judicial center of the kingdom. Philip drew into royal service townsmen and professional lawyers, usually of urban background and fiercely royalist in their sympathies and loyalties.

In order to increase revenues, Philip began to regularize the principle of the royal right to tax his subjects, at first in cases of the defense of the realm in emergencies, and later on a routine basis. In matters of taxation, Philip and his agents dealt with provincial assemblies, because of the strongly localized traditions of legal and financial administration that had prevailed in France during the acquisition of so many new territories. Thus, the large national assemblies that Philip called in Paris in 1303 and 1308—the Estates-General—never acquired the financial or judicial powers of the English Parliament.

Philip IV's financial demands strained every royal resource and led him into areas where no French king had acted before. Although the status of the Jews in France had sharply declined under Louis IX, it became much worse during Philip's reign. In 1306, Philip confiscated Jewish money and property and expelled all unbaptized Jews from the kingdom, as his contemporary, Edward I, had done in England in 1290. Philip increased his demands for money and even claimed the right to tax the clergy. Pope Boniface VIII protested Philip's actions, and after a long, drawn-out battle between the two (to be discussed later in this chapter), Philip gained the power to tax the clergy as well as the laity.

Yet for all of his fiscal rapacity and opposition to traditional clerical privileges, Philip IV was not irreligious. Rather, his sense of religion appears to have been inseparable from his awareness of the mission of Christian France and the spiritual obligations his kingship imposed on him. Cold, impersonal, and distant, he was nevertheless driven by a vision of France as a holy land, and its people and king as particularly favored by God. His propagandists and also his subjects appear to have agreed with him. His great appeals to the kingdom were answered favorably by a population whose resources were strained to the utmost by royal demands. The people's acceptance of regular royal taxation marked an important step in the creation of new royal resources and in the growth of their loyalty to the king and the kingdom.

When Philip died in 1314, the kingdom had survived the military, financial, and ecclesiastical crises of his reign, testimony to the achievements of Philip and his royal ancestors. But within a few years, the kingdom faced another great crisis, one from which it was not able to extricate itself as quickly as it had in the early years of the fourteenth century. Philip was succeeded in order by his three short-lived sons, Louis X (1314–1316),

Philip V (1316–1322), and Charles IV (1322–1328). At the death of Charles IV in 1328, the succession to the throne became a major problem for the first time since 987. The aristocracy's resistance to royal centralization complicated the issue and sent France into the fourteenth century facing what the historian Raymond Cazelles has termed the "crisis of royalty" at the end of the eleven generations of Capetian kings.

THE NEW ORDER: THE CONFLICT BETWEEN POPES AND TERRITORIAL MONARCHS

The Great Interregnum of the kingdom of Germany ended with the election of Rudolf of Hapsburg as king of the Romans in 1273. Rudolf and his imperial successors, with the striking exception of Louis of Bavaria (r. 1314–1347), remained content to exercise their limited powers in Germany and Austria and to build their family domains and influence. The popes had succeeded in removing Sicily from the Staufer dynasty in 1268 through the agency of Charles of Anjou, brother of Louis IX of France, who became king of Sicily in that year. But Charles's rule in Sicily and South Italy excited fear of his power on the part of the Roman curia and resentment on the part of his Sicilian subjects. In 1282, the population of Palermo massacred the French garrison, a revolt known as the Sicilian Vespers, and precipitated a general conflict throughout the northern Mediterranean world. This conflict lasted until the Treaty of Caltabellotta in 1302, which awarded the island of Sicily to the royal house of Aragon and mainland South Italy to the Angevin successors of Charles of Anjou.

Charles of Anjou's grandnephew was Philip IV the Fair, who, in addition to the considerable debts inside his kingdom, faced popular resentment toward France's participation in ecclesiastical vendettas and the diplomatic intricacies of the papal elections during the years 1292–1305. After a two-year vacancy following the death of Pope Nicholas IV in 1292, the saintly hermit Peter Morone was elected pope. Although many hopes were pinned to Morone, who took the papal name of Celestine V, he was largely controlled by the Angevin court at Naples, where he spent his entire brief pontificate, and the burden of the papacy proved too much for him. To the shock of everyone, he resigned the office in December 1294. His successor was an old, wily, and talented papal bureaucrat, Benedetto Gaetani, who took the name Boniface VIII.

It was precisely over questions of royal financial needs and practices that the great quarrel between Philip and Boniface was launched. Although papal permission had long been required in order for temporal rulers to tax their clergy (and even then only in cases of dire necessity), thirteenth-century rulers had often neglected this rule. Facing a war with England and a vexing problem in Flanders, Philip issued new demands for taxes from the clergy in 1296. Boniface responded with a papal letter directing the French bishops not to pay. This letter, *Clericis laicos*, condemned the abuse of temporal authority, and although its legal provisions were on solid ground, its tone was rather more categorical than suited Philip. In the same year, Philip prohibited the export of any money at all, including papal revenues, from France. In 1297, in the letter *Romana mater*, Boniface qualifiedly suspended the provisions of *Clericis laicos* for France, and in a later letter of the same year, *Etsi de statu*, he withdrew slightly from his earlier position.

In 1297, Boniface had proclaimed the canonization of Louis IX of France, but in that same year, Boniface faced difficulties on several fronts. An influential segment of the college of cardinals, supported by a rival family to that of Boniface, denounced him as a usurper, and Boniface resorted to the unfortunate device of proclaiming a Crusade against them. Disappointed supporters of Celestine V further accused Boniface of canonical irregularity. In 1298, Boniface published his great lawbook, the *Liber Sextus*, part of which included his own texts justifying papal resignation and the procedures for providing a successor to a still-living former pope, and in 1300, he announced the Jubilee Year, a period in which the pilgrimage to Rome was surrounded with particular spiritual benefits. By 1301, both parties appeared to have recovered from the earlier encounter, and the success of the Jubilee Year must have been encouraging to Boniface. So many pilgrims thronged the narrow streets of Rome that the officials of the city were forced to invent the one-way street.

In 1301, however, the second conflict broke out. Philip arrested the bishop of Pamiers, Bernard Saisset, for treason and heresy, condemned him, and wrote to Boniface requesting papal confirmation of his action. Boniface could legitimately have modified his position on taxation, but he could not relax the canonical sanctions against any layman who presumed to try to convict a bishop. Boniface therefore refused, called a council at Rome for 1302, and wrote Philip a long letter, *Ausculta fili,* in which he carefully cautioned the king against abusing the age-old liberties of the Church. Philip's propagandists circulated a forged version of the letter in which Boniface was made to appear to have claimed complete temporal and spiritual authority in France. This was one of the first documents in modern propaganda warfare. In addition, in 1302, Philip called a large assembly of nobles, clergy, and people—the first Estates-General in the history of France—to solicit public support in his quarrel with the pope.

By the end of the year, Boniface replied with the bull *Unam sanctam,* a long, detailed, and wholly traditionalist exposition of papal authority. This bull, one of the most famous documents in the history of the relations between the papacy and the monarchy, elicited no counterarguments from Philip's supporters. Instead, Guillaume de Nogaret, Philip's chief minister, denounced Boniface as a heretic and blasphemer and marched into Italy, where he took the pope captive at Anagni and attempted to force him to repudiate his earlier statements and resign the papacy. Although he was released before he was forced to do this, Boniface died a few weeks later, and the questions of the relations between France and the papacy were momentarily suspended.

With the accession of Clement V (1305–1314) the relations between France and the papacy were slowly restored, but at a formidable price to the latter. The excommunications against Nogaret and others were lifted, and Philip was formally praised for his devotion in the bull *Rex Gloriae* of 1311. The pope formally repudiated some of Boniface's arguments in *Clericis laicos, Ausculta fili,* and *Unam sanctam,* and Clement had to work very hard to prevent Philip from engineering a church council that would pronounce Boniface VIII an antipope. These concessions weakened the direct authority of the popes after Clement V, and they presaged an even more remarkable incident, the royal destruction of the Order of the Knights Templar.

In one sense, Boniface's concern over Philip's claim may well have come from his fear that the territorial monarchies in general were acquiring too much direct power over the clergy in their kingdoms. After all, the machinery of governance and communications was more direct and influential within England or France than throughout all of Christendom, and events of the fourteenth and fifteenth centuries proved such that monarchical control over clergy appealed to local churchmen and was therefore a significant threat to the universal claims of the papacy.

No event suggests more clearly the threat constituted by a temporal power than the affair of the Templars. This order, having earned the praise of Bernard of Clairvaux in the twelfth century and having acquired an attractive reputation in the Holy Land, had expanded its role in Europe, particularly in the fields of banking and Crusade financing. The wealth of the Templars and their virtual independence from governmental institutions made them an attractive target for the financially needy Philip, and their growing concern with financial affairs and their own privileges, as well as the failures of the crusade movements during the thirteenth century, had doubtless weakened their standing in the eyes of many Christians. Between 1307 and 1314, Philip undertook to destroy the order and confiscate its property. In 1307, his campaign began with the arrest of the Templars on charges of heresy and unspecified, but enormous and horrible vices. By 1310, a number of Templars had been burned at the stake as heretics, and in 1314, the grand master of the order, Jacques de Molai, was executed. The financial resources of the Templars were confiscated by the crown, although it could not keep them in the end, and papal approval was elicited with difficulty after royal pressure was exerted on Clement V in the matter of Boniface VIII and the other troubles of the first decade of the fourteenth century. Although not all subjects of Philip IV, clergy and laity, concurred in the destruction of the Templars, the king's success marked, along with his successful conflict with the papacy, one significant moment in the status of temporal, nonimperial authority in European history. The powers of the king, enhanced by new administrative agents, financial resources, unquestioned Christian orthodoxy, and the growing cult of the kingdom of France itself, were both more immediately visible and more directly effective.

None of these crises destroyed the traditional authority of the pope, nor did they weaken his theoretical claims to the leadership of Christian society. The struggle between the popes and the kings of France was not that between an "archaic" church and the "modern" state, but rather between spiritual and temporal authorities in the new circumstances of the late thirteenth and early fourteenth centuries. In this sense, both powers were still traditional powers. The authority of the clergy and the papacy still counted for much throughout the fourteenth century, and continued to do so until the eighteenth century. Temporal authority, however, with its resources, claims, and spiritual justification, now increasingly defined the terms of the new relationship, but still left ample room in which spiritual authority continued to function effectively.

16

Reason and Imagination
in the Thirteenth Century

THE TRIUMPH OF ARISTOTLE

One of the most important aspects of the new learning of the twelfth century was
western Europeans' access to Muslim and Greek scientific and philosophical thought.
With the expansion of Christian power in Iberia, signaled by the capture of Toledo in
1085, clerical scholars in Iberia and then in Sicily began the process of translating the
works of some of the most important thinkers in both alien cultures, first from Arabic
and later directly from Greek. Peter the Venerable (above, Chapter 12), abbot of the
monastery of Cluny, even commissioned a translation of the *Qur'an* into Latin in the
mid twelfth century. Among the works of Arabic scholars available to Europeans in Latin
versions by the end of the twelfth century, were Arabic translations of Greek philosophy,
and the original philosophical and scientific ideas of Ibn Sina (Avicenna to the Latins:
980–1037) on medicine and philosophy, al-Khwarizmi (d. 850) on mathematics, and
Alhazen (d. 1039) on optics. In addition, the Latins received from the Arabs much
Greek scientific and philosophical literature, particularly the scientific and philosophical
works of Aristotle, with the great commentary of the Muslim philosopher Ibn Rushd
(Averroes to the Latins: 1126–1198).

It is something of a paradox that the work of these thinkers, most of them
Muslims, had a far greater impact on Latin Christians than on later Islamic thought. This
question in turn leads to the problem of comparative intellectual history—why and how
did the three parallel civilizations of the period deal with similar areas of culture so

differently? Although much of ancient Greek thought had always been available in the Byzantine world, it had also been assimilated and Christianized early, and Byzantine theology had little interest in philosophy beyond this. Byzantine intellectuals, most of them resident in Constantinople and moving in the society of the capital and court circles, concentrated their secular studies exclusively on literature written in the language of ancient Attic Greek, not the contemporary version of Greek, demotic, that was the everyday language of Byzantines. Religion within the empire and in missionary enterprises outside it concentrated on the liturgy and the gospel, not the wider apparatus of secular thought and learning.

In the Muslim world after the ninth century, learning was sharply divided between religious and nonreligious subjects. Although several caliphs patronized centers of learning for nonreligious subjects like the great House of Wisdom in Baghdad under the translator Hunayn ibn-Ishaq (ca. 809–863), science and speculative philosophy could only be pursued and supported by individual personal or family interest. Several devotional movements in early Islam did attempt to use philosophical ideas and arguments in religious matters, most notably in the field of *falsafah,* the Arabic word for "philosophy." Thinkers like al-Kindi (ca. 800–ca. 866) adapted neoplatonic thought in order to devise a philosophical system that would lead to the same truths as the revealed *Qu'ran.* Most of the thinkers who pursued *falsafah* had had scientific educations and served as court physicians or civil servants, and these were the thinkers whose discovery in western Europe ignited a new interest in philosophical theology. But they had few successors in the Muslim world. Religious teachers and rulers disliked the novelties of philosophical speculation—one caliph, on being told that his city held a great library of ancient thought, replied that if the books of philosophy agreed with the *Qu'ran* they were unnecessary and if they did not, they were blasphemous. In either case, they were to be destroyed. The Almoravid and Almohad rulers of Islamic Iberia were uniformly hostile to philosophical speculation. The popular movement of Sufi mysticism did not require a philosophical theology. Finally, although a number of rationalist thinkers also taught in religious and law schools, *madrasas,* their philosophical work was marginalized in them and the Muslim world never developed the secular schools that would have institutionally sustained and developed the new organization of knowledge. In short, comparative intellectual history must consider both the content of ideas and the social and cultural settings in which they and their thinkers exist. In Muslim law, for example, only a human being could be considered a legal person but, in western law, a corporation could be a legal person; therefore, there could be no incorporated schools—universities—in the Muslim world unless individual rulers permitted them, but no rulers did.

The less organized Latin west, however, took to the new learning eagerly, as the careers of Otloh of St. Emmeram, Guibert of Nogent, and Peter Abelard demonstrate. For a while, as in the cases of Otloh and Guibert, monastic schools could absorb and apply some of this knowledge, but in time, its content and techniques exceeded what monastic schoolmasters were willing to tolerate, largely because they thought that monks did not need it. There is a law of academic inertia that says that schools tend to continue doing what they were originally established to do, and can only with difficulty be inspired to do something else. The monastic school was so crucial to the training of monks that it had little need to change its curriculum. The cathedral school accommodated itself to the new learning more easily, but ultimately it was the combination of these with the schools of private masters like Abelard that invented the organizational and institutional form of the new learning—the universities.

For the new Aristotelian-inspired studies affected the curriculum and ultimately the organization of knowledge into distinct disciplines. Early in the twelfth century, Hugh, the schoolmaster of the house of canons of St. Victor on the left bank of the Seine in Paris, wrote a treatise called the *Didascalicon,* an attempt to inventory the legitimate and illegitimate subjects of knowledge. Hugh's inventory was original and in many ways novel—for instance, he included an interesting discussion of the mechanical arts, rarely considered intellectually respectable before his time. The organization of knowledge raised questions about entire fields of study and what should be taught and learned in them. Gradually, the study of ethics was joined to that of grammar, while the new natural philosophy of Aristotle was attached to logic. Dissatisfaction with the conventional schema of the seven liberal arts led to three further changes. First, some of the liberal arts, notably grammar and rhetoric, became preliminary subjects and eventually dropped out of some university curricula altogether. Second, the subjects of the quadrivium, along with logic, increased in importance. Third, by the thirteenth century the Aristotelian "sciences"—physics, ethics, and metaphysics—became subjects in their own right and were added to the arts. Thus was created the original category of "arts and sciences." By the early thirteenth century, not only was academic learning a profession practiced in corporate universities with specialized professional curricula and technical vocabularies, but the old arts curriculum was largely dominated by the study of logic and natural philosophy. Those old liberal arts that did not lend themselves to the requirements of the new disciplines of theology and law tended to be downgraded into merely preparatory subjects; those that did, grew to dominate the study of the arts and sciences and to shape European thought in many areas. The division of faculties within the early universities is an indication of the new organization. Although not all universities possessed all faculties, the ideal four were Arts, Medicine, Law, and Theology.

In different medieval universities, of course, the new subjects produced different results. Oxford became prominent in natural philosophy and mathematics, chiefly through the influence of its first chancellor, Robert Grosseteste. Paris concentrated on theology and metaphysics, and Montpellier on medicine. Orleans, on the other hand, maintained a respected school of rhetoric, and the University of Bologna became the greatest of medieval schools of law.

The faculties of the arts and sciences, by now separated from the faculties of medicine, theology, and law, treated their own specialized subjects with a new freedom and often with a disregard for both tradition and theological caution. Thus, several thirteenth-century thinkers outside the theology faculty came under attack from theologians who accused them of sharing not only Aristotle's beliefs in natural philosophy but also his pagan ideas about the uncreatedness of the world. They were also charged with failing to account properly for such doctrines as that of the Trinity or the theological virtue of Charity. Growing friction between theology and philosophy led to several incidents of rivalry within the thirteenth-century universities. In early thirteenth-century Paris, for example, secular arts masters bitterly resented the arrival of Franciscan and Dominican scholars in university teaching chairs of theology. This rivalry was one of the dominant themes at Paris throughout the century. In addition, the arts faculty was censured several times during the 1200s for teaching philosophical doctrines that ran counter to scripture and Christian truth. In 1277, Etienne Tempier, the bishop of Paris, issued a condemnation of 219 propositions that he claimed were erroneously being taught at Paris by the arts faculty. The condemnation later played a very important role in redirecting philosophy away from pure Aristotelianism, although a strong and articulate school of philosophers committed to the teaching of Aristotle and his Arabic commentator Averroes flourished through the fourteenth century.

It is impossible to overestimate the impact of Aristotelian thought on thirteenth-century western Europe. The historical rediscovery and wide circulation of the work of an earlier thinker is not, of course, itself a cause of intellectual change, but rather a sign that change is already taking place and that the thinker's work appeals because it is consistent with that change. The work of Aristotle and his Arabic commentators was appealing to western Europeans because it enhanced their desire to understand the created world as an avenue toward understanding divine truth. Twelfth-century thinkers had long claimed that there were two sources of knowledge of the divine—the book of revelation, scripture, and the book of the world, each approached through faith, *fides,* and reason, *ratio.* Different styles of theological argument placed different values on each of these books, but those who defended the study of the world argued that since God had created the world and had given man reason, any discoveries about the world by the proper use of reason would necessarily lead to a better understanding of God and would not be incompatible with the revelations of faith. Other thinkers were not so sure. In short, Aristotle had offered the detailed picture of an intelligible universe, the heavens distinguished from the realm of nature, a description of the operation of sentient, animate, rational beings, a plausible account of the nature of the intellect, and a means of understanding being itself. At first, his teachings seemed to richly complement earlier Christian doctrines, to recognize in creation itself a dignity it had hitherto lacked. As noted above, Aristotle's distinction between the *substance* of a thing and its appearance, its *accidents,* gave theologians of the eucharist and the members of the Fourth Lateran Council the new technical term, *transubstantiation.* The "Arabized" Aristotle became the presiding genius of the created world.

As western Europeans received them, Aristotle's works fell roughly into eight groups: a group of treatises on logical reasoning that dealt extensively with the use of language and the uses of logic was collectively called the *Organon,* or "tool," consisting of preliminary works on elementary logic, the so-called "old logic," that had been translated by Boethius and long been known; a group of more complex treatises known as the "new logic"; a group of treatises on the physical world that dealt with what was called natural philosophy; a group of works dealing broadly with psychology; two important and widely used treatises on ethics; equally influential treatises on economics and political philosophy; and a substantial treatise on metaphysics. An eighth area, Aristotle's treatise on poetics, did not become known in Europe until much later.

The logical works of Aristotle that had not been translated by Boethius, notably the *Posterior Analytics,* had been integrated into the curriculum of the eleventh- and twelfth-century schools under the subject of dialectic. It was this "new logic" that troubled Otloh and other primarily monastic thinkers. But the remainder of Aristotle's corpus of writings—and the important Arabic commentaries on it, as well as original works of Arabic science and philosophy (some of which Europeans attributed erroneously to Aristotle)—dealt with subjects that were not so easily accommodated to the standard academic curriculum. Natural philosophy, ethics, metaphysics, and politics required an expanded curriculum, just as they influenced learned attitudes toward the naturalness of the created universe and the dignity of nature and humanity. They challenged the Platonic-Augustinian tradition of thought that remained skeptical of the value of knowledge of the world, material reality, and human efforts to understand them, and focused on the invisible forms and ideas in the mind of God that were more perfect, and hence more "real," than their crude and imperfect earthly copies. The new material from Greek and Arabic thinkers argued instead for the regularity, coherence, and intelligibility of material creation and, by extension, even the domestic and social institutions of human life.

Because much of the thought of late antiquity that had originally transmitted Aristotle to the Latin West, including the work of Boethius, had been devoted to proving that Aristotle and Plato were in essential agreement, there was little initial resistance to the reception of more Aristotelian texts from the middle of the twelfth century on. Aristotle's works of natural philosophy offered a systematic and consistent set of physical principles that were then applied elsewhere to different aspects of human nature and activity. Aristotle's *Physics,* for example, analyzed motion in terms of changes in some of the categories that the logical texts had established. It then considered innate tendencies in terms of actuality and potentiality in matter that were realized by motion. In Aristotelian physics, motion was a key concept, and the doctrine of motion and of movers (including that of the ultimate "unmoved mover," which appealed to both philosophers and theologians) laid the groundwork for both physics and mechanics.

Aristotle's other works of natural philosophy—*On Generation and Corruption, On the Heavens,* and *On Meteorology*—offered an account of the physical universe, its structure, its inhabitants, and human psychology that appealed very strongly to thirteenth-century thinkers. Aristotle divided the "skies" into a realm of nature, physics, and one of metanature, the heavens. His doctrines of motion and matter accounted for the movement of planets and apparent lack of movement of the stars, and they also accounted for the possibility of an "unmoved mover" beyond the stars. Aristotle's treatises of natural philosophy made both the earth and the heavens intelligible without apparently violating major Christian beliefs.

His treatise *On the Soul* distinguished among the different life forces of sentient, animate, and rational beings. For Aristotle, the soul and body are one, as are form and matter. Only in the function of the active intellect, an idea much developed by Averroes, which is shared by all rational beings and is not individualized, do humans have a power of conceptualization and reasoning that distinguishes them from other life forms.

For Aristotle and his followers, metaphysics was the supreme science. It is the study of being and virtue, as well as that of the four causes of all things: the material, formal, efficient, and final. Since God could be identified as the final cause of all things, Aristotelian thought again appeared consistent with much of Christian doctrine. These "causes" are based on Aristotle's sense of the purposefulness of all change in nature.

Aristotle's Arabic commentators were often not distinguished by Europeans from Aristotle himself. Islamic philosophers had already identified the "unmoved mover" with God and the active intellect with the prophetic spirit of Muhammad. Avicenna had added the dimension of necessity and contingency in distinguishing between God and creation. This theological-philosophical approach to Aristotle by the Arabic natural philosophers and theologians appealed equally to Christians, and not only Aristotle's natural philosophy, but his work on metaphysics, ethics, and politics was swept along in its train.

The texts of Aristotle generally served thirteenth-century Europe well. They argued for the dignity and intelligibility of the material world, the naturalness of human society and the state, and the secular virtue of social obligations and the rational use of public power. But although they were long held authoritative, they were not always accurate, and they and their popularity troubled thinkers from the late thirteenth century on (see below, Ch. 18). In other areas, they reinforced ideas that were already powerful. One instance of this is the popularity and authority of Aristotelian biology and gynecology.

Aristotle defined being as the imposition of form on matter. Aristotelian biological doctrine held that the generation of the human being began when menstrual blood (passive matter) was given form by male semen, the perfect union of the two producing a male, the imperfect union producing a female or a monster. Male seed was also assumed to impose rational characteristics to the fetus, which developed a soul slowly, absorbing both astrological and divine influences because of its combination of material and spiritual existence. Christian theologians read Aristotle on human gestation in the light of the long history of their theories of female inferiority to the male and their fear of unbridled lust and the passions generally, which they thought represented the dangerous realm of matter and therefore disordered reason in terms of both excess and deficiency.

This ambiguous attitude toward sexual reproduction colored virtually all discussions of both human sexual relations and the psychological and physiological character of men and women, consistently to the disadvantage of women. When the masculine was identified with the mind and spirit—the nobler parts of the human being—the feminine was identified with the flesh and carnal passions, considered the inferior aspects of human nature. Aristotelian physiology even offered directions for being assured of begetting male children: Intercourse immediately following the menstrual period tended to beget males; intercourse later in the cycle tended to produce females, monsters, or no children at all, for it was thought to impose male form upon unfresh and tainted matter. On this point, Aristotle was, of course, dead wrong. But he was authoritative, and no one conceived that he might be wrong, although a number of thinkers criticized Aristotle on other points where his conclusions might be more readily challenged by available evidence.

Menstruation was regarded as a form of pollution, and many of the rules of Jewish scripture regarding sexual purity and pollution were adopted by Christian theologians and canon lawyers. Women were regarded as enjoying twice the sexual pleasure of men, and of possessing far more intense carnal desires than men. The act of sexual intercourse was considered more fatiguing and injurious for men, who had only one means of expelling the buildup of semen, since it was also thought that women had the additional means of purging their bodies by menstruation.

In this instance, the new science of Aristotle and his Arabic commentators served to confirm the highly ambiguous and frequently misogynistic attitudes of learned European males. What about female medical practitioners? Statistics are hard to come by and unreliable when found, but those that are most respected suggest that in France and England about one percent of known medical practitioners were women, and perhaps half of one percent midwives. At the important medical center at Salerno, a number of women practitioners and medical writers are recorded, the most famous of whom was the twelfth-century Trota, to whom were later attributed a great number of medical treatises that passed under the general name of "Trotula." These female practitioners were not limited to gynecology, nor were they limited to the treatment of women exclusively; and male practitioners certainly undertook to deal with at least some gynecological problems, particularly fertility.

But the experience of actual practitioners, male or female, does not seem to have affected the view of human gestation depicted in the Aristotelian biological writings. Aristotle was as influential in his errors as in his insights. And his influence spread quickly, widely, and through orthodox religious and philosophical channels, although it was not entirely unquestioned.

Aristotelian logical method created the form of academic teaching and disputation in both philosophy and theology, the scholastic method. When a teacher or student had arrived through study at a philosophical or theological conclusion, he (there were no university women) was expected to pose a question, usually in the form, "Whether or not. . . ." He began by stating the position with which he was going to disagree. He had to list all of the possible objections to his own conclusion, supported by authoritative texts. These could not be weak arguments, but the strongest arguments possible, and he was not allowed to misrepresent or mischaracterize them. The scholar would then use a single text to question these and to serve as the hinge that turned toward his own conclusion. This text was usually introduced by the phrase *sed contra*, "but against (the preceding arguments)." The scholar then expounded his own position, citing the authoritative evidence that he had used to reach it. But even at this point, he wasn't finished; he was then obliged to refute each of the original arguments against his conclusion that he had cited in the first place.

Here is an example. In his *Commentary on the Sentences of Peter Lombard (Book II, distinction 7, question 3),* Thomas Aquinas deals with the question of whether Christians are permitted to seek the aid of demons. Aquinas begins by citing apparently authoritative texts, including one by Saint Paul, that indicate that Christians may seek the aid of demons. As a *sed contra* text, Aquinas cites Deuteronomy 18:10–12, in which God commands that all enchanters and sorcerers be executed, and a text from Augustine that those who seek demonic aid are sinners. Aquinas then concludes that those things that are beyond nature and the capacity of human faculties are to be asked only of God, and that anyone who asks from a creature (the demon) that which can only be asked of God is guilty of idolatry. Aquinas ends by refuting the original arguments that he had cited at the beginning. The scholastic method could be applied to virtually any subject or question. When used in philosophy or theology, it linked elementary Aristotelian logic with the most complex questions that could be asked—and it made academic intellectual exchange lively, disputatious, tough, and demanding.

It is against this background that the career of Albert the Great, or Albertus Magnus (1193–1280), can best be understood. Albert was born at Lauingen in Germany, entered the Dominican order, and lived at the Dominican convent in Cologne until he was sent to study in Paris in 1240, where two years later he assumed the Dominican chair of theology, which he held until 1248. From 1242 until his death, Albert virtually became the new model of a learned churchman. From Paris, he returned to Cologne to lecture at the Dominican house. He traveled up and down central Europe, from Rome to the Baltic Sea, as head of the German province of the Dominican order. He became bishop of Regensburg and served in other administrative capacities throughout Europe. He attended the Second Council of Lyons in 1274, where he defended some of the work of his greatest pupil, Thomas Aquinas, and he repeated his defense at Paris during the attacks on Aquinas associated with the condemnations of 1277. Although Albert occupies a central place in the history of medieval thought, his career was also that of a competent administrator and experimental scientist.

Albert's greatest efforts were directed at assimilating the body of Aristotle's natural philosophy into a plan of Christian learning without conflicting with revelation and dogma. To do so, Albert distinguished two spheres of knowledge. Theology, he said, dealt with supernatural things and was reached by faith; philosophy dealt with natural things and was reached by reason. Albert argued that these two kinds of knowledge and two ways of knowing were not incompatible, for they led to the same faith and the same truth. Although Albert thought that much of revelation lay outside the realm of reason, he argued that certain topics could be studied by both theology and philosophy. Albert's *Commentary on the Sentences of Peter Lombard* is one of the landmarks of thirteenth-century theology. In his later works, which tended to treat philosophy more than theology, Albert attempted to create a system of natural philosophy that could be tested by reason and experience and proved by purely rational means without dependence on revelation and theology. In at least one instance, Albert demonstrated that Aristotle was wrong, when he pointed out that, contrary to the philosopher's assertion that women had shorter lifespans than men, in Albert's own age, women tended to outlive men. By sharpening the distinction between theology and philosophy, Albert, heavily influenced by Aristotle, created one sphere in which reason could claim legitimate autonomy.

THOMAS AQUINAS AND BONAVENTURE

The new mendicant orders of the thirteenth century produced not only preachers, saints, and pastoral missions to the populations of the towns, but also scholars. By the 1250s, the theology faculty at the University of Paris was dominated by teachers who were members of these two orders. Of these, the two greatest were Thomas Aquinas, a pupil of Albert the Great, and Bonaventure, the most influential representative of Franciscan learning in the thirteenth century.

Thomas Aquinas was born around 1225 to the family of the lords of Aquino in southern Italy. He studied at the monastery of Monte Cassino from 1230 to 1239, and in the arts faculty of the University of Naples. In 1244, against his family's strong opposition, Thomas joined the Dominican order, began his theological studies under Albert the Great at Cologne, and was sent to Paris to study scripture in 1245. After his studies, he began to lecture on the text of scripture, then on Peter Lombard's *Book of Sentences,* just as Albert and other theologians had. A commentary on Peter Lombard's work was the standard doctoral thesis in theology. Aquinas' *Commentary on the Sentences* was his first great work. Although Aquinas was prepared to be received by the higher faculty of theology, both he and the Franciscan Bonaventure had to wait, because of secular masters' opposition to the rise of the orders in the university.

Bonaventure was born Giovanni di Fidanza in Italy in 1221. He took his religious name when he entered the Franciscan order around 1240, and he studied at Paris with the great English Franciscan theologian Alexander of Hales (1170–1245). After a distinguished teaching career at Paris, Bonaventure was elected minister general of the Franciscan order, became the official biographer of Francis of Assisi, and was made a cardinal in 1273. He died at the Second Council of Lyons in 1274.

Although Thomas and Bonaventure were both affected by the resentment in Paris against the rise of the mendicant orders in the theology faculties, they were not similar thinkers. Aquinas followed his teacher Albert in taking the path of Aristotle and in creating a sphere of activity in which reason was supreme and perfectly consistent with faith. Bonaventure, on the other hand, was far less an Aristotelian, adhering instead to the older tradition of Augustinian Platonism. Thomas, for example, argued that the question of whether the world was created or eternal could not be answered by reason and therefore had to be answered by faith, which stated that God had created the world. Bonaventure, on the other hand, argued that reason can and does prove that the world was created and could not be eternal. Bonaventure scorned many of the claims made on behalf of reason by the Aristotelians, and argued for the primacy of mystical knowledge.

The two thinkers also revealed their differences in their works. Those of Aquinas were chiefly either academic treatises or occasional pieces dealing with philosophy. His *Summa Against the Gentiles* was requested by Raymond of Penafort, the great Aragonese canon lawyer turned missionary, in order to provide missionaries to the Muslims with logical arguments for Christian faith that did not depend on revelation. His *Summa Theologiae* was a vast introductory textbook of both philosophy and theology, the monument to Aristotelianism in its Christian form. Bonaventure, besides his academic works, was a contemplative theologian, and his little work *The Mind's Journey to God* is a masterpiece of contemplative theology. Somewhat ironically, Bonaventure's work as minister general of the Franciscan order took him out into the world and its affairs far more than the restricted academic career of Aquinas.

The careers of Aquinas and Bonaventure reflect merely two of the many sides of the rapidly changing world of thirteenth-century thought and testify to the enduring influence of Plato, Aristotle, and Saint Augustine on that world. In spite of their differences, however, which also reflect some of the differences between their two orders, these two thinkers together suggest much of the variety and power of the philosophical revolution of the thirteenth century.

GOTHIC ENGINEERING AND ARCHITECTURE

One result of the triumph of Aristotelianism was a new degree of confidence in the assertion made by many thinkers that the created universe was intelligible in terms of geometry and mathematics. No one ever took more literally the phrase from Wisdom (11:21): "Thou hast disposed all things according to measure, number, and weight" than the architects of twelfth- and thirteenth-century western Europe. A new interest in mathematics (and the gradual adoption of Arabic numerals and mathematical place notation, especially as calculating scripts, in the late twelfth and thirteenth centuries) influenced both technology and aesthetics and carried the concept of the intelligibility of nature into yet other areas. Twelfth- and thirteenth-century thinkers and artists often considered, and sometimes pictorially represented, God as a kind of geometer-craftsman using mathematical principles and aesthetic criteria to create and providentially sustain the universe. A famous manuscript illumination of the twelfth century shows God setting out to create the world with a geometer's compass in his hand; another of the thirteenth century shows two angels rotating the universe by means of celestial cranks. Neither of these depictions is naive; both represent a courageous attempt to represent immaterial reality as analogous to rational, material principles.

This elevation of the dignity and intelligibility of the material world carried over into theology as well. The impact of Aristotelian natural philosophy and metaphysics on Christian theology was not so much a revolution as a shift in emphasis. Chapter 57 of the Benedictine *Rule* had permitted monks who were craftsmen to work at their crafts as long as they had their abbot's permission and did not take excessive pride in their work. Around 1120, Theophilus, a monk who believed in the inherent dignity of all labor dedicated to God, wrote a rational account of many artistic processes, *On the Various Arts*. Perhaps the most eloquent expression of this new respect for material creation is the sculpture on the north porch of Chartres cathedral showing a seated, infinitely compassionate and tender God molding Adam out of amorphous clay; Adam's human nature takes visible, physical shape under God's own hands. In this portrayal of creation the soul and body of a human being are undifferentiated visually. Thus, Aristotelian influences extended into theology and the arts, taking up an old strand of Christian thought.

The Faces of God: The Creation of Adam. This sculptured group, from the north porch of Chartres cathedral, is a stunning expression of the Creator's love for his creation and emphasizes its physical and material aspects. (Caisse Nationale des Monuments Historique et des Sites)

Theophilus' treatise reveals a wealth of artistic talent and rationality in the ideal monastery, but that talent was exercised chiefly in manuscript copying, illumination, painting, metal sculpture, and the coloring of glass. The greater building arts were probably beyond the capacities of a single group of monks or a single chapter of a cathedral, except for some aspects of design and later decoration of the finished church building. The achievements of Romanesque architects and engineers, however, had revolutionized architecture. In addition, other aspects of building craftsmanship had greatly improved. The increasingly professional use of geometrical principles of design, the development of complex tools such as cranes and hoists, and improved jointing work and stone dressing all contributed to the high quality of the building crafts in the twelfth and thirteenth centuries. These techniques had been developed, not only in the construction of that "white robe of churches," mentioned in Chapter 12, but also in the many roads, bridges, town and castle walls, and public buildings that had gone up in the twelfth century.

Durham Cathedral, Nave. The nave of Durham cathedral is a fine example of the transition from Romanesque to Gothic church architecture. (British Tourist Authority)

The high degree of technical expertise worked out in Romanesque church architecture was enhanced by new design elements in such Romanesque buildings as the cathedrals of Autun in France and Durham in England. At Autun (1120–1132) the pointed arch, contrasting with the round arches of traditional Romanesque style, first appeared in a major church building in western Europe. Durham cathedral (1093–1104) featured the ribbed vault. Thus, two of the most characteristic features of the style called Gothic appeared in late Romanesque churches. The third main structural element was the flying buttress, which permitted the weight of the roof to be transferred from the walls of the nave to the buttress, thus allowing the walls themselves to be made thinner with more room for windows. Modern photoelastic modeling has shown that even the elaborate stone pinnacles on many flying buttresses served to compress the stone below them in order to prevent lateral sliding.

The first church to combine these components, which permitted the height of the building to increase greatly and the structural role of walls and columns to be transformed, was the new church at the monastery of St. Denis, constructed by Abbot Suger around 1140.

The monastery of St. Denis was the religious institution associated most closely with the kings of France. Suger himself, while still abbot, was made regent of the kingdom during the absence of King Louis VII on the second crusade. The chronicles of St. Denis were the closest to an official history of the monarchy that France possessed, and St. Denis was the burial place of the Capetian dynasty. Therefore, Suger's decision to build a new church was an act of public importance; he was the regent of the kingdom, the biographer of the late King Louis VI, and one of the ablest churchmen and councillors in the kingdom. The new church was to be no mere monastic center; it was the spiritual center of royal France, a pilgrimage site, and the physical illustration of the new twelfth-century spirituality.

Suger was inspired by the great churches that most twelfth-century western Europeans knew or knew of—Hagia Sophia at Constantinople and the Temple of Solomon. As he built, almost certainly with the aid of a master builder, the inspiration of these remote buildings became embodied in a structure that employed the newest and most effective techniques that the twelfth century knew. By building the vaults on cross-ribs (arches that stretched diagonally from one column to another and crisscrossed at the center of a bay consisting of four columns), Suger was able to lighten the load of the ceiling. By using pointed arches, he was able to deflect the weight of the roof directly onto much thinner support columns. The use of these two techniques meant that the height of the church could be greatly increased and that the thick, formidable walls, piers, and columns of the Romanesque churches could be replaced with slender walls, pierced by windows and light, and slender columns, and greater interior height. The aesthetic experience was wholly different from that of the earlier Romanesque style.

The problems of organizing a large-scale building project are illuminated not only by this great new church itself but by Suger's treatise *De administratione,* in which he recounts the story of its creation. Suger tells of the decision to renovate an older, venerated monastery church and the problems of getting stone of the right quality and timbers large enough for his purposes, and of course, raising the necessary funds. Organizing the labor on this church and others like it was a considerable task. A master builder had to be found who had both the technical expertise and the managerial skills to administer the whole project. Masons, carpenters, roofers, metalworkers, glassmakers, and sculptors had to be brought together, often from great distances. For them, the work site became a living site for several years. By the mid twelfth century, practical geometry was essential, not necessarily for the patron of a project such as St. Denis but certainly for the master builder. He had to translate suggestions into sketches and mathematically perfect them by basing them on a single modular measurement, multiples and subdivisions of which became the actual measurements of the design. Sometimes other buildings besides the older church had to be demolished for a new, larger church. The entire project, from plans and early demolitions to the final dedication, could take as long as thirty years.

The Choir and South Transept of Notre Dame, Paris. The most famous, if not the most beautiful of all Gothic churches, was, like many others, an urban church. A long structure, its short transept is barely noticeable. The lowered façade, pointed arches, and great rose window are characteristic of the Gothic style. (French Government Tourist Office)

And they consumed timber and stone on an enormous scale. Many of the great churches were at least three hundred feet long. The interior arches of the cathedral of Beauvais rose to 161 feet—before they collapsed and had to be rebuilt slightly shorter at 155 feet. Until the development of structural steel, these were the highest mortared stone arches it was possible to build. Church towers, too, rose very high. The spire of Strasburg cathedral rose 466 feet from the ground. Between 1050 and 1350, several million tons of stone were quarried in France to build eighty cathedrals, 500 large churches, and tens of thousands of parish churches. More stone was quarried in France during these three centuries than at any comparable period in the history of ancient Egypt, including the period of the building of the Great Pyramid.

The organization and financing of the work, the integration of the new building with others nearby, and the quality of engineering and building techniques were striking. A finished Gothic church such as St. Denis, or the slightly later cathedrals of Chartres, Amiens, and Notre Dame, was the result not only of a new spirituality and aesthetic sense but of applied geometry, engineering, and construction skills of a very high order. Several historians have pointed out that these cathedrals and monastic churches were the first examples in the western world of monumental architecture produced by free, paid laborers. The professional dignity, literacy, and cosmopolitanism of the Gothic architects and engineers help explain the spread of Gothic architectural principles and the high regard in which the technical achievements of great builders were held.

The aesthetics and engineering of Gothic architecture are its most striking aspects to one unfamiliar with them. Less clear, but no less important, is the spiritual ideal that the aesthetics and engineering skills of the patrons and builders shaped into physical form. Beneath their high roofs, whose weight was distributed onto slender columns and external buttresses, Gothic churches were full of light. The walls were filled not with

Reims Cathedral, Façade. One of the richest Gothic facades, that of Reims cathedral, held particular meaning, since it was the church in which the kings of France were crowned. (Foto Marburg/Art Resource, NY)

thick stone and small windows, but with great windows of stained glass, providing images of light and color to those inside. The ceilings soared far higher than any most people had ever seen or could imagine. Light and the impression of fragility of the church fabric, immense height, and the delicacy of window traceries and sculpture are the aesthetic dimensions of Gothic architecture.

In twelfth-century theology, the church building was symbolic both of the Church as a whole and of paradise. The elaborately decorated west fronts of twelfth- and thirteenth-century churches were specifically designed to lead the eye and mind of those entering them into a spiritual state in which they could benefit from the experience of the liturgy. The two main features of Gothic architecture, light and the visibility of structural elements, also played a spiritual role. The light suggested the principle of creation and the gifts of the Holy Spirit; the visible structural members emphasized the order, unity, and coherence of the Church, of belief, and of the spiritual community. The dignity and majesty of the greatest Gothic churches conveyed as well the gifts and richness of a loving God. As a work of art, of engineering, and of spirituality the Gothic church illustrates the link between reason and imagination in the Gothic world.

Chartres Cathedral, Nave. The opening of the walls, the great height of the interior, and the rose window all suggest the great enthusiasm for Chartres that is reflected in literature from the twelfth century to the twentieth. (Bildarchiv Foto Marburg/Art Resource, NY)

THE KNIGHT AND THE LADY
BETWEEN GOD AND THE WORLD

The new schools and the new churches of the late twelfth and thirteenth centuries were not the only institutional expressions of reason and imagination in the Gothic world. Cities and aristocratic and royal courts also developed new cultural forms, which are reflected in the arts and literature, in building styles, and in styles of life. The ideal of behavior, status, and values among the higher and lower nobility in the late twelfth century acquired a distinctive name of its own, which appeared first in France and quickly spread to the rest of Europe: *courtois, höflich, cortese,* "courtly—in the manner of those at court." Courtly manners, ethics, dress, skills, and values grew out of, and sharply contrasted with, the rough life of the warrior and warlord. Next to the man who was brave, *preux,* there emerged the ideal of the man who was both brave and properly behaved, the *prudhomme.* By the thirteenth century, the way of life of the ideal courtier, whether wealthy lord or individual knight, was considered by such different figures as King Louis IX of France and the German poet Wolfram von Eschenbach to be the ideal noble layman's counterpart to the monk's daily round of prayer and liturgy.

But courtly life and values represented something more than a cultural style. The configuration of noble households and families was changing in the twelfth and thirteenth centuries, and political life was often savage and turbulent. The ideals of courtly behavior must be considered against a backdrop of reality that demonstrates them only as ideals that tried to glamourize these circumstances and rationalize the transition to new kinds of social and emotional dimensions of noble life.

It is necessary to consider the social reality against which the ideals of courtliness were developed and expressed. Courtly literature and books of advice either entirely ignore the lives of ordinary people with their extensive poverty, their scorned status at the very bottom of the orders of society, or the dangers that they routinely faced from brutal lay and clerical lords and their soldiers. The Latin word for "courtly," *curialis,* like the word for urban culture, *urbanus,* "urbane," were both contrasted in the twelfth, thirteenth, and fourteenth centuries with the dismissive term *rusticitas,* "rusticity," or "boorish peasant simplemindedness." Courtly literature enhanced this contrast by highly idealizing the life of the court. Reality, as people well knew, was something completely different. Even the home of court itself, the castle, in the words of one historian, consisted of:

> *Tight, gloomy spaces . . . unimaginably primitive hygenic conditions, a lack of light and heating, the absence of expert medical care, an unhealthy diet, rough table manners, degrading sexual behavior toward women: this was the reality. . . . Lordship expressed itself all too often as mere oppression and exploitation of the weak. Sales of offices and bribery were common practices. Justice was won by the person who could either pay more or who prevailed in a judicial duel through sheer brute force. Warfare was only in the slightest degree directed toward the exercise of knightly military skills—pillaging and plundering were the customary techniques.*[1]

[1]Joachim Bumke, *Courtly Culture: Literature and Society in the High Middle Ages,* trans. Thomas Dunlap (Berkeley-Los Angeles and London: University of California Press, 1991; reprint, Woodstock and New York: The Overlook Press, 2000), 2.

Courtly ideals thus constituted a counterreality, singling out individual isolated and infrequent moments in the real life of the nobility (the great court feast, the procession, the marriage ceremony, the occasion of knighting, those very rare moments when kings actually put on their crowns and displayed themselves in majesty to awed subjects, or a king's formal arrival and departure at different places on his itinerary) and implying that these were an everyday norm of social intercourse. Courtly literature did not describe what was, but how certain levels of society preferred to think about what was.

One example is the emergence of the noblewoman as the object of erotic and amatory pursuit and conquest. In many of the poems, tales, and longer romances that courtly society generated is the motif of the young man whose heart is kindled with passion, usually for the lady of his lord. Since conjugal love was thought to be more restrained than passionate, erotic love, these tales gave a respectable dimension to eroticism—coming (as it was thought to) from an uncontrollable passion generated by the vision of the feminine object on the masculine gaze. The motif indeed allows for the social and domestic superiority of the woman and the submissive status of the lover, but it also allows for the woman to subject the lover to a highly intricate code of etiquette and to set tests, which the lover fulfills and thereby earns a reward from the lady. Because of the lady's superior status and the dangers of being discovered, the lovers are compelled to an elaborately deceptive code of public behavior, although the conclusion of the lover's passionate courtship is clearly intended to be sexual.

This motif, cultivated by courtly society and written in the vernacular (and hence understandable even to those who could not read) may represent a shared fantasy of high- and lower-born members of that society and may have also served as often as a focus for proper behavior as a fantasy of knightly males who themselves would not have had wives and often had little prospect of obtaining one without their lord's support. It allowed for a temporary role reversal in the initial domineering female and the submissive male, and this reversal allowed for the depiction of psychological states and public behavior that reflected the interests and psychology of important aspects of courtly society.

Courtly society dealt with far more than experimental eroticism. The existence of courtly households required the articulation of statuses and the status, wealth, and reputation of one court over those of others. The late twelfth and thirteenth centuries saw elaborate definitions of noble status, and the development of coats of arms and rules for knightly conduct may all be regarded as manifestations of the efforts of both the higher and lower nobility to come to terms with a rapidly changing world. In the literature of these courts, a secular lay life, an ideal for knights possessing a dignity equal to that of the clergy, was first expressly enunciated. The heavy-handed fighting man of the tenth century and the greedy warlord of the eleventh, who had to do hard penance for killing and whose hopes for salvation were few, slowly turned into the knight, whose initiation into knighthood paralleled the entry into religious life of the clergy. The knight's brotherhood with all other knights discreetly obliterated real social and economic differences among the nobility. The character of a *prudhomme,* as Louis IX once observed, was so dignified and meritorious that merely to say the word "filled the mouth."

The elevation of knightly status and the elaboration of courtly culture are perhaps best reflected in the term gentleness. In the late thirteenth and early fourteenth centuries, this concept, with its complex earlier meanings in the literature of love and knightly conduct, became imbued with an ethical dignity that was close to religious virtue and constituted a major landmark in the history of social ideas and relationships. This slow process of transformation of the human concept of self had some of its roots in the changing conceptions of the relations between man and God in the devotional revolution of the eleventh and twelfth centuries, and other roots in the formulation of a secularized ideal of gentlemanly conduct. In this process, which later extended from the courts to the towns and contributed much to an increasing emphasis on human dignity, idealized courtly culture played a considerable role. The knight, like other social types, made a contribution far greater than his picturesqueness, quaintness, and archaic dignity; he helped in his own way to seek a measure of lay life that satisfied both material circumstances and the high demands of moral theology. The knight and the court, just as much as the townsman, merchant, free peasant, and ecclesiastical critic, constitute part of the variety of secular experience that established the legitimacy of lay status in early Europe. Far from being remote, idealized, picturesque institutions, the idealized courts of the thirteenth century legitimated with a new ideal of the self a life of hard activity and much insecurity. Lords, courtiers, retainers, clergy, and poets in these courts absorbed influences from the world outside and created a sense of order and ethical conduct that accommodated their own status and an increasingly secularized world.

The Latin and vernacular love poetry of the twelfth and thirteenth centuries has several themes in common with other kinds of literature, much of it originally clerical in its emphasis on self-knowledge, whether that knowledge was to be found in Peter Abelard's interest in the role of intention in judging the sinfulness or innocence of an act, or in the treatises on friendship by such monastic writers as Ailred of Riveaulx, the English Cistercian monk who turned Cicero's views on friendship into the language of twelfth-century spirituality. For the clerics, too, self-knowledge necessarily meant self-improvement. The individual who explored the inner life, whether that of the emotions or that of the conscience in confession, was regarded as superior. Theologians valued contrite repentance more than routine penance; devotional writers insisted on the emotional bonds between humans and God, not merely on the formal bonds of worship and obedience to the law. The surprising number of twelfth-century autobiographies also reflects a heightened awareness of an inner life, and thus a new kind of psychology.

Part of the new vernacular love poetry of the twelfth century can thus be understood as one further reflection of a concern for the self, its relation to others, and the changes made in it by different emotions. The sophisticated erotic poetry of southern France (along with the bawdy songs and stories that the same poets often turned out) found in the amatory emotions a topic eminently suited to the values of an aristocracy whose life and culture were changing from the harsh and blunt ideals of the eleventh century to a more mannered and stylized court life.

Birth, training, and the acceptance of a place in the retinue of a great lord made a knight; but knightly status alone was not sufficient to prove a man's quality. Certain ideal virtues had to be added to noble birth in order to make a true knight. Constancy in love, the capacity for love itself, gentleness, humility, bravery, and above all, the capacity of the "gentle" heart to experience these emotions made the nobly born knight worthy of the love of the nobly born lady. Proponents of such a view argued that love in the courtly setting indicated that the heart was gentle; a gentle heart indicated elevation above the common run of human beings. When a knight loved "gently," he became a better person, and his superiority had to be recognized by others in his society.

A literary setting different from those of the *chansons de geste* (epic poems of heroism and war like the earlier *Song of Roland*) was needed for the expression of these values. Writers began to adapt Greek and Roman stories, and then they discovered King Arthur. The legends of King Arthur, scattered obscurely through saints' lives and piecemeal histories, suddenly began to attract a great interest after the mid twelfth century, especially in the imaginative *History of the Kings of Britain,* written by Geoffrey of Monmouth around 1150. The Champagne poet Chretien de Troyes wrote a number of remarkable works in the second half of the twelfth century, in which the court of Arthur served as a focus for knightly adventures that had far more to do with what a modern critic would call the search for an identity than with battles against Saracens or endless feuds over property, privilege, and offended honor that characterized the heroic earlier *chansons de geste*. In this world of Arthurian romance, personal identity was discovered through the solution of problems posed by adventure. The court represented order, stability, established identity, and public recognition. Outside the court—in the forests, lakes, and deserts of the literary landscape—lurked the elements of temptation, disorder, uncertainty, paradox, and unintelligibility. There, outside the court, the knight discovered who he was, and his trials legitimized him when he returned to the court to tell his story. In the thirteenth century, the stories of Arthur's court expanded. The theme of the Holy Grail, introduced under Cistercian influence, reflects the elevation of knighthood to sacral status. By the early thirteenth century, the great *Prose Vulgate* had begun to piece together all the stories linked to Arthur. Versions of this work are found in most European languages. By the mid fifteenth century in England, the Arthurian corpus had become a great mine of secular themes, one that contributed political as well as emotional dimensions to Thomas Malory's great epic *Morte d'Arthur.*

The romance based on Arthurian materials expressed a spectrum of courtly concerns. Early in the thirteenth century, Gottfried von Strassburg produced the brooding *Tristan and Isolde,* which explored the tensions between loyalty to a legitimate lord and erotic passion. Among his contemporaries were the great German poets Wolfram von Eschenbach, whose *Parzival* and *Willehalm* contained new speculations on secular values and personal religious doubts, and Hartmann von Aue, whose *Der Arme Heinrich* and *Gregorius* included analyses of the layman's devotion and the conflict between role and conscience. The love lyrics of Languedoc, the center of lyric vernacular poetry in southern France, were echoed in Germany, Italy, Sicily, and England.

The history of the tenth-century explorations and settlements in Iceland and Greenland later created a Scandinavian literature of adventure and social conflict—the sagas. These are spare narratives written in the late twelfth and thirteenth centuries whose concern is often with the corrosive tensions between good intentions and unanticipated and usually tragic results. The greatest of the sagas, *The Saga of the Burning of Njall,* is easily comparable to the best of the better-known European literary works.

Scandinavian mythology, from pagan antiquity to the thirteenth century, is described in the *Eddas*, long, complex poems exploring the remote pagan Scandinavian past in the light of thirteenth century concerns. In Kievan Russia, the *Song of Igor's Campaign* was the twelfth-century counterpart to the heroic literature of Scandinavia, early Germany, northern France, and the Spain of the *Song of el Cid*.

Folk literature circulated throughout the European world. Its stories, including those from Islamic, Byzantine, and Buddhist sources, made their way into Latin as well as the vernacular literatures, and they contributed to the language of emotional discourse. In the thirteenth century, the Franciscan influence, reflected in the *Little Flowers of St. Francis*, a collection of appealing and sentimental stories about the personality of Francis of Assisi, extended to other forms of narrative. As we have seen, the new devotional revolution of the twelfth and thirteenth centuries produced different types of saints and holy men, clerical and lay, such as Bernard of Clairvaux, Thomas Becket, and Francis of Assisi. Their distinctive lives and personalities expanded the genre of biography. The lives of women saints contributed to the continued exploration of the self in an otherwise traditional genre. *Fabliaux*—comic stories that satirized both townsmen and knights—laid the foundation for the wide range of humorous and often scatological tales of the fourteenth century, particularly those of Boccaccio, Sachetti, and Geoffrey Chaucer.

There existed also a vast body of literature of which much less is known. Popular songs, tales, verses, and moralizing stories are often neglected by scholars because of their dubious value as "great literature." Yet to the historian of culture, they reflect life and interests no less than do the more formally recognized works. The collections of miracle stories of Caesarius of Heisterbach at the beginning of the thirteenth century and of saints' lives by James of Varazze at the end of the century, *The Golden Legend*, were read by Europeans for centuries. The *exempla*, moral tales used to illustrate and enliven sermons, offer frequent insights into popular life and interests. The stories, jokes, and scurrilous verses quoted in chronicles and memoirs of such thirteenth-century writers as Salimbene offer glimpses of general life that are found nowhere else. Here is Salimbene passing along a popular contemporary verse about some of the worst scourges of humanity—the flea, the gnat, and the bedbug:

> *Three awful creatures annoy and vex,*
> *Regarding no tenderness and no sex,*
> *Nailing all to the cross of their ending –x:*
> *Pulex, Cimex, Culex.*
> *In balmy weather, a constant affliction,*
> *And force can't avail, nor malediction.*
> *With a great leap, flea pulex has vanished from sight,*
> *And gnat culex escapes by its volatile flight,*
> *Bedbug cimex surely by the devil's instigation*
> *Has built-in resistance to any fumigation.*[2]

[2] *The Chronicle of Salimbene de Adam*, trans. Joseph L. Baird, Giuseppe Baglivi, and John Robert Kane (Binghamton, NY: Medieval and Renaissance Texts and Studies, 1986), 584.

From moralizing tales and popular proverbs to outright scatology, medieval vernacular literature is a widely varied and rich window into life beyond the imaginary court. For the interested reader, these materials heighten and illuminate a level of culture that is attained only incompletely in more formal documents and works of philosophy.

Perhaps two final examples will serve to illustrate. *The Song of the Nibelungs* is a thirteenth-century epic poem written in Bavaria and based on materials and events that date, in their Latin form, from the sixth and seventh centuries. It is the tale of the warrior Siegfried, his people, and his wife, Kriemhild, the sister of Gunther, Siegfried's enemy. After Gunther has arranged Siegfreid's murder, Kriemhild plots revenge, and the ensuing action draws in the whole historical and legendary world; Attila the Hun, Theoderic the Ostrogoth, and the heroes of the old Latin and German sagas all appear. Yet the Nibelung poet does not revel in the wealth of legend, literary tradition, folklore, and violence he presents, but relentlessly focuses the action and diversity in a masterly way on the theme of Kriemhild's revenge. The classification of this work somewhere among the heroic sagas, *chansons de geste,* and romances reflects both the high command of literary skill that had been reached throughout Europe by the thirteenth century and the complex relationships between medieval vernacular literature and early European society.

The Song of the Nibelungs preserves some of the older aspects of heroic literature while emphasizing many of the newer—particularly in its depiction of Kriemhild's psychology. Another work, written around the same time in France, shows another side of courtly values. Around 1235, a French poet named Guillaume de Lorris wrote the first 4000 lines of a poem that he called *The Romance of the Rose.* The poem was in the popular form of a dream-vision, in which the poet dreams he is in a garden peopled by personifications of human behavioral traits—characters with such names as Sir Mirth, the lord of the garden, his lady Dame Gladness, and a helpful figure named Fair-Welcome. The dreamer falls in love with a rose in the heart of the garden (the symbol of a young woman), but his attempts to reach the Rose are blocked by the personified vices of Shame and Jealousy. These abstractions in the allegorical garden are in one sense all part of a refined analysis of the psychological state of what the author considered the proper way of falling in love.

The Romance of the Rose was immensely popular throughout the thirteenth century. At the end of the century, another poet, Jean de Meun, completed the poem with another 18,000 lines. But the approaches of the two poets were remarkably different. Guillaume de Lorris was a gentle idealist. His figures are painted lightly and gracefully, and the theme of proper love is morally linked to the theme of the proper social life. Jean de Meun, however, knew other kinds of twelfth- and thirteenth-century thought, and his long continuation of the poem drew upon the methods and interests of academic and legal culture as well. Personifications of various psychological states and human attributes give long and contradictory speeches and argue violently. At the end of the poem, after a military siege of the Rose's castle, described by a master of the language of military siege tactics (Jean de Meun had also translated the fourth-century Roman military manual by Vegetius, the *De re militari,* into French), the Lover wins the Rose, and elevated though they are by the literary courtship, the conclusion is clearly sexual.

Jean de Meun brought a different mind and different values to the elegant poem of Guillaume de Lorris. It is nevertheless striking that the courtly setting, developed by twelfth-century poets and continued by thirteenth-century romancers, became an appropriate and effective setting for his scholastic diatribe.

The *Song of the Nibelungs* and *The Romance of the Rose* encompass a wide range of thirteenth-century courtly literature. Its knightly characters, caught between God and the world, developed an ethos that appeared for a time to satisfy the demands of both, based as it was upon the creative power of love, personal loyalty and conduct, and devotion to God. Even though other cultural values soon clamored for recognition in different settings, courtly literature survived until the eighteenth century. In it, the European aristocracy had found its perfect mirror.

COURT AND CITY IN THE WORLD OF DANTE ALIGHIERI

Others besides the courtly nobility found new sets of values in the twelfth and thirteenth centuries, sometimes adapting courtly values for themselves. In northern Italy, France, Flanders, and Germany townspeople created a distinctly urban culture, the liveliest manifestations of which are the large cities of northern Italy—in Lombardy, Tuscany, and Venetia. The term that people used to describe this new urban culture—the *vita civile,* or civic life—is as important as the new courtly culture. Like that culture, with which it shared many values, the *vita civile* represented a predominantly lay approach to the definition and ordering of the good life.

The cities of northern Italy present a variegated picture at the turn of the fourteenth century. They differed widely in size and constitutional structure, in dependence upon or alliance with other, more powerful towns, in financial, commercial, and diplomatic affairs, in the degree of city control of social and economic life both within the city walls and in the rural area surrounding the city—the *contado,* with its peasant communities of sharecroppers and tenant farmers—in the degree of civic consciousness, and in levels of education and artistic patronage. They were small societies, but their inhabitants were densely packed together, and the degree of political energy required to mobilize their resources and conduct policy, their high consciousness of the dangers of the surrounding world, and their attempts to control ecclesiastical authority all reflect their precocious development as political societies. The wealth brought in from trade, industry, and finance, the necessity of having a "foreign" policy and a militia, the needs of public financing, and the sense of independence reflected by the phrase of a later lawyer, "the city, a prince unto itself," made many of these cities resemble later kingdoms. The political instability and constitutional crises to which the cities were usually prone reflect not so much political immaturity as political creativity. After the church, the northern Italian towns may be said to have created the first European protostates.

Population and economic growth, the long struggles for independence, and the very experience of living within the physical city contributed to the development of an urban culture that expressed itself in various ways, from education to history writing, from architecture to public ceremonies. The necessities of town government produced the great town halls and walls that still survive in many of even the smallest towns, as do the carefully planned and maintained public squares. Pride in the physical appearance of the city dates from very early in communal history, and statutes protecting its physical fabric and quality of life, from measures concerning hygiene to those dealing with aesthetics, appear in the statute books of many towns. When Venetians decided that glassmakers were making the town air unfit to breathe, the city ordered the entire industry to move across the lagoons to Murano, where it remains today. The towns were responsible, too, for church building. Citizen committees raised the finds, managed the work, and commissioned the artists who decorated the churches. The contacts many cities had with Byzantium and the east and with France and the north and west brought many diverse influences into the towns, and those contributed to the selection and planning of buildings and the artistic themes embodied in them. The cities knew and hired individual artists by reputation, and many of the greatest works of Duccio di Boninsegna, Arnolfo di Cambio, and Giotto were done on civic commissions. The decoration of churches expressed the spiritual values of the town, and the decoration of public buildings expressed the town's sense of its own history and self-image.

There is no more striking example of the liveliness of urban artistic patronage than the series of frescoes produced by Ambrogio Lorenzetti in the Palazzo Publico of Siena in 1338–1340. His frescoes on the subject of good and bad government, the city of war and the city of peace, offer a vast and extraordinarily detailed exposition of the self-image of the city of Siena. Theological personifications and political abstractions are set against a highly intricate depiction of the life of the city and its inhabitants, from masons and carpenters to farmers, traders, hunters, and governing officials. Outdoors, in the towns themselves, fountains, piazzas, public buildings, streets, and bridges provided opportunities for the city to enhance its beauty and reinforce visually and physically the sense of belonging to a well-ordered society.

Ideas, artistic and literary styles, and new forms of urban devotion were other contributors to the *vita civile*. The courts of southern France and of Frederick II of Sicily gave birth to literary influences that, adapted by urban Italian poets, shaped the *dolce stil nuovo*, "the sweet, new style," in which amatory, ethical, and philosophical themes were blended in Italian vernacular poetry of a very high order. Lively satirical lyrics and short tales found eager audiences in the towns. So did the stories about Francis of Assisi and his followers, as well as the Latin and vernacular town histories that began to appear early in the thirteenth century. The earliest and one of the greatest of these was the *Chronicle* written by the Franciscan Salimbene of Parma about the personalities and events of his day—and his often very strong opinions about them. At the end of the thirteenth century, Dino Compagni (1266–1324) of Florence wrote a *Chronicle of Events Occurring in His Own Time*, a vivid account of personalities and political crises in Florence at the end of the thirteenth and beginning of the fourteenth centuries. The Florentine merchant, Giovanni Villani (1270–1348), wrote a *Chronicle* of Florentine and world history that constitutes an important landmark in the lay writing of history.

This lively cultural world appealed to the eyes, ears, and especially the minds of townspeople in the thirteenth and fourteenth centuries, and it appealed to their spirits as well. Eminent laymen listened to lectures in the Dominican church of Santa Maria Novella in Florence or the Franciscan church of Santa Croce. These two great churches, the cathedral of Santa Maria dei Fiore, and the third circle of the city walls of Florence were all built in the lifetime of Dante Alighieri (1265–1321), the greatest of all Italian poets and men of letters. At the turn of the fourteenth century, cities such as Florence had an air not of antiquity but of striking modernity. The new fabric of Florence literally went up and took shape under the eyes of the writers, artists, and preachers who were the most eloquent praisers and critics of the city and its life. Old, narrow streets were widened; cramped, poor neighborhoods were torn down to make room for spacious public squares; small, old family houses were replaced by new family palaces, and the towers of the nobles, when they caused too much political trouble at the wrong time, were dramatically leveled to the ground.

Associations for the building of churches, drinking and gaming clubs, youth associations, craft guilds, literary circles, and religious confraternities—communal organizations of piety—divided and subdivided the social and cultural life of the towns. By the fourteenth century, the life of the city had come to include distinctively urban forms of religious devotion. The culture of the townsman as well as the culture of the knight and noble acquired a spiritual dimension that enhanced the secular activities that sustained the worlds of court and city.

No single figure represents—indeed transcends—the cultural world of the northern Italian towns more strikingly than Dante Alighieri, and no single literary or artistic work reflects the intellectual and political movements between 1150 and 1300 in greater detail and artistic force than his great poem, *The Comedy* (the adjective "Divine" was added by a much later commentator on the poem). Dante was born in 1265 to a family that claimed descent from earlier Florentine nobility but had recently come down in the world, although in Dante's youth his father had experienced a brief period of economic prosperity through moneylending. But its status certainly remained modest, indicated by Dante's marriage to Gemma di Manetto, a member of only a minor branch of the princely Donati family who brought a very small dowry with her. But even minimal social respectability afforded many opportunities to Florentine citizens. Dante was able to afford to pursue a course of literary studies, probably in Florence, and in 1289, he fought in the cavalry arm of the Florentine militia in its defeat of the rival city of Arezzo at the battle of Campaldino. By that date, his earliest literary work, several lyric poems, had attracted the attention of a talented and influential group of Florentine writers, and his friendships with poets in other cities and with the great noble Florentine lyric poet Guido Cavalcanti, and the encyclopedist Brunetto Latini date from these years.

Dante was thus exposed both to a wide literary circle and to the new sensibility expressed in contemporary love lyrics. In his own life, a young woman, presumably Bice Portinari, later the wife of Simone dei Bardi, a prominent citizen of Florence, became his ideal; after her death in 1290, Dante wrote a short account of her role in his personal spiritual and intellectual development in verse and prose, *La Vita Nuova* (The New Life), which he completed in 1292. Not only are the verses in this work the indication of a major poetic talent, but the development of Bice into Beatrice, Dante's own spiritual guide, foreshadows her role in the *Comedy* and represents a highly original transformation of the older courtly motif of passionate love between a man and a woman—this time into a powerful spiritual force through which the woman raises the man spiritually to heights he would be unable to achieve without her.

Dante's development during this period was not solely that of a poet and philosopher. Between 1295 and 1300, he was elected to various high political offices in Florence and, like other men of letters, he enrolled in the guild of apothecaries and physicians. Membership in a guild was essential for holding political office, and there is no evidence that Dante was ever a practicing pharmicist or physician.

The constitutional life of Florence became highly unstable during Dante's terms of public service. In many Italian cities, groups of local political rivals identified themselves in terms of the rival groups of supporters of popes or emperors in the conflicts of the twelfth and thirteenth centuries. Nominal supporters of the popes called themselves Guelfs (after the Welf family), and nominal supporters of the emperors called themselves Ghibellines (after the battle cry of the Staufer dynasty, "*Waiblingen!*" the name of one of their castles). In most cases, however, what divided rivals within a city were local political interests rather than the larger-scale issues of papal-imperial relations. Most cities were either entirely Guelf or entirely Ghibelline. After several experiments and revolts, Florence had become a Guelf city shortly after Dante was born, and it remained Guelf. But in the late 1290s, two rival groups within the city began to call themselves White and Black Guelfs, and the White Guelfs often allied themselves with Ghibelline cities and other groups of White Guelfs in other cities. Dante became increasingly sympathetic to the White Guelf cause, especially in light of the dangers he and others perceived from the territorial ambitions of Pope Boniface VIII. Boniface, the Black Guelfs of Florence, and the royal house of France were involved in complex intrigues, and Dante's term as one of the six priors, the highest governmental offices in the city, between June and August 1300, revealed to him the dangers that the city faced. In 1301, while Dante was serving as a representative of the Florentine government in Rome, the Black Guelfs, supported by Boniface VIII and the French prince Charles of Valois, seized power in Florence, attacked their enemies, and banished Dante from the city in absentia, citing several charges of political corruption on his part that would have resulted in his execution had he returned.

From 1302 to 1304, Dante wandered throughout northern Italy, serving as an adviser to the exiled White Guelf faction in its quest to restore itself to power in Florence. However, Dante broke with his fellow exiles, whose shortsightedness, greed, and self-interest he later denounced bitterly in the *Comedy*. Between 1304 and 1310, he wandered even more widely, moving from court to court and aristocratic patron to aristocratic patron, experiencing the pain of exile, separation from his family, and the fitful patronage of local princes. The early years of his exile produced the unfinished treatise on the Italian vernacular, *De vulgari eloquentia*, and the long, unfinished collection of philosophical poems and prose commentaries, *Il Convivio* (The Banquet).

When the emperor Henry VII (r. 1310–1313) descended into Italy in the hope of restoring order to the faction-ridden cities, Dante joined his cause and became a spokesman of nonpartisan imperial rule. Dante's letters on behalf of Henry VII contain a distinctly prophetic strain, as if Henry VII were the last hope for peace in Italy, and his later letters, written when Henry had died and his cause had failed, contain bitter denunciations of those whom Dante held responsible not only for the emperor's failure but for the chaos of Italian life. Dante had reached the idea that without social and political order in the world, the opportunities for ordinary people to lead virtuous active lives were greatly diminished. Dante thus identified a just political order with the economy of salvation, a theme echoed in the *Comedy.*

From 1310 to his death in September, 1321, Dante lived at the courts of various patrons, most notably that of Can Grande della Scala at Verona and that of Guido da Polenta at Ravenna, where he died after a diplomatic mission to Venice, and where he is buried. During the last decade of his life, and possibly earlier, he worked on the *Comedy,* a vast vision of hell, purgatory, and heaven in which he organized and analyzed the events and personalities of his life and his time with a vast intelligence and one of the greatest poetic voices the world has ever known.

The first section, or *cantica,* of the poem, *Inferno,* opens on Good Friday in the year 1300 with a character named Dante, who has lost his moral bearings and finds himself in a dark forest, his way blocked by savage animals. The spirit of the Roman epic poet Vergil appears and informs Dante that he had been on the verge of death and damnation when a woman in heaven, Beatrice, had asked Vergil to lead Dante back to life and the right moral path. Their journey leads down through all the levels of Hell, depicted as a perverted upside-down city, until they reach the awful lake of ice at the very botton, in which the monstrous, three-headed Satan is imprisoned. Dante's use of a pagan poet for such a Christian purpose was audacious, and Vergil may be understood in part to represent human reason and will unaided by divine grace—that is, the qualities that human beings themselves can develop on their own, whether Christians or not.

After climbing down the sides of Satan (and observing that they had somehow begun to climb *upwards* after they had passed the center of the earth), Vergil and Dante ascend a narrow tunnel that brings them out onto the shores of an island set in the southern ocean, and the second *cantica,* the *Purgatorio,* begins. Purgatory, too has its surprises: Its guardian is the pagan Roman suicide, Cato the Younger, whom Dante sees as a symbol of the freedom of human moral choice. Vergil and Dante then climb the great mountain of Purgatory, each of whose levels purges one of the seven deadly sins. When they reach the top, Vergil disappears, and as Dante steps into the Garden of Eden, the Earthly Paradise, he meets Beatrice, who becomes his guide in the third *cantica,* the *Paradiso.* After they move through the heavens, Dante is afforded a direct vision of God, and the poem ends. Throughout the *Comedy,* Dante encounters hundreds of characters, including devils, centaurs, monsters, demons, Satan, saints, historical figures, angels, giants, and finally, when Bernard of Clairvaux has taken Beatrice's place as his guide, the vision of God. There is nothing in any literature quite like the *Comedy,* so it can hardly be called typical of anything except the genius of a particular poet, philosopher, and prophet who cried out against the injustice of his world and offered in its place a setting of perfect justice and the perfecting of human nature.

Dante attempted to negotiate with Florence several times for his return to the city, but the parties never reached terms that Dante could accept. His exile and pilgrimage became for him a metaphor of injustice. *Exul immeritus,* "an undeserving exile," he called himself, condemning in passionate and eloquent language the disorder of justice that in his vision prevented humankind from governing itself properly. One of his last works, written in 1217, was a philosophical defense of the necessity of a world emperor, the *De Monarchia,* "The Treatise on Monarchy." From his exile there emerged the great poem that embodies his visionary genius. Citizen, scholar, man of letters, philosophical lover, and exile, Dante illuminates, not as a type but as a distinctive, compelling individual, the life of the cities in which he lived and the force of the culture that he shared and helped shape.

PART VI CHRISTENDOM AND EUROPE, 1325–1500

17

Apocalypse Then? Crisis and Recovery in the Thirteenth and Fourteenth Centuries

THE FOUR HORSEMEN OF THE APOCALYPSE AND PROPHETIC CHRISTIANITY

The book of *Apocalypse,* or *Revelations,* the last canonical book of the Christian Bible, describes a vivid scenario of the end time of the world, the second coming of Christ, and the last judgment. Although Christians were certain that the events described in the Apocalypse were going to happen, they also knew that they were not permitted to predict when they would occur. But the scenario also contained signs that could be interpreted by the wise, and periodically some writers and preachers professed to see the signs of the end in their own time or in the immediate future. One of the most striking images of the Apocalypse was that of the Four Horsemen who were let loose to afflict the earth. Scriptural commentators identified them as death, famine, pestilence, and war. The art of the fourteenth and fifteenth centuries abounds with depictions of these figures, and pictorial representations of the last judgment appear in large numbers in the twelfth and thirteenth. From the fourth century, other nonscriptural elements came to be added to the final scenario, one of the most influential of which was the figure of the Antichrist, whose persecutions would herald the beginning of the end. Another was the idea of the ferocious peoples of Gog and Magog, who were thought to have been confined in the distant east by Alexander the Great, but would break out and swarm into the west as another sign of the end times.

In addition, other prophecies and legends began to circulate that implied both threats and assistance from the world outside western Europe. In the mid twelfth century, there appeared the legend of "Prester John" (John the Priest), a Christian king originally located in Asia, and later in Ethiopia, who would lead his people against Muslim forces. The legend appears to have been based on an actual ruler in Asia, many of whose subjects were Nestorian Christians. Like the prophecies and legends, a number of events of the thirteenth and early fourteenth centuries made it seem to many Europeans that the signs of the end now abounded, for some of them were indeed ariving from the legendary ends of the earth.

THE SILK ROAD AND THE ROADS OF WAR

Until the thirteenth century, most Europeans shared the sketchy idea of the wider Eurasian, Indian, and African worlds beyond Europe and the Mediterranean that had characterized late Roman geography and ethnography. They also applied what knowledge they had in speculating on such problems as the size and shape of the earth, its habitable and uninhabitable areas, that had emerged from centuries of commentary on the book of Genesis. For instance, they believed that the equatorial zone was so hot that humans could not pass through it into the southern hemisphere. Therefore, since Jesus had come to save all peoples, it was not possible that humans could inhabit the southern hemisphere. Within the habitable northern hemisphere, however, there were many different peoples, as well as wonders and monsters, many of them also drawn from the literary tradition of Pliny, Strabo, and other Roman sources. Some came from the twelfth-century revival of interest in the legends and tales of Alexander the Great. These images of monstrous and mysterious peoples survived into the seventeenth century; as the world became more familiar, Europeans simply relocated the monstrous races into more distant and unreached parts of the earth. The tradition was still lively in Shakespeare's day, when Othello told of,

> . . . my travels' history,
> Wherein of antres vast and deserts idle,
> Rough quarries, rocks, and hills whose heads touch heaven,
> It was my hint to speak—such was the process;
> And of the Cannibals, that each other eat,
> The Anthropophagi, and men whose heads
> Do grow beneath their shoulders.

Such creatures also survived in literature, particularly travel accounts and instructional literature, long after the fifteenth century. When Gerald of Wales (ca. 1146–1223) wrote his *History and Topography of Ireland* around 1185, for example, he made a point of including Irish wonders and marvels for the edification of King Henry II of England, since geography, even fabulous geography, was one of the subjects considered suitable for a king's learning and amusement.

The only truly impressive body of geographical knowledge developed between the ninth and the thirteenth centuries, that of Muslim geographers, was unknown in western Europe. For many learned men, geography was a minor subdivision of theology, teaching that Jerusalem was the center of the world, that Europe occupied precisely one quarter, Africa another quarter, and Asia a half. They thought that Africa was much shorter north to south than it is, and that it was connected by land to India in its southern parts. The Mediterranean Sea and the Nile and Don Valleys neatly divided the sections of the world in such a way as to distinguish the three parts of the earth by drawing the waters that separated them in the shape of a letter T within the large circle representing River Ocean that surrounded all the lands. The resulting T-O maps constituted the basis of symbolic geographical knowledge.

But from the thirteenth century on, Europeans' knowledge of geography became distinctly less fabulous as the rest of Eurasia emerged, at first militarily, then economically, into European awareness. Europe's new geography lesson may be considered in terms of three elements: the Silk Road, the steppe peoples from northern China to the Black Sea, and the creation of the Mongol empire.

The western and eastern ends of the Eurasian land mass are characterized by the forests and plains of western Europe and the coastal forests of China. Between these forested areas there extends a series of very different geophysical and climatic areas. From the Tropic of Cancer to the Arctic Circle, south to north, central Eurasia consists of a series of hot deserts, mid-latitude deserts, a belt of steppe grasslands, coniferous forests, and the bleak tundra of northern Siberia. In those areas where the desert touches the grasslands are some of the world's highest mountains, driest deserts, the most extreme winter and summer temperatures on earth, and a string of oases that enabled merchants and pilgrims to move from east to west and west to east from at least as early as 1000 B.C.E. These were also the areas in which sedentary agricultural societies interacted with the nomadic steppe pastoralists.

The string of oases and trading cities and the many roads that linked them are called the Silk Road, since silk was the most valuable product that was transported from China to the West, although many other things also traveled with it. The earliest silk found in Egypt dates from around 1000 B.C.E., and the first in western Europe from around 700 B.C.E. The Silk Road, which actually consists of different sets of routes that flourished at different times, extended from Chang-an in northern China to Baghdad and the Black Sea. The routes shifted because of periodical political dangers and also because of the attraction of different markets at different times. Although silk, gold, and paper were the best-known products, since the high risks of such travel made higher-value goods the most profitable, agricultural developments, technologies, religious beliefs, and ideas all traveled the routes with them.

The Silk Road was most safely traversed by large caravans drawn by horses, mules, and donkeys, and, in the deserts, camels. Some historians have called these caravans moving cities, traveling around thirty miles per day, traveling, often with military escorts, along well-known routes, stopping at familiar oases, trading at each, restocking themselves, then moving on to the next oasis, or *caravanseray*. Since caravans provided the safest means of travel, diplomatic missions were often attached to them, as were traveling craftsmen, artists, scholars, translators, missionaries, and pilgrims.

Along these routes, and by means of the great caravans, many religions spread out across Eurasia as well. Buddhism spread from India to China, especially during the seventh century. After the centers of Nestorian Christianity (above, Chapter 4) were absorbed into the Sasanid Persian empire, Nestorian communities moved east with Persian culture, so that Christians who arrived in central and east Asia in the thirteenth century found other Christians already there, strengthening the rumors about Prester John. When Islamic armies conquered Persia in the mid seventh century, Islam, too, moved with merchants and political rulers eastward along the Silk Road and ultimately came to dominate it.

From earliest recorded history, a number of political societies in these areas acquired land and power and then were absorbed into newer polities. The Sogdians in Uzbekistan were absorbed by the Caliphate of Baghdad in the eighth century; in the ninth century, the Uighur Khanate dominated the area to the south of Lake Baikal; in the tenth century, Samanid rulers controlled the land eastward from Khorasan through Transoxiana to Fergana; in the eleventh century, the vast Ghaznavid empire ruled from the Caspian Sea to Kabul in modern Afghanistan and Delhi in India. Around 1200, the Ghurid empire extended from Nishapur to the Bay of Bengal, creating the Muslim Sultanate of Delhi, which transformed the world of Hindu India. Occasionally, Chinese rulers exerted considerable power from the eastern end of the Silk Road, although the Chinese defeat by a Muslim army at Talas in 751 limited Chinese influence to the east of the Tarim Basin. The travelers along the Silk Road had to know where political and military power lay ahead of them and around them.

The strongest forces in this world, however, were the armies of the steppe nomads. At the western end of the steppe belt we have met some of them already (above, Chapter 9)—Pechenegs, Bulgars, Magyars, Cumans, and the Khazars, whose khanate was broken by the combined forest-steppe power of the Kievan Rus in the late tenth century. But later Kievan princes had to deal with newer steppe peoples, the Kipchak, comprised of Cumans and Polovtsii, in the early twelfth century. In the Islamic world, the rise of the Seljuk Turks brought the same kind of warriors into the caliphate of Baghdad in the eleventh century (above, Chapter 12).

The most powerful of all the steppe peoples, however, were the Mongols. All steppe military societies of any size were confederations of many groups, unstable systems of alliances of lords and their followers, whose composition and loyalty shifted frequently. One such federation, that of the Mongols, was put together by a young leader originally named Temüjin (ca. 1165–1227), and in 1206 acclaimed by his followers as Chinggis (or "Universal") Khan. Having come to power by securing the loyalty of his followers by generosity and the capitulation of his enemies by terror, Chinggis Khan reorganized the Mongol armies, so that the military unit and not the small tribe held the soldier's first loyalty. The Mongol army of around 130,000 men under ninety-five commanders launched military campaigns only after careful planning, having collected detailed intelligence concerning enemy strength and weakness, and their own tactical movements were closely cordinated by means of couriers and signal arrows. The armies were composed of heavily armed cavalry and larger numbers of tough, well-trained, ordinary soldiers, lightly armed with spears and strong, compound bows. Their tactics were marked by tough internal discipline, coordination of different kinds of forces, and continuous movement—if Chinggis Khan had not kept the new armies occupied with expansion, they would probably have turned on each other. Military techniques that were not originally possessed by nomadic steppe armies, notably siegecraft, were learned as the armies moved.

In 1209, Chinggis launched an attack on the Hsia-Hsia of northwest China. He attacked and conquered much of northern China itself in 1215. In 1219, Chinggis turned his armies into central Asia, reaching Bukhara in 1220 and Samarkand shortly after. Cities and princes who surrendered to the Mongols were usually spared, but those that resisted were destroyed, their inhabitants killed or enslaved, and their property looted. The calculated news of Mongol terror worked in Chinggis' favor; as a Mongol army approached, their opponents knew very well what would be the consequences of unsuccessful resistance. In 1223, a Mongol army crossed the Caucasus mountains, defeated a coalition of Kipchak and Rus forces, and Chinggis then turned back east toward China, where he died in 1227.

He was succeeded by his chosen son Ogodei (r. 1228–1241), who completed the conquest of northern China by 1234 and then turned his forces west, defeating a large Kipchak army in 1235, sending the remnants fleeing into Hungary, where they received permission to settle. Ogodei's forces then turned against the Rus in 1237/8, using newly learned siegecraft against the cities of Ryazan, Moscow, and Vladimir. Moving south, they captured Kiev in 1240. The army then divided, one branch moving into Poland, where it defeated an army of Poles and Teutonic Knights at Liegnitz in 1241, and a second invading Hungary, whose king, Bela IV, it defeated in the same year. News of the horrors of Mongol tactics preceded them rapidly. Many sources observe that no one knew anything about the Mongols, neither whence they came nor why. Some sources had it that they were indeed the peoples of Gog and Magog, released from their prison in deepest Asia and let loose on Christian Europe as one of the signs of the end time.

When news of the death of Ogodei reached the Mongol commanders in the west in 1242, they moved their armies back east to settle the succession. Their departure from central and eastern Europe, however, probably also had to do with the new kinds of terrain that they encountered. Although Mongol armies were the most powerful in the world, they also depended on open grasslands and a large supply of horses for remounts, and the steppe pastures ended in Hungary. It is doubtful that the Mongols could have sustained a military campaign of several years in the more heavily forested lands of western Europe.

The succession to Ogodei was debated and fought over until 1251, when his son Mongke succeeded and sent his brother Hulagu into Persia, where Hulagu destroyed Baghdad in 1258, killing the last Abbasid caliph. Although the Mongol advance into Syria was halted by their defeat at the hands of the Mamluk sultans of Egypt at the battle of Ayn Jalut in 1260, they did establish the Ilkhanate of Persia and Iraq. At the same time, the armies of Mongke and his brother Khubilai began the conquest of southern

Sung China, which was completed in 1279. Khubilai began the building of the new capital at Beijing. Mongol rule in China lasted until the rise of the Ming dynasty in 1360. The Mongol khanates in Persia and Russia lasted until the fifteenth century.

The achievements of Mongol armies in the west attracted the attention and concern of both popes and kings. Pope Innocent IV (1243–1254) dispatched the Dominican friar Giovanni del Pian Carpine to the Great Khan on a remarkable diplomatic mission in 1245–1247, which the diplomat recorded in a detailed and fascinating text. King Louis IX of France dispatched the friar William of Rubruck in 1253–1255. Other papal emissaries followed, and their reports began to provide western Europeans with information concerning the east that circulated widely. The work of Giovanni del Pian Carpine was written into the large universal history by Vincent of Beauvais shortly after his return; the great thirteenth-century English chronicler Matthew Paris included it; and even the chronicle of Salimbene repeated some of it.

Since the Mongols ruled Eurasia from Persia and Russia to the China Sea, they imposed a tough, orderly rule across their lands, established efficient courier services, and permitted free travel and religious proselytizing. A stream of legates, missionaries and merchants followed Pian Carpine into central and eastern Asia after 1247. As early as 1260, two Venetian brothers, Maffeo and Nicolo Polo, left the Venetian settlement in the Crimea and traveled with their merchandise to the Mongol court at Sarai on the Volga River. They then made their way to Bukhara, and in the company of one of Khubilai Khan's envoys, to Shangtu in China. In 1269, they returned to the west with messages and gifts from Khubilai to the pope. They took their son and nephew, Marco, on another journey to China, which they reached for the second time in 1275. The Polo brothers had begun as merchants, but their first experience in China turned them into gentleman ambassadors.

After spending eighteen years in China, Marco Polo returned to Italy in 1295, a year after the Franciscan John of Monte Corvino arrived in Beijing, whose first Christian bishop he became in 1307. Marco settled in Venice as a moderately wealthy citizen. During a war between Venice and Genoa in the late 1290s, Marco was captured and imprisoned in Genoa until 1299. While in prison, Marco Polo shared a cell with a down-at-heel writer of chivalric romances, Rustichello of Pisa, and he told Rustichello about his adventures in China. Rustichello, never one to miss a good story, wrote up Marco's stories in a book, called *The Divisions of the World,* which became popularly known as *Il Milione,* "The Million," because of the fabulous wealth it described. Two centuries later, when Christopher Columbus began to make his plans to reach China by sailing westward, he knew the book.

The Mongol wars had been followed by the "Mongol peace" which opened eastern Asia to western Europeans for the first time and familiarized them with it. In 1340, Francesco Balduccio Pegolotti wrote a treatise on commerce commonly called *La practica della mercatura.* "The Practice of Business," in which he described very soberly and confidently all the things a merchant needed to know in order to do business in Mongol territories, from the steppes north of the Black Sea to China. The work included a remarkable description of the overland route, which Pegolotti found to be much more secure than it had ever been before or ever has been since.

After the middle of the fourteenth century, however, the increasingly unstable political conditions in central and eastern Asia associated with the rise of the Ming dynasty in China and the empire of the Ottoman Turks in the west (below, Chapter 20), reduced the appeal of direct travel to Asia over lands and seas no longer controlled by friendly or at least neutral rulers. As the Mongol window slowly closed, however, the memory of China remained powerful, and it remained in European minds for the next two centuries.

As terrible as the Mongols had usually been, and continued to be in Russia and Persia for the next two centuries, they had clearly also not been the peoples of Gog and Magog or the Four Horsemen of the Apocalypse. But in the fourteenth century, other candidates for that title appeared.

THE BLACK HORSEMAN: HUNGER

I looked, and there was a black horse! Its rider held a pair of scales in his hand, and I heard what seemed to be a voice in the midst of the four living creatures saying, "A quart of wheat for a day's pay, and three quarts of barley for a day's pay. (Rev. 6:5–6)

The mild climate that Europe had enjoyed since 100 B.C.E., began to change in the thirteenth century. This did not mean instantly colder temperatures, shorter summers, and more severe winters. The signs of change came, rather, in increasingly unpredictable weather patterns. Extremely good years were followed by inexplicably bad ones; a series of heavy rains that rotted crops and leached the earth might last for several years, to be followed by improved weather for a decade or more; intermittent severe conditions might freeze or inundate vineyards and grain fields for a season or two. Under such conditions, seedbeds were washed away, fields submerged, grain rotted, fish traps were wrecked, dikes were washed away, meadows became too wet to mow, turf too soggy for cutting and impossible to dry, and quarries flooded. Good land became sodden and produced few crops; marginal land became impossible to work.

The effects of such changes were felt most quickly in the former marginal lands that required intensive cultivation and whose margin of productivity was small in the best of times. Famine had been a constant danger, even in periods of prosperity, and from 1290 on, it appears to have occurred more regularly. Although from 1309 to 1314, extremely poor crops and a series of long, destructive rains posed a threat of famine in a few places, the general shortage of food everywhere and the immediate impact of climatic change on marginal land mark the first of the fourteenth-century crises. The tenuous balance between population and agricultural productivity was particularly threatened. As a result of earlier population growth, farm size was reduced as parents divided their land among more children. Rents increased as landlords encouraged tenants to compete for available land. The yield-to-seed ratio of even the best-tended and most productive fields was relatively low, and even a small decline in that ratio had serious consequences for the total agricultural output of a region. Modern yield-seed ratios are around 200:1 or 300:1; an excellent thirteenth-century ratio would be 10:1, and the usual would be 3:1. On lands requiring intensive labor for prevention of erosion or maintenance of drainage, a higher population level was needed than elsewhere; agricultural output had to remain high if it was to sustain that population.

The famine was greatest from 1315 to 1317. Grain prices soared astronomically. Regions that depended on distant places for their food suffered a drastic population loss—as high as 10 percent in some towns, and the yield-to-seed ratio fell, in some cases by half. The 1315/17 famine was the greatest that Europe experienced, but it was not the only one. The fragile agricultural system, even if it had achieved its potential output, had nevertheless proved incapable of feeding Europe without profound revision. Moreover, nearly every succeeding decade of the fourteenth century witnessed either regional or more widespread famine, and hunger became a universal and perennial scourge for the first prolonged period since the end of antiquity. Farms and whole villages were often abandoned.

Hungry people die or move. In the fourteenth century, land that could no longer be worked—because of soil exhaustion, population loss, the ravages of war, or the frequency and extent of pestilence—was abandoned. The fourteenth century produced an increasing number of deserted farming settlements, many of which were never settled again. People moved to monasteries, towns, or more productive regions, there to seek food through charity, wage labor, or the assumption of servile status. The migrations provoked by famine raised other problems. The new arrivals could contribute little to the quality of town or city life, and they strained urban food supplies. As we will see later in this chapter, fourteenth and fifteenth century warfare also disrupted agricultural life. And on the heels of famine and war followed pestilence.

The dangers of reduced harvests, rising grain prices, and widespread famine are many. Death by starvation is not the only consequence of famine, nor is it the most far-reaching. Early Europeans knew little about the different properties of foods, and medieval nutrition was barely adequate even in the best of times. The wealthy tended, even as late as the seventeenth century, to eat more animal protein and fewer vegetables than they needed, and the poor tended to eat far less animal protein. Because these foods were more readily available, the poor ate far more vegetables and starch. Animal protein, always expensive, was usually available only in late fall and early winter, when animals were slaughtered. As winter progressed, meat was salted more and more heavily and spiced to prevent spoiling.

Besides producing such diseases as gout, a diet of too much meat raises the dangers of a host of other diseases and severe vitamin deficiency. Wealthy or moderately prosperous Europeans ran these risks until well into modern times. On the other hand, a deficiency of animal protein produces tuberculosis, dysentery, and other illnesses, and stunts growth substantially. Vitamin deficiency generally produces enormously painful and chronic conditions—scurvy, rickets, and gallstones. Thus the European diet, even in the most prosperous of years, created physiological imbalances that afflicted many people, although their causes were not generally known until the eighteenth century.

Starvation and malnutrition raised equally severe problems. The period between 1300 and 1850 witnessed the greatest effects of malnutrition on the greatest number of people. Starvation and malnutrition kill the old and the weak and, as we now know, damage those who experience them in childhood. The disruption of even a minimally nutritious diet places great stress on the body, creating a loss of energy, slackness of muscles, slow, clumsy movements, lower body temperature, anemia, a reduction of peripheral blood flow, diarrhea, dehydration, and lowered resistance to cold. The psychological consequences include depression and despair, increasing hatred of aliens and the prosperous groups, and widespread complaints about dysfunctional social institutions, inducing social disorder and violence. They produce a drastic change in the demographic composition of society. The number of old and sick drops, infant mortality increases, and the birthrate decreases. Women die during their most fertile years. Those who survive, leave the area, taking with them another generation, one that will be born elsewhere. Thus, the depopulation of many farms, villages, and towns does not last merely for the duration of the period of famine, but for two or three generations, and sometimes forever.

THE PALE HORSEMAN: PLAGUE

I looked and there was a pale green horse! Its rider's name was Death, and Hell followed him; they were given authority over a fourth of the earth to kill with sword, famine, and pestilence, and by the wild animals of the earth. (Rev. 6:8)

Those who suffer malnutrition lack resistance to disease. Widespread starvation and malnutrition had already begun to reduce the population of Europe when the next of the Four Horsemen—pestilence—struck with unprecedented fury. It struck a population weakened by hunger and lack of resistance, crowded into cities, more mobile than in any period of Europe's history since the fifth and sixth centuries, and thus extremely vulnerable to contagion—a principle it did not understand—carried by a bacillus that was not identified until 1918.

The history of widespread epidemic disease and human society has only recently begun to be written. The great plague described by Thucydides in Athens during the Peloponnesian War, the plague brought back to Italy by Marcus Aurelius' troops in the late second century C.E., and the great plague that struck Constantinople and the West in 542/3—these were the most striking, best-known, and remembered epidemics in early European history. Although the great epidemics of cholera, smallpox, and influenza in nineteenth- and twentieth-century Europe have been better described and analyzed than earlier epidemics, the plague of 1348/50, and its subsequent outbreaks between the mid fourteenth and the late seventeenth centuries, stands as the most memorable and destructive of all. Although its ravages were regional, it reduced the aggregate population of Europe by at least one third, completely depopulated some regions and towns, and further aggravated the earlier effects of agricultural disaster, famine, and population loss that had begun by the last years of the thirteenth century. It was also a prodigious test of the resiliency of European society. The recovery of fifteenth-, sixteenth-, and seventeenth-century Europe in terms of population, agricultural output, and living conditions offers eloquent testimony to the vigor and recuperative powers of that society. The roots of this recovery surely lay in the agricultural, technological, and economic innovations of the tenth through the early fourteenth centuries.

Bubonic plague is generally thought to be the product of the bacillus *yersinia pestis,* which lives in the blood stream of the flea, *xenopsylla cheopsis,* which in turn lives in the coat of the black rat (*rattus rattus*). This combination thrived best in warm and moist environments, and it appears to have grown and disappeared historically in cycles, from the 3.9-year rat-cycle, to larger cycles of twenty, up to three hundred years. The etiology of the plague begins when the flea, whose sucking mechanism is blocked when laden with *yersinia pestis,* repeatedly bites a rat in order to consume the blood it needs. The repeated bites kill the rat, and the fleas transfer to humans, transmitting the bacillus into the human, producing a pustule (a bubo, hence the name bubonic plague for this form of the disease) which necroses to a blackish plaque after a day of high fever. In the following days, large abcesses form in the lymphatic system nearest to the original inoculation, in the armpits, groin, and lower abdomen. The patient is then subject to neurological and psychological disturbances as the nervous system is afflicted; digestion becomes difficult, and dark blotches appear on the skin as a result of subcutaneous hemorrhaging. If the buboes suppurate within a week, the patient may survive. If they do not, thirty to forty percent of those infected die by the second day; fifty to ninety percent die by the end of the first week, and eighty to ninety percent die by the third week.

When the plague creates abscesses in the lungs, the pneumonic form of plague is contracted. After a one- to three-day incubation, the fever is not as high as in the bubonic form, but the pulse varies drastically, respiratory difficulties ensue, sputum increases, neurological disorders are manifested, the patient falls into a coma and gradually suffocates. All those infected in this way die within two to three days, with an average life expectancy of 1.8 days. Pneumonic plague is highly contagious. Coughing, expectoration, and sneezing spread the bacillus into the air (in cool and damp atmospheres, the bacillus can linger in the air), creating a zone of contagion up to about fifteen yards.

When the bacillus infects the bloodstream directly, the plague assumes its septicemic form, and the patient dies before buboes have a chance to appear. In its three forms—bubonic, pneumonic, and septicemic—the plague was, until the twentieth century, the most devastating epidemic disease known to humans. The cycle that struck in 1348 did not end until the late seventeenth century, and the black rat was not driven out of Europe and replaced by the less plague-hospitable brown rat until the eighteenth century. Only with the invention of modern antibiotics, has the possibility of breaking the great plague cycles become possible.

The cycle of plague that struck western Europe in 1348 seems to have originated in Asia and to have struck first in China around 1333. By 1340, it had reached Lake Baikal in Siberia, and by 1346, it had crossed the Caucasus and struck the Crimea, at Caffa, the great port center on the Black Sea. Carried by black rats on an Italian fleet from the Black Sea to the Mediterranean, the plague struck first in Europe in Messina and Sardinia in 1347. The next year it hit Genoa and Venice, the greatest ports of the west, simultaneously. From the ports, the plague followed the trade routes. In February

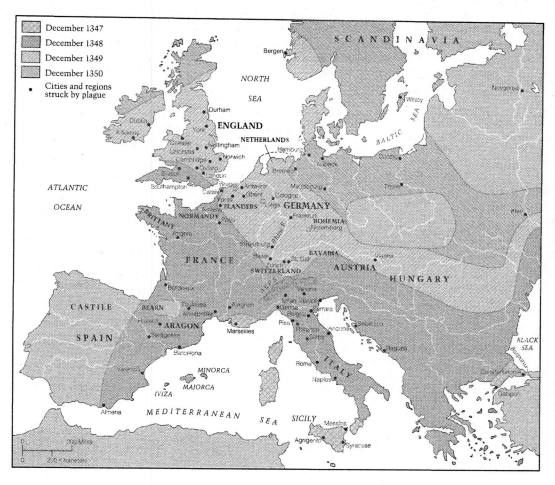

Spread of Black Death.

1348, both Lucca and Avignon reported outbreaks, and two months later Siena and Perugia in Italy and Cerdana and Rousillon in southwestern France were struck. In May, Ancona, Orvieto, and Rimini in Italy and Barcelona and Catalonia in Spain were afflicted, followed in July by Paris and Antioch and a year later by Germany and Tunisia. By September of 1349, the plague had reached England, by 1350 Prussia, Bremen, and the eastern Netherlands, and by 1351/2 western Russia. The indescribably swift spread of plague, its erratic destructiveness of human life, and the utter incomprehension of European society not only provoked severe loss of life and economic disruption on a vast scale, but struck the European Christian mind and imagination with a terrible force. The consequences of the plague were echoed in literature, devotional styles, and the visual arts, as well as in depopulated farms and villages, devastated cities, and disordered economic institutions. Moreover, survival of the 1348/51 crisis did not guarantee immunity to later outbreaks.

THE WHITE HORSEMAN: WAR

I looked, and there was a white horse! Its rider had a bow; a crown was given to him, and he came out conquering and to conquer. (Rev 6:2)

Famine and plague strike most severely at those least able to provide for themselves. In fourteenth- and fifteenth-century Europe, a society in which material resources had been stretched to their limits, a series of wars broke out between 1337 and the late fifteenth century. Their duration and character were different from those of earlier wars, which had consisted generally of infrequent pitched battles between small armies that were not assembled for long periods of time. Such wars usually troubled the noncombatant population relatively little, because they did little permanent damage. The wars of England and France, Castile, and northern Italy in the fourteenth and fifteenth centuries, however, had a different character. Recurring campaigns made battlefields out of plowed fields year after year. Some essential components of agricultural life, such as mills and barns, could not be quickly replaced, because they required substantial capital and labor investment. The temporary, but often regular, destruction of crops and the prolonged effects of the destruction of mills and barns framed the circumstances of warfare. An invading fourteenth-century army, rather like a small expeditionary force, struck into enemy territory on a swift raid, a *chevauchée*, supporting itself from enemy land, capturing enemy towns, and destroying opposing forces. The invaded country, its inhabitants temporarily crowded into fortified towns and castles barely large enough to contain them, could only destroy the food in its own fields so that it did not fall into enemy hands, and hold out until the invaders, frustrated and hungry, moved on. The open country of northern France was particularly vulnerable to this kind of warfare, and the frequent slowing down of military campaigns by prolonged sieges increased the dangers to the noncombatant population considerably. Enemy armies, particularly when they wished to demoralize a hostile population, would themselves destroy fields and crops, exact large ransoms and bribes, and fail to keep their armies from looting.

The duration, frequency, and style of warfare proved particularly disastrous to noncombatants, and so did the composition of fourteenth-century armies. Soldiers were paid little, and their pay was frequently late if it came at all. Soldiers were usually recruited from the poorer and less stable elements of society, and regarded military activity as a means of self-enrichment. Prisoners were taken for ransom, towns and castles were plundered, and agricultural lands were held for tribute. Financial needs usually demanded that armies be disbanded as soon as possible, and large bands of discharged soldiers wandered around the countryside during truces, plundering and terrorizing the population. These groups, called *routiers* in the fourteenth century and *écorcheurs* in the fifteenth, posed continual problems. Sometimes they were reabsorbed into armies when the wars broke out again, and sometimes they sold themselves to the highest bidder in local conflicts. France and Italy were plagued the most severely by them, until the end of the fifteenth century.

Closely related to the activities of discharged or deserted soldiers was the increasing prevalence of banditry in the late fourteenth and fifteenth centuries. *Écorcheurs* took over territory around fortified places they had captured on their own, demanded ransom from those they kidnapped, demanded entire harvests, and required "protection" payments from all whose lives they touched. Impoverished and undisciplined lords of castles found it profitable to raid neighboring areas, particularly after acquiring some military experience—and probably some military personnel—in the numerous wars of the fourteenth century. Both nobles and displaced peasants sometimes formed their own bands or joined larger gangs in the French provinces and the north of England. Finally, robber bands seem to have formed among the poor, as well as among individuals of yeoman status.

A final aspect of late medieval warfare ought to be discussed. Earlier wars had been fought by professional knights and men-at-arms, and were caused by the arguments of princes and kings. They were small in scale and generally short. By the fourteenth century, however, wars touched the noncombatant population more regularly, not only through their destructiveness, but through their financing and recruitment as well. The affairs of kings and princes drew upon a wider circle of resources and personnel. The organization of late medieval warfare and its power to mobilize extensive social and material resources made war a more prominent part of both social and economic history, and an important part of political and constitutional history as well.

Philip IV the Fair of France won his first conflict with Pope Boniface VIII on the grounds that a king's obligation to defend his kingdom overrode his conventional obligations to churchmen and their finances. As other kings and rulers found that financing warfare was growing more and more expensive, they, too, tended to neglect traditional restraints in their dealings, not only with the Church but with their other subjects. Royal administrators, judges, and tax collectors had made the king's power known throughout his kingdom; so now did military recruiters and suppliers. In this way, then, late medieval warfare made people more aware that they were the subjects of a territorial monarch and that this status entailed increasingly substantial obligations.

THE RED HORSEMAN: FINANCIAL COLLAPSE AND RECOVERY

And out came another horse, bright red; its rider was permitted to take peace from the earth, so that people would slaughter one another; and he was given a great sword. (Rev. 6:4)

Among the earliest consequences of the changes in material life between 1270 and 1350 in the agricultural sector of the economy, were the stabilization and decline of cereal grain prices, a rise in the prices of manufactured or crafted goods, a considerable jump in the prices of commercial agricultural products, and an increase in the size of sheep herds at the expense of agricultural land. The new mobility of peasant families and the new demands for labor contributed to changing patterns of inheritance among the peasant population, and to the practice of leasing vacant land at a fixed rent for a short period and subcontracting a labor force to work it. High urban labor costs and the search for cheap sources of power by the urban craft guilds led entrepreneurs to take different stages of wool production into the countryside, where they found an unregulated labor force in need of income. In much of England, western Germany, the Low Countries, and Savoy, the growth of rural craft industry became prominent. The material crises of the fourteenth century opened much land to the profitable vocation of sheep raising, and in Castile an organization of wealthy sheepherders, the Mesta, grew quickly after 1273. Great herds of fine merino sheep were driven north across the vast Castilian table-land in the spring and south in the fall. Although the dominance of sheep herding restricted the development of the Castilian agricultural economy, it also put the valuable long-staple merino wool on the international market, where it competed successfully with English wool.

To the peasants who survived famine, plague, and war, the new economic opportunities were in some places considerable. The price of labor in a reduced labor force had gone up. If old lords were unwilling to renegotiate the price and conditions of service, other lords or even prosperous peasant proprietors would. Statutes against wage increases, like the English Statute of Laborers of 1351, proved incapable of controlling labor costs, and there appeared thriving peasant agricultural entrepreneurs who became employers of the available rural wage labor. The old haphazard scattering of settlements on good land and bad that had spread unchecked between the tenth and the fourteenth centuries began to be tightened into compact new villages. Field systems were reorganized. Farms grew larger, often owned and worked by a single peasant family with its own employees and servants. The standard definition of a peasant—as opposed to a servile—agricultural economy is, "family labor on family land." These peasants were increasingly resentful of demands made by old lords and royal tax agents, and of the successful enterprise of townspeople and middlemen that seemed to keep grain prices down and allow the towns to grow rich at the expense of rural labor. Sometimes lords reforested their lands to produce timber and charcoal for a market, other lords converted their land to a pastoral economy, less labor-intensive than farming. The new conditions of rural enterprise and the markets of the wider world contributed to the heightened tensions of society.

The good fortune of some peasants must not obscure the miserable lot of others. Wage laborers had been forced to trade the security of servile tenure for the economic and social instability of a world in which there was opportunity both to earn and to lose money—or never to earn a living wage. The increase in the number of wage laborers in the countryside who had no possessions or security, led to a widening of the economic spectrum of the peasant population and to a differentiation of social and economic relationships. For instance, the cereal-grain farmer was generally closer to his employees and servants than the commercial farmer or the stock raiser. The new conditions of economic exchange further eroded the old social and economic bonds of dependence and security that had characterized much of rural society before the mid fourteenth century.

The crisis in grain prices and the growth of industry in the fourteenth and fifteenth centuries increased the spread of commercial agriculture. Barley and hops for the brewing of beer brought better prices than wheat and rye. Flax, hemp, woad, madder-fiber, and other dye crops all increased in value as wheat prices remained stable or declined.

The Walled City, Carcassonne. Built in the thirteenth century, primarily as a trading and manufacturing center, Carcassonne was extensively restored in the nineteenth century. The restoration has perhaps given it a more quaint and romantic look than it originally possessed; it was far more busy than picturesque. (Peter Buckley/Pearson Education/PH College)

Some of the changes in late medieval agriculture ultimately proved beneficial. The retreat of grain cultivation to good land rather than marginal or poor land concentrated the remaining labor force on the most productive lands. The increase in crop rotation and the generally greater proportion of leguminous crops meant that the soil received more nitrogen, animal and human diets improved, and land that grew grain crops after having produced legumes required somewhat less animal manure to fertilize it. The cultivation of fodder crops, which increased after the fourteenth century, decreased the frequency of necessary fallow periods, in many areas from one year in three to one year in five or six.

The city was the module of nonagricultural society, and although its population generally remained small and its political significance often dwindled in the face of the increased power of royal authority, it remained the hub of the European economy. Moreover, between the fourteenth and the seventeenth centuries, the city replaced the rural castle as the seat of royal government. In spite of the catastrophies in the agricultural, industrial, and commercial sectors of the fourteenth- and fifteenth-century economy, the importance of the city increased. While territorial monarchies were being shaped, the cities became the critical components of larger states, and the life of the late medieval city influenced the psychology, politics, and economy of larger regions. The study of the nonagricultural sectors of the late medieval European economy begins, then, with the cities.

The density of population in a medieval city permitted the concentration not only of a productive labor force, but of economic activities on both a large and a small scale. Venice, Genoa, Milan, and Florence became the principal centers in Italy of international trade and finance; in England, London and Bristol; in Germany, Nuremburg and Augsburg; in Flanders, Ghent, and Bruges; in the south of France, Marseilles and Avignon; and in northern Europe, the Hanseatic towns of Danzig, Riga, Stralsund, Rostock, Lübeck, Hamburg, and Bremen. These were the international as well as the regional centers of the European economy, and they controlled the economy in their immediate vicinity: Venice, the Adriatic Sea and increasingly, the towns in the Trevisan March; Genoa, the Ligurian coast and what is now the Riviera, with a growing influence in southern Spain; Milan and Florence, the center and north of Italy; London and Bristol, the productive wool trade of southeastern and southwestern England. In international affairs, these cities prospered because of their strong coinage, the exclusivity of their control, and the supporting services they offered their merchants and bankers. In regional affairs, their strong political control of the countryside and their relative prosperity made them local capitals as well. Powerful rulers of large territories transformed such cities as Paris, London, Dijon, Avignon, and Naples into political capitals, thereby enhancing their economic prominence and drawing people to them. Although many medieval cities preserved their traditional character and their customary political divisions, the economic boom of the twelfth and thirteenth centuries, the growing concentration of political authority, and the stabilizing of local and long-distance trade and finance caused the greatest cities to grow even greater.

Sophisticated and extensive recording and accounting systems created new kinds of information about the economy. Public as well as commercial finances were watched more carefully and more expertly. In the fifteenth century, the kingdom of France produced the first modern budget constructed according to sound accounting principles. A good example of this new economic instrumental rationality is to be found in the history of early European banking. The word "bank," like the legal term "bench," derives from the Latin *bancus,* the bench on which simple bankers and judges did their work. But neither law nor finance remained simple. Large amounts of capital in the hands of Italian merchant bankers of the thirteenth century were let in the form of large loans, sometimes to individuals or companies, but more often to those who could offer more substantial security—the rulers of the principalities and territorial monarchies. As we shall see, the fiscal and political crises of the early fourteenth century caught European rulers with antiquated fiscal systems in a dilemma: Rulers had come to depend on large loans as a regular part of their revenue, and the retarded development of public finance in the late thirteenth and early fourteenth centuries met the new flood of private commercial capital and engorged it indiscriminately.

The large amounts of capital available to underfinanced rulers in the late thirteenth and early fourteenth centuries led them to borrow on anticipation of revenues, to assign future revenues to their creditors, and to issue monopolies inconsiderately. Even these unwise measures failed to produce enough money for repaying debts or covering current expenses, and they further decreased operating revenues. Consequently, during the 1330s and 1340s, the kings of England and France, faced with extensive financial needs because of their mobilization for war, refused many of their obligations to the Italian and Flemish bankers who had loaned them money. Thus, in addition to demographic, epidemic, and military crises, Europe experienced a financial crisis of previously unheard-of dimensions. Banking companies whose revenues had been committed to government loans quickly failed. The great banking houses of Siena collapsed in 1339; in 1343 and 1346, the great Florentine banks of the Peruzzi and the Bardi went under, as did the third largest Florentine bank, that of the Acciaiuoli. The crisis of the great early banking houses not only incapacitated public finance for most of the century and turned the rulers of Europe to new means of raising money, it also transformed banking itself. Investments in even the most wealthy territorial monarchies had proved to be no more secure than investments in private enterprises. Banks had to take two steps: first, to find a way of minimizing their risks, and, second, to find new investments for their diminished capital.

Until the seventeenth century, the banking houses that survived the crash of the mid fourteenth century generally operated on a smaller scale than their great predecessors. The new banks that rose in the wake of the mid fourteenth-century failures—in Italy, those of the Medici in Florence with branches in other cities, the *Casa di San Giorgio* in Genoa, and the *Banco di San Ambrogio* in Milan—became semipublic, absorbing shares of the increasingly common funded debts (publicly guaranteed, interest-paying bonds) of the cities and acquiring political power in their cities that made their investments more secure than they had been in the thirteenth century. The surviving banks and the newer institutions were aided by an increasing tendency to make monetary values homogeneous over wider regions. With this alignment of currencies, one of the most vexing and time-consuming activities of early medieval money changers and bankers was slowly overcome. Some areas also insisted on evaluating different currencies according to a stable gold standard determined according to purity and weight. Currency speculation had long provided a profitable area of investment, but unstable currency had increased economic risks, and "bad money" persisted in driving out "good money." The great stable coins of the twelfth and thirteenth centuries—the Byzantine *solidus,* the Venetian *ducat,* the Florentine *florin*—all succumbed in the fourteenth century. By the end of the fourteenth century, Italian banks had begun to issue paper currency, but the spread of this new form of money was slow and irregular. Early modern Europe operated on a metallic currency, and the scarcity or promiscuity of bullion considerably altered the economic activity of regions, cities, and kingdoms.

The history of the wool industry in the fourteenth and fifteenth centuries illuminates one aspect of late medieval trade: shifts in the areas of production, finishing, and sale, and the consequent economic, social, and political changes in those areas that lost and those that gained from such shifts. The rise of the English cloth industry, its relative freedom from restriction, the decline of Flanders, and the weakening of Italian trade all suggest an aspect of late medieval economic life that has long been misunderstood—the economic reorganization within a complex system that many historians have insisted must be labeled uniformly as a decline. To be sure, there is remarkable evidence of many sorts of decline—from financial to agricultural—during this period. But there are also compelling indications that the rearrangement of the European economy—from finance to agriculture—not only increased prosperity in some places and among some social groups, but ultimately laid the groundwork for the social and economic changes of the seventeenth and eighteenth centuries. The new freedom of different kinds of entrepreneurs, new means of record keeping and accounting, the increasingly prominent role of political authority in economic activity, and the rapidly changing prosperity of many areas offer a confusing picture, but not one that can casually be labeled as uniform decline. Regional variations were still the predominant characteristic of European economic life until well into the eighteenth century, and the decline of one region, town, or family usually meant the rise of another.

Most of these economic changes were misunderstood: They were interpreted as acts of God, as signs of the corruption of political or ecclesiastical authority, as the result of greed (the predominant vice in moral theology), or as the consequences of a world turned upside down. Economic complaints were joined indiscriminately to other kinds of complaints, and sometimes to the literary or artistic preoccupations of late medieval society. The resulting picture of unrelieved gloom and totally unchecked self—interest is a common portrayal, but certainly not a uniformly accurate one. It does little justice to those who, in bettering their lot, however novel and incomprehensible their activities, did attempt to be useful to society, to serve their rulers loyally, to be good Christians, and to accommodate as best they could the deepest and most enduring values their society held.

* * *

Famine, plague, war, and economic disruption were not the Four Horsemen of the Apocalypse any more than the Mongols had been. For all of their measurable impact, what is most striking about western Europe's response was its powers of recovery.

18

Clergy and Laity

CHRISTENDOM AND EUROPE

From the time of its coinage by Popes Nicholas I and John VIII in the ninth century, the term *christianitas*—"Christendom"—had been used to designate both any individual's Christian identity and also the religious, and fraternal identity of all who professed Christianity. It also came to mean those lands where Christians lived and where Christian practices prevailed—as early as the ninth century, Carolingian writers had termed Charlemagne's lands the *imperium Christianum,* "the Christian empire."

The conversion of northern and parts of eastern Europe, the conquests by Christian rulers and peoples in the Iberian Peninsula, the Crusader States in Syria and Palestine, and parts of the North African coast, also suggested, following Christ's injunction to the apostles, that not only should Christendom expand, but that it could expand and that it had expanded already. But Christendom did not exactly coincide geographically with Europe. Thirteenth- and fourteenth-century Europeans also discovered that Christendom could shrink, that some lands once confidently thought Christian had ceased to be so. Most important, from the late thirteenth century on, the actual territory controlled by Christians began to coincide more and more exactly with geographical ideas about the boundaries of Europe. From the fifteenth century on, the term Europe began to replace Christendom in common usage, having acquired both a cultural and a geographical meaning.

There were many reasons why "Europe" replaced "Christendom." Among them are: the loss of Christian territory outside continental Europe, the changing relations between Christian and non-Christian peoples within Europe, the appearance of the Mongols—and both the threats that they posed to the wealth and abundance of Europe and the avenues that they opened into eastern Asia—and an increasing geographical sense of just how vast the world was and how small a part of it the Christian peoples of Europe occupied.

In the face of these events, some of the basic institutions of Christendom changed. In spite of propaganda and the urging of popes and preachers, the Crusades that followed the fall of Acre in 1291 tended to be smaller in scale and limited in purpose to defending the frontiers of Europe, matters that were of greater importance to those who lived near the frontiers—and to those who continued to regard the Crusades as appropriate occasions for performing penance and experiencing adventure—than to those who, having less hope of recapturing Jerusalem, grew less inclined to participate in Crusades that brought them to no Holy Land. With the failures in North Africa and Syria-Palestine, where the Mamluks of Egypt and the Ilkhans of Persia kept a firm hold on their territories until the sixteenth century, a new boundary had been drawn for Christendom. With the fall of Constantinople to the Ottoman Turks in the middle of the fifteenth century (below, Chapter 20), the ambiguous Byzantine presence was also removed from the orbit of Christendom.

In other parts of southern Europe, however, Christian rulers and peoples also gained territory. From the eighth century on, the Iberian Peninsula had been one of the very few places in Europe besides Rus in which large non-Christian populations lived side by side with Christians, in both the Islamic kingdoms and in those of the Christians. From the twelfth century on, the pace of the Christian conquest quickened, and over the next three centuries, much of the Peninsula had been won by Christian kings and their armies. If Syria-Palestine and much of Anatolia, Greece, and the Balkans were removed from Christian hands, most of the Iberian Peninsula and eventually eastern Europe came into them.

As was the case along the southern edge of Christendom, however, in northern Europe there was a gain of both territory and Christians as well as a loss. Although Christian kingdoms had existed in Hungary, Bohemia, and Poland since the tenth century (above, Chapter 11), many large territories extending northward to the Baltic Sea had not been Christianized, either by Slavs or by the expanding northern German territorial principalities. From the thirteenth century on, German princes launched military enterprises in the form of crusades against the Prussians, Livonians, and Estonians. In addition, with the marriage of the Christian Polish princess Jadwiga to Prince Jagiello of Lithuania in 1386, the Christianization of Lithuania began and was quickly completed. The last substantial non-Christian territory and people in the north of Europe had now become Christian. By the late fourteenth century, Christendom and Europe, with the exception of the strong Mongol presence in Russia, had become virtually identical.

The coincidence of Christendom and geographical Europe cast the world beyond those borders in a new light. No longer was there a realistic hope of expanding the powers of Christian rulers, but there was the hope of exerting the spirit of Christianity in a missionary effort of conversion. Moreover, legends of Christian peoples beyond the lands ruled by Muslims and Mongols remained attractive, particularly those centered on the legendary Christian ruler Prester John. But as Christians began to travel overland to Asia, they found no Prester John, although they did find large numbers of peoples they had never heard of before, including, much to their surprise, real Nestorian Christians whom they promptly suspected of being heretics. In this context, a new missionary and conversion spirit arose, heightened by a sense that prophecies circulating through Europe since the twelfth century were about to be fulfilled.

Arnald of Villanova, a lay theologian, physician, and counselor of popes and kings, wrote on prophecy and the coming end of the world. Among the strongest influences on Arnald was the conviction that a new age of the world had begun when new spiritual men would convert Jews and Muslims without the need of the sword or temporal power. This view had been developed in the writings of the late twelfth-century Calabrian monk Joachim of Fiore (above, Chapter 16), who had redesigned prophetic history in such a way that the Trinity, not the six ages, dominated the patterns of time. The Age of the Father preceded the birth of Christ; the Age of the Son (and the Church) followed it; in its turn, the Age of the Son would be followed by the Age of the Holy Spirit, not an age of fear and trembling before the last things, but an age of tranquility, guided by holy men in a religious order. Many of Joachim's ideas were adapted by a strict group of Franciscans, who identified his final prediction with Francis of Assisi and their own wing of the Order of Friars Minor. These thinkers, the Spiritual Franciscans, played a prominent role in the thirteenth and fourteenth centuries, running afoul of popes and inquisitors, but also providing a perspective for criticism of the institutionalized church and the Franciscan order.

The historical failure of the Crusade movement and new idealistic hopes about the immediate future converged to create a new vision of the future, a vision whose emphases on reform, the coming of the millennium, and the miraculous conversion of non-Christians became common topics of discussion in many clerical and lay circles.

One of the most striking figures in this movement was the Catalan noble Ramon Llull (1232–1316). A gifted poet and a prosperous man, Llull was moved by the example of Francis of Assisi around 1263. Renouncing marriage and the world, he learned Arabic, founded training schools for missionaries, and became a missionary to Muslims himself. Llull attended school in Italy and Paris, patronized the Franciscans, founded schools for training missionaries and teaching them Arabic, and produced many literary works of great influence. He died, possibly in North Africa, on a conversion mission. His ideas and works continued to circulate widely, and he is one of the most important figures in late medieval devotional literature.

Such aspects of Christian practice and theory as the problem of the rights of non-Christians, the conversion movements, and the problem of the reunion of the divided Greek and Latin churches dominated much of Christian thought from the mid thirteenth to the mid fifteenth century. The emotional pitch of this concern was very high, for lay people and clerics alike feared that their efforts had been too few and that hope for reform had dawned too late. The Council of Vienne in 1312 decreed that schools of Arabic and other non-Christian languages ought to be established, and popes and lawyers attempted to institutionalize these concerns in their decretals and administrative practices. At a very different level, such laymen as Arnald of Villanova and Ramon Llull responded to these same concerns in their own inventive ways. Behind both institutional and personal activity lay the fear that the last age of the world was coming soon, or was already upon humanity. A prophetic mentality was echoed in many places in the fourteenth and fifteenth centuries, and it forms a characteristic background to the hope, fearful anticipation, and sense of duty that mark the efforts of so many thinkers between the mid thirteenth and mid fifteenth centuries. It also shaped the attitudes with which people responded to the crises of the later fourteenth century—the revolt against Aristotle and Aquinas, the failure of Greek and Latin reunion, the Avignon papacy, the Great Schism, the conciliar movement, and the new forms of devotion that grew up in the fourteenth and fifteenth centuries.

THE ECCLESIASTICAL STRUCTURE: NORMATIVE RELIGION

By the fourteenth century, both the administrative structure of the Latin church and its normative definition of Christianity in theology, pastoral care, and canon law were highly articulated. At the head of the community of Christians was the pope. Although a number of critics of papal authority produced eloquent arguments against some aspects of that authority and even professors of canon law explored its limits, there was no alternative to it in a world believed to be hierarchically ordered, with spiritual affairs ranked higher than temporal affairs. Even the church council, which challenged papal authority in the fifteenth century (below, this Chapter), had to be convened and presided over by the pope. The financial, secretarial, and legal components of the papal household were by far the most advanced in Europe, and papal legates and judges-delegate supplemented their work. But even high papal theory and institutions had their limitations.

When no council sat, Christendom was directed by the metropolitan archbishops and their descending network of subordinates—bishops, archdeacons, deans, and parish priests. Monasteries and religious orders like the mendicants were given special papal protectors, tying them directly to the pope. Bishops were instructed to visit the institutions of their dioceses, although few did so regularly. The carefully kept visitation records of Eudes Rigaud (d. 1275), the extraordinarily energetic Franciscan archbishop of Rouen in Normandy, reveal the limits to what even the most dedicated pastoral bishop could hope to accomplish by visitations.

The training of parish clergy varied widely, from short apprenticeships to rural clergy to years of study at the universities. Certain conditions made recruitment of clergy difficult: the development of other career opportunities for males; the sudden increase of Christian-controlled territories that required more clergy; depopulation because of famine, war, or plague; and the attractions of nonparochial priestly functions like that of household chaplain or chantry priest. The only sure tests of the extent of clerical education were the rules that various dioceses set for priestly ordination—how many years of study and the mastery of what kinds of knowledge were required, even if these could not always be enforced. There were no seminaries for formal training; most priests seem to have had some elementary education, acquired the ability to read Latin, and perhaps studied at a cathedral school, whose chancellor was expected to provide theological instruction within the diocese. It is impossible to coordinate the high expectations of clergy displayed by councils and synods, at least since the Fourth Lateran Council in 1215, with the actual experience of the majority of clergy in the following three centuries.

However well- or ill-educated they were, parish priests were expected to know the rites required to perform the sacraments and to know the mass by heart. They had to teach their congregations the creed and the essential prayers layfolk had to know. When they preached, they were expected to explain the Ten Commandments and other doctrinal matters that affected laypeople—the Seven Deadly Sins, the Seven Corporal Works of Mercy, and the Works of Spiritual Comfort. They were expected to observe the cults of local saints and both the universal and local church calendars.

Perhaps the most demanding aspect of the priestly profession was the sacrament of penance. This required considerable sensitivity to pastoral psychology, since it entailed the examination of the sinner's conscience guided by the priest and the imposition of the appropriate penance. The manuals for confessors, which began to appear in the late twelfth century, are among the most revealing texts of the interaction between clergy and people that we have. Pastoralism, of course, involved not only religious instruction and the administration of the sacraments, but also ecclesiastical discipline. On the ordinary level, such discipline was administered in the privacy of the individual confession of sins, the "internal forum" of conscience. For more grievous sins, the powers of absolution of the parish priests might be insufficient, and the penitent might be required to attend the "external forum," a hearing before the episcopal judicial official, usually the archdeacon. In cases of public dissent and heresy, the bishop's court had jurisdiction, and among the manuals of clerical instruction there also appeared manuals of inquisitorial procedure.

From the thirteenth century on, the theology faculties of the universities, particularly that of the University of Paris, became the preeminent teaching authorities in the Latin west. Although few parish clergy attended such schools, those scholars who did attend, even for a short time, experienced lively debate over theological propositions, a rigorous training in formal logic, and familiarity with the standard textbooks of the masters, from Peter Lombard's *Book of Sentences*, to the works of Aquinas and Bonaventure. Theology even worked its way into the subordinate arts faculties, and sometimes arts debates generated objections from professional theologians.

However incomplete and inefficient the actual operation of normative religion may have been, the design of the church, from pope, council, prelates, and universities down to the ordinary parish priest or individual monk or mendicant, was hierarchical and systematic. But even hierarchy and system were occasionally open to revision. The fourteenth and early fifteenth centuries witnessed a number of occasions for such revision. The first of them was the revolt against Aristotle and Aquinas.

THE REVOLT AGAINST ARISTOTLE AND AQUINAS

From the first appearance of Aristotle's works of natural philosophy and metaphysics in the late twelfth century, opposition to Aristotelian thought developed among Christian theologians, just as it had among earlier Muslim theologians. Aristotle's picture of an uncreated universe and a single collective intellect for the human race, his neglect of charity, the failure of his theology to account for the Trinity, and the theory attributed to him that God acted from necessity rather than freedom, encountered bitter opposition from many theologians and led to the condemnation of many of his works and ideas (and their Arabic commentaries and developments) from 1210 to 1277. Indeed, the condemnation of many Aristotelian and Averroistic theses by Stephen Tempier, the bishop of Paris, in 1277, has often been considered the watershed of early European intellectual history. But others besides theologians had attacked Aristotle, and even the expositions of Albertus Magnus and Thomas Aquinas came under heavy fire, from outside and inside the Dominican order.

Roger Bacon (1214–1292), a teacher of natural philosophy and a lay member of the Franciscan order, bitterly attacked Parisian scholars for their unthinking acceptance of Aristotelian natural philosophy. Other natural philosophers, including Robert Grosseteste, developed original scientific approaches to problems that Aristotle had generally left unsolved or had treated inadequately, such as the nature of rainbows and the problem of local motion. The condemnations of 1277, which were primarily theological and aimed at reasserting the absolute liberty of God from Aristotelian necessity, were also important for prying loose Aristotelian authority in general and consequently permitting the work of such natural philosophers as Grosseteste and Bacon to have an impact in the schools with much greater independence.

The condemnation of many Aristotelian and Thomistic principles at the University of Paris in 1277 produced a revolt not only against a theology based on Aristotle, but against Aristotelian natural philosophy as well. Although a few schools, notably those of theology and natural philosophy at the University of Padua, remained close (too close, many thought) to Aristotelianism and Averroism, and although the Dominican order tried (ultimately successfully) to preserve the authority and reputation of Thomas by having him canonized in 1323, among other things, a number of thinkers set off in new directions in both theology and natural philosophy.

John Duns Scotus (1265–1308), an immensely complex theologian in the Augustinian and Franciscan traditions, criticized the Aristotelian tendency to make God less transcendent by attributing to him rationality and a kind of intelligibility that made him accessible to human reason but also appeared to diminish divine transcendence. Duns Scotus argued that such a view of God diminished God's transcendence and majesty. He therefore emphasized the power of the divine will, which could not be analyzed according to rationalist principles, rather than divine reason, and he asserted the ultimate unknowability of God. Reason, Duns Scotus argued, can give no reliable information about God at all.

Although William of Occam (1285–1349), whose studies focused on logic and cognition, criticized much of Duns Scotus' work, he agreed that God was transcendent, omnipotent, and infinitely free. Only faith and revelation tell us about God's nature and will. Reason, on the contrary, informs us only of the observable world. Occam argued that there are three types of human knowledge: intuition, abstraction, and faith. Intuition and abstraction are the realm of reason; faith is the realm outside of reason. Although Occam's rationalism may appear to represent a step backwards in its reversion to a mystical theology from a rational one, it is probably more accurate to regard his and Scotus' theology as correcting a theological movement toward rationalism that seemed to them to have gone too far—to have made God comprehensible in purely rational terms. On the other hand, by insisting on the supremacy of reason in the field of observable phenomena, Occam posited a new and independent degree of authority to rational and scientific analysis of the physical world. Having deprived reason of all power to inform us about God, Occam gave it every power to inform us about the phenomenal world. Since in Scotus' and Occam's theology, God's will may interrupt the operation of the phenomenal world at virtually any time, reason describes only the regular operation of that world before God intervenes. Occam and other thinkers thus worked out the important distinction between the absolute and ordained powers of God. In terms of absolute powers, God could, of course, do anything; but in terms of ordained powers (those powers that God himself has put into nature), God operated in nature according to laws that he himself had established. According to Occam, God had made a covenant with humanity, allowing humanity to expect that God would act consistently. That covenant represented God's ordained power.

Occam replaced Aristotelian realism with a rigorous form of nominalism—the theory that what we know by intuition is only the individual thing, not characteristics that it may share with others. Abstract categories are at best only probable conclusions; what we know securely is only the concrete. Occam also dismissed Aristotle's four causes—material, efficient, formal, and final—in favor of the principle of the economy of explanation. This principle, known as "Occam's Razor," states that explanations need contain no more causes than are necessary to account for the immediate behavior of phenomena.

Out of this division of religious and philosophical consciousness, reflected in other theologians and scientists between the fourteenth and the seventeenth centuries, there emerged the twin currents of divine voluntarism and rational authority in explanations of the material world. In the case of voluntarism, God's will, unbounded and incomprehensible, characterized the Divinity. Mystical and negative theology, mystical devotion, pious private prayer, interior spiritual development, a revival of symbolic thought and expression, and a new interest in contemplation came to characterize religious sensibility after the mid fourteenth century. Some of its most dramatic manifestations may be seen in the writings of the German Dominican Meister Eckhart (1260–1328) and in the Flemish mystic Jan Ruusbroec (1293–1381), in the writings of the school known as the *Devotio Moderna,* "the modern devotion," and in the writings of a number of Beguines in the Low Countries, particularly Hadewijch and her followers.

In the case of natural philosophy, Scotus and Occam opened the door to the idea that if reason is of no value in ascertaining truths about God, it may be of supreme and uncontestable value in ascertaining truths about the observable world. If reason has no validity in clarifying the spiritual realm and must thereby defer to faith, revelation, and mysticism, conversely these three may not validly ascertain truths about the material world. This last point, developed more fully by thinkers of the fifteenth and sixteenth centuries, created a much smaller realm, but a much more manageable and verifiable one, for rational empiricism. Finally, both voluntaristic theology and rational empiricism, having developed in common as a reaction to Aristotelianism and Aquinas, were mutually acceptable to each other. One finds many late medieval thinkers of a strongly mystical theological bent holding obviously rational ideas about the material world.

While Franciscans were attacking Aristotle and Aquinas, several fourteenth-century thinkers revived the thought of Augustine into a dominant influence. Thomas Bradwardine, archbishop of Canterbury (d. 1349), relied heavily on Augustine's writings in his treatise *On the Cause of God Against Pelagius*, which emphasizes the importance of faith rather than human effort in the achievement of salvation. Bradwardine was also associated with a group of mathematicians at Merton College, Oxford, and in his scientific studies of dynamics and local motion, he strongly criticized Aristotelian dynamics and brought to bear on Aristotle's generally nonmathematical physics a new mathematical sophistication that further eroded the prestige of Aristotelian natural philosophy.

Thus, the revolt against Aristotle and Aquinas gave new impetus to the evolution of theology and natural philosophy alike. The marvelous synthesis of Aquinas came under attack from many directions, and the vast resources of theological thought and feeling, as well as the new interest in experimental natural philosophy—incompatible as these movements may appear to a modern mind—shaped the spiritual and scientific direction of later European thought and began to forge the links (which historians are still exploring) between the early and modern worlds.

THE POPES AT AVIGNON

Not only did Greek and Latin Christianity fail to find union, but internal changes in the governance of the Latin Church itself marked the fourteenth and fifteenth centuries. The long residence of the popes in Avignon was perhaps the most striking manifestation of these changes.

Boniface VIII died at Rome in 1303. His successor, Benedict XI (1303–1304), died at Perugia. According to the rules for papal elections set down by Gregory X in the late thirteenth century, the cardinals assembled to elect Benedict's successor in Perugia, where the pope had died. Benedict's successor, Clement V (1305–1314), was not in Italy when he was elected, and was crowned pope in Lyons. Clement's urgent wish to mediate the quarrel between the kings of England and France and to prevent Phillip IV from staging a posthumous trial of Boniface VIII, along with his presiding at the Council of Vienne in 1311/12 kept Clement out of Italy; the press of business and turbulence in Italy kept his successor, John XXII, in the south of France. From the pontificate of John XXII (1316–1334), the popes took up residence in the city of Avignon, in which they purchased first the bishop's palace and, in 1348, the city itself from its owner, the king of Naples, a papal vassal.

To a great extent the Avignon residence aided the papacy in its task of directing the spiritual life of Christendom. It is ironic that although the popes at Avignon were more disposed, better equipped, and more efficiently financed for the task of directing Christian society than ever before, their residency there was regarded by many as the "Babylonian captivity" of the papacy. There were reasons for this. The increasing friction between the kings of France and England always tended to place the mediating popes in great disfavor with parties who opposed their activities. The struggle between the Avignon popes and the emperor Louis of Bavaria (1314–1347) has often been regarded as high-handed and autocratic on the part of the popes. Indeed, the Avignon residency was long widely heralded by contemporaries and later historians as the symbol of the breakup of Christendom. Only recently have scholars clarified its real accomplishments, estimated the dedication of popes and curia, and begun to regard the work of some of the fourteenth-century popes as highly as it deserves.

The Avignon popes put papal, financial, and administrative practices on a sounder footing than ever before. They enlarged the number of administrative officers from around two hundred in the thirteenth century to around six hundred in Avignon. The palace of the Popes at Avignon appears to have been designed and built specifically to facilitate papal business; it may be regarded as the first building in Europe constructed specifically to house large-scale administrative and governmental functions. The care with which papal archives and records were kept, the intelligent design and decoration of the palace, and the increasing consistency of papal policy during this period mark the Avignon papacy as a time of vigorous application of rationality to the stubborn problems of rule rather than as a captivity, a concession to the kings of France, or the expression of a frustrated monarchical political theory.

In Avignon, abstract theory about papal authority gave way to concrete practice. Successive popes claimed and exercised the right to control more and more appointments to ecclesiastical offices throughout Europe. The old papal practice of imposing taxes for the crusade developed into the practice of regularly taxing the holders of benefices—an important step toward modern state taxation powers long before secular kingdoms were able to impose such taxation. The popes themselves, and most of their officials, were lawyers, increasing the juristic character of papal government.

As the fourteenth century wore on, pressures on the popes to return to Rome grew stronger. But now the enormity of the task of moving the greatly enlarged papal administration, household, and records (as well as the households of cardinals) postponed such a move (except for a very brief visit by Pope Urban V from 1367 to 1370) until 1377. Gregory XI (1371–1378) returned to Rome because he wished to use the prestige of a pope in Rome to call another crusade, but he hastened his return when the city-republic of Florence launched a war against the papal states, the so-called "War of the Eight Saints," named after the eight ruling officers of the city of Florence. The conflicting opinions concerning the return of the papacy to Rome proved to be the prelude to a great crisis, the double papal election of 1378. Gregory XI died at Rome in 1378, and the sixteen cardinals, most of them from the kingdom of France, elected his successor at a conclave held in Rome. Pressure from the people of Rome, who cried that "We want a Roman, or at least an Italian," struck fear into the cardinals, who hastily elected Bartolomeo Prignano, the archbishop of Bari, as Pope Urban VI.

THE GREAT SCHISM AND THE CONCILIAR MOVEMENT

Urban's furious temper and outspoken contempt and high-handed treatment of the curia, however, led a dissident group of eleven cardinals to flee Rome, denounce the papal election as uncanonical, and elect another pope, Cardinal Robert of Geneva, who established himself back in Avignon. These two popes, the "Roman" Urban VI (1378–1389) and the "Avignonese" Clement VII (1378–1394), divided the Christian Latin world into two conflicting camps. Charles V of France recognized his cousin Clement VI, as did his allies. Richard II of England recognized Urban VI, as did his allies. Individual prominent Christians, including two who were later canonized as saints, divided their loyalties. Catherine of Siena (1347–1380), the mystic and papal critic, sided with Urban. Vincent Ferrer (1350–1419), the influential Dominican preacher, sided with Clement. The rivalry between two claimants to the papal throne greatly eroded the nonpartisan status of the papacy in mediating international conflicts, diverted the popes' attention from the needs of Christendom to those of diplomacy, and led to a virtual duplication of papal governing apparatus as each pope strove to force his rival and his rival's supporters to capitulate.

In spite of widespread efforts at mediation between the two parties, the schism endured. Catherine of Siena wrote bitter letters denouncing those who sustained the Avignon residence and those who perpetuated the Schism, including the male ecclesiastical hierarchy. A number of individuals left the path of ecclesiastical careerism to establish new devotional movements, including Gert Groote, who established the Brothers and Sisters of the Common Life and the Congregation at Windesheim, the center of the *Devotio Moderna*. Various steps were taken by kings, theologians, canon lawyers, and prelates to pressure the two sides to compromise. Between 1399 and 1403, the king of France declared a "subtraction of obedience" from both sides and gave the French church an early experience of independence from Rome that, in the form of special agreements between the king of France and later popes, was to help create the highly autonomous Gallican church of the sixteenth and seventeenth centuries.

In 1409, a council at Pisa assembled by cardinals who had defected from both papal claimants deposed both papal rivals and elected yet another pope, Alexander V, thereby widening the contest to a field of three. When the three papal claimants died, their supporters elected successors, prolonging the Schism. The years between 1409 and 1415 were spent in a series of dramatic attempts to resolve their conflicting claims, and only the persistence of many prelates, the universities, and the emperor Sigismund (d. 1437) determined the direction in which a solution to the dilemma might be found. It was decided that this, the greatest of all ills in the history of the Church, must be solved—could only be solved—by an ecumenical Church council. The council, called to meet at Constance in 1415, was to be the Church's last opportunity to restore unity to a faction-ridden world and to place once more a single universal pope on the throne of Peter. The council also recognized the need to speed up church reform and to combat several newly discovered heretical movements, of which the most important was that of the Bohemian followers of Jan Hus, the Hussites.

The Council of Constance (1414–1418) finally did manage to remove the three contending popes and elect a fourth pope, Martin V (1417–1431), who spent his pontificate trying to restore the pope's rights and security in the city of Rome and recover the papacy's lost prestige throughout Europe. The council also executed, by burning, the Bohemian ecclesiastical reformer John Hus, who was accused of unorthodox views on the Church hierarchy, excessive criticism of clerical abuses, and heresy. Hus had been a major figure in Bohemian spiritual and cultural life, however, and after his execution, Bohemia was torn by civil wars until 1434.

Finally, the council mandated that general councils be called regularly. But the suggestion of the most extreme supporters of this view, the Conciliarists, that a General Council might be superior to a pope and that a pope could be forced to convene a council, generated papal opposition to the notion of regular councils. From the pontificate of Martin V on, the popes grew more preoccupied with settling affairs within the Papal States and Italy, ruling the Church alone with the help of the curia, and restoring papal Rome. By opposing the calling of councils, Martin V and his successors helped to turn the loyalties of many churchmen to local temporal powers instead of to Rome. Up to the beginning of the sixteenth century, these popes found that the return to Rome and the local political rivalries in the papal states and northern Italy occupied far more of their time and attention than they could readily spare from dealing with the remnants of a universal Christian society and its pressing spiritual and material needs.

VARIETIES OF DEVOTION: LIVED RELIGION

The idea of Christendom as a geographic term designating those lands in which king and clergy guided peoples who possessed a set of common religious beliefs and observances was only one meaning of the term. Another meaning was that of the quality of being a Christian, and for most people, that quality was learned and practiced in one's immediate locality. By the late thirteenth century, this locality was organized as the parish. The parish supervised the beginning, middle, and end of the Christian life in its administration of the sacraments of baptism, penance, the eucharist, marriage, the last rites, and burial in the parish cemetery. The parish and its priest taught the rudiments of the religious life through the media of liturgy, preaching, and confession—after 1215, a mandatory annual practice for all Christians—and penance. The content of normative belief was reiterated in simple creeds, taught by memorization to a largely nonliterate public.

Beyond this local sacramental life, the sermons of popular preachers played a more and more important role. The Dominican Order had been founded as the Order of Preachers, and dynamic individual preachers appeared throughout Europe in the fourteenth and fifteenth centuries. Vincent Ferrer (ca. 1350–1419) was one of the best known of these, as was the fiery Franciscan, Bernardino of Siena (1380–1444).

The individual experience of becoming—and being—a Christian was a common experience throughout most of Europe. The organization of the religious life—from the public observance of the ecclesiastical calendar to the administration of the sacraments, the common celebration of universal and local feast days, and the last rites and local burial—was also a common and public experience, shared by whole communities that did not often encounter non-Christians. Only in Russia, where the Mongol presence was extensive, and the Iberian Peninsula, with many Muslim and Jewish inhabitants, were there significant numbers of non-Christians mingled with Christian populations.

By the fourteenth century, the world of ordinary lay people, ecclesiastical specialists such as parish priests, preachers, canon lawyers, and theologians, and the mediating and regulating offices of the ecclesiastical hierarchy had shaped a religious culture that paid attention to the affairs of this world and also defined and aspired to the sacred. The mental images in which people conceived of such issues as sin and penance, baptism and salvation, were those of kin and fraternity—kinship with Christ, the Virgin, and the saints, and fraternity with fellow Christians on an earth that abounded in occasions for hostility and violence. The sins of avarice, pride, and anger were particularly worrisome because they tended to drive people apart.

Images of unity and fraternity also sharply defined those who were not brothers and sisters—Jews, Muslims, lepers, heretics, and those thought to practice magic or witchcraft on their fellow Christians. The fourteenth and fifteenth centuries witnessed ferocious attacks on the outsider—the enemy—just as it emphasized the brotherhood of true Christians in sacramental and social bonds.

Attempts at Church reform are surprisingly numerous after 1350, and the intensity of the laity's search for spiritual comfort and assurance is notable. Fourteenth-century English bishops, for example, made substantial attempts to administer their dioceses and care for the spiritual life of their congregations. The appearance of such guides for parochial clergy as William of Pagula's *The Priest's Eye* in the early fourteenth century and John Mirk's *Instructions for Parish Priests* in the fifteenth mark the first stages of the slow process by which thirteenth-century theology, morality, and canon law began to filter down to the parish level, and there generate a pastoral revolution, just as the influence of the Franciscans and Dominicans was beginning to wane. The early fourteenth-century compendium by John of Freiburg, the *Summa Confessorum,* became the standard handbook of theology for most fourteenth- and fifteenth-century clergy with any pretense to learning at all. In the mid fourteenth century, Pope Benedict XII made an extensive effort to reform monasticism, the first such attempt since the Cistercian revolution two centuries before, and the last until the mid sixteenth century. In a number of instances, particular religious houses or groups of houses within a religious order transformed their way of life into a much stricter form, which they called "Observant."

In the fourteenth century, a pastoral ideal took shape that is perhaps best illustrated by the parson in Geoffrey Chaucer's *Canterbury Tales*, a figure idealized, but certainly not invented by Chaucer himself. A genuine sense of responsibility for the souls of individual Christians at all levels of society—aided by ideals of clerical behavior, handbooks of instruction for laity and clergy alike, and helps for sermon writing and delivery—was one of the greatest legacies of the thirteenth century. That sense of responsibility was sometimes impossible to activate, however, and it is more remarkable in isolated centers than in dioceses with consistently applied and supervised regulations.

The fourteenth and fifteenth centuries also witnessed a new sophistication and acuteness of conscience on the part of many individuals, laity as well as clergy. Religious guilds and confraternities spread through the towns as urban spiritual needs came to be perceived as different from the needs of the rural population. The Brethren of the Common Life at Deventer in the Netherlands offers an example. A devoted organization of lay people from all walks of life, they explored the inner spiritual life by means of pietist contemplation, the most popular example of which was the little book called *The Imitation of Christ,* by Thomas à Kempis. Brigit of Sweden, Catherine of Siena, and Bernardino of Siena—among the most remarkable religious figures of the fourteenth and fifteenth centuries—shared this concern for devotional purity and feared its pollution by secular abuses and the temptations of the world.

Another powerful force in the religious sensibility of the period was the increasing capacity of the European vernacular languages. Although creeds, prayers, and sermons had always been part of vernacular expression, Latin Christian society heard masses and other forms of the liturgy in Latin, and the formal administrative affairs of the Church, as well as all higher learning and learned law, were conducted in Latin. The universality of the Latin language made it easier for universal institutions such as the papacy and universities to draw on a wide range of people for their administrators and other personnel. Latin was also a linguistic reflection of a kind of Christian European unity. Finally, Latin permitted complex thought to find expression at a time when vernacular languages were not sufficiently developed to do so.

The European vernacular languages developed quickly and irregularly after the eighth century. Two generations after Charlemagne the Frankish language was giving way to Old French and Old High German. But vernacular linguistic development reflected the particularization of Europe. In the territory of France, for example, the language of the north, the *langue d'oil,* was very different from the language of the south, the *langue d'oc* (the terms derive from the different forms of the word for "yes": *oui* in northern and present-day French [from the Latin *hic*], *oc* in the south [from the Latin *hoc ille*], whence the teritorial term Occitania for the region). But dialects and smaller regional differences also survived, as did the different languages of Catalan in the southwest and Breton in Brittany.

A variant of the *langue d'oil* traveled with the Normans to England in 1066 and helped create the Anglo-Norman language of the Norman aristocracy, which displaced vernacular Old English to a socially inferior status. The Anglo-Norman tongue contributed to the shaping of yet another language, Middle English, which emerged in the twelfth century. Not until the reign of King John (1199–1216) could a post-Conquest king of England speak English. Not until 1349, was English used as a medium of teaching, and not until 1362 was it made the language of law. In the latter year, English was first used in a speech in Parliament. What has been called the triumph of English took place between 1350 and 1400.

The slow development and great variety of vernacular languages, and the slow formation of more widely understood literary vernaculars, made churchmen hesitant to permit translations of Scripture into European vernaculars on the often justified grounds that theological errors and mistranslations might crop up as a result of linguistic deficiency or the failure of the reader or hearer to understand the rules for the different levels of interpretation of scripture. But much devotional literature, especially after 1200, did make its way into common languages. Stories about Francis of Assisi, stories for use in sermons, meditative literature, and poetry all conveyed religious sentiments to wider circles of people. By the fourteenth century, the desire for vernacular Bibles had inspired several English translations and versions in other languages as well. John Hus wrote several pieces of religious literature in Czech, thereby stabilizing a standard form of literary Czech. Martin Luther's German bible did much the same for literary German early in the sixteenth century. Vernacular biographies of Jesus also appeared, supplementing the Latin Gospels. The coming of age of the European languages had a great impact on religious sentiment and expression, particularly in the work of preachers, during the fourteenth and fifteenth centuries.

A heightened sense of pastoral obligation, a broad awareness of the need for reform, the insistence on self-awareness through confession, the spread of religious fraternities and devotional movements, the growing self-consciousness of the laity, and the rise of vernacular religious literature—all are eloquent testimony to the spiritual condition of Europe in the fourteenth and fifteenth centuries. The fragmented ecclesiastical organization of the fifteenth century could not deal adequately with these movements as a whole and had only occasional contact with them in particular localities. The death of the learned and humanist pope Pius II (1458–1464) as he was setting out on a crusade against the Ottoman Turks (below, Chapter 20)—the first great humanist pope setting out on the last Crusade—may well have marked an end to one formal phase in the history of the idea of Christendom.

19

Power and Order

DEBATES ABOUT POWER AND ITS LEGITIMACY

By the thirteenth century, the various intellectual disciplines of Christian Europe—rhetoric, theology, canon law, philosophy, learned law, and the writing of history—had each come to deal with problems of the proper ordering of society and the place of legitimate political authority in it. Since everyone agreed that God had created the cosmos as the supreme form of order, human societies were expected to reflect the cosmos in their own search for orderliness. Although each intellectual discipline approached political theory from a different perspective and asked different questions about it, most political theory now agreed with the observed facts of political life and the religious and ethical theories that usually framed discussions of the legitimate sources and uses of public power and the earthly, as well as the spiritual, purpose of human society.

To most political thinkers, monarchy, tempered by divine law, was the ideal form of human government. Most political thinkers also recognized that monarchy might be misused—either by tyrants or by incompetent kings—and that some constraints on monarchy were a part of theories of legitimacy. Thinkers argued that the king's duty included both the maintenance of Christian society and the well-being of society: the maintenance of justice, peace, and material prosperity. The impact of Aristotle's ideas on politics in the thirteenth century was great, precisely because twelfth-century thinkers had already begun to consider such topics as the naturalness of society and the state, the common good, the limits of legitimate authority, and the rights of subjects in the face of injustice or oppression—as well as inventing the idea of human rights independently of any polity. Dante's *Comedy* and *Monarchy* carried a profound political message, that the world was ruled best when it was ruled by a single emperor, and the late thirteenth and fourteenth centuries produced a number of innovative and original examples of constitutional experiments as well as works of theory.

One of the best examples of the potential of political discourse in the late thirteenth- and fourteenth-century Europe is Marsiglio of Padua's treatise *The Defender of the Peace*, completed in 1324. Marsiglio (1275–1342) set out to solve the problem of the loss of civil peace in the Italian cities of the late thirteenth and fourteenth centuries, a problem that inspired some of the most dramatic and influential political discourse in European history and gave Italian writers a predominance in political theory until the end of the sixteenth century. Marsiglio drew upon the political thought and culture of the northern Italian cities, which had had to justify their independence, not only from ecclesiastical authority (as had Philip the Fair of France), but also from imperial authority. The Italian city-republics, consequently, made greater and wider use of Aristotelian political theory than did most transalpine thinkers, and they discovered and wrote much earlier than others about an organic concept of the political community. *The Defender of the Peace* is therefore the first European political treatise to offer a comparative vocabulary of political concepts and constitutional principles applicable to all political communities in general, not merely to particular monarchies, the Holy Roman Empire, or individual city-republics.

For Marsiglio, as for Aristotle and Aquinas, political order is a natural and beneficial attribute of human society. Its end is the formation of a new kind of political community, one whose members participate freely and productively in a society ordered on the basis of civic peace. Marsiglio's analysis of such a society is certainly not "liberal" or "democratic" in the modern sense of the term, but it may truly be called philosophically liberal. He drew upon many diverse strands of earlier political thought and the unique experience of Italian city-republics, to describe a universal set of political principles based on the overriding rights of an essentially lay community. That community also constituted the true church and had the right to elect the leader of that church, either collectively or by means of a designated human legislator. For Marsiglio, papal authority was delegated to incumbent popes by the Christian community and had no validity in and of itself.

Marsiglio ran afoul of Pope John XXII, who declared his work heretical (Dante's treatise on *Monarchy* was the only one of the poet's works also condemned for heretical political ideas), and Marsiglio spent much of his life at the imperial court of Louis of Bavaria. So did William of Occam, whose views, like those of Marsiglio, located ecclesiastical legitimacy in the laity and clergy, disputing the claims of popes and councils. For a short time in the early fourteenth century, the court of Louis of Bavaria produced the most original political philosophy in Europe. The work of Marsiglio and Occam was simplified and circulated by publicists, and its influence lasted well into the seventeenth century.

Others besides Marsiglio of Padua addressed political questions, and they usually wrote with a sense of urgency, a need to provide legitimate doctrine for real societies with real problems. It is in the fourteenth century, for example, that arguments about the nature and character of citizenship appear with great frequency in works of political theory, following the theologians', lawyers', and philosophers' distinctions between the individual, mortal body of the king and the representative, immortal body politic of the realm, which the king also possesses. At the level of the individual and the state, late medieval political thought reflected both real theory and real life, speculation and experience, their issues, and the stakes at risk. The political culture of the fourteenth and fifteenth centuries gave them even more opportunities to do this.

EMPERORS, KINGS, PRINCES, AND CITIES IN GERMANY

The disappearance of the Staufer dynasty left the Empire without an emperor and Germany without a king. The period between the death of Frederick II in 1250 and the election of Rudolf I of Hapsburg in 1273 is generally termed the Great Interregnum, although two rival candidates were simultaneously elected in 1257, and one of them, Richard of Cornwall, brother of Henry III of England, pressed his claim until his death in 1272. During this period, a number of elements dramatically transformed the constitutional structure of the kingdom of Germany.

One of the most striking of these elements was the breakup and dissipation of the vast Staufer properties throughout Germany. These properties and the public rights attached to them consisted of lands, rights of taxation in cities, a number of fiscal rights in particular districts, and forests, taxes from Jews, and the revenues of a number of courts of law. As these were taken over by individuals and cities, they constituted a steady drain on royal resources. Later rulers also contributed to this drain by selling imperial offices, pledging lands to creditors, and failing to develop such alternate revenues as taxation. From 1273 on, the kings of Germany were forced once again to depend on their own personal resources and those they could acquire through legal, military, or dynastic policies.

A second important element was the regularization of the number and character of those who elected the king and emperor into a recognized electoral college, ultimately a separate order of nobles within the kingdom, lower only than the king himself, and in many ways sharers in the royal power. The first mention of a specific group of people empowered "by law" to elect the king occurs in a document written on behalf of the candidacy of Otto IV in 1198. In 1198, sixteen nobles claimed to be the legal lay electors, but in 1356, the emperor Charles IV established the number at seven: three ecclesiastical electors and four lay electors. The ecclesiastical electors were the archbishops of Mainz, Trier, and Cologne, who were also the chancellors of Germany, Burgundy, and Italy, respectively and rulers of the oldest archbishoprics in German lands. The four lay electors were the Count Palatine of the Rhine, the duke of Saxony, the Margrave of Brandenburg, and the King of Bohemia. The electoral dignity became hereditary in their families. The four lay electors had also performed certain ceremonial functions in the royal court, those of steward, marshal, chamberlain, and cupbearer.

The final number of four lay electors has long posed a problem for historians: Why these four and not, for example, the Duke of Bavaria (who in fact contested an electoral role until the fourteenth century) or other powerful nobles? The most recent argument put forth to explain the number of lay electors is very persuasive. The historian Armin Wolf has argued that these were the surviving male descendants and representatives of the female lines of the Ottonian, or Saxon, dynasty that ended in the male line in 1024, thus casting the old debate about election and inheritance in a new light: Although the kings became clearly electable, they were elected by electors whose position was hereditary. From 1257 until the publication of the Golden Bull of 1356, the powers of the electors, their status among the nobility, their relation to the king, and the inviolability of their lands were made more and more precise by law. By the middle of the fourteenth century, they constituted an order that had no parallel elsewhere in Europe.

Thus, the tasks that faced Rudolf of Hapsburg (1273–1291) were formidable, and they were increased by the powerful rivalry of King Ottakar of Bohemia, who had added to his domains the large and important territories of Carinthia, Lower Austria and Styria. During a long conflict, Rudolf declared these territories to be vacant imperial fiefs, and Ottakar refused to pay homage to the king for them. At the battle of the Marchfeld in 1278, Rudolf was victorious, and he transferred these territories to his son, Albert, thus beginning the Hapsburg rule in Austria that lasted until 1918. From 1273 on, the Hapsburgs became one of the most powerful German noble families, providing kings in Albert I (1298–1308) and Albert II (1438–1439) and an emperor, Frederick III (1440–1493). But the success of Rudolf of Hapsburg also determined the electors to seek out other candidates for the throne, and throughout the fourteenth century, the Wittelsbach and Luxemburg Dynasties contended with the Hapsburgs and with each other as the rulers of Germany, Austria, and Bohemia. Imperial history in the fourteenth and fifteenth centuries became the history of the rivalry among these three families.

From the death of Rudolf I in 1291 a series of emperors invoked grand ideals, but they achieved their greatest successes as dynasty-builders. The history of the Hapsburg, Wittelsbach, and Luxemburg Dynasties is much more important in their own lands—Austria, Bavaria, and Bohemia—than in the history of the German kingdom or empire.

By the middle of the fourteenth century, the "German lands," as the kingdom was commonly called, had been constitutionally and territorially transformed. On the frontiers as well, new pressures were felt. The sons and successors of Charles IV, Wenzel (1378–1400) and Sigismund (1411–1437), of the Luxemburg Dynasty, concentrated largely on Bohemian and Hungarian affairs. Sigismund's involvement in the attempts at Church reform and reunion at the Council of Constance, efforts which were recognized as the emperor's unique responsibility as the head of Christian society, nevertheless cost him dearly in prestige and power. At the western edge of the empire, the growing influence of France and the power of the Duchy of Burgundy (see below, this chapter) eroded royal power there and alienated considerable noble loyalty.

For all of its economic vitality, the settlement of new lands in the north and east, the planning of towns and villages, and the establishment of a lively and productive trading network, the kingdom of Germany remained fragmented politically, and the developments in the late thirteenth and fourteenth centuries preserved and regularized that fragmentation. Even the more ambitious reigns of Frederick III (1440–1493) and

Maximilian I (1493–1519), which established the Hapsburg Dynasty firmly upon the imperial throne, failed to consolidate the divided kingdom. The political experimentation of the fourteenth and fifteenth centuries left hundreds of principalities, towns, and greatly weakened emperors to divide the riches and the people of a vastly expanded Germany. The political vigor that in other states focused on centralizing governance and developing various sentiments of national identity, remained focused in the German lands on local princely and ecclesiastical authority.

THE HUNDRED YEARS' WAR: ENGLAND AND FRANCE

Rivalry among Italian city-republics, the conflict between the Wittelsbach emperor Louis of Bavaria and Pope John XXII, and the political growth and development of most territorial monarchies in the fourteenth and fifteenth centuries are all manifestations of the political problems that concerned Marsiglio of Padua and other political theorists. But there is no better or broader example of the relation between old and new political theory and old and new political experience than the long war between the rulers of England and France that lasted from 1337 to 1453 and acquired the dramatic but erroneous name of the Hundred Years' War. Like most early European conflicts, it began as a private war between rival kings. It ended by consuming resources and people on a national scale, transforming the political culture of its participants, and influencing the affairs of other powers drawn into it.

The heavy hand of Edward I of England had suppressed rebellions against his father, Henry III, controlled the turbulent English aristocracy during his own reign, established (for a short time) the supremacy of the English king in Scotland, and intervened in the affairs of the turbulent French province of Flanders. Flanders, with its prosperous cities of Ghent, Bruges, and Ypres, was a key trading partner for English wool, and its wealthy and independent-minded citizens regularly contended with both the count of Flanders and his lord, the king of France, for their economic and political independence. In 1302, for example, an army organized by the Flemish cities defeated the army of Philip IV at Courtrai. Although the king of France reasserted his authority in 1305 in the treaty of Atlis-sur-Orge, the territories in Flanders remained ready to revolt any time they considered their economic and political interests threatened. The counts of Flanders themselves often turned to England when threatened by the power of their own lords, the kings of France. English intervention in Flanders, particularly during the struggle between Edward I and Philip IV, had far greater consequences than English intervention in Scotland. One reason for this was the location of Flanders. The northernmost province of the kingdom of France, Flanders was also the gateway into the counties of Holland and Zeeland to the north and to the territories of Brabant and Hainault to the east and south—the latter two technically part of the old duchy of Lower Lorraine and belonging, in theory at least, to the jurisdiction of the king-emperor of the German lands.

But the death of strong kings was inevitably the signal for a resurgence of the aristocracy and a reconsideration of both domestic and foreign policy, especially when faced

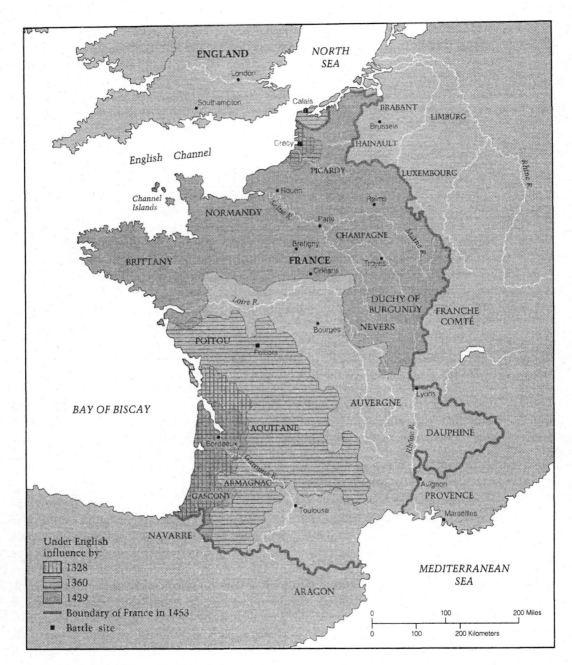

The Hundred Years' War and English rule in France.

with the prospect of a weaker successor. Upon Edward's death and the increasingly perceived political incompetence of his successor, Edward II (1307–1327), the Scots, under Robert I (1306–1329), the Bruce, successfully asserted independence from England, defeating an English army at the Battle of Bannockburn in 1314. Aristocratic discontent and the alienation of his queen, Isabella, led to Edward II's deposition and murder and the placing of his young son, Edward III (1327–1377), on the throne in his place. Edward III was far more able and had far fewer opponents than his father.

In France, the succession crises of 1314–1328 led to the replacement of the direct Capetian Dynasty by the cadet Valois branch of the dynasty in the person of Philip VI (1328–1350). But the agreement of the great princes of France on Philip VI was not uncontested. Philip VI was the son of Charles of Valois (d. 1325), the brother of Philip IV of France. Edward III of England was the grandson of Philip IV through his mother, Isabella of France. Edward could claim direct descent, and Philip only collateral descent (from a junior branch of the house of Capet) in the Valois line, although his grandfather had been Philip III of France. Edward was also the closest surviving male relative of the last Capetian king, Charles IV, while Philip VI was only his cousin. In strict dynastic terms, Edward III had the better claim. To confuse matters further, the last three Capetian kings had left daughters, whose rights to succeed to the crown of France were passed over by the great princes, although one of them, Joan, daughter of Louis X, was allowed to inherit the crown of Navarre in 1328.

Although the question of the right of a female to succeed to the throne of France did not come up—Edward III's mother, Isabella of France, never claimed a right to succeed—the question of whether a right to succeed could pass through a woman to her son raised a problem that was exacerbated when, in 1332, Joan of Navarre and her husband, Philip of Evreux, had a son, later king Charles the Bad of Navarre, who claimed that his right to the French crown was superior to that of Edward III. But Charles's claim also passed through a woman. In effect, the French princes had made a constitutional decision, not only ignoring the possibility that a woman might rule France, but denying that any claim to the throne of France could descend through a woman to her son. Publicists of this view referred to the old Salic law of the early Franks for historical support, although the claim was extremely weak.

Edward did not assert a claim to Philip's throne immediately, performed homage to the king for his lands in Gascony, and turned his attention to English affairs. The political instability of England during the early reign of Edward III and the lack of unanimity in France about Philip's legal title to the throne exacerbated a number of structural elements in the governance of France and eventually led to Edward's making a claim on the French throne and to war with England. Large segments of France were ruled by virtually independent dynasties of nobles—Brittany, Aquitaine, and Flanders. Other large territories were given as appanages to royal children, especially the duchies of Burgundy and Bourbon and the counties of Artois, Alençon, and Evreux. The financial resources of the kings of France were thus considerably reduced at a moment when the number of wars they fought increased, royal expenses rose, royal arsenals—particularly those at Narbonne and Rouen—became more costly, the pay of soldiers rose, the size of armies grew bigger, and tax collections failed. One resource of the kings of France had been gross confiscations—of the property of expelled Jews in 1306, and of some of the wealth of the Order of Templars in 1313. Kings had also attempted to manipulate the metallic content and value of the coinage. Several historians have argued that at the death of Philip IV in 1314, the kingdom of France was at the zenith of its power—but also at the absolute limits of its economic and political capacities.

The succession crises of 1314–1328 emphasized the limited resources of the French crown and the structural dangers to the kingdom. The three territories of Brittany, Aquitaine, and Flanders were closely tied to the interests of the king of England, as was the commerce of Flanders. That part of Aquitaine known as Gascony had been in the English king's hands since the Treaty of Paris in 1259. In 1337, however, Philip VI confiscated the duchy of Gascony from Edward III, and Edward III undertook a campaign against the king of France in Flanders, the most expensive military enterprise of any English king in history to that date. The opening salvos of the Hundred Years' War took place in Flanders, culminating in the combined naval-infantry victory of the English at Sluys in 1340.

But Flanders did not long remain the main theater of war. In 1337, and again in 1340, Edward III finally claimed the crown of France. His claims to legitimacy were made in a period of financial crisis and aristocratic ascendance, and they influenced governmental policy in such territories as Gascony and Brittany, which, although they were in France, were either ruled or strongly influenced by England. In 1341, a disputed succession to the duchy of Brittany created another arena for English and French royal conflict, as did the pressing of the French king's claims to Gascony, the English-ruled enclave in southwestern France.

The English occupation of Gascony represented virtually all that was left of the once extensive Angevin empire. Technically, the king of England was vassal to the king of France for his lordship of Gascony, but the roles of lord and vassal became very strained in the thirteenth and fourteenth centuries when both happened to be kings. Theorists on both sides argued that "the king shall be no man's vassal." The kings of England had long administered Gascony in much the same way that they administered other crown possessions to which they had absolute authority. Moreover, Gascon wine was part of a complex English economy that included free access to Flemish wool centers, Breton salt processing, and Portuguese trade. The conflict between lord and vassal over Gascony is simply one way of looking at a set of problems that possessed equally critical economic and diplomatic dimensions. The lord-vassal relationship, if pressed too strictly, was no longer capable of accommodating these problems adequately.

The French pressure on Gascony and the English claim to the French throne heightened tensions between the two monarchs, which were exacerbated by the French alliance with Scotland. In 1340, the English destroyed a French fleet at Sluys, and from then until the Treaty of Bretigny in 1360, the English kept the upper hand in the war. England launched armed expeditions into France, winning pitched battles at Crécy and Poitiers in 1346 and 1356, capturing the Channel Islands in 1345, and the great port of Calais in 1347. The battle of Poitiers resulted in the humiliating English capture of King John II of France and their holding him in England for an enormous ransom. But in spite of significant victories, the war proved difficult to control and very expensive. Moreover, both kingdoms were devastated by the Black Death of 1348. The early English triumphs helped strengthen the prestige and the power of Edward III, but the French losses, culminating in the capture of King John II in 1356, precipitated intense factionalism among the nobility, and in 1356–1358, a social revolution in Paris itself, the *Jacquerie,* led by Robert LeCoq, bishop of Laon, and Etienne Marcel, provost of the merchants of Paris.

The reign of Charles V (1364–1380) witnessed significant improvements for France. Between the capture of his father John II, and John's death in 1364, Charles was the regent of France. In that capacity, he first subdued the rebels of 1358 and then successfully negotiated his father's ransom and release. By 1369, Charles's administrative and financial reforms had allowed him to resume the war, in which he profited from the senility of Edward III, the deaths of Edward's son, the Black Prince, in 1376, and of Edward III himself in 1377, and the minority of the Black Prince's son, Richard II (1377–1399), to gain a truce. Charles's fiscal and military reforms were only part of his success. His artistic and literary patronage helped inaugurate the role of the French crown as a leader in intellectual and artistic, as well as political, life.

However, Charles's son Charles VI (1380–1422) was a minor at his accession, and his long reign was also troubled by his periodic insanity after 1392. While the great noble families were contending for power over Charles VI, John the Fearless, Duke of Burgundy (1404–1419), in a dramatic step against his rivals for control of the French king, allied with England. Because the Duchy of Burgundy had been linked to the County of Flanders through the marriage of John's father Philip the Bold (1384–1404) and Margaret de Male, hereditary countess of Flanders, the potential for a new and greatly expanded Burgundian state considerably upset the conventional balance of power (below, this Chapter). Upon the English resumption of the war in 1415, then, France was plunged into far greater misery than it had experienced from 1340 to 1360.

England had made little use of its early victories in the war, and forces of discontent built during the last years of the disabled Edward III. The loss of the king's popular and widely admired son, the Black Prince, and the troubled minority of Richard II permitted great nobles, particularly Edward III's younger brother John of Gaunt, duke of Lancaster, to assume ascendancy over the crown and the young king and create the economic policies that helped precipitate the Peasants' Revolt of 1381. Richard II's peace policy and his intelligent but autocratic attempts to restore royal control over the government and nobles led to his deposition and murder in 1399, the usurpation of the throne by Henry IV (1399–1413), son of John of Gaunt, and the beginning of the royal house of Lancaster, a cadet branch of the Plantagenets.

Henry V (1413–1422), facing rebellions in the north and discontent at home, reopened the war with France in 1415, and the English forces sustained a major victory at Agincourt in 1415. At the Treaty of Troyes in 1420, Henry V's title to the throne of France was guaranteed. When Charles VI of France died in 1422, he left a shattered kingdom with an English king on its throne, an empty treasury, bitter resentment against the Crown and the higher nobility, and a legally disinherited son, Charles, ruling a small part of southern France from an empty, borrowed palace in the old city of Bourges.

Between 1415 and 1453, the tone of the war changed. The length of the conflict, its social and economic costs and consequences, the political instability that ensued, and the character of the fighting made it considerably more savage than earlier stages of the war, and France, the invaded land, bore the brunt of these effects first. The complete and efficient occupation of a conquered nation is difficult in the present, and it was impossible in the fifteenth century. Although England began the fifteenth century by ruling most of northern France, it had neither the population nor the ability to "occupy" the kingdom, nor could it support indefinitely an expensive expeditionary force in an economically depleted country. Intimidation of the population had become a matter of English policy, and the economic and social consequences of this intimidation influenced the character of English rule. Thus, as the character of the war changed and the costs of war mounted, opportunities for dissension increased considerably, whether over traditional problems such as privilege and status or over novelties such as the burden of taxes and the less tangible circumstances of shifting fortunes. In addition, the increasing number of mercenary companies of soldiers raised the level of violence throughout France and neighboring lands, particularly when these armies were temporarily disbanded and had to support themselves without a princely or royal paymaster.

Nor did the images of chivalric warfare with which nobles liked to amuse themselves correspond with the actual conduct of the war. Cannon began to be used at the end of the fourteenth century, requiring both new kinds of fortification and new siege equipment and tactics. Increasingly, kings turned to mercenary troops, either independent companies under their own leaders (some of whom were nobles trying to augment their income) or troops recruited and paid directly by the kings. At the level of nobility, enemies were treated with the respect that their high status required, but the ordinary soldiers were brutally maimed and slaughtered, and the civilian population was treated no differently by the same nobles who were so considerate of each other.

Victories also stirred the opinions of a wider public in England, since returning soldiers brought back hostages for large ransoms, booty, and stories of valor and adventure. The reigns of Edward III and Henry V were long celebrated in English history because of these early victories and the image of a nation in arms that later writers imagined.

France's internal stresses between 1340 and 1430 prefigured the internal conflicts of 1380 to 1480 in England. The shifting aims of war, changing political circumstances, and mutual reluctance of France and England to surrender, respectively, sovereignty and the claim to the French throne, revealed that there was no clear way of ending the conflict that might satisfy all interested parties.

PATTERNS OF RECOVERY: FRANCE

In spite of England's initial triumphs, the toll of prolonged war and the poverty of English institutional response to its social and economic crises threatened its hold on France. Not the least important element of French resistance was the disinherited prince himself. Charles VII (1422–1461), weakened by the Treaty of Troyes and suffering from the added imputation of illegitimacy, was an unlikely reformer. Sickly, personally unattractive, completely unwarlike, and dominated by powerful and ruthless favorites, he helplessly witnessed the English armies proceed south from 1422 to 1428 through Maine and Anjou toward his temporary residence in Bourges. But in 1428, French military resistance stiffened. Among the complex causes for this new resistance was the astonishing appearance of a sixteen-year-old peasant girl named Joan "of Arc" from Domremy, a small town on the frontier of Lorraine and Champagne. Arriving at Charles's court at Chinon in 1429, Joan claimed that Saints Michael, Catherine, and Margaret had "told me of the pitiful state of France and told me that I must go to help the King of France." In April, Joan and the leaders of the French army relieved the English siege of Orleans, the gateway to Bourges and the south of France, a battle in which Joan showed great courage and was wounded. In July, Charles was able to proceed to Rheims for his coronation. But in further pursuing the war, Joan was captured by the Burgundian allies of England (see next section) in 1430, tried by an irregular ecclesiastical court, condemned as a relapsed heretic, and burned at the stake in 1431.

But Joan's execution did not substantially weaken France. The recent victories over the English and renewed diplomatic relations with the duke of Burgundy, Philip the Good, managed to strengthen Charles's cause. In 1434, the legitimacy of Charles VII's birth was affirmed by the Council of Basel, and in 1435, at the Congress of Arras, he was formally reconciled with Philip the Good (1419–1467), successor to John the Fearless as duke of Burgundy. By 1453, Charles had won back northern France, Normandy, and Gascony and had begun to implement many of the reforms instituted by his grandfather, Charles V. In 1456, he initiated the overturning of the verdict of heresy on Joan of Arc. The last years of Charles's reign were spent restoring royal fiscal and political dominion over a drastically weakened kingdom against the discredited nobility and the rebellious burghers. When he died in 1461, Charles VII had laid the foundations for the growth of monarchical power and national order.

Joan "of Arc" was the most dramatic, but not the most efficient, servant of Charles VII. Over the long process of recovery and reform, Charles was also served by the great financier Jacques Coeur. A wealthy merchant of Bourges, Coeur traveled and traded in the Mediterranean and returned to France to be made master of the royal mint at Paris in 1436. In 1437, Charles made Coeur his treasurer, and in this post, Coeur became the king's chief commercial and financial entrepreneur. Coeur helped restore the financial stability of the French Crown, and his own private trading network helped open the Mediterranean to French trade, in which Coeur also had a hand, trading cloth, salt, silver, copper, leathers, and furs. Like many successful traders, he operated money exchanges as well. Coeur grew so wealthy that he was personally able to lend Charles 200,000 gold crowns in 1449, enabling the king to begin the reconquest of Normandy. The services of Joan and Jacques Coeur gave Charles VII the epithet by which he is known to history, Charles le Bien Servi—Charles the Well-Served.

Charles's son Louis XI (1461–1483) built upon his father's successes in striking ways. A rebel against Charles as a youth, Louis had lived a complex and anxious life for many years. Of this period, Louis' biographer Philip de Commines once remarked: "What he did in his youth, when he was a fugitive from his father under the Duke of Burgundy, was very valuable to him, for he was compelled to please those of whom he had need, and this benefit taught him the meaning of adversity." Louis' capacity for finding out information, dissembling his real intentions, and controlling the French nobles gave him the nickname of "the Spider King," a reputation that Louis himself did little to discourage.

But Louis also worked. Commines elsewhere remarked: "I think that if all the good days he enjoyed during his life, days in which he had more pleasure and happiness than hard work and trouble, were carefully numbered, they would be found to be few; I believe one would find twenty days of travail and worry for every one of ease and pleasure." Louis fully developed the use of royal authority to alleviate the economic problems of his kingdom. He encouraged industries and domestic trade, continued his father's practice of abolishing internal tolls and tariffs, and sponsored fairs that brought the money of others into France and prevented a financial drain on the kingdom. On the other hand, Louis continually collected old taxes and levied new ones. He waged economic warfare abroad and practiced economic protectionism at home.

Louis XI was one of the first monarchs in European history to possess an accurate sense of the potential economic power of the royal government in alliance with a national economy. At his death in 1483, France had greatly improved its economic position, both internally and in relation to other kingdoms, the great nobles had generally been humbled, and the income of the Crown had nearly quadrupled. Charles VII had left Louis an income of 1,800,000 pounds per year. Louis left his successor, Charles VIII, an income of 4,700,000 pounds per year, a full treasury, a strong diplomatic position, a kingdom at peace, and a restored throne.

"I, A WOMAN, DARE"

The case of Joan ("of Arc" was her father's surname, but she did not use it, calling herself only "Joan the Maid"), an illiterate young peasant woman from Domremy, not only stirred the sluggish Charles VII of France and greatly vexed the English, but it also inspired a poem, the *Ditié de Jehanne d'Arc* (*The Tale of Joan of Arc*), written by Christine de Pizan. Christine was born either in the Venetian Republic or in Bologna, probably in 1365. She moved with her father to France in 1368, where he had been invited to serve as astrologer to King Charles V. She married a minor official at the royal court in 1380. Upon the death of her husband in 1390, Christine was left a twenty-five-year-old widow with three small children to raise and very little money.

Christine had come from and married into a circle of literate, educated men, and was literate and learned herself, although apparently without formal education. But she was a remarkably quick student, having read both Boethius' *Consolation of Philosophy* and Ovid, as well as a substantial learned and popular literature. She was one of the first writers in France to mention the work of Dante. She may at first have become a copyist of manuscripts for patrons, a profession that required an accomplished and disciplined script, and she occasionally wrote verses for her own spiritual consolation. Soon, however, certainly by the 1390s, her lyric poems began to attract a wider audience, some of them criticizing the male-dominated themes of courtly love by focusing on the theme of deceived and abandoned women, and on the sorrows of being a widow—at the time, an original topic. In 1402, Christine participated in a literary dispute over the *Romance of the Rose,* taking the position that it slandered women, and leading her into more ambitious literary ventures. Her great work, *The Book of the City of Ladies,* continued her defense of women, this time by emphasizing their contributions to civilization and extensively discussing the problems they faced in organizing their world. These and Christine's other works inspired her to write what was probably her last work, a poem in praise of Joan, who seemed to her an ideal subject for her long argument on behalf of women and feminine identity.

The *Ditié* had another purpose. Written in 1429, when it appeared that Joan and Charles VII would soon occupy Paris and permit Christine's return to the city from which she had been exiled since 1418, the poem praises Joan for raising Christine's own prospects of return, and praises Charles VII for promising a period of peace and prosperity to France. The poem is thus political on the large scale as well as in praise of Joan the individual. Christine says that Joan's career reflects not only divine providence, but God's particular favor toward France. Joan is identified with a number of Old Testament heroines; her achievements are miracles, and thus a proof of divine favor. But Christine also raises the political theme; not divine providence alone, but the character of France and its monarchy are also her theme. For Christine displays a broad and complex political vision, comprised of anti-English sentiments, but also devotion to France and its kings and her expectation of the recovery of the prosperity of France.

Christine links her theme of the defense of women to her other political concerns. She emphasizes Joan's youth in order to show how Joan surpasses all other heroines. Joan's achievements have not only saved France, but have saved womankind, as well as exemplifying the importance of women in their own right, rather than as appurtenances to the male-dominated chivalric world. The *Ditié* was a kind of summing-up of Christine's long concerns with philosophy, politics, religion, and the defense of women with a woman's voice. As Christine once wrote, anticipating much of the criticism that she foresaw her work and thought might generate:

> *Let no one accuse me of unreason, of arrogance or presumption, for daring, I, a woman, to challenge and answer back so subtle an author* [*Jean de Meung, the author of the* Romance of the Rose] *or for diminishing the praise due his work, when he, one man on his own, has dared to slander and reproach the entire female sex without exception.*

The figures of Joan and Christine illustrate other aspects of the partial recovery of France—and, in a wider sense, of Europe—from the silences that had been generated by a long tradition of misogyny and the concealment of women and women's lack of a feminine and public voice.

PATTERNS OF RECOVERY: ENGLAND

England recovered politically less quickly than France, and in a different way. The overstrained English governmental institutions were not improved by Lancastrian rule, and the collapse of the English occupation of France, coupled with the early death of Henry V in 1422 and the long minority of Henry VI (1422–1461), precipitated political and military struggles over royal power that lasted nearly to the end of the fifteenth century.

The costs of the wars had been enormous compared with the decreasing political and financial returns from English victories, and the resulting strain imposed on English royal finances had led to violent clashes within the high aristocracy and to arguments that the king should "live of his own"—his normal financial income and the returns on his properties—and respect the privileges of the nobility without tapping their purses. The reign of Henry VI witnessed fiscal and political collapse, and the reversals of English fortune in France plunged England into the dynastic conflicts commonly called the Wars of the Roses (1454–1485). The red rose was the emblem of the house of Lancaster, the white rose that of the house of York.

Edward of York deposed Henry VI and assumed the crown for himself as Edward IV (1461–1483). Upon Edward's death, his brother, Richard of Gloucester, claimed the protectorship of Edward's son, Edward V (r. April–June, 1483) and his brother, whom he confined in the Tower of London. They were never heard of again, and Richard seized the throne and ruled as Richard III (1483–1485). The opposition Lancastrians, however, assembled an army and engaged the army of Richard on Bosworth Field, where he was killed. The crown went to Henry Tudor (as Henry VII, 1485–1509), who married Elizabeth, the surviving daughter of Edward IV, technically uniting the dynasties of the roses. Henry's rule was restrained in England, since his enemies had been defeated and taxes lowered, but his diplomatic vision extended widely. His daughter Margaret married James IV Stuart of Scotland, establishing the Tudor dynasty's connection to the Stuart dynasty, which bore fruit in 1603, when Margaret's great-grandson James VI of Scotland succeeded her niece Elizabeth I Tudor as King James I of England. Henry VII's eldest son, Arthur, was married to Catherine of Aragon, daughter of Ferdinand of Aragon and Isabella of Castile. Upon Arthur's death, Catherine became the first wife of his younger brother, Henry, who became Henry VIII in 1509. These three marriages did much to shape the histories of England, Scotland, and Spain over the next two centuries.

But the economic, military, and social consequences of these over-romanticized wars turned out to be quite small. The changes of dynasty that placed Edward IV on the throne in 1461 and then Henry VII in 1485 were accompanied by the increasing ability of the English monarchs after 1461 to learn indeed for a time how to "live of their own" and capitalize on the end of expensive foreign wars, to reorganize royal finances, and to restrain aristocratic factionalism in favor of a stable, but not particularly strong, royal rule. England's recovery was also achieved at the expense of the vast English territorial claims in France. Except for the city of Calais, the Channel became the dividing line for the two kingdoms from the late fifteenth century on.

THE GREAT DUCHY OF THE WEST:
THE BURGUNDIAN LOW COUNTRIES

The scope and pressures of the Hundred Years' War, especially in the County of Flanders and the western German territories of Hainault and Brabant help to account for the appearance of a remarkable principality in the late fourteenth and fifteenth centuries, Burgundy, "The Great Duchy of the West." Almost from the outset of the great conflict between France and England, other powers were drawn into the contest. England attempted to interfere in Flanders and France in Scotland. England and France both interfered in the struggle between Pedro the Cruel of Castile and the successful rebel, Henry of Trastàmara. The king of Bohemia, John of Luxemburg, son of the emperor Henry VII and father of the emperor Charles IV, was killed by the English at the battle of Crécy while fighting on the side of France. But there is no greater example of the opportunities, as well as the new kinds of alliances, that the Hundred Years' War offered to ambitious princes than the case of Valois Burgundy.

One of the techniques developed by the French monarchy in the thirteenth and fourteenth centuries in order to bind together the different children of the king, was the creation of the *appanage*. The *appanage* was an extraordinary territorial lordship, sometimes over a recently acquired province, given to younger sons of the royal family as a means of maintaining for them a respectable status in the world while at the same time binding the new territories more closely to the royal dynasty. After the rule of several generations descended from the original recipient, however, some of these *appanages* became as troublesome to the kings as the other great principalities of other great families not related to the dynasty. The story of fifteenth-century Burgundy is a classic example of an *appanage* run wild that gradually turned into an independent princely state.

Ever since its days as a virtually independent territory at the end of the Carolingian period, Burgundy had been a prosperous, largely rural principality, part of which came under the rule of the German kings and emperors, and part of which was ruled by dukes who were often very closely related to the royal house of France. Its principal city, Dijon, was small, and its economy largely agricultural, producing chiefly the excellent wines that were—and still are—sent across Europe.

At the death of Duke Philip de Rouvres in 1361, King John II of France claimed the duchy and got part of it, although another part descended to Margaret of Flanders. When John II died in 1364, he left his part of the duchy of Burgundy to his youngest son, Philip the Bold, who married Margaret of Flanders in 1369, thereby not only reuniting Burgundy but also adding the immensely wealthy and troublesome territories of Flanders to his lands, and creating two great principalities extending nearly from the Alps to the North Sea between the kingdoms of Germany and France, separated only by Lorraine. Philip, nicknamed the Bold (1342–1404) because of his heroic conduct at the battle of Poitiers in 1356, became one of the great princes of France, a strong influence on his royal brother, Charles V, and on his young and unstable nephew, who later became Charles VI (1380–1422).

Philip's son and successor, John the Fearless (1404–1419), inherited his father's wealth and power. Philip's other children married into neighboring noble families, and both Philip and John the Fearless received enormous revenues from the French Crown as well as their various princely revenues from their possessions in Flanders and Burgundy.

Bitter rivalry arose between John the Fearless and the other great princes of France, particularly over the question of who was to control Charles VI during that king's increasingly frequent periods of insanity. John the Fearless was apparently responsible for the assassination in 1407 of his greatest rival, the Duke of Orleans, and John's bitter hatred of his other opponents led him to support Henry V of England when Henry invaded France in 1415. In 1419, John himself was assassinated. His son, Philip the Good (1419–1467), continued the English alliance, cemented at the Treaty of Troyes in 1420, in which Henry V's claim to the throne of France was recognized. After the death of Charles VI in 1422, Philip the Good, Duke of Burgundy, was a vastly more powerful figure in France than the young and uncrowned dauphin Charles, who possessed only an empty treasury and few allies, and who had been legally disinherited by his father Charles VI, who had also denied the legitimacy of Charles's birth. The young "King of Bourges," as Charles was sarcastically called, appeared insignificant compared to his prosperous and successful cousin, Philip of Burgundy and Flanders.

Although the many different territories ruled by Philip the Good in his different (and entirely distinct) capacities of Duke of Burgundy, Count of Flanders, and other titles posed all of the problems of localism, variety, and inconsistency that often accompanied personal empire-building in the later Middle Ages, the dukes of Burgundy were generally successful in establishing their customary rights of governance and revenue throughout their lands, and they devised an impressive court to rule over all of them. So much did they deftly employ ceremony and political ritual along with force, that some historians have referred to their rule as a "theater-state," in which impression and illusion played roles equal to that of power and military force. They used and adapted some of the governmental techniques developed in the kingdom of France, which had also grown strong by acquiring territories with different histories, institutions, and traditional forms of limitation on the powers of their princes.

The combination of territories that the Dukes of Burgundy inherited, acquired by marriage, and conquered was the most diverse of any medieval state. Although Burgundy was largely agricultural, containing only a few small cities, the County of Flanders was part of the most economically prosperous and densely populated area north of Italy. Its two major cities, Ghent and Bruges, were the second and third largest cities north of the Alps (the first was Paris). The county held still other substantial cities, and these were largely merchant- and crafts-dominated, contained a substantial manufacturing base—based on their virtual monopoly on finishing raw English wool—and served as centers of commerce with the cities of northern Italy and the great trading network along the Rhine and the Baltic Sea. Such a territory was difficult to rule, as the long history of struggles between the cities and the counts, and those between the counts and the kings of France, indicate. The Flemish towns were ruled by a broader group of citizens than anywhere else in Europe, were difficult to govern, and had long-worked-out principles of insisting on their own consent to taxation—and of rebelling when their liberties were infringed. Both in Flanders and Brabant, the cities prided themselves on the custom of the *Joyeuse Entrée*, the *Blijde Inkomst*—the formal promise to respect the town's traditional liberties and privileges made by a new count upon his first formal entry into a city. In 1356, a *Joyeuse Entrée* was forced upon the Duke and Duchess of Brabant by the entire territory. The terms of this agreement required that the duchy not be divided, that only Brabanters could hold government office, and that the prince could not make war or coin money without the consent of his subjects. It is virtually the earliest written constitution in European history.

In addition to Flanders, the Dukes of Burgundy slowly acquired comital and ducal rights over other territories, notably Luxemburg, Limburg, Namur, Brabant (with its cities of Brussels and Leuven) and Hainault, as well as the independent cities of Antwerp and Mechelen. They usually managed to place candidates of their choice in the Prince-Bishoprics of Liège and Utrecht, and they exerted influence on the important northern counties of Holland and Zeeland and the Duchy of Guelders.

To balance all of their different titles, rights, and complex territories was an immensely difficult task for the Dukes of Burgundy, but the rewards for doing so successfully were great—the ducal income was enormous and ducal patronage was lavish. Poets, manuscript illuminators, sculptors, tapestry-weavers, musicians, and the great fifteenth-century Flemish painters all enjoyed ducal patronage on a scale unknown elsewhere in Europe. By the mid fifteenth century, the Dukes of Burgundy were as powerful and respected as any rulers in Europe. Their prestige in turn helped them to govern their various territories.

The greatest creation of the dukes of Burgundy was the ducal court. A successful and prestigious court was one of the most important tools any ruler had, both for display and admiration and for asserting control over a varied and often violent and ambitious nobility. By the beginning of the fifteenth century, many of the royal courts that had dominated Europe earlier were either in decline or politically divided. The Bohemian court of Prague declined after the death of Charles IV; that of Vienna was still being developed; that of Paris had been greatly diminished by warfare and political rivalry, and that of Westminster by the straitened circumstances of the kings. The creation of the ducal court of Burgundy gave the dukes access to most of the political talent in their territories, and their patronage supported some of the greatest artists of fifteenth-century Europe. Located originally in the city of Dijon, but later moved to Flanders, the court of the dukes of Burgundy became an instrument of administration as well as display, patronage, and diplomacy. Its reputation grew rapidly, and its style and manner influenced the other courts of Europe down to the sixteenth century. In addition, the dukes developed a talented and loyal cadre of educated noble and nonnoble servants, an able and salaried group of domestic officials, and an efficient and usually full treasury, managed from the city of Lille.

The administrative side of the court was complemented by its social side. The dukes attracted and bound to themselves the nobility from throughout their dominions and abroad, thus weakening local resistance to their centralizing powers, and they blended the various regional nobilities by arranging their marriages. The Dukes also created the knightly Order of the Golden Fleece in 1430, the most prestigious military order in Europe, thus creating yet another means of tying their different noble subjects and more distant admirers more closely to their own rule.

Poets, chroniclers, and writers of romances all found patronage at Dijon, and visual artists, then still considered mere domestic servants in most of the rest of Europe, were treated with respect by their ducal master. Some of the best examples of early Netherlandish painting, for example, the sculptures by Klaas Sluter and the great Baerze-Broderlam altarpiece for the Charterhouse at Champmol, the burial place of the dukes, were produced for the ducal court of Burgundy. The painters Jan Van Eyck and

Rogier Van Der Weyden did some of their greatest work on ducal commission. And the duke's officials followed suit. Philip the Good's great Chancellor, Nicholas Rolin, not only had his own portrait painted by Van Eyck, but commissioned the great *Last Judgment* from Van Der Weyden for the hospital he founded at Beaune, not far from Dijon. If the Low Countries rivaled Italy for the greatest painters of the fifteenth century, they were surpassed nowhere in their musicians. Gilles Binchois, Guillaume Dufay, Jakob Obrecht, and Petrus Alamire were the most renowned European musicians of their century, all commissioned by both ducal and other patrons.

But the success of the Great Duchy of the West also depended on the weakness of France, English economic needs, and the indifference of the empire. When the tide of war turned in favor of France, the dukes lost much of their influence at the French royal court. From the reign of John the Fearless, the Dukes of Burgundy turned their attention more and more toward their northern territories, the Burgundian Low Countries. Originally, the dukes had referred to their Burgundian lands as "the lands over here," and to their northern territories as "the lands over there," because they spent most of their time in Burgundy or Paris. But as they acquired more and more territory in the north, the terms were reversed—Flanders and the northern territories became "the lands over here," and Burgundy became "the lands over there." With each new acquisition of territory in the Low Countries, the northern interests of the dukes increased. John the Fearless and Philip the Good spent most of their time in their Low Countries territories, staying variously at Ghent, Bruges, Mechelen, and Brussels.

In 1435, Philip the Good was formally reconciled with Charles VII of France at the Congress of Arras. With the growing strength of the French recovery, Philip's successor, Charles the Bold (1461–1477), turned his attention to the lands on his eastern flank and engaged in immensely expensive military campaigns, draining the ducal treasury and alienating many of his taxpaying subjects. Charles's agreement with Edward IV of England to invade France in 1461 alienated Louis XI of France, who stirred up further resistance to Charles within Charles's own dominions. Charles also encountered strong opposition from the great cities of the duchy, toward which he had often behaved ruthlessly. Louis XI allied himself with Charles's enemies in Austria and Switzerland, and after a series of dismally unsuccessful military campaigns, Charles was killed at the Battle of Nancy in 1477.

But Charles's death did not diminish the cultural splendor of the ducal court or cause the disappearance of Burgundy. He left a widow and an heiress. His widow, Margaret of York, sister of the English king Edward IV, worked heroically and successfully on behalf of the interests of her stepdaughter to preserve her rights in the Low Countries. Charles's daughter, Mary of Burgundy, lost some of her Burgundian lands to Louis XI, but she also married Maximilian of Austria, the future emperor. Although much of the great dynastic lordship forged by Philip the Bold and made powerful and independent by John the Fearless and Philip the Good, was dismantled as an independent state by the laws of lordship and inheritance, Mary of Burgundy (r. 1477–1482) brought her rich northern lands into the Hapsburg orbit. Although she died young as the result of a fall from a horse, Maximilian provided a generally stable regency for their children, Margaret of Austria and Philip, later Philip the Fair (1482–1509), until they came of age. When Margaret and Philip married two of the children of Isabella of Castile and Ferdinand of Aragon, they set the stage for yet another dynastic union whose consequences, like those of the Tudor marriages in Scotland and Spain, troubled and largely dominated Europe for the next two hundred years: the vast Hapsburg territories that combined Flanders, Brabant, Hainault, Holland and Zeeland, part of the old duchy of Burgundy, and the mighty Crown of a united Spain, and allied its rulers by blood to the emperors and their domains in southern Germany, Bohemia, Austria, and Hungary. Although the Great Duchy of the West had passed into history more quickly than it had arisen, it had greatly influenced the internal dynamic and resources of the southern Low Countries, a dynamic that long survived it and that underlies the later history of the Netherlands and Belgium.

20

Frontiers and Horizons

THE WORLD ON THE LAST DAY

Byzantine resistance to western demands for ecclesiastical reunion, factional quarrels within the empire, and the vastly diminished resources of the restored empire of Michael VIII Palaeologos after 1261, had reduced Byzantine power considerably. A fifteenth-century English chronicler who had observed Emperor Manuel II's visit to the west in 1399–1402 asking for aid, sadly commented, "How grievous it was that this great Christian prince should be driven by the Saracens from the furthest East to these furthest Western islands to seek aid against them. . . . Oh God, what dost thou now, ancient glory of Rome?" In the fourteenth century, the vigorous kings of Serbia, particularly Stephen Dusan (1331–1355), had already threatened the empire's existence, and the growth of Catalan and Aragonese power at the same time in the eastern Mediterranean, further reduced Byzantine strength. But the greatest and final threat came from the rising power of the Ottoman Turks.

The Turkic peoples had left the scrub lands of the Eurasian steppe in the ninth century, converted to Islam, and moved slowly westward. Some of them, the Seljuks, had conquered Anatolia on the eve of the First Crusade (above, Chapter 12) and dominated much of the Islamic Near East until the late twelfth century.

In 1327, Osman I (1280–1324), the leader of another Turkic people, conquered the Byzantine city of Bursa, on the Sea of Marmara, the Byzantine western end of the Silk Road, and began to expand into Anatolia and the Balkans. Ottoman troops also served as mercenaries in Christian armies. The Catalan Grand Company brought the first Ottoman mercenaries into Europe, and they also served in the Byzantine army in 1341. But Ottoman leaders soon perceived the weaknesses of the Byzantine empire. Osman's successor, Orhan Gazi (r. 1324–1359) led his people across the Sea of Marmara into Thrace, whose capital city, Edirne (Adrianople), they captured in 1362. Sultan Murad I (r. 1360–1369) defeated an army of Serbians and Hungarians at the Maritsa river, thus alerting western Europe to the Ottoman threat. But neither the Byzantines nor local Balkan powers were able to coordinate their resistance to the Ottomans, who skillfully exploited the differences among their Christian enemies. Control of the Black Sea and new influence in the Ukraine and Poland, as well as in the Balkans and most of Hungary, now passed into the hands of the sultan. In 1389, Ottoman forces allied with Bulgarians and some Serbian nobles defeated Serbian and Kossovar armies on the Field of Blackbirds, near the town of Pristina in Kossovo, and they defeated a large crusading army at Nicopolis in 1396—the battle at which John the Fearless of Burgundy acquired his nickname in a lost cause. Ottoman armies assaulted Constantinople itself in 1396 and 1422. Only the interruption of Ottoman expansion by the Mongol armies of Tammerlane (1336–1405) delayed the fall of Constantinople after the Christian defeat at Nicopolis. In 1453, when Mehmet II assaulted the city by sea and land with vast armies and massive artillery pieces manned by German and Hungarian gunners, the city was defended by only five thousand troops and two thousand foreigners. The Ottoman assault finally breached the Theodosian walls on May 29, and Constantine XI, the last emperor, died fighting in the streets of the sacred city.

After Constantinople was taken, other cities and territories fell in its wake. Athens fell in 1456, Serbia in 1459, Trebizond in 1461, Bosnia by 1466, and Albania in 1468. The great city became the capital of a new Turkish empire. For many centuries, Constantinople had been referred to simply as *hi stan polein*—"to the city"; the Turks simply Turkicized the pronunciation of this Greek phrase and called the city Istanbul.

Sultan Selim I (r. 1512–1520) conquered Syria, Arabia, and Egypt. During the reign of Suleiman the Magnificent (r. 1520–1566), Hungary lost its independence at the battle of Mohacs in 1526, and Vienna was first besieged in 1529. The eastern political and cultural borders of Europe had suddenly become very clear indeed.

Pope Pius II (1458–1464) complained of Europe's failure to restore Constantinople and blamed the particularism of the Latins for their reluctance to challenge the new Turkish lords of southeastern Europe. Latin Europe indeed fought later battles against the Turks, but these were largely defensive battles in southeastern Europe, where the Ottoman threat lasted at least until the Treaty of Carlowitz in 1699, and the consequences of its Balkan conquests last into the twenty-first century. The last emperor was dead, and the new Christian patriarch of Constantinople, George Scholarios, Gennadios II, was an appointee of the sultan, who enthroned the new patriarch in the Church of the Holy Apostles in January, 1454, in exactly the same ceremony that Byzantine emperors had used, and took the Orthodox Church under his protection.

Only very small enclaves preserved something of the vanished Byzantine past. But the power of Byzantine civilization survived in other places: in Venice, whose very fabric

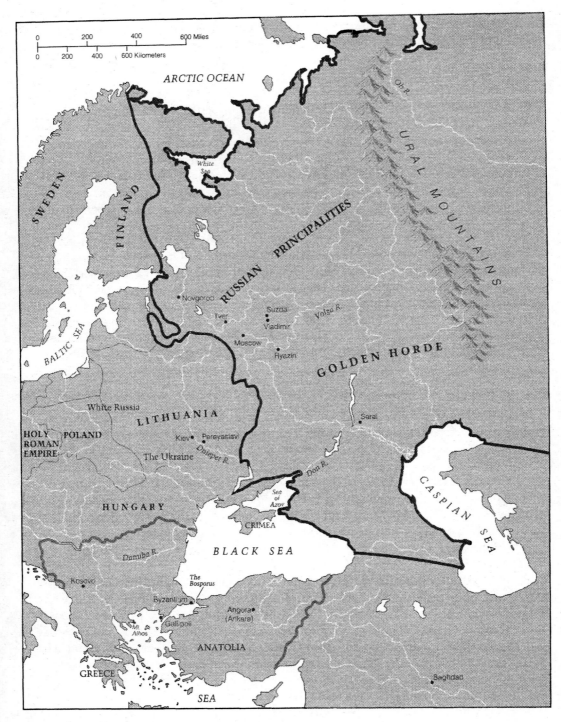

Mongol and Ottoman Turkish invasions of eastern Europe.

was built from Byzantine influences; in Muscovy, which became the heir of Byzantine religious orthodoxy and culture, ultimately calling itself "The Third Rome"; in the new intellectual interest in the Greek language and Greek scholarship in western Europe; and in the somber and mysterious pictures painted in faraway Spain in the sixteenth century by the Greek painter Domenikos Theotokopoulos—*El Greco,* "the Greek."

THE THIRD ROME

The Mongol occupation of Russia and the Ukraine had virtually cut those lands off from both Byzantium and the West (above, Chapter 17). In 1300, the metropolitan of Kiev established himself in Vladimir, to the north of Kiev, and then in 1328, in the town of Moscow. The Russian revival of the fourteenth century that brought it once again into active contact with Byzantium began with the rise of the principality of Muscovy and signaled a change in the relations between the Russians and the Byzantines. Muscovy's greater distance from Constantinople, its long period under Mongol domination, and its ecclesiastical rivalry with Lithuania all helped weaken the bonds between Byzantium and the most faithful of its cultural dependents. The alternations between Greek and Russian metropolitans of Kiev after 1250, however, helped maintain relations between the two peoples, and the steady stream of Russian pilgrims to Constantinople continued to testify to the great city's religious attraction in the north. In addition to its rivalry with Lithuania over the question of the metropolitan, however, Muscovy also began to criticize Constantinople itself after 1439, when the emperor John VIII accepted Latin Christianity. The Council of Florence, at which union between the Greek and Latin churches was proclaimed, seemed to the Russians a sacrilegious breach of the true faith. The Greek metropolitan of Kiev, Isidore, was arrested after he attempted to introduce the Latin rite upon his return to Muscovy. In 1448, a synod of Russian bishops took the unprecedented step of electing a metropolitan of Kiev without Byzantine initiation. Although this step must be considered in terms of Russian resistance to Byzantine unionization, it may also be considered as a reflection of the vigor and increasing sense of independence of the Russian church.

The rule of Grand Duke Ivan III (1462–1505) traditionally marks the full coming of independence to Muscovy. Ivan brought Italian architects to begin building the Kremlin in Moscow. Under Ivan's energetic and ambitious rule, the breakup of the Mongol khanate and the diversion of Lithuanian interests to the west were both exploited to Muscovy's advantage. By the mid fifteenth century, the Golden Horde had splintered into three separate khanates, one at Kazan, one in the Crimea, and a third on the lower Volga. In 1480, Ivan III rejected the sovereignty of the Golden Horde and became the first grand duke of Muscovy to assume his rulership without Mongol permission. He soon began to exert Muscovite control over other northern Russian principalities. Between 1456 and 1478, the great city of Novgorod, hitherto dependent on its economy and its Lithuanian neighbors for support, fell to Ivan's armies. The rise of Muscovy to the domination of all Russia had begun.

The strained ecclesiastical relations between Russia and Byzantium in the fourteenth and fifteenth centuries, the vigor of the principality of Muscovy, and the success of Grand Dukes Vasili (1425–1462), and Ivan III in the face of Lithuanian, Polish, Mongol, and other Russian opposition all led to the development of considerable economic and political power within the Muscovite state, as well as to a fierce sense of pride and divine approval. Thus, in 1460, the metropolitan of Moscow could firmly observe that Constantinople had fallen because of God's disapproval of the union of the Greek and Latin churches at the Council of Florence in 1439. Like the earlier rulers of Serbia, Bulgaria, and the Romanian principalities, the grand dukes of Muscovy began to adopt the outward signs of Byzantine imperial rule. In 1472, partly through the agency of the pope, Ivan III married Zoe Palaeologina, the niece of the last Byzantine emperor. Although the pope may have hoped through this marriage to effect the 1439 provisions in Russia, Ivan and the empress, renamed Sophia, adopted an elaborate Byzantine court ceremonial and the imperial device of the double-headed eagle. Under this rule, the grand dukes of Muscovy began to evolve into the tsars of Russia (tsar is the Russian equivalent of Caesar). Muscovite self-confidence went even further in certain areas. In 1492, Moscow was proclaimed the "New Constantinople"; in 1510 the monk Philotheus of Pskov declared it the "Third Rome."

THE FIRST ROME

As the Muscovite principality claimed its place as the third in the sequence of centers of Christendom, many western European thinkers also turned to the idea of Rome, but not in search of a successor state to old Rome and Constantinople. From the twelfth century on, western Europeans had begun to acquire a greater appreciation of some of the achievements of ancient Roman culture and civilization. This new appreciation was not exclusively the result of greater familiarity with ancient Latin literature, although reading the classics was certainly one important part of it. Rome still contained its ancient buildings and churches, many of them restored over the preceding centuries by popes, emperors, and local religious communities and nobles.

To be sure, the considerable literary achievements of European writers in the twelfth century had also led some writers to take great pride in the achievements of their own time. Chrétien de Troyes, the greatest of the French writers of knightly romances, went so far as to claim for France the sum total of all the virtues of the past:

> *Greece once had, for chivalry,*
> *The greatest honor, and for clergy.*
> *Then chivalry passed on to Rome,*
> *And clergy too. But now their home*
> *Is France.*

Next to the papal ideal of the *translatio imperii*, the translation of legitimate empire from Rome to Germany, and the university ideal of the *translatio studii*, the translation of learning from the east to the west, there emerged the secular idea of the translation of culture, not merely from the lands of the east to those of the west but from the societies of antiquity to those of twelfth- and thirteenth-century western Europe.

Europeans also discovered that antiquity held treasures that had not yet been fully appreciated. Among these were the writings of the fourth-century Church Fathers, particularly Jerome and Augustine. Besides the theology of the Fathers, however, fourteenth-century thinkers discovered their Latin prose style, which was modeled on the clarity and elegance of earlier Latin writers like Cicero. Just as philosophers were drawn away from Aristotle toward Plato, so theologians and writers were drawn from the thirteenth-century scholastic thinkers to the eloquent Church Fathers. Because the Fathers themselves had been strongly influenced by Plato, the works of that philosopher began to be translated into Latin, most of them for the first time. The fifteenth century saw the acquisition of other Greek manuscripts by Latins, some of them from Constantinople and from Greek scholars traveling in western Europe. The new interest in the thought of Plato and other Greeks also led to greater study of the Greek language in western Europe, first in northern and southern Italy and later across the Alps.

But the primary linguistic focus of fourteenth- and fifteenth-century thinkers was Latin, and their initial purpose was both rhetorical and moral. Perhaps the most characteristic of the new thinkers was the Florentine scholar and man of letters Francesco Petrarca (1304–1374), whose importance lies as much in his later influence as in his own considerable achievements. Petrarca was raised in Avignon and was sent to study law at the universities of Montpellier and Bologna. Unlike many of his contemporaries, however, Petrarca felt no love for the law nor for what he perceived as the immorality of most lawyers. Indeed, he bitterly criticized the technical jargon, not only of legal studies but of logic and medicine as well. Petrarca's ambitions were literary rather than legal, and he never finished his legal studies. From early in life, he had studied Latin, particularly the prose of Cicero, which he admired immensely and read more carefully than anyone had before him. Petrarca's excellent ear for the intricacy and subtlety of Ciceronian Latin was matched by a careful eye and a critical intelligence of considerable merit. As he read, he became aware of the errors that had crept into ancient texts because of scribal carelessness or incomprehension over many centuries of recopying. Petrarca began to search for more and more manuscripts, developing his study of Latin philology and textual editing to a new level. These two activities led to Petrarca's own development of a fine Latin prose style, flexible and elegant, which stood in sharp contrast to the plodding formality of much of the academic and professional language he had come to despise. Petrarca's interest in searching out manuscripts not only turned up more Latin literature than had previously been known to exist, but brought to light literary works that had been little used since the twelfth century as well as formerly unknown manuscript versions of known works.

The renovation of Latin prose and the beginning of the search for antiquity through the study and collection of ancient manuscripts were two of Petrarca's most important achievements. But his real greatness lay in two other areas. Having rejected the profession of law—and indeed the very idea of a profession in the fourteenth-century sense—Petrarca became a poet and man of letters, perhaps the first such figure in European history. But he did not do so solely out of a love for literature. In Cicero's and

Augustine's works, Petrarca found a personal and social moral theory that appealed to him far more strongly than the academic theology and social ideas of his contemporaries, and he insisted that the study of Latin and the practice of letters had a primarily moral end. His early works investigate his own personality. Clarity, eloquent language, friendship, and cultivated leisure—these for Petrarca were the elements of the ideal life, and he pursued them in his own life and writings, particularly in his many letters and treatises addressed to a wide range of friends and correspondents. In so doing, he opened a new vista not only on scholarship and literature but on individual and social morality.

This practical use of the Latin classics, coupled with Petrarca's thoroughgoing Christian values, immensely influenced the next several generations of scholars and writers north and south of the Alps. By claiming for Roman morality a degree of virtue that no Christian writer had ever accorded it, Petrarca opened new avenues for later generations to explore, especially in literature and moral thought. This combination of Latin literary study, exact scholarship, and the ideal of the life of dignified leisure in semi-retirement has generally been labeled "humanism," and Petrarca was acclaimed the first humanist by later scholars. As we have seen, Cicero himself had defined the liberal arts, and chiefly literature, as those arts befitting a free man—that is, a leisured, conscientious Roman citizen with aristocratic status and good taste. Cicero's idea of humane studies strongly appealed to Petrarca's secularized psychology, and although strong claims have been made for a medieval ideal of humanism, tradition still attributes to Petrarca the title of the first humanist.

Petrarca's interest in ancient Rome did not end with imitating its literary language and appreciating its morality. On his visits from Avignon to Rome (where he was awarded the ancient laurel crown for poets in 1341), Petrarca was stunned by the desolation of the city, abandoned by its popes (who were still in Avignon) as it had once been abandoned by its ancient emperors. When a young Roman, Cola di Rienzo (1313–1354), created a revolutionary government in the city and designated himself its tribune—the ancient civic title of Rome's Republican leaders—Petrarca praised Cola eloquently. Even Cola's early death and the failure of his "Roman Republic" did not dissuade Petrarca from his fascination with the ancient greatness and present desolation of the city. Rather, it led him to the study of history. In 1343, two years after his poetic coronation amid the ruins of Rome, Petrarca wrote to his friend Giovanni Colonna:

> As we walked over the walls of the shattered city of Rome, or sat there, the fragments of the ruins were under our very eyes. Our conversation turned toward history, which we appear to have divided up between us in such a way that in modern history you, in ancient history I, seemed the more expert. Ancient were called those events that took place before the name of Christ was celebrated in Rome and adored by the Roman emperors. Modern, however, were called the events from that time to the present.

Petrarca's sense of a major division of history, marked by the Christianization of the Roman Empire in the fourth century, was the result of his veneration of ancient Latin literature and morality and his distaste for much of what succeeded them. But it proved to be very influential in the following three centuries, when Petrarca's own role in "reviving" the culture of antiquity was regarded as the beginning of a rebirth—in French, a *renaissance*—of the world of antiquity. As closely related as his thought was to the devotional and scholarly trends of the fourteenth century, Petrarca's vision of history was later regarded conveniently as itself beginning a new age in European civilization, the "Age of the Renaissance."

But the rediscovery of the first Rome was not an achievement of Petrarca alone, nor of Italian scholars exclusively. Richard de Bury, tutor to King Edward III of England and author of the *Philobiblon,* was also a fine Latin scholar, collector of manuscripts, and connoisseur of Roman civilization. In the fifteenth century, a number of Italian humanists came to England, and English scholars studied under humanist teachers in Italy. Humphrey, Duke of Gloucester (1391–1447) commissioned the copying of classical manuscripts in Italy to be sent to him in England (he left many of these to the university of Oxford), and he even invited the Italian humanist Tito Livio Frulovisi to write a biography of the duke's brother, King Henry V. In France, the great moralist Nicholas de Clamanges (ca. 1360–1437) shared the literary and cultural interests of Petrarca, Richard de Bury, and other humanists. By the end of the fourteenth century, the new interest in Latin literature and the moral philosophy of ancient Roman and Greek civilization that had been created by Petrarca and others had brought the first Rome before the eyes of curious and interested Europeans.

By revealing, sometimes painfully, the differences between the civilization of ancient Rome and that of fourteenth- and fifteenth-century western Europe, the humanists sharpened Europeans' sense of the complex nature of the past as they began to provide more and more accurate information about that past. The image of the first Rome gradually became grander, more dignified, and more profound than contemporary culture, and European thinkers began to speak of Petrarca's "modern history" as if it represented a great decline from the glories of Rome. For the next three hundred years, that period of the European past extending from the fourth to the fourteenth century had to defend itself against the formidable attacks of the humanists, as one by one its own achievements were either ignored or dismissed as errors. With the rediscovery of the first Rome, there also occurred the invention of the Middle Ages.

ANCIENTS AND MODERNS

Those writers who praised the virtues of ancient Greece and Rome at the expense of the Middle Ages, made possible another point of view, one that regarded the fifteenth century and later as superior even to the glories of Greece and Rome. Such a view grew out of certain late-medieval achievements in culture and technology. By the seventeenth and eighteenth centuries, the debate between those who praised Greece and Rome as the greatest cultural achievements of humanity and those who claimed that distinction for the period between the fifteenth and eighteenth centuries had produced a literary and philosophical argument that is generally called the Quarrel Between the Ancients and the Moderns. Although ancients and moderns both used examples from literature, morality, the arts, and the sciences in their arguments, the moderns had an edge that the ancients could not claim—the results of late-medieval and early-modern developments in geography and technology.

As we have seen in earlier chapters, one of the most distinctive features of early medieval society was its free use of new techniques and machines to open the forests and scrublands of northern Europe to extensive agricultural development. But the development of new techniques in agriculture and new sources of nonanimal and nonhuman power was not the only contribution to the arguments of the moderns against the ancients. Much more striking was the application of machines from one area of economic activity to others— from the farm to the cloth mill, from the rural monastery to the smithy, from the grain mill to the sawmill. The best historian of medieval European technology, Lynn T. White Jr., has argued persuasively that one of the most distinctive features of medieval European culture is precisely this machine mindedness, the assimilating ability and willingness of Europeans that made them the most technologically developed people in the world at the end of the Middle Ages: "During the later Middle Ages there was a passion for the mechanization of industry such as no culture had known. . . . The Europe which rose to global dominance about 1500 had an industrial capacity and skill vastly greater than that of any of the cultures of Asia—not to mention Africa or America—which it challenged." The windmill and the printing press were simply two of the many machines that made Europeans, however great their reverence for Greece and Rome, vastly different from their ancient predecessors.

"Every day new arts are discovered," observed a Florentine preacher in 1306. Friar Giordano da Pisa particularly admired (as scholars and other people have ever since) the invention of eyeglasses, which had taken place around 1280. He went on to note

> There are even many arts which have not yet been discovered. Every day you could find one, and there would still be new ones to find. . . . It was not twenty years since there was discovered the art of making spectacles which help you to see well, which is one of the best and most necessary arts in the world. I myself saw the man who discovered and practiced it, and I talked with him.

As White concisely observes, "Here was a mood without historical precedent: . . . the invention of invention as a total project. It was the mood of Europe's technicians from the later thirteenth century onwards."[1] Although White and other historians of technology and science have differed over which qualities in European culture of the period between the sixth and the fourteenth centuries made Europeans so machine minded, most agree that the causes are cultural, the product of distinctive human attitudes toward labor, the material world, mathematics, and efficiency. Not only did Europeans borrow, modify, and invent machines, but they also put them into works of art and imagination.

And they spread them. Individual technological developments were spontaneously invented in several different places. Communication was another integral part of European technological development. From the thirteenth to the seventeenth century, most of the improvements in land communication and transport consisted of refinements of techniques that had been developed in the twelfth and thirteenth centuries. New techniques in harnessing and shoeing horses, more maneuverable wagons with better suspension, and improvements in road and bridge building brought European

---

[1] Lynn T. White, Jr., *Medieval Religion and Technology: Collected Essays* (Berkeley and Los Angeles: University of California Press, 1978), p. 221.

technology in this field to a state that remained essentially static until the extensive road-building programs and the development of the steam engine in the eighteenth century. Networks of information, in merchants' companies and in kingdoms and other political units, improved the regularity and speed of some communications. By the early fourteenth century, cart roads were being built in the alpine passes, and in 1480, gunpowder was used in the Tyrol to blast rock for the widening of roads. Slowly the pack animal gave way to the wagon, the track to the road. The increasingly sedentary character of large governments made capital towns and cities centers of new communications networks, from papal Avignon in the fourteenth century to Vienna and Madrid in the sixteenth.

As the means of sending information and goods improved in this period, so did the means of preserving information. The increasingly wide use of paper and the invention of movable type illustrate Europe's considerable capacity for importing and adapting techniques from other cultures. Papermaking technique had come to Islamic Spain from

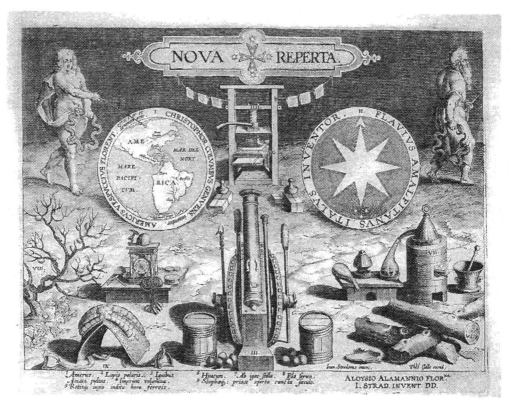

Nova Reperta, engraved by Theodore Galle, a graphic depiction of geographical and technological discoveries unknown to the Greeks and Romans. Besides the Americas, the devices include gunpowder and cannon, a distillation device, the saddle and stirrups, and the printing press. (Title page, Nova Reperta, sixteenth-century engraving. Photo Courtesy of John M. Wing Foundation, The Newberry Library, Chicago)

China, and with the Christian conquest of Valencia in 1258, paper entered the world of European communications, becoming both cheaper and more durable in the fourteenth and fifteenth centuries, when better quality cotton cloth was used in its manufacture. By then, the price of paper was one-sixth the price of parchment—and considering that a single bible required between two and three hundred animal skins, the saving was considerable. China had also invented the technique of block printing: cutting script onto the surface of blocks of wood or other substances and impressing these on paper. Fifteenth-century Europeans adapted this technique in the manufacture of playing cards, and then went on to invent movable metal type, first at Mainz in the 1455 forty-two-line Bible attributed to Johann Gutenberg. Type and paper also required ink, and European printers appear to have developed an oil-based ink, which flows smoothly when applied to metal, perhaps from the contemporary use of new, oil-based paints by artists. The new technology also required capital, an increased investment in printing, and the growth of a literate public. All of these propelled the book trade into a prominent place in fifteenth- and sixteenth-century economies and cultural life. Not only books, of course, but laws, newsletters, and official and unofficial printed matter of all kinds helped accelerate the dissemination of information.

The fifteenth century also saw a number of frequent large-scale public assemblies, from regional gatherings to the great international congresses and councils, like the Councils of Constance (1415–1417) and Basel (1431–1437) and the Congress of Arras in 1435, where Duke Philip the Good of Burgundy and King Charles VII of France were reconciled. These assemblies drew people together from remote corners of Europe and then returned them to their places of origin, their heads full of what they had seen, read, and heard.

By 1360, after more than a century of development, fully operative mechanical clocks had come into use. Once developed, they were widely incorporated in public buildings, first at the church of St. Eustorgio in Milan in 1309 (just three years after Giordano da Pisa's sermon in praise of eyeglasses), and by 1370, in the palace of King Charles V of France. As in other aspects of social and cultural relations, notably weights, measures, and coinage on the one hand and practical and speculative mathematics on the other, towns and lay authorities in general transformed the measuring and proclamation of time.

Besides affecting productivity, measurement, good order, and peace, European technology transformed the face of war. Cavalry was still important for the prestige of the mounted warrior, but it also still possessed shock value, and in need, cavalrymen could fight dismounted. The use of infantry, however, increased, and the assembly, training, arming, and paying an army of professional or mercenary infantry contributed to the increasing costs of war. With the higher proportion of infantry and the appearance of more highly developed missiles, the armor of the horseman also changed. Required to deflect missiles, pikes, swords, lances, and maces, armor now became full iron and steel plate, replacing the older chain mail. Armor was also strengthened by improved metallurgy, so that by 1400, a good set of plate armor could stop the arrow from a longbow, although it probably could not stop a bolt from the improved fifteenth-century crossbow.

But it could be redesigned to improve the deflecting function of its surface, a practice that became essential with the introduction of gunpowder. Gunpowder was brought to Europe from China at the end of the thirteenth century, and by the fourteenth, it was being used on a very small scale in warfare. The development of heavy metal casting in the manufacture of bells soon provided a means of containing gunpowder and projectile in a single cannon. The use of the cannon—at first as a kind of superior catapult and then quickly adding the more mobile capacity of field artillery—increased during the 1400s, and by the end of that century, the mobility and destructiveness of field cannon were causing great consternation among those who depended on thick castle walls to protect them from the enemy. The guns burst the walls, and the inhabitants had to find ways to redesign them. By making the walls thinner, but building out from them angle bastions that would deflect cannon fire and cover the breaches in the walls by means of enfilading fire, military architects transformed the thick-walled medieval castle into the geometrically calculated star fort of early-modern Europe. They did so by mathematical calculations that were just as careful as the calculations necessary in making large guns and projectiles.

From the heavy plow to the cannon, from the water mill to the angle bastion, from the water clock to the mechanical clock, European technology knew little of the conventional divisions of medieval, renaissance, and early-modern history. As the "moderns" knew well, the technical achievements and the technology mindedness of Europeans were very different from those of the ancient Greeks and Romans.

"HERE THERE BEE TYGRES"

Marco Polo was alleged to have brought back great wealth with him to Venice. Thirty years earlier, regular Genoese and Venetian fleets had for the first time sailed out of the Mediterranean Sea and into the Atlantic to make commercial connections with the trade networks of northern Europe. In 1291, two brothers of Genoa, the Vivaldi, had outfitted several ships and sailed west out of the Mediterranean to seek new trade routes to the west coast of Africa. The records of missionary and merchant travels to Asia, the establishment of regular maritime contact between the Mediterranean and the Atlantic, and the mystery and interest generated by such adventures as those of the Vivaldi, who disappeared, and Marco Polo, whose story quickly became widely known, suggest a new interest by many Europeans not only in the wonders of the unknown parts of the world but also in the possible economic value of the products of the unknown world. The time between the papal missions to the Mongols of John del Pian Carpine in 1245–1247 and William of Rubrouck in 1253–1255 (above, Chapter 18) and the establishment of regular sailing routes to the west was very brief. By the 1270s, others had begun to travel to Asia.

In turning to the western Mediterranean, and then to the Atlantic, Genoa assumed a more prominent role than Venice, whose interests remained concentrated in the eastern Mediterranean.

During the thirteenth century, as Venice and Genoa were making their economic and political triumphs in the East, the rulers of the kingdom of Aragon were establishing their power not only southward in the eastern Iberian Peninsula into Valencia, but also eastward across the Mediterranean. During the thirteenth century, the rulers of Aragon and their subjects, often in loose alliance, captured the Balearic Islands and Sardinia, and acquired the island of Sicily in 1302. In these lands, they developed a colonial economy, in which the Genoese participated. In the Iberian Peninsula itself, the rulers of both Aragon and Castile extended their conquests southward, to the southern edge of the peninsula, capturing Cadiz in 1268 and Seville in 1291, acquiring in the process the largest populations of non-Christians of any European state, and gaining access to both the Mediterranean Sea and the Atlantic Ocean.

Unlike the Venetians, the Genoese worked most successfully within territories largely ruled by others, and they moved into the Aragonese and Castilian kingdoms easily and smoothly. The deep-water ports of southern Spain were necessary for their large commercial ships and served as useful stopping points on the Genoese route northward through the Atlantic and the English Channel, established since 1277. Along the Mediterranean-Atlantic route, the Genoese shipped alum (necessary for the cloth-finishing processes of the northern textile industry), sugar, and the sweet wines for which northern Europeans were eager.

By the late fourteenth century, the Mediterranean-Atlantic routes had raised Castilian and especially Portuguese interests in yet another area, North Africa. Ever since the tenth century, the Maghreb, the western coast of North Africa, had been the northern destination of the gold caravans that originated in Ghana and crossed the western edge of the Sahara to Ceuta, Oran, Algiers, and Tunis. Copper and salt also came up this route. These products, along with North African wheat, enriched the North African cities and made them attractive—for trade, conquest, or both—to other Mediterranean powers from Norman Sicily in the twelfth century, to the Italian maritime cities in the thirteenth and fourteenth, to the Crusading army of Saint Louis of France in 1270, and finally to the Castilian and Portuguese rulers in the fourteenth and fifteenth centuries.

In the fourteenth century, the gold of the Sudan became a particularly important prize among Christian and North African Muslim powers, and Christians began to obtain clearer information about its sources. A Majorcan portolan map of 1339 noted, "Below the Sahara, on the banks of a river that is the Niger, there is a king whose riches are counted in gold; it is the king of Mali." One chronicler's account of Jaume Ferrer's voyage to West Africa in 1346 stated that his purpose was "to go to the river of gold." By the mid fourteenth century, Europeans knew that the source of the gold traded in the cities of the Maghreb was in the West African part of the Sudan and that it was extracted from rivers by black men, about whom a number of legends had circulated among Muslim traders. Europeans also knew that there were powerful, advanced black kingdoms in West Africa whose strength rested on their rulers' control of the gold trade. The great kings of Ghana and Mali controlled access to the gold-mining natives and permitted only their own subjects to trade salt for gold, which they then carried north and traded to the North African caravan merchants.

The greatest of all black Muslim rulers of this period was, as the Majorcan map of 1339 had observed, the king of Mali. By 1375, when Abraham Cresques drew his great Catalan atlas, the brief reference of 1339 had been expanded to a large picture of the black king seated on a throne, holding a globe and (somewhat improbably) the royal scepter of France with a fleur-de-lis at its end. The new legend read, "This black lord is called Musa Melly, lord of the blacks of Guinea. This king is the richest and most noble

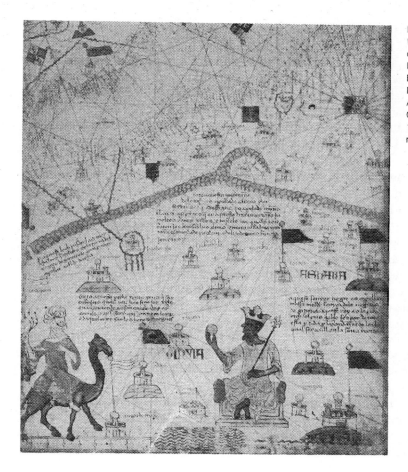

Mansa Musa, ruler of Mali, the splendor and generosity of whose pilgrimage to Mecca in 1324 astonished both Egyptian and Arab Muslims. From the Catalan Atlas made by Abraham Cresques on Majorca in 1375. (Cliché Bibliotheque nationale de France—Paris)

lord by reason of the abundance of gold that is found in his country." The black king of the 1339 and 1375 Catalan maps was Mansa Musa, who had made a pilgrimage in 1321 to Mecca. There, his display of wealth and piety astonished his Muslim coreligionists.

The financial crisis of the late fourteenth century had drastically increased Europeans' need for gold, and the new knowledge of the sources of West African gold raised the possibility of circumventing the Saharan-Maghreb trade routes by sailing directly to the source of the gold. The new maritime importance of Castile and Portugal on the Mediterranean-Atlantic trade routes, the new security of Christian Iberia, and the production of sugar cane in the eastern Atlantic islands had greatly increased Iberian maritime experience and skill and had also brought the enterprising commercial genius and technological skills of Genoa to bear on the peninsula.

The central, but still obscure, figure in the first Portuguese voyages to the west coast of Africa was Prince Henry the Navigator (1394–1460), the son of King John I of Portugal. Little different in world-view or character from other fifteenth-century princely knights, Henry appears to have been particularly interested in the legends of mysterious lands in Africa, especially the reports that Prester John, the legendary Christian king, was to be found in Africa, perhaps in Ethiopia. Interested in measuring the extent of Muslim power and imbued with the Crusade mentality that had driven the earliest stages of the *reconquista,* Henry also thought that his own dynasty and kingdom might be the first to tap African gold at its source. With this mixture of motives—none of which was particularly "scientific" or "modern"—Henry spent vast sums of his own wealth in assembling at Sagres a group of cartographers, scholars, and sailors of all faiths and many languages. Henry was driven by an important youthful experience. In 1415, when he was twenty-one, a military expedition under his father had captured Ceuta on the North African coast, the first Christian landfall in Muslim Africa. For the rest of his life, Henry considered that event the beginning of Portuguese expansion, as much for the injury to Islam as for any particular increases in scientific knowledge that it might promote. By 1431, Portuguese fleets had discovered and settled in the Azores and Henry, armed with royal and papal privileges to carry on the *reconquista* in Africa, had begun his annual dispatches of fleets to the west coast of Africa. Shortly after mid century, Portuguese sailors landed in Guinea and began to exploit the gold reserves and the large numbers of slaves, a right that had once belonged exclusively to the Muslim Sahara caravans. By the time Henry died, he had fulfilled many of his ambitions. Gold had begun to flow into Portugal, and just before his death, Portugal had issued its first gold coin, appropriately called the *crusado.*

The beginning of Portuguese exploitation of the Gold Coast of Africa had two remarkable consequences; the direct acquisition by the Portuguese of a new source of gold, and the beginning of the trade in black slaves that was to remain a source of income first in Mediterranean Europe and later, and to a much greater degree, in the ranching, agricultural, and mining settlements in the New World.

Africa offered not only gold, copper, salt, and slaves, but also the islands of the eastern Atlantic, which became essential bases for Mediterranean and Atlantic sailors who wished to sail down the western coast. By the middle of the fourteenth century, the Canaries, Madeira, most of the Azores, and the Cape Verde Islands had become known to Europeans, and their conquest, too, had begun. The evidence of maps and sailing charts is reliable from the late fourteenth century, and the European conquest of these islands was complete by the late fifteenth century. The eastern Atlantic islands were important, not only as stopping points on the route to western Africa but also because of their position in relation to the Atlantic Ocean's wind systems. These islands are located at the eastern end of the most climatically favorable route for sailing west—between 35 and 42 degrees north latitude. From them, the trade winds and ocean currents flow westward for nine months of the year. Thus, although the Vivaldi brothers had been lost trying to circumnavigate Africa in 1291, as was the Catalan Jaume Ferrer in 1346, after the middle of the fourteenth century, the northwest edge of Africa increasingly became the central point, not only for further African exploration but also for the crossing of the Atlantic.

During this period, marine engineering had developed as rapidly, and in as complex a manner, as had conquest and trade, and it stood out in sharp contrast to the lack of development of land transportation. As long as it was forced to remain within the upward limits of animal and human power, land transportation remained generally unchanged between the thirteenth and the nineteenth centuries. On the sea, however, technological and economic influences quickly expanded Europeans' capacities for long-distance travel. Early European ships were of two types, neither very satisfactory. The round-bottomed cog with a square sail was roomy but slow, and the long, narrow, oar-powered galley was fast but had too large a crew for the profitable transport of cargo. In the fourteenth century, the great hulk was developed in the Baltic. It had a greater carrying capacity but no more speed. At the beginning of the fifteenth century, however, the caravel appeared. The stern rudder, the increased proportion of beam to length, the use of two masts, one of which carried a triangular lateen-rigged Mediterranean sail, the superior hull construction, the reduced crew, and the enormous cargo capacity of around four hundred tons produced the most efficient ship the West had ever known and the most profitable ship afloat. It was also the fastest. The caravel's speed under full sail was exceeded only slightly by the clipper ships of the nineteenth century. By the end of the fifteenth century, not only had sail gone far to replace oar, but the upward limits of commercial sailing speed had very nearly been reached.

Marine technology and practical navigation quickly outstripped geography and cartography. Celestial navigation and the geographical and cartographical knowledge that characterizes more recent marine technology and theory did not come for a century. But the compass, the minutely accurate local sailors' charts called portolans, and practical trigonometry for course correction—all of which developed by the end of the thirteenth century—gave European mariners impressive tools. Baltic, North Sea, and Atlantic sailing routes had all been developed by the end of the thirteenth century. During the Spanish *reconquista* sugar-cane-producing settlements on the Atlantic islands of the Canaries and Madeira developed in imitation of the Venetian and Genoese colonies in the eastern Mediterranean. In spite of these practical achievements, however, knowledge of geography and ethnography was still restricted to the descriptions of Marco Polo and the fabulous accounts of Sir John Mandeville's alleged travels in the Near East between 1332 and 1366, which featured semihuman creatures and the catchall warning *hic sunt leones,* "here there bee tygres," as the Elizabethans later translated it. Not until Poggio Bracciolini's *Dialogue on Geography,* written in 1447/8, was there an attempt to link learned geography with the practical experience of travelers and sailors. Indeed, there was no word for "explorer" in any European language.

The short-range and immediate interests of Genoa and the Iberian kingdoms had established not only an Atlantic linkage between southern Europe and the Mediterranean and the northern worlds, but they also had begun to open up the long-closed world of northwestern and Western Africa and the even larger world beyond the eastern Atlantic islands. The first of these achievements transformed the economic and political history of Europe; the second presented problems on a scale too vast and complex for any satisfactory solution. From the appearance of the Mongols on, Europeans were brought face to face with new kinds of human beings and a world immensely larger—although increasingly accessible—than they had ever imagined. Asians, Black Africans, and Canarians posed problems of anthropology that Europeans had only a crude means of perceiving and identifying, and the discussions of the "human nature" of these new peoples created categories of thought that were later transferred to the still newer worlds of North and South America, and policies of behavior toward them whose consequences are still felt in the twenty-first century.

Finally, although Europeans gained a surprising knowledge of the size of the world, they also discovered that they could reach new parts of it in periods of time that were not unthinkable. Columbus' first voyage, from Gomera in the Canary Islands to Santo Domingo in the Caribbean, took thirty-two days, about twice as long as it had taken Columbus to sail from Palos in Spain to Gomera itself. Not only was the western edge of the Atlantic bounded by promising islands—whether these lands were more Canary Islands, China, or an unknown land mass took some time to discover—but these lands could be reached by existing marine technology, on familiar ships, sailed by routinely trained men. These lands and seas could be mapped, and people far from the voyages or settlements could learn from the maps. Europeans encountered the wider world of the fifteenth and sixteenth centuries provincially prepared, but infinitely ambitious, and much of the rest of later history is the result of that encounter.

Epilogue

Empress Europa and Her Ambassadors

Conventional literary and pictorial representations of Europa usually showed the legendary kidnapping by the bull. But in the sixteenth century, a different kind of image of Europa appeared: Europa the continent personified as a queen. Gone were the bull, the seascape, and the island. In their place there stood a regal, richly gowned woman, alone, wearing a crown, and carrying a scepter and a symbol of abundance. The favorable comparison of Europe with other parts of the world became a frequent topic in fifteenth- and sixteenth-century geographical representations. The title page of the *Theatrum Orbis Terrarum* of Abraham Ortelius of 1572 depicted a crowned, elegantly gowned Europa, but this time sitting on a throne both literally and figuratively higher above the partly dressed female personifications of Africa and Asia in the central register, and far above the nude America and the incompletely discovered Tierra del Fuego in the lowest register.

In 1550, the Protestant Hebraic scholar Sebastian Münster (1489–1552) published a second edition of his vast, richly illustrated and mapped geographical commentary, the *Cosmographia Universalis,* which he had originally published in German in 1544. In it he praised Europe, which, "though smaller than other parts of the world, is the most populous, fertile, and cultivated." Europe has become an empress whose body parts are a map of Europe, oriented toward the west. The head and the imperial crown is Spain and Portugal; the arms are Italy and Denmark, with Sicily as an imperial orb held by the Italian arm; France and Germany are the bosom. The Danish arm holds a scepter, from which flies a banner, comprised of Ireland, Scotland, and England. The lower parts of her body are Hungary, Poland, Lithuania, Macedonia, and Bulgaria. Scandinavia outside Denmark does not form part of the body, and Asia and Africa are clearly separated from her. The myth of Europa was hereafter confined to classical scholarship; but Empress Europa had work to do and servants eager to do it for her.

In 1533, the Augsburg painter Hans Holbein the Younger painted the portrait of two young French ambassadors in London, the noble Jean de Dinteville (1504–1555) and the bishop-elect of Lavaur, Georges de Selve (1509–1541). The painting, *The Ambassadors,* and the personified map-portrait of Europa, serve as convenient objects around which to draw together many of the themes in this book.

Jean de Dinteville, on the left in the painting, was the ambassador of King Francis I (1515–1547) to England. He came from an old noble family near the city of Troyes in Champagne, was the local lord of the town of Polisy, and held the ancient office of bailli of Troyes. The prominence of French nobility in royal service was apparent in the early

Empress Europa, from Sebastian Muenster, Cosmographia, published at Basel in 1588. Here the conventional female personification is imposed on and identified with the lands of Europe. (The Granger Collection, New York)

Hans Holbein: The Ambassadors (1533) (© National Gallery, London)

sixteenth century, and the lay noble, rather than the cleric alone, participated in those royal affairs that touched other parts of the world as well as the operation of the kingdom itself. Georges de Selve, son of the president of the Parlement of Paris, was one of six brothers, five of whom were ambassadors in the service of the king of France. He had been the king's ambassador to the Diet of the Holy Roman Empire and was visiting de Dinteville in London at the time he commissioned the portrait. Inscriptions in the portrait indicate clearly that de Selve was twenty-five at the time and Dinteville twenty-nine.

The portrait itself had come of age in the fifteenth century, as the vast surviving number of portraits of individuals remind us, and from that period on, it is possible to see the figures of history in ways that were virtually impossible earlier. In general, medieval artists, like medieval biographers, tended to portray an ideal type rather than a particular individual, to glorify or caricature rather than to depict realistically. But the artistic triumphs of the Romanesque and Gothic movements allowed greater artistic freedom and a greater degree of naturalism. By the end of the thirteenth century, first in tomb sculptures and later in portraits of the donors of churches, there is a clear attempt to record the actual physical appearance of individual subjects. The Dukes of Burgundy and their Chancellor, Nicholas Rolin, have themselves left us many portraits, as well as portraits of their female relatives and children. Holbein's portrait catches an important aspect of late medieval artistic technique and taste.

The office of Holbein's subjects had emerged out of the earlier offices of papal legate, personal messenger, and herald. The status and functions of these individuals had become more regularized and more recognized in the early fifteenth century. In 1436, Bernard du Rosier, later bishop of Toulouse, completed the first analysis and description of diplomacy in European history, *The Short Treatise About Ambassadors*. It is difficult for a modern reader to imagine a world of strong and thoroughly governed states touching each other's borders and necessarily having business with each other but not possessing a regular network of formal and informal communications. Such a practice, though, was the invention, first of the papacy, and in the fourteenth and fifteenth centuries, of the western European states that imitated papal practice. Among the earliest and best-known records of this new institution are the reports of Venetian ambassadors, for Venice, like the papacy, had business everywhere and demanded information as much as any larger power—more information, indeed, than many. The circumstances of late medieval states, and their unique capacity to borrow from tradition—from Roman law, canon law, chivalric practice, political expediency, elaborate ceremony, and public relations—combined to form the idea, the status, and the office of the late-medieval ambassador. Holbein's painting shows us an institution that grew out of many different sources, and that by the early sixteenth century was a recognized, but not always welcome, figure in the political and diplomatic world of western Europe.

On the two levels of the table that occupies the center of Holbein's painting is a collection of objects that illustrate, literally and symbolically, the ambassadors' world—those on the upper level are associated with the heavens, and those on the lower, with the earth. Each of the astronomical and navigational instruments in the picture can be identified, either with objects whose maker is known and that are presently in the world's museums, or with common types known to have been made around the time of the portrait. Holbein was fascinated with measuring devices, and their presence here both reflects our earlier notice of the tool-mindedness of early Europeans and suggests just how wide the world of the ambassadors had become.

The late fifteenth-century voyages of Vasco da Gama and Columbus had immensely widened that world and shown that the ancient Greeks and Romans had not known about the new continents, and Europeans in turn began to produce instruments and maps to measure and describe it. The celestial globe by de Dinteville's left hand matches the terrestrial globe by his left leg, which prominently shows the location of his French home, Polisy. The book in front of the terrestrial globe has also been identified: It is Peter Apian's *Well-Grounded Instruction in All Merchant's Arithmetic.* Apian was a professor of mathematics and astronomy in Bavaria, and he made the celestial globe that can be seen on the higher level of the table.

The open book in front of the lute shows on one page the German words and music of Martin Luther's translation of the hymn *Veni Sancte Spiritus,* "Come, Holy Spirit," a popular hymn in both reformed Lutheran and Roman Catholic churches. It was a hymn particularly associated with Church councils, and by extension, with universal harmony under the guidance of the Holy Spirit. The lute, too, was a symbol of musical, and hence universal, political harmony, and its broken string, meticulously depicted by Holbein, suggests the discord of states in Europe. When William Shakespeare, in *Troilus and Cressida,* wished to describe the chaos that comes upon human society when the hierarchical order is dissolved, he also used the familiar musical metaphor:

> *The heavens themselves, the planets, and this center*
> *Observe degree, priority, and place,*
> *Insisture, course, proportion, season, form,*
> *Office and custom, all in line of order. . . .*
> *How could communities,*
> *Degrees in schools, and brotherhoods in cities,*
> *Peaceful commerce from dividable shores,*
> *The primogenitive and due of birth,*
> *Prerogative of age, crowns, sceptors, laurels,*
> *But by degree, stand in authentic place?*
> *Take but degree away, untune that string,*
> *And, Hark! What discord follows.*

Harmony in music and harmony in the affairs of men and women was a medieval commonplace that later centuries preserved and used themselves, in spiritual as well as human affairs. The fifteenth-century Dutch music theorist Johannes Tinctoris once wrote that Jesus Christ was the greatest of all musicians, because he had brought into harmony the great discord between God and humankind.

Running diagonally from left to right in the center of the picture's lowest register is a distorted human skull. Sitters for portraits were frequently depicted with a skull, the symbol—and reminder—of human mortality. The only victory over human mortality, as all Christians knew, was the Cross, which is depicted half-concealed in the very upper left-hand corner of the portrait. The skull is drawn in the technique known as anamorphosis—the representation of an object or person by a conscious distortion of perspective which, when viewed from a specific angle, becomes normal again. Holbein's picture, like many others before and after, is thus capable of being "read" as well as viewed. It preserves many of the themes and characteristic features of the culture that took form in the preceding centuries.

This book began with some predecessors of de Dinteville and de Selve—the Phoenician and Greek sailors and migrants who set out westward across the Mediterranean sea to found colonies, spread their way of life and thought among other peoples, and gain wealth and land for themselves and the geographers who recorded the information they provided—and the Romans, who politically ordered that world and spread some of it to transalpine Europe and elsewhere around the Mediterranean. By the early sixteenth century, new geographers had to account for two new continents that neither Greeks nor Romans had known, which they named after a human being—the Italian navigator Amerigo Vespucci. By the beginning of the sixteenth century, Europeans were ready to step out across a far wider sea than the Mediterranean, regardless of whether or not the people who lived beyond it were ready for them. The peoples who encountered the European explorers, colonists, soldiers, missionaries, conquistadors, and ambassadors have been dealing ever since, in one way or another, with the consequences of their visits. Parts of the land laws hammered out in twelfth- and thirteenth-century Castile still survive in the laws of Latin America, Texas, and California. The institutional descendants of Henry II's grand jury still assemble in Canada, Australia, Hong Kong, and the United States. The medieval university still has not been replaced as the most efficient means of organizing and disseminating knowledge. States and ambassadors still wrangle about the means of restoring concord to a discordant world. The difference between the world into which the Phoenicians, Greeks, and Romans stepped and that of the explorers, traders, and ambassadors of Empress Europa between the thirteenth and sixteenth centuries, is one measure of the achievement of those early Europeans. It is a powerful and impressive measure. For de Dinteville and de Selve and others like them stepped not only into a far wider world, but into time itself. And the culture they brought with them was the foundation of the modern world.

Bibliography

This bibliography covers large areas, but it is far from exhaustive, even of the materials in English-language scholarship. Much crucial scholarship on the subject is not in English, although that is not listed here. The bibliography is arranged both chronologically and topically; the sections at the end of each chapter in earlier editions of this book entitled Further Reading have been incorporated here into a single bibliography. This Bibliography begins with several general topics and continues chronologically, following the sequence of **Parts** in the book, and **chapters** within parts, with general topical bibliography included in those **Parts** in which the subject is first, or most extensively, discussed, and indicated in **bold**. For example, all of the bibliography for Byzantium and Islam is listed under **Part II (Chapters 4–5)**, but the bibliography for **Military History** is on p. 452. The bibliography under each **Part** is followed by a list of **Sources in Translation** (after **Part III** only selectively). Most of the works cited below also contain extensive bibliographies to their date of publication. Finally, it should be remembered that the divisions within this bibliography are for the sake of convenience, and many of the works listed under a single heading could as easily fit into other sections. I have tried to separate sections for convenience, but the diligent reader should look widely, rather than narrowly, at all of these references. Included in the running bibliography at appropriate places are topical bibliographies that range across the entire period covered by the book. These are:

The Name and the Idea

On the term "medieval" and its (usually erroneous) modern usages, Fred C. Robinson, "Medieval, the Middle Ages," *Speculum* 59 (1984), 745–756. *Speculum* is the journal of the Medieval Academy of America and publishes articles and book reviews in all disciplines. On the debated character of the name, Timothy Reuter, "Medieval: Another Tyrannous Construct?" *The Medieval History Journal* 1 (1998), 25–45. *The Medieval History Journal,* published in New Delhi, often prints studies of the wider Eurasian world during the period. On Europe/Europa, see under **Part VI (Chapters 17–20).**

Some of the great figures in shaping medieval studies are considered in Helen Damico and Joseph Zavadil, eds., *Medieval Scholarship: Biographical Studies on the Formation of a Discipline,* 3 vols. (New York: Garland, 1997–2000), and Kelly Boyd, ed., *Encyclopedia of Historians and Historical Writing* (London and Chicago: Fitzroy Dearborn, 1999). There is an excellent collection of studies on the subject, John Van Engen, ed., *The Past and Future of Medieval Studies* (Notre Dame and London: University of Notre Dame Press, 1994).

Guides to Medieval Studies

Two excellent introductions to the general character of medieval studies and the types of sources and methodology for dealing with them are R. C. Van Caenegem and F. L. Ganshof, *Guide to the Sources of Medieval History* (Amsterdam: North Holland Publishing Co., 1978), and J. M. Powell, ed., *An Introduction to Medieval Studies* (Syracuse, NY: Syracuse University Press, 1976, rev. ed. 1993). The best introduction to historical method with a focus on early Europe is Martha Howell and Walter Prevenier, *From Reliable Sources: An Introduction to Historical Methods* (Ithaca, NY, and London: Cornell University Press, 2001).

Two very informative examples of current research and scholarly debate treating the entire period are Lester K. Little and Barbara H. Rosenwein, eds., *Debating the Middle Ages: Issues and Readings* (Oxford and Malden, MA: Blackwell, 1998), and Peter Linehan and Janet L. Nelson, eds., *The Medieval World* (London and New York: Routledge, 2001).

Medieval Internet Search Devices/Directories:

The Labyrinth: http://www.georgetown.edu/labyrinth/

Argos: A Limited Area Search of the Ancient and Medieval Internet: http://argos.evansville.edu/

The WWW Virtual Library History Index: Medieval Europe http://www.msu.edu/~georgem1/history/medieval.htm

The Online Reference Book for Medieval Studies http://orb.rhodes.edu/

Encyclopedias and Dictionaries

J. R. Strayer, ed., *The Dictionary of the Middle Ages,* 13 vols. (New York: Charles Scribner's Sons, 1982–1989), of which several supplementary volumes are in progress; André Vauchez, in conjunction with Barrie Dobson and Michael Lapidge, eds., *Encyclopedia of the Middle Ages,* trans. Adrian Walford, 2 vols. (Chicago and London: Fitzroy Dearborn Publishers, 1997–2000). A number of scholarly encyclopedias in their most recent editions contain useful information for the historian: E. A. Livingstone, ed., *The Oxford Dictionary of the Christian Church,* 3rd ed. (Oxford:

Oxford University Press, 1997); *The New Catholic Encyclopedia* (New York: McGraw-Hill, 1967 second ed., Detroit: Gale, 2003); Jacob Neusner, Alan J. Avery-Peck, and William Scott Green, eds., *The Encyclopedia of Judaism*, 3 vols. (New York: Continuum, 1999); H. A. R. Gibb et al., eds. *Encyclopedia of Islam: New Edition*, 10 vols. (Leiden: Brill, 1960–1998). There are also a number of specialized national, area, and topical encyclopedias for the medieval period.

Bibliographies

L. J. Paetow, *A Guide to the Study of Medieval History*, rev. ed. (Cambridge, MA: Mediaeval Academy of America, 1931); and Gray C. Boyce, *Literature of Medieval History, 1930–1975: A Supplement to Louis John Paetow's "A Guide to the Study of Medieval History"*, 5 vols. (Millwood, NY: Kraus, 1981). For more recent bibliography, *International Medieval Bibliography* (Leeds: University of Leeds School of History, 1967–; Turnhout, BE: Brepols, 1995–).

Source Materials in English Translation

C. P. Farrar and Austin P. Evans, *Bibliography of English Translations From Medieval Sources* (New York: Columbia University Press, 1946), has been continued by M. A. Ferguson, *Bibliography of English Translations From Medieval Sources, 1944–1968* (New York: Columbia University Press, 1973). There are many fine collections of source materials in both independent volumes and anthologies. Two extensive collections are Patrick J. Geary, *Readings in Medieval History*, 2nd ed. (Peterborough, ON: Broadview, 1997), and Alfred J. Andrea, *The Medieval Record: Sources of Medieval History* (Boston and New York: Houghton Mifflin, 1997).

A number of publication series contain extensive materials in translation, particularly the series *The Middle Ages*, since 1970 published by the University of Pennsylvania Press (which also distributes the useful series from the Liverpool University Press, *Translated Texts for Historians*), and the publications of the series *Medieval Academy Reprints for Teaching* (MART), published by the University of Toronto Press. The Columbia University Press has published several updated translations of original sources from its great series, *Records of Western Civilization*. The series *Medieval Institute Publications*, Western Michigan University, Kalamazoo, MI, publishes a number of important volumes, particularly the productions of *The Consortium for the Teaching of the Middle Ages, Inc.* (TEAMS). The website of the Manchester University Press www.medievalsources.co.uk has an excellent series of sources in translation online.

Atlases and Historical Geography

Richard J. A. Talbert, ed., *Barrington Atlas of the Greek and Roman World* (Princeton and Oxford: Princeton University Press, 2000); Angus Mackay, with David Ditchburn, eds., *Atlas of Medieval Europe* (London and New York: Routledge, 1997); Thomas Cussans et al., eds. *The Times Atlas of European History*, 2nd ed. (London: Times Books, 1998). Also useful for the wider world is Geoffrey Barraclough, ed., *The Times Atlas of World History* (Maplewood, NJ: Hammond, 1978, 5th ed. 1999). R. A. Butlin and R. A. Dodgshon, eds., *An Historical Geography of Europe* (Oxford: Clarendon, 1998).

For the history of cartography, J. B. Harley and David Woodward, eds., *The History of Cartography*, Vol. I, *Cartography in Prehistoric, Ancient, and Medieval Europe and the Mediterranean*, (Chicago: University of Chicago Press, 1987), and the website http://www.henrydavis.com/MAPS/LMwebpages/LML.html

Computers

Anne Gilmour-Bryson, ed., *Computer Applications to Medieval Studies* (Kalamazoo, MI: Medieval Institute, 1984).

Film and Videotape

The Media Centre, University of Toronto, has produced a number of excellent videotapes dealing with many different aspects of medieval culture. Video documentaries, especially those on commercial cable networks, are rarely reliable. On movies, Stuart Airlie, "Strange Eventful Histories: The Middle Ages in the Cinema," in Linehan and Nelson, eds., *The Medieval World* (above, p. 430), 163–183, and John Aberth, *A Knight at the Movies: Medieval History on Film* (London: Routledge, 2003).

Chronology and Calendars

A good extensive chronology is that of R. L. Storey, *Chronology of the Medieval World, 400–1491* (New York: D. McKay, 1973). For England, there are fine guides by F. M. Powicke and E. B. Fryde, *Handbook of British Chronology,* 2nd. ed. (London: Royal Historical Society, 1961), and C. R. Cheny, *Handbook of Dates for Students of English History* (London: Royal Historical Society, 1945). There is also much useful information in Elias J. Bickerman, *Chronology of the Ancient World,* 2nd ed. (Ithaca, NY: Cornell University Press, 1980); Bonnie Blackburn and Leofranc Holford-Strevens, *The Oxford Companion to the Year* (Oxford: Oxford University Press, 1999); Bridget Ann Henisch, *The Medieval Calendar Year* (University Park, PA: The Pennsylvania State University Press, 1999).

The Physical Environment

For the grand and long geological story, the intelligent and beautiful book by Ron Redfern, *Origins: The Evolution of Continents, Oceans and Life* (Norman, OK: University of Oklahoma Press, 2001) is a stunning introduction. Useful for all historians is Jared Diamond, *Guns, Germs, and Steel: The Fates of Human Societies* (New York and London: W. W. Norton, 1997). For the whole of Eurasia, Peter Golden and Michael Adas, *Nomads and Sedentary Societies in Medieval Eurasia* (Washington, DC: American Historical Association, 1998), and Denis Sinor, ed., *The Cambridge History of Early Inner Asia* (Cambridge: Cambridge University Press, 1990).

For climate, see E. LeRoy Ladurie, *Times of Feast, Times of Famine* (New York: Doubleday, 1971); and T. M. L. Wigley, M. J. Ingram, and G. Farmer, eds., *Climate and History* (Cambridge: Cambridge University Press, 1985).

A brilliant and very influential example of working these kinds of data into historical argument is Fernand Braudel, *The Mediterranean and the Mediterranean World in the Age of Philip II,* 2 vols. (New York: Harper & Row, 1972). But Braudel should now be balanced by Peregrine Horden and Nicholas Purcell, *The Corrupting Sea: A Study of Mediterranean History* (Oxford: Blackwell, 2000), and the brilliant review article by Brent Shaw, "Challenging Braudel: A New Vision of the Mediterranean," *Journal of Roman Archaeology* 14 (2001), 419–453. On Medieval Europe specifically, Lester J. Bilsky, ed., *Historical Ecology: Essays on Environment and Social Change,* Part III (Port Washington, NJ: Kennikat Press, 1980) and Alfred W. Crosby, *Ecological Imperialism: The Biological Expansion of Europe, 900–1900* (Cambridge and New York: Cambridge University Press, 1986). On forests, Roland

Bechmann, *Trees and Man: The Forest in the Middle Ages,* trans. Kathryn Dunham (New York: Paragon House, 1990). On fisheries, Richard C. Hoffmann, "Economic Development and Aquatic Ecosystems in Medieval Europe," *American Historical Review* 101 (1996), 630–669.

Archaeology

Rainer Berger, ed., *Scientific Methods in Medieval Archaeology* (Berkeley-Los Angeles: University of California Press, 1970), and the ongoing research published in the journal *Medieval Archaeology.* Good examples of specialized work are M. W. Barley, ed., *European Towns: Their Archeology and Early History* (New York: Academic Press, 1977); Kathleen Biddick, ed., *Archaeological Approaches to Medieval Europe* (Kalamazoo, MI: Medieval Institute, 1984); and Klaus Randsborg, *The First Millennium in Europe and the Mediterranean: An Archaeological Essay* (Cambridge: Cambridge University Press, 1991).

Medieval History: Narrative Surveys

The most comprehensive recent survey may be found in Volumes XIII and XIV of *The Cambridge Ancient History* and the ongoing *New Cambridge Medieval History:* Averil Cameron and Peter Garnsey, eds., *The Cambridge Ancient History,* Vol. XIII, *The Late Empire, A.D. 337–425* (Cambridge: Cambridge University Press, 1998); Averil Cameron, Bryan Ward-Perkins, and Michael Whitby, eds., *The Cambridge Ancient History,* Vol. XIV, *Late Antiquity: Empire and Successors, A.D. 425–600* (Cambridge: Cambridge University Press, 2000); Rosamund McKitterick, ed., *The New Cambridge Medieval History,* Vol. II, *c.700–c.900* (Cambridge: Cambridge University Press, 1995). The first great individual history of medieval Europe—and in the opinion of many, still both the greatest and the crankiest—is Edward Gibbon, *The Decline and Fall of the Roman Empire,* the most complete edition of which is that of J. B. Bury (London: Methuen, 1909–1914). On Gibbon, Rosamund McKitterick and Roland Quinault, eds., *Edward Gibbon and Empire* (Cambridge: Cambridge University Press, 1997). The most recent general survey is William Chester Jordan, *Europe in the High Middle Ages* (London: Penguin, 2002). The best recent short history is Barbara H. Rosenwein, *A Short History of the Middle Ages* (Peterborough, ON: Broadview Press, 2001).

Part I (Chapters 1–3)

A brilliant short and well-illustrated treatment of the material covered in Parts I and II of this book is Peter Brown, *The World of Late Antiquity* (London: Thames & Hudson, 1971; reprint W.W. Norton, 1978). A longer and more systematic treatment is A. H. M. Jones, *The Later Roman Empire,* 2nd ed., 2 vols. (Baltimore: Johns Hopkins University Press, 1986). The most useful guide is G. W. Bowersock, Peter Brown, Oleg Grabar, eds., *Late Antiquity: A Guide to the Postclassical World* (Cambridge, MA, and London: Harvard University Press, 1999), the second part of which is a small encyclopedia of the period. A perceptive and original survey is Peter Brown, *The Rise of Western Christendom: Triumph and Diversity AD 200–1000* (Oxford/Malden, MA: Blackwell, 1997).

For Rome, Fergus Millar, *The Roman Empire and Its Neighbors* (London: Weidenfeld & Nicholson, 1967); Karl Galinsky, *Augustan Culture: An Interpretive Introduction* (Princeton: Princeton University Press, 1996); Clifford Ando, *Imperial Ideology and Provincial Loyalty in the Roman Empire* (Berkeley-Los Angeles: University of California Press, 2000). For the center of Roman power, Fergus Millar, *The Emperor in the Roman World* (Ithaca, NY, and London: Cornell University Press, 1977).

On the frontiers, C. R. Whittaker, *Frontiers of the Roman Empire* (Baltimore: Johns Hopkins University Press, 1994), and Steven K. Drummond and Lynn H. Nelson, *The Western Frontiers of Imperial Rome* (Armonk, NY: M. E. Sharpe, 1993). There are many studies of individual Roman European provinces.

For the European world inside and outside the Empire, Barry Cunliffe, ed., *The Oxford Illustrated Prehistory of Europe* (Oxford and New York: Oxford University Press, 1994); Cunliffe, *Greeks, Romans and Barbarians* (London: Methuen, 1988); Herbert Schutz, *The Prehistory of Germanic Europe* (New Haven, CT: Yale University Press, 1983); Malcolm Todd, *The Northern Barbarians, 100 B.C.–A.D. 300* (1975; reprint, Oxford: Basil Blackwell, 1987); Peter S. Wells, *Farms, Villages, and Cities: Commerce and Urban Origins in Late Prehistoric Europe* (Ithaca, NY, and London: Cornell University Press, 1985); idem, *The Barbarians Speak: How the Conquered Peoples Shaped Roman Europe* (Princeton, NJ: Princeton University Press, 1999); Klaus Randsborg, *The Birth of Europe: Archaeology and Social Development in the First Millennium A.D.* (Rome: L'Erma di Bretschneider, 1989); Lotte Hedeager, *Iron-Age Societies: From Tribe to State in Northern Europe, 500 B.C. to A.D. 700* (Oxford and Cambridge, MA: Blackwell, 1992).

For the East, Fergus Millar, *The Roman Near East, 31 B.C.–A.D. 337* (Cambridge, MA: Harvard University Press, 1994). On Tacitus, Ronald Martin, *Tacitus* (London: Batsford, 1981).

"Race" and "Ethnicity"

A popular account of the Roman view of Romans and non-Romans is that of J. P. V. D. Balsdon, *Romans and Aliens* (Chapel Hill: University of North Carolina Press, 1979). More recently, David Noy, *Foreigners at Rome: Citizens and Strangers* (London: Duckworth, 2000). Lloyd A. Thompson, *Romans and Blacks* (Norman, OK: University of Oklahoma Press, 1989); Frank Snowden, Jr., *Before Color Prejudice: The Ancient View of Blacks* (Cambridge, MA, and London: Harvard University Press, 1991). Steven A. Epstein, *Speaking of Slavery: Color, Ethnicity, and Human Bondage in Italy* (Ithaca, NY, and London: Cornell University Press, 2001), is excellent. On the problem of using the modern conception of "race" in historical description for the Middle Ages, see the special number of *The Journal of Medieval and Early Modern Studies* 31 (2001), *Race and Ethnicity*. For the related problem of ethnogenesis, see below under **Part III (Chapters 6–9)**, and Walter Pohl, with Helmut Reimetz, *Strategies of Distinction: The Construction of Ethnic Communities, 300–800* (Leiden: Brill, 1998); Giorgio Ausenda, ed., *After Empire: Towards an Ethnology of Europe's Barbarians* (Woodbridge, UK, and Rochester, NY: Boydell and Brewer, 2002); Patrick J. Geary, *The Myth of Nations: The Medieval Origins of Europe* (Princeton, NJ: Princeton University Press, 2002); Andrew Gillet, ed., *On Barbarian Identity: Critical Approaches to Ethnicity in the Early Middle Ages* (Turnhout BE: Brepols, 2002); James M. Muldoon, *Identity on the Medieval Irish Frontier* (Gainesville: University Press of Florida, 2003).

*   *   *

On Trajan and Hadrian, Lino Rossi, *Trajan's Column and the Dacian Wars* (Ithaca, NY, and London: Cornell University Press, 1971), and A. D. Divine, *Hadrian's Wall* (Boston: Gambit, 1969). On Hadrian and Rome, Maria Taliaferro Boatwright, *Hadrian and the City of Rome* (New Haven, CT: Yale University Press, 1988), and idem, *Hadrian and the Cities of the Roman Empire* (Princeton: Princeton University Press, 2000).

Immensely original and stimulating is Jaś Elsner, *Imperial Rome and Christian Triumph: The Art of the Roman Empire A.D. 100–450* (Oxford and New York: Oxford University Press, 1998).

There are several recent studies in Roman social history and the history of women in the ancient world: Philippe Aries and Georges Duby, eds., *A History of Private Life,* Vol. I, *From Pagan Rome to Byzantium,* ed. Paul Veyne (Cambridge, MA: Harvard University Press, 1987); Susan Treggiari, *Roman Marriage* (New York: Clarendon Press of Oxford University Press, 1991); Suzanne Dixon, *The Roman Family* (Baltimore: Johns Hopkins University Press, 1992); Sarah B. Pomeroy, *Goddesses, Whores, Wives and Slaves: Women in Classical Antiquity* (New York: Schocken, 1975); Jane F. Gardner, *Women in Roman Law and Society* (London: Croom Helm, 1986). Aline Rousselle, *Porneia: On Desire and the Body in Antiquity* (Oxford: Blackwell, 1988).

On the crisis and Rome's response, Ramsay MacMullen, *The Roman Government's Response to Crisis, A.D. 235–337* (New Haven, CT: Yale University Press, 1976); Timothy D. Barnes, *The New Empire of Diocletian and Constantine* (Cambridge, MA: Harvard University Press, 1982); Stephen Williams, *Diocletian and the Roman Recovery* (New York: Methuen, 1985), and Ramsay MacMullen, *Constantine* (New York: The Dial Press, 1969; reprint, New York: Harper & Row, 1971). On gentile Greco-Roman religion, Ramsay MacMullen, *Paganism in the Roman Empire* (New Haven, CT, and London: Yale University Press, 1981); J. H. W. G. Liebeschutz, *Continuity and Change in Roman Religion* (Oxford: Clarendon Press, 1979); Arnaldo Momigliano, *The Conflict Between Paganism and Christianity in the Fourth Century* (Oxford: Oxford University Press, 1963); Polymnia Athanassiadi and Michael Frede, eds., *Pagan Monotheism in Late Antiquity* (Oxford: Clarendon Press, 2000); Garth Fowden, *Empire to Commonwealth: Consequences of Monotheism in Late Antiquity* (Princeton, NJ: Princeton University Press, 1993).

Jews in Late Antiquity and Medieval Europe

The most accessible reference work is Jacob Neusner, Alan J. Avery-Peck, and William Scott Green, eds., *The Encyclopedia of Judaism,* 3 vols. (New York: Continuum, 1999).

The great study of the Jews in the Roman world is that of Emil Schurer, *The History of the Jewish People in the Age of Jesus Christ,* 3 vols., rev. ed. (Edinburgh: T. and T. Clark, 1973–1987). The new edition, edited by Geza Vermes and others, is not yet complete. See also Alan F. Segal, *Rebecca's Children: Judaism and Christianity in the Roman World* (Cambridge, MA: Harvard University Press, 1986); Peter Schäfer, *Judeophobia: Attitudes towards Jews in the Ancient World* (Cambridge, MA, and London: Harvard University Press, 1997) and see below, p. 437; A classic work on Judaism and Hellenism is that of Martin Hengel, *Judaism and Hellenism* (Philadelphia: Fortress Press, 1981). The place of Jews in Roman imperial law is illuminated in Amnon Linder, *The Jews in Roman Imperial Legislation* (Detroit, MI: Wayne State University Press, 1988), and for the later period, Linder, *The Jews in the Legal Sources of the Early Middle Ages* (Detroit, MI: Wayne State University Press, 1997). The great parallel collection is that of Schlomo Simonsohn, *The Apostolic See and the Jews: Documents,* 6 vols. (Toronto: Pontifical Institute of Mediaeval Studies: 1989–1991).

Volumes III–VIII of Salo W. Baron's *A Social and Religious History of the Jews,* 2nd ed. (New York: Columbia University Press, 1957), deal with most of the Middle Ages and represents the work of one of the greatest modern historians. The most exhaustive work on the early period is Bernard S. Bachrach, *Early Jewish Policy in Western Europe* (Minneapolis: University of Minnesota Press, 1977). Among particularly useful detailed studies is Joshua Starr, *The Jews in the Byzantine Empire, 641–1204* (Athens: Verlag der Byzantinisch-Neugriechisechen Jahrbücher, 1939), reprint, New York: Burt Franklin, 1970).

A new general history is Mark R. Cohen, *Under Crescent and Cross: The Jews in the Middle Ages* (Princeton, NJ: Princeton University Press, 1994). Robert Chazan has considered the important outbreak of anti-Judaic violence in connection with the First Crusade: Robert Chazan, *European Jewry and the First Crusade* (Berkeley-Los Angeles: University of California Press, 1987).

A classic study of the roots of anti-Semitism is Joshua Trachtenberg, *The Devil and the Jews: The Medieval Conception of the Jew and its Relation to Modern Antisemitism* (New Haven, CT: Yale University Press, 1943).

Gavin Langmuir, *History, Religion, and Antisemitism* (Berkeley-Los Angeles: University of California Press, 1990), and idem, *Toward a Definition of Antisemitism* (Berkeley-Los Angeles: University of California Press, 1990) are the works of a major American historian. Particularly important are the studies of David Berger, *The Christian-Jewish Debate in the High Middle Ages* (Philadelphia: Jewish Publication Society, 1979); Jeremy Cohen, *The Friars and the Jews* (Ithaca, NY: Cornell University Press, 1982); idem, ed., *Essential Papers on Judaism and Christianity in Conflict: From Late Antiquity to the Reformation* (New York: New York University Press, 1991); idem, ed., *From Witness to Witchcraft: Jews and Judaism in Medieval Christian Thought* (Wiesbaden: Harrassowitz, 1996); idem, *Living Letters of the Law: Ideas of the Jew in Medieval Christianity* (Berkeley-Los Angeles: University of California Press, 1999); Robert Chazan, *Daggers of Faith: Thirteenth-Century Christian Missionizing and Jewish Response* (Berkeley-Los Angeles: University of California Press, 1988); Miri Rubin, *Gentile Tales: The Narrative Assault on Late Medieval Jews* (New Haven, CT, and London: Yale University Press, 2001); Robert E. Lerner, *The Feast of Saint Abraham: Medieval Millenarians and the Jews* (Philadelphia: University of Pennsylvania Press, 2001); John Edwards, *The Jews in Christian Europe, 1400–1700* (London and New York: Routledge, 1988).

The most thorough study of a single Jewish community in the Middle Ages is S. D. Goitein, *A Mediterranean Society: The Jewish Communities of the World as Portrayed in the Documents of the Cairo Geniza,* Vol. I, *Economic Foundations;* Vol. II, *The Community* (Berkeley-Los Angeles: University of California Press, 1968, 1971). Equally important in studying the impact of Judaism on a very different kind of society is D. M. Dunlop, *History of the Jewish Khazars* (Princeton, NJ: Princeton University Press, 1954).

*   *   *

For early Christianity, Angelo Di Berardino, ed., *Encyclopedia of the Early Church* (New York: Oxford University Press, 1992), and Everett Ferguson et al., *Encyclopedia of Early Christianity* (New York and London: Garland, 1990). Specialized atlases are also very useful: F. Van Der Meer and Christine Mohrmann, *Atlas of the Early Christian World* (London: Nelson, 1958), and Henry Chadwick and G. R. Evans, *Atlas of the Christian Church* (New York: Facts on File, 1987).

On the "historical" Jesus, the work of Geza Vermes is important, most recently, *The Religion of Jesus the Jew* (London: SCM, 1993), and Paula Fredriksen, *From Jesus to Christ* (New Haven, CT, and London: Yale University Press, 1988).

On the early communities of Christians, Howard Clark Kee, *Who Are the People of God? Early Christian Models of Community* (New Haven, CT, and London: Yale University Press, 1995), and Wayne A. Meeks, *The First Urban Christians* (New Haven, CT, and London: Yale University Press, 1983). On the impact of Christianity, Robin Lane Fox, *Pagans and Christians* (New York: Viking, 1986); Robert L. Wilken, *The Christians as the Pagans Saw Them* (New Haven, CT, and London: Yale University Press, 1984); Ramsay MacMullen, *Christianizing the Roman Empire* (New Haven, CT, and London: Yale University Press, 1984); R. A. Markus, *Christianity in the Roman World* (London and New York: Thames & Hudson, 1974).

On the history of sacred architecture, L. Michael White, *Building God's House in the Roman World: Architectural Adaptation among Pagans, Jews, and Christians* (Baltimore, MD: Johns Hopkins University Press, 1990).

On Christian anti-Judaism, Robert L. Wilken, *John Chrysostom and the Jews* (Berkeley-Los Angeles: University of California Press, 1983), and Arnaldo Momigliano, *On Pagans, Jews, and Christians* (Middletown, CT: Wesleyan University Press, 1987). On the Christian appropriation of Palestine, P. W. L. Walker, *Holy City, Holy Places? Christian Attitudes to Jerusalem and the Holy Land in the Fourth Century* (Oxford: Clarendon Press, 1990), and E. D. Hunt, *Holy Land Pilgrimage in the Later Roman Empire AD 312–460* (Oxford: Clarendon Press, 1982).

On the question of the body and gender, Ross Kraemer, cited below, and A. Cameron and A. Kuhrt, eds., *Images of Women in Late Antiquity* (London: Croom Helm, 1983); Gillian Clark, *Women in Late Antiquity: Pagan and Christian Lifestyles* (Oxford: Clarendon Press, 1993); Peter Brown, *The Body and Society: Men, Women and Sexual Renunciation in Early Christianity* (New York: Columbia University Press, 1988); Elizabeth Clark, *Women in the Early Church* (Wilmington, DE: Glazier, 1983); Jo Ann McNamara, *A New Song: Celibate Women in the First Three Christian Centuries* (New York: Haworth, 1983); Joyce E. Salisbury, *Church Fathers, Independent Virgins* (London and New York: Verso, 1991); On the important genre of saints' lives as historical sources, Joyce E. Salisbury, *Perpetua's Passion: The Death and Memory of a Young Roman Woman* (New York: Routledge, 1997), and Lynda L. Coon, *Sacred Fictions: Holy Women and Hagiography in Late Antiquity* (Philadelphia: University of Pennsylvania Press, 1997), and below, under **Part III (Chapters 6–9)**.

On normative Christianity, Joseph H. Lynch, *The Medieval Church: A Brief History* (London and New York: Longman, 1992). On Gnosticism, Giovanni Filoromo, *A History of Gnosticism* (Oxford: Basil Blackwell, 1988).

On the ascetic life, Philip Rousseau, *Pachomius: The Making of a Community in Fourth-Century Egypt* (Berkeley-Los Angeles: University of California Press, 1986), and Rousseau, *Ascetics, Authority and the Church in the Age of Jerome and Cassian* (Oxford: Clarendon Press, 1978); Susanna Elm, *Virgins of God: The Making of Asceticism in Late Antiquity* (New York: Oxford University Press, 1994) C. H. Lawrence, *Medieval Monasticism,* 2nd ed. (London and New York: Longman, 1989).

On Augustine, Peter Brown, *Augustine of Hippo* (Berkeley-Los Angeles: University of California Press, 1969); Alan D. Fitzgerald, ed., *Augustine Through the Ages: An Encyclopedia* (Grand Rapids, MI, and Cambridge: Eerdmans, 1999); Garry Wills, *Saint Augustine* (New York and London: Penguin, 1999). On Jerome, J. N. D. Kelly, *Saint Jerome* (London: Duckworth, 1975). On Ambrose, Neil B. McLynn, *Ambrose of Milan: Church and Court in a Christian Capital* (Berkeley-Los Angeles: University of California Press, 1994).

Much of both pagan and Christian late antiquity has been illuminated by the works of Peter Brown: *The World of Late Antiquity* (cited above); *The Cult of the Saints: Its Rise and Function in Late Antiquity* (Chicago: University of Chicago Press, 1981); *The Body and Society* (cited above); *Power and Persuasion in Late Antiquity: Towards a Christian Empire* (Madison: University of Wisconsin Press, 1992).

In general, Averil Cameron, *The Mediterranean World in Late Antiquity AD 395–600* (London: Routledge, 1993), and P. S. Barnwell, *Emperor, Prefects, & Kings: The Roman West, 395–565* (Chapel Hill: University of North Carolina Press, 1992). On Rome, Richard Krautheimer, *Rome: Profile of a City, 312–1308* (Princeton, NJ: Princeton University Press, 1980; rpt. Princeton, 2000), Peter Llewellyn, *Rome in the Dark Ages* (New York and Washington: Praeger, 1971); Bertrand Lançon, *Rome in Late Antiquity: Everyday Life and Urban Change,* trans. Antonia, Nevill (New York: Routledge, 2001).

On the rise of Constantinople, Richard Krautheimer, *Three Christian Capitals: Topography and Politics* (Berkeley-Los Angeles: University of California Press, 1983); David Talbot Rice, *Constantinople: From Byzantium to Istanbul* (New York: Stein & Day, 1965); for the eastern perspective, Walter Emil Kaegi, *Byzantium and the Decline of Rome* (Princeton, NJ: Princeton University Press, 1968).

On the migrants and invaders, J. Hubert et al., *Europe of the Invasions* (New York: Braziller, 1969); Herwig Wolfram, *The Roman Empire and Its Germanic Peoples,* trans. Thomas Dunlap (Berkeley-Los Angeles: University of California Press, 1997); Patrick Amory, *People and Identity in Ostrogothic Italy 489–554* (Cambridge: Cambridge University Press, 1997); Walter Pohl, ed., *Kingdoms of the Empire: The Integration of Barbarians in Late Antiquity* (Leiden: Brill, 1997); D. H. Green, *Language and History in the Early Germanic World* (Cambridge: Cambridge University Press, 1998).

On the Huns, Otto Maenchen-Helfen, *The World of the Huns* (Berkeley-Los Angeles: University of California Press, 1975). On the Goths, Herwig Wolfram, *History of the Goths* (Berkeley-Los Angeles: University of California Press, 1988), and Peter Heather, *Goths and Romans AD 332–489* (New York: Oxford University Press, 1992). On the Franks, Edward James, *The Franks* (Oxford: Basil Blackwell, 1988).

For the response of the Theodosian dynasty, Noel Q. King, *The Emperor Theodosius and the Establishment of Christianity* (New York: Westminster Press, 1962); J. F. Matthews, *Western Aristocracies and the Imperial Court, AD 364–425* (Oxford: Clarendon Press, 1975). On the world of Galla Placidia, Stewart I. Oost, *Galla Placidia Augusta* (Chicago: University of Chicago Press, 1968), and Kenneth G. Holum, *Theodosian Empresses: Women and Imperial Dominion in Late Antiquity* (Berkeley-Los Angeles: University of California Press, 1982).

On Boethius, Margaret Gibson, *Boethius: His Life, Thought and Influence* (Oxford: Blackwell, 1981), and for Cassiodorus, James J. O'Donnell, *Cassiodorus* (Berkeley-Los Angeles: University of California Press, 1979).

A brilliant study of the transformation of the city is that of Brian Ward-Perkins, *From Classical Antiquity to the Middle Ages: Urban Public Building in Northern and Central Italy* (Oxford: Oxford University Press, 1984). For the important province of Gaul, Raymond Van Dam, *Leadership and Community in Late Antique Gaul* (Berkeley-Los Angeles: University of California Press, 1985, and his *Saints and Their Miracles in Late Antique Gaul* (Princeton, NJ: Princeton University Press, 1993); Claire Stancliffe, *St. Martin and His Hagiographer* (Oxford: Oxford University Press, 1983).

PART I (Chapters 1–3): Sources in Translation

For the entire period, Michael Maas, ed., *Readings in Late Antiquity: A Sourcebook* (London and New York: Routledge, 2000); Julius Caesar, *Seven Commentaries on The Gallic War, with an Eighth Commentary by Aulus Hirtius,* trans. Carolyn Hammond (Oxford and New York: Oxford University Press, 1996); Tacitus, *Germania,* ed. and trans. J. B. Rives (Oxford: Oxford University Press, 2001); Naphtali Lewis and Meyer Reinhold, ed. and trans., *Roman Civilization,* 2 vols. (New York: Columbia University Press, 1951–1955); Ross Shepard Kraemer, *Maenads, Martyrs, Matrons, Monastics: A Sourcebook on Women's Religions in the Greco-Roman World* (New York: Oxford University Press, 1988); idem, *Her Share of the Blessings: Women's Religions among Pagans, Jews, and Christians* (New York: Oxford University Press, 1992); Boethius, *The Consolation of Philosophy,* trans. V. E. Watts (London and New York: Penguin Books, 1969); Cassiodorus Senator, *An Introduction to Divine and Human Readings,* trans. Leslie Webber Jones (New York: Columbia University Press, 1946; reprint, New York: W. W. Norton, 1969); Cassiodorus, *Variae,* trans. S. J. B. Barnish (Philadelphia: University of Pennsylvania Press, 1992); Robert Chazan, *Church, State, and Jew in the Middle Ages* (New York: Behrman House, 1980); Edward Peters, *Heresy and Authority in Medieval Europe* (Philadelphia: University of Pennsylvania Press, 1980); Karl F. Morrison, *The Church in the Roman Empire, University of Chicago Readings in Western*

Civilization, Vol. III (Chicago: University of Chicago Press, 1986); Brian Croke and Jill Harries, *Religious Conflict in Fourth-Century Rome* (Sydney: Sydney University Press, 1982); Thomas F. X. Noble and Thomas Head, *Soldiers of Christ: Saints and Saints' Lives from Late Antiquity and the Early Middle Ages* (University Park: The Pennsylvania State University Press, 1995).

Part II (Chapters 4–5)

Byzantium and Greek Christianity

The best introductions are those of Alexander Kazhdan and Giles Constable, *People and Power in Byzantium: An Introduction to Modern Byzantine Studies* (Washington, DC: Dumbarton Oaks, 1982); Alexander P. Kazhdan, ed., *The Oxford Dictionary of Byzantium,* 3 vols. (Oxford: Clarendon, 1991); Angeliki E. Laiou and Henry Maguire, eds., *Byzantium: A World Civilization* (Washington, DC: Dumbarton Oaks, 1992); Cyril Mango, ed., *The Oxford History of Byzantium* (Oxford: Oxford University Press, 2002). A comparative study is Judith Herrin, *The Formation of Christendom* (Oxford: Blackwell, 1987).

The most recent full history is Warren Treadgold, *A History of the Byzantine State and Society* (Stanford: Stanford University Press, 1997). A shorter version is Treadgold, *A Concise History of Byzantium* (New York: Palgrave, 2001). Other brief accounts are Robert Browning, *The Byzantine Empire* (Washington, DC: Catholic University of America Press, 1992); Michael Angold, *Byzantium: The Bridge from Antiquity to the Middle Ages* (London: Weidenfeld and Nicholson, 2001); John Haldon, *Byzantium: A History* (London: Tempus, 2001).

For the sixth century, J. Moorhead, *Justinian* (London: Harlow, 1994); John W. Barker, *Justinian and the Later Roman Empire* (Madison: University of Wisconsin Press, 1966); Robert Browning, *Justinian and Theodora* (London and New York: Thames & Hudson, 1987); James Allan Evans, *The Empress Theodora: Partner of Justinian* (Austin: University of Texas Press, 2002); Alan Cameron, *Circus Factions* (Oxford: Clarendon Press, 1977); Averil Cameron, *Procopius and the Sixth Century* (Oxford: Oxford University Press, 1989). For the crucial seventh century, J. F. Haldon, *Byzantium in the Seventh Century: The Transformation of a Culture* (New York: Cambridge University Press, 1990); Mark Whittow, *The Making of Byzantium, 600–1025* (Berkeley-Los Angeles: University of California Press, 1996).

There are excellent studies of the governing groups of the East Roman Empire by Liz James, *Empresses and Power in Early Byzantium* (London: Continuum, 2002); Judith Herrin, *Women in Purple: Rulers of Medieval Byzantium* (London: Weidenfeld and Nicholson, 2002); Michael Angold, *The Byzantine Empire, 1025–1204* (New York: Longman, 1984), and idem, ed., *The Byzantine Aristocracy, IX–XIII Centuries* (Oxford: British Archeological Reports, 1984). On the end of the Empire, see Donald Nicol, *The Immortal Emperor: The Life and Legend of Constantine Palaiologos, Last Emperor of the Romans* (Cambridge: Cambridge University Press, 1994), and below, under **Part VI (Chapters 17–20).**

On Constantinople, David Talbot Rice, *Constantinople: From Byzantium to Istanbul* (New York: Stein & Day, 1965). On art, David Talbot Rice, *Byzantine Art* (Harmondsworth, UK: Penguin, 1968), and the splendid and learned catalogue of the great 1997 exhibit at the Metropolitan Museum in New York, Helen C. Evans and William D. Wixom, eds., *The Glory of Byzantium: Art and Culture of the Middle Byzantine Era, A.D. 843–1261* (New York: The Metropolitan Museum of Art, 1997).

On religion, the chapters by Hans-Georg Beck in Friedrich Kempf et al., eds., *The Church in the Age of Feudalism* (New York: Herder & Herder, 1969), and George Every, *The Byzantine Patriarchate, 451–1204* (London: Society for the Promotion of Christian Knowledge, 1947).

Byzantium's impact on neighboring societies is outlined in the important study by Dimitri Obolensky, *The Byzantine Commonwealth* (London: Weidenfeld and Nicolson, 1971).

On culture and ideas, Alexander Kazhdan and Ann Wharton Epstein, *Change in Byzantine Culture in the Eleventh and Twelfth Centuries* (Berkeley-Los Angeles: University of California Press, 1985).

Islamic History

P. M. Holt, Ann K. S. Lambton, and Bernard Lewis, eds., *Encyclopedia of Islam;* idem, *The Cambridge History of Islam*, 2 vols. (Cambridge: Cambridge University Press, 1970); John L. Esposito, ed., *The Oxford Dictonary of Islam* (New York: Oxford University Press, 2002); idem, ed., *The Oxford History of Islam* (New York: Oxford University Press, 1999).

On the Arabian peninsula, Glen W. Bowersock, *Roman Arabia* (Berkeley-Los Angeles: University of California Press, 1983), and Irfan Shahid, *Byzantium and the Arabs in the Sixth Century* (Washington, DC: Dumbarton Oaks Publications, 1995). For pre-Islamic Arabian history F. E. Peters, ed., *The Arabs and Arabia on the Eve of Islam*, Vol. III of *The Formation of the Classical Islamic World*, General Editor, Lawrence I. Conrad (Aldershot, UK, and Brookfield, VT: Ashgate/Variorum, 1999). Albert Hourani, *A History of the Arab Peoples* (Cambridge, MT: Harvard University Press, 1991; reprint, New York: MJF Books, 1991); Ira Lapidus, *A History of Islamic Societies* (Cambridge: Cambridge University Press, 1988; 2nd ed., Cambridge, 2001).

On the Prophet, F. E. Peters, *Muhammad and the Origins of Islam* (Binghamton: State University of New York Press, 1990); Michael Cook, *Muhammad* (Oxford and New York: Oxford University Press, 1983); Hugh Kennedy, *The Prophet and the Age of the Caliphates* (London and New York: Longman, 1986); Harald Motziki, ed., *The Biography of Muhammad: The Issue of the Sources* (Leiden, Boston, and Cologne: Brill, 2000).

Besides the translation of the *Qur'an* by Arberry, cited in the text, see also *The Qur'an: A Modern English Version,* trans. Majid Fakhry (Reading, UK: Garnet, 1997). For reference, Jane Dammen McAuliffe, ed., *Encyclopedia of the Qur'an,* Vol. I (Leiden, Boston, and Cologne: Brill, 2001); Michael Cook, *The Koran: A Very Short Introduction* (Oxford: Oxford University Press, 2000); Michael Sells, *Approaching the Qur'an: The Early Revelations* (Ashland, OR: White Cloud Press, 1999).

For the *hadith,* Maulana Muhammad Ali, *A Manual of Hadith* (Lahore, Pak: The Ahmadiuyya Anjuman Ishaat Islam, n.d. [1951]); Thomas Cleary, trans., *The Wisdom of the Prophet: Sayings of Muhammad, Selections from the Hadith* (Boston and London: Shambhala, 2001).

On the holy city and the pilgrimage, F. E. Peters, *Mecca: A Literary History of the Muslim Holy Land* (Princeton, NJ: Princeton University Press, 1994), and idem, *The Hajj: The Muslim Pilgrimage to Mecca and the Holy Places* (Princeton, NJ: Princeton University Press, 1995). The most stimulating study of the early period is Marshall Hodgson, *The Venture of Islam: Conscience and History in a World Civilization,* Vol. I, *The Classical Age of Islam* (Chicago: University of Chicago Press, 1974).

For the early caliphate, Wilferd Madelung, *The Succession to Muhammed: A Study of the Early Caliphate* (Cambridge: Cambridge University Press, 1997); the best study of the early conquests is that of Fred M. Donner, *The Early Islamic Conquests* (Princeton, NJ: Princeton University Press, 1981), and of the armies, Hugh Kennedy, *The Armies of the Caliphs: Military and Society in the Early Islamic State* (London: Routledge, 2002).

Prominent in important revisionist scholarship are John Wansborough, *Quranic Studies* (Oxford: Oxford University Press, 1977), and idem, *The Sectarian Milieu* (Oxford: Oxford University Press, 1978); Richard W, Bulliet, *Islam: The View from the Edge* (New York: Columbia University Press, 1994); Patricia Crone and Michael Cook, *Hagarism: The Making of the Islamic World* (Cambridge: Cambridge University Press, 1977); Patricia Crone, *Slaves on Horses: The*

Evolution of the Islamic Polity (Cambridge: Cambridge University Press, 1980); Patricia Crone and Martin Hinds, *God's Caliph: Religious Authority in the First Centuries of Islam* (Cambridge: Cambridge University Press, 1986); G. R. Hawting, *The Idea of Idolatry and the Emergence of Islam: From Polemic to History* (Cambridge: Cambridge University Press, 1999).

For law, Wael B. Hallaq, *A History of Islamic Legal Theories: An Introduction to Sunni Usul al-fiqh* (Cambridge: Cambridge University Press, 1997); George Makdisi, *The Rise of Colleges: Institutions of Higher Learning in Islam and the West* (Edinburgh: Edinburgh University Press, 1981).

For political thought, Antony Black, *The History of Islamic Political Thought: From the Prophet to the Present* (New York: Routledge, 2001), and F. I. J. Rosenthal, *Political Thought in Medieval Islam* (Cambridge: Cambridge University Press, 1962).

On material culture and the economy, see Andrew M. Watson, *Agricultural Innovation in the Early Islamic World* (Cambridge: Cambridge University Press, 1988); George F. Hourani, *Arab Seafaring* (Princeton, NJ: Princeton University Press, 1995); A. H. Hourani and A. M. Stern, eds., *The Islamic City* (Philadelphia: University of Pennsylvania Press, 1970); D. S. Richards, ed., *Islam and the Trade of Asia* (Philadelphia: University of Pennsylvania Press, 1971).

On the translation movement from Greek to Arabic, F. E. Peters, *Aristotle and the Arabs* (New York: New York University Press, 1968), and two studies by Norman Daniel: *The Arabs and Medieval Europe* (London: Longman, 1975), and *The Cultural Barrier: Problems in the Exchange of Ideas* (Edinburgh: Edinburgh University Press, 1975). For philosophy, Majid al-Fakhry, *A History of Islamic Philosophy* (New York: Columbia University Press, 1983).

There is much related material in several essays included in K. M. Setton, ed., *A History of the Crusades*, Vols. I and II, 2nd ed. (Madison: University of Wisconsin Press, 1969). On the Muslim perspective, see Amin Maalouf, *The Crusades Through Arab Eyes* (New York: Schocken, 1985), and especially the massive study by Carole Hillenbrand, *The Crusades: Islamic Perspectives* (New York: Routledge, 2000). See also below, **Part IV (Chapters 10–12); Part VI (Chapters 17–20)**. An intelligent and helpful contemporary comparative study is John L. Esposito, *What Everyone Needs to Know About Islam* (Oxford and New York: Oxford University Press, 2002).

Part II (Chapters 4–5): Sources in Translation

Deno John Geanakoplos, *Byzantium: Church, Society, and Civilization Seen through Contemporary Eyes* (Chicago: University of Chicago Press, 1984).

Procopius, *The Secret History*, trans. G. A. Williamson (Baltimore: Penguin, 1966).

Harry Turtledove, trans., *The Chronicle of Theophanes* (Philadelphia: University of Pennsylvania Press, 1982).

George T. Dennis, trans., *Maurice's Strategikon* (Philadelphia: University of Pennsylvania Press, 1984).

Michael Psellus, *Fourteen Byzantine Rulers*, trans. E. R. A. Sewter (Harmondsworth, UK, and Baltimore: Penguin, 1966).

Cyril Mango, *The Art of the Byzantine Empire* (Toronto: University of Toronto Press, 1986).

Bernard Lewis, ed. and trans., *Islam: From the Prophet Muhammad to the Capture of Constantinople*, 2 vols. (New York: Oxford University Press, 1987).

Part III (Chapters 6–9)

Rosamund McKitterick, ed., *The New Cambridge Medieval History*, Vol. II, *c.700–c.900* (Cambridge: Cambridge University Press, 1995), and Timothy Reuter, ed., Vol. III, *c.900–c.1024* (Cambridge: Cambridge University Press, 1999), and the journal, *Early Medieval Europe* (1992–).

The new series *The Short Oxford History of Europe* includes a very useful volume edited by Rosamond McKitterick, *The Early Middle Ages* (Oxford: Oxford University Press, 2001).

On the political structure of Italy in the period, T. S. Brown, *Gentlemen and Officers: Imperial Administration and Aristocratic Power in Byzantine Italy, A.D. 554–800* (London: British School at Rome, 1984); Chris Wickham, *Early Medieval Italy: Central Power and Local Society* (London: Macmillan, 1981); Thomas F. X. Noble, *The Republic of St. Peter* (Philadelphia: University of Pennsylvania Press, 1984); Neil Christie, *The Lombards* (Cambridge, MA: Blackwell, 1994).

The best introduction to the world of Gregory I is R. A. Markus, *The End of Ancient Christianity* (Cambridge: Cambridge University Press, 1990), and idem, *Gregory the Great and His World* (Cambridge: Cambridge University Press, 1997). On the popes, Jeffrey Richards, *The Popes and the Papacy in the Early Middle Ages 476–762* (Boston: Routledge & Kegan Paul, 1979). The best study of Gregory's thought and writings is Carole Straw, *Gregory the Great: Perfection in Imperfection* (Berkeley-Los Angeles: University of California Press, 1988).

On Frankish Gaul, Patrick Geary, *Before France and Germany: The Creation and Transformation of the Merovingian World* (New York and Oxford: Oxford University Press, 1988); Edward James, *The Franks* (Oxford and New York: Basil Blackwell, 1988); For East *Francia*, Matthew Innes, *State and Society in the Early Middle Ages: The Middle Rhine Valley, 400–1000* (Cambridge: Cambridge University Press, 2000); Richard Fletcher, *The Barbarian Conversion from Paganism to Christianity* (Berkeley-Los Angeles: University of California Press, 1999).

On Ireland, Michael J. O'Kelly, *Early Ireland: An Introduction to Irish Prehistory* (Cambridge: Cambridge University Press, 1989); Kathleen Hughes, *The Church in Early Irish Society* (Ithaca, NY: Cornell University Press, 1966); Dáibhí Ó Cróinín, *Early Medieval Ireland 400–1200* (London and New York: Longman, 1995).

On Britain, Henry Mayr-Harting, *The Coming of Christianity to England* (New York: Schocken: 1972; reprint, University Park: Pennsylvania State University Press, 1991).

On the Iberian Peninsula, Edward James, ed., *Visigothic Spain: New Approaches* (Oxford: Clarendon Press, 1980); Roger Collins, *Early Medieval Spain: Unity in Diversity, 400–1000* (New York: St. Martin's Press, 1983); Rachel L. Stocking, *Bishops, Councils, and Consensus in the Visigothic Kingdom, 589–633* (Ann Arbor: University of Michigan Press, 2000).

On thought and literature, Pierre Riché, *Education and Culture in the Barbarian West*, trans. John Contreni (Columbia: University of South Carolina Press, 1976).

For the rural economy, Georges Duby, *The Early Growth of the European Economy: Warriors and Peasants from the Seventh to the Twelfth Century* (Ithaca, NY: Cornell University Press, 1974); Adriaan Verhulst, *The Carolingian Economy* (Cambridge: Cambridge University Press, 2002); Jean Chapelot and Robert Fossier, *The Village and House in the Middle Ages*, trans. Henry Cleere (1985); David Herlihy, *Medieval Households* (Cambridge, MA: Harvard University Press, 1985); Leopold Genicot, *Rural Communities in the Medieval West* (Baltimore, MD, and London: Johns Hopkins University Press, 1990).

Religion and culture are treated in J. M. Wallace-Hadrill, *The Frankish Church* (Oxford: The Clarendon Press, 1983), and Ytzhak Hen, *Culture and Religion in Merovingian Gaul, A.D. 481–751* (Leiden, New York, Cologne: E. J. Brill, 1995). For the problem of conversion and sanctity, Felice Lifshitz, *The Norman Conquest of Pious Neustria: Historiographic Discourse and Saintly Relics 684–1090* (Toronto: Pontifical Institute of Medieval Studies, 1995).

On the complex question of rulership, D.A. Binchy, *Celtic and Anglo-Saxon Kingship* (Oxford: Clarendon Press, 1970); J. M. Wallace-Hadrill, *Early Germanic Kingship in England and on the Continent* (Oxford: Clarendon Press, 1971); P. H. Sawyer and I. N. Wood, eds., *Early Medieval Kingship* (Leeds: School of History, University of Leeds, 1977); Janet L. Nelson, *Politics and Ritual in Early Medieval Europe* (London: Hambledon Press, 1986); idem, *The Frankish*

World 750–900 (London and Rio Grande, OH: Hambledon, 1996); idem, *Rulers and Ruling Families in Early Medieval Europe: Alfred, Charles the Bald, and Others* (Aldershot, UK, and Brookfield, VT: Ashgate/Variorum, 1999); Frans Theuws and Janet L. Nelson, eds., *Rituals of Power: From Late Antiquity to the Early Middle Ages* (Leiden, Boston, and Cologne: Brill, 2000). Merovingian rulership is treated in Ian Wood, *The Merovingian Kingdoms, 450–751* (London and New York: Longman, 1994), and Paul Fouracre, *The Age of Charles Martel* (London and New York: Longman, 2000).

On the problem of violence, Guy Halsall, ed., *Violence and Society in the Early Medieval West* (Woodbridge, UK, and Rochester, NY: Boydell, 1998), and Warren Brown, *Unjust Seizure: Conflict, Interest, and Authority in an Early Medieval Society* (Ithaca, NY, and London: Cornell University Press, 2001).

On Gregory of Tours, Giselle de Nie, *Views from a Many-Windowed Tower* (Amsterdam: Rodopi, 1987), and especially Walter Goffart, *Narrators of Barbarian History (A.D. 550–800): Jordanes, Gregory of Tours, Bede, and Paul the Deacon* (Princeton, NJ: Princeton University Press, 1988).

For England in the late seventh and eighth centuries, James Campbell, ed., *The Anglo-Saxons* (London: Penguin, 1992). On the religious context, David Rollason, *Saints and Relics in Anglo-Saxon England* (Oxford: Basil Blackwell, 1989); Nicholas Brooks, *The Early History of the Church of Canterbury* (Atlantic Highlands, NJ: Humanities Press, 1984); Peter Hunter Blair, *The World of Bede* (London: Secker & Warburg, 1970); Paul Meyvaert, *Benedict, Gregory, Bede and Others* (London: Variorum, 1977); James Campbell, *Essays in Anglo-Saxon History, 500–1100* (London: Variorum, 1986).

On early Frankish history, the classic study by J. M. Wallace-Hadrill, *The Long-Haired Kings* (New York: Barnes & Noble, 1962; reprint, with new bibliography by Roger Collins, Oxford: Blackwell, 1996). See also the work of Geary, Wood, Fouracre, and Gerberding cited below, pp. 447–48. The most comprehensive recent survey of Carolingian political history is that of Rosamund McKitterick, *The Frankish Kingdoms under the Carolingians, 751–987* (London and New York: Longman, 1983); Karl F. Morrison, *The Two Kingdoms* (Princeton, NJ: Princeton University Press, 1964).

Rosamund McKitterick, *The Frankish Church and the Carolingian Reforms, 789–895* (London: Royal Historical Society, 1977) is a detailed study of the ecclesiastical side of the period. Important, and visually stunning, accounts of one aspect of Carolingian culture are: the masterpiece of Walter Horn and Ernest Born, *The Plan of St. Gall* (Berkeley-Los Angeles: University of California Press, 1979) and the survey by Richard Sullivan, "What Was Carolingian Monasticism? The Plan of St. Gall and the History of Monasticism," in *After Rome's Fall: Narrators and Sources of Early Medieval History. Essays Presented to Walter Goffart*, ed. Alexander Callander Murray (Toronto and Buffalo: University of Toronto Press, 1998), 251–287.

For Italy, Thomas F. X. Noble, *The Republic of St. Peter*, and J. T. Hallenbeck, *Pavia and Rome: The Lombard Monarchy and the Papacy in the Eighth Century* (Philadelphia: American Philosophical Society, 1982).

On Carolingian Europe, Donald Bullough, *The Age of Charlemagne* (New York: Putnam's, 1966); idem, *Carolingian Renewal: Sources and Heritage* (New York: St. Martin's Press, 1991); Pierre Riché, *The Carolingians: A Family Who Forged Europe*, trans. Michael Idomir Allen (Philadelphia: University of Pennsylvania Press, 1993); F. L. Ganshof, *The Carolingians and the Frankish Monarchy* (Ithaca, NY: Cornell University Press, 1971); Louis Halphen, *Charlemagne and the Carolingian Empire* (Amsterdam: North Holland Publishing Co., 1977); Roger Collins, *Charlemagne* (Toronto and Buffalo: University of Toronto Press, 1998).

On broad aspects of intellectual life, Walter Goffart, *The Narrators of Barbarian History (A.D. 550–800): Jordanes, Gregory of Tours, Bede, and Paul the Deacon* (Princeton, NJ: Princeton

University Press, 1988); Rosamond McKitterick, ed., *Carolingian Culture: Emulation and Innovation* (Cambridge: Cambridge University Press, 1994), and Bernhard Bischoff, *Manuscripts and Libraries in the Age of Charlemagne* (Cambridge: Cambridge University Press, 1994).

The most detailed study of the imperial coronation of Charlemagne is that of Robert Folz, *The Coronation of Charlemagne, 25 December 800* (London: Routledge & Kegan Paul, 1974).

Important studies of the ceremonial aspects of late antique early medieval kingship are: Sabine G. MacCormack, *Art and Ceremony in Late Antiquity* (Berkeley-Los Angeles: University of California Press, 1981); Michael McCormick, *Eternal Victory* (Cambridge: Cambridge University Press, 1985).

On Louis the Pious, Peter Godman and Roger Collins, eds., *Charlemagne's Heir* (Oxford: The Clarendon Press, 1991). For the later history of Carolingian Europe, Rosamund McKitterick, *The Frankish Kingdoms under the Carolingians, 751–987* (London and New York: Longman, 1983), and for particular divisions, Timothy Reuter, *Germany in the Early Middle Ages, 800–1056* (London and New York: Longman, 1991); Jean Dunbabin, *France in the Making, 843–1180* (New York: Oxford University Press, 1985); Barbara M. Kreutz, *Before the Normans: Southern Italy in the Ninth and Tenth Centuries* (Philadelphia: University of Pennsylvania Press, 1991).

Studies of individual rulers vary in availability and quality. Charles the Bald has attracted more recent scholarly attention than others. See Margaret Gibson and Janet Nelson, eds., *Charles the Bald: Court and Kingdom* (London: British Archeological Reports, 1981), and Janet L. Nelson, *Charles the Bald* (Harlow, UK: Longman, 1993).

Recent early histories of modern nations have begun to cast off twentieth-century spectacles and analyze ninth- and tenth-century society in terms more consistent with ninth- and tenth-century mentalities. The most important aspect of this period, however, is the self-awareness and power of the aristocracy. The most important collection of studies of the aristocracy is Timothy Reuter, ed., *The Medieval Nobility* (New York: North Holland, 1979).

A stunning depiction of mentality is Heinrich Fichtenau, *Living in the Tenth Century: Mentalities and Social Orders*, trans. Patrick J. Geary (Chicago and London: University of Chicago Press, 1991).

On Scandinavia and the Vikings, Philip Pulsiano and Kirsten Wolf, eds., *Medieval Scandinavia: An Encyclopedia* (New York: Garland, 1993); Birgit Sawyer and Peter Sawyer, *Medieval Scandinavia: From Conversion to Reformation, circa 800–1500* (Minneapolis and London: University of Minnesota Press, 1993); Thomas A. DuBois, *Nordic Religions in the Viking Age* (Philadelphia: University of Pennsylvania Press, 1999); P. H. Sawyer, *Kings and Vikings: Scandinavia and Europe, A.D. 700–1100* (New York: Methuen, 1982); David M. Wilson, ed., *The Northern World: The History and Heritage of Northern Europe, AD 400–1000* (New York: Harry N. Abrams, 1980); Peter Foote and David M. Wilson, *The Viking Achievement: The Society and Culture of Early Medieval Scandinavia* (New York: St. Martin's Press, 1990); William W. Fitzhugh and Elizabeth I. Ward, eds., *Vikings: The North Atlantic Saga* (Washington DC: Smithsonian Institute Press, 2000); R. I. Page, *Chronicles of the Vikings* (London: British Museum, 2000).

For Iceland, Orri Vésteinsson, *The Christianization of Iceland* (Oxford: Oxford University Press, 2001); Kirsten Hastrup, *Culture and History in Medieval Iceland* (Oxford: Clarendon Press, 2000); William Ian Miller, *Bloodtaking and Peacemaking: Feud, Law, and Society in Saga Iceland* (Chicago and London: University of Chicago Press, 1990).

On the character of Ottonian East *Francia*, Karl J. Leyser, *Rule and Conflict in an Early Medieval Society: Ottonian Saxony* (Bloomington: Indiana University Press, 1979); Karl J. Leyser, *Medieval Germany and Its Neighbours, 900–1250* (London: Hambledon Press, 1982); Fredric L. Cheyette, ed., *Lordship and Community in Medieval Europe* (New York: Holt, Rinehart, 1968). The art is lucidly discussed in Henry Mayr-Harting, *Ottonian Book Illumination* (London: Harvey

Miller, 1999) and Adam S. Cohen, *The Uta Codex* (University Park: The Pennsylvania State University Press, 2000); John W. Bernhardt, *Itinerant Kingship and Royal Monasteries in Early Medieval Germany* (Cambridge: Cambridge University Press, 1993); Stefan Weinfurter, *The Salian Century: Main Currents in an Age of Transition,* trans. Barbara Bowlus (Philadelphia: University of Pennsylvania Press, 1999).

On early central and eastern Europe, Florin Curta, *The Making of the Slavs* (Cambridge: Cambridge University Press, 2001); P. M. Barford, *The Early Slavs* (Ithaca, NY, and London: Cornell University Press, 2001); A. P. Vlasto, *The Entry of the Slavs into Christendom* (Cambridge: Cambridge University Press, 1970); Boris Gasparov and Olga Raevsky-Hughes, eds., *Christianity and the Eastern Slavs,* 3 vols. (Berkeley-Los Angeles: University of California Press, 1993–); Geoffrey Barraclough, ed., *Eastern and Western Europe in the Middle Ages* (London: Thames & Hudson, 1970); Charles W. Bowlus, *Franks, Moravians, and Magyars: The Struggle for the Middle Danube, 788–907* (Philadelphia: University of Pennsylvania Press, 1995).

Norman Davies, *God's Playground: A History of Poland,* Vol. I (New York: Columbia University Press, 1982); Tadeusz Manteuffel, *The Formation of the Polish State: The Period of Ducal Rule, 963–1194,* trans. Andrew Gorski (Detroit: Wayne State University Press, 1982); Miklós Molnár, *A Concise History of Hungary,* trans. Anna Magyar (Cambridge: Cambridge University Press, 2002). Simon Franklin and Jonathan Shepard, *The Emergence of Rus 750–1200* (London and New York: Longman, 1996); David Christian, *A History of Russia, Central Asia and Mongolia,* Vol. I, *Inner Asia from Prehistory to the Mongol Empire* (Oxford and Malden, MA: Blackwell, 1998). See also below, under **Political, History, Regional,** *Central Europe; Slavic Europe.*

Women's History

On women in antiquity and late antiquity, see the references in **Part I,** above, p. 435.

General reference in Katherine M. Wilson and Nadia Margolis, eds., *Women in the Middle Ages: An Encyclopedia* (New York: Routledge, 2001), and Christiane Klapisch-Zuber, ed., *A History of Women in the West,* Vol. II, *The Silences of the Middle Ages* (Cambridge, MA: Harvard University Press, 1992). For the early period, Suzanne F. Wemple, *Women in Frankish Society: Marriage and the Cloister, 500–900* (Philadelphia: University of Pennsylvania Press, 1981); Lisa M. Bitel, *Women in Early Medieval Europe, 400–1000* (Cambridge: Cambridge University Press, 2002); Pauline Stafford, *Queens, Concubines, and Dowagers: The King's Wife in the Early Middle Ages* (Athens: University of Georgia Press, 1984).

An excellent guide to historiography is Susan Mosher Stuard, ed., *Women in Medieval History and Historiography* (Philadelphia: University of Pennsylvania Press, 1987), with an extensive and up-to-date bibliography. Individual collections of studies are in Susan Mosher Stuard, ed., *Women in Medieval Society* (Philadelphia: University of Pennsylvania Press, 1976), and in Derek Baker, ed., *Medieval Women, Studies in Church History: Subsidia,* Vol. I (Oxford: Basil Blackwell, 1978). For art, Madeline H. Caviness, *Visualizing Women in the Middle Ages: Sight, Spectacle, and Scopic Economy* (Philadelphia: University of Pennsylvania Press, 2001). On gynecology, Monica H. Green, *The Trotula: A Medieval Compendium of Women's Medicine* (Philadelphia: University of Pennsylvania Press, 2001).

The debunking of one famous myth may be seen in Alain Boureau, *The Lord's First Night: The Myth of the* Droit de Cuissage, trans. Lydia G. Cochrane (Chicago and London: University of Chicago Press, 1998), and that of another, in Alain Boureau, *The Myth of Pope Joan,* trans. Lydia G. Cochrane (Chicago and London: University of Chicago Press, 2001).

On women writers, see Peter Dronke, *Women Writers of the Middle Ages* (New York: Cambridge University Press, 1984); For individual examples, Barbara Newman, *Sister of*

Wisdom: St. Hildegard's Theology of the Feminine (Berkeley: University of California Press, 1987; supp. ed., Berkeley and Los Angeles: University of California Press, 1989); Anne L. Clark, *Elizabeth of Schönau: A Twelfth-Century Visionary* (Philadelphia: University of Pennsylvania Press, 1992); Renate Blumenfeld-Kosinsky, ed., *The Collected Writings of Christine de Pizan*, trans. Renate Blumenfeld-Kosinski and Kevin Brownlee (New York: W.W. Norton, 1997).

Research on medieval women has focused on particular places and circumstances. For general surveys, see Shulamith Shahar, *The Fourth Estate: A History of Women in the Middle Ages* (London: Methuen, 1983), and the essays collected in Rosemary Thee Morewedge, ed., *The Role of Women in the Middle Ages* (Albany: State University of New York Press, 1975); Jenny Jochens, *Old Norse Images of Women* (Philadelphia: University of Pennsylvania Press, 1996); Penelope D. Johnson, *Equal in Monastic Profession: Religious Women in Medieval France* (Chicago and London: University of Chicago Press, 1991); Clarissa W. Atkinson, *The Oldest Vocation: Christian Motherhood in the Middle Ages* (Ithaca, NY: Cornell University Press, 1991).

Important studies of feminine consciousness and its devotional forms are those by Caroline Bynum, *Jesus as Mother: Studies in the Spirituality of the High Middle Ages* (Berkeley-Los Angeles: University of California Press, 1982), and *Holy Feast and Holy Fast: The Religious Significance of Food to Medieval Women* (Berkeley-Los Angeles: University of California Press, 1987), and Barbara Newman, *From Virile Woman to WomanChrist: Studies in Medieval Religion and Literature* (Philadelphia: University of Pennsylvania Press, 1995); idem, *God and the Goddesses: Vision, Poetry, and Belief in the Middle Ages* (Philadelphia: University of Pennsylvania Press, 2003).

On various kinds of female authority, see Mary Erler and Maryanne Kowaleski, eds., *Women and Power in the Middle Ages* (Athens: University of Georgia Press, 1987); Theodore Evergates, ed., *Aristocratic Women in Medieval France* (Philadelphia: University of Pennsylvania Press, 1999); Carol Adams, Paula Bartley, Hilary Bourdillon, and Cathy Loxton, eds., *From Workshop to Warfare: The Lives of Medieval Women* (Cambridge: Cambridge University Press, 1984). Susan L. Smith, *The Power of Women: A "Topos" in Medieval Art and Literature* (Philadelphia: University of Pennsylvania Press, 1995). The extensive study by Martha Howell, *Women, Production, and Patriarchy in Late Medieval Cities* (Chicago: University of Chicago Press, 1986) is a model of its kind.

On queenship, John Carmi Parsons, *Medieval Queenship* (New York: St. Martin's, 1993). On sanctity, Jane Tibbetts Schulenberg, *Forgetful of their Sex: Female Sanctity and Society, ca. 500–1100* (Chicago and London: University of Chicago Press, 1998), and McNamara, *Sainted Women* (below, p. 447).

A set of unique devotional communities is described in Walter Simons, *Cities of Ladies: Beguine Communities in the Medieval Low Countries, 1200–1565* (Philadelphia: University of Pennsylvania Press, 2001).

The Body, Sexuality, and Gender

On the body, Sarah Kay and Miri Rubin, *Framing Medieval Bodies* (New York: St. Martin's Press, 1994), and Caroline Walker Bynum, *Fragmentation and Redemption: Essays on Gender and the Human Body in Medieval Religion* (New York: Zone Books, 1992), and idem, *The Resurrection of the Body in Western Christianity, 200–1336* (New York: Columbia University Press, 1995) and above, p. 437; Sergio Bertelli, *The King's Body: Sacred Rituals of Power in Medieval and Early Modern Europe*, trans. R. Burr Litchfield (University Park: The Pennsylvania State University Press, 2001); Agostino Paravicini Bagliani, *The Pope's Body*, trans. David S. Peterson (Chicago and London: University of Chicago Press, 2000).

On sexuality, Joan Cadden, *The Meanings of Sex Differences in the Middle Ages: Medicine, Science, and Culture* (Cambridge: Cambridge University Press, 1993); Pierre J. Payer, *Sex and the*

Penitentials (Toronto: University of Toronto Press, 1984); Payer, *The Bridling of Desire: Views of Sex in the Later Middle Ages* (Toronto: University of Toronto Press, 1993); James A. Brundage, *Law, Sex, and Christian Society in Medieval Europe* (Chicago and London: University of Chicago Press, 1987); Joyce E. Salisbury, *Sex in the Middle Ages* (New York: Garland, 1991); Dyan Elliott, *Spiritual Marriage: Sexual Abstinence in Medieval Wedlock* (Princeton, NJ: Princeton University Press, 1993); Vern L. Bullough and James A. Brundage, *Sexual Practices and the Medieval Church* (Buffalo: Prometheus Books, 1982); Mary F. Wack, *Lovesickness in the Middle Ages* (Philadelphia: University of Pennsylvania Press, 1990); Dyan Elliott, *Fallen Bodies: Pollution, Sexuality, and Demonology in the Middle Ages* (Philadelphia: University of Pennsylvania Press, 1999).

On prostitution, Leah Lydia Otis, *Prostitution in Medieval Society* (Chicago: University of Chicago Press, 1985); Jacques Rossiaud, *Medieval Prostitution* (Oxford: Basil Blackwell, 1988); Ruth Mazo Karras, *Common Women: Prostitution and Sexuality in Medieval England* (New York and Oxford: Oxford University Press, 1996).

On gender and masculinities, Thelma S, Fenster and Clare A, Lees, eds., *Gender in Debate from the Early Middle Ages to the Renaissance* (New York, Palgrave, 2002); Jeffrey Jerome Cohen and Bonnie Wheeler, eds., *Becoming Male in the Middle Ages* (New York: Garland, 1997); Ruth Mazo Karras, *From Boys to Men: Formations of Masculinity in Late Medieval Europe* (Philadelphia: University of Pennsylvania Press, 2002).

On homosexuality, John Boswell, *Christianity, Social Tolerance, and Homosexuality: Gay People in Western Europe from the Beginning of the Christian Era to the Fourteenth Century* (Chicago: University of Chicago Press, 1980).

PART III (Chapters 6–9): Sources in Translation

E. Peters, *Monks, Bishops, and Pagans* (Philadelphia: University of Pennsylvania Press, 1975).

Alexander Callander Murray, ed. and trans., *From Roman to Merovingian Gaul: A Reader* (Peterborough, ON: The Broadview Press, 2000).

J. N. Hillgarth, ed., *Christianity and Paganism, 350–750: The Conversion of Western Europe* (Philadelphia: University of Pennsylvania Press, 1986).

Gregory of Tours, *The History of the Franks,* trans. Lewis Thorpe (Harmondsworth, UK, and New York: Penguin, 1974).

Gregory of Tours, *Glory of the Martyrs,* trans. Raymond Van Dam (Liverpool and Philadelphia: Liverpool University Press and University of Pennsylvania Press, 1988).

Gregory of Tours, *Glory of the Confessors,* trans. Raymond Van Dam (Liverpool and Philadelphia: Liverpool University Press and University of Pennsylvania Press, 1988).

Gregory of Tours, *Life of the Fathers,* trans. Edward James (Liverpool and Philadelphia: Liverpool University Press and University of Pennsylvania Press, 1986).

Paul Fouracre and Richard Gerberding, ed. and trans., *Late Merovingian France: History and Hagiography, 640–720* (Manchester and New York: Manchester University Press, 1996).

J. M. Wallace-Hadrill, trans., *The Fourth Book of the Chronicle of Fredegar with its continuations,* (London and New York, Thomas Nelson, 1960).

Jo Ann McNamara and John E. Halborg, with E. Gordon Whatley, eds. and trans., *Sainted Women of the Dark Ages,* (Durham, NC, and London: Duke University Press, 1992).

Katherine Fischer Drew, *The Laws of the Salian Franks* (Philadelphia: University of Pennsylvania Press, 1991).

Ephraim Emmerton, trans., *The Letters of Saint Boniface,* intro. Thomas F. X. Noble (New York: Columbia University Press, 2000).

P. D. King, *Charlemagne: Translated Sources* (Lancaster, UK: University of Lancaster, 1987).

Paul Edward Dutton, ed., *Carolingian Civilization: A Reader* (Peterborough, ON: Broadview Press, 1993).

Paul Edward Dutton, ed. and trans., *Charlemagne's Courtier: The Complete Einhard* (Peterborough, ON: Broadview Press, 1998).

Bernhard Walter Scholz, trans., *Carolingian Chronicles,* (Ann Arbor: University of Michigan Press, 1972).

H. R. Loyn and J. Percival, *The Reign of Charlemagne* (New York: St. Martin's Press, 1975).

Janet L. Nelson, trans., *The Chronicle of St. Bertin* (Manchester: Manchester University Press, 1991).

Timothy Reuter, trans., *The Annals of Fulda* (Manchester: Manchester University Press, 1992).

Boyd H. Hill, Jr., *Medieval Monarchy in Action* (New York: Barnes & Noble, 1972).

David Warner, trans., *Ottonian Germany: The Chronicon of Thietmar of Merseburg* (Manchester: Manchester University Press, 2001).

Marcelle Thiebaux, ed. and trans., *The Writings of Medieval Women* (New York: Garland, 1987).

Elizabeth A. Petroff, ed., *Medieval Women's Visionary Literature* (New York: Oxford University Press, 1986).

Karen Cherewatuk and Ulrike Wiethaus, *Dear Sister: Medieval Women and the Epistolary Genre* (Philadelphia: University of Pennsylvania Press, 1993).

Part IV (Chapters 10–12)

For the whole period, R. I. Moore, *The First European Revolution, c.970–1215* (Oxford and Malden, MA: Blackwell, 2000).

Georges Duby, *Rural Economy and Country Life in the Medieval West,* trans. Cynthia Postan, fwd. Paul Freedman (Philadelphia: University of Pennsylvania Press, 1999); Del Sweeney, ed., *Agriculture in the Middle Ages: Technology, Practices, and Perceptions* (Philadelphia: University of Pennsylvania Press, 1995); Paul Freedman, *Images of the Medieval Peasant* (Stanford: Stanford University Press, 1999). J. A. Raftis, ed., *Pathways to Medieval Peasants* (Toronto: University of Toronto Press, 1981), is an excellent collection of studies dealing with many aspects of peasant life; Wendy Davies, *Small Worlds: The Village Community in Early Medieval Brittany* (London: Duckworth, 1995). On households, David Herlihy, *Medieval Households* (Cambridge, MA: Harvard University Press, 1985), and on houses and settlements, Jean Chapelot and Robert Fossier, *The Village and House in the Middle Ages* (Berkeley-Los Angeles: University of California Press, 1985). Peasant life is now treated extensively in Robert Fossier, *Peasant Life in the Medieval West* (Oxford and New York: Basil Blackwell, 1988); Leopold Genicot, *Rural Communities in the Medieval West* (Baltimore, MD: Johns Hopkins University Press, 1990); Barbara A. Hanawalt, *The Ties That Bound: Peasant Families in Medieval England* (New York and Oxford: Oxford University Press, 1986).

There is considerable lucid discussion of the communal and corporate character of both villages and cities in Susan Reynolds, *Kingdoms and Communities in Medieval Europe, 900–1300* (Oxford: Clarendon Press, 1984). On cities, Susan Reynolds, *An Introduction to the History of English Medieval Towns* (New York: Oxford University Press, 1977); Adriaan Verhulst, *The Rise of Cities in North-West Europe* (Cambridge: Cambridge University Press, 1999) and David Nicholas, *The Growth of the Medieval City: From Late Antiquity to the Early Fourteenth Century* (New York: Longman, 1997); idem, *The Later Medieval City* (New York, Longman, 1997). Different approaches and perspectives are reflected in Harry A. Miskimin, David Herlihy, and A. L. Udovich, eds., *The Medieval City* (New Haven, CT: Yale University Press, 1977).

The term "feudalism" is now properly on the wane among historians of medieval Europe. There are useful illustrative essays in Fredric L. Cheyette, ed., *Lordship and Community in*

Medieval Europe (New York: Holt, Rinehart, 1968). The classic argument against the term is Elizabeth A. R. Brown, "The Tyranny of a Construct: Feudalism and Historians of Medieval Europe," *American Historical Review* 79 (1974), pp. 1063–1088. The most formidable criticism is Susan Reynolds, *Fiefs and Vassals: The Medieval Evidence Reinterpreted* (Oxford: Oxford University Press, 1994).

On the Peace and Truce of God, Thomas Head and Richard Landes, eds., *The Peace of God: Social Violence and Religious Response in France around 1000* (Ithaca, NY, and London: Cornell University Press, 1992).

On East *Francia,* Stephan Weinfurter, *The Salian Century,* trans. Barbara Bowlus (Philadelphia: University of Pennsylvania Press, 1999); I. S. Robinson, *Henry IV of Germany, 1056–1106* (Cambridge: Cambridge University Press, 1999); Karl Hampe, *Germany under the Salian and Hohenstaufen Emperors* (Totowa, NJ: Rowman and Littlefield, 1973).

On West *Francia,* Jean Dunbabin, *France in the Making, 843–1180* (New York: Oxford University Press, 1985), and Marcus Bull, ed., *France in the Central Middle Ages, 900–1200* (Oxford: Oxford University Press, 2002).

On Anglo-Norman England, the works of David C. Douglas: *William the Conqueror* (Berkeley-Los Angeles: University of California Press, 1967); *The Norman Achievement* (Berkeley-Los Angeles: University of California Press, 1969); *The Norman Fate* (Berkeley-Los Angeles: University of California Press, 1977); John Le Patourel, *The Norman Empire* (Oxford: Clarendon Press, 1976). On the kings, Frank Barlow, *William Rufus* (Berkeley-Los Angeles: University of California Press, 1983); C. Warren Hollister, *Henry I,* ed. and comp. Amanda Clark Frost (New Haven and London: Yale University Press, 2001); Judith A. Green, *The Government of England under Henry I* (Cambridge: Cambridge University Press, 1986).

On Iberia, in addition to the works by Collins and O'Callaghan, see Bernard F. Reilly, *The Kingdom of Leon-Castilla under Queen Urraca* (Princeton, NJ: Princeton University Press, 1982); idem, *The Kingdom of León-Castilla under Alfonso VI* (Princeton, NJ: Princeton University Press, 1988); idem, *The Kingdom of León-Castilla under King Alfonso VII, 1126–1157* (Philadelphia: University of Pennsylvania Press, 1998), and the excellent cultural history of R. A. Fletcher, *St. James's Catapult: The Life and Times of Diego Gelmirez of Compostela* (Oxford: Clarendon Press, 1984). On stress between Muslims and Christians, Kenneth Baxter Wolf, *Christian Martyrs in Muslim Spain* (Cambridge: Cambridge University Press, 1988).

On southern Italy and Sicily, see below, under **Political History,** Regional, *Sicily and South Italy* p. 461. Important scholarly studies are H. E. J. Cowdrey, *The Age of Abbot Desiderius* (Oxford: Clarendon Press, 1983), and G. A. Loud, *Church and Society in the Norman Principality of Capua, 1058–1097* (Oxford: Clarendon Press, 1985).

On religious reform in general, Gerhart Ladner, *The Idea of Reform* (Cambridge, MA: Harvard University Press, 1959); Gerd Tellenbach, *The Church in Western Europe from the Tenth to the Early Twelfth Century* (Cambridge: Cambridge University Press, 1993); and the essays in Adriaan H. Bredero, *Christendom and Christianity in the Middle Ages* (Grand Rapids, MI: William B. Eerdmans, 1994).

On monasticism, two general surveys are especially valuable: Wolfgang Braunfels, *Monasteries of Western Europe: The Architecture of the Orders* (Princeton, NJ: Princeton University Press, 1972), and C. H. Lawrence, *Medieval Monasticism* (New York: Longman, 1984).

On Cluny, Barbara Rosenwein, *Rhinoceros Bound: Cluny in the Tenth Century* (Philadelphia: University of Pennsylvania Press, 1982); idem, *To Be the Neighbor of St. Peter: The Social Meaning of Cluny's Property, 909–1049* (Ithaca, NY, and London: Cornell University Press, 1989), and H. E. J. Cowdrey, *The Cluniacs and the Gregorian Reform* (Oxford: Clarendon Press, 1970). On Citeaux, Constance Berman, *The Cistercian Evolution: The Invention of a Religious Order in Twelfth-Century Europe* (Philadelphia: University of Pennsylvania Press, 2000).

Two useful studies of other forms of religious life are Henrietta Leyser, *Hermits and the New Monasticsm: A Study of Religious Communities in Western Europe, 1000–1150* (London: Macmillan, 1984), and Ann K. Warren, *Anchorites and Their Patrons in Medieval England* (Berkeley-Los Angeles: University of California Press, 1985).

On the Investiture Conflict, Uta-Renata Blumenthal, *The Investiture Controversy: Church and Monarchy from the Ninth to the Twelfth Century* (Philadelphia: University of Pennsylvania Press, 1988), and the classic work Gerd Tellenbach, *Church, State and Christian Society at the Time of the Investiture Contest* (Oxford: Basil Blackwell, 1948). A detailed balanced account is Karl F. Morrison, *Tradition and Authority in the Early Church, 300–1140* (Princeton, NJ: Princeton University Press, 1969). On Gregory, H. E. J. Cowdrey, *Pope Gregory VII* (Oxford: Clarendon Press, 1998). On the period after Gregory VII, see H. E. J. Cowdrey, *The Age of Abbot Desiderius, Montecassino, the Papacy and the Normans in the Eleventh and Twelfth Centuries* (Oxford: Clarendon Press, 1983). On the polemical debates, I. S. Robinson, *Authority and Resistance in the Investiture Contest* (New York: Holmes & Meier, 1978).

On pilgrimage, Debra J. Birch, *Pilgrimage to Rome in the Middle Ages* (Woodbridge, UK, and Rochester, NY: Boydel and Brewer, 1998); Maryjane Dunn and Linda K. Davidson, *Pilgrimage in the Middle Ages: A Research Guide* (New York: Garland, 1996); Vera and Helmut Hell, *The Great Pilgrimage of the Middle Ages* (New York: Clarkson N. Potter, 1967); Jonathan Sumption, *Pilgrimage: An Image of Medieval Religion* (Totowa, NJ: Rowman and Littlefield, 1976); Diana Webb, *Pilgrims and Pilgrimage in the Medieval West* (New York: Palgrave, 2002); Barbara N. Sargent-Baur, ed., *Journeys Toward God: Pilgrimage and Crusade* (Kalamazoo, MI: The Medieval Institute, 1992).

On crusade, Carl Erdmann, *The Origin of the Idea of Crusade* (Princeton, NJ: Princeton University Press, 1977); Edward Peters, ed. and trans., *The First Crusade* (Philadelphia: University of Pennsylvania Press, 1971; 2nd ed. Philadelphia: University of Pennsylvania Press, 1998); Jonathan Riley-Smith, *The First Crusade and the Idea of Crusading* (Philadelphia: University of Pennsylvania Press, 1986); idem, *The Crusades: A Short History* (New Haven, CT, and London: Yale University Press, 1987); idem, ed., *The Oxford Illustrated History of the Crusades* (Oxford and New York: Oxford University Press, 1997); see also the references above, to **Part IV, Chapter 12** p. 449, and Angeliki E. Laiou and Roy Parviz Mottahedeh, eds., *The Crusades from the Perspectives of Byzantium and the Muslim World* (Washington, DC: Dumbarton Oaks, 2001); Thomas Madden, ed., *The Crusades: The Essential Readings* (Oxford and Malden, MA: Blackwell, 2002).

On a distinctive crusading phenomenon, the military orders, see Malcolm Barber, *The New Knighthood: A History of the Order of the Temple* (Cambridge: Cambridge University Press, 1990); Helen Nicholson, *The Knights Templar: A New History* (London: Sutton, 2001); and idem, *The Knights Hospitaller* (Woodbridge, UK: Boydell, 2000). See also below, **Part V (Chapters 13–15)** and **Part VI (Chapters 17–20).**

Economic History

Michael McCormick, *Origins of the European Economy: Communications and Commerce, A.D. 300–900* (Cambridge: Cambridge University Press, 2001) is highly original and well written. The most comprehensive study is the older collaborative work by J. Clapham et al., eds., *The Cambridge Economic History of Europe,* Vols. I–III (Cambridge: Cambridge University Press, 1941–1961). This work is being revised under the new joint editorship of M. M. Postan and J. Habbakuk; Vol. II, *Trade and Industry in the Middle Ages,* ed. M. M. Postan and Edward Miller, appeared in 1987. See also Norman J. G. Pounds, *An Economic History of Medieval Europe* (New York: Longman, 1974); still extremely informative is Robert L. Reynolds, *Europe Emerges* (Madison: University of Wisconsin Press, 1961).

For the early period, see McCormick, and Georges Duby, *The Early Growth of the European Economy: Warriors and Peasants from the Seventh to the Twelfth Centuries* (Ithaca, NY: Cornell University Press, 1974). The famous thesis of Henri Pirenne concerning the nature of the early medieval economy is discussed in A. F. Havighurst, ed., *The Pirenne Thesis*, 3rd ed. (Lexington, MA: D. C. Heath, 1976). The most recent contribution is that of Richard Hodges and David Whitehouse, *Mohammed, Charlemagne, and the Origins of Europe: Archaeology and the Pirenne Thesis* (Ithaca, NY: Cornell University Press, 1983). There is an excellent new survey by Adriaan Verhulst, *The Carolingian Economy* (Cambridge: Cambridge University Press, 2002).

For the economic takeoff of the tenth and eleventh centuries, Robert S. Lopez, *The Commercial Revolution of the Middle Ages, 950–1350* (Cambridge: Cambridge University Press, 1976); Edwin S. Hunt and James M. Murray, *A History of Business in Medieval Europe, 1200–1550* (Cambridge: Cambridge University Press, 1999); Peter Spufford, *Power and Profit: The Merchant in Medieval Europe* (London: Thames and Hudson, 2002); E. A. Ashtor, *A Social and Economic History of the Near East in the Middle Ages* (Berkeley-Los Angeles: University of California Press, 1976). For one kingdom, Christopher Dyer, *Making a Living in the Middle Ages: The People of Britain, 850–1520* (New Haven, CT, and London: Yale University Press, 2002).

For the later Middle Ages, Harry A. Miskimin, *The Economy of Early Renaissance Europe* (New York: Cambridge University Press, 1975). In general, Carlo M. Cipolla, ed., *The Middle Ages,* Vol. I of *The Fontana Economic History of Europe* (London: Collins/Fontana, 1972), and idem, *Before the Industrial Revolution* (New York: W.W. Norton, 1976, 2nd ed. 1980).

On money, two books by Peter Spufford, *Money and Its Uses in Medieval Europe* (Cambridge: Cambridge University Press, 1987), and *Handbook of Medieval Exchange* (London: Royal Historical Society, 1986). For one important location, Alan M. Stahl, *Zecca: The Mint of Venice in the Middle Ages* (Baltimore, MD, and London: The Johns Hopkins University Press, 2000).

On perceptions of economic change, Richard Newhauser, *The Early History of Greed* (Cambridge: Cambridge University Press, 2000); Lester K. Little, *Voluntary Poverty and the Profit Economy in Medieval Europe* (Ithaca, NY, and London: Cornell University Press, 1978); Joel Kaye, *Economy and Nature in the Fourteenth Century* (Cambridge: Cambridge University Press, 1998).

Social History

The classic work in medieval social history is Marc Bloch, *Feudal Society* (Chicago: University of Chicago Press, 1961). It should be compared now with Georges Duby, *The Chivalrous Society* (Berkeley-Los Angeles: University of California Press, 1977), and idem, *The Three Orders: Feudal Society Imagined* (Chicago: University of Chicago Press, 1980). Examples of modern approaches may be found in David Herlihy, *The Social History of Italy and Western Europe, 700–1500* (London: Variorum, 1978); John W. Baldwin, *Masters, Princes and Merchants: The Social Views of Peter the Chanter and His Circle,* 2 vols. (Princeton, NJ: Princeton University Press, 1970); Hans-Werner Goetz, *Life in the Middle Ages* (Notre Dame, IN: Notre Dame University Press, 1993). On the complex question of wealth and poverty, see Michel Mollat, *The Poor in the Middle Ages: An Essay in Social History* (New Haven, CT: Yale University Press, 1986).

The best general introduction to medieval slavery is Ruth Mazo Karras, *Slavery and Society in Medieval Scandinavia* (New Haven, CT: Yale University Press, 1988).

On private life, the ambitious and important work edited by Philippe Aries and Georges Duby, Vol. II, *Revelations of the Medieval World,* ed. Georges Duby (Cambridge, MA: Harvard University Press, 1988).

On the shape of the individual human life, see J. A. Burrow, *The Ages of Man* (New York: Clarendon Press of Oxford University Press, 1986), and Elizabeth Sears, *The Ages of Man: Medieval Interpretations of the Life Cycle* (Princeton, NJ: Princeton University Press, 1986).

Transportation and Technology

Albert C. Leighton, *Transport and Communication in Early Medieval Europe, A.D. 500–1100* (Newton Abbot, UK: David & Charles, 1972); Norbert Ohler, *The Medieval Traveller*, trans. Caroline Hillier (Woodbridge, UK, and Rochester, NY: Boydell, 1989); J. R. S. Phillips, *The Medieval Expansion of Europe*, 2nd ed. (Oxford: Clarendon, 1998), and below **Part VI (Chapters 17–20)**.

There are a number of good general histories of technology, a subject long neglected but extremely important in early European history. Two particularly lively studies are Lynn White, Jr., *Medieval Technology and Social Change* (Oxford: Oxford University Press, 1962), and White's scholarly essays: *Medieval Religion and Technology* (Berkeley-Los Angeles: University of California Press, 1978). Two other studies also offer considerable information: Edward J. Kealey, *Harvesting the Air: Windmill Pioneers in Twelfth-Century England* (Berkeley-Los Angeles: University of California Press, 1987), and George Ovitt, Jr., *The Restoration of Perfection: Labor and Technology in Medieval Culture* (New Brunswick, NJ: Rutgers University Press, 1987). Pamela O. Long, *Technology, Society, and Culture in Late Medieval and Renaissance Europe, 1300–1600* (Washington, DC: American Historical Association, 2000) is a useful short account. Idem, ed., *Science and Technology in Medieval Society* (New York: The New York Academy of Sciences, 1985) is a fine collection of essays on particular topics.

Military History

Geoffrey Parker, ed., *The Cambridge Illustrated History of Warfare in the West* (Cambridge: Cambridge University Press, 1996); Kurt Rauflaub and Nathan Rosenstein, eds., *War and Society in the Ancient and Medieval Worlds: Asia, The Mediterranean, Europe, and Mesoamerica* (Cambridge, MA, and London: Harvard University Press, 1999); Anne Nørgård Jørgensen and Birthe L. Clausen, *Military Aspects of Scandinavian Society in a European Perspective, AD 1–1300* (Copenhagen: Publications of the National Museum, 1997); Philippe Contamine, *War in the Middle Ages*, trans. Michael Jones (Cambridge, MA, and Oxford: Blackwell, 1984). *The Journal of Medieval Military History* (2002–) is the best journal in which to look.

Bernard S. Bachrach, *Early Carolingian Warfare: Prelude to Empire* (Philadelphia: University of Pennsylvania Press, 2001); John France, *Victory in the East: A Military History of the First Crusade* (Cambridge: Cambridge University Press, 1994); idem, *Western Warfare in the Age of the Crusades, 1000–1300* (Ithaca, NY, and London: Cornell University Press, 1999); R. C. Smail, *Crusading Warfare, 1097–1193*, 2nd ed. (Cambridge: Cambridge University Press, 1995); Christopher Marshall, *Warfare in the Latin East, 1192–1291* (Cambridge: Cambridge University Press, 1992).

Kelly DeVries, *Medieval Military Technology* (Peterborough, ON: Broadview, 1992); Randall Rogers, *Latin Siege Warfare in the Twelfth Century* (Oxford: Clarendon Press, 1992); Richard W. Kaeuper, *War, Justice, and Public Order: England and France in the Later Middle Ages* (Oxford: Oxford University Press, 1988); idem, *Chivalry and Violence in Medieval Europe* (Oxford and New York: Oxford University Press, 1999). And below, **Part VI (Chapters 17–20)**.

On the theory, Frederick H. Russell, *The Just War in the Middle Ages* (Cambridge: Cambridge University Press, 1975); Thomas Patrick Murphy, ed., *The Holy War* (Columbus: The Ohio State University Press, 1976); Peter Partner, *God of Battles* Princeton, NJ: Princeton University Press, 1997).

Outside Europe, Erik Hildinger, *Warriors of the Steppe: A Military History of Central Asia 500 B.C. to 1700 A.D.* (Cambridge, MA: DaCapo, 1997).

The Latin Church

The most extensive general history is that edited by Hubert Jedin and John Dolan, *Handbook of Church History,* Vols. I–IV (Freiburg: Herder; London: Burns & Oates; New York: Seabury, Vol. I, 1965; Vol. II, 1980; Vol. III, 1969). Vol. I is Karl Baus, *From the Apostolic Community to Constantine* (1965); Vol. II is Karl Baus, Hans-Georg Beck, Eugen Ewig, and Hermann Vogt, eds., *The Imperialist Church from Constantine to the Early Middle Ages* (1980); Vol. III is Friedrich Kempf, Hans-Georg Beck, Eugen Ewig, and J. A. Jungmann, eds., *The Church in the Age of Feudalism* (1969); Vol. IV is Hans-George Beck, Karl A. Fink, Josef Glazik, Erwin Iserloh, and Hans Wolter, eds., *From the High Middle Ages to the Eve of the Reformation* (1980). The translator of all volumes is Anselm Biggs.

The best atlases are F. Van Der Meer and Christine Mohrmann, eds., *An Atlas of the Early Christian World* (London: Nelson, 1958), and H. Jedin, K. S. Latourette, and J. Marten, eds., *Atlas zur Kirchengeschichte,* (Freiburg: Herder and Herder, 1970).

The most recent short accounts are Joseph H. Lynch, *The Medieval Church: A Brief History* (London and New York: Longman, 1992), and F. Donald Logan, *A History of the Church in the Middle Ages* (London: Routledge, 2002).

On doctrine, the vast work of Jaroslav Pelikan, *The Christian Tradition: A History of the Development of Doctrine,* Vols. I–IV (Chicago: University of Chicago Press, 1971–1986): Vol. I, *The Emergence of the Catholic Tradition* (1971); Vol. II, *The Spirit of Eastern Christendom* (1974); Vol. III, *The Growth of Medieval Theology* (1978); Vol. IV, *Reformation of Church and Dogma* (1984).

On liturgy, Thomas J. Heffernan and E. Ann Matter, eds., *The Liturgy of the Medieval Church* (Kalamazoo, MI: The Medieval Institute, 2001).

Among shorter studies of particular periods are, Henry Chadwick, *The Early Church* (Baltimore, MD: Penguin, 1967); R.W. Southern, *Western Society and the Church in the Middle Ages* (Baltimore, MD: Penguin, 1970). Both are superbly readable and reliable, although selective in their approach. For later periods, J. M. Wallace-Hadrill, *The Frankish Church* (Oxford: Clarendon, 1983); Gerd Tellenbach, *The Church in Western Europe from the Tenth to the Early Twelfth Century,* trans. Timothy Reuter (Cambridge: Cambridge University Press, 1993); Colin Morris, *The Papal Monarchy: The Western Church from 1050 to 1250* (Oxford: Clarendon, 1989).

On the popes, Philippe Levillain, ed., *The Papacy: An Encyclopedia* 3 vols. (London and New York: Routledge, 2001); Eamon Duffy, *Saints and Sinners: A History of the Popes* (New Haven, CT, and London: Yale University Press, 1997); Bernhard Schimmelpfennig, *The Papacy,* trans. James Sievert (New York: Columbia University Press, 1992); Agostino Paravicini Bagliani, *The Pope's Body,* trans. David S. Peterson (Chicago and London: University of Chicago Press, 2000); I. S. Robinson, *The Papacy, 1073–1198: Continuity and Innovation* (Cambridge: Cambridge University Press, 1990). On one important pope, John C. Moore, ed., *Pope Innocent III and His World* (Aldershot, UK, and Brookfield, VT: Ashgate, 1999).

Richard Krautheimer, *Rome: Profile of a City* (Princeton, NJ: Princeton University Press, 1980), is a rich account of the papal city, as are Robert Brentano, *Rome before Avignon* (Berkeley-Los Angeles: University of California Press, 1990), and Herbert L. Kessler and Johanna Zacharias, *Rome 1300: On the Path of the Pilgrim* (New Haven, CT, and London: Yale University Press, 2000), the latter two richly illustrated.

Particular aspects of papal theory are treated in Kenneth Pennington, *Pope and Bishops: The Papal Monarchy in the Twelfth and Thirteenth Centuries* (Philadelphia: University of Pennsylvania Press, 1984); Christopher Ryan, ed., *The Religious Roles of the Papacy: Ideals and Realities, 1150–1300* (Toronto: Pontifical Institute of Mediaeval Studies, 1989); Peter Partner,

The Lands of St Peter: The Papal State in the Middle Ages and the Early Renaissance (Berkeley-Los Angeles: University of California Press, 1972). See also below, **Part V (Chapters 13–16)** and **Part VI (Chapters 17–20)**.

For the later Middle Ages, see the excellent studies by Steven Ozment, *The Age of Reform, 1250–1550* (New Haven, CT: Yale University Press, 1980); Francis Oakley, *The Western Church in the Later Middle Ages* (Ithaca, NY: Cornell University Press, 1979); R. N. Swanson, *Religion and Devotion in Europe, c. 1215–c. 1515* (Cambridge: Cambridge University Press, 1995).

PART IV (Chapters 10–12): Sources in Translation

Jacqueline Murray, ed., *Love, Marriage, and the Family in the Middle Ages* (Peterborough, ON: Broadview, 2001).

Robert S. Lopez and Irving Raymond, *Medieval Trade in the Mediterranean World* (New York: Columbia University Press, 1955).

Theodor Mommsen and Karl F. Morrison, trans., *Imperial Lives and Letters of the Eleventh Century*, intro. Karl F. Morrison (New York: Columbia University Press, 2000).

Edward Peters, ed., *The First Crusade,* 2nd ed. (Philadelphia: University of Pennsylvania Press, 1998).

Paul J. Archambault, trans., *A Monk's Confession: The Memoirs of Guibert of Nogent,* (University Park: The Pennsylvania State University Press, 1996).

Lambert of Ardres, *The History of the Counts of Guines and Lords of Ardres,* trans. Leah Shopkow (Philadelphia: University of Pennsylvania Press, 2001).

Galbert of Bruges, *The Murder of Charles the Good,* trans. J. B. Ross (reprint, Toronto and Buffalo: University of Toronto Press, 1982).

Pamela Sheingorn, ed. and trans., *The Book of Sainte Foy* (Philadelphia: University of Pennsylvania Press, 1995).

PART V (Chapters 13–16)

On Romanesque art, Kenneth John Conant, *Carolingian and Romanesque Architecture* (Baltimore, MD: Penguin, 1974). Walter Cahn, *Romanesque Bible Illumination* (Ithaca, NY: Cornell University Press, 1982) is an excellent study of nonarchitectural Romanesque art.

On the intellectual tradition, Marcia Colish, *Medieval Foundations of the Western Intellectual Tradition* (New Haven, CT, and London: Yale University Press, 1997). On schools and scholars generally, Robert L. Benson and Giles Constable, eds., with Carol Lanham, *Renaissance and Renewal in the Twelfth Century* (Cambridge, MA: Harvard University Press, 1982); Peter Dronke, ed., *A History of Twelfth-Century Philosophy* (Cambridge: Cambridge University Press, 1988); D. E. Luscombe, *Medieval Thought* (Oxford: Oxford University Press, 1997); John Marenbon, *Early Medieval Philosophy (480–1150): An Introduction* (London and New York: Routledge, 1988), and *Later Medieval Philosophy (1150–1350)* (London and New York: Routledge, 1987).

On Anselm, R. W. Southern, *Saint Anselm: A Portrait in a Landscape* (Cambridge: Cambridge University Press, 1991), and on Lanfranc, Margaret Gibson, *Lanfranc of Bec* (Oxford: Clarendon Press, 1978). On Guibert, Jay Rubinstein, *Guibert of Nogent: Portrait of a Medieval Mind* (New York and London: Routledge, 2002). On Abelard, Leif Grane, *Peter Abelard* (New York: Harcourt Brace Jovanovich, 1970); D. E. Luscombe, *The School of Abelard* (Cambridge: Cambridge University Press, 1969); Michael T. Clanchy, *Abelard: A Medieval Life* (Oxford and Malden, MA: 1997).

On women writers and the epistolary genre, see above, under **Part III (Chapters 6–9)**.

The centrality of biblical study is treated in the classic work of Beryl Smalley, *The Study of the Bible in the Middle Ages* (Notre Dame, IN: Notre Dame University Press, 1964).

On universities, Hilde De Ridder-Symoens, ed., *A History of the University in Europe,* Vol. I, *Universities in the Middle Ages* (Cambridge: Cambridge University Press, 1992). On the risks, Heinrich Fichtenau, *Heretics and Scholars in the High Middle Ages, 1000–1200,* trans. Denise Kaiser (University Park: The Pennsylvania State University Press, 1998). On the origins, Stephen Ferruolo, *The Origins of the University: The Schools of Paris and Their Critics, 1100–1215* (Stanford: Stanford University Press, 1985).

Dispute Settlement and Law

On the complex matter of dispute settlement, the essays in John Bossy, ed., *Disputes and Settlements: Law and Human Relations in the West* (Cambridge: Cambridge University Press, 1983) and Wendy Davies and Paul Fouracre, eds., *The Settlement of Disputes in Early Medieval Europe* (Cambridge: Cambridge University Press, 1986) are essential. On the judicial ordeal, Robert L. Bartlett, *Trial by Fire and Water: The Medieval Judicial Ordeal* (Oxford: Clarendon Press, 1986). On law and literacy, *Michael Clanchy, From Memory to Written Record,* 2nd ed. (Cambridge, MA: Blackwell, 1993).

Manlio Bellomo, *The Common Legal Past of Europe, 1000–1800,* trans. Lydia G. Cochrane (Washington, DC: The Catholic University of America Press, 1995) surveys the whole period; James A. Brundage, *Medieval Canon Law* (London and New York: Longman, 1995), and Richard Helmholz, *The Spirit of Classical Canon Law* (Athens, GA, and London: University of Georgia Press, 1996) are excellent introductions to canon law. Wilfried Hartmann and Kenneth Pennington, eds., *A History of Medieval Canon Law,* is forthcoming. On one form of legal procedure, Edward Peters, *Inquisition* (New York: Free Press, 1988; reprint Berkeley-Los Angeles: University of California Press, 1989).

For English law, J. H. Baker, *An Introduction to English Legal History,* 3rd ed. (London and Boston: Butterworth's, 1990); Patrick Wormald, *The Making of English Law: King Alfred to the Twelfth Century,* Vol. I, *Legislation and its Limits* (Malden, MA: Blackwell, 1999); John Hudson, *The Formation of the English Common Law: Law and Society in England from the Norman Conquest to Magna Carta* (London and New York: Longman, 1996).

Languages and Literacy

W. B. Lockwood, *A Panorama of Indo-European Languages* (London: Hutchinson, 1972), and Philippe Wolff, *Western Languages A.D. 100–1500* (New York: McGraw-Hill, 1971).

On various periods, Rosamond McKitterick, *The Uses of Literacy in Early Medieval Europe* (Cambridge and New York: Cambridge University Press, 1990), and idem, *The Carolingians and the Written Word* (Cambridge and New York: Cambridge University Press, 1989). On literacy and its problems, the brilliant work of Brian Stock, *The Implications of Literacy* (Princeton, NJ: Princeton University Press, 1983).

Thought and Learning

Colish, *Medieval Foundations,* cited above p. 454, is now the standard work. Good general introductions to the early period are M. L. W. Laistner, *Thought and Letters in Western Europe, A.D. 500–900,* 2nd ed. (Ithaca, NY: Cornell University Press, 1957); Pierre Riché, *Education and Culture in the Barbarian West,* trans. John Contreni (Columbia: University of South

Carolina Press, 1976); Philippe Wolff, *The Awakening of Europe* (Baltimore, MD: Penguin, 1968). M.-D. Chenu, *Nature, Man and Society in the Twelfth Century* (Chicago: University of Chicago Press, 1968), is a classic collection of studies revealing thought in action, as is, in a different way, Alexander Murray, *Reason and Society in the Middle Ages* (Oxford: Clarendon Press, 1978).

Anders Piltz, *The World of Medieval Learning* (Totowa, NJ: Barnes & Noble, 1981), is an excellent description of the subjects of study and their method, as are the essays in David Wagner, ed., *The Seven Liberal Arts in the Middle Ages* (Bloomington: Indiana University Press, 1983). On the social establishment of learning, see John Van Engen, ed., *Learning Institutionalized: Teaching at the Medieval University* (Notre Dame, IN, and London: University of Notre Dame Press, 2000), and Jacques Verger, *Men of Learning in Europe at the End of the Middle Ages,* trans. Lisa Neal and Steven Rendall (Notre Dame, IN, and London: University of Notre Dame Press, 2000).

Mathematics, Science, and Medicine

Loren C. MacKinney, *Early Medieval Medicine With Special Reference to France and Chartres* (Baltimore, MD: Johns Hopkins University Press, 1937), and idem, *Medical Illustrations in Medieval Manuscripts* (Berkeley-Los Angeles: University of California Press, 1965) constitute a good introduction to the history of medieval medicine; each includes bibliographic guides. B. Lawn, *The Salernitan Questions* (Oxford: Oxford University Press, 1963), is a good introduction to the conceptualization of medical and scientific problems in the Middle Ages. C. H. Talbot, *Medicine in Medieval England* (London: Oldbourne, 1967), is extremely wide ranging and informative. The work of Nancy Siraisi is essential: *Medieval and Early Renaissance Medicine: An Introduction to Knowledge and Practice* (Chicago and London: University of Chicago Press, 1990), and for a particular place, Michael McVaugh, *Medicine Before the Plague* (Cambridge: Cambridge University Press, 1995).

An extensive bibliography may be found in Edward Grant, *A Sourcebook in Medieval Science* (Cambridge, MA: Harvard University Press, 1974).

For all of these fields, see David Lindberg, ed., *Science in the Middle Ages* (Chicago: University of Chicago Press, 1978), and idem, *The Beginnings of Western Science* (Chicago and London: The University of Chicago Press, 1992).

Some of the important work of Anneliese Maier is available in English in Steven Sargent, ed. and trans., *On the Threshold of Exact Science* (Philadelphia: University of Pennsylvania Press, 1982).

There is a fine introduction to mathematical theory and practice generally in Michael S. Mahoney's essay "Mathematics," in *Science in the Middle Ages,* ed. David C. Lindberg (Chicago: University of Chicago Press, 1980). A good survey of the Muslim contribution is Ali Abdullah Al-Daffa', *The Muslim Contribution to Mathematics* (London: Kazi Publications, 1977).

The relation of mathematics to other sciences is considered in Edward Grant and John E. Murdoch, eds., *Mathematics and Its Applications to Science and Natural Philosophy in the Middle Ages* (Cambridge: Cambridge University Press, 1988).

* * *

There are a number of good introductions to the topic of the religious life of the laity in medieval Europe: Bernard Hamilton, *Religion in the Medieval West* (London and Baltimore, MD: Edward Arnold, 1986) offers a handy survey of doctrine, institutions, and the life of ordinary Christians. Rosalind and Christopher Brooke, *Popular Religion and the Middle Ages* (London and New York: Thames & Hudson, 1984) discusses a variety of popular religious practices. Benedicta

Ward, *Miracles and the Medieval Mind: Theory, Record, and Event, 1000–1215* (Philadelphia: University of Pennsylvania Press, 1982) is a detailed and enlightening study of one category of devotion. Jacques Le Goff, *The Birth of Purgatory* (Chicago: University of Chicago Press, 1984), studies another. Patrick Geary, *Furta Sacra: The Theft of Relics in the Central Middle Ages* (Princeton, NJ: Princeton University Press, 1978; 2nd ed. Princeton, 1990) studies a particular aspect of devotion and economics.

On one important aspect of the relationship between the spiritual and the social identity, Joseph Lynch, *Godparents and Kinship in Early Medieval Europe* (Princeton, NJ: Princeton University Press, 1986).

On the Mendicant Orders, Rosalind B. Brooke, *The Coming of the Friars* (New York: Barnes & Noble, 1975); M.-H. Vicaire, *Saint Dominic and His Times,* trans. Kathleen Pond (Green Bay, WI: Alt, 1964).

On dissent and heresy, the extensive references and texts in Walter L. Wakefield and Austin P. Evans eds. and trans., *Heresies of the High and Late Middle Ages* (New York: Columbia University Press, 1969); Edward Peters, *Heresy and Authority in Medieval Europe* (Philadelphia: University of Pennsylvania Press, 1980). There are good discussions in; R. I. Moore, *The Origins of European Dissent* (New York: St. Martin's Press, 1977); Malcolm Lambert, *Medieval Heresy,* 3rd ed. (Oxford and Malden, MA: Blackwell, 2002). Excellent detailed studies are Walter L. Wakefield, *Heresy, Crusade and Inquisition in Southern France, 1100–1250* (Berkeley-Los Angeles: University of California Press, 1975); James B. Given, *Inquisition and Medieval Society* (Ithaca, NY, and London: Cornell University Press, 1997); Mark Pegg, *The Corruption of Angels: The Great Inquisition of 1245–1246* (Princeton, NJ: Princeton University Press, 2001).

The problem of new forms of coercion has been taken up in different ways in Edward Peters, *Inquisition* (New York: Free Press, 1988), and R. I. Moore, *The Formation of a Persecuting Society* (Oxford: Basil Blackwell, 1987). A regional study of high quality is that of Richard Kieckhefer, *Repression of Heresy in Medieval Germany* (Philadelphia: University of Pennsylvania Press, 1979).

On various other uses of the Crusades, Benjamin Z. Kedar, *Crusade and Mission* (Princeton, NJ: Princeton University Press, 1984), and, on papal diplomacy, James M. Muldoon, *Popes, Lawyers and Infidels* (Philadelphia: University of Pennsylvania Press, 1979).

Popular Culture

Two recent studies have begun to lay out the dimensions of popular culture in medieval Europe; both are by the Soviet historian Aron Gurevich: *Categories of Medieval Culture* (Boston: Routledge & Kegan Paul, 1985), and *Problems of Medieval Popular Culture* (Cambridge: Cambridge University Press, 1988). One popular form of devotion is considered in Miri Rubin, *Corpus Christi* (Cambridge: Cambridge University Press, 1991). For sources, there is the excellent book by John Shinners, *Medieval Popular Religion, 1000–1500* (Peterborough, ON: Broadview, 1997).

Political Theory and History

The Cambridge History of Medieval Political Thought c.350–c.1450, J. H. Burns, ed., (Cambridge: Cambridge University Press, 1988) is fundamental. Medieval political units did not always coincide with modern political societies, nor did they possess the same components. The creation of the modern state, or nation-state, was not their purpose, and they need not be regarded as somehow deficient when they did not create states. But they did think, often profoundly, about the nature and purpose of power and political life. For the general character of political life and thought in general, Fredric L. Cheyette, ed., *Lordship and Community in Medieval Europe: Selected Readings* (New York: Holt, Rinehart, 1968; reprint, Huntington, NY: Krieger, 1975); Beryl Smalley, ed., *Trends in*

Medieval Thought (New York: Barnes & Noble, 1965); Joseph Canning, *A History of Medieval Political Thought* (London and New York: Routledge, 1996); Antony Black, *Political Thought in Europe 1250–1450* (Cambridge: Cambridge University Press, 1992). For the early period, see above, **Part III (Chapters 6–9)**, and **Part IV (Chapters 10–12)**.

Recent research in political history has focused on both the development of political theory and doctrines and the establishment of communities at different social levels. On theory, the concise summary of Brian Tierney, *Religion, Law, and Constitutional Thought, 1150–1650* (Cambridge: Cambridge University Press, 1982). Tierney's work may be supplemented by Joseph R. Strayer, *On the Medieval Origins of the Modern State* (Princeton, NJ: Princeton University Press, 1970), and there is a fine study of the alternatives available to medieval Europeans in Antony Black, *Guilds and Civil Society in European Political Thought from the Twelfth Century to the Present* (Ithaca, NY: Cornell University Press, 1984). Although it deals primarily with the period 1300–1500, there is much important information in Bernard Guenée, *States and Rulers in Later Medieval Europe* (Oxford: Basil Blackwell, 1985). The most recent general study is Kenneth Pennington, *The Prince and the Law 1200–1600: Sovereignty and Rights in the Western Legal Tradition* (Berkeley-Los Angeles: University of California Press, 1993).

On the idea of empire, Robert Folz, *The Concept of Empire in Western Europe from the Fifth to the Fifteenth Century* (London: Edward Arnold, 1969). On the Papacy, see above, under **The Latin Church.**

Susan Reynolds, *Kingdoms and Communities in Western Europe, 900–1300* (Oxford: Clarendon Press, 1984) reassesses the experience of collective political participation and mentalities on all levels of medieval society. Antony Black, *Guilds and Civil Society* (Ithaca, NY: Cornell University Press, 1984), contrasts two different and powerful views of political systems.

Classic works on kingship and constitutionalism are Ernst Kantorowicz, *The King's Two Bodies* (Princeton, NJ: Princeton University Press, 1957); on representative institutions, Antonio Marongiu, *Medieval Parliaments: A Comparative Study* (London: Eyre & Spottiswoode, 1968); Gaines Post, *Studies in Medieval Legal Thought: Public Law and State, 1100–1322* (Princeton, NJ: Princeton University Press, 1964); Michael Wilks, *The Problem of Sovereignty in the Later Middle Ages* (Cambridge: Cambridge University Press, 1963). Anne Duggan, ed., *Queens and Queenship in Medieval Europe* (Woodbridge, UK, and Rochester, NY: Boydell, 1997); idem, *Kings and Kingship in Medieval Europe* (London: King's College, 1993).

New work is illustrated by Thomas N. Bisson, ed., *Cultures of Power: Lordship, Status, and Process in Twelfth-Century Europe* (Philadelphia: University of Pennsylvania Press, 1995), and Fredric L. Cheyette, *Ermengard of Narbonne and the World of the Troubadours* (Ithaca, NY, and London: Cornell University Press, 2001).

Political History: Regional

Balkans: John V. A. Fine Jr., *The Early Medieval Balkans* (Ann Arbor: University of Michigan Press, 1983); Fine, *The Late Medieval Balkans* (Ann Arbor: University of Michigan Press, 1987).

Central Europe: above, **Part III (Chapters 6–9),** and Lisa Wolverton, *Hastening Toward Prague: Power and Society in the Medieval Czech Lands* (Philadelphia: University of Pennsylvania Press, 2001).

Crusader States and the Mediterranean: See the bibliography in Jonathan Riley-Smith, *The Crusades: A Short History* (New Haven, CT: Yale University Press, 1987). For the Latin kingdom of Jerusalem, Jean Richard, *The Latin Kingdom of Jerusalem*, 2 vols. (New York: North Holland, 1979). On the Islamic states, Robert Irwin, *The Middle East in the Middle Ages: The Early Mamluk Sultanate, 1250–1382* (Carbondale: Southern Illinois University Press, 1986).

Eastern Europe: see above, **Part III (Chapters 6–9),** and S. C. Rowell, *Lithuania Ascending: A Pagan Empire within East-Central Europe, 1295–1345* (Cambridge: Cambridge University Press, 1994), and below, **Part VI (Chapters 17–20),** and also below, *Slavic Europe.*

England: See the bibliography above, **Part IV, Chapters 11** and **15.** The series edited by David C. Douglas, *English Historical Documents* (New York: Eyre & Spottiswoode, 1955–), is a collection of extensively annotated source materials in translation. Recent work is listed in the Cambridge University Press series *Bibliographical Handbooks.* Especially useful are the volumes edited by Michael Altschul (1969), Bertie Wilkinson (1977), and DeLloyd J. Guth (1978). A standard work is Edgar B. Graves, *Bibliography of English History to 1485* (Oxford: Oxford University Press, 1975). The best short survey is C. Warren Hollister, *The Making of England 55 B.C. to 1399* (Lexington, MA, and Toronto: D.C. Heath, 1992). For the aftermath of the conquest, Brian Golding, *Conquest and Colonisation: The Normans in Britain, 1066–1100* (New York, 2001); Barbara Harvey, *The Twelfth and Thirteenth Centuries* (Oxford: Oxford University Press, 2001). For the Angevins, W. L. Warren, *Henry II* (Berkeley-Los Angeles: University of California Press, 1973), and Frank Barlow, *Thomas Becket* (Berkeley-Los Angeles: University of California Press, 1986); John Gillingham, *The Angevin Empire,* 2nd ed. (Oxford and New York: Oxford University Press, 2001); idem, *Richard I* (New Haven, CT, and London: Yale University Press, 1999); W. L. Warren, *King John* (New Haven, CT, and London: Yale University Press, 1997); S. D. Church, ed., *King John: New Interpretations* (Woodbridge, UK: Boydell, 1999); J. C. Holt, *Magna Carta,* 2nd ed. (Cambridge: Cambridge University Press, 1992); D. A. Carpenter, *The Minority of Henry III* (London: Methuen, 1990); idem, *The Reign of Henry III* (London and Rio Grande, OH: Hambledon, 1996); Sandra Raban, *England under Edward I and Edward II 1259–1327* (Oxford and Malden, MA: Blackwell, 2000); Anthony Tuck, *Crown and Nobility: England 1272–1461,* 2nd ed. (Oxford and Malden, MA: 1999).

France: For all aspects of medieval France, William W. Kibler and Grover A. Zinn, eds., *Medieval France: An Encyclopedia* (New York and London: Garland, 1995). There is no comprehensive history of medieval France in English. On specific periods, Jean Dunbabin, *France in the Making, 843–1180* (Oxford and New York: Oxford University Press, 1985); Marcus Bull, ed., *France in the Central Middle Ages 900–1200* (Oxford: Oxford University Press, 2002); John W. Baldwin, *The Government of Philip Augustus* (Berkeley-Los Angeles: University of California Press, 1986); William Chester Jordan, *Louis IX and the Challenge of the Crusade* (Princeton, NJ: Princeton University Press, 1979), and Joseph R. Strayer, *The Reign of Philip the Fair* (Princeton, NJ: Princeton University Press, 1980). For the later period, P. S. Lewis, *Later Medieval France: The Polity* (New York: St. Martin's Press, 1968). For the countryside, Marc Bloch, *French Rural History* (Berkeley-Los Angeles: University of California Press, 1970).

German Lands: For the early period, Timothy Reuter, *Germany in the Early Middle Ages c. 800–1056* (London and New York: Longman, 1991). Written from a European perspective, Horst Fuhrmann, *Germany in the High Middle Ages, c. 1050–1200* (Cambridge: Cambridge University Press, 1986) is intelligent and eloquent. On the later period, F. R. H. Du Boulay, *Germany in the Later Middle Ages* (New York: St. Martin's Press, 1983); Otto Brunner, *Land and Lordship: Structures of Governance in Medieval Austria,* trans. with intro. Howard Kaminsky and James Van Horn Melton (Philadelphia: University of Pennsylvania Press, 1992); and two works edited by Gerald Strauss, *Manifestations of Discontent in Germany on the Eve of the Reformation* (Bloomington: Indiana University Press, 1971), and *Pre-Reformation Germany* (New York: Harper & Row, 1972).

On the German ministerials, John Freed, *Noble Bondsmen: Ministerial Marriages in the Archdiocese of Salzburg, 1100–1343* (Ithaca, NY: Cornell University Press, 1995); Benjamin Arnold, *German Knighthood, 1050–1300* (Oxford: Clarendon Press, 1985). For the Hansa, Philippe Dollinger, *The German Hansa* (London: Macmillan, 1970). The most recent study of the great opponent of Barbarossa is that of Karl Jordan, *Henry the Lion* (New York: Oxford University Press, 1986).

Hungary: Nora Berend, *At the Gate of Christendom: Jews, Muslims, and "Pagans" in Medieval Hungary* (Cambridge and New York: Cambridge University Press, 2001). Specialized studies offer much more recent scholarship: Erik Fugedi, *Kings, Bishops, Nobles and Burghers in Medieval Hungary*, ed. J. M. Bak (London: Variorium, 1986), and idem, *Castle and Society in Medieval Hungary (1000–1437)* (Budapest: Akademiai Kiad, 1986).

Ireland: In general, see R. F. Foster, ed., *The Oxford History of Ireland* (Oxford and New York: Oxford University Press, 1989); Michael J. O'Kelly, *Early Ireland: An Introduction to Irish Prehistory* (Cambridge: Cambridge University Press, 1988); Kathleen Hughes, *The Church in Early Irish Society* (Ithaca, NY: Cornell University Press, 1968); Donncha O'Corrain, *Ireland Before the Vikings* (Dublin: Gill and Macmillan, 1972); Francis John Byrne, *Irish Kings and High-Kings* (London: Batsford, 1973); Art Cosgrove, ed., *A New History of Ireland*, Vol. II, *Medieval Ireland, 1169–1534* (Oxford: Clarendon Press, 1987; 2nd ed. 1993); a volume in the ongoing series edited by T. W. Moody, F. X. Martin, and F. J. Byrne, *A New History of Ireland* (Oxford and New York: Oxford University Press, 1976–). See also James Lydon, *Ireland in the Later Middle Ages* (Dublin: Gill and Macmillan, 1973); and idem, *The Lordship of Ireland in the Middle Ages* (Dublin: University Press of Ireland, 1972).

Italy: J. K. Hyde, *Society and Politics in Medieval Italy, 1000–1300* (New York: St. Martin's Press, 1969); Gino Luzzato, *An Economic History of Italy* (New York: Barnes & Noble, 1961); Daniel Waley, *The Italian City-Republics* (New York: McGraw-Hill, 1969); John Larner, *Italy in the Age of Dante and Petrarch, 1216–1380* (New York: Longman, 1980); Chris John Wickham, *Early Medieval Italy* (Totowa, NJ: Barnes & Noble, 1982); Marvin Becker, *Medieval Italy* (Bloomington: Indiana University Press, 1980).

Low Countries: see below, **Part VI (Chapters 17–20)**.

Scandinavia: Philip Pulsianzo and Kirsten Wolf et al., eds., *Scandinavia: Medieval Scandinavia: An Encyclopedia* (New York and London: Garland, 1994); Birgit and Peter Sawyer, *Medieval Scandinavia: From Conversion to Reformation, circa 800–1500* (Minneapolis and London: University of Minnesota Press, 1993); David M. Wilson, *The Northern World: The History and Heritage of Northern Europe, AD 400–1100* (New York: Harry N. Abrams, 1980). There is little recent literature on individual Scandinavian states. See Palle Lauring, *A History of the Kingdom of Denmark*, 4th ed., (Copenhagen: Host, 1973). An important source is available in Peter Fisher, trans., *Saxo Grammaticus: The History of the Danes* (Totowa, NJ: Rowman and Littlefield, 1979).

Other important studies include Jesse L. Byock, *Medieval Iceland: Society, Sagas, and Power* (Berkeley-Los Angeles: University of California Press, 1988); Ruth Mazo Karras, *Slavery and Society in Medieval Scandinavia* (New Haven, CT: Yale University Press, 1988); William Ian Miller, *Bloodtaking and Peacemaking: Feud, Law, and Society in Saga Iceland* (Chicago and London: University of Chicago Press, 1990); Kirsten Hastrup, *Culture and History in Medieval Iceland* (Oxford: Clarendon Press, 1985).

Scotland: A. F. Smyth, *Warlords and Holymen: Scotland AD 80–1000* (Toronto and Buffalo: University of Toronto Press, 1984); G. W. S. Barrow, *Kingship and Unity: Scotland, 1000–1306* (Toronto and Buffalo: University of Toronto Press, 1981); Alexander Grant, *Independence and Nationhood: Scotland, 1306–1469* (Toronto and Buffalo: University of Toronto Press, 1984); Jenny Wormald, *Court, Kirk, and Community: Scotland, 1470–1625* (Toronto and Buffalo: University of Toronto Press, 1981). A good popular history is John L. Roberts, *Lost Kingdoms: Celtic Scotland and the Middle Ages* (Edinburgh: Edinburgh University Press, 1997). On rule, Marjorie O. Anderson, *Kings and Kingship in Early Scotland* (Edinburgh and London: Scottish Academic Press, 1980). On society, K. J. Stringer, ed., *Essays on the Nobility of Medieval Scotland*

(Edinburgh: John Donald, 1985). On one example of Scotland in the world, Alan MacQuarrie, *Scotland and the Crusades, 1095–1560* (Edinburgh: John Donald, 1985).

   Sicily and South Italy: Barbara Kreutz, *Before the Normans: Southern Italy in the Ninth and Tenth Centuries* (Philadelphia: University of Pennsylvania Press, 1991); G. A. Loud, *The Age of Robert Guiscard: Southern Italy and the Norman Conquest* (Harlow, UK: Pearson Education, 2000); Hubert Houben, *Roger II of Sicily: A Ruler Between East and West* (Cambridge: Cambridge University Press, 2002); Donald Matthew, *The Norman Kingdom of Sicily* (Cambridge and New York: Cambridge University Press, 1992). Steven Runciman, *The Sicilian Vespers* (Cambridge: Cambridge University Press, 1958), addresses the late thirteenth century. For the period of Frederick II, see Ernst Kantorowicz, *Frederick II* (New York: Ungar, 1957), and David Abulafia, *Frederick II: A Medieval Emperor* (Oxford and New York: Oxford University Press, 1988). On the aftermath, Jean Dunbabin, *Charles I of Anjou: Power, Kingship, and State-Making in Thirteenth-Century Europe* (London and New York: Longman, 1998), and Clifford Backman, *The Decline and Fall of Medieval Sicily: Politics, Religion, and Economy in the Reign of Frederick III* (Cambridge: Cambridge University Press, 1995).

   Slavic Europe: Florin Curta, *The Making of the Slavs: History and Archaeology in the Lower Danube Region, c.500–700* (Cambridge: Cambridge University Press, 2001); A.P. Vlasto, *The Entry of the Slavs into Christendom* (Cambridge: Cambridge University Press, 1970); Geoffrey Barraclough, ed., *Eastern and Western Europe in the Middle Ages* (New York: Harcourt Brace Jovanovich, 1970). For Poland, Alexander Gieysztor et al., eds., *History of Poland,* 2nd ed. (Warsaw: Polish Scientific Publishers, 1979); Tadeusz Manteufel, *The Formation of the Polish State: The Period of Ducal Rule, 963–1194* (Detroit, MI: Wayne State University Press, 1982). For the later period, Paul W. Knoll, *The Rise of the Polish Monarchy: Piast Poland in East Central Europe, 1320–1370* (Chicago: University of Chicago Press, 1972); Richard C. Hoffmann, *Land, Liberties, and Lordship in a Late Medieval Countryside* (Philadelphia: University of Pennsylvania Press, 1990), and Piotr Gorecki, *Economy, Society, and Lordship in Medieval Poland, 1100–1250* (New York: Holmes & Meier, 1992).

   Spain: See J. Vicens Vives, *Approaches to the History of Spain* (Berkeley-Los Angeles: University of California Press, 1970); J. F. O'Callaghan, *A History of Medieval Spain* (Ithaca, NY: Cornell University Press, 1975); Bernard Reilly, *The Medieval Spains* (Cambridge and New York: Cambridge University Press, 1993); D.W. Lomax, *The Reconquest of Spain* (New York: Longman, 1978); Bernard F. Reilly, *The Contest of Christian and Muslim Spain, 1031–1157* (Cambridge, MA, and Oxford: Blackwell, 1992); Joseph O'Callaghan, *Reconquest and Crusade in Medieval Spain* (Philadelphia: University of Pennsylvania Press, 2003); J. N. Hillgarth, *The Spanish Kingdoms, 1250–1516,* Vol. I, *The Precarious Balance, 1250–1410,* and Vol. II, *The Castilian Hegemony, 1410–1516* (New York: Oxford University Press, 1976, 1978) J. R. L. Highfield, *Spain in the Fifteenth Century* (New York: Harper & Row, 1972); Thomas F. Glick, *Islamic and Christian Spain in the Early Middle Ages* (Princeton, NJ: Princeton University Press, 1978); A. Chejne, *Muslim Spain* (Minneapolis: University of Minnesota Press, 1974); L. P. Harvey, *Islamic Spain 1250 to 1500* (Chicago and London: University of Chicago Press, 1990), and R. I. Burns, *The Crusader Kingdom of Valencia,* 2 vols. (Cambridge, MA: Harvard University Press, 1967).

   On one important aspect of the Conquest, R. I. Burns, S. J., *Muslims, Christians, and Jews in the Crusader Kingdom of Valencia: Societies in Symbiosis* (Cambridge, MA: Harvard University Press, 1984). James William Brodman, *Ransoming Captives in Crusader Spain* (Philadelphia: University of Pennsylvania Press, 1986) is an excellent study of a complex topic. For later medieval Spain, there is an extensive bibliography in Edward Peters, *Inquisition* (New York: Free Press, 1988), 320–325. See also Peter Linehan, *Spain, 1157–1300* (Cambridge, MA, and Oxford: Blackwell, 1990).

On Aragon and Catalonia, Thomas N. Bisson, *The Medieval Crown of Aragon: A Short History* (New York: Oxford University Press, 1987), and Archibald R. Lewis, *The Development of Southern French and Catalan Society, 718–1050* (Austin: University of Texas Press, 1965).

Switzerland: E. Bonjour, H. S. Offler, and G. R. Potter, *A Short History of Switzerland* (Oxford: Clarendon Press, 1952); and Thomas A. Brady Jr., *Turning Swiss: Cities and Empire, 1450–1550* (Cambridge: Cambridge University Press, 1985).

Wales: Wendy Davies, *Wales in the Early Middle Ages* (Leicester: Leicester University Press, 1982); David Walker, *Medieval Wales* (Cambridge: Cambridge University Press; 1990); and R. R. Davies, *Conquest, Coexistence, and Change: Wales, 1063–1415* (Oxford: Clarendon Press, 1987).

*   *   *

On medieval thought in the thirteenth through fifteenth centuries, Norman Kretzman, Anthony Kenny, and Jan Pinborg, eds., *The Cambridge History of Later Medieval Philosophy* (Cambridge: Cambridge University Press, 1982); and John Marenbon, *Later Medieval Philosophy (1150–1350): An Introduction* (New York: Routledge & Kegan Paul, 1987).

On Aristotelian and other theories of sexuality and gestation, Claude Thomasset, "The Nature of Woman," in Christiane Klapisch-Zuber, *A History of Women in the West,* Vol. II, *Silences of the Middle Ages,* 43–69 (above, p. 445).

The literature on philosophy and theology in the thirteenth century is vast, and the beginning student will want as easy a guide through it as possible. M.-D. Chenu, *Toward Understanding St. Thomas,* trans. A. M. Landry and D. Hughes (Chicago: Henry Regnery, 1964), is an ideal student's guide to the period in general as well as to Aquinas himself. A good recent biography of Aquinas is James Weisheipl, *Friar Thomas d'Aquino: His Life, Thought and Work* (New York: Doubleday, 1974). For Bonaventure, see J. Guy Bougerol, *Introduction to the Works of St. Bonaventure,* trans. José de Vinck (Paterson, NJ: St. Anthony Guild Press, 1965).

On Gothic architecture, Jean Bony, *French Gothic Architecture of the 12th and 13th Centuries* (Berkeley-Los Angeles: University of California Press, 1983). For a single example, Robert Branner, *Chartres Cathedral* (New York: W.W. Norton, 1969). The wonderful children's book by David Macaulay, *Cathedral: The Story of Its Construction* (Boston: Houghton Mifflin, 1973), is a mine of easily accessible information.

On the complex problem of knighthood and chivalry, Georges Duby's essays, *The Chivalrous Society* (Berkeley-Los Angeles: University of California Press, 1980). The essential study of the origins of courtly culture is now that of C. Stephen Jaeger, *The Origins of Courtliness: Civilizing Trends and the Formation of Courtly Ideals, 939–1210* (Philadelphia: University of Pennsylvania Press, 1985), as is the substantial work by Joachim Bumke, *Courtly Culture: Literature and Society in the High Middle Ages,* trans., Thomas Dunlap (Berkeley: University of California Press, 1991; reprint, Woodstock, NY, and New York: Overlook, 2000). On chivalry as a topic of research, Maurice Keen, *Chivalry* (New Haven, CT: Yale University Press, 1984), and Constance Brittain Bouchard, *"Strong of Body, Brave, and Noble": Chivalry and Society in Medieval France* (Ithaca, NY, and London: Cornell University Press, 1998).

On the *vita civile* and Dante, see John Larner, *Italy in the Age of Dante and Petrarch, 1216–1380* (New York: Longman, 1980); Rachel Jacoff, ed., *The Cambridge Companion to Dante* (Cambridge: Cambridge University Press, 1993), and Richard Lansing, ed., *The Dante Encyclopedia* (New York and London: Garland, 2000). Charles T. Davis, *Dante's Italy and Other Essays* (Philadelphia: University of Pennsylvania Press, 1984) illuminates Dante's moral and political world. Three studies by Patrick Boyde are indispensable: *Dante Philomythes and Philosopher: Man in the Cosmos* (Cambridge: Cambridge University Press, 1981); *Perception and Passion in Dante's Comedy* (Cambridge: Cambridge University Press, 1993); *Human Vices and Human Worth in Dante's Comedy* (Cambridge: Cambridge University Press, 2000). A contemporary account of Dante's city is now available: Daniel E. Bornstein, ed. and trans., *Dino Compagni's Chronicle of Florence* (Philadelphia: University of Pennsylvania Press, 1986). A good detailed study of the interweaving of poetry and politics is Joan M. Ferrante, *The Political Vision of the Divine Comedy* (Princeton, NJ: Princeton University Press, 1984).

The best general history of thirteenth-century Europe is that of John H. Mundy, *Europe in the High Middle Ages, 1154–1309* (New York: Longman, 1973, 3rd ed. New York: Longman, 2000). Mundy's study of the High Middle Ages also contains important aspects of the history of women, as does the volume of essays made in his honor: Julius Kirschner and Suzanne F. Wemple, eds., *Women of the Medieval World* (Oxford: Basil Blackwell, 1985).

Part V (Chapters 13–16): Sources in Translation

Betty Radice, trans., *The Letters of Abelard and Heloise* (Baltimore, MD: Penguin, 1974).

Constant J. Mews, *The Lost Love Letters of Heloise and Abelard: Perceptions of Dialogue in Twelfth-Century France* (New York: Palgrave, 1999).

Lynn Thorndike, *University Records and Life in the Middle Ages* (New York: Columbia University Press, 1944; reprint, New York: W.W. Norton, 1975).

Richard Dales, *The Scientific Achievement of the Middle Ages* (Philadelphia: University of Pennsylvania Press, 1973).

R. I. Moore, *The Birth of Popular Heresy* (New York: St. Martin's Press, 1975).

Walter L. Walefield and Austin P. Evans, eds. and trans., *Heresies of the High Middle Ages* (New York: Columbia University Press, 1991).

Joseph L. Baird, Giuseppe Baglivi, and John Robert Kane, trans., *The Chronicle of Salimbene de Adam* (Binghamton, NY: Medieval and Renaissance Texts and Studies, 1986).

Ewart Lewis, *Medieval Political Ideas*, 2 vols. (New York: Knopf, 1954).

Brian Tierney, *The Crisis of Church and State 1050–1300* (Englewood Cliffs, NJ: Prentice Hall, 1964; reprint, Toronto and Buffalo: University of Toronto Press, 1988).

Richard Kaeuper and Elspeth Kennedy, *The Book of Chivalry of Geoffroi de Charny: Text, Context, and Translation* (Philadelphia: University of Pennsylvania Press, 1996).

Dante Alighieri, *The Divine Comedy*, trans., with commentary, Charles S. Singleton, 6 vols. (Princeton, NJ: Princeton University Press, 1970–1975).

Part VI (Chapters 17–20)

On the whole period, Denys Hay, *Europe in the Fourteenth and Fifteenth Centuries* (New York: Longman, 1966); George Holmes, *Europe: Hierarchy and Revolt, 1320–1450* (New York: Harper & Row, 1975); John Hale, Roger Highfield, and Beryl Smalley, eds., *Europe in the Later Middle Ages* (Evanston, IL: Northwestern University Press, 1965); Margaret Aston, *The Fifteenth Century* (New York: Harcourt Brace Jovanovich, 1968); F. R. H. Du Boulay, *An Age of Ambition* (New York: Viking, 1970); David Abulafia, *The Western Mediterranean Kingdoms, 1200–1500: The Struggle for Dominion* (London and New York: Longman, 1997).

On the apocalyptic mentality, Richard K. Emmerson and Bernard McGinn, *The Apocalypse in the Middle Ages* (Ithaca, NY, and London: Cornell University Press, 1992); Bernard McGinn, *Antichrist* (San Francisco, CA: Harper San Francisco, 1994; reprint, New York: Columbia University Press, 2000).

William Chester Jordan, *The Great Famine: Northern Europe in the Early Fourteenth Century* (Princeton, NJ: Princeton University Press, 1996).

David Herlihy, *The Black Death and the Transformation of the West,* ed. with intro. Samuel Klein Cohen (Cambridge, MA, and London: Harvard University Press, 1997). William McNeill, *Plagues and Peoples* (New York: Doubleday, 1976); and the brilliant cultural study by Millard Meiss, *Painting in Florence and Siena after the Black Death* (New York: Harper & Row, 1964). On a particular region, John Hatcher, *Plague, Population and the English Economy, 1348–1530* (London: Macmillan, 1977).

On warfare, see above, **Military History**, and J. F. Verbruggen, *The Art of Warfare in Western Europe During the Middle Ages* (Amsterdam: North Holland Publishing Co., 1977); Kenneth Fowler, ed., *The Hundred Years' War* (New York: St. Martin's Press, 1971); Malcolm Vale, *The Origins of the Hundred Years War: The Angevin Legacy, 1250–1340* (Oxford: Clarendon, 1996). The most exhaustive history of the Hundred Years' War has been begun by Jonathan Sumption, *The Hundred Years War: Trial by Battle* (Philadelphia: University of Pennsylvania Press, 1990); idem, *The Hundred Years War II: Trial by Fire* (Philadelphia: University of Pennsylvania Press, 1999).

On the changing concepts of Christendom and Europe, Denys Hay, *Europe: The Emergence of an Idea* (New York: Harper, 1966); Karl J. Leyser, "Concepts of Europe in the Early and High Middle Ages," *Past & Present* 137 (1992), 25–47; Anthony Pagden, ed., *The Idea of Europe from Antiquity to the European Union* (Cambridge: Cambridge University Press, 2002). On the changing territorial character, Robert Bartlett, *The Making of Europe: Conquest, Colonization and Cultural Change 950–1350* (Princeton, NJ: Princeton University Press, 1993).

On the later Crusades and the Near East, Donald Queller, *The Fourth Crusade,* 2nd ed., with Thomas Madden, (Philadelphia: University of Pennsylvania Press, 1997); James M. Powell, *The Anatomy of a Crusade, 1213–1221* (Philadelphia: University of Pennsylvania Press, 1986) and Maureen Purcell, *Papal Crusading Policy, 1244–1291* (Leiden: Brill, 1975), and, for criticism, Elizabeth Siberry, *Criticism of Crusading, 1095–1274* (Oxford: Clarendon Press, 1985). On the crusades of the fourteenth century, Norman Housley, *The Avignon Papacy and the Crusades, 1305–1378* (Oxford: Clarendon Press, 1986); idem, *The Later Crusades from Lyons to Alcazar, 1274–1580* (Oxford and New York: Oxford University Press, 1992).

On the Baltic, William Urban, *The Baltic Crusade* (DeKalb: Northern Illinois University Press, 1975), and Urban, *The Prussian Crusade* (Lanham, MD: University Press of America, 1980); Michael Burleigh, *Prussian Society and the German Order* (Cambridge: Cambridge University Press, 1984). On the great Baltic-Rhineland-English trading network, Philippe Dollinger, *The German Hansa* (London: Macmillan, 1964).

For the peoples of Eurasia and North Africa generally, Archibald R. Lewis, *Nomads and Crusaders* (Bloomington and Indianapolis: Indiana University Press, 1988), and Richard C. Foltz, *Religions of the Silk Road* (New York: St. Martin's Griffin, 1999). And for the steppe peoples, Peter B. Golden, *An Introduction to the History of the Turkic Peoples: Ethnogenesis and State-Formation in Medieval and Early Modern Eurasia and the Middle East* (Wiesbaden: Harrassowitz, 1992); David Christian, *A History of Russia, Central Asia, and Mongolia,* Vol. I, *Inner Eurasia from Prehistory to the Mongol Empire* (Oxford and Malden, MA: 1998); Donald Ostrowski, *Muscovy and the Mongols: Cross-Cultural Influences on the Steppe Frontier, 1304–1589* (Cambridge: Cambridge University Press, 1998); John Fennell, *The Crisis of Medieval Russia: 1200–1304* (Oxford and Malden, MA: Blackwell, 1983).

For the Mongols in western Asia and Russia, David Morgan, *The Mongols* (Oxford: Basil Blackwell, 1986); Paul Ratchnevsky, *Genghis Khan* (Oxford: Blackwell, 1991); J. A. Boyle, *The Mongol World Empire 1206–1370* (London: Variorum, 1977); and Charles J. Halperin, *The Tatar*

Yoke (Columbus, OH: Slavica, 1986), and idem, *Russia and the Golden Horde: The Mongol Impact on Medieval Russian History* (Bloomington: University of Indiana Press, 1987).

Most general histories of late medieval Europe deal in some way with the problems of reform, reunion, and prophecy discussed in the first section of this chapter. Several works, however, are good guides to some of the most interesting aspects of the period. E. Randolph Daniel, *The Franciscan Concept of Mission in the High Middle Ages* (Lexington: University Press of Kentucky, 1975), and Marjorie Reeves, *The Influence of Prophecy in the Later Middle Ages* (Oxford: Oxford University Press, 1969), offer sensitive treatments of the prophetic mentality from a wide variety of sources. Delno C. West, ed., *Joachim of Fiore in Christian Thought*, 2 vols. (New York: Burt Franklin, 1975), is a good collection of essays on different aspects of one influential thinker. An example of the popularity of prophecy is Robert E. Lerner, *The Powers of Prophecy: The Cedars of Lebanon Vision from the Mongol Onslaught to the Dawn of the Enlightenment* (Berkeley-Los Angeles: University of California Press, 1983), and idem, *The Feast of Saint Abraham: Medieval Millenarians and the Jews* (Philadelphia: University of Pennsylvania Press, 2001).

On formal thought, John Marenbon, *Later Medieval Philosophy* above, p. 462, which contains an excellent bibliography, as does Norman Kretzmann, Anthony Kenny, and Jan Pinborg, eds., *The Cambridge History of Later Medieval Philosophy* (Cambridge: Cambridge University Press, 1982). An excellent study of Ockham is that of Marilyn McCord Adams, *William Ockham*, 2 vols. (Notre Dame, IN: Notre Dame University Press, 1987).

On the Avignon papacy, Yves Renouard, *The Avignon Papacy, 1305–1403* (London: Faber & Faber, 1970). On the outbreak of Schism. Walter Ullmann, *The Origins of the Great Schism* (London: Burns, Oates & Washburn, 1948; reprint, Hamden, CT: Archon Books, 1973).

On the Hussite revolt, Howard Kaminsky, *A History of the Hussite Revolution* (Berkeley-Los Angeles: University of California Press, 1967); Matthew Spinka, *John Hus: A Biography* (Princeton, NJ: Princeton University Press, 1968).

Fine recent general studies of the period are Francis P. Oakley, *The Western Church in the Later Middle Ages* (Ithaca, NY: Cornell University Press, 1980); Steven Ozment, *The Age of Reform* (New Haven, CT: Yale University Press, 1980); and most recently, John Van Engen, "The Church in the Fifteenth Century," in Thomas A. Brady Jr., Heiko A. Oberman, and James D. Tracy, eds., *Handbook of European History 1400–1600: Late Middle Ages, Renaissance, and Reformation*, Vol. I (Leiden and New York: E. J. Brill, 1994), 305–330. On the pastoral concerns of the period, Leonard E. Boyle, *Pastoral Care, Clerical Education and Canon Law, 1200–1400* (London: Variorum, 1981).

The theme of fraternity is well laid out in John Bossy, *Christianity in the West, 1400–1700* (New York: Oxford University Press, 1985). Some of the most important devotional literature is translated and analyzed in Bernard McGinn, *Meister Eckhart and the Beguine Mystics* (New York and Mahwah, NJ: The Paulist Press, 1994); Mother Columba Hart, *Hadewijch: The Complete Works* (New York and Ramsey, NJ, and Toronto: The Paulist Press, 1980); James A. Wiseman, *John Ruusbroec: The Spiritual Espousals and Other Works* (New York and Mahwah, NJ: The Paulist Press, 1985); and John Van Engen, ed., *Devotio Moderna: Basic Writings* (New York and Mahwah, NJ: The Paulist Press, 1988).

The general framework of the place of religion in medieval life has also been reassessed in the excellent and wide-ranging study by John Van Engen, "The Christian Middle Ages as an Historiographical Problem," *American Historical Review* 91 (1986), 519–552.

Antony Black, *Political Thought in Europe 1250–1450* (Cambridge: Cambridge University Press, 1992), and Brian Tierney, *Religion, Law, and the Growth of Constitutional Thought, 1150–1650* (Cambridge: Cambridge University Press, 1982) are the best introductions to the transmission of late medieval political theory through the early modern period, and are important correctives to most studies of the political theory of the Renaissance and Reformation. Ernst H. Kantorowicz, *The King's Two Bodies* (Princeton, NJ: Princeton University Press, 1957), is a classic work, as is Margaret Aston, *The Fifteenth Century* (London and New York: Thames & Hudson, 1968). An excellent recent topical study is J. H. Burns, *Lordship, Kingship, and Empire: The Idea of Monarchy 1400–1525* (Oxford: Clarendon Press, 1992).

On Germany, see the works of F. R. H. Du Boulay, *Germany in the Later Middle Ages* (New York: St. Martin's Press, 1983); Joachim Leuschner, *Germany in the Late Middle Ages* (New York: North Holland, 1980), and Gerald Strauss, ed., *Pre-Reformation Germany* (New York: Harper & Row, 1972).

On Joan of Arc, see Régine Pernoud, *Joan of Arc by Herself and Her Witnesses,* trans. Edward Hyams (New York: Stein & Day, 1982); idem, with Marie-Véronique Clin, *Joan of Arc: Her Story,* trans. and rev. Jeremy duQuesnay Adams, ed. Bonnie Wheeler (New York: St. Martin's, 1998); Charles T. Wood, *Joan of Arc and Richard III: Sex, Saints, and Government in the Middle Ages* (New York and Oxford: Oxford University Press, 1988); Bonnie Wheeler and Charles T. Wood, eds., *Fresh Verdicts on Joan of Arc,* (New York: Garland, 1996). There is an exhaustive bibliography by Nadia Margolis, *Joan of Arc in History, Literature, and Film* (New York: Garland, 1990). For Christine, there is a good biographical study by Charity Cannon Willard, *Christine de Pizan: Her Life and Works* (New York: Persea Books, 1984).

For France's recovery, see P. S. Lewis, ed., *The Recovery of France in the Fifteenth Century* (New York: Harper & Row, 1972). On England, see J. R. Lander, *The Wars of the Roses* (New York: Capricorn, 1967), and H. S. Bennett, *The Pastons and Their England* (Cambridge: Cambridge University Press, 1970).

There is much value in the work of P. S. Lewis, *Essays in Later Medieval French History* (London: Hambledon, 1985); M. G. A. Vale, *Charles VII* (London: Eyre Methuen, 1974); Richard W. Kaeuper, *War, Justice, and Public Order: England and France in the Later Middle Ages* (Oxford: Clarendon Press, 1988).

On courtly culture generally, see the essays in A. G. Dickens, ed., *The Courts of Europe: Politics, Patronage and Royalty, 1400–1800* (New York: McGraw-Hill, 1977), and Ronald G. Asch and Adolf M. Birke, eds., *Princes, Patronage, and the Nobility: The Court at the Beginning of the Modern Age, ca. 1450–1650* (Oxford: Oxford University Press, 1991).

There is now an excellent history of Flanders: David Nicholas, *Medieval Flanders* (London and New York: Longman, 1992). Johan Huizinga's classic work, *The Waning of the Middle Ages* Eng. trans. (London: E. Arnold, 1924; reprint, Garden City: Doubleday, 1953); new English trans. as *The Autumn of the Middle Ages* by Rodney J. Payton and Ulrich Mammitzsch (Chicago: University of Chicago Press, 1996) must be read with both caution and scepticism, and M. G. A. Vale, *War and Chivalry* (London: Duckworth, 1981) should be consulted for its critique. On the lively character of the towns, Barbara Hanawalt and Kathryn Ryerson, eds., *City and Spectacle in Medieval Europe* (Minneapolis: University of Minnesota Press, 1992). On the literary culture of Holland, the brilliant work of Frits Pieter Van Oostrom, *Court and Culture* (Berkeley-Los Angeles: University of California Press, 1992).

The best studies of Burgundy in English are those of Walter Prevenier and Wim Blockmans, *The Burgundian Netherlands* (Cambridge and New York: Cambridge University Press, 1986), superbly illustrated, and Wim Blockmans and Walter Prevenier, *The Promised Lands: The Low Countries under Burgundian Rule, 1369–1530* (Philadelphia: University of Pennsylvania Press, 1999).

On Byzantium, see Donald M. Nicol, *The Last Centuries of Byzantium, 1261–1453* (London: Hart-Davis, 1972), and *The End of the Byzantine Empire* (New York: Holmes & Meier, 1981). See also the well-told story of Steven Runciman, *The Fall of Constantinople, 1453* (Cambridge: Cambridge University Press, 1965). The best survey of early Ottoman Turkish history is Halil Inalcik, *The Ottoman Empire: The Classical Age, 1300–1600* (London: Weidenfeld & Nicholson, 1973).

For Muscovy, see J. L. Fennell, *The Crisis of Medieval Russia 1200–1304* (London and New York: Longman, 1983), and Fennell, *The Emergence of Moscow, 1304–1359* (Berkeley-Los Angeles: University of California Press, 1968); Nancy Shields Kollman, *Kinship and Politics: The Making of the Muscovite Political System, 1345–1547* (Stanford, CA: Stanford University Press, 1987); and Gustav Alef, *Rulers and Nobles in Fifteenth-Century Muscovy* (London: Variorum, 1983).

On Eastern and East-Central Europe, Jean W. Sedlar, *East-Central Europe in the Middle Ages, 1000–1500* (Seattle: University of Washington Press, 1994); and Gabor Klaniczay, *Holy Rulers and Blessed Princesses: Dynastic Cults in Medieval Central Europe* (Cambridge: Cambridge University Press, 2002).

On the city of Rome after the Avignon papacy, J. A. F. Thomson, *Popes and Princes, 1417–1517* (Boston: George Allen & Unwin, 1980).

On the humanist movement, Albert Rabil, ed., *Renaissance Humanism: Foundations, Forms, and Legacy,* 3 vols. (Philadelphia: University of Pennsylvania Press, 1988); Ronald G. Witt, *"In the Footsteps of the Ancients": The Origins of Humanism from Lovato to Bruni* (Leiden and Boston: Brill, 2000).

On the growing interest in travel and its literature, see Scott D. Westrem, ed., *Discovering New Worlds: Essays on Medieval Exploration and Imagination* (New York and London: Garland, 1991); and Mary B. Campbell, *The Witness and the Other World: Exotic European Travel Writing, 400–1600* (Ithaca, NY, and London: Cornell University Press, 1988). The best account of the development of Mediterranean-Atlantic expansion is now that of Felipe Fernandez-Armesto, *Before Columbus: Exploration and Colonization from the Mediterranean to the Atlantic, 1229–1492* (Philadelphia: University of Pennsylvania Press, 1987), with extensive references. On Columbus, see William D. Phillips Jr. and Carla Rahn Phillips, *The Worlds of Christopher Columbus* (Cambridge: Cambridge University Press, 1992); and Felipe Fernandez-Armesto, *Columbus* (Oxford and New York: Oxford University Press, 1991). For the European response to the discoveries, Fredi Chiappelli, ed., with Michael J. B. Allen and Robert L. Benson, *First Images of America* (Berkeley-Los Angeles: University of California Press, 1976). For the impact on conceptions of humanity, Anthony R. Pagden, *The Fall of Natural Man* (Cambridge: Cambridge University Press, 1982).

A. G. Dickens, ed., *The Courts of Europe* (New York: McGraw-Hill, 1977), portrays the ambassadors' world, as does Donald Queller, *The Office of Ambassador in the Middle Ages* (Princeton, NJ: Princeton University Press, 1967). John North, *The Ambassadors' Secret: Holbein and the World of the Renaissance* (London: Hambledon, 2002) brilliantly uses Holbein's painting as a window on the European world of the early sixteenth century.

Maritime History

The best general account, with an excellent bibliography, is now that of Archibald R. Lewis and Timothy Runyon, *European Naval and Maritime History, 300–1500* (Bloomington: Indiana University Press, 1985). Several earlier works of Archibald R. Lewis remain indispensable: *Naval Power and Trade in the Mediterranean, A.D. 500–1100* (Princeton, NJ: Princeton University Press, 1951); and *The Northern Seas, AD. 300–1100* (Princeton, NJ: Princeton University Press, 1958). There is a readable account in Vincent Cassidy, *The Sea Around Them* (Baton Rouge: Louisiana State University Press, 1968); and a good survey in Pierre Chaunu, *European Expansion in the Later Middle Ages* (New York: North Holland, 1978). See also G. J. Marcus, *The Conquest of the North Atlantic* (London: Boydell and Brewer, 1988). Specialized studies are collected in

Arne Bang-Andersen, Basil Greenhill, and Egil Harald Grude, eds., *The North Sea: A Highway of Cultural Exchange, Character, History* (Oslo: Norwegian University Press, 1985); and John H. Pryor, *Geography, Technology and War* (Cambridge: Cambridge University Press, 1988).

On marine technology, see Richard W. Unger, *The Art of Medieval Technology: Images of Noah the Shipbuilder* (New Brunswick: Rutgers University Press, 1991); and on the economic role of the ship, Unger, *The Ship in the Medieval Economy 600–1600* (London and Montreal: Croom Helm and McGill-Queen's University Press, 1980).

The finest survey of the preparation for the Atlantic crossing, dealing with many other related topics as well, is Felipe Fernandez-Armesto, *Before Columbus* (Philadelphia: University of Pennsylvania Press, 1987), the best account of the events leading to Columbus' first voyage.

PART VI (Chapters 17–20): Sources in Translation

Bernard McGinn, *Visions of the End: Apocalyptic Traditions in the Middle Ages,* rev. ed. (New York: Columbia University Press, 1998).

Rosemary Horrox, ed. and trans., *The Black Death* (Manchester and New York: Manchester University Press, 1994).

Norman Housley, ed. and trans., *Documents on the Later Crusades, 1274–1580* (New York: St. Martin's Press, 1996).

Francis Woodman Cleaves, trans., *The Secret History of the Mongols* (Cambridge, MA: Harvard University Press, 1982).

Christopher Dawson, *Mission to Asia* (Toronto: University of Toronto Press, 1980).

Renate Blumenfeld-Kosinski and Kevin Brownlee, trans., *The Selected Writings of Christine de Pizan* (New York and London: W.W. Norton, 1997).

Louise Ropes Loomis, *The Council of Constance,* ed. John H. Mundy and K. M. Woody (New York: Columbia University Press, 1961).

Marsiglio of Padua, *Defensor Pacis,* trans. Alan Gewirth (New York: Columbia University Press, 1951–1956; reprint, Toronto: University of Toronto Press, 1980).

Gerald Strauss, *Manifestations of Discontent in Germany on the Eve of the Reformation* (Bloomington: Indiana University Press, 1971).

Appendix

POPES AND RULERS

The following tables contain the names and dates of popes and rulers of medieval European states. Tables II–VI are in genealogical form, although not all family members are shown.

TABLE I. THE MEDIEVAL POPES

Sylvester I, 314–335
Mark, 336
Julius I, 337–352
Liberius, 352–366
Damasus I, 366–384
Siricius, 384–399
Anastasius I, 399–401
Innocent I, 401–417
Zosimus, 417–418
Boniface I, 418–422
Celestine I, 422–432
Sixtus III, 432–440
Leo I the Great, 440–461
Hilary, 461–468
Simplicius, 468–483
Felix III, 483–492
Gelasius I, 492–496
Anastasius II, 496–498
Symmachus, 498–514
Hormisdas, 514–523
John I, 523–526
Felix IV, 526–530
Boniface II, 530–532
John II, 533–535
Agapitus I, 535–536
Silverius, 536–537
Vigilius, 537–555
Pelagius I, 555–561
John III, 561–574
Benedict I, 575–579
Pelagius II, 579–590
Gregory I the Great,
590–604
Sabinianus, 604–606
Boniface III, 607
Boniface IV, 608–615
Deusdedit, 615–618
Boniface V, 619–625
Honorius I, 625–638
Severinus, 640
John IV, 640–642
Theodore I, 642–649
Martin I, 649–655
Eugenius I, 654–657
Vitalian, 657–672
Adeodatus, 672–676

Donus, 676–678
Agatho, 678–681
Leo II, 682–683
Benedict II, 684–685
John V, 685–686
Conon, 686–687
Sergius I, 687–701
John VI, 701–705
John VII, 705–707
Sisinnius, 708
Constantine, 708–715
Gregory II, 715–731
Gregory III, 731–741
Zacharias, 741–752
Stephen II, 752–757
Paul I, 757–767
Stephen III, 768–772
Adrian I, 772–795
Leo III, 795–816
Stephen IV, 816–817
Paschal I, 817–824
Eugenius II, 824–827
Valentine, 827
Gregory IV, 827–844
Sergius II, 844–847
Leo IV, 847–855
Benedict III, 855–858
Nicholas I the Great,
858–867
Adrian II, 867–872
John VIII, 872–882
Marinus I, 882–884
Adrian III, 884–885
Stephen V, 885–891
Formosus, 891–896
Boniface VI, 896
Stephen VI, 896–897
Romanus, 897
Theodore II, 897
John IX, 898–900
Benedict IV, 900–903
Leo V, 903
Sergius III, 904–911
Anastasius III, 911–913
Lando, 913–914
John X, 914–928

Leo VI, 928
Stephen VII, 928–931
John XI, 931–935
Leo VII, 936–939
Stephen VIII, 939–942
Marinus II, 942–946
Agapitus II, 946–955
John XII, 955–964
Leo VIII, 963–965
Benedict V, 964–966
John XIII, 965–972
Benedict VI, 973–974
Benedict VII, 974–983
John XIV, 983–984
John XV, 985–996
Gregory V, 996–999
Sylvester II, 999–1003
John XVII, 1003
John XVIII, 1004–1009
Sergius IV, 1009–1012
Benedict VIII, 1012–1024
John XIX, 1024–1032
Benedict IX, 1032–1044
Sylvester III, 1045
Benedict IX, 1045
Gregory VI, 1045–1046
Clement II, 1046–1047
Benedict IX, 1047–1048
Damasus II, 1048
Leo IX, 1049–1054
Victor II, 1055–1057
Stephen IX, 1057–1058
Nicholas II, 1059–1061
Alexander II, 1061–1073
Gregory VII, 1073–1085
Victor III, 1086–1087
Urban II, 1088–1099
Paschal II, 1099–1118
Gelasius II, 1118–1119
Calixtus II, 1119–1124
Honorius II, 1124–1130
Innocent II, 1130–1143
Celestine II, 1143–1144
Lucius II, 1144–1145
Eugenius III, 1145–1153
Anastasius IV, 1153–1154

TABLE I. (CONT.)

Adrian IV, 1154–1159
Alexander III, 1159–1181
Lucius III, 1181–1185
Urban III, 1185–1187
Gregory VIII, 1187
Clement III, 1187–1191
Celestine III, 1191–1198
Innocent III, 1198–1216
Honorius III, 1216–1227
Gregory IX, 1227–1241
Celestine IV, 1241
Innocent IV, 1243–1254
Alexander IV, 1254–1261
Urban IV, 1261–1264
Clement IV, 1265–1268
Gregory X, 1271–1276
Innocent V, 1276

Adrian V, 1276
John XXI, 1276–1277
Nicholas III, 1277–1280
Martin IV, 1281–1285
Honorius IV, 1285–1287
Nicholas IV, 1288–1292
Celestine V, 1294
Boniface VIII, 1294–1303
Benedict XI, 1303–1304
Clement V, 1305–1314
John XXII, 1316–1334
Benedict XII, 1334–1342
Clement VI, 1342–1352
Innocent VI, 1352–1362
Urban V, 1362–1370
Gregory XI, 1370–1378
Urban VI, 1378–1389

Clement VII, 1378–1394
Boniface IX, 1389–1404
Benedict XIII, 1394–1423
Innocent VII, 1404–1406
Gregory XII, 1406–1415
Alexander V, 1409–1410
John XXIII, 1410–1415
Martin V, 1417–1431
Eugenius IV, 1431–1447
Nicholas V, 1447–1455
Calixtus III, 1455–1458
Pius II, 1458–1464
Paul II, 1464–1471
Sixtus IV, 1471–1484
Innocent VIII, 1484–1492
Alexander VI, 1492–1503

TABLE II. THE FRANKISH KINGDOMS AND EMPIRE, 680–987

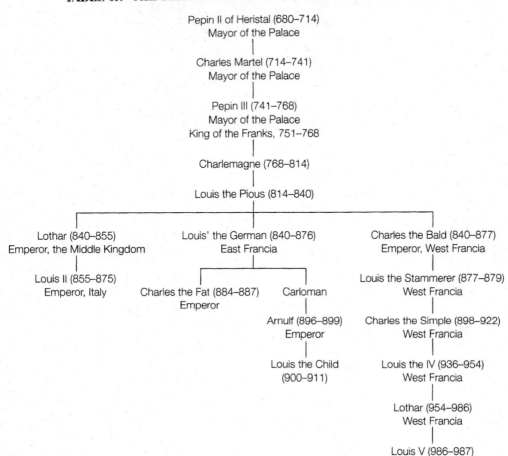

Pepin II of Heristal (680–714)
Mayor of the Palace

Charles Martel (714–741)
Mayor of the Palace

Pepin III (741–768)
Mayor of the Palace
King of the Franks, 751–768

Charlemagne (768–814)

Louis the Pious (814–840)

Lothar (840–855)
Emperor, the Middle Kingdom

Louis' the German (840–876)
East Francia

Charles the Bald (840–877)
Emperor, West Francia

Louis II (855–875)
Emperor, Italy

Charles the Fat (884–887)
Emperor

Carloman

Louis the Stammerer (877–879)
West Francia

Arnulf (896–899)
Emperor

Charles the Simple (898–922)
West Francia

Louis the Child
(900–911)

Louis the IV (936–954)
West Francia

Lothar (954–986)
West Francia

Louis V (986–987)

TABLE III. THE SAXON, SALIAN, AND STAUFER SUCCESSION
IN EAST FRANCIA AND THE EMPIRE, 919–1268

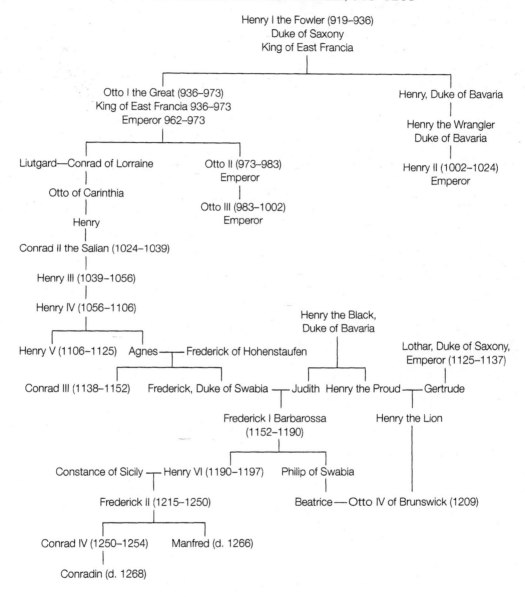

TABLE IV. THE CAPETIAN AND VALOIS SUCCESSION IN WEST FRANCIA AND FRANCE, 987–1498

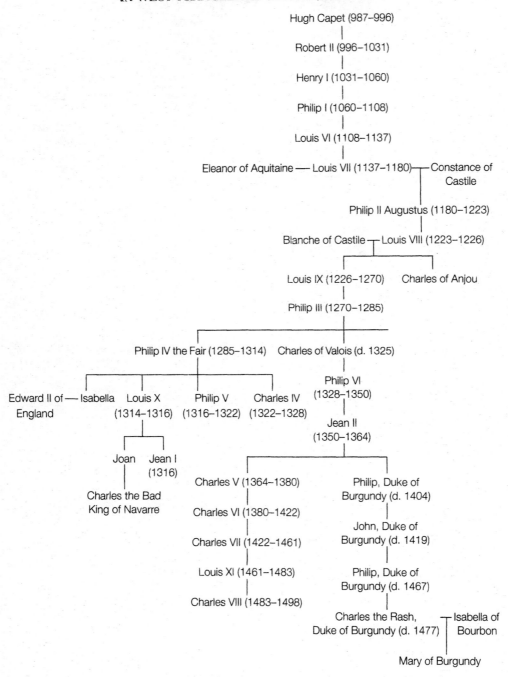

Hugh Capet (987–996)

Robert II (996–1031)

Henry I (1031–1060)

Philip I (1060–1108)

Louis VI (1108–1137)

Eleanor of Aquitaine — Louis VII (1137–1180) — Constance of Castile

Philip II Augustus (1180–1223)

Blanche of Castile — Louis VIII (1223–1226)

Louis IX (1226–1270)   Charles of Anjou

Philip III (1270–1285)

Philip IV the Fair (1285–1314)   Charles of Valois (d. 1325)

Edward II of — Isabella   Louis X   Philip V   Charles IV   Philip VI (1328–1350)
England   (1314–1316) (1316–1322) (1322–1328)

Jean II (1350–1364)

Joan   Jean I (1316)

Charles the Bad King of Navarre

Charles V (1364–1380)   Philip, Duke of Burgundy (d. 1404)

Charles VI (1380–1422)   John, Duke of Burgundy (d. 1419)

Charles VII (1422–1461)   Philip, Duke of Burgundy (d. 1467)

Louis XI (1461–1483)

Charles VIII (1483–1498)

Charles the Rash, Duke of Burgundy (d. 1477) — Isabella of Bourbon

Mary of Burgundy

TABLE V. ANGLO-SAXON, NORMAN, AND PLANTAGENET ENGLAND, 871–1485

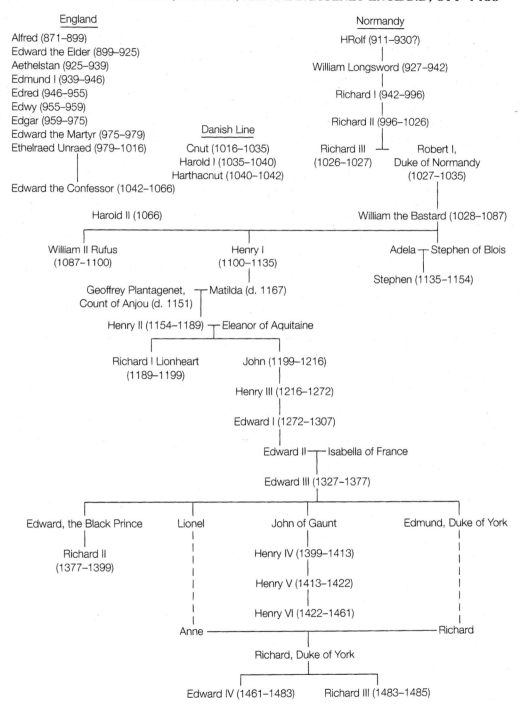

England

Alfred (871–899)
Edward the Elder (899–925)
Aethelstan (925–939)
Edmund I (939–946)
Edred (946–955)
Edwy (955–959)
Edgar (959–975)
Edward the Martyr (975–979)
Ethelraed Unraed (979–1016)

Edward the Confessor (1042–1066)

Danish Line

Cnut (1016–1035)
Harold I (1035–1040)
Harthacnut (1040–1042)

Normandy

HRolf (911–930?)

William Longsword (927–942)

Richard I (942–996)

Richard II (996–1026)

Richard III (1026–1027)

Robert I,
Duke of Normandy
(1027–1035)

Harold II (1066)

William the Bastard (1028–1087)

William II Rufus (1087–1100)

Henry I (1100–1135)

Adela — Stephen of Blois

Stephen (1135–1154)

Geoffrey Plantagenet, — Matilda (d. 1167)
Count of Anjou (d. 1151)

Henry II (1154–1189) — Eleanor of Aquitaine

Richard I Lionheart (1189–1199)

John (1199–1216)

Henry III (1216–1272)

Edward I (1272–1307)

Edward II — Isabella of France

Edward III (1327–1377)

Edward, the Black Prince

Richard II (1377–1399)

Lionel

Anne

John of Gaunt

Henry IV (1399–1413)

Henry V (1413–1422)

Henry VI (1422–1461)

Richard, Duke of York

Edmund, Duke of York

Richard

Edward IV (1461–1483)

Richard III (1483–1485)

TABLE VI. THE LATER EMPERORS AND KINGS OF GERMANY, 1273–1519

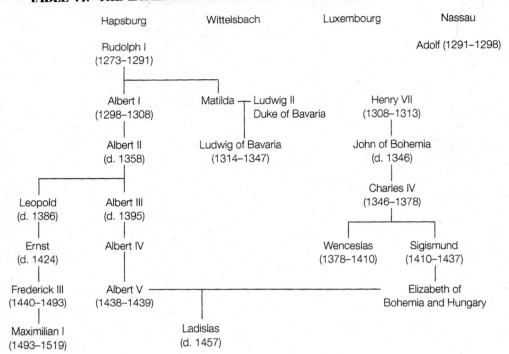

Hapsburg   Wittelsbach   Luxembourg   Nassau

Rudolph I (1273–1291)

Albert I (1298–1308) — Matilda — Ludwig II Duke of Bavaria

Henry VII (1308–1313)

Adolf (1291–1298)

Albert II (d. 1358)

Ludwig of Bavaria (1314–1347)

John of Bohemia (d. 1346)

Charles IV (1346–1378)

Leopold (d. 1386)

Albert III (d. 1395)

Ernst (d. 1424)

Albert IV

Wenceslas (1378–1410)   Sigismund (1410–1437)

Frederick III (1440–1493)

Albert V (1438–1439)

Elizabeth of Bohemia and Hungary

Maximilian I (1493–1519)

Ladislas (d. 1457)

Index